Communicating in the Workplace

Sixth Canadian Edition

Margaret Francis-Dombeck

Professor
Centennial College of Applied Arts and Technology
Scarborough, Ontario

Sue C. Camp, Ed.D.

Associate Professor of Business Administration
Broyhill School of Management
Gardner-Webb University
Boiling Springs, North Carolina

Marilyn L. Satterwhite

Business and Technology Division
Danville Area Community College
Danville, Illinois

McGraw-Hill
Ryerson

Toronto Montréal Boston Burr Ridge, IL Dubuque, IA Madison, WI New York San Francisco
St. Louis Bangkok Bogotá Caracas Kuala Lumpur Lisbon London Madrid Mexico City
Milan New Delhi Santiago Seoul Singapore Sydney Taipei

Communicating in the Workplace
Sixth Canadian Edition

ISBN: 0-07-090814-1

4 5 6 7 8 9 10 TRI 0 9 8 7 6 5

Printed and bound in Canada

Vice President, Editorial and Media Technology: Patrick Ferrier
Sponsoring Editors: James Buchanan/Leanna MacLean
Marketing Manager: Sharon Loeb
Developmental Editor: Sandra de Ruiter
Production Coordinator: Andrée Davis
Supervising Editor: Anne Nellis
Copy Editor: Cat Haggert
Cover Design: Sharon Lucas
Cover Image Credit: Brian Jensen/Stock Illustration Source
Interior Design: Greg Devitt
Composition: Jack Steiner Design
Printer: Tri-Graphic Printing

National Library of Canada Cataloguing in Publication

Francis Dombeck, Margaret M
     Communicating in the workplace / Margaret M. Francis Dombeck. — 6th Canadian ed.

Includes bibliographical references.
ISBN 0-07-090814-1

1. English language—Business English. 2. English language—Rhetoric. 3. Business communication. I.
Title.

PE1408.S763 2003   808'.06665   C2003-901626-9

Brief Contents

Contents

Welcome to the Sixth Canadian Edition of *Communicating in the Workplace*. Technological changes continue to provide faster and varied ways in which to communicate. Communication any time to anywhere has become commonplace. What has not changed, however, is the need for exceptional communication skills. While technology provides us with different communication media, for example, text chat, e-mail, and voice mail, the success of your communication continues to rely on the ability to use excellent verbal, and written communication skills. In addition, you require an understanding of how factors such as nonverbal communication, cultural diversity, and ethics influence business communication.

Communicating in the Workplace, *Sixth Canadian Edition*, is designed to help you achieve success in your business communications. Therefore, this edition not only retains the comprehensive, detailed approach of previous editions, but also contains revised, updated information and new topics such as nonverbal communication, voice mail, plagiarism, and customer communication methods. Review exercises are included for each chapter, providing opportunities for individual and team work, and researching topics on the Internet.

Highlights of New Content and Text Reorganization

The chapters have been grouped into *Units* to assist curriculum planning.

- *Learning Outcomes* are provided for each chapter.
- **▶ Key Terms** Each Section of a chapter begins with *Key Terms*.
- The Section Assessment feature includes Review of Key Terms and *Discussion Points*, as well as the familiar *Practical Application* and *Editing Practice* exercises.
- Recognizing that most workplaces function in team settings, each *Practical Application* now contains a *Teamwork Exercise* to facilitate working collaboratively in groups to solve an issue or research a topic.
- Chapter reviews have been added. Each Chapter Wrap-up contains a *Summary*, two *Cases, Communicating in Your Career*, and *On the Web*. The Summary provides a review of the main points in the chapter, while the other exercises provide opportunities for research, writing, and discussion.
- *Canadian content* has been substantially increased, especially in the case studies and research exercises.

- **Oops**
  MEMORY HOOK
  The popular "*Memory Hook*" and "*Oops*" features assist students in identifying and avoiding common communication errors.

Major changes to chapter contents include:

- Chapter 1, **Exploring Communication**, provides a comprehensive introduction to communication issues. It includes new introductory topics on the elements of communication, types of communication, and barriers to effective communication, expanded coverage of ethics in communication, and a discussion of global communication issues.

- Chapter 2, **Developing Oral Communication Skills**, includes nonverbal communication and how to plan and manage an effective meeting.

- In Chapter 3, **Exploring Language Elements**, the sentence has its own section. This chapter now includes verbs and predicate agreement.

- Chapter 4, **Mastering Nouns and Pronouns**, have additional examples throughout to increase clarity and enhance comprehension.

- Chapter 5, **Expanding Language Skills**, contains a new section on predicate adjectives and expanded coverage of adverbs.

- Chapter 6, **Applying the Mechanics of Style**, has news sections on predicate usage and comma splices and the section on commas has been moved so that it precedes the sections on semicolons, colons, and dashes.

- Chapter 7, **Sharpening Writing Skills**, now contains information on proofreading within the "Revising and Editing" section.

- Chapter 8, **Writing Business Correspondence—Pt. 1**, has an increased emphasis on writing e-mail messages.

- Chapter 9, **Writing Business Correspondence—Pt. 2**, contains several new letter samples.

- Chapter 10, **Writing Reports, Minutes, and News Releases**, includes new information on plagiarism and referencing, as well as additional illustrations for report preparation.

- Chapter 11, **Improving Communication with Customers**, has been completely revised and approaches customer communication from the viewpoint of satisfying customers' major needs for respect, resolution of their requests, and speed and convenience.

- Chapter 12, **Communicating in Employment Situations**, has been substantially revised. These revisions include expanded coverage of interview types and preparation, and new information on assembling a portfolio.

Acknowledgments

Most of the credit for this book must go to the U.S. authors, Sue C. Camp and Marilyn L. Satterwhite, whose work forms the basis of this text.

We wish to thank the following educators for their valuable comments and feedback on this Canadian edition. Many of the changes were based on their thorough and constructive reviews.

Sheila Barkley	Conestoga College
Nancy Barry	Georgian College
Joe Benge	Camosun College
Gary Bouchard	Cambrian College
Debra Brech	Sheridan College
Gloria Cott	Northern Alberta Institute of Technology
Liesje DeBurger	Durham College
Carol Evans	Saskatchewan Institute of Applied Science and Technology
Barbara Graham	St. Clair College
Linda Large	Canadore College
Helen MacDonald	Nova Scotia Community College
Terry Macklem	Oulton's College
Colleen Morrison	College of the North Atlantic
Sandy Nemcko	Niagara College
Nancy Oike	Douglas College
Barry Sutherland	Fanshawe College

Thanks go to Cat Haggert for editing this text. In addition, this edition has been made possible by the support, organization, insight, and assistance of the following people at McGraw-Hill Ryerson in Whitby, Ontario: James Buchanan, Sandra de Ruiter, and Anne Nellis.

Biography

Margaret Francis-Dombeck has dedicated her working life to teaching, and related activities. A graduate of the University of South Australia, she taught in Australian high schools for six years before arriving in Canada in the early 70s. Margaret has been a professor at Centennial College in Toronto since 1974. Throughout her teaching career, she has taken leave to gain further business experience and enhance her teaching abilities, working at firms in Australia, England, and Canada. Margaret has also been very involved in educational writing, and her accomplishments include: co-authoring curriculum materials in Kuwait, and developing graduation standards for several Ontario community college programs. At Centennial College, she has authored a number of texts in subjects such as customer service and contact-centre communications.

Chapter 1

Exploring Communication

Chapter Learning Outcomes

**After successfully completing
this chapter, you will have
demonstrated the ability to:**

▶ name the types of communication and their purposes;
▶ list and briefly discuss the components of the communication process;
▶ give examples of communication barriers and state strategies to overcome these barriers;
▶ explain the importance of listening, reading, and writing skills;
▶ distinguish between external and internal business communication and outline the flow of information within an organization;
▶ name and outline the functions of the six Cs of communication;
▶ define ethics and identify ethical behaviours;
▶ communicate in a socially-acceptable manner by eliminating discriminatory actions and behaviours;
▶ give examples of ways in which interpersonal skills are used to ensure effective communication;
▶ outline factors to consider when communicating globally.

Michelle works as a part-time assistant in the Archives Department at the Hometown Public Library while attending college. Her principal duties are to help patrons research their genealogy and use microfilm readers as well as to conduct research for e-mail research requests from across the country.

Michelle's supervisor, Roberta, is the director of the Reference Department, which is located in a separate part of the building. Michelle and Roberta communicate mostly by e-mail and telephone messages.

On the occasions when they meet face-to-face, Roberta rarely initiates a greeting. When they meet to discuss a problem, Roberta often interrupts Michelle as she speaks, waving her finger at Michelle in a dominating way. Michelle becomes upset and finds it hard to concentrate on what Roberta is saying.

When Roberta sends Michelle notes of instruction, she sometimes leaves words out, making it difficult to understand the notes. In addition, Roberta often contradicts written instructions she had given earlier.

Michelle is frustrated with the miscommunication that occurs between her and Roberta. Her frustration reaches a breaking point when Roberta reprimands Michelle for the way she had distributed information for a computer training course Roberta was conducting for other library employees. Michelle wasn't sure how to distribute the information. She vaguely remembered Roberta giving some instructions. Finally she decided to post the announcement on the notice board in the reception area, since Roberta was always reminding her to be cost-conscious. When Roberta saw the announcement on the notice board, she became very angry and told Michelle she should have sent e-mail to each employee.

As you read Chapter 1, identify some of the communication problems that Michelle and Roberta have, and think about how the problems could be eliminated or minimized.

Elements of Communication

To be human is to communicate, speak and relate to other human beings.

—Beverley McLachlin, Chief Justice, Supreme Court of Canada

Communication, very simply defined, is the exchange of information. It is a vital part of our everyday lives, beginning at birth. Very early in life, we learn to communicate our needs. A baby, for example, learns that crying makes a parent or caregiver respond quickly with attention, a dry diaper, food, or all three. As a child develops, the way he or she communicates becomes more complex. Speaking, listening, reading, writing, and even observing become part of the communication process.

Today, in addition to traditional methods of communication such as letters and telephone conversations, communicating by electronic media—for example, e-mail, voice mail, pagers, PDAs (personal digital assistants), and video-conferencing—is becoming increasingly common. Each of those media allows people in different locations to exchange messages quickly and conveniently. This increased use of electronic media is changing communication practices, especially with regard to ethics and confidentiality.

Types of Communication

Communication can be divided into three main categories: oral, written, and nonverbal.

Oral Communication

Oral communication uses spoken words to exchange ideas and information. Examples of oral communication include one-on-one conversations, meetings, voice-mail messages, and teleconferencing. Spoken messages can be sent instantaneously, and they usually result in some immediate feedback. The disadvantage of oral communication is that there is often little opportunity to reflect on what is said. There is also no written record.

Written Communication

Written communication can include letters, faxes, memos, e-mails, reports, news releases, tables, diagrams, charts, and graphs. Written communication provides proof that the information was exchanged. The disadvantage of written communication is that immediate feedback may not always be possible.

Nonverbal Communication

Nonverbal communication is communication without words. Nonverbal communication is an important form of communication. Think about it. Without saying a single word, you can express your feelings with body language—gestures, facial expressions, and body movements or positions.

Many times, the nonverbal message is stronger and therefore more believable than the verbal message. The nonverbal message also may reinforce or contradict the verbal message. An example would be talking to someone who said she wasn't in a hurry but kept glancing at her watch.

Good communicators combine oral and nonverbal communication techniques to make their communication more effective. When this combination is faulty, the effect is easy to spot. Have you ever listened to a speaker who was an authority on a subject, but whom you considered boring because the speaker used very little nonverbal expression? Even if the subject interested you, you probably found it hard to keep your mind on the speech. Nonverbal communication can add emphasis and depth to spoken words and can even tell you whether or not to believe a speaker. Nonverbal communication plays an important role in the clear, effective exchange of messages. Chapter 2 gives further information on nonverbal communication.

Purposes of Communication

The first step in planning any message is to determine the purpose of your communication.

Recall for a moment what you said to various family members, friends, and school or business associates today. Each question you asked, each statement you made—from "How do you feel today?" to "I just found a ten-dollar bill!"—falls into at least one of the following four main purposes of communication.

To inquire. "When did you get your new cell phone?"

To inform. "This phone was a birthday gift."

To persuade. "You can access your e-mail with this phone."

To develop goodwill. "Thank you for helping me select my new phone."

You will learn how to plan business messages and to determine the purposes of such messages in Chapters 8, 9, and 10.

Components of Communication

What can a speaker communicate if there is no one to listen? Keep in mind that communication can take place only if you have *both* a sender and a receiver. Each time you have a conversation with someone or exchange written messages, you should be aware of each component of the communication model as illustrated in Figure 1.1.

The six basic components of communication are:

1. *Message sender.* The sender composes the intended message. The sender could be a writer, a speaker, or a person who sends a nonverbal message through gestures and body language.
2. *Actual message.* The actual message may be written, oral, or nonverbal, or it may combine two or more types of communication. It may or may not be the message the sender intended.

3. *Message transmission.* The message can be sent or delivered in a variety of ways. Written messages can be sent in the form of letters, memorandums, and reports. Written messages could also be sent electronically using fax machines or electronic mail. Oral messages can be delivered through face-to-face conversations, meetings, presentations, and through telephone conversations and voice mail. Nonverbal messages include gestures, facial expressions, and other forms of body language.

4. *Message receiver.* The receiver takes in, or receives, the message. The receiver's knowledge, interest, and emotional state will affect how the message is received.

5. *Message interpretation.* The receiver interprets the message. The interpretation may be different from the intended message or the actual message.

6. *Feedback.* The sender and the receiver respond to each other in writing, orally, nonverbally, or in a combination of these ways.

As you can see from Figure 1.1, communication is a complex process. The sender wishes to deliver an idea or information. To make the message clear, the words chosen and the manner of delivery must be as accurate and precise as possible. In face-to-face communication the sender uses words, body language, and voice qualities. In telephone communication, there is no body language to assist the communication process, making voice qualities and the words used even more important. In written communication, the sender must rely completely on the words, the organization of the message. and its visual presentation.

The sender must think about the purpose of the communication. Does he or she want to persuade or to request help? What does the sender want the receiver to think or do? What image of himself or herself does the sender want to project? The sender must also consider the audience or receiver. How much does the receiver already know about this topic? What is the receiver's attitude towards this topic? What benefits or objections can be anticipated? What information is necessary? How will the message affect the receiver? How should the message be adapted to meet the needs of the receiver?

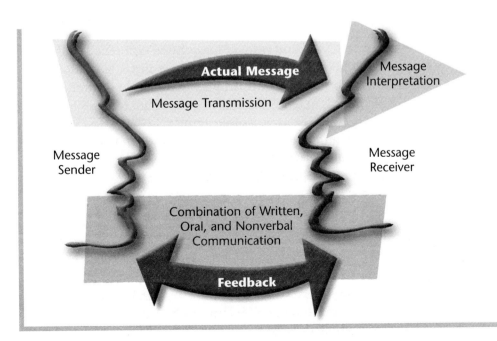

◀ **Figure 1.1 Communication Components**
Communicating in teams is an important aspect of internal communication.

Thinking Critically.
How could team members apply the information shown in this illustration to communicate effectively?

The sender may need to check that the intended message has been received; that is, did the receiver interpret the message in the way the sender intended? To check for this common understanding, the sender can observe the receiver's body language, ask questions, paraphrase the receiver's comments, and verify important details.

In addition, to ensure clear communication it is necessary to consider what communication barriers are present and how these may be overcome.

Barriers to Effective Communication

Communication barriers are factors that interfere with communication and might negatively affect the intended message. Barriers include environmental and physical distractions, emotional distractions, and cultural and language differences. Such distractions draw the receiver's attention away from the message, thus creating barriers to effective communication. The resulting lack of concentration can lead to incomplete communication by message senders and erroneous conclusions by message receivers.

Environmental and physical distractions are usually easier to prevent in a speaking or a listening situation because the surroundings can often be controlled or changed by the sender or the receiver. For example, room temperature, seating arrangements, and background noise are environmental factors that can usually be controlled. Physical distractions can be caused by such things as uncomfortable seating, tiredness, and poor health.

Emotional distractions on the part of the receiver can prevent him or her from concentrating on, and giving full attention to, the communication. Emotional distractions may include thinking about a personal matter or allowing an emotion such as anger to influence how you interpret a message. A written message containing errors can also cause an emotional distraction, because the receiver reacts negatively and possibly begins to discount the importance of the message or the sender.

Barriers such as language differences, inattention, and misunderstanding caused by different interpretations of a word or an expression can have a negative influence on the communication process. In today's multicultural society, it is important to be sensitive to cultural diversity when using any form of communication. An awareness of, and respect for, cultural differences will help you to avoid miscommunications. For example, people in Canada and Japan may have different ideas about what constitutes politeness in a letter.

Selecting the correct words to use is particularly important in cases in which there might be a language barrier, for example, if the receiver's first language is not English. Use of slang and jargon in communicating with people who do not understand the terminology can also cause a barrier to communication. If the receptionist tells the international caller, Mr. Wong, that Mrs. Wyatt can't take his call because she's *tied up* in a meeting, Mr. Wong could interpret the message literally (Mrs. Wyatt is *tied with ropes to a chair* in the meeting).

Language and Communication Skills

Every businessperson is involved in some form of communication with others and must be able to use language effectively to send and receive messages. Words are the major tools of language, and they must be chosen carefully to express the intended meaning. How well the sender of the message uses these tools and how well the receiver interprets their use are major factors in the effectiveness of the message.

As a message sender, you must communicate facts, ideas, opinions, and instructions in a coherent manner, with a minimum of effort, and with clarity, confidence, and knowledge. To do this, you must have a broad vocabulary and the ability to spell, pronounce, and select the correct words. You must be able to speak and write clearly, concisely, and without error. As a message receiver, you must also be able to read and listen with understanding. Both the sender and the receiver share the responsibility for effective communication.

In spoken communication, word choice, grammar, pronunciation, and listening are also factors in effective communication. A receiver may be distracted by incorrect grammar, incorrect pronunciation, or misused words and, consequently, he or she may not receive the intended message. For example, a diner may focus on the errors, rather than the message, when a server says, "We *done* the meal as *good* as we could so a 15-per cent *gratitude* would be appreciated."

In written communication, something as simple as using the wrong word, making a spelling or grammatical error, using an incorrect format, or misusing a punctuation mark may change the intended meaning of the message. Even if the receiver understands the message, his or her opinion of the sender's intelligence and credibility may be negatively influenced by the error. For example, a receiver may not do business with a company because of a poorly written sales letter. The receiver may feel that if a company is careless about its letters it may also be careless about filling orders promptly and accurately.

Each of these language tools is discussed more fully in later sections of this book. Keep in mind, however, that these tools apply not only to writing but also to reading, listening, and speaking. If the communication process is to be successful, the message sender must be an effective writer or speaker, and the receiver must be an effective reader or listener.

Combining the Communication Skills in Your Social, Educational, and Professional Lives

Effective comunication is an essential ingredient of successful family, social, and business relationships. A communication breakdown can lead to misunderstandings and serious problems in our personal and business lives, while good communication skills have a positive affect on relationships.

Learning to be a successful, effective communicator is somewhat like learning to be a good basketball player or a good musician. Once you have learned the basic skills, you become better and better as you practise the skills and gain confidence.

Listening, speaking, reading, and writing are important and useful skills in and of themselves. When used together, they reinforce each other, producing a higher, more efficient level of communication. Each of the four skills can be strengthened by being combined with the others. Take listening, for example.

Listening Skills

Listening involves concentrating on what you hear. It is one of the primary means of receiving information.

Formal communications training focuses on writing skills, but over 50 per cent of our communication time is usually spent on listening. In addition, listening is the fundamental skill required in establishing relationships. However, in spite of its importance, we often forget to focus on listening in the communication process. Help with developing listening skills is given in Chapter 2.

The problem with listening is that if you miss something or forget part of what you heard, you cannot replay the message (unless, of course, you have recorded it). When you know something about the subject, however, when you have "read up on it" or "done your homework," you will find it easier to grasp the information presented orally. Reading, then, can reinforce listening; it helps you gain more from what you hear.

Speaking can also reinforce your listening skills. Good listeners ask questions to clarify points and elicit additional information. Speaking can also be used as a memory aid. Repeating a person's name right after you hear it, for example, will help you remember the name.

Writing reinforces listening skills on an ongoing basis. You jot down the name and address of a restaurant someone recommends, or you take a phone message for a co-worker. You take notes when your supervisor explains how a job should be done. You can then refer to your notes when you need them.

Your Social Life. In a social setting, good listeners—those who understand what the speaker is saying and why—are much in demand. We often choose a good listener as a friend: someone to turn to when we want to talk about our problems or fears or to share our triumphs or joys. Good listeners often reap the benefit of the experience of others and enjoy the satisfaction of close, personal relationships.

Your Educational Life. Good listening skills help you absorb an instructor's lectures, explanations, and directions for assignments. The process of taking notes on the oral information enhances listening. Your notes provide a record of the information you received and enable you to review the information at a later time.

Your Professional Life. Excellent listening skills enhance job performance. In business you need to listen in a great variety of situations; for example, telephone and face-to-face conversations, voice-mail messages, training sessions, informal and formal meetings. As a newcomer in an organization, listening carefully will provide you with information about how the organization works, about relationships among co-workers, and about the details of your job.

Kristen was daydreaming about her weekend and not paying attention when the instructor announced that class would not meet tomorrow. Kristen was the only student who showed up the next day.

Peanuts ©. Reprinted by permission of United Features Syndicate.

There is a close relationship between effective listening and productivity in the workplace. Effective listening means that you grasp information the first time it is spoken, or that you take steps to ensure that you have received the message correctly. Busy executives require assistants and colleagues to develop excellent listening skills so that information does not have to be repeated and so that it is acted on correctly. Time is lost and problems are caused when people do not follow instructions or fail to hear important information. For example, someone who did not listen carefully to instructions about backing up files caused a major problem for his organization when the server was replaced and the old files were deleted.

You can see how listening is assisted by the other communication skills when you consider how Lynn Shearer uses these skills in her job as an administrative assistant in a social service agency. Listening is an important part of Lynn's job. She attends staff meetings where she listens to case workers and senior staff discussing current problems and cases. To help her remember what was discussed and what she's been assigned to do, Lynn takes notes. She enters her notes on a computer, creating a permanent record and handy reference. In the meetings Lynn often hears references to articles, books, or legislation. She finds that background reading helps her understand discussions at meetings. Lynn also uses her speaking skills in her job. She asks questions and supplies requested information at the staff meetings, and she spends some time each day on the telephone, answering questions and providing information about the agency. Lynn has discovered that reading, writing, and speaking have helped her become a more effective listener.

Use these strategies to enhance and reinforce your listening skills:

- *Read* to gain background information.
- *Repeat* a person's name when you are introduced to someone.
- *Ask* questions to clarify information.
- *Take* good notes.

Speaking Skills

Speaking can be an excellent way to transmit information. Speaking also comes into play as part of being a good listener. You provide feedback by letting the speaker know you understand, by offering advice, by asking for more details, or by paraphrasing to make sure you understand the message.

Your Social Life. You use your speaking skills to share your thoughts, wants, accomplishments, and feelings with others. You also ask questions to gain information and show interest.

Your Educational Life. Asking questions, summarizing information, and expressing ideas are important parts of the learning process. Your spoken feedback tells your instructor what information you understand and what information needs clarification. Your speaking skills will help you master the course material.

Your Professional Life. Communicating by speaking is an important skill in the work world. Let's look at how Andrea Rosado uses speaking on her job as a paralegal. Andrea spends a good portion of her day speaking with lawyers, other paralegals, and clients. She makes telephone inquiries regarding legal cases she's working on, and she engages in discussions with lawyers and colleagues.

Reading, writing, and listening skills support Andrea's speaking skills. Andrea knows that reading is an essential part of her job. She must analyze the facts of a case and conduct research to identify laws, judicial decisions, and legal articles that may have a bearing on the case. Andrea uses her writing skills to prepare legal documents and legal correspondence. Listening is also an important skill for Andrea. As a paralegal, she must listen to clients to obtain information and she must listen to instructions from her supervising lawyer.

Reading Skills

Reading is one of the principal means of obtaining information. The information may be in printed form, such as a book or magazine, or in electronic form on a computer screen. Reading is an efficient way to learn because it allows you to control the flow of information. You can reread a passage you have not fully understood, and you can take notes which will help you when reviewing the material. Reading allows you to skip over material you don't need.

Your Social Life. Reading newspapers, magazines, and books helps you broaden your knowledge and understanding of the world and become a more interesting person. Reading gives you more information and ideas to share with others.

Your Educational Life. In any kind of educational setting, reading is one of the principal means of gaining course-related information.

Reading skills are important for students at every level. Take Jim Hamid for example. Jim works for a travel agency during the day and attends a community college at night. Jim found the reading assignments for some of his courses difficult at first. However, things improved when he started taking notes on his reading. Taking notes helped Jim organize and remember the information. These notes made studying for exams easier, since Jim could review his notes rather than the entire text.

Jim discovered that he gets more out of a class when he has read the assignment ahead of time. The lectures help him review basic material and clarify difficult points. Jim has also found that he likes participating in discussions when he is prepared for class. Talking about the material in class reinforces Jim's reading and helps him master the material.

Your Professional Life. Reading will be part of any job, starting with the employment forms you must read when you are hired. Memos, letters, reports, computer manuals, schedules, procedures manuals, and policy manuals are a few of the documents that will require reading skills.

Writing Skills

Writing skills are important for creating and communicating information. The major advantage of writing is that it provides a physical record that can be used for reference and, if necessary, as proof.

Your Social Life. Writing is probably the communication skill that is least used in our personal lives today. Many of us tend to make a telephone call rather than write a personal letter to a friend who lives some distance away. However, we need to know how to write a note of appreciation or to express condolences to a friend or family member.

In addition, we all have to use our writing skills when we take care of personal-business correspondence, such as letters or e-mail messages of request, complaints, and notification of a change of address. Committing your personal business to writing gives you a record of the communication.

Your Educational Life. Excellent writing skills can help you earn higher grades on research papers and tests. Writing about a subject helps you learn because you must think about the material and organize the information you have before you can start writing.

Your Professional Life. On the job, you use your writing skills to compose e-mail messages, notes on a client's file, memos, letters, and reports. In many jobs writing is a supporting skill, but in some jobs such as that of newspaper reporter or author, writing is the primary skill. Writing, via some form of electronic communication, will become an increasingly important part of our lives in the future.

The Value of Good Communication Skills

Good communication skills will be a great asset in your ongoing learning process. With the rapid rate of technological advancements, you can expect to have several different jobs during your working life. There will be new skills to learn and new technology to master. Your communication skills are tools that will help you to adapt to a variety of work situations.

Using the four communication skills in various combinations will strengthen your ability to communicate. Let's see how Renee Chu uses all four communication skills in her job. Renee works as a reporter on the *Centennial Times*. She has always liked to write and now has a chance to write full-time. Renee, though, has found that listening, speaking, and reading skills are also crucial in writing newspaper articles.

For example, Renee had to read the minutes of last year's council meetings to get the history of the new recycling program. She found that she needed more information about recycling plans in other communities and the technology involved. Renee spent the morning in the public library, reading and taking notes. Next, she wanted to find out what various city officials and citizens thought about the new program. Was the proposed program worth the expense? Would it really help cut down the amount of garbage? Would the plastic bottles be processed and reused as promised? Renee drew up a list of questions before conducting her first interview. When Renee asked the questions, she listened carefully to the answers and took notes.

Renee then assembled the material for her story. She was able to plan what she was going to say before she sat down at the computer to write.

When analyzing Renee's job, you see how the four communication skills are interconnected. Though you may use one skill more often than the others, those other skills play vital supporting roles. Each of the communication skills—listening, speaking, reading, and writing—is strengthened and reinforced by the other skills.

Review of Key Terms

1. Name and briefly describe the types of *barriers* that interfere with communication.
2. What is the role of *feedback* in communication?

Practical Application

1. One communication skill is featured in each of the following examples. Explain how one or more of the other skills might be used in each situation to reinforce the main skill.
   a. Listening to a neighbour's complaints about a barking dog.
   b. Speaking to a group about the pros and cons of two popular software programs.
   c. Writing a report about public opinion on local property tax rates.
   d. Listening to an adviser in the school placement office explain what papers you will need to take when you go for a job interview.
   e. Reading several consumer and photography magazines in the library that evaluate compact cameras. (You want to buy a compact camera.)
2. Today, immediately after a conversation with a fellow student or students, analyze what was said by jotting down answers to the following questions:
   a. What was the sender's intended message?
   b. What was the sender's actual message?
   c. What was the receiver's interpretation of the message?

   Compare notes to determine if all messages are the same. If not, discuss what factors may have influenced the message.

Editing Practice

Spelling Alert! Write or key each of the following sentences, correcting the spelling errors. A sentence may have more than one misspelled word.
1. The rest of you order is back ordered and should be hear in 7 to 10 days.
2. Although Joaquin maled the package last week, Alicia has not recieved it yet.
3. Your plane is quit late.
4. Ms. Lamay finaly wraped up her project.
5. With the car radio blaring, Bryan past the hospital quite zone.

Discussion Points

1. Describe the differences between oral, written, and nonverbal communication. Why is each type of communication essential to effective communication?
2. Describe several ways in which you will use different types of communication skills in your chosen career.

Applying Your Communication Skills in Business

If you can't write your idea on the back of my calling card, you don't have a clear idea.

—David Belasco, producer of Broadway musicals

▶ **Key Terms**

No matter what your job is, your working day is basically a constant flow of information. As an employee, you will communicate with customers or clients, co-workers, and managers in a variety of settings. You will communicate one-on-one and as part of a team. You will communicate not only by giving information but also by listening to or reading information provided by others. This listening and reading keeps you informed and enables you to tap into an endless supply of ideas and solutions.

Imagine that you are an employee who has made suggestions for improvement in the department or company. How would you feel if your supervisor listened to your ideas and actually put some of them into effect? You would probably feel great. You might respond by working even harder than you were working before. You would have experienced effective communication.

Flow of Communication

Communication not only links members of a certain department but also serves as a vital link between people in different departments. In a company each department functions as a link in the communication chain. If one or more of the links are broken or missing, information is missing, incomplete, or incorrect.

Upward communication is communicating with people who rank above you. **Lateral** or **horizontal communication** is communicating with people who are at the same rank or level as you. **Downward communication** is communicating with people who rank below you. The direction your communication is flowing will influence how you communicate—the words you use and the method you choose.

Not only does good communication make a company operate efficiently, but it also creates a sense of unity—a team spirit—and a striving for common goals among employees.

Figure 1.2 ▶
Flow of Communication Within an Organization

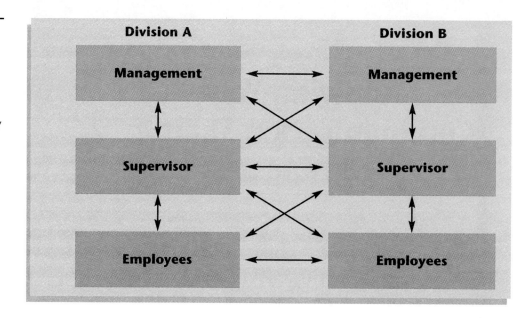

Figure 1.2 illustrates the flow of communication within an organization and shows the directions in which communication can travel. The arrows at both ends of a line show that communication flows both ways.

Types of Business Communication

Communication that takes place in a company or an organization falls into two categories: internal communication and external communication. The tone used in internal communication usually differs from that used in external communication. Tone, as it applies to business communication, usually refers to the general manner of expression or effect of a written document, conversation, discussion, or speech.

Internal Communication

Internal communication is the transmittal of information between and among persons within a business or organization. Within a company, internal communication is used to accomplish company goals and objectives. Managers must, for example, let employees know when and why a specific job must be done. On the other hand, nonmanagement personnel use communication for understanding and clarifying how a specific job must be done. Non-management personnel communicate to convince management that their knowledge and personal attributes qualify them for pay increases or promotions. Other examples of internal communication include suggestions for improving products and services, and guidelines for completing a process.

Internal communication may be carried out with people in the same department, in other departments, and at other company locations.

Also, employees may communicate individually or as members of a team. Internal communication may include face-to-face conversations, telephone calls, e-mail messages, and brainstorming ideas at a meeting.

In internal communication, a person's tone may be friendly and informal. As an employee, you must assess a situation and use the most appropriate tone. For instance, when telling a colleague about an idea you have to make your department more productive, you would use different words, different phrasing, and a different tone than if you were making the same suggestion to the vice president of your company.

External Communication

External communication is the transfer of information to and from people outside the company. The goal of most external communication is to persuade the recipients to respond favourably to company needs. A sales letter, for example, tries to get a potential customer to buy a product or a service. A job listing tries to attract qualified personnel to fill a certain position.

In external communication, a person's tone is usually more formal. Using the right tone in external communication is more challenging than using the right tone in internal communication because you are representing your company as well as yourself. Often, customers and clients will transfer their opinions of you and your communication skills to the company itself. They will base opinions not only on what you say or write but also on your appearance and manner. In other words, the whole package counts.

Although your physical appearance may not be so important as the content of what you say or write, your appearance creates a first impression. Keep in mind that the first impression you create will often influence how closely your customer or client will pay attention to what you have to say. As a result, your appearance (or the appearance of your communication) can work either for you or against you.

The Six Cs of Business Communication

Effective business communication meets the test of the six Cs—it is clear, complete, concise, consistent, correct, and courteous. The six Cs apply to any communication situation, whether you are speaking or writing, and whether you are communicating with someone inside or someone outside your organization. Using the six Cs will make your communication coherent and easy to follow.

Misunderstandings can arise when someone uses the wrong word. Consider this statement made by an employee in a hotel:

"Please leave your values at the front desk."

Clear

It isn't enough to communicate so you can be understood; you must communicate so clearly that you cannot be misunderstood. Being specific rather than vague is a way to meet this test. If you leave your car for "routine service," will you be upset when you receive a bill for $368? Asking the service department to call you if the car will require more than $100 worth of service work would eliminate this miscommunication.

Complete

Complete communication includes enough details so that the recipient will not need to ask for more information. Imagine receiving a notice from your doctor for a return visit on Tuesday at 3 p.m. Which Tuesday would you go? To be complete, a communication should answer the following questions: Who? What? Where? When? Why? and How? or How much?

Concise

Unnecessary words hamper communication because the extra words used to express the idea or thought clutter the message. The following sentence is wordy: "I am writing this letter to inform you that your airline tickets will be mailed ten days before your scheduled departure." A more concise version is more effective: "We will mail your airline tickets to you ten days before your scheduled departure." You've eliminated seven words, and none of the meaning is lost from the original message.

Consistent

All communication should be consistent in fact, treatment, and sequence. Consistency in *fact* refers to agreement with a source document or an established fact. For example, an open house scheduled for April 31 should be questioned since April has only 30 days. Consistency in *treatment* means treating similar items the same way. An example of consistent treatment would be using the courtesy title (*Mr., Mrs., Miss,* or *Ms.*) with the names of all recipients of a letter or indenting all paragraphs in a letter. Consistency in *sequence* refers to the arrangement of listings such as alphabetical, chronological, or numerical. Imagine a telephone book that is not arranged in alphabetical order. If a workshop is scheduled for three days, the dates should be given in chronological order (the order in which they occur), for example, May 3, May 6, and May 10.

Correct

All the information in a message should be accurate—the content, spelling, capitalization, grammar, spelling, and punctuation.

Courteous

Your communication should use the you-attitude instead of the I-attitude. This means keeping the reader or listener in mind when you write or say something. Use positive words instead of negative words, and use tactful language. Use formats (lists, short paragraphs, tables) that are easy to read and comprehend.

The six Cs of effective communication

Clear	Consistent	To recall the six Cs, remember this sentence: Clara gave clear, complete, and concise directions on how to greet customers in a consistent, correct, and courteous way.
Complete	Correct	
Concise	Courteous	

Applying Interpersonal Skills

Interpersonal skills, also known as human relations skills, involve the ability to understand and deal with people in such a way that a favourable relationship and goodwill are maintained. This ability to interact with others effectively is a key part of your emotional intelligence. The social skill component of emotional intelligence is demonstrated through managing relationships and building networks, and the ability to find common ground and build rapport.

Workers need to possess good communication skills in order to be competitive in the changing workplace and in the global economy. Practising the human relations techniques described in this section will help you improve your communication skills.

Use the You-Attitude. Using the *you-attitude* when writing and speaking helps build goodwill and helps maintain an environment of friendliness. The you-attitude means putting your reader or listener first and being considerate of the other person. An example of the you-attitude is "For your convenience, we are extending our hours until 7 p.m."

The *I-attitude* is the opposite of the you-attitude; it is putting your own interests, well-being, and comfort ahead of anyone else's. An example of the I-attitude is "I have decided to extend our hours until 7 p.m."

Demonstrate a Positive Attitude. A good communicator demonstrates a positive attitude by building good working relationships with peers, superiors, subordinates, customers, and clients. Showing enthusiasm about your job and your organization, cooperating with others, and controlling your emotions are ways to demonstrate a positive attitude.

Be a Good Listener. A good communicator is also a good listener. It is important to listen carefully and to let the speaker know you are interested. Ask questions when you are unsure of the content of the message, and take notes when appropriate.

Maintain Confidentiality. A good communicator understands the importance of confidentiality. This means releasing information to authorized personnel only and releasing information at the appropriate time—not early and not late. Also, do not spread rumours—even if you believe they are true.

Be Considerate. Treat others as you would like to be treated. A good communicator is courteous, honest, and patient in dealing with other people and respects the opinions of others. This means using tact and diplomacy. It also means using words and terms that your receiver understands. Another way to show courtesy is to be prompt in answering correspondence and in returning telephone calls.

Review of Key Terms

1. How is *upward communication* different from *lateral* or *horizontal communication?*
2. What is the difference between *external* and *internal communication?*

Practical Application

1. For each of the following situations, write a paragraph about what combination of communication skills you would use and why.
   a. Applying for a job advertised in the want-ad column in the newspaper that gives a box number for reply.
   b. Receiving a message on your voice mail to call an employer to set up an appointment for a job interview.
   c. Preparing a research paper on a topic about which you have limited knowledge.
   d. Conducting a workshop on refinishing furniture (assume you are not an expert).
2. Choose one human relations technique and prepare a team presentation on how this technique can be used to improve communication. Consider including a brief role play.

TEAMWORK

Editing Practice

Which of the six Cs of communication is violated in each of the following sentences?
1. We would like to take this opportunity to welcome all retirees.
2. We demand that you make a payment now.
3. The pictures will be sent separately.
4. The sales manager told the associate that he would not attend the meeting.
5. The new Zellers store will have the ribbon-cutting ceremony on Wednesday, August 28.
6. The prices will be $2, $6, and $4.

Discussion Points

1. Study Figure 1.2. With whom do employees and supervisors in the two divisions directly communicate?
   Why do you think it is inappropriate for an employee to communicate directly with management? What communication problems could this cause?
2. How can speech and appearance provide a tone of a company you represent? Brainstorm examples of both positive and negative tones.

Ethical and Socially Acceptable Business Communications

An act has no ethical quality unless it is chosen out of several choices.

—William James

Ethics

Ethics are the moral principles of right and wrong by which a person is guided. The issue of ethics doesn't surface unless there are choices to be made. For example, if you find a wallet without identification on the floor in a store, you have several choices. Those choices include (1) walking away and leaving the wallet on the floor, (2) turning the wallet in to the customer service desk, (3) putting the wallet in your pocket and leaving the store with it, (4) taking out and keeping any money that was in the wallet and leaving the wallet on the floor, and (5) taking out and keeping any money that was in it and then turning the wallet in to the customer service desk. The ethical person will choose option two; the unethical person will choose from among the other options.

Being ethical also means working toward the good of all rather than toward the good of a specialized group at the expense of some other group. Many organizations develop a written **code of ethics** so that employees and customers have a written record of the philosophy of the group. A code of ethics states the goals of the organization in terms of how it operates and how it treats customers and competitors. An example from the Winnipeg Police Service is provided in Figure 1.3. Some companies have all their employees sign a statement of business ethics.

We often hear about business practices being legal and being ethical. What is the difference? Laws determine whether or not something is legal. The goal of every business communicator should be to conduct all business in a legal and ethical manner. It is possible for an activity to be legal but unethical. For instance, suppose you purchase a camera from a store with a 30-day return policy with the intention of using it for your vacation and then returning the camera for a full refund. Your behaviour would be legal but unethical.

Winnipeg Police Service

Police Officer's Code of Ethics

As a police officer, I recognize that my primary obligation is to
serve the public effectively and efficiently by protecting lives and
property preventing and detecting offences, and preserving peace
and order. I will faithfully administer the law in a just, impartial,
and reasonable manner, preserving the equality, rights, and privileges of citizens as afforded by law. I accept that all persons rich
or poor, old or young, learned or illiterate, are equally entitled to
courtesy, understanding, and compassion. I will not be disparag-
ing of any race, creed, or class of people. In the performance of
my duties, I acknowledge the limits of my authority and promise
not to use it for my personal advantage. I vow never to accept gra-
tuities or favours or compromise myself or the service in any way.
I will conduct my public and private life as an example of stability, fidelity, morality, and without equivocation adhere to the same
standards of conduct which I am bound by duty to enforce. I will
exercise self-discipline at all times. I will act with propriety
toward my associates in law enforcement and the criminal justice
system. With self-confidence, decisiveness, and courage, I will
accept all the challenges, hardships, and vicissitudes of my profession. In relationships with my colleagues, I will endeavour to
develop an "esprit de corps". I will preserve the dignity of all persons and subordinate my own self - interests for the common
good. I will honour the obligations of my office and strive to
attain excellence in the performance of my duties.

Treating Others with Honesty and Fairness

One way of incorporating ethics into business communication is to be honest
and fair, and to treat other persons as you would like to be treated. A new sales
associate with no previous retail experience was advised by her hardware
manager that a certain brand of mediocre-quality tools paid a higher commission
rate than the top-quality tools. (A *commission* is a fee paid to the sales associate
as a result of the sale.) The manager suggested making the following response
to prospective customers who asked about the quality of the mediocre brand:
"It is a very popular item." This statement implies that the tools are a good
quality. While it is not a lie, the statement is misleading—and unethical.

Stating Facts Instead of Opinions

Business communication should be ethical and communicate information
that is true. Another way of incorporating ethics into business communication
is to use objective language and verifiable information. For example, suppose

you are asked for a recommendation about a former employee's dependability for a job. Instead of saying "Sally will not be dependable," say "Our attendance records show that Sally missed work 11 times in the last three months." Stating a verifiable fact instead of your opinion lets the receiver form his or her own opinion of Sally. Many human resources departments have strict guidelines in place that specify how to respond to these queries.

Another example of providing honest, verifiable information occurs when a company requests a reference check on a prospective employee. Information about this person's attendance record, academic qualifications, and length of employment with a previous organization gives verifiable fact rather than opinion.

Providing Full and Accurate Details

Ethical business communication should not withhold information that could cause the communication to be misinterpreted. Deliberately withholding information about the dangers of a product, and misleading the public by misrepresenting facts are examples of unethical communication.

For example, if a tire manufacturer fails to inform customers about defects in certin sizes of tires, this is unethical communication.

A more subtle example of unethical communication occurs in the following situation. An environmental group releases data indicating the city water is unsafe to drink at the same time that the water company releases data indicating the city water is safe to drink. The water company tests samples of water at the water company and in homes throughout the city. The environmental group tests water at points along feeder waterways, just downstream from a golf course that uses fertilizer and other chemicals to enhance the appearance of the grass on the golf course. Both groups are accurately reporting the results of their tests. However, drinking water should be tested after it has been processed, treated, and released by the water company to homes and businesses. Clearly, since the two groups are using different sources for their data, the test results are different. Which group is releasing ethical communication?

Here are some other examples of the type of unethical communication you might encounter on the job: (1) Your supervisor asks you to "adjust" some figures in a report to make the results look better; (2) you work in the lab of a company that makes no-fat cookies, but you know they contain some fat; (3) your city promotes recycling to appeal to environmentalists, but you know that the "recycled" materials really go to the landfill with the rest of the garbage.

Maintaining Confidentiality

Confidential information is private or secret and should be released only to people with a proven need to know. Confidentiality is another important aspect of ethics. Right-to-privacy laws have been passed to legislate confidentiality in certain instances. For example, medical records, lawyers' client files, and banking and financial records are considered confidential information. Businesses and industries that develop new products and technologies, such as the electronics and pharmaceutical industries, have confidential information that should not fall into the hands of competitors.

Avoiding Discrimination in Communication

When you are communicating, it is important to avoid discrimination in what you say and do. *Discrimination* is the act of treating or judging someone on a basis other than that of individual merit. **Discriminatory language** refers to the biased statements and terms that are unfairly used to set an individual or group apart from others.

Behaving in an ethical manner obviously means avoiding discrimination. In addition, discrimination is also illegal in Canada and contravenes the law set out in the Charter of Rights and Freedoms, which became part of the Canadian Constitution in 1982. The Equality Rights section of the Charter states that "Every individual is equal before and under the law and has the right to the equal protection and equal benefit of the law without discrimination based on race, national or ethnic origin, colour, religion, sex, age or mental or physical disability."

In keeping with this law, the Treasury Board of the Canadian government published "Fair Communication Practices" in 1990 as part of its *Treasury Board Manual, Information and Administrative Management, Appendix E.* This document gives guidelines for using language that eliminates sexual stereotyping, ensures fair and representative depiction of ethnic and visible minorities, Aboriginal peoples, and people with disabilities. These guidelines seek to ensure that communications demonstrate courtesy and respect for all, regardless of gender, origin, or disability.

Develop the habit of using gender-neutral words and inclusive (nondiscriminatory) words to avoid offending any person or groups and to demonstrate respect for all people.

Use Gender-Neutral Words

Gender-specific words indicate male or female. Such **gender-bias words** show favouritism toward or imply a greater importance of one gender over another. Gender-specific words and expressions are not appropriate in today's business communication. Instead, use gender-neutral words that don't emphasize male or female.

Avoid expressions such as "He's the best man for the job," which implies that men are more capable than women. Instead, say "He's the best person

A politician is only as good as his latest scandal.

(Politicians are only as good as their latest scandal.

OR

A politician is only as good as his/her latest scandal.)

[Adapted from the Writer's Block Calendar.]

Gender-Specific	Gender-Neutral
businesswoman	business person, business worker
chairman	chairperson
fireman	firefighter
foreman	supervisor
housewife	homemaker
mailman	mail carrier
newsman	newscaster, reporter
salesman	sales associate, salesperson
spokesman	spokesperson
stewardess	flight attendant
weatherman	weather reporter

for the job." Similarly, avoid a phrase such as "executives and their wives," which implies that all executives are male. A more neutral statement would be "executives and their partners."

Use Inclusive Language

As human beings, we have a need to feel included in groups and activities and to be treated with respect. Communication must therefore use **inclusive language**—language that does not single out people who have different characteristics, beliefs, values, and attitudes from your own.

Use unbiased and inclusive language when communicating—especially when referring to a person's physical or mental condition, race, religion, age, and so on. It is important to be aware of people's differences and to appreciate the richness provided in Canadian society by their diversity. Always use bias-free language. Some words have negative connotations or meanings. For example, *handicapped* is more negative than *physically challenged*. Here are some guidelines for using inclusive language.

1. Describe people in terms of their skills and abilities, not in terms of their gender, race, cultural background, appearance, religion, age, or physical challenges.

   Not: My assistant has great computer skills and is "easy on the eyes" too.
   Better: My assistant has great computer skills.

   Not: A well-informed Asian doctor conducted the 10 a.m. tour.
   Better: A well-informed doctor conducted the 10 a.m. tour.

2. Don't make assumptions about people based on their gender, race, cultural background, looks, religion, age, or physical challenges.

   Not: David did well at the Vancouver sales office because he is Chinese.
   Better: David did well at the Vancouver sales office.

   Not: Elderly clients are grumpy and hard to deal with.
   Better: Some clients are grumpy or hard to deal with.

3. Use preferred terms for members of different groups.

   Asian (Do not use *Oriental* and be specific if possible: for example, *Japanese, Chinese*).

   English, Welsh, Scottish, Irish (Not all the British are English. Some are Welsh, Scottish, or Irish.)

   Jewish (Do not use *Hebrew*, which refers to a language, or *Israelite*, which is a biblical term. Also, not all Israelis are Jews.)

   Muslim (Avoid using *Muhammadan. Moslem,* however, is acceptable. Remember that not all Muslims are Arabs; and not all Arabs are Muslim.)

   Aboriginal people (Canadian Indian) may also be acceptable, but not *Indian*, which is used for natives of India. It is best to be as specific as possible: for example, Indian, Inuit, and Mètis peoples of Canada.

4. Use preferred terms to describe specific conditions.

Not:	Better:
crazy, weird	eccentric, offbeat
deaf and dumb	hearing- and speech-impaired
handicapped, disabled, crippled	physically challenged
retarded	developmentally delayed

Avoiding Stereotyping and Prejudice

Stereotyping is a simplified and standardized conception or image of a person, group, etc. Stereotyping is often negative and based on false or incomplete information. It is often a result of a belief that one's own ethnic group or culture is superior to other ethnic groups or cultures. Such a belief is called ethnocentrism.

A **prejudice** is a negative attitude about an individual, a group, or a race, or about its supposed characteristics. Prejudices are conclusions that are drawn without sufficient facts.

Some examples of stereotypes are:

Individual or Group	Stereotype
overweight people	lazy; overeat
people with poor grammar	lower class; uneducated; dumb
Asian people	intelligent; industrious: bad drivers
young black people	good athletes
women	nurturing; emotional
men	non-domestic; good math/spatial skills; insensitive
tall, slender women	would make good models
people who talk slowly	dumb
homeless people	alcoholics; crazy
lawyers	untrustworthy; mercenary

Your view or interpretation of events and people is based on your personal experiences and on information you have heard or read. If you have had a negative experience with your first contact with someone from a group, you tend to assume all people in this group are the same. For example, if your first experience with a motorcycle rider was a bad one where the person was a gang member, had numerous tattoos, wore black leather, and used excessive profanity, you would probably have a negative opinion of motorbike riders from that point on. Whereas, if your first experience of the community of motorcyclists was at a fundraiser they sponsored for seriously-ill children, and you observed how hard they worked to raise the money, you would probably have a positive opinion of bikers in general.

A physically challenged person on TV made the comment that he resented people saying he was "tied to" his wheelchair. He made the point that his wheelchair enables him to get to most places the rest of us do.

Discriminatory Actions

You can offend another person with your actions as well as words. People who are blind are frequently spoken to in a loud voice. Remember, they are vision-impaired, not hearing-impaired. Likewise, people who wear a hearing aid frequently find that others speak to them as though they were hearing-impaired. The hearing aid usually corrects the hearing problem. Moreover, if the volume of speaking is much above normal, the voice of the speaker is distorted, and the volume on the hearing aid will need to be adjusted.

People who don't speak English aren't deaf; they just don't understand. Don't shout; speaking louder won't help them understand, but speaking a little more clearly and slowly may help.

As you communicate in school and at work, strive to use language that is inclusive and not biased. Doing so will help you to avoid misunderstandings and to treat others equally and fairly.

Review of Key Terms

1. How are *ethics* incorporated into business communications?
2. How can you avoid *discrimination* in writing?
3. What are *gender-biased* words? Give two examples and explain why each is unacceptable.

Practical Application

1. Rewrite each of the following sentences, correcting the biased and discriminatory language. A sentence may have more than one error.
   a. The old mailman was very dependable.
   b. My girl Friday is a cute brunette and has excellent telephone skills.
   c. Her Catholic parents always stressed the importance of honesty.
   d. The blind teacher made three important points at the meeting.
   e. Danny Jones, the black quadriplegic, sang the national anthem at the ceremony.
   f. Murray is definitely the best man for the job.
   g. The salesman gave us a free gift for completing the credit application.
   h. His Vietnamese mother was a strict disciplinarian.

2. Mary's family comes from Newfoundland. Mary likes her job at a large accounting firm in Toronto, but sometimes overhears jokes about people from Newfoundland. Although the jokes are not directed at her, she is offended by them. What should Mary do?

TEAMWORK

Editing Practice

Spelling Alert! Correct any spelling errors in the following sentences.

1. Mr. Downing felt his bussiness math was the most valuable skill he had learned in school.
2. Accruels and defferals are difficult aspects of the accounting procedure.
3. Mrs. Soong does reel esate apraisals in addition to teaching at the college.
4. The whether was so cold that most of the plants died.
5. The hotel manager made an extra effort to acommodate the huricane victims.

Discussion Points

1. Comment on the following statement: "Withholding information cannot be classified as unethical communication because no communication has taken place." Support your answer by relating it to the definition of ethics.
2. Give some examples of confidential information and describe how this information must be handled.

Global Communications

The newest computer can merely compound, at speed, the oldest problem in the relations between human beings, and in the end, the communicator will be confronted with the old problem of what to say and how to say it.

—Edward R. Murrow, broadcast news journalist

Choosing a Communication Method

Technology offers a variety of options for communicating spoken and written messages. Many factors should be considered when choosing a technology tool for a communication. These considerations include not only items such as cost, speed, and quality, but also the needs and preferences of those receiving your communications. An awareness of, and sensitivity to, differences arising from such things as geographical location, language, and cultural differences are important factors in your appropriate use of technology.

Technology provides us, as communicators, with choices. However, technology does not change our need to carefully analyze each situation on its individual merits, plan and compose our messages with care, and choose our transmission media to derive the maximum return on our efforts. Automatically choosing the latest technology does not necessarily guarantee that you will get the desired response.

Time and Speed

Time refers to how fast you can get a message to its intended receiver. The speed with which a message or document reaches its intended receiver is affected by both preparation time and delivery time.

One advantage of using e-mail or fax technology is that a message can be delivered after office hours. Oral presentations generally take a significant amount of time to prepare and present, but if a presentation is videotaped, it can be reused making the initial time and cost worthwhile.

Quality

Quality shows in the ability to deliver a professional-looking message. There are times when the most important factor is not that the message look nicely printed on bond paper, but that there is simply a hard copy of record.

Quality is especially important when you are sending a message to someone outside the organization. Written messages should be formatted attractively, with appropriate paragraphing and use of white space. Both written documents and e-mail messages should be checked for correctness.

Confidentiality

When transmitting any document, you need to determine whether the document contains restricted information. For example, a performance appraisal must be transmitted in a way that maintains confidentiality.

It is vital to safeguard log-in information that provides access to e-mail and voice-mail messages.

Personalization

You need to know the customers you serve. Some people want the human touch in their dealings with organizations. A person who feels comfortable with technology will see voice mail as a normal business practice and will leave a message and wait for the call back. The person who disdains the "cold, impersonal" machine may simply hang up, thinking "If I'm not important enough to have a person take my call, forget it!"

Hard Copy Availability

It may be critical to have a written record of a document or message. Technologies that use a paper-based document such as word processing and fax automatically provide a hard copy of any document that is transmitted. Some legal restrictions may apply to the acceptability of faxes. Check first if you are faxing legal or other sensitive documents.

What about e-mail? E-mail messages can easily be printed from the screen and then filed, but otherwise they do not leave a hard copy. They can, however, remain electronically filed.

Message Complexity

If a message is complex, you would be wise to send a written document. When a message covers a number of points or deals with complex issues, most people like to have a hard copy of the message to refer to in subsequent messages or conversations. If an issue or concern is simple and easy to understand, voice mail, the telephone, or e-mail may be the most expedient way of conveying the message. Even a simple message needs to be followed up with the information in writing if the consequences could be far-reaching.

Communicating Around the World

Through advances in technology and telecommunications our world is expanding each day. Our messages can travel to almost any part of the world in a matter of minutes, seconds—even nanoseconds! As we communicate on an increasingly global basis, it is crucial that we understand the people we communicate with and the culture they live in. **Culture** refers to the customs, beliefs, lifestyles, and practices of a group of people.

Cross-cultural communication means communicating—either in writing or verbally—with people who are from a culture different from your own. To communicate effectively, you must understand and respect cultural

You may also want to make souvenirs for your guest to take home as memorandums.

(mementos)

differences and be adaptable. Many of the same principles of cross-cultural communication need to be observed in both **domestic** and **international communication**. *Domestic* refers to one's own country, while *international* communication goes beyond one's national boundaries or viewpoints and involves two or more countries. An example of an international company would be a law firm or an advertising agency that has branches, business dealings, or employees in more than one country.

When working with people from different cultural, religious, and ethnic groups, keep in mind these guidelines.

- Research the customs of the communities in which you do business.

- Keep note of significant religious holidays that affect the company's employees and clients.

- Do not make comments or jokes based on cultural or religious practices.

- Do not imitate cultural language expressions or accents in an attempt to be friendly.

We need to be aware of, and respect, cultural preferences and beliefs different from our own. This includes being aware of significant religious holidays. For example, if a business conference is scheduled at the same time as the Jewish High Holy Days of Rosh Hashana or Yom Kippur, Jewish members would be placed in an awkward position.

It is also critical to know the business protocol in a country where you and your company do business. A lack of such knowledge can easily result in behaving in an impolite or disrespectful fashion. In Japan, for example, business cards are considered very important and are treated with care. Cards are presented face up and accepted with both hands, and it is considered very disrespectful to write on a person's business card.

Time Zones

From British Columbia and the Yukon in the west, to Newfoundland in the east, Canada spans six time zones. These time differences must be taken into consideration with some forms of domestic communication. When it is 9 a.m. in Montreal, it is 6 a.m. in Vancouver, 7 a.m. in Calgary, 8 a.m. in Winnipeg, 10 a.m. in Halifax, and 10:30 a.m. in Newfoundland. If you begin work at 9 a.m. in Halifax and need to talk to a colleague in your Vancouver office, you must calculate the time difference.

Similarly, time zones must be considered when making international calls. If you work in Winnipeg and wish to call London, England, during regular business hours, there is a time difference to be considered, usually six hours, depending on changes for daylight savings time in England and Manitoba.

The widespread use of voice mail, fax, and e-mail has freed us from many of the time difference restrictions, as information can be sent or received at any hour using these methods.

Holidays

People from diverse cultural and religious backgrounds make up our Canadian population, and a variety of festivals and celebrations have been included on the Canadian calendar. For example, Chinese New Year, which

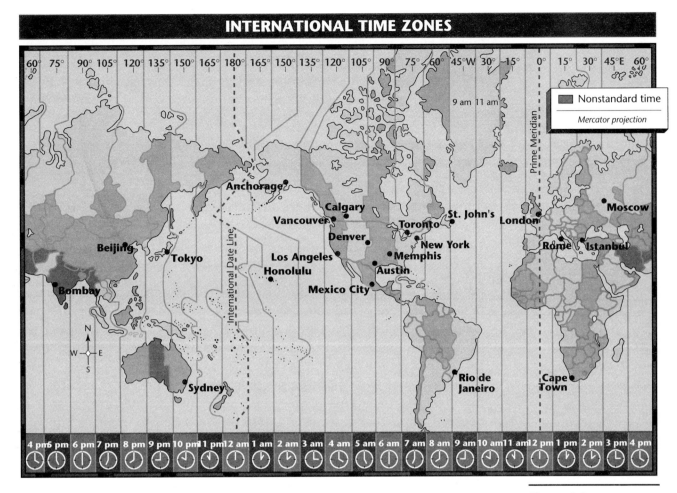

INTERNATIONAL TIME ZONES

Nonstandard time

Mercator projection

Figure 1.4
World Times Zones
Map of International Time Zones. The earth's surface is divided into 34 time zones.

Thinking Critically. *How might a lack of knowledge about time zones hinder international communications?*

is governed by the cycle of the moon, can occur any time between January 20 and February 19. Different provinces also celebrate special days. For example, Quebec's unique summer holiday is St. Jean Baptiste Day on June 24. On this same date, Newfoundland celebrates Discovery Day.

Other countries celebrate different holidays from the ones celebrated in Canada, and businesses are closed on different days. For example, Canada Day and Thanksgiving are Canadian holidays; those two holidays are normal working days in other countries. Likewise, other countries have their own national holidays. Even though Canada celebrates St. Patrick's Day informally, in Ireland it is a legal holiday. May Day on May 1 is a legal holiday in Great Britain. A holiday similar to our Canada Day is celebrated on different dates in these other countries:

U.S.A. (Independence Day)	July 4
Greece (Independence Day)	March 25
Italy (Liberation Day)	April 25
Japan (Constitution Day)	May 3
India (Independence Day)	August 15
France (Bastille Day)	July 14
Mexico (Independence Day)	September 16
Germany (Unification Day)	October 3

Microsoft Corporation committed an oops in a Spanish-language version of its Microsoft Word software program. The thesaurus for the program suggested that *maneater, cannibal,* and *barbarian* could be substituted for the Spanish term for *black people.* The program also equated Indians with man-eating savages. Microsoft promised to correct the software.

—The Wall Street Journal

Language

Although English is widely recognized worldwide as the language of business, English is a second language for people in most other countries. Slang, clichés, and jargon make English one of the most complex languages in the world. When communicating with people in other countries, follow these guidelines:

- **Keep figures of speech and clichés to a minimum.** For example, instead of *right as rain*, use *right*. Instead of *to add insult to injury*, use *in addition* or *moreover*.

- **Avoid using cute, fancy, or trendy terms for standard English words.** For example, instead of *legal eagle*, say *lawyer*.

- **Use specific terms.** Instead of *just a little way down the road*, use *5 kilometres*. Instead of *unsanitary conditions*, say *unsafe drinking water*.

- **Be aware of multiple definitions of words.** Some words carry more than one meaning and may be confusing to someone whose first language isn't English. For example, the word *bug*, may refer to an insect, the flu, or a computer-software virus. The word *break* in the sentence *There was a break in the negotiations* can refer to an opening (opportunity for agreement) or a halt (the stopping of talks). Make sure the context makes the meaning clear. This problem is especially troublesome in speech because words that are spelled differently may be pronounced similarly: for example, *sum* and *some*, or *bough* and *bow*.

- **Avoid any form of slang or jargon.** Canadian slang, such as *bad* meaning *good, cool* meaning *in style,* and *awesome* meaning *good, great,* or *excellent,* would be confusing to a person whose first language isn't English.

- **Avoid using abbreviations or acronyms.** An *abbreviation* is a shortened form of a word or phrase. *St.* is an abbreviation for either Street or Saint; *Blvd.* is an abbreviation for Boulevard. An *acronym* is a word formed from the first letter or letters of each word in the phrase, such as *PIN* for *p*ersonal *i*dentification *n*umber or *radar* for *ra*dio *d*etecting *a*nd *r*anging. Acronyms may be unfamiliar, and abbreviations can stand for more than a single term. For example, does the abbreviation *IRA* mean *Irish Republican Army* or does it mean *individual retirement account?* Does *St.* mean *Street* or *Saint?*

- **Use visual aids.** Wherever possible use visual aids to clarify your message. A map, a sketch, or a picture usually enhances verbal or written communication.

If your message must be translated, be aware that many English words do not have an exact translation. Many companies have learned the hard way that some translations cause problems. In his book *The Tongue-Tied American* (Continuum Publishing Corporation, New York, 1980, pp. 6, 7 and 32), Paul Simon gives these examples of problem translations:

- Chevrolet would have a hard time selling its Nova model in Latin American countries. In Spanish, the phrase *no-va* literally means "It does not go."

- General Motors' slogan "Body by Fisher" translates to "Corpse by Fisher" in Flemish.
- The slogan "Come alive with Pepsi" translates to "Pepsi brings your ancestors back from the grave" in Chinese and translates to "Come alive out of the grave" in German.
- Parker pen put on a sales campaign in South America. A less-than-accurate Spanish translation promised buyers that the new ink in the pen would prevent unwanted pregnancies.
- Schweppes Tonic Water advertisements in Italy translated as "bathroom water."
- Cue toothpaste, a Colgate-Palmolive product, was advertised in France with no translation errors but *Cue* happens to be the name of a widely circulated pornographic book.

Because of these kinds of translation problems, companies sometimes change product names or slogans before marketing products in other countries.

Business Etiquette

Many cultures have a high regard for formality and social rules. In Canada most people are very time conscious and view punctuality as important. In some other cultures, however, it is not considered rude to be quite late for an appointment or to keep a person waiting for a long time. In fact, in some cultures arriving early or on time is considered rude.

Customs in various countries regarding clothing styles, greetings, and eye contact are also different. Some examples include the following:

- **Clothing styles.** Women in some cultures do not appear in public with their faces uncovered, while other cultures accept quite skimpy attire in public.
- **Greeting others.** In some cultures men kiss each other on the cheek or bow from the waist when they meet rather than shake hands as men and women do in Canada. A woman being introduced in the business world in Canada shakes hands; in another cultural setting she may not do so, especially if she is being introduced to a man in a Middle Eastern country.
- **Eye contact.** In some cultures it is considered extremely rude to have direct eye contact with people to whom you are talking. By contrast, in Canada direct eye contact is expected; lack of eye contact is interpreted as disinterestedness, unfriendliness, or perhaps even dishonesty.

Measurements and Currency

Canada and much of the world uses the metric system (a decimal system of measures using units such as metres, kilograms, litres, kilometres, and so on) for measurement. The United States uses U.S. customary units of measurement (that is, feet, pounds, gallons, and miles).

Most countries have their own currency. For example, Japan has the yen; South Africa, the rand; and Mexico, the peso. Twelve European countries have established a common currency called the euro. The exchange rate, the ratio at which the principal unit of two currencies can be traded, fluctuates daily.

Marilyn and Bill had recently arrived in Belgium for a four-month stay to help with the start-up of a new plant. The first Saturday, they were invited to a company party at 6 p.m. at a local restaurant. They arrived about ten minutes before six and were surprised to find they were the first guests. They became worried when no one else had arrived by 6:20 p.m. Finally, at 6:35 p.m. the first guests arrived, and by 7:05 p.m. most guests were present and the group sat down to eat. In Belgium, arriving late is the custom, but Marilyn and Bill were embarrassed by not knowing this custom.

Review of Key Terms

1. *Cross-cultural communication* occurs in both *domestic* and *international business communication.* Please explain this statement.

Practical Application

1. For each of the following tasks, decide which communication technology would be the most appropriate for the situation. Be prepared to explain the reasoning behind your choice.

   a. A manager needs to warn two employees that their performance is below company standards.

   b. A national sales manager wants to notify sales representatives (57 of them) that their most popular product will no longer be produced, but a new and improved product will be replacing it.

   c. The chairman of the office technology committee needs to notify committee members of the next meeting and supply them with an agenda for that meeting.

2. On July 14, Maria Hong discovers she needs to telephone the Paris office to explain that the merchandise they ordered will be two weeks late. She know that the receptionist speaks English. Maria has never made an overseas phone call. What does she need to know before she places the call?

3. Choose a country that you would like to research. Imagine that your employer will be travelling there on business. Write a brief summary of the country that describes its customs in business clothing and social etiquette, its national holidays, its time zone, its currency, and any other important information your employer should know.

TEAMWORK

Editing Practice

Proper proofreading involves checking the spelling of each word and the meaning of the word within the sentence. Proofread the following paragraph. Make a list of all the errors. Then rewrite or type the paragraph so that it is free of errors.

Inter-culturel experiences are important to help us understand people form all parts of the world. We tend to assume that everyone has the same beleifs, customs, and practises that we do. Being aware of these diferences will help us to be more tolerant and understanding of people from other cultures and contries.

Discussion Point

How does jargon or slang interfere with cross-cultural communication?

Chapter 1 Wrap-Up

SUMMARY

▶ Communication can be divided into three main categories: oral, written, and nonverbal. Using these communication categories, we inquire, inform, persuade, and develop goodwill. This process involves a sender and a receiver who send, receive and interpret messages, and provide each other with feedback.

▶ Communication barriers interfere with the communication process. These barriers include emotional and physical distractions, and cultural and language differences.

▶ Effective communication is an essential ingredient of successful family, social, and business relationships. It involves using listening, speaking, reading, and writing skills.

▶ Internal communication within an organization flows in a predetermined pattern to achieve the objectives of that organization. External communication involves communicating with people outside your organization and is usually more formal in tone.

▶ All communication should satisfy the six Cs of communication by being clear, complete, concise, consistent, correct, and courteous.

▶ Interpersonal, or human relations, skills assist communication by building and maintaining favourable relationships and goodwill.

▶ Ethical communications are honest, fair, provide full and accurate details, and respect confidentiality.

▶ Socially acceptable communications avoid using discriminatory and biased language, stereotyping, and displaying prejudice.

▶ Global communication requires you to choose a suitable communication method, to be aware of time zones, holidays, systems of measurements, and currency in other areas. It also involves using clear language that is free of jargon and respects the business etiquette of other cultures.

CASE 1.1

Pete works for Soft-Tech, a Canadian software company in British Columbia that is involved in international business. Last week, Pete attended a company seminar titled "The Clumsy Canadian." The aim of the seminar was to make employees aware of appropriate—and inappropriate—behaviour when dealing with people from other areas or cultures.

CASE 1.1 continued

The seminar leader used actual examples of serious communication problems that had prompted management to offer the seminar. Some of the examples were as follows:

1. An employee from the Vancouver office, where everyone wore casual clothes, dressed in blue jeans, boots, and a flowered shirt for a meeting with officers of a major bank customer in Vancouver.

2. Victoria plant employees frequently tried to return calls to a major New York customer after 3 p.m. British Columbia time.

3. A conference call was scheduled on May 1 with a vendor in England.

4. At a meeting with some Aboriginal prospective clients, the company engineers talked down to the band representatives. The band was run as a multimillion-dollar corporation, and the representatives were the chief executive officer (CEO) and the chief financial officer (CFO).

For each of these examples, suggest more appropriate ways to handle the situation.

CASE 1.2

In May 2000, a tragic disaster occurred—the water supply in Walkerton, a town in Ontario's rural heartland, became contaminated with E. coli bacteria. Seven people died from drinking contaminated water and thousands more became seriously ill. A lengthy inquiry ensued to determine what went wrong. The human suffering, the economic impact, and the social impact were enormous. In this town of 5000 people, everyone knew someone who had died or was sick. It was estimated that the water tragedy cost at least $155 million, if human suffering was factored in. In the early days of this disaster, the town's local medical officer of health stunned Canada by claiming that this tragedy could have been prevented. Dr. Murray McQuigge stated that the Walkerton Public Utilities Commission had known for several days that there was a problem with the water before they informed the public.

What is your personal opinion about the ethical position of ignoring or withholding facts and information?

Communicating in Your Career

To maintain a competitive edge in a career, people read—they read about new concepts, new products, and even new regulations.

Why is it important to read about what is happening in your profession on a regular basis? What kinds of material could you read to keep up to date in your chosen career?

On the Web

How does non-verbal communication differ around the world? Examine Web of Culture for gesture tips. Go to **http://www.webofculture.com/previews/ gestures_preview.asp**.

Key Terms

Chapter 2

Developing Oral Communication Skills

Chapter Learning Outcomes

After successfully completing this chapter, you will have demonstrated the ability to:

▶ outline the role of oral communication in business and the forms of oral communication;
▶ give examples of techniques for successful telephone communication;
▶ explain the role of nonverbal communication and speech qualities in effective communication;
▶ outline strategies for overcoming listening barriers and using effective listening techniques;
▶ plan and conduct a meeting;
▶ deliver both formal and informal presentations;
▶ list the qualities of good visual aids and explain how technology can facilitate their use.

As Margaret Reilly enters the reception area of the Maritime Building, she is greeted by the warm smile and friendly voice of the receptionist asking, "May I help you?" She replies, "I'm Margaret Reilly. I have a ten o'clock appointment with Ms. Truillo, the director of marketing."

"Ms. Truillo's office is on the fifth floor, Suite 528. She is expecting you; I'll let Ms. Truillo know that you are on your way to her office," the receptionist responds. She then directs Margaret to an elevator.

The director of marketing has expressed an interest in having Margaret's company develop presentations for Maritime's sales and marketing campaigns.

As Margaret steps from the elevator a young man approaches her. "Good morning, Ms. Reilly; I'm Bradley Smith, Ms. Truillo's administrative assistant. Ms. Truillo will be with you as soon as she completes a conference call. Please make yourself comfortable. Would you like a cup of coffee or tea?"

While she waits, Margaret notices several associates quietly engaged in telephone conversations. In one corner, someone is explaining and demonstrating how to operate a new photocopier. Margaret notices that the demonstration is being interpreted into sign language for one of the office associates. In a glass-enclosed conference area, a small group is seated around a conference table, participating in a teleconference. Then, as Margaret is shown into Ms. Truillo's office, she realizes how fortunate she is to have had training in oral communication. She is about to make a presentation to an important potential client.

As you read Chapter 2, identify some strategies that Margaret could use to make a successful oral presentation.

Basics of Oral Communication

▶ **Key Terms**

▶ "warm" transfer
▶ "dead" air
▶ voice-mail greeting

Our voice is both a window and a mirror. The words we use are a mirror, reflecting the way the world touches us. The way we say those words is a window into our hearts and minds.

—Goldie Hawn, actor

As you saw in the case at the beginning of the chapter, Margaret was convinced of the importance of oral communication in the business world. This conviction, however, grew after her visit to the Maritime Company. From the receptionist who greeted her in the lobby to the director of marketing, information was continually being transmitted orally from one employee to another; from employees to customers and vendors; and from customers, vendors, and other outsiders to employees of the firm. The success of any business organization depends, to a very large degree, upon the success of its members in making themselves understood and in persuading others to accept their ideas.

The Role of Oral Communication in Business

Although written communication is important in transacting business, oral communication is used more often and by more people. Some business positions require the use of oral communication almost exclusively, and the people who fill these jobs are hired on the strength of their ability to speak well. For example, sales associates, administrative assistants, customer service representatives, paralegals, and medical assistants must be highly skilled in oral communication. Whatever the job title, all business professionals make extensive use of oral communication in carrying out their job responsibilities.

Your ability to speak clearly, correctly, and convincingly will play a vital role in helping you achieve your success in the business world. In many work-related situations, you will do much of the talking. You will seek to solve problems; you will be assigned to project teams; you will participate in and conduct meetings and small-group discussions; you will speak to supervisors and colleagues, to the public, and to business and professional groups. In your daily contacts with those inside and outside your organization, you will use oral communication to make requests, provide instructions, and give information.

Business professionals use oral communication in a variety of ways and settings. Professionals depend upon oral communication when engaged in activities such as the following:

- *Explaining or reporting to supervisors, subordinates, and associates on the same level.* Report to a supervisor about the status of a project. Direct a subordinate to complete a task. Work with peers as part of a team.
- *Giving information to customers and potential customers.* Answer face-to-face or telephone inquiries about items or services offered by your company. Give presentations describing products and services provided.
- *Acquiring information necessary to conduct the everyday affairs of business.* Speak with vendors and suppliers to request information about products or order supplies. Speak with outside consultants such as accountants, lawyers, and computer specialists.
- *Participating in meetings.* Meet with all personnel levels to discuss current and future projects. Meet with consultants or customers to discuss products and services. Meet with teams to complete an assigned project.
- *Participating in informal discussions with fellow employees.* Ask coworkers to contribute for flowers for a hospitalized colleague. Plan recreational functions for employees. Attend an informal social event for employees.
- *Giving instruction to an individual or a group.* Train new employees. Instruct customers in the use of newly purchased products. Instruct patients in caring for themselves.
- *Interviewing employees and prospective employees.* Interview job applicants. Participate in performance appraisals.
- *Participating in social-business conversations.* Engage in conversation with representatives from civic and professional organizations. Congratulate associates and business acquaintances on their accomplishments.
- *Giving formal speeches before groups.* Give a speech before a civic group. Talk to students (elementary, high school, or college level) about your work experience.

These are just a few examples of oral communication activities that take place every day in professional settings—activities that rely for their success almost wholly upon effective oral communication.

Forms of Oral Communication

Oral communication occurs in many different forms; some used more frequently than others. Among the most commonly used methods of oral communication are the following:

- *Face-to-face conversations.* Interviews, sales, social-business situations, informal discussions with coworkers.
- *Group discussions or meetings.* Employee group discussions, team meetings, meetings of business and professional organizations.
- *Telephone conversations.* Discussions with a colleague, a supervisor, a customer, or a supplier.

- *Voice-mail messages.* Recording a telephone message for someone to hear later.
- *Formal speeches.* Debates; panels; addresses to employees, the public, customers, or professional groups.
- *Instruction.* Conducting orientation and training sessions for employees.
- *Dictation and recording.* Dictating letters and memos for transcription, or recording meetings electronically.
- *Using voice recognition software.* Bypassing the traditional keyboard method of entry by using voice recognition technology to enter text or data into a computer.

Each of these forms of oral communication requires a slightly different technique. The difference may be (1) the amount and kind of preparation, (2) the manner in which the voice is projected, or (3) the style in which the speaker makes the presentation. For example, speaking over the telephone requires a knowledge of how far to position the telephone mouthpiece or headset microphone from the lips and how much the speaker's voice should be projected. Leading a meeting requires knowledge of parliamentary procedure. Speaking to a large group requires experience with a microphone. Teaching a class requires that the instructor know how to ask questions properly. Participating in a team meeting requires the ability to think quickly and to put your thoughts into understandable language without hesitation.

Communicating One-on-One

High on the list of communication activities for most business employees is communicating orally on a one-on-one basis. The opening case study for this chapter describes a variety of situations in which business people use speaking skills to effectively perform daily tasks.

Business employees talk with colleagues in their own departments, with their supervisors, with top management, and with service personnel many times during the working day. In addition, many employees talk either on the telephone or in person with individuals outside the company—customers, patients, clients, sales representatives, suppliers, visitors, and various people requesting or giving information. Many business employees depend heavily on their oral communication skills to earn their living—sales representatives, personnel interviewers, and customer service representatives are just a few examples.

Use the following suggestions as guidelines for communicating effectively on a one-on-one basis, whether speaking to someone in person or over the telephone.

Listen Attentively

Listening attentively and showing interest in the other person are just two attributes of a good communicator. In a one-on-one or telephone conversation, you alternate between the roles of speaker and listener. As a speaker, part of your responsibility is to listen to what the other person says, to be courteous, and to get the necessary information. For example, a sales associate should listen to a customer's inquiry or complaint in order to know how to answer the customer. A medical assistant needs to ask questions and then listen to the patient's responses to find out about the patient's illness. Section 2.3 gives detailed information on effective listening techniques.

Use the Person's Name

Be certain that you clearly hear the name of the person whom you have met or talked with on the telephone for the first time. Repeat the name right after it is given to you. "I'm happy to meet you, Mr. Zolner."

If you aren't absolutely sure of the person's name, ask that it be repeated. You can say, "I didn't hear your name clearly," or "How do you pronounce (or spell) your name?" Then, after hearing the name, pronounce it aloud to fix it in your mind.

Whenever it is appropriate, use the name once or twice during the conversation. "Yes, I understand, Mr. Zolner."

Finally, always be sure that you say the person's name in your good-bye: "Good-bye, Mr. Zolner. Thank you for calling ABC Company."

Permit Others to Talk

Don't do all the talking. Give the other person a chance to talk, while you listen attentively. Watch for signs that the other person wants to say something or is becoming bored and not listening carefully. No matter how interesting you think the conversation is or how well informed or articulate you think you are, you must give your listener a chance to speak. Otherwise, you will not keep the listener's attention and respect. For example, you might ask questions to let the listener know you are interested in receiving feedback.

Compliment When Appropriate

Compliments are always welcome, so compliment someone whenever the occasion is appropriate. Paying a compliment is especially effective during tense situations. For example, compliment an employee for work well done or for loyalty. However, never pay a compliment unless you can do so honestly and convincingly. Insincerity is easily detected.

Keep Conversations Concise

Since time is valuable, you should keep your conversations to the point. If you are asked for opinions, give them clearly and concisely. Being concise, however, does not mean being brusque. Try to sense the amount of information the situation calls for and act accordingly. Most people do not want to hear unnecessary details or to listen to prolonged excuses for your inability to do something they have requested. Give enough information to satisfy the listener. If you are in doubt, the best policy is to keep your conversations short.

Establish the Best Atmosphere

One way to establish good relations with colleagues and customers is to create a relaxed, conversational atmosphere. You can accomplish this in one-on-one conversations by sitting or standing so that there are no physical barriers between you and the listener. Focus on the conversation. Giving the other person your undivided attention shows courtesy and respect.

Communicating by Telephone

Since the speaker and the listener in a telephone conversation are unable to see each other, they must depend entirely upon their voices to communicate friendliness, interest, and a willingness to be helpful.

The manner in which a customer is treated on the telephone is just as important as good written communication is in developing goodwill—sometimes even more important. All employees create a public image of the company they represent by the manner in which they speak to current and potential clients and customers. A curt or rude employee can cause a business to lose both potential and existing customers. In a telephone conversation, the associate must, through the words and tone used, make listeners feel that their interests are important and that the company wants them to be satisfied.

The telephone is one of the most important communication media in business. You must use it with great skill, whether you are speaking to callers from inside or outside the organization.

Although we are familiar with using the telephone, we may not be using it properly. Some of the following suggestions may seem obvious. Nevertheless, you should read them carefully and follow them whenever you use the telephone for either personal or business use.

Guidelines for Telephone Communications

- *Be courteous.* Remember to use "please" and "thank you". Listen attentively, and don't interrupt. Your tone of voice should convey friendliness and interest. Personalize the call by using the other person's name; this is especially important when talking to a customer.
- *Speak clearly and at a suitable pace.* When giving telephone numbers or other details that the other person will need to write, speak more slowly. Speak directly into the mouthpiece or, if using headphones, make sure that the microphone is properly placed (about the width of two fingers from your mouth).
- *Provide a* **"warm"** *transfer.* If you must transfer the call to someone else, ask the other person's permission to transfer the call. Give the name and extension of the person to whom you are transferring the call, in case the transfer does not go through. Relay to the next person any information already discussed, so that the caller does not have to repeat details. Stay on the line to announce the transfer.
- *Use hold correctly.* Ask the other person's permission before putting him/her on hold. When you come back on the line, thank him/her for holding.
- *Avoid* **"dead"** *air.* Acknowledge comments with an occasional "Yes", "I see", or some other short comment so that the other person knows you are listening. If there is waiting time while you perform a task such as looking up information, explain what you are doing.
- *Make notes.* Write down points you need to remember or follow-up action that must be taken.
- *Verify important details.* Check details such as telephone numbers, account numbers, dates, and names. You should repeat these out loud as they are given to you to make sure you are recording them correctly. If

unsure of the spelling of a person's name, ask him or her to spell it for you.

Receiving Telephone Calls

- *Answer promptly.* You should answer no later than the third ring, and preferably sooner.
- *Greet the caller, and identify yourself.* This pleasantness is achieved both by the words you use and by the tone of your voice. If you know who the caller is, use a greeting such as "Good morning, Mr. Ackley" or "Hello, Abigail." If you do not know who the caller is, identify yourself first: "Ms. Cheney speaking" or "Phyllis Cheney." When answering the telephone for a department, identify both the department and yourself: "Engineering Department, Phyllis Cheney speaking."
- *Close effectively.* If necessary, summarize important points and/or action that will be taken. Offer additional help; for example, "Is there anything else I can help you with today, Ms. Smith?" Thank the caller; for example, "Thank you for calling Acme Tire," or "Thank you for your business." Allow the caller to hang up first.

Making Telephone Calls

- *Plan the call.* A little preparation will save both time and money. This preparation is also important because you may need to leave a voice-mail message.
- *Identify yourself and state the purpose of your call.* For example, "My name is Walter Chen. I would like to speak to the person in charge of adjustments."

Voice Mail

Everyone in business uses voice mail, but often the messages are not clear or complete. Many voice-mail messages ramble and include unnecessary details. Voice mail falls into two categories—**voice-mail greetings** telling callers you are not available, and voice-mail messages left for other people.

Recording a Voice-Mail Greeting

Use the following guidelines when you record a message telling callers you are not available.

- Include your *name* and the name of your *business organization or department.*
- Use *business language.* For example, "Hi" is not professional.
- Include any *special directions* for leaving messages; for example, instructions for marking the message "urgent."
- If appropriate, provide a number where the caller can receive *immediate attention.*
- Keep the message *concise and clear.*
- Speak at a *pace* that is easy to listen to.
- Make sure your *voice tone* is pleasant. There should be a "smile" in your voice.
- If possible, let callers know *when you will return calls;* for example, by the end of the business day.

- *State the information you require;* for example, "Please leave your name, telephone number, and the reason for your call."
- After recording your message, *replay it* to make sure that it conforms to these guidelines. Re-record until you are satisfied.

Leaving Voice Messages for Co-Workers and Customers

Did you ever become impatient or annoyed when retrieving your voice mail? If you did, it was probably because the message was too long, or disorganized, or the person's voice was hard to understand. To ensure that the voice messages you leave are effective, use the following guidelines.

- *Start with your name, business affiliation, or department.* If you are calling inside the company, your name may be sufficient. If the other person does not know you, spell your name if you think they'll have trouble with it.
- *Prepare.* Before you dial, assume that you will get voice mail. Be prepared to deliver a message that covers each point you want to mention. Make notes before you call. If you are prepared, your message will be clear, will flow smoothly, and will contain all the necessary information.
- *Keep your messages brief.* People retrieving voice mail want to do so as efficiently as possible. A short, well-organized message will increase your chances of getting what you need.
- *Slow down when you give your phone number, or other numbers or amounts.* Pretend you're writing the number as you say it. Most callers rush this part of the message, forcing the recipient to replay the message.

Review of Key Terms

1. Explain how you would provide a *"warm" transfer* on the telephone.
2. What is *"dead" air*? How can you avoid its occurrence?

Practical Application

1. Indicate the oral communication activities that you think would be typical for each of the following positions:
   a. Administrative assistant
   b. Paralegal
   c. Medical assistant
   d. Accountant
   e. Sales representative

2. Under three headings—Home, School, Business—list the oral communication activities that you think would be typical.

3. You are an administrative assistant for Ronald Quinn, the president of Quick-Read Books, a discount book publisher. Mr. Quinn has placed you in charge of making arrangements for a conference with Quick-Read's main suppliers to be held at your company's headquarters next month. One of your responsibilities is to contact the suppliers and arrange for their travel and hotel accommodations. Outline the notes you would make to prepare for making the calls. Include details such as the dates, times, and information on how to reach you.

4. Practise reading aloud the following instructions for talking on the telephone so that you do not sound as though you are reading the material or have memorized it. Then make a tape recording of your presentation to determine if you achieved your goal. Review the tape to see if you enunciated distinctly.

    Clear enunciation is extremely important if you wish to be understood by the listener. Each word and each syllable must be pronounced distinctly. Your voice should be well modulated, and you should move your lips, tongue, and jaw freely. Hold the mouthpiece about an inch from your mouth, speaking directly into the receiver. Keep your mouth free of gum, candy, and other objects that could affect your pronunciation or cause you to slur your words. You can usually tell if your words are being heard clearly by the number of times the listener asks you to repeat what you have said.

5. Critique the following voice-mail message. Does it follow the suggestions given in this section for recording a voice mail greeting? Write an improved version.

    "Hi, this is Ilanda Tosie at ExecuSearch. Sorry I can't talk to you right now; I'm either away from my desk or on another call. Please leave me a detailed message and I'll get back to you. Thanks for calling. If you need someone to help you right away, you can dial zero to get back to Reception and they'll connect you with someone. Have a good day."

6. Without using any gestures or diagrams, each team member should give oral directions for one of the following situations:
   a. How to get from your classroom to the campus library.
   b. How to get to the nearest bus stop (or the parking lot) from your classroom.
   c. How to fold a letter for insertion in a standard-sized envelope.
   d. How to reboot a computer.
      Provide constructive feedback that will improve the directions.

7. Each team member should orally describe an object in the classroom without telling the other team members what the object is. If the object is described clearly, the team should be able to identify it.

Editing Practice

Spelling and Vocabulary.   Correct the following sentences. Some contain spelling errors and some test vocabulary.

1. How will the new policy effect office morale?
2. What plans does your company have for deposal of used paper?
3. Which proceedures apply to this job?
4. Let's plan a luncheon to celabrate Pat's promotion.
5. What was the occassion for the early closing of the store?
6. The new computer equiptment arrived this morning.
7. Have you recieved the specifications yet?
8. The new superviser was formally introduced to the employees today.
9. I adviced the new employee to take a public speaking course.
10. On which sight will the new factory be build?

Discussion Points

1. What are some of the guidelines you should use when communicating one-on-one in a business situation?
2. Courtesy is a vital part of effective business communications. A number of educators are concerned about the increasing use of bad language and the decline in civility.
   What is civility and how is it reflected in speech?
3. Check out one of the following Web sites and bring one or two interesting points to the class for discussion: **www.crazydogtravel. com/language. html; www.WordsCanHeal.org.**

▶ **Key Terms**

Nonverbal Communication and Speech Qualities

Every move you make, I'll be watching you.

—Sting, The Police

Nonverbal communication, simply defined, is communicating without words; it is the conscious and subconscious use of actions, behaviours, and interactions with one's surroundings, which convey a message.

Without realizing it, communicators send numerous nonverbal messages every day. Note the occurrences of nonverbal and verbal communication in the following scenario:

> Raoul, president of the student association, entered the classroom with a woman in smart business attire. Raoul was well-groomed and neatly dressed in freshly-pressed pants, matching sweater, and newly polished shoes. As Raoul warmly and respectfully introduced the visitor to the class, her friendly smile acknowledged the participants.
>
> With a sense of excitement, Raoul explained that the visitor was a lawyer who was going to be on campus every Wednesday morning to advise students on legal matters. He was excited because the student association had been trying for some time to make these arrangements. A number of students looked at each other with questioning looks when Raoul made this announcement. The lawyer greeted the class and complimented the student association on this new initiative. She added that she had noticed some puzzled looks and offered to answer any questions about her role on campus.

A positive attitude was conveyed nonverbally by the Raoul's warm and respectful manner and the visitor's friendly smile. Their appearance made an immediate nonverbal statement about their professionalism. The audience members sent a nonverbal message to Raoul and the visitor when they "looked at each other with questioning looks." The lawyer observed this nonverbal message and was able to respond effectively.

The Importance of Nonverbal Communication

Most people agree that actions speak louder than words. Our friends, coworkers, and others often attach more meaning to our nonverbal messages than they do to our verbal messages, because they feel nonverbal messages more accurately reflect attitudes and feelings. For example, suppose two employees are vying for the same promotion to branch manager. When the promotion decision is announced, the employee not getting the promotion congratulates the new branch manager and says, "I'm happy for you." However, his nonverbal facial expression might communicate disappointment about the promotion. Professional courtesy and protocol has compelled the person who did not get the promotion to congratulate the new branch manager. Reading the true feelings of disappointment in his face, the new branch manager takes the opportunity to respond warmly and sincerely, and crosses the room to shake hands. The nonverbal communication these two shared speaks volumes more than the words they exchanged.

A fundamental reality exists in human nature regarding verbal and nonverbal communication. When nonverbal cues contradict verbal cues, people tend to trust their reading of the nonverbal cue. It is easier for people to modify what they say than to modify their nonverbal behavior. Therefore, the nonverbal information you broadcast will have a major influence on the first impressions people form of you and in the subsequent development of personal and professional relationships.

Categories of Nonverbal Communication

Nonverbal communication can be divided into five categories.

Paralanguage

Paralanguage includes nonverbal communication, such as tone, pitch, quality, rate of speech, laughing, crying, belching, and even hesitating or sighing. Paralanguage can help reinforce a verbal message. For example:

- A father says, "awww" to his daughter who has just fallen.
- An ill student with a scratchy voice calls her professor to let him know she will not be able to give her presentation.
- A customer clears his throat to let a busy cashier know he is ready to check out.

Body Language (Kinesics)

Physical attributes such as appearance, facial expressions, eye contact, gestures, and posture all contribute to **body language** or **kinesics.** Here are examples of body language.

- *Physical appearance* includes clothes, jewelry, and grooming. People form impressions about a person's attitudes, personality, and status in the business world by observing physical appearance. Wearing the appropriate clothing to specific events demonstrates taste and style. Wearing jeans to a formal dinner would convey that the person has poor judgment. A speaker's physical appearance often sets the stage for the acceptance or non-acceptance of the speaker's words. A person who makes a good physical impression quickly gains the interest of listeners.
- *Facial expressions* indicate our emotions: happy, sad, confused, angry, etc. A relaxed, pleasant, interested expression will create a favourable atmosphere for communicating, while a wrinkled brow and downturned

mouth will do the opposite. Eye contact is important in the Canadian culture, conveying confidence, honesty, and interest in the conversation.
- *Gestures* can express many things: a friendly wave to say hello, a frantic wave from a trader on a stock exchange floor signalling a wish to buy shares, and a supervisor holding his hand up to defer questions in a meeting. Some gestures can be distracting. For example, while talking do not distract your listeners by pulling at your clothing, toying with an object such as a paper clip or eye glasses, or putting your hands to your face or hair.
- *Posture* sends a nonverbal message. Standing or sitting erect denotes that you are paying attention to the matter at hand. Leaning forward conveys increased interest, while leaning back, especially with arms and/or legs crossed, conveys disinterest or a feeling of discomfort or defensiveness. Regardless of how tall you are, always stand up to your full height. Good posture makes you appear more professional and confident.

Environment

Our environment communicates many different messages. Environmental factors of nonverbal communication include objects in our surroundings, or the surroundings themselves. For example:

- A large desk in a corner office with windows communicates status within an organization.
- Fast-food restaurants are usually designed to move customers through quickly, using bright colours and plastic seating that is comfortable for about 10 minutes.
- Some organizations arrange product catalogues or sales awards in the reception area. This is done to give visitors a positive first impression.
- Colour communicates many different messages. Many hospital delivery rooms are painted in soothing colours to relax expectant parents.

Touch

Touch, or **haptic communication**, is a primary method for achieving connection with people, indicating intention, or expressing emotion. Like other factors of nonverbal communication, the use of touch is culturally bound. Consider the following:

- In a business setting, the most appropriate form of haptic communication is the handshake. A limp handshake can communicate nervousness or a feeling of inferiority; a firm handshake communicates confidence.
- Haptic communication is status-driven. That is, a manager may give an employee an encouraging pat on the back, but not vice versa.
- People in business must avoid touch that could be considered condescending or sexual harassment. Sexual harassment is any unwanted verbal or physical action related to sex.

Space

Space, as it relates to nonverbal communication, is the physical distance maintained with others. How you use space to communicate depends upon cultural norms, your relationship with the receivers of your communication, and the activities involved.

James recently conducted a business meeting in Japan. When greeting his Japanese colleagues, he held out his hand for a handshake as his colleagues bowed. James did not realize that the custom in Japan is to usually bow instead of shaking hands.

For North Americans, space generally falls into four categories:

- *Intimate distance.* From physical contact to 18 inches. This distance is reserved for personal expression with those we know well.
- *Personal distance.* From 18 inches to three feet. This distance is used for casual and friendly conversations.
- *Social distance.* From three feet to seven feet. This distance is used in the workplace for business-related conversations, small meetings, and social functions. It is also used for other conversations that are not personal in nature.
- *Public distance.* From seven feet and beyond. This distance is usually for public speaking. Obviously, this distance in a personal conversation would constitute a huge communication barrier.

CHECKUP 1

Answer *T* for *True* and *F* for *False* for the following questions.

1. A positive attitude cannot be conveyed through nonverbal communication.

2. Another term for body language is kinesics.

3. Nonverbal communication is composed totally of body language.

4. In a Canadian business setting, shaking hands is the most appropriate form of haptic communication.

5. Your relationship with the person/s with whom you are communicating in a face-to-face conversation will be the one factor that determines your use of physical space.

6. In the Canadian business world, personal distance is used for work-related conversations.

7. The absence of nonverbal communication can deliver a negative message.

8. When nonverbal cues contradict verbal cues, people tend to trust their reading of the nonverbal cues.

9. Paralanguage can help reinforce a verbal message.

10. Body language and environment both affect communications.

Speech Qualities

The quality of speech—how something is said—may have greater impact than what is actually said. The quality of speech is determined by the following voice attributes.

- Volume
- Pitch
- Tone
- Tempo
- Enunciation
- Pronunciation

Volume

For oral communication to be effective, the message must be clearly heard. Sufficient **volume**, achieved through good breath control, is important. If your voice is too soft and you have trouble being heard, practise breathing deeply and controlling your breath with your diaphragm and abdominal muscles, just as a singer does. The large abdominal cavity should be used to store a supply of air that can be released evenly to produce a clear, sustained tone. How much force you must use is determined by the acoustics in the room in which you are talking, the size of your audience, and whether or not you are using a microphone or other device to amplify your voice.

Pitch (Voice Level)

A speaker's voice should have a pleasing pitch. **Pitch** refers to the level of a sound on a musical scale. Practice can help correct the shrillness of a voice that is pitched too high or the excessive resonance of a voice that is pitched too low. Another pitch-related problem is the constant pitch that results in a monotone. An effective speaker varies the pitch of his or her voice to help communicate the message. **Intonation**, the rising and falling of voice pitch, can indicate that a statement is being made, that a question is being asked, or that a speaker is pausing.

A drop in pitch usually signals finality or determination and is, therefore, used at the end of a declarative sentence. For example, in reading the following sentence you should close with a drop in pitch.

I cannot *possibly* respond to all of the e-mails by 5 p.m. (Emphasize the word *possibly*.)

A rise in pitch can signal a question or an expression of suspense, doubt, or hesitation. Read the following sentences, closing with a rise in pitch.

What *more* can I do? (Emphasize *more*.)

I'm so sorry I can't give you the answer today, *but* I will *definitely* give it to you next week. (Emphasize the words *but* and *definitely*.)

Gliding the pitch up and down, or down and up, usually expresses sarcasm or contempt, as in the slang expression "Oh, yeah?"

The most important aspect of pitch is variation. Variation of pitch not only helps hold listeners' attention but also helps listeners know the exact meaning intended by the speaker. A rise in pitch can stress important words. Using the same pitch for each element can stress comparisons; pitching the first element high and the second low, on the other hand, can denote contrasts.

Notice the different shades of meaning that emerge as you read the following sentences and emphasize the italicized words.

Tony gave her the special assignment. (Tony did, not someone else.)

Tony *gave* her the special assignment. (She did not earn it.)

Tony gave *her* the special assignment. (Only she was given the special assignment.)

Tony gave her the *special* assignment. (The particular, or special, assignment.)

Tony gave her the special *assignment*. (The special thing he gave her was the assignment, not something else special.)

Tone

The **tone** of your voice often reveals your attitudes and feelings. A pleasant and cheerful tone is desirable because it will have a good effect on your listeners. On the telephone, the tone of your voice must substitute for your facial expression. In addition, you can use variation in tone, as well as in volume and pitch, to add interest to your speaking voice. The kind of tone you use should be appropriate for the words and ideas you are expressing.

Tempo

Tempo, the rate at which you speak, should be varied to avoid extremes in either direction. Most people tend to speak too rapidly. Although you should not speak so rapidly that words are not understood, neither should you speak so slowly that your listeners lose concentration. Regulate your rate of speaking so that you can say each word clearly.

A good speaking rate is 125 words a minute; oral reading rates tend to run slightly faster—about 150 words a minute. To determine what a rate of 125 words a minute sounds like, read aloud the paragraph below in a half minute. Reread the paragraph as many times as necessary until you achieve the desired rate. At the end of 15 seconds, you should be at the diagonal line. Use this line as a guide to either increase or decrease your speaking rate.

A good speaker talks slowly enough to be understood by the listeners and speaks in a pleasant voice, articulating and pronouncing each word correctly and distinctly. To develop a good / speaking voice, you must spend sufficient time practising the elements of good speech. An effective speaker is a definite asset to a business and will usually find more opportunities for advancing in the job. (64 words)

Changing the rate contributes to variety, as well as to clarity. Important words and ideas should be spoken slowly, while unimportant words or phrases should be spoken more rapidly.

Try to speak in thought units so that you can assist the listener in interpreting your words. If the sentence is short, the thought unit can be the entire sentence, as in "My job is very exciting." When there are several thought units within a sentence, pause slightly after each thought group, as in "My job is very exciting; / but I must admit, / some days are almost too exciting."

Use pauses to stress major points. By pausing between major points or after important statements, you add variety and emphasis to the points you want your listeners to remember.

Enunciation and Pronunciation

In business—and even in social situations—it is important for all business employees, particularly those who have face-to-face or telephone contact with customers, to speak clearly and correctly.

The terms enunciation and pronunciation are closely related, but they do have slightly different meanings. Understanding the difference between the two terms and practising problem words or difficult words will help you improve your speech.

Enunciation

Enunciation refers to the distinctness or clarity with which you articulate or sound each part of a word. For instance, saying "offen" for *often* or "gonna" for *going to* are examples of careless enunciation. Careless enunciation often occurs in *ing* words, such as "willin" for *willing* and "askin" for *asking*. Also, when we speak rapidly, most of us have a tendency to run words together, dropping some of the sounds. Saying "didjago" for *did you go,* and "meetcha"

for *meet you,* are examples. A person who slurs too many words is likely to be misunderstood, particularly over the telephone, on transcribing equipment, or when using voice recognition software. It is annoying for both the listener and the speaker if the listener must ask the speaker to repeat something several times. When using voice recognition software, an incorrect word or words will be entered. Such difficulties can often be avoided if we simply speak more slowly and distinctly.

Pronunciation

Pronunciation refers either to the sound that the speaker gives to letters or letter combinations that make up a word, or to the way in which the speaker accents the word. Note the following examples of mispronunciation and correct pronunciation.

Incorrect Pronunciation	Correct Pronunciation
pro•*noun*•ci•a•tion	pro•*nun*•ci•a•tion
li•*ba*•ry	li•*bra*•ry
com•par´•able	com´•par•able

Of course, there are regional differences in pronunciation; and, in addition, a number of words have more than one acceptable pronunciation. In the latter case, the dictionary lists the preferred pronunciation first.

Many difficulties in pronunciation arise because some letters or combinations of letters are pronounced one way in some words and another way in others. For example, the combination *ow* has an "oh" sound in *know* but an "ow" sound (as in *ouch*) in *now.*

Other difficulties in pronunciation arise because a letter may be sounded in some words and silent in others. For example, *k* is sounded in the word *kite*, but it is not sounded in such words as *know* and *knee*. Consult the dictionary whenever you are in doubt about the pronunciation of a word.

Pronunciation errors are most likely to occur with (1) unfamiliar words, (2) words of foreign origin, (3) names, and (4) multisyllable words. Such errors tend to distract the listener and may give the impression that the speaker is careless or uneducated. The business employee who is eager to succeed does not wish to be marked with either of these labels.

Review of Key Terms

1. How can *nonverbal communication* affect a speaker's message?
2. What is the difference between *enunciation* and *pronunciation*? How do they affect oral communication?

Practical Application

1. Reread the case at the beginning of this chapter. Assume that you are a candidate for Margaret Reilly's job. List your strengths and weaknesses, including such factors as your personality, the first impression you make on others, your personal appearance, your facial expressions, and your mannerisms. Briefly comment on each of these factors. Would you be a likely candidate for this position? Why or why not? Would it be possible for you to overcome any deficiencies that you perceive that you have?

2. Think of certain situations in which your nonverbal communication sent a loud message to the listener. For example, consider your nonverbal cues when being interviewed, getting a speeding ticket, going on a first date, or presenting an oral report. Write a paragraph in which you list your strengths and weaknesses in relation to the kind of impression you make on others with your personal appearance, your facial expression, and your mannerisms.

3. Politicians, business leaders, and television journalists should be aware of how their nonverbal communication may affect their audience. Watch a television show or video clip of one of these professionals giving a speech or delivering news. Look for nonverbal factors—both pro and con—that affect their speaking effectiveness. Prepare notes on how nonverbal communication made the message more, or less, effective.

4. Read each of the following sentences aloud three times. Each time, emphasize a different word in the sentence to change the meaning of the sentence.
   a. Michael mailed the letter yesterday morning.
   b. I liked Los Angeles more than any other city we visited on our trip.
   c. Did you see Hosea at the banquet this week?
   d. If possible, please arrive earlier on Tuesday.
   e. Please forgive me for arriving so late.

5. Read the following sentences silently once or twice. Then, standing in front of the class or a group of fellow students, read them aloud from beginning to end. Strive for appropriate use of volume, pitch, tone, and tempo. Enunciate clearly and pronounce all the words correctly. Try to keep your eyes on the audience as much as possible.

   TEAMWORK
   a. Barry is never late for work, if he can avoid it.
   b. I doubt very much that I will be able to attend the booksellers convention next week.

    c.   No, in my opinion, the new computer does not perform as efficiently as the old one.

    d.   What difference does it make whether or not I attend your cousin's graduation next Tuesday?

    e.   Do you really think that he will deliver the main speech at the awards banquet?

6.   Form a group with two other class members. Familiarize yourselves with the following paragraphs by reading them silently twice. Then read one paragraph aloud each while the other group members evaluate the speech qualities. Provide each other with constructive feedback. Repeat the process, concentrating on improving your speech qualities by using the constructive feedback.

TEAMWORK

    a.   When you are communicating face-to-face on a one-on-one basis, don't do all the talking. Give the other person a chance to talk while you listen attentively. Watch for signs that the other person wants to say something or is becoming bored and not listening carefully. No matter how interesting you think the conversation is or how well informed and articulate you think you are, you must give your listener a chance to speak. Otherwise, you will not keep his or her attention and respect.

    b.   Most people take telephone usage for granted—and this is one of the reasons so many office workers are ineffective telephone communicators. Too many employees assume that a business telephone conversation is the same as a personal telephone call. Actually, the telephone is one of the most important communication media in business, and you must use it with great skill, especially when you are talking with outside callers and with superiors in the office.

    c.   Nearly every speech of any length is brightened considerably by touches of humour and by human interest narratives. Of course, such stories should not dominate the speech. Observe the following rules: Use stories and jokes that add interest to the subject or illustrate a particular point. Before telling a joke to an audience, test it on friends to make sure it has a punchline. Make sure that stories and jokes do not offend or embarrass the audience. And finally, time your stories to make sure that they are not too long.

Editing Practice

Copying amounts of money, form numbers, dates, and other figures often results in errors because of reading mistakes. Proofread the copied list (B) to determine if any items have been copied incorrectly.

List A	List B
1. 789836B	789863B
2. 43287v698	43287V698
3. $2786.54	2786.54
4. S768R3456J789	S768R3546J789

Discussion Points

1. Provide examples of people you know, such as friends, family, or instructors, using nonverbal language to convey a positive message. How did these nonverbal cues affect your reaction to the message?

2. Discuss how nonverbal cues can be misinterpreted. In your discussion, include how cultural differences play a role.

Improving Listening Skills

▶ **Key Terms**

▶ hearing
▶ listening
▶ interpreting
▶ retaining
▶ passive listening
▶ active listening
▶ listening barriers
▶ external noise
▶ internal noise

We have been given two ears and but a single mouth in order that we may listen more and talk less.

—Zeno of Citium, Greek philosopher

Listening is an integral part of the communication process, yet it is often taken for granted. Excluding sight, listening is the main way of learning what is going on in your surroundings. Active listening provides you with vital information and signals. Listening is a primary means of gathering information and is crucially necessary in your life and your work.

Effective listening is an important workplace skill. If you are prepared to listen, you are more likely to receive the information you need from friends, instructors, coworkers, and supervisors. Employees with excellent listening skills are more likely to do accurate work, avoid misunderstandings, make sales, and develop good relationships with coworkers and customers.

Often, we think just because we have ears, we can listen. *Listening,* however, is a mental function requiring active concentration and involving perception. *Hearing,* on the other hand, is the physical function of detecting sound. Those who are hearing impaired "listen" to sign language. That is, they receive the sign language and use their perception to analyze and give meaning to the communication just received.

The Listening Model

As shown in Figure 2.1, the listening model has four components:

1. **Hearing**—the physical ability to perceive sounds. For example, you may hear a nearby conversation or the hum of a computer without focusing on these sounds.
2. **Listening**—the act of filtering out distractions to allow you to comprehend the meaning of sounds. For example, when you ask someone a question you then listen for a response.
3. **Interpreting**—a mental function whereby you analyze the sounds that you comprehended. You relate what you have heard to information and experiences with which you are familiar.
4. **Retaining**—the act of remembering the interpreted sounds for later use.

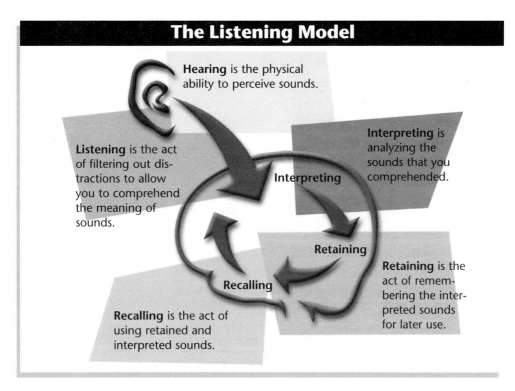

The Listening Model

Hearing is the physical ability to perceive sounds.

Listening is the act of filtering out distractions to allow you to comprehend the meaning of sounds.

Interpreting

Interpreting is analyzing the sounds that you comprehended.

Retaining

Retaining is the act of remembering the interpreted sounds for later use.

Recalling

Recalling is the act of using retained and interpreted sounds.

◀ **Figure 2.1**
The Listening Model
The listening model involves five elements.

Thinking Critically.
Which are most challenging for you?

As you can see from the listening model, you do not choose which sounds you will hear. You do, however, decide on which sounds you focus your attention. Then you assign meaning and importance to these sounds.

Types of Listening

There are two types of listening: passive and active. The difference between these two kinds of listening is the level of the listener's involvement.

Passive Listening

Passive listening means concentrating at a low level and absorbing just enough of the speaker's words to stay involved in a conversation or speech. Passive listeners actually understand or remember little of what is said. Often, passive listeners let the speaker's inflection or tone of voice signal when they should react by nodding, smiling, or saying, "I see." Such reactions can suggest that the speaker has a listener's attention even though that may not be the case.

Passive listening is appropriate only when you listen for pleasure and when it doesn't matter whether or not you retain what you hear. This would be the case, for example, if you were sitting in a comfortable chair reading a magazine, listening to music.

In these situations, you listen passively because you don't need to register every piece of sound information you hear. Often, you use the music as background noise and listen attentively only when you hear something—for example, your favourite song—that suddenly captures your attention.

Active Listening

Active listening uses a high level of concentration because you are listening for information. In school or in the workplace, active—not passive—listening is appropriate. Listening carefully to an instructor's explanation of an assignment or to your supervisor's directions about the procedure to follow for performing a particular task, are examples of active listening.

Workplace conversations are filled with names, dates, places, prices, requests, and suggestions, and each has its level of importance and priority. Active listening is required to gather accurate, complete, and relevant information. The computer programmer, for example, must listen to the company accountant to understand what is needed in the new accounting program. The administrative assistant must listen to which specific data is needed prior to setting up a new database. The travel agent must listen for the customer's preferences, times, dates, and destinations for booking a trip. The medical assistant must hear the doctor's exact instructions for patient care. Team members must listen actively to information, ideas, and opinions to participate effectively in team discussions, activities, and decision making.

Listening Barriers

Listening barriers, unless recognized and overcome, disrupt the communication process. These barriers can be classified in the following way.

Physical and Environmental Listening Barriers

These barriers affect the listener's physical comfort and well-being. Some examples are: poor health (headache or other pain), feeling tired, and negative factors in the work environment (poor lighting, too much heat or lack of heat, uncomfortable seating, a cluttered work space, poor acoustics, noise, etc.) **External noise** includes sounds from conversations, radios, televisions, machinery, and so on. **Internal noise** includes distractions such as pain, fatigue, preoccupation with other thoughts, worry, or a personality conflict with the speaker.

Attitudinal Listening Barriers

These barriers involve the listener's attitude towards the speaker in particular and towards himself/herself and others in general. Some examples are: becoming annoyed when people speak too slowly, too quickly, or with an accent; thinking that you know more than the speaker and/or other people in general; prejudging the speaker because of his or her appearance or ethnic background. Effective listeners focus on the speaker's message. They make an effort to learn something from the speaker. They believe that diversity provides an opportunity to share different viewpoints and that people with a different background may have a new and interesting point of view.

Emotional Listening Barriers

Most people's listening is worst in emotional situations. Knowing this, it is necessary to make a greater effort to focus on listening to overcome emotional listening barriers. Emotions such as feeling upset, impatient, or angry can create listening barriers. Some examples are: being upset about and preoccupied with personal problems; feeling stressed and pressured, and therefore impatient; and becoming defensive. Once you become defensive you have decided that you are right and the other person is wrong, and that you therefore don't need to continue listening.

Phyllis was preoccupied with her mother's recent illness and was passively listening to her supervisor, Gail, ask her to make hotel reservations for a visiting consultant. Phyllis, not paying attention, wrote down the wrong date. As a result, Phyllis failed to reserve a hotel room for the consultant, and she had some explaining to do to Gail.

Listening Checklist

- Have you had your hearing tested recently?
- Do you try to filter out distracting sights and sounds when you are listening to someone?
- Do you avoid interrupting speakers before they finish expressing their thoughts?
- Do you avoid doing something else—such as reading—while trying to listen?
- Do you always look at the person who is talking to you?
- When people talk to you, do you try to concentrate on what they are saying?
- Do you listen for people's ideas and feelings as well as for factual information?
- Do you believe that you can learn something from others?
- If something is unclear, do you always ask the speaker to repeat or explain information?
- Do you ever refuse to listen because you do not agree with the speaker's ideas?
- Do you ever stop listening because you do not like a speaker's appearance or mannerisms?
- Do you ever think about what you will say next while another person is talking?
- Do you ever have to ask the speaker to repeat some important information because you cannot remember what was said?
- Do you ever let your mind wander because you believe that what the speaker is saying will not interest you?
- Do you sometimes stop listening because you feel that you need to spend too much time and effort to understand what the speaker is saying?

◀ **Figure 2.2**
Listening Checklist
The listening checklist allows you to evaluate your listening abilites.

Thinking Critically.
Which question did you find most difficult to answer? Explain.

Language Listening Barriers

These barriers include the listener's ability to comprehend what the speaker is actually saying, and the listener's reaction to the words that are used. Some examples are: unfamiliar words (the listener does not understand the vocabulary used by the speaker); and emotionally laden or "charged" words being used by the speaker, causing the listener to react negatively. The listener should make a note of unfamiliar words or terms. These can be looked up in a dictionary or questions can be asked which will help to clarify understanding. This then becomes a useful way of increasing vocabulary as well as understanding of a particular topic. Although emotionally charged words are unfortunate, a good listener should be aware that it is highly unlikely that the speaker meant to cause offence. Focusing on these words may cause the listener to miss important information that follows.

Listening Techniques

The following techniques will help you improve your listening skills by overcoming listening barriers and increasing your ability to actively listen.

Prepare Yourself Physically and Mentally

Physical Preparation

- If you are experiencing any hearing difficulties, schedule a hearing examination with a medical professional.
- In a conference setting, choose a seat location that limits distracting sights and sounds, has suitable lighting, and where you can easily see the speaker.
- Prepare any equipment you are using—PDA, laptop, etc. Make sure it is fully charged and ready to use.

Mental Preparation

- Create a receptive frame of mind. Good listeners clear their minds of extraneous thoughts—meeting deadlines, making car payments, scheduling a dental appointment, deciding where to eat lunch, making plans for the weekend—so their minds are open to receive the speaker's message.
- Develop your vocabulary. Effective listening in the workplace often requires expanding your vocabulary. Almost every field has its own lexicon or specialized vocabulary, and the listener must master this vocabulary to understand the material under discussion. Collect and learn new and useful words so they become part of your own vocabulary.
- Determine your listening objectives. Know why you are attending a meeting, training session, or conference. What are the expected outcomes? For example, imagine that you will be attending a session to learn how to design Web pages for your company. What level of expertise is expected from you after the session? Are you expected to learn enough about Web page construction to teach the process to your co-workers?
- Find out the subject matter to be covered in a meeting, training session, or conference, and learn something about it before you attend the session. This preparation will give you a frame of reference that helps you absorb the information that you will hear.

Listen Actively

Concentrate

Working efficiently means absorbing and comprehending a speaker's words without having to ask the speaker to repeat what has been said. Give the speaker your undivided attention. Do not continue with another physical or mental task, such as working at your computer or thinking about another subject. Stop what you are doing and focus on the speaker. Dividing your attention is bad manners, interferes with the listening process because you are distracted, and signals a preoccupation with other matters. Concentrate on the speaker and the message and try to block out any distractions such as background noise. Continued practice at blocking out distracting sounds improves mental focusing capabilities.

Sometimes you will encounter speakers with unusual voices or accents. In these instances, very active and focused listening is required to adapt to the challenging characteristics of the speakers' voice. In situations like these, maintaining your mental focus on the speaker's message is your main priority.

Listen with a Positive Attitude

Don't prejudge a speaker on the basis of personal characteristics such as mannerisms, voice, speech patterns, or appearance. Good listeners must not confuse the speaker's message with the manner of speaking or the speaker's appearance.

To be an effective listener, you don't have to agree with the speaker. However, you do have to believe the speaker has something useful to offer.

In the business world, the employee who wants to do a good job will listen carefully to the supervisor's explanations and directions. To be productive, supervisors also need to listen carefully to workers' problems and needs. Good listeners learn to listen even when they don't want to listen.

Do Not Interrupt

As a listener you may be tempted to interrupt the speaker to express your opinion or to share information. However, interrupting a speaker is bad manners and also may cause the speaker to lose his or her train of thought. Wait until the speaker has finished making a point, and then respond with an appropriate comment. Often people do not really listen because they are looking for an opportunity to interrupt the other person. Once you start thinking about what you want to say, active listening has ceased.

Use Body Language to Indicate Listening

Use nonverbal cues to communicate your interest in what the speaker is saying. To send a positive non-verbal message, face the speaker and establish eye contact. Lean forward slightly in your chair and avoid crossing your arms and legs. Nod to indicate understanding or agreement, and smile or use other appropriate facial expressions. Even when the speaker cannot see you, you will listen more effectively when your posture indicates active listening.

Listen for Feelings

A speaker's tone of voice and body language will provide information about feelings. These clues will tell a sensitive listener whether or not the speaker is, for example, happy, upset, sarcastic, or sincere. As discussed previously, if the speaker's body language conflicts with what he or she is saying, the body language provides you with the accurate clue concerning what the speaker really thinks or feels.

Make Efficient Use of Available Time

The average person can say 125 to150 words a minute, but a good listener processes 300 or more words a minute. Because of this ability to understand faster than people speak, listeners tend to relax and listen to only part of what is being said. However, missing a sentence or even a single word can change the speaker's message.

This extra time should be spent on mental activities that will help you retain the speaker's message. These activities are summarized in the following Memory Hook.

Identify Ideas and Relationships

As you begin to grasp the speaker's ideas, look for relationships among them.

One method to help you retain the content of a speaker's message is to think of the strategies represented by the letters in the sentence "IS A FACT":

Identify—Identify the speaker's ideas and connections among the ideas.

Summarize—Summarize the main points of the message.

Assess—Assess the correctness or validity of the message.

Formulate—Formulate appropriate questions.

Associate—Associate the speaker's ideas with other known concepts.

Consider—Consider specific ways the information might be used.

Take notes—Take notes to assist in better recall.

For example, which idea is most important? Do the other ideas support the main one? What is the speaker leading up to? Can you anticipate what the speaker is going to say next? What cues does the speaker give to show relationships among the ideas?

Imagine listening to the following excerpt from a speech:

Two major costs in a vacation to Alaska are airfare and hotel accommodations. For instance, if your plane ticket is $700 per person and your hotel room is $150 per night for two people, an eight-day trip for two will start at $2,600. Of course, there are other costs such as meals, tours, and souvenirs.

Note the first sentence, in *italics*, contains the main idea. The word *major* is a cue to the importance of that first sentence. In the next sentence, the speaker also uses the phrase *for instance* as a cue to indicate that what follows will support the main idea. Experienced speakers use verbal cues such as these to emphasize important ideas. Examples of verbal cues are: This concept is important; Remember how to apply this information; The most important thing is …; Another consideration; On the other hand; Finally; In summary.

Listen for vocal cues such as pauses and changes in volume or tone of voice, as well as nonverbal cues such as such as gestures, nodding or shaking the head, or counting on their fingers, that speakers use to indicate main points. They also reinforce points by writing them on flip charts or using visual aids such as handouts, overhead transparencies, or computer-generated slide shows. All of these cues help you identify the speaker's ideas and see the interrelationships among them.

Summarize Main Points

As you listen, summarize the speaker's words by paraphrasing them in your own words. By reducing the speaker's message to its most basic terms, you will be able to understand and remember the message better. The following example shows how you might paraphrase the speaker's points in your own words.[1]

---

[1] Lois Schneider Farese, Grady Kimbrell, and Carl A. Woloszyk, *Marketing Essentials,* 2nd ed., Glencoe/McGraw-Hill, New York, 1997, p. 183.

What the Speaker Says

Empathy is the essence of customer-oriented selling. Empathetic salespeople are able to see things from a customer's point of view and to be sensitive to a customer's problems. For example, such a salesperson might say, "I can understand why you feel that way. If I were in your situation, I would feel the same."

But the salesperson must be sincere in this. Customers are astute and can tell when salespeople don't mean what they say. When customers sense that you have their best interests at heart, they let down their defenses and begin really listening to you.

Your Summary of the Speaker's Points

Salespeople should see the situation from the customer's point of view, and be empathetic and sincere in their comments.

Assess the Message

As you summarize the speaker's message and see the organization and the relationship structure of the speaker's ideas, you will probably find yourself beginning to agree or disagree with the speaker. When this happens, try to trace your response to the speaker's reasons or arguments. Ask yourself if the arguments and ideas of the speaker really lead to his or her conclusions. Also, determine if the speaker is trying to convince you with reason or to persuade you by pleading, coaxing, or insisting. Make sure you are in favour of the speaker's views for substantive and tangible reasons, not just because they are presented with humour, enthusiasm, or charm.

Formulate Questions

Formulating questions helps you stay focused on what the speaker is saying. You might ask questions of the speaker to clarify a point that is unclear or to determine if you have interpreted the material correctly. In a conference setting, most speakers indicate a specific time for questions. Some allow questions during the session. Other speakers prefer to answer questions at the end of the session. Make a note of your questions for use at the appropriate time.

Associate Ideas with Familiar Concepts

As you listen to the speaker's ideas, relate this information to what you already know about the topic or related topics. Doing so allows you to quickly grasp the information presented by the speaker. For example, suppose you are listening to a sales presentation on the functions of several fax machines. As you listen to the speaker, you would want to think about and compare the functions discussed with those of your present fax machine.

Consider Ways to Use the Information

One of the best ways to personally integrate a speaker's message is to determine how you can best use the information in the message. For example, if you are responsible for handling customer inquiries, you can directly benefit from listening to your supervisor's explanation of a new procedure for dealing with customers.

Take Notes

You are most likely to take notes in meetings or in a lecture or conference setting. As discussed in Chapter 1, taking notes is an excellent way of recording spoken information for future reference. Notes, however, should be more than just aids to memory. They should also be tools that help the listener concentrate on the speaker's message.

CHECKUP 1

Answer *T* for *True* and *F* for *False* for the following questions.

1. When you paraphrase a speaker's thoughts, you put them in your own words.
2. Speakers may use body language to reinforce certain points.
3. A speaker can talk twice as fast as a listener can comprehend spoken words.
4. Having your hearing checked is one way to physically prepare yourself to listen.
5. The general vocabulary you developed in high school is adequate for effective listening on the job.
6. Listening is the physical function of detecting sound.
7. People choose which sounds they will hear.
8. Listening is an acquired skill.
9. The difference between active and passive listening is the level of the listener's involvement.
10. Even good listeners occasionally lose their focus when they should be listening.

Review of Key Terms

1. What is the difference between *hearing* and *listening*?
2. What is the difference between *active listening* and *passive listening*?
3. How can a good listener avoid *internal noise*?
4. How can you be an effective listener during a *teleconference*?

Practical Application

1. Answer the following questions.
   a. Describe the five facets of the listening model.
   b. Name five barriers to effective listening. List some strategies for overcoming these barriers.
   c. Explain how preparation could enhance your listening skills at a conference.

2. A good listener is able to distinguish between facts and opinions. Identify each of the following statements as a fact or an opinion.
   a. The article I read on energy conservation was biased.
   b. Andrew was told that his car needs two new tires.
   c. If you park on the street from 9:00 a.m. to 5:00 p.m., your car will be towed away.
   d. Wearing a suit to a job interview will give the interviewee more self-confidence.
   e. The price of those tires is too high.

3. Think back to a recent occasion when someone told you how to do something new. Did you listen carefully and understand fully what you were supposed to do, or did you realize a few minutes later that you had actually missed or misunderstood certain steps in the directions? Suppose you had to ask for the directions to be repeated. Refer to the information on listening barriers to determine what may have prevented you from hearing all of the directions the first time.

4. Listen to a short article or story read by the instructor. Then write a brief summary of the information. Compare your summary with that of several classmates. What discrepancies exist? What listening behaviours may account for these discrepancies?

5. Select one or two areas of employment. List five specialized vocabulary words from each area that you might hear on the job. Define all terms and present the specialized vocabulary to the class.

6. Listen to a specific news broadcast assigned by your instructor. Take notes and bring them to class. Compare your notes with the notes of several classmates. Determine if there are any discrepancies between your notes and the notes taken by your classmates. What are some factors that may account for the discrepancies?

7. Write a description of a job situation that demonstrates some of the listening techniques presented in this section. Include examples of poor listening skills. Role-play the case for the class. Classmates should identify good and poor listening techniques that they observed.

TEAMWORK

Editing Practice

Speaking Contextually.   Each of the following sentences contains a word that is not used correctly. Replace the incorrect words.

1. The speaker's presentation had an amazing affect on the audience.
2. We need the corporation of everyone in the office.
3. The defendant is to be arranged in court next week.
4. Tom accused the company of infringing on his patent rights.
5. Discrimination of confidential information is prohibited.

Discussion Points

1. How can a person improve his or her listening skills?
2. Do you agree with the following statement? Why or why not?
    "The listener is responsible for listening even when the speaker is boring."
3. "It went in one ear and out the other." What does this common saying mean, and how does this meaning relate to the definitions of hearing and listening?

Communicating in Meetings

● TOPICS

▶ Planning Meetings

▶ Managing Meetings

▶ Participating in Meetings

Are meetings held because "Two heads are better than one"?

—Anonymous

▶ **Key Terms**

▶ standing committee

▶ ad hoc committee

▶ minutes

▶ agenda

▶ directives

▶ *Robert's Rules of Order*

▶ parliamentary procedure

▶ motion

Meetings are among the most important ways to exchange ideas and report information within businesses. A meeting may involve a supervisor and an employee, several employees at various levels, and employees and vendors or customers. With an increase in global competition, many businesses are adopting a team approach to conducting business. Using the team approach helps involve employees at all levels in planning and decision making. Rather than working independently, employees work in groups in which they share ideas and responsibilities.

As a business communicator, you are likely to have frequent opportunities to participate in a variety of capacities in many types of meetings. You might be selected as a member of a **standing** (permanent) **committee** that meets regularly, such as a planning committee or a finance committee. You may also serve on an **ad hoc** (temporary) **committee** formed for a particular purpose, such as a committee appointed to study employee grievances or to plan the company's 25th anniversary celebration. You may be selected as chairperson of one of these committees, with the responsibility for planning and conducting the meetings.

After attending meetings during working hours, many business professionals often go to meetings and serve on other committees outside the company—for example, in professional, cultural, social, religious, political, sporting, and civic groups.

Planning Meetings

The success or failure of a group meeting is very often determined by preparation. Skilful planning can turn an ordinary meeting into an extremely positive experience for each participant. Without careful advance work, the most promising meeting can result in a waste of time for everyone.

Determine the Reason for the Meeting

Unless a specific group is required to meet on a regular basis, it is up to the meeting chairperson to decide if a meeting should be called. For example, if you wish to distribute information, a meeting may not be necessary. It may be more efficient to send an e-mail or memo with attachments. Meetings should be held when the exchange of ideas from different people needs to be processed to make decisions.

Determine the Meeting Participants

Meetings are time consuming and expensive because they take the participants away from their usual tasks and responsibilities. Consequently, you want to include only those people who have direct input to the causes, results, solutions, or impact of the discussions and the resulting decisions. Invite those who have the knowledge of the issues, the creativity to solve them, and the authority to put the decisions made into action.

Prepare Thoroughly

A successful meeting or conference requires that the leader or leaders prepare adequately and make all the necessary arrangements. Preparations should include determining the starting time, the length, and the site of the meeting; the names of those who are to attend; the objectives to be accomplished at the meeting; and potential problems.

Notification of a meeting is usually done by e-mail or memo. The message should include the time, date, and location of the meeting. You should attach a copy of the meeting agenda and a copy of the minutes for the previous meeting (if not already distributed). The **minutes** of a meeting are the official record of the meeting proceedings. An **agenda** is a list of the topics to be discussed and the names of the people who are to lead the specific discussions. It usually specifies the name of the group and the date, time, and place of the meeting. Sometimes the agenda also specifies the anticipated ending time of the meeting. Refer to Figure 2.3 for a sample agenda. Some tips for agendas follow:

Tips for Agendas

- Send the agenda prior to the meeting, allowing sufficient time for the group members to prepare for participation.
- List topics in the order in which they will be discussed. Include the names of the people responsible for each agenda item to alert them to be especially prepared for that particular topic.
- Under "New Business," list the most important items first in case there is not enough time to discuss them all.
- If meeting length is a concern, include a suggested time limit for each discussion item to encourage completion of the agenda.

Check the Meeting Site

Arrangements for the meeting site must be planned so that the room, the furniture, and the equipment to be used are set up in time for the meeting. The following is a list of routine tasks associated with meeting preparations.

To start the meeting promptly, check the room at least 45 minutes before the scheduled time to ensure that everything is ready. By checking in advance, you can take care of any problems before the meeting begins and thereby

◀ Figure 2.3
An Agenda
An agenda lists the topics
to be discussed at a
meeting.

Thinking Critically. *How
can an agenda help all
parties present at the
meeting?*

BAXTER AND BRADSHAW, INC.

AGENDA

Quarterly Sales Meeting

Tuesday, April 18, 20—
9 A.M.–10 A.M.

Conference Room #2

Call to order	Tracy Dillard
Approval of minutes of January meeting	George Sanders

Old Business:
    a. Report on new incentive
        compensation plan   Melinda Regan

    b. Review of customer
        service survey results   Steve Horowitz

New Business:
    a. Review of previous
        January, February, and
        March sales   Jared Adams

    b. Recommendations
        for proposed new
        sales territories   Teresa Atkins

    c. Report on college
        intern applications   Brooke Kinkaid

Adjournment

Routine Meeting Site Tasks

- Reserve a meeting room with enough tables and chairs.
- Make sure that the meeting room is clean and ready for use.
- For small meetings, arrange seating so that participants have eye contact with one another, such as around a conference table.
- Make needed adjustments to the ventilation, room temperature, and lighting.
- Request any special equipment, such as a computer, an overhead projector, a slide projector, or multimedia projection equipment.

continued on page 70

Routine Meeting Site Tasks *continued*

- Check all equipment to make sure that it is working properly and have an extra bulb for the projection equipment.
- Check to see that electricity receptacles are accessible for your equipment. Bring extension cords if they are needed.
- Place packets of documents needed at the meeting at each person's place. Or, you can have them at the door ready for distribution when meeting participants arrive.
- Arrange for a meeting recorder to take the minutes.
- Request any special services needed for participants. For example, you may need an interpreter for a deaf participant or a note-taker for a visually impaired participant.
- Arrange for refreshments if appropriate.

avoid delays. Problems are more easily solved if they are discovered in a timely fashion.

Arrive Early

The leader of the meeting should arrive a few minutes early to check the facilities and to set an example for the participants. Arriving early also gives the leader a chance to greet the participants and offer them a copy of the agenda. Even though everyone should have an advance copy of the agenda, not everyone will remember to bring it to the meeting. Extra copies of reports or other papers to be discussed should also be available, even though copies may have been distributed in advance.

Managing Meetings

Being able to run a meeting smoothly is an acquired skill. The following guidelines provide a basis for developing this important skill.

Establish a Businesslike Atmosphere

The chairperson or facilitator sets the tone of the meeting. If the leader begins late or is slow to start the meeting, the participants are likely to lose whatever enthusiasm they may have had when they arrived at the meeting. It is best to start a meeting at the scheduled time, even though there may be latecomers. This shows respect for the participants' time and encourages punctual attendance at future meetings.

Facilitate the Discussion

The good leader talks as little as possible and draws out the opinions and ideas of the participants. The leader's function is not to show how much he or she knows but to steer the discussion in the proper direction. An experienced leader knows that the greater the participation—that is, the more minds constructively working on issues—the better the chances of accomplishing the meeting objectives.

Encourage Participation

Everyone invited to a meeting should be able to make some contribution to the discussion. Sometimes, ground rules are needed to encourage the members of the group to participate. The leader of the meeting should make it clear that individuals are not allowed to interrupt the person who is speaking. Also speakers should know that they will be able to express their ideas without being criticized or attacked.

Some people are shy and will not say anything unless they are encouraged to speak. The leader should call on these people in a manner that will offer them encouragement; for example, "Marcia, you have had a lot of experience in advertising. What do you think of José's design for the product label?" or "Ken, we would be interested in having the benefit of your experience in designing the home page for our Web site."

A leader can encourage positive participation by complimenting a speaker who has made a worthwhile contribution; for example, "Thank you, Isaac, for that timesaving suggestion," or "That's a great idea, Ms. Kraft. Can you tell us a little more about how you think that plan would work?"

Comments of this type are effective when they are obviously sincere. Negative comments, on the other hand, discourage participation and should be kept to a minimum and be presented so tactfully that they do not discourage others from making suggestions. "If that idea could be implemented in a cost-effective way, our problem would be solved." This statement tactfully says that the idea will not work because it costs too much.

Discourage Excessive Talkers

In any group there will always be one or two people who want to do all the talking. Unless these individuals are listed on the agenda as principal contributors, they should not be permitted to take over the discussion. A leader should be firm in preventing a single person from dominating the meeting. "That's very interesting, Thad, but I think we ought to hear what Hannah thinks," or "Let's get back to you a little later, Helen; I think we would all be interested in hearing as many points as we can in our brief meeting."

Keep the Discussion Pertinent

Meetings sometimes tend to get off topic. All too often, a subject comes up that is of genuine personal interest to some or all meeting participants but has little or no bearing on the main topic. When side issues begin to waste valuable time, they must be cut off tactfully by the leader and the discussion must be brought back on track. "That certainly was an interesting experience, Robin, but let's get back to our discussion on safety in the parking garage. Yolanda, when will the new video cameras be installed?"

Usually you can keep the discussion on track with tactful comments, but if someone is attempting to monopolize the discussion and is off topic, your comments need to be more direct. "Sandy, time is getting away from us, and we want to avoid having to call another meeting to settle this problem. Do you have any specific solutions?"

Summarize Periodically

The group leader should always listen attentively but does not need to comment except, perhaps, to stimulate further discussion. "Excellent—that's an interesting point. I gather that you think this schedule will be more effective than the one we have been following. Is that a correct assumption?" Above all, the leader should not tear down ideas or argue with participants; doing so will only discourage others in the group from expressing themselves. The leader of the meeting is only one member of the group; thus it is poor practice for the leader to judge every idea expressed instead of letting other members of the group participate.

From time to time, the chairperson should summarize the major points that have been presented. "We all seem to agree that we should not add more people to each team at the present time. Instead, you feel we should create one more team. Is that correct? Let's discuss how tasks can be re-assigned. Brian, do you have any suggestions about the tasks that could be assigned to the new team?"

Know When to Conclude

If the chairperson has prepared the agenda carefully and has conducted the meeting efficiently, the meeting should end close to the time scheduled for adjournment. If the discussion seems likely to extend beyond the closing time and it is important to continue, get the approval of the group; for example, "It is five minutes before twelve, and it looks as though we won't get out of here by noon. Shall we continue the discussion, or would you rather schedule another meeting for tomorrow?"

Complete After-Meeting Tasks

After the meeting, the recorder should prepare the minutes and distribute them as soon as is feasible. (Information on writing minutes is given in Chapter 10). E-mails or memos should be written to those who were assigned special responsibilities at the meeting. **Directives** (formal authorizations for changes) should be composed, signed, and sent to those responsible for implementing the decisions that were made. The chairperson should make notes on his or her calendar as a reminder to verify that these special responsibilities have been completed and the decisions have been implemented.

Conducting Formal Meetings

Many groups conduct their meetings on a formal basis, following parliamentary rules. If you are elected to office in such a group, you should read *Robert's Rules of Order*, the standard guide to *parliamentary procedure.*

Parliamentary procedure is a set of rules for conducting meetings. These rules allow everyone to be heard and decisions to be made in an orderly manner. Widely used at business meetings and public gatherings, these rules can be adapted to fit the needs of a business, club, or organization. Organizations using parliamentary procedure usually follow a fixed order of business that determines the agenda. For example, the order of business may be as follows:

1. Call to Order
2. Roll Call of Members Present
3. Minutes of Last Meeting
4. Officers' Reports
5. Committee Reports
6. Special Orders (unfinished business previously noted for discussion at this meeting)
7. Unfinished Business (from previous meetings)
8. New Business
9. Announcements
10. Adjournment

Important decisions are reached by making, seconding, discussing, and voting on motions. A **motion** is a proposal that the entire membership take action or a stand on an issue. It is proposed ("moved") by one member and must be supported ("seconded") by another member; if not, the motion is lost. After being seconded, the motion is discussed and finally a vote is taken. Although not all members may vote in favour of a motion, once it has been adopted ("carried") by a majority of the members it becomes official policy.

Participating in Meetings

Everyone invited to participate in a group discussion has an obligation to contribute his or her best thinking and suggestions. Here is an opportunity to exhibit your interest in, and knowledge about, the work you are doing. Too often, time and money are wasted because so many employees take meetings for granted and do not contribute their maximum effort to the discussion. They often come to a meeting unprepared, uninterested, and uninspired.

Jon motioned that the policy be approved.

(moved)

The six basic rules for participating effectively in both informal and formal meetings are:

1. Prepare for the meeting.
2. Express opinions tactfully.
3. Make positive contributions.
4. Be courteous.
5. Keep remarks concise and pertinent.
6. Take notes.

Prepare for the Meeting

The first rule for effective participation in a meeting is to come prepared. Learn all that you can about the topics to be discussed at the meeting. If there is an agenda, study each item carefully and learn more about those topics which are unfamiliar to you. For example, if the subject of employee absenteeism is to be discussed, be sure that you know what the current company procedures are for dealing with absenteeism, as well as the advantages and disadvantages of these procedures. You may refer to books or articles dealing with this topic or examine company forms that are currently in use. In addition, you might get the opinions of knowledgeable people who will not be present at the meeting.

Being prepared also means coming to a meeting with a set of well-founded opinions. Opinions that are worth listening to in a business meeting are the ones backed up by facts. People are often opposed to a new idea merely because they don't know enough about it. Make certain that you can supply facts that will support your opinions and that will help convince others of the validity of your position.

Express Opinions Tactfully

Be tactful in expressing your opinion. Often, opposing points of view can cause strong disagreement. No matter how strongly you may feel, your chances of winning support from those with an opposing viewpoint are better if you are tactful in presenting your views.

Never tell someone that he or she is wrong—*wrong* is a strong term, and your right to use it requires indisputable evidence. Acknowledge the other person's point of view and show your respect for it. Then present your own ideas. For example, don't say, "You're wrong, and here's why." Instead, you could say "Your point of view certainly has merit, Henri. However, I have doubts because…"

In expressing yourself, separate facts from opinions. Label as facts only those statements for which you have solid evidence. Opinions should be signalled by such words as "it seems to me," "as I understand it," or "in my opinion."

Make Positive Contributions

Many meetings are held for the purpose of solving problems, and problems cannot be solved in a negative atmosphere. Approach a problem with the attitude that the only way to solve it is to present as many ideas as possible. No one should immediately veto an idea; instead, each person should try to see the idea's merits and to enlarge upon the idea's possibilities, no matter how weak the idea may seem at first. To dismiss ideas before they are fully aired is not only rude but also extremely disheartening to those who are genuinely trying to reach intelligent solutions.

Be Courteous

The ideal meeting is one in which everyone participates freely. A speaker who monopolizes the discussion will discourage the participation of others. Even though you may be more knowledgeable about the topic than anyone else in the group, never display your knowledge in an offensive, overbearing manner.

More victories have been won in group discussion by modesty and tact than will ever be achieved by aggressiveness. Don't jump in while others are speaking; wait your turn patiently. Show interest in what others are saying. You will win more support by listening and taking notes than by interrupting, regardless of how inane the remarks may seem to you.

Courteous group members do not (1) resort to sarcasm when they disagree with someone, (2) interrupt the person who is talking, (3) fidget, (4) gaze into space, or (5) carry on side conversations with other members of the group while someone else is speaking. If someone interrupts you while you are speaking, say something like "Please let me finish," and continue with the point you are making.

Keep Remarks Concise and Pertinent

Some participants in a meeting take a roundabout route to reach the point they want to make. They ramble endlessly. If you have something to say, get to your point quickly. Meetings become boring and unproductive when participants insist on relating personal preferences, experiences, and opinions that have little or no bearing on the discussion at hand.

Take Notes

It is a good idea to develop the habit of taking notes at meetings, because the act of taking careful notes (1) keeps you alert, (2) tells speakers that you consider their remarks worth remembering, and (3) provides a valuable reference source both during and after the meeting. Take notes not only on what the speaker is saying but also on what you want to say when it is your turn to speak. Jot down your key remarks in advance so that your comments are well organized and complete.

Avoid Substituting Note Taking for Active Listening

Occasionally, listeners will just "try to get it all down on paper," while promising themselves that they will review their notes later. When this happens, the listener transfers the information directly to paper without thinking about what was said. As a result, very little learning takes place because thinking is at the core of attentive listening and note taking.

If possible, compare your notes with those of a colleague. This comparison should help fill in gaps for both of you.

Review Your Notes Within 24 Hours

Read your notes as soon as possible after taking them. Reading your notes soon after taking them will enable you to include any necessary explanations or additions while the information is still fresh in your mind. A significant amount of memory loss takes place after 24 hours.

Highlight Major Points

Use a highlighter pen or underscoring to emphasize major points in your notes. Some people have a tendency to colour virtually the entire page with a highlighter. This practice defeats the purpose of highlighting. Highlight only the major points.

Key and Print Notes as a Learning Strategy

If the material is unusually hard to master, you may choose to key your notes and possibly expand on them while the information is still fresh in your mind. Keying the information helps you learn it, and having a neat printout makes your notes easier to read, study, and share with others.

Review of Key Terms

1. What is the difference between a *standing committee* and an *ad hoc committee*?
2. Under what circumstances would you use *Robert's Rules of Order*?

Practical Application

1. Evaluate your ability to conduct a meeting, using as guidelines your previous experience, if any, and the qualities you consider necessary in an effective leader of group discussions.
2. Interview a person who frequently attends meetings. Determine what she/he finds are the positive and negative aspects of these meetings. Discuss possible solutions for the negative points. Write a short report on your findings, or bring your notes to class for a group discussion.
3. The following negative statements were made by a meeting leader. Replace each statement with comments that will encourage participation.
   a. "We tried that before and it didn't work."
   b. "I don't think most people will agree with that."
4. Each team will select a subject for an ad hoc committee. Choose a chairperson for your committee and then develop a list of topics related to your subject. Create an agenda, using the sample agenda in this section and assign responsibility for each topic. Give team members time to write notes about their topics. Then role-play the meeting, with the chairperson bringing the meeting to order and leading the meeting. Then evaluate your meeting. What worked well? What could be improved, and how?

Editing Practice

Correct the spelling errors in the following message.

   Please plan to attend a meeting of the Personel Committee on Thrusday, September 15 at 8:30 a.m. I am preparing the ajenda; please foreward any topics you would like included. The minutes of the last meeting are atached. Please revue them carefully.

Discussion Points

1. How would you set up your classroom to be used as a meeting room by 10 people? What other preparations would you make for the meeting?
2. Note taking during meetings is important. What techniques can you use to avoid writing down everything the speaker is saying?

Making Presentations

To keep an audience's attention, make sure your speech is full of visual images. Examples are an excellent means of creating pictures.

—Phyllis Martin, in *A Word Watcher's Handbook*

▶ **Key Terms**

▶ rhetorical question
▶ document camera
▶ design templates
▶ animation
▶ slide transitions

Most professionals routinely make presentations as part of their job. They may also be asked to introduce and thank speakers at a conference or special event. Presentations could include addressing a student group that is touring their facility, making a formal sales presentation to a prospective client, or explaining a proposed policy to senior management. Being able to develop and make formal and informal presentations is an important business skill. Following the suggestions provided in this section will help you improve your presentation skills.

The Importance of Developing Presentation Skills

For many business professionals, the ability to speak effectively to groups is necessary for career success.

A business executive may be expected to represent the company before professional organizations and many different cultural, civic, religious, and educational groups. The executive's speaking duties at work may include speaking to members of one's own organization at employee meetings, at board meetings, or at stockholders' meetings.

However, even those who are not top executives often are called upon to participate in activities involving speeches before either large or small groups—instructing subordinates, reporting to an executive committee, introducing a speaker, explaining a new company policy to a group of employees, or hosting a group of visitors.

An effective speech should convey a message clearly and convincingly and, at the same time, it should build goodwill. Since nearly everyone is called upon at one time or another to "say a few words" to an audience, every business professional should be prepared to represent his or her company in a way that will reflect favourably.

Introducing and Thanking a Speaker

A brief, informative introduction sets the stage for the speaker and the presentation. In introducing and thanking a speaker, observe the following points.

1. Use an appropriate, brief introduction.
2. Set the stage for the speaker.
3. Keep your eyes on the audience.
4. End with the speaker's name.
5. Make closing remarks brief and appropriate.

Use an Appropriate, Brief Introduction

The audience has come to hear the speaker, not the person who is introducing the speaker. Therefore, keep the introduction short—not more than two or three minutes in length. Avoid giving specific information on the topic; the speaker will do that.

When you are introducing a speaker, avoid such trite expressions as, "The speaker for this evening needs no introduction," "I give you Professor Renee Christof," or "Without further ado, I present Dr. Moses Znaimer."

Set the Stage for the Speaker

Find out from the speaker's friends, associates, or assistant some personal traits or achievements that do not appear in the usual sources. Although you should have a complete resumé supplied to you itemizing the speaker's experience, education, and attainments, you do not need to use all this information. An audience is quickly bored by a straight biographical presentation, no matter how impressive. Give only the most significant dates, positions, and accomplishments. You need only to convince the audience that the speaker is qualified to speak on the topic assigned, is worth knowing, and has something important to say.

Keep Your Eyes on the Audience

Do not turn from the audience to face the speaker you are introducing—always keep your eyes on the audience. After you have made the introduction, wait until the speaker has reached the lectern before seating yourself.

End with the Speaker's Name

Many successful toastmasters recommend that you not mention the speaker's name until the very end of the introduction. During the introduction refer only to "our speaker." Then, at the end of the introduction, say something like, "It is my pleasure to present General Martin MacKenzie."

Make Closing Remarks Brief and Appropriate

At the end of the speaker's remarks, someone on the platform or at the speaker's table should assume the responsibility for thanking the speaker and closing the meeting. If the speech was a particularly effective one, you may say with sincerity, "Thank you, General MacKenzie, for your most enlightening and inspiring message. We are most appreciative. Members of the audience, the meeting is adjourned."

On the other hand, if the speech has been average or even disappointing, as indicated by the audience reaction, you may close by merely saying, "Thank you, Dr. Kingsley, for giving us your ideas on how to manage a multinational sales force. Members of the audience, thank you for coming to our meeting, and good night."

Under no circumstances should you prolong the closing remarks. If the speech was a good one, there is nothing more you can contribute to its effectiveness. If the speech was a poor one, the audience is probably anxious to leave.

Preparing for a Presentation

Preparation is the key to a good presentation. You have an obligation to prepare and to deliver a presentation that will be worthwhile for your audience.

Analyzing Your Audience

One of the first steps in preparing for a presentation is to analyze your audience. You should learn everything you can about your audience, including their knowledge of, and interest in, the subject. Doing so helps you plan what to say. The following tips will help you analyze your audience.

1. Determine the occasion for your presentation. Is it a staff meeting? birthday dinner? retirement banquet?
2. Tailor every presentation to the audience and to the occasion or theme of the meeting.
3. Respect your audience. This includes remaining within your allotted time. Using more time than allowed is discourteous. A good speaker knows the requirements of the program and adapts to them.
4. Put yourself in the shoes of the people who will be listening to your presentation and ask, "Would this speech be interesting to me?"
5. Find out such things as gender, job titles, education, interests, and general age range of the audience.
6. Find out how many people will attend so that you can prepare enough handouts.
7. Determine how much your audience knows about your topic. Your audience may know much about your topic or very little.
8. Choose the appropriate level of communication. Do not use specialized terminology that the audience may not understand. If you cannot avoid using these terms, explain them and include them in a handout.

Developing Your Speech

The second step in preparing a presentation is developing your speech. Whatever your topic, you should always have a strong introduction and conclusion. A brief but strong introduction grasps your audience's attention and gives a clear understanding of what you intend to talk about. You may choose to use a rhetorical question, a startling fact, or a true story to introduce your topic. A **rhetorical question** is a question that is posed—with no expectation of a response—to stimulate thought about a specific topic.

The body of your presentation should have substance for your listeners. You should develop your points and support them. Be careful to avoid

Figure 2.4 ▶
Breakdown of a
Presentation

Thinking Critically.
If you are making a
10-minute presentation to
the class, how much time
should you spend on your
introduction and
conclusion? Do you think
this is reasonable? Why or
why not?

Part	Purpose	Percentage of Time
Introduction	Tell them—briefly—what you are to cover; stimulate interest in the topic	15%
Body	Tell the content to be conveyed	70%
Conclusion	Tell them what you told them; summary and positive ending	15%

information overload. Most audiences will remember about five major points. You may want to use a handout to reinforce your major points.

Your concluding remarks should be well prepared, and you should end on a positive note. Remember that your audience, during these last critical minutes, is formulating a lasting impression of you and your presentation. A strong conclusion summarizes your major points and helps the audience remember what you said. Note the chart in Figure 2.4. It suggests an amount of time for each major part of your presentation.

Here are some tips to help you develop your speech.

Content

1. Determine the purpose for your presentation, and make sure that it is clear in your mind.
2. Brainstorm ideas about the subject and outline your presentation, keeping the organization simple.
3. Write your ideas about the subject in words that your audience can understand.
4. Do whatever research is necessary. A good guideline is to know ten times more about your subject than you are able to say during the allotted time. This extra knowledge will help you field questions and feel self-confident.

Clarity

1. Be specific, avoid making too many broad generalizations, and stay on your subject.
2. Don't try to ad-lib or add material on the spot.
3. Use repetition as an effective way to emphasize main points.
4. Summarize after each main point.
5. Explain difficult points as you go along, and define unfamiliar terms the first time that you mention them.
6. Do not use abbreviations, acronyms, or technical terms that are unfamiliar to the audience.
7. Bring the presentation to a deliberate conclusion. Re-emphasize the basic message, and summarize your main points.
8. Even though the audience is not reading your presentation, it is a good idea to use the readability function in your word processing software to estimate the grade level of the content. Then, make any necessary adjustments to target your presentation to the appropriate level for your audience.

Treatment

1. Try to give an overall impression of the subject rather than just facts and figures. The audience will get bored if all you do is give statistics.
2. Use illustrations and examples to help your audience relate to your content.
3. Use human-interest stories and phrases that appeal to the senses and tend to create pictures in the minds of your audience.

Humour

1. Use humour only if you are comfortable with it. Omit telling jokes if you know that you always forget the punchline or that no one ever laughs at your jokes.
2. Remember that starting with a joke is risky. If the joke bombs, recovering is almost impossible.
3. Use humour only if it pertains to your topic.
4. Do not make fun of an individual or group of individuals. If you are questioning whether to use a specific joke, the rule of thumb is don't use it.
5. If there are humorous aspects to your subject, make reference to them. Humour can be a true story that has a humorous side. A speaker telling how to give CPR might say, "When you first see a person lying down, check to see if he or she is breathing. I almost gave CPR to a person who was simply sleeping."

When trying to decide whether or not a certain anecdote, joke, or story would be appropriate, use the following general rule:

When in doubt, leave it out!

-MEMORY HOOK-

Getting Ready

After you have analyzed your audience and developed your presentation, you should prepare your notes and rehearse. Speakers, just like musical performers and actors, should practise before the actual presentation. Here are some tips to help you get ready for the presentation.

1. Develop speaking notes from the text of your presentation.
2. If possible, use presentation software such as PowerPoint for your speaking notes or outline. This frees you from referring to hard copy and the accompanying distraction of shuffling note cards or papers. It also provides freedom of movement because you are not restricted by the use of a lectern or table for your speaking notes. Attractive slides help keep your audience focused on the message and make it easier for them to absorb the information. Always prepare a backup set of overhead sheets in case you have computer or projection problems.
3. Print your notes on index cards, not full sheets of paper. Sheets of paper look unprofessional, and even the slightest movement of papers will cause noise, which will be amplified if you are using a microphone.
4. Use large print (14 to 16 point) on your note cards, which will allow you to see the text easily. The distance from the lectern to your eyes will probably be slightly greater than your normal reading distance.
5. Use a brightly coloured highlighter pen to mark important points.

6. Don't put your notes on the podium ahead of time. The speaker before you may inadvertently remove them.

7. Indicate on your note cards the visual aid that should be used at that particular point in the presentation.

8. Practise until you feel confident and can coordinate your visual aids with your presentation. Practice is the key to success, especially if it is your first presentation. Rehearse at least three times; a good guideline is three to six times. Rehearse in front of a mirror, or in front of a friend or family member. Ask your helper to makes notes on strengths and areas for improvement. Stress that you are looking for constructive criticism that will help you improve your presentation. Memorize the opening so that you can concentrate on making contact with your audience.

9. Rehearse for timing. Plan what you can cut if it becomes necessary and what you can add if you finish ahead of schedule.

10. If possible, rehearse in the room in which you will be presenting with the equipment you will be using.

11. Practise with a microphone if you will be using one.

12. Videotape your presentation to detect and fine-tune details such as speaking too fast, speaking without expression, and using distracting mannerisms.

13. Remember that skipping meals before you speak can take the edge off your energy level. Overeating can cause you to become sluggish.

14. Determine the best location for visual aids.

15. Make sure the audience can hear you. Ask for a microphone if you know that you have difficulty projecting your voice in a large room.

16. Examine podium lighting to make sure you can read your notes.

17. Adjust the room temperature if possible. Set the temperature a few degrees below the comfortable level. The temperature will rise when people assemble in the room.

18. Make sure that all equipment is working properly.

19. Send a copy of your resumé or a brief autobiographic sketch to the person introducing you. Take an extra copy with you to the presentation.

Number your note cards for a speech. If you drop them, they can easily be put back into the correct order.

Conveying a Professional Image

Now that you have finished your preparation, you should be concerned with conveying a professional image during your presentation. Audience members start forming their opinions of you as soon as they see you. Use your best manners, be sure that you are dressed appropriately, and demonstrate a professional image as you enter the room and walk to the podium.

The following tips should help you convey a professional image.

1. Be real, be sincere, be yourself. Being pompous or arrogant destroys audience rapport.

2. Remember that much of your message is communicated nonverbally through your posture, tone of voice, expressions, gestures, and attire.

3. Be well-groomed. Make sure that your hair is neat and your clothes are fastened.
4. Decide what you will wear for your presentation in time to have your garments pressed or cleaned.
5. Select clothes and accessories that look professional. Wear comfortable shoes that are appropriate for the occasion.
6. Use appropriate facial expressions.
7. Avoid mannerisms that take your listener's attention away from your content. Avoid rocking back and forth, standing on one foot, chewing gum, or jingling keys or coins.
8. Use relaxed, natural movements and appropriate gestures. Lean toward your audience, not away from it.
9. Walk confidently to the podium or front of the room, and stay poised throughout your presentation.

Delivering Your Presentation

Now, you are ready to actually deliver your presentation. You should greet your audience and convey your pleasure at being asked to speak to them by smiling and using a friendly tone. In greeting your audience, you should observe the courtesies that are dictated by the formality of your speaking situation. For example, at a committee meeting, you might say, "Madam Chair and Committee Members." A simple "Good morning" would be appropriate in casual circumstances.

Probably, the most-mentioned audience expectation is that the speaker not read his or her presentation. A second expectation is that the speech be useful or engaging. The third expectation is that the speaker should end on time. The smart speaker, when assigned 45 minutes, plans on 35 to 40 minutes. If there are 5 to 10 minutes left, this time may be used to answer questions. Following are some suggestions for improving your delivery.

1. Deliver your presentation; don't read it. Reciting from memory or reading a presentation makes you seem insincere, apprehensive, and unprepared.
2. Print your outline on note cards. Writing out every word on note cards will confuse you during the presentation.
3. Radiate energy, be enthusiastic, and be sincere.
4. Maintain eye contact. Focus on one person for several seconds, letting the person sense that you are talking to him or her. Then, focus on someone else in another segment of the room.
5. Speak at a slow, deliberate pace, and pause occasionally. Silence can be an effective way to get your audience's attention.
6. Concentrate on your words so that you do not slur your speech.
7. Properly pronounce words, use correct grammar, and choose appropriate vocabulary.
8. Stay focused and keep ideas moving.
9. Adjust your volume to enable everyone in the room to hear you.
10. Speak to your audience, not to your visual aid. Face your audience. Don't turn your back as you explain visuals.
11. Repeat important points. Audience members are more likely to remember details that they hear more than once.

Put prompts or reminders to yourself on your note cards. For example, you could put a smiley face to remind you to have a pleasant expression. You could write SLOW UP! on several cards if you have a tendency to speak too fast. A clock drawing would remind you to check your time.

12. Avoid fillers such as *uh* and *um,* and clichés such as "to make a long story short" or "That reminds me of a story…"
13. Monitor expressions and nonverbal cues to determine if your audience is confused, listening, disagreeing, or bored. Respond by adjusting your presentation accordingly.
14. Use appropriate gestures to emphasize major points.
15. Coordinate content and visual aids. Do not show a visual aid until you are ready for your audience to see it.
16. Anticipate potential noise such as people talking in the halls. When noise occurs, keep your composure and pause for the noise to end.
17. Stay within your assigned time limit.
18. Leave time for questions from your audience.

Fielding Questions

Cultivate a positive attitude about questions from your audience. Good questions can help clarify important concepts, identify misunderstandings from audience members, and recognize specific areas that they want to know more about. Most presentation situations offer a question-and-answer period. When someone asks you a question, acknowledge the person and listen closely to the question. Following are some guidelines for fielding questions.

1. At the beginning of your presentation, tell your audience your preference for handling questions—at the end or as they occur throughout the presentation. An inexperienced speaker may prefer handling questions at the end.
2. If you like handling questions throughout the presentation, you may want to stop at convenient points and ask for questions.
3. Repeat the questions for the audience members who may not have heard them. Restating the question gives you time to formulate your response.
4. Ask for clarification if a question is unclear to you.
5. Give brief, direct answers to questions.
6. Try to anticipate possible questions by the audience, and think of answers in advance.
7. If you don't know the answer to a question, offer to find the answer and forward it. Ask the person to leave a business card with the question on the reverse side.
8. Stay calm and polite if you receive antagonistic questions. Avoid displaying negative emotions. If the audience member continues to be confrontational, offer to talk with the person after the session ends.

Managing Stage Fright

What are the symptoms of stage fright, or speaker's anxiety? Some speakers report cold hands, sweaty palms, shaky knees, or a quivering voice. Others sense a pounding heart. Most experienced and inexperienced speakers have anxiety when addressing a group of people. Experienced speakers, however, value the benefits produced by anxiety and attempt to convert it into a positive energy that keeps them sharp and alert during their presentations.

Good advice for managing stage fright used to appear on the lid of a popular brand of mayonnaise: "Keep cool, but don't freeze."

If you experience stage fright, remember that nervousness is normal and that you are not alone in this emotion. Most people list the fear of speaking in public as their number one fear. Experienced speakers do not eliminate stage fright, but they learn how to live with it and how to manage it. Following are some suggestions for managing anxiety.

1. Prepare adequately. The key to conquering stage fright is preparation.
2. Master your content and visual aids to boost your self-confidence.
3. Because much of the anxiety comes as you begin your presentation, make sure that you are especially prepared with a very strong opening.
4. Go to the meeting room early, and talk with members of your audience. Introduce yourself to those whom you do not know, and have an informal conversation with those you already know.
5. While in the rest room or other private place, loosen up by bending from the waist and letting your hands and arms hang limp.
6. Just before you go to the podium, take three deep breaths to help you relax.
7. When you are speaking, focus on your topic and your audience.
8. Develop a positive attitude toward speaking. Speak every time you have the opportunity, whether at school, work, club meetings, or other social or religious functions.

Evaluating Your Presentation

After each presentation, you should evaluate yourself. Also, ask a friend or co-worker if he or she will constructively criticize your presentation. Be receptive to any suggestions. Try to complete the evaluation within two to three days after the presentation, while you still clearly remember the details. This self-evaluation process will help you become a better speaker. Here are some evaluation techniques.

1. Seek constructive criticism of your presentation from people you respect.
2. Maintain a good attitude about negative comments.
3. Profit by your mistakes, and convert them into a learning experience.
4. Note any segments getting several questions. It is possible that your content was incomplete or unclear in this particular area.
5. List any changes you would make if you were presenting the same topic soon.
6. Compare yourself with others who spoke on the same program.
7. List your assets and liabilities that are related to speaking.
8. Accept as many opportunities to present as possible. Each speaking experience and subsequent evaluation will help you improve your presentation skills.
9. Keep a presentation file. The file will be helpful should you be asked to speak to the same group again or to another group on the same or a similar topic. Include your evaluation in this file.

Visual Aids

Creating useful and appropriate visual aids is vital for presentation success. Visual aids should help convey your message, keep your audience focused, and improve retention of your subject matter.

Visual aids can include electronic slide shows, 35 mm slides, handouts, overhead transparencies, videos, traditional photographs, scanned or digital photographs, demonstrations, objects, samples, flip charts, and skits. Some presentations might use a combination of the mentioned methods. For example, a presentation on how to give CPR might include electronic slides giving the statistics on the number of lives that can be saved using this procedure. Then, using a dummy, the presenter might demonstrate how to administer CPR.

Basic Guidelines for Visual Aids

Visual aids should support and enhance your presentation and reduce the amount of effort that your listener needs to understand what you are saying. In other words, visual aids should help convey your message. Suppose, for example, you were doing a presentation on credit card abuse and your visual aids consisted of a stack of credit cards and your most recent statement. Would the credit cards and the statement help convey your message? No, everyone has seen credit cards and statements. Neither aid would help convey the message about the huge amount of credit debt accumulated by people who overextend their purchases based on their current salaries. Facts and figures in an electronic slide show would be a good choice to convey the details about credit card abuse.

Your content, your presentation location, and the equipment available will determine the best visual aid to help you get your points across. Remember, the quality of your visual aids strongly influences your audience's perception of you. Strive for professional-looking quality.

One of the basic rules of communication also applies to the preparation of visual aids. The KISS rule should be emphasized. KISS stands for *Keep It Short and Simple*. For example, when preparing handouts, slides, and other printed visuals, use key words instead of complete sentences. In addition to simplicity, you should keep the visuals uncluttered.

Use an appropriate number of visuals in relation to the length of your presentation. Saturating your presentation with visuals loses an audience. Remember that visual aids are not the presentation and that good visuals are not a substitute for good content. Impressive visual aids will not disguise content that lacks substance.

Visual aids should be easily read from any location in the room. For that reason, posters are usually ineffective for a group of more than ten people. Passing around samples is also ineffective for large groups, because the distribution causes a distraction and, in most instances, the speaker is finished before the samples reach everyone in the room.

Make sure that you do not stand between your audience and the visual aid. Also make sure that you do not talk to your visual aid but face your audience. You should, however, quickly glance at your visual as soon as it is displayed to make sure that it is indeed there and is positioned correctly.

Integrating the visual aids throughout the presentation—as opposed to clustering them at the beginning or end of the presentation—helps sustain your audience's attention. Use a variety of visual aids in long presentations. This tactic helps keep your audience's attention.

Always practice your presentation with your visuals. Putting everything together smoothly takes much practice. Always number your visuals and indicate on your note cards when the visual should be shown.

Handouts

Experienced speakers recommend that you give your audience at least one handout. Having something to take away from the presentation helps the audience remember you and your topic. Always include contact information such as your name, postal address, e-mail address, and fax and telephone numbers on your handouts.

Handouts are a good choice for visual aids when the information is too complex or too small to be projected onto a screen. They are also useful when you want audience members to evaluate the material or react to the content at a later date.

If you are going to use your handouts during your presentation, ask someone to distribute the handouts for you, preferably as audience members enter the room. This saves time and avoids the distraction of distributing them during your presentation. If your handout will not be used during your presentation, distribute them as your audience is leaving. You could also choose to have your audience download the handouts from your Web site.

Numbering or colour-coding handout pages makes it easier for audience members to locate a specific page when you refer to it during your presentation: "Please find page 7," or "Please turn to the blue page in your handouts." It is helpful to leave generous margins on handouts for additional notes. Many presenters provide miniature slide printouts to make note taking easier for listeners.

Multimedia Rooms and Projectors

Corporations often have multimedia rooms for meetings and presentations. These rooms use a combination of equipment. The presenter stands at a console that houses a computer and the other needed equipment. Some rooms have rear projection capabilities; others have a projector mounted from the ceiling that can be activated from the console.

From the console, the presenter can show transparencies and project hard-copy documents using the document camera. The **document camera** projects a photograph, a drawing, or the printed page onto the screen. The presenter, from the console, can also play a videotape or access an Internet connection or a cable television show. Additionally, anything on the computer screen, such as an electronic slide show, can also be projected.

The quality of multimedia equipment varies. Several companies make portable equipment that can be transported in a rolling case to different locations within the firm or to distant locations.

Using Presentation Software

Presentation software such as PowerPoint will let you generate electronic slides that can be used as visual aids during a presentation or as a presentation that will run automatically. Automatic slide show presentations have many uses because they run uninterrupted and can be left unattended. For example, a college admissions staff developed an automatic slide show to be used when the staff visits high schools to recruit students. Using a notebook computer, the slide show runs continuously on a television monitor at the admissions booth during college fairs. Parents and students can observe the show while they are waiting to talk with an admissions counselor.

Additionally, presentation software can be used to write, edit, and print the speaker's outline or notes, as well as to produce professional-looking handouts. You can also use the software to print miniature copies of your slides to be used as part of your notes or to distribute as handouts to your audience to facilitate note taking. One of the major advantages of using presentation software is that you can update your electronic slides within a few moments. This convenient updating is particularly helpful for sales representatives who use PowerPoint presentations when making sales calls.

Presentation software provides design templates to make slide show creation easy for the novice. **Design templates** are preformatted layouts that let you add text, while keeping layout, colour, fonts, etc., consistent. You can add clip art, animation, or slide transitions to make your visual aids more interesting. The clip art gallery, provided with your software, is a collection of simple drawings that can be used to illustrate your slides. In addition to the clip art that comes with the presentation software, there are Web sites that provide a variety of clip art that can be used in your electronic slides.

Slides can be animated in several ways. **Animation** is a feature that lets parts of the slide—titles, bulleted items, and clip art—arrive on the screen at different times. For example, the title would appear first, the clip art next, and then each bulleted item would be added one at a time as the speaker talks about each one. Slide transitions are another presentation software feature. **Slide transitions** are special effects that introduce each slide as it appears on the screen. Examples would be sounds announcing the next slide or special visual effects like having the slide fade in or out.

The following checklist will help you prepare and use an electronic slide show.

Checklist for Presentation Software Visual Aids

- Make sure all information on the graphics is correct and up-to-date.
- Use an appropriate number of visuals in relation to the length of your presentation. Oversaturating your presentation with visuals loses an audience. Project each slide for about 30 seconds.
- Use colour effectively to make your visuals more interesting and pleasing to the eye. Avoid red and green. Most people who are colour-blind find these colours difficult to read.
- Keep slides simple and uncluttered. Slides that require lengthy explanations are ineffective.
- Limit each slide or transparency to three to four lines of text; seven lines should be the maximum.

- Use block lettering, not fancy or script type. Limit type styles to three per visual. Using more than three styles complicates the visual.
- The three preferred font sizes are 36, 24, and 18. A size 18 font should be the smallest font that you use.
- Use uppercase and lowercase letters. Solid capitals are hard to read.
- Use bullets to emphasize important points.
- Vary the visuals. Use a combination of pictures, graphs, and cartoons.
- Use a limited number of special features on each slide. Too many pictures, animations, and transitions can detract from your content.
- Test visual aids on the equipment that you will be using during the presentation.
- Complete your remarks about a transparency or PowerPoint slide before showing the slide. Once the slide goes up, your audience will focus on it rather than on what you are saying.

Anticipating Problems

No matter how much you prepare and how well you are organized, situations can develop over which you have no control. Anticipate as many of these situations as you can and plan how you will handle the situation.

One of the most common problems with technology is the incompatibility of software. For example, a slide show that works perfectly on your office computer may not work in the hotel conference room if two different software applications are involved.

Other problems include such frustrating situations as the following:
- The bulb burns out in your projector.
- The projection equipment malfunctions.
- The slide carousel jams.
- Your handouts were lost in transit.
- There is a power outage.

Prepare backup visuals; for example, transparencies for your slide show or slide miniatures as handouts. Here is some more good advice: Be able to give your presentation without visual aids if necessary.

You, your content, and the manner in which you deliver the content are the presentation. Prepare and rehearse—these are the keys to successful presenting.

Review of Key Terms

1. When beginning a speech, how can a *rhetorical question* help set the stage?
2. How can *design templates* aid in creating a slide show?
3. When would you want to use *animation* in an electronic slide show?

Practical Application

1. Identify a person whom you feel is an excellent speaker. List at least five reasons for your selection.
2. Prepare and present a three-minute informal presentation to your class on how to do something; for example, how to change a flat tire or how to set a formal table. Use visual aids. As you present, try to make each person in your audience feel as though you are talking individually to them.
3. a. Prepare and present a five-minute formal presentation to your class on a topic related to your intended career. Research of your topic must be evident in your presentation. Use visual aids. To give you experience in fielding questions, open the floor for questions at the end of your presentation.

   b. Ask your teacher and class members to evaluate your presentation. Do your own evaluation. Compare and discuss the evaluations.
4. You will introduce your instructor at a dinner for the graduates of your class and their guests. Ask your instructor to select a topic and to supply needed biographical information. Be sure to use an appropriate attention-getting introduction that will encourage the audience to listen.
5. Interview someone in the field of education, human resources, or staff development and find out what kinds of visual aids are used. Find out if more advanced technological aids are being introduced and what the advantages and disadvantages are to using these tools. Write a brief essay about your findings for your instructor.
6. Prepare and deliver a short presentation about your campus. Include some form of visual aid—electronic slides, 35 mm slides, overhead transparencies, videos, handouts, etc. List your preparation and presentation steps, and assign duties to each team member. Remember to rehearse your presentation using the visuals.

Editing Practice

Editing for Context. Replace the word in each sentence that does not fit the context.

1. The threat of a tax audit compiled us to consult with our accountant.
2. Did you receive all the items listed on the manifest?

3. His actions did not ward our taking any steps at this time.
4. Their quite concerned about environmental issues.
5. Sign the affidavit where indicted.
6. Please call the personal office to arrange a preliminary interview.
7. All the employees will benefit tremulously from the changes.
8. The error demented our confidence in his ability.
9. We attended to complete the project by Saturday.
10. To countenance serious problems, we must make drastic budget cuts.

Discussion Points

1. Discuss how audience and content play a role in the development of a presentation. How does content dictate the treatment of a topic? Should humour be used in all speeches?

2. When should a presenter use handouts? What are some guidelines in using handouts?

3. "A picture is worth a thousand words." What does this mean, and how does this meaning relate to the use of visual aids in a presentation?

Chapter 2 Wrap-Up

SUMMARY

▶ Business professionals rely on effective oral communication skills in performing a great variety of tasks. When preparing for any oral communication, analyze your audience and adapt your nonverbal communication and voice qualities to their particular needs and wants. Especially in one-on-one exchanges in person or over the telephone, it is important to listen attentively, speak concisely, and give the other person your undivided attention.

▶ Effective telephone communication also requires following a number of guidelines such as providing a "warm" transfer, verifying important details, and greeting the caller. When using voice mail, you should record a professional greeting and leave concise, complete messages.

▶ Nonverbal communication is communicating without words. Nonverbal communication plays a major part in the forming of first impressions and in the subsequent development of a relationship. The categories of nonverbal communication are paralanguage, body language, environment, touch, and space.

▶ The quality of your speech is determined by volume, pitch, tone, tempo, enunciation, and pronunciation. Enunciation refers to the distinctness or clarity with which you articulate words, while pronunciation refers to the sound that the speaker gives to letters or letter combinations of a word or to the way in which a speaker accents a word.

▶ Listening is a primary means of gathering information. Active listening is appropriate when you need to remember the information you hear. An active listener will concentrate, maintain eye contact, and take notes. Barriers to active listening may be physical and environmental, attitudinal, emotional, or language barriers. To improve listening skills, you should prepare physically and mentally, listen with a positive attitude, avoid interrupting, listen for feelings, and make efficient use of available time. This time can be used on such activities such as assessing the message and formulating questions.

▶ A meeting organizer should consider the reason for the meeting and the participants' background, as well as thoroughly prepare an agenda and send it ahead of time. The effectiveness of the meeting is based on the leader's ability to know how to lead a discussion, summarize ideas presented, and encourage participation. The leader of the meeting should always follow up on critical actions approved in the meeting. To effectively participate in a meeting, you should prepare, make positive, tactful statements, and keep your remarks concise and pertinent.

▶ When introducing and thanking a speaker, you should keep your comments brief and set the stage for the speaker.

▶ The ability to speak to groups is an important skill for many business professionals. You should prepare by analyzing your audience, and then developing and rehearsing your speech. When giving a presentation you should convey a professional image, deliver your presentation (not read it), allow time for questions, and end on time. A professional presentation utilizes effective visual aids and electronic presentation mediums like Pow-erPoint. Follow the *Keep It Short and Simple* (KISS) guideline for preparing visual aids.

CASE 2.1

You are the marketing director for Pfizer, a leading pharmaceutical company. You have been asked to coach one of your marketing interns who will compose a speech to present to her business communication class.

Some of the most commonly used prescription drugs the company has developed are Zoloft, Viagra, and Lipitor, each of which pulls in profits of more than $1 billion. You don't want the intern to make the speech too complex. What would be your advice to the intern for the class presentation based on the tips presented in Chapter 2?

CASE 2.2

Many companies have offices worldwide, which frequently makes it difficult to communicate on an immediate basis. MasterCard International has resolved this problem by using advanced video conferencing to communicate with its executives. Meetings can be scheduled without employees ever leaving the building. This method of communicating saves the company time and money that would otherwise be spent on international travel.

What skills covered in this section do you think employees must use to make these video conferences productive?

Communicating in Your Career

You are a financial consultant for Royal Investments Canada. You have a client who has requested an in-home consultation with him and his 75-year-old mother. She is interested in investing her money so that her grandson has a trust fund for college. What content and delivery aspects should you consider when preparing for the initial phone conversation with the client and the subsequent meeting with the client and his mother?

On the Web

1. Toastmasters International is a worldwide organization dedicated to helping individuals improve their public speaking and communication skills. Toastmasters has many clubs throughout Canada. Visit *www.toastmasters. org* to find the club nearest to you, to read about the benefits of membership, and to study the Speaking Tips.

2. Research *Robert's Rules* by either

   a. Using a search engine such as Google.com to search for information on *Robert's Rules.* Find information that gives an introduction to *Robert's Rules of Order* and answer the following questions: What are the four basic types of motions? What are the procedures for voting on a motion?

   b. Using *www.robertsrules.com* find information on the basics of parliamentary procedure. What topics are covered? Then go to the Question and Answer Forum, choose two questions and study the answers.

   Make notes so that you can share the information with the class or write a short report for your instructor.

Key Terms

active listening	57	interpreting	56	retaining	56
ad hoc committee	67	intonation	50	rhetorical question	79
agenda	68	listening	56	*Robert's Rules of*	
animation	88	listening barriers	58	*Order*	72
body language		minutes	68	slide transitions	88
(kinesics)	47	motion	73	space	48
"dead" air	41	nonverbal		standing committee	67
design templates	88	communication	46	tempo	51
directives	72	paralanguage	47	tone	50
document camera	87	parliamentary		touch (haptic	
enunciation	51	procedure	72	communication)	48
external noise	58	passive listening	57	voice-mail greeting	42
hearing	56	pitch	50	volume	49
internal noise	58	pronunciation	52	"warm" transfer	41

Chapter 3

Exploring Language Elements

Chapter Learning Outcomes

After successfully completing this chapter, you will have demonstrated the ability to:

▶ identify the eight parts of speech;

▶ distinguish between sentences and fragments;

▶ correctly use regular and irregular verbs;

▶ apply the principles of subject-verb agreement.

Ashley had been working as administrative assistant to Mr. Bisram, the head of the shipping department, for about two years. When the administrative assistant to the company president retired, Ashley applied for the position. Ashley was disappointed when she did not get the promotion and asked Mr. Bisram if he knew the reason.

Mr. Bisram was quite candid. He reminded Ashley that her performance evaluations had indicated that she was weak in grammatical skills and that the reports and letters she produced always had to be corrected for grammatical errors.

Ashley decided that she would not be passed over for the next available promotion. She bought a communications text, began to review it immediately and placed it beside her dictionary in the office as a ready reference. After confirming that her company had a tuition reimbursement policy, Ashley enrolled in a grammar course at the local community college.

Ashley's grammar skills improved. Her next performance evaluation was positive and included a note about Ashley's efforts to refresh her grammar skills to improve her job performance.

Ashley's efforts paid off. She got the next available promotion, which included a salary increase.

As you read Chapter 3, identify areas of grammar usage in which you could improve. Like Ashley, plan what you will do to strengthen your language skills.

The Parts of Speech

I am the Roman king, and am above grammar.

—Sigismund, Holy Roman emperor

▶ **Key Terms**

In the case study at the beginning of the chapter, Ashley found out that, unlike the emperor whose quotation introduces this section, she was not above grammar. Just the opposite. Ashley discovered that understanding basic grammar terms and knowing how to use grammar correctly gave her a firm base on which to create effective communications.

The many thousands of words in our language can be grouped into eight categories: nouns, pronouns, verbs, adjectives, adverbs, prepositions, conjunctions, and interjections. These categories are called the parts of speech. Each part of speech has certain characteristics, one of which is how the words from the category function in a sentence. Let's begin with nouns.

Nouns

The word *noun* is derived from a word meaning "name." A **noun** is the *name* of a person, place, thing, idea, concept, or quality. Nouns may be proper or common. A proper noun names a specific person, place, or thing. A common noun names a general person, place, or thing. The list on the following page gives examples of proper and common nouns.

In a sentence, nouns function as subjects, direct objects, indirect objects, objects of a preposition, appositives, and complements. These functions will be discussed in this chapter.

Pronouns

Pronouns are words that *replace* nouns. Examples include *I, you, he, it, we, they, me, her, us, them, my, its, your, his, mine, our,* and *their*. Pronouns add variety to our speech and our writing and provide us with shortcuts. Some examples are:

She asked Jason to order new stationery. (Another way of saying "*Maria* asked Jason to order new stationery.")

She gave *them* the keys to *their* offices. (Another way of saying "*The administrative assistant* gave *Fred and Mary* the keys to *Fred's and Mary's* offices.")

Since pronouns replace nouns, they also function as subjects, direct objects, indirect objects, objects of prepositions, appositives, and complements.

Common & Proper Nouns	
Proper	**Common**
Persons: Ms. Rodchester Hampton, Lisa	associates students
Places: Laurentian Mountains West Coast	universities restaurant
Things: CN Tower Nortel Networks Corporation	videocassettes computers
Ideas, concepts, or qualities: Buddhism Taoism	democracy courage

◀ **Figure 3.1**
Common and Proper Nouns
This table shows common and proper nouns.

Thinking Critically.
How does knowing the difference between common and proper nouns affect your communications with others?

CHECKUP 1

Identify the nouns and pronouns in the following sentences. Label each noun (*N*) and each pronoun (*P*).

1. Can we order tickets for a play in Toronto?
2. I am sure Jasmin Lee will make our reservation if we ask her.
3. They bought the software in Ottawa last month.
4. You and I will meet next Tuesday to discuss the new budget.
5. She plans to visit Edmonton and Banff to tour the sights.
6. Sol and Chris tell me the Maritimes is their favourite part of the country.

Verbs

Verbs are words that express action, a state of being, or a condition. Verbs that express an obvious action are called "**action verbs**" because they give sentences life. Some examples are:

Our company *imports* Swiss chocolate and *uses* it in various desserts. (*Imports* and *uses* are action verbs.)

Ms. Platt *bought* one Swiss chocolatier's inventory and *shipped* it to our New Brunswick plant. (*Bought* and *shipped* are action verbs)

Some verbs do not indicate an obvious action but express a condition or a state of being. These verbs are called **linking verbs**. Linking verbs include forms of the verb *to be*, such as *am, is, are, was, were, be,* and *been*. Linking verbs also include the sense verbs *look, feel, sound, taste,* and *smell,* as well as the verbs *appear* and *become*. Some examples are:

Of course, I *am* delighted about Indira's promotion, but her parents *are* thrilled. (*Am* and *are* are verbs that show state of being.)

Mario *will be* an assistant manager in April. By that time Kathy *will have been* a manager for 12 years. (*Will be* and *will have been* are verbs. Note that each consists of more than one word.)

In a sentence, verbs function as predicates. You will learn about predicates later in this chapter.

CHECKUP 2

Identify the verbs in the following sentences.

1. John seems happy about his new job.
2. Heidi was planning a new brochure for these products.
3. Janice hired two new assistants after she promoted John.
4. Mr. Vernon has been in Halifax for about two weeks.

Now supply a verb for each blank in the following sentences and indicate whether it is an action verb or a linking verb.

5. Adriana _____ her college diploma requirements in May and _____ her new job two months later.
6. She _____ proud of her diploma and her new job.
7. Adriana _____ every evening during the two weeks before her exams.
8. Her parents _____ proud of her and _____ her graduation ceremony.

Adjectives

Adjectives *describe* nouns and pronouns by limiting, or making more specific, the noun or pronoun. Another word for limiting is *modifying*.

Adjectives may show what kind of, which one, or how many. Some examples are:

What kind of: *hectic* schedule, *interesting* article, *expensive* equipment

Which one: her *former* supervisor, *that* report, *those* folders

How many: *one* employee, *several* clients, *few* tickets

The words *a*, *an*, and *the* are special types of adjectives called *articles*. *A* and *an* are indefinite articles because they do not identify a specific item. *The* is a definite article because it identifies a specific item.

When an adjective describes a noun, the adjective usually precedes the noun. When an adjective describes a pronoun, the adjective generally follows a linking verb or a sense verb. Some examples are:

She was *impatient* with the slow growth of her investment. (The adjective *impatient* describes the pronoun *she*.)

She feels *ill*. (*Ill* describes the pronoun *she*.)

Adjectives that follow linking verbs and sense verbs can also describe nouns.

Caterina feels *ill*.

The group was *nervous* before its presentation.

Adverbs

Adverbs are also *modifiers*; like adjectives, adverbs *describe* or *limit* adjectives, verbs, or other adverbs. They specify *how, when, where, why, in what manner*, and *to what extent*. Some examples are:

Jean was *unusually* calm during the meeting yesterday. (The adverb *unusually* modifies the adjective *calm*.)

Herb *nearly* fell on his face as he tripped over the telephone cord. (The adverb *nearly* modifies the verb *fell*.)

Note that many adverbs end in *ly* and are therefore very easy to identify. Some examples are:

sure*ly*	immediate*ly*	bad*ly*
sudden*ly*	successful*ly*	happi*ly*

We form these adverbs by adding *ly* to the adjectives *sure, sudden, immediate, successful, bad,* and *happy.* Note that with *happy,* the "y" changes to "i."

Although most words that end in *ly* are adverbs, not all adverbs end in *ly.* Here are some adverbs that do *not* end in *ly:*

always	very	well	then
not	soon	here	never
much	quite	there	almost

CHECKUP 3

Identify the words in parentheses as either adjectives or adverbs.

1. They were (excited) about graduation.
2. The (beautiful) weather (here) attracts (many) tourists each summer.
3. Frank will forward the shipment (immediately) to the (new) construction site.
4. Several (experienced) police officers are (eagerly) waiting to start the investigation.
5. A (professional) presentation (always) includes (attractive) visual aids.
6. The (last) person whom we interviewed was (more) qualified than we had expected.

Prepositions

Prepositions are *connecting words that show the relationship between a noun or pronoun and other words in a sentence.* The following words are commonly used prepositions:

about	between	over	throughout
at	beneath	of	toward
against	beyond	off	up
across	concerning	on	upon
after	down	onto	under
above	during	out	until
around	except	regarding	underneath
but	for	respecting	past
before	from	since	with
by	in	to	within
below	into	through	without
beside			

Choosing the Correct Preposition

Choosing the correct preposition often causes difficulty. Certain words are followed by certain prepositions. Here is a list of frequently used combinations.

accompanied *by* **a person:** Susan was *accompanied by* her brother.

accompanied *with* **something:** Jay's speech was *accompanied with* slides.

account *for* **something or someone:** I find it hard to *account for* his attitude.

account *to* **someone:** I will have to *account to* my supervisor for the lost files.

agree *on* or *upon* **(to reach an understanding):** We have *agreed on* the price.

agree *to* **(to accept another person's plan):** Will you *agree to* their terms?

agree *with* **(concur with a person or an idea):** I *agree with* Henry.

angry *with* or *about* **something:** Sue was *angry about* the timetable change.

angry *with* **someone:** Bill is *angry with* me.

apply *for* **a position:** Ryan will *apply for* the manager's job.

apply *to* **someone or something:** I have *applied to* the engineering program at the Fraser Institute.

argue *about* **something:** We *argued about* the arrangements for Uwe's party.

argue *with* **a person:** Jean is *arguing with* Ahmed.

beneficial *to:* Regular exercise is *beneficial to* your health.

compare *to* **(assert a likeness):** She *compared* my writing *to* E.B. White's. (She said I wrote like E.B. White.)

compared *with* **(analyze for similarities and differences):** When she *compared* my writing *with* E.B. White's, she said that I had a similar kind of humour but that my sentences lacked the clean and easy flow of White's material.

confer *on* or *upon* **(give to):** The Governor General *conferred* the Order of Canada *on* Liona Boyd.

confer *with* **(talk to):** Teresa *conferred with* her team.

conform *to:* These blueprints do not *conform to* the plans we discussed. (preferred to *with*)

consists *in* **(exists in):** Happiness largely *consists in* being contented with what you have.

consists *of* **(is made up of):** The recipe *consists of* flour, eggs, and butter.

convenient *for* **(suitable):** These rubber boots are *convenient for* gardening.

convenient *to* **(near at hand):** Our business is *convenient to* public transit.

correspond *to* **(agree with):** This shipment does not *correspond to* our order.

correspond *with* **(exchange written correspondence with):** Justine *corresponds with* her cousin in Quebec by e-mail.

deal *in* **goods and services:** Our company *deals in* heavy equipment.

deal *with* **a person or organization:** Our company *deals with* Scotiabank.

differ *about* **something:** We *differ about* ideas on bringing up children.

differ *from* **something else:** Your sweater *differs from* the one in The Bay window.

differ *with* **someone:** I *differ with* Norah over the solution to question 10.

different *from:* This shampoo is *different from* the one I usually use.

different *than:* I view the matter in a *different* way *than* you do. (Although different from is normally preferred, than is acceptable in order to avoid sentences like "I view the matter in a different way from the way in which you do.")

identical *with*: This $100 jacket is *identical with* one advertised for $150. (not identical to)

independent *of*: He wants to be *independent of* his family's money. (not independent from)

interested *in*: We are *interested in* buying a house on Elm Street.

retroactive *to*: This salary increase is *retroactive to* May 1 (not retroactive from).

speak *to* (tell something to): You should *speak to* them about your holiday plans.

speak *with* (discuss with): It was good to *speak with* you yesterday.

Superfluous Prepositions

Omit prepositions that add nothing to the meaning. Here are some examples.

Where is she [at]?

Where did that paper go [to]?

The new applicant seems to be [of] about sixteen years of age.

She could not help [from] laughing.

His office is opposite [to] hers.

Why don't we meet [at] about one o'clock? [or, Why don't we meet at one o'clock?]

The carton apparently fell off [of] the truck.

The strike is now over [with].

Necessary Prepositions

Conversely, do not omit essential prepositions. Here are some examples.

I need to buy a couple *of* books. (Not: I need to buy a couple books.)

Of what use is this gadget? (Not: What use is this gadget?)

We don't stock that type *of* filter. (Not: We don't stock that type filter.)

He has a great interest *in*, as well as a respect *for*, fine antiques. (Not: He has a great interest, as well as a respect *for*, fine antiques.)

She frequently appears in movies, *in* plays, and on television. (Not: She frequently appears in movies, plays, and on television.)

Note: The preposition *of* is understood in expressions such as *what colour cloth* and *what colour shoes*.

Prepositions are always used in phrases, as shown in the following examples.

Preposition	Prepositional Phrase
in	in May, in the morning
for	for Helene, for us
by	by the parking lot, by tomorrow morning
of	of the company, of my supervisor
from	from Ms. Chu, from me
to	to the park, to my friend

Prepositional phrases are frequently used in sentences. A prepositional phrase contains an *object*, which is a person or thing that receives the action of the verb. Some examples are:

The pilot left here *after the meeting* and went directly *to the airport.*

At the airport she boarded the plane *with her crew.*

The horse leaped *over the fence, across the ditch,* and *over the hedges.*

Conjunctions

Conjunctions are words that *join words, phrases,* or *clauses.* **Coordinating conjunctions** connect words, phrases, or clauses of equal rank. Note how the co-ordinating conjunctions *and, but, or,* and *nor* are used in these sentences.

Rebecca *and* Jayne attended the convention in Quebec. (*And* joins two words—the nouns *Rebecca* and *Jayne.*)

Their friends did not go to the bar *but* to the gym. (*But* joins two prepositional phrases).

He will visit the construction site, *or* he will go to the architect's office. (*Or* joins two independent clauses.)

The defendant would not respond to their accusations, *nor* did she offer to answer any of their questions. (*Nor* joins two independent clauses.)

Subordinating conjunctions join subordinate clauses to main clauses; they indicate that the clause that follows is subordinate to the main clause. Common subordinating conjunctions are *when, where, after, before,* and *if.* Note the use of subordinating conjunctions in the following sentences:

We must collect all the facts *before* we make a decision.

When the team meets next week, we will rehearse our presentation.

If we book by September 30, we can save $200 on this vacation package.

CHECKUP 4

Identify each word in parentheses as either a preposition (*P*) or a conjunction (*C*).

1. The letter (from) Mr. Delaney explained the reason (for) the cancellation.
2. Elise (and) Paula went (to) the electronics show (in) Calgary (with) their manager.
3. Bob likes the baker (on) the corner, (but) Katja prefers the one (on) Connors Street.
4. Glen did not order more (of) these toys, (nor) has he ordered anything else (through) our purchasing department (during) September.
5. (With) Ms. Jankowski's approval, the seminar will begin (on) Wednesday (or) Thursday.

Interjections

Interjections are words *used alone* that *express an extremely strong feeling.* Interjections are often followed by exclamation marks, as shown in the following examples.

Congratulations! All your hard work has finally paid off handsomely. (Note that the interjection *Congratulations* is treated as an independent sentence.)

Yes! We are delighted to accept your invitation.

Wait! Don't send that e-mail!

Review of Key Terms

1. How does a *pronoun* take the role of a *noun*?
2. What are *prepositions* and why are they important?

Practical Application

1. Identify each word in parentheses as a <u>noun</u>, <u>pronoun</u>, <u>verb</u>, <u>adjective</u>, <u>adverb</u>, <u>preposition</u>, <u>conjunction</u>, or <u>interjection</u>.
    a. (Trainees) should be encouraged (to) ask questions.
    b. (Suggestions) are (always) welcome in this organization.
    c. A (special) bonus will be given to employees if (their) suggestions are implemented.
    d. Stacy Moreno (and) Jack Kemper have (already) received bonuses for their (recycling) suggestions.
    e. (Congratulations!) You have (won) the computer sales contest (for) our district.
    f. (Astrotech) finished second, (but) CompFast performed (very) poorly.
    g. (In) 2010, (Winnipeg) (or) Regina will host (our) (national) conference.
    h. It is a (difficult) task to choose between these cities, but (we) will make the selection (in) October.
    i. I (personally) (believe) that Vancouver would be the best (location) (for) our national meeting.
    j. The (players) (knew) the rules (before) (they) (entered) the game.
2. Form a group. Identify five items in the classroom. List these nouns and use one or more adjectives to describe each noun. Write five sentences, with each sentence including one of your nouns and its adjectives. Identify the parts of speech in each sentence. Share your sentences with the class and explain the parts of speech.

TEAMWORK

Editing Practice

Correct any spelling errors in the following excerpt from an e-mail message: Here are the sales figures for January, <u>Feburary</u>, and March. If their is any posible explanation for the sales delcine in March, I would appreciate that information before noon tomorow. We frequently expereience declines in February sales but not in March.

Discussion Points

1. How are action verbs different from linking verbs?
2. Compare the role and characteristics of adjectives with the role and characteristics of adverbs.

▶ **Key Terms**

▶ subject

▶ simple subject

▶ compound sub-
   ject

▶ predicate

▶ independent
   clause

▶ dependent clause

▶ prepositional
   phrase

▶ infinitive phrase

▶ verb phrase

▶ sentence

▶ sentence
   fragment

The Sentence

There is no better feeling than when you write something you know is a piece of you and that, at some point, is going to communicate with someone else.

—Alanis Morissette, singer and songwriter

The parts of speech are used to form sentences, the basic units we use in reading, writing, and speaking. Therefore, our ability to use and to understand sentences determines our ability to communicate.

A sentence is a group of words that expresses a complete thought and contains a subject and a predicate. (An interjection such as "Yes!" "No!" or "Congratulations!" may be used as an elliptical expression that stands for a sentence. An *elliptical expression* can represent a complete statement or command and may be an answer to a question.) *The subject and the predicate are the key elements needed to build a sentence.* Let's look at subjects first.

Subjects

The **subject** of a sentence names (1) the person or persons speaking, (2) the person or persons spoken to, or (3) the person(s) or thing(s) spoken about. A subject is usually a noun or pronoun. Here are a few examples.

1. **Who is speaking:**

I approved the proposal yesterday. (*I* is the complete subject of the sentence, the person who is speaking.)

2. **Who is spoken to:**

You have been selected to attend the training session, Fred. (The subject *You* identifies the person spoken to, Fred.)

Open a chequing account. (Here the subject is still *you,* but this sentence is an *imperative sentence*—an order. In such sentences, the speaker usually directly addresses the person spoken to; therefore, it is clearly understood that the subject is *you.*)

3. **Who or what is spoken about:**

Anthony is the manager of the Customer Relations Department. (Who is spoken about? Answer: *Anthony,* the subject of the sentence.)

He bought the condominium in July. (Who is spoken about? Answer: *He*, the subject of the sentence.)

In the last example, the person spoken about is referred to by the pronoun *He*.

Now that we have seen examples of *who* is spoken about, let's see examples of *what* is spoken about:

This insurance policy covers loss by fire and theft. (What is spoken about? Answer: *This insurance policy*.)

It covers loss by fire and theft. (What is spoken about? *It*, a pronoun that substitutes for the complete subject *This insurance policy*. *It* is the subject of the sentence.)

That disk belongs to Nicole. *Those disks* belong to Clarence. (*That disk* and *Those disks* are the complete subjects. *That disk* is the thing spoken about; *Those disks* are the things spoken about.)

CHECKUP 1

Identify the subjects of the following sentences. Determine whether each subject is (1) the person or persons speaking, (2) the person or persons spoken to, or (3) the person(s) or thing(s) spoken about.

1. Amir Gammal will be given the award.
2. William Ko-Chen will be the top sales agent for the month.
3. I feel that the price for repairing my car is too high.
4. The reports will be finished by November 15.
5. Emilio and Dana will share the real estate commission.

Simple Subjects

The **simple subject** is the main word in the complete subject—the core of the subject. Some examples are:

The owner of these buildings is Vince Panetta. (The complete subject is *The owner of these buildings*. The main word, or simple subject, in this complete subject is *owner*.)

Two former partners in the Wolfe & Crowell accounting firm are scheduled to meet with us today. (The complete subject of this sentence is *Two former partners in the Wolfe & Crowell accounting firm*. Within this complete subject, the simple subject is *partners*.)

Because the subject of the first example is *owner*, not *buildings*, the correct verb must be *is*. Because the subject of the second example is *partners*, not *firm*, the correct verb must be *are*. As you can see, only by knowing how to find the simple subject will you be sure to make subjects and verbs agree.

Compound Subjects

A **compound subject** is two or more equal subjects joined by a conjunction such as *and*, *but*, *or*, or *nor*.

The drivers and loaders in our company have announced that they will indeed strike if their demands are not met. (The complete subject is *The drivers and loaders in our company*. The main words in this complete subject are *drivers* and *loaders*, which are joined by the conjunction *and*. The compound subject is *drivers and loaders*.)

A cruise to the Bahamas or a one-week vacation in Cancun is going to be the first prize. (The complete subject is *A cruise to the Bahamas or a one-week vacation in Cancun*. The two main words in this complete subject are *cruise* and *vacation,* which are joined by the conjunction *or.* The compound subject is *cruise* or *vacation*.)

Every time you identify the subject correctly, you simplify your work in identifying the predicate.

CHECKUP 2

Identify the simple subject or the compound subject for each sentence.

1. All employees submitted suggestions for solving the problem.
2. One seminar participant asked about tuition reimbursement programs for employees.
3. Has Harrison or Margaret made our flight reservations?
4. Four comprehensive folders on the Nelson case are filed in the cabinet beside my desk.
5. Two hair salons and a grocery store have shown interest in renting your building.

Predicates

The **predicate** is the part of the sentence that tells what the subject is or does, or what is done to the subject. The simple predicate is the main verb of the sentence plus any helping verbs, usually the various forms of the verb "to be." The complete predicate is the simple predicate and all the words that modify it. Some examples are:

Mr. Navini will organize the teams for the project. (The complete predicate is *will organize the teams for the project.* The simple predicate is *will organize,* which is what Mr. Navini will do.)

Farret and Hope are the managers of these departments. (The complete predicate is *are the managers of these departments.* The simple predicate is *are,* which tells what Garret and Hope are.)

CHECKUP 3

Identify the complete predicate in each of the following sentences.

1. People from 30 countries attended the conference in Victoria.
2. Our firm offers an excellent benefits package to all employees.
3. Winnie Lee is the manager of our Legal Department.
4. The three-year warranty on this printer expires next month.
5. This filing system uses colour-coded labels.

Normal Order: Subject and Then Predicate

The normal order of a sentence is subject first, then predicate. Some examples are:

Four members of the council were at last night's meeting of the zoning board. (The complete subject *Four members of the council* precedes the complete predicate, which is *were at last night's meeting of the zoning board.* Therefore, this sentence is in *normal* order.)

At last night's meeting of the zoning board were *four members of the council.* (The words are the same, but the order is different. Now the predicate precedes the subject. This sentence, therefore, is *not* in normal order. It is in *inverted* order.)

Most questions are phrased in inverted order, not normal order. An example is:

Has Alex checked on the estimated cost of this brochure? (Why is this question in inverted order? The subject is *Alex,* and part of the verb—the word *Has*—precedes the subject. Normal order would be, *Alex has checked on the estimated cost of this brochure.*)

Now let's see why it is important to be able to distinguish between normal order and inverted order. What, if anything, is wrong with this sentence?

Where's the disks that Peter left for us?

Many people almost automatically start sentences with *Where's, There's,* and *Here's,* even when these words are incorrect. Normal order quickly points out the error:

The disks that Peter left for us is where? (Simply put, "The disks…is where?" *Disks is* is incorrect; we must say "*Disks are.*" Thus the correct form for the question is, Where are the disks that Peter left for us?)

It is important to spot inverted order not only in questions, but also in statements. Note this sentence:

On the shelf in my office is the disks that Peter left for us. (In normal order, this sentence reads: "The blank disks that Peter left for us is on the shelf in my office." The subject *disks* is plural and does not agree in number with the verb *is,* which is singular. This error is masked by the inverted order. The original sentence should read, The blank disks…are….)

CHECKUP 4

Read each of the following sentences carefully. Then (1) change any inverted sentence to normal order, (2) write the complete subject of each independent clause, and (3) underline the simple or compound subject of that clause.

1. Eve and Eric Norton plan to use their basement as a business office.
2. While the basement is being renovated, the Nortons will rent space on Queen Street.
3. Although the renovation will be quite expensive, the Nortons have a loan with a low interest rate.
4. Located at the top of the hill are the only other houses on Saugeen Road.
5. On the south border of the property are a bridge and a lake.

Types of Sentences

You use sentences to make statements, ask questions, state a command or request, and express strong feeling. There are four types of sentences to serve these purposes.

You don't have no excuses for using a double negative.

(any excuses)

—From *The Writer's Block* Calendar

Type of Sentence	Definition	Example
Declarative	Makes a statement	You are wise.
Interrogative	Asks a question	How old are you?
Imperative	States a command or request	Proofread the letter.
Exclamatory	Expresses strong feeling	I can't believe it!

CHECKUP 5

Identify each of the following sentences as declarative (*D*), interrogative (*INT*), imperative (*IMP*), or exclamatory (*E*).

1. Who attended the conference? *INT*
2. Please give me the latest sales figures by tomorrow. *Imp*
3. Both Stefanie and Boyd are candidates for the job. *Dec*
4. Congratulations on winning the award! *Exc*
5. Connie answered my question. *Dec*

Clauses and Phrases

Words that are grouped together are classified as a *clause* if the group of words includes both a subject and a predicate. A group of related words that does *not* have both a subject and a predicate is called a *phrase*.

Clauses

A clause is a group of words containing both a subject and a predicate. If the clause expresses a complete thought and can stand alone as a complete sentence, it is an **independent clause.** If the clause cannot stand alone, it is called a **dependent clause.**

Review the following sentence. Note that the sentence has a subject and a predicate and *can* stand alone. The sentence is an *independent* clause.

James Northrop is a well-known expert in computer networking. (The subject is *James Northrop,* and the predicate is the rest of the sentence. Because this group of words can stand alone, this is an independent clause.)

Now read the clause that follows. It has a subject and predicate but cannot stand alone. Therefore, it is a *dependent clause.*

If Ms. Tanaka accepts the nomination. (The subject of this clause is *Ms. Tanaka,* and the complete predicate is the rest of the clause. But does this group of words make sense? No. This is a *dependent clause.* More information is required if this group of words is to make sense.)

Dependent clauses cannot stand alone as sentences; therefore, they must be joined to independent clauses for their meaning to be complete.

If Ms. Tanaka accepts the nomination, she must resign her present position. (*She must resign her present position* is an independent clause. Thus the dependent clause, *If Ms. Tanaka accepts the nomination,* is correctly joined to an independent clause.)

CHECKUP 6

Determine which of the following groups of words are sentences and which are dependent clauses that are incorrectly treated as sentences. For each dependent clause, suggest an independent clause that would complete it.

1. Because Claire Hunt, the head nurse, will not return until next week, Thursday's meeting has been cancelled. *dependent / Indep*
2. Claire and Joel will draw up the nurses' schedules. *independent*
3. Before the nurses meet to discuss their patients. *dependent*
4. If Claire does not hire another nursing assistant by May 1. *dependent*
5. When Florence meets with the nursing staff in her hospital. *dependent*

Phrases

A *phrase* is a group of words that has neither a subject nor a predicate. As you study the following three kinds of phrases, note that none has a subject or a predicate.

Prepositional Phrases. A prepositional phrase consists of a preposition, an object, and any modifier of the object. Phrases such as *for the associates, among the interns, with Sean Murphy, in the office, at the meeting, between you and me,* and *from Dr. Holzman,* are prepositional phrases. The nouns and pronouns at the end of prepositional phrases are not subjects; they are objects of the prepositions.

As you read the following examples, note how prepositional phrases can be used (1) as adjectives, (2) as adverbs, and (3) as nouns.

1. As adjectives:

The woman *with the clipboard* is Suzanne Chung. (Which woman? The prepositional phrase *with the clipboard* describes the noun *woman.* Therefore, this prepositional phrase serves as an adjective.)

2. As adverbs:

Dirk sent the letter *to the chairperson.* (Sent it where? The prepositional phrase *to the chairperson* answers the question "Where?" This prepositional phrase serves as an adverb.)

3. As nouns:

After 5 o'clock is the best time to meet. (The prepositional phrase *After 5 o'clock* serves as the noun or subject of the sentence.)

Infinitive Phrases. An *infinitive* is the "to be" form of a verb: *to drive, to study, to analyze, to review, to compute, to keyboard, to be, to have, to do,* and so on. An **infinitive phrase** includes the infinitive and any other words that are related to it. Infinitive phrases may be used (1) as nouns, (2) as adjectives, and, less frequently, (3) as adverbs.

1. As nouns:

To develop sound training programs is the objective of this department. (The complete infinitive phrase is *To develop sound training programs;* the phrase is the subject of the verb *is.*)

2. As adjectives:

Sheila McGuire is the manager *to ask.* (Here the infinitive phrase *to ask* modifies the noun *manager* and therefore serves as an adjective.)

3. As adverbs:

Pat bent down *to tie her shoelaces.* (Bent down for what reason? Here the infinitive phrase answers the question "Why?" The infinitive phrase *to tie her shoelaces* therefore serves as an adverb.)

Because infinitives begin with the word *to,* they may sometimes be confused with prepositional phrases beginning with the word *to.*

Infinitive	Prepositional Phrase
to keyboard	to the committee
to review	to Professor Grant
to accept	to me

Remember that an infinitive is the *to* form of a *verb.* Test by using the infinitive as a verb: *I keyboard, you review, they accept.*

Verb Phrases. In a **verb phrase**, two or more verbs work together as one verb. In such cases, the main verb is always the last verb in the phrase; the other verbs are helping (or auxiliary) verbs. Some common helping verbs are *is, are, was, were, can, could, has, had, have, should, will,* and *would.*

The engineer *will complete* the calculations by noon tomorrow. (*Will complete* is a verb phrase. The main verb is *complete; will* is a helping verb.)

By noon tomorrow the calculations *will have been completed.* (The main verb is *completed,* the last word in the verb phrase. *Will have been* is a helping verb.)

The shipment *should arrive* tomorrow morning. (The main verb is *arrive,* the last word in the verb phrase; *should* is a helping verb.)

Verb phrases are often interrupted by adverbs, as shown in the following examples. Do not be misled by such interruptions.

The engineer will *soon* be showing his calculations to the traffic consultant. (The verb phrase *will be showing* is interrupted by the adverb *soon.*)

The traffic consultant has *already* been told about possible delays on metropolitan bus routes. (The verb phrase *has been told* is interrupted by the adverb *already.*)

CHECKUP 7

Identify the words in parentheses as prepositional phrases (*PP*), infinitive phrases (*IP*), or verb phrases (*VP*).

1. The chef's recipe (will be submitted) (to the award committee) (by next Monday).
2. Mr. Heffner wants (to taste the recipe) when he goes (to the award dinner) (with Alma Brady).
3. (To become a chef) (at André's), you (must have had) at least five years' experience (at a three-star restaurant).
4. Several cooking classes (have been scheduled) (for André's best customers).
5. (To attend the cooking classes), customers (have been asked) (to pay) (in advance).

Sentence Fragments

A sentence is a group of words that expresses a complete thought and contains a subject and a predicate. When the writing is an incomplete thought, it is called a **sentence fragment.** You can distinguish between a complete sentence and a fragment by applying the "no sense/no sentence" rule. An example is:

Emily Clark wants to attend the conference because the topic is creating web pages. (This is a complete thought. This group of words makes sense. This is a sentence.)

If, however, you try to split off part of the sentence, you create a fragment.

Emily Clark wants to attend the conference. Because the topic is creating web pages. (The first group of words is a sentence. The words *Because the topic is creating web pages* do not make sense by themselves; they form a dependent clause or fragment of a sentence. The word *because* leads us to expect more.)

In the preceding example, the word *because* begins a clause that cannot stand alone. Note that the following words often introduce dependent clauses (clauses that cannot stand alone):

after	before	provided that	when
although	even if	since	whenever

as	for	so that	where
as if	how	than	wherever
as soon as	if	that	whether
as though	in order that	unless	while
because		until	why

CHECKUP 8

Identify each group of words as a sentence or a fragment. Then rewrite each fragment to make it a complete sentence.

1. If Mr. Bartoli decides to sign the contract. *fragment*
2. Because two signatures are required for cheques over $500. *fragment*
3. Our vice president initiated the policy in 1989. *Sentence*
4. Although Sam's passport was valid at that time. *fragment*
5. Maureen or Elliot will be chosen as our new safety officer. *Sentence*

Review of Key Terms

1. What is the role of a *subject* in a sentence? What is the role of a *predicate* in a sentence?
2. How can a reader distinguish between a *sentence* and a *fragment*?
3. What is the difference between a *phrase* and a *clause*?

Practical Application

1. Identify each *word* in parentheses as a noun, pronoun, verb, adjective, adverb, preposition, conjunction, or interjection. For each *phrase* in parentheses, identify the phrase by writing *VP* (verb phrase), *IP* (infinitive phrase), or *PP* (prepositional phrase).
   a. (Trainees) should be encouraged (to ask questions).
   b. (Suggestions) are always welcome (in this organization).
   c. A special bonus (will be given) (to employees) if their suggestions are implemented.
   d. Stacy Moreno (and) Jack Kemper have (already) received bonuses for their (recycling) recommendation.
   e. (Hooray!) (We) have just (won) the computer sales contest (for) our district.
   f. (Astrotech) finished second, (but) CompFast performed (very) poorly.
   g. (In 1999), (Winnipeg) (or) Regina will be the site of (our) (national) conference.
   h. (To choose between these cities) is a (difficult) task, but (we) will make the selection (in) October.
   i. I (personally) (believe) that Vancouver would be the best (location) (for our January national meeting).
   j. The (players) (should have known) the (rules) before (they) (entered) the game.

2. Identify the following clauses as *D* (dependent) or *I* (independent).
   a. When an increasing number of firms are striving for global competitiveness.
   b. Before we see a significant upturn in the economy.
   c. One of the most important signs that we have seen in terms of consumer buying power.
   d. Discount retailers are winning the battle.
   e. While more aggressive managers are searching for multitalented employees.
   f. The manufacturing sector has been hardest hit.
   g. To the degree to which trainees will take direction.
   h. If they really want Carlotta Morris to approve the merger.
   i. As soon as the results of the taste test have been tabulated.
   j. In about a week we should know which brand was the top choice.

3. Read each of the following sentences carefully. Then, (1) change any inverted sentence to normal order, (2) write the complete subject of each independent clause, and (3) underline the simple or compound subject of that clause.
   a. Frank and Emily Simpson plan to renovate their office space as a dance studio.
   b. As soon as the renovation is completed, their three assistants will begin teaching lessons there.
   c. Students and their parents will tour the new studio during a reception on August 25.
   d. Although renovating the basement is quite expensive, First Branch Bank has agreed to lend the couple most of the needed money.
   e. While the basement is being renovated, Frank will be getting estimates on paving the gravel parking lot at the back of the building.
   f. Prior to the opening of the dance studio, the Simpsons and their assistants will install a new sound system.
   g. In late July or early August, Mr. and Mrs. Simpson will sell their old studio.
   h. Their real estate agent has found a buyer for the old studio.

4. For each item below, (1) write (*S*) sentence or (*F*) fragment. For each fragment, add the words needed to change the fragment to a complete sentence.
   a. What is your address?
   b. As soon as we receive the loan application.
   c. The two people in the accounting department who do that work.
   d. The supervisors and associates agree with your suggestion.
   e. Can you remember how to use the presentation software?
   f. Where are the photographs for the Supershop advertisement?
   g. Although this system was in effect between 1962 and 1991.
   h. At the November trade show in St. John's, they will be able to examine our new software.
   i. Locked in the green cabinet are all the old files.
   j. Until Mr. Nicholson agrees to the reorganization plan that you submitted last April.

5. Choose a newspaper or magazine photograph that everyone in the group likes. Brainstorm a list of words or phrases that describes the photograph, its mood, and the team's feeling toward it. Then, use those words to write a descriptive paragraph about the photograph and your own reaction to it. Include active verbs, adjectives, adverbs, and interjections in your description.

TEAMWORK

Editing Practice

As a Matter of Fact... Proofreading requires us to look not only for errors in grammar, spelling, and punctuation, but also for inconsistencies and errors in facts. Read and correct the following excerpt from a business memo.

On September 31 we mailed Mr. Benson a cheque for $200, but we omitted the 8 per cent sales tax on this total as well as the shipping charge of $10. Please send Mr. Benson a cheque for $18 to cover the additional cost of the tax on $200 and the shipping expense.

Discussion Point

How can inverted sentence order create problems in agreement?

Verbs

Good business communication is marked by words that form a sharp, clear meaning in the mind.

—*Basic Business Communication*

▶ **Key Terms**

▶ regular verbs

▶ helping (auxiliary) verbs

▶ verb tenses

▶ irregular verbs

▶ "being" verbs

▶ transitive verbs

▶ direct object

▶ indirect object.

▶ intransitive verb

Among the most serious and the most common errors we make as we speak and write are *verb tense* errors. Yet forming most verbs correctly is very easy, because most verbs follow one simple pattern, as you will see in the first half of this section. The verbs that do not follow this regular pattern are the ones that cause problems; these irregular verbs are discussed in depth in the second part of this section.

Identifying Verbs

As you read in Section 3.1, *a verb is a word that describes an action, a condition, or a state of being.* The verb in a sentence is referred to as a *predicate.* The following examples illustrate action verbs and two types of linking verbs.

Action

Edith *signed* the agreement.

They *landed* on time at 4:15 p.m.

I *will speak* to the administrative assistants this morning.

Ms. Russo *is writing* the draft now.

Bob *will be running* in the Toronto marathon.

The verbs *signed, landed, will speak, is writing*, and *will be running* all describe actions.

Condition

Edith *seems* pleased with the new clauses in the agreement.

They *felt* better on the ground.

The administrative assistants *became* restless during my talk.

Ms. Russo *appears* to be a good writer.

Bob *grew* thirsty during the Toronto marathon.

The verbs *seems, felt, became, appears*, and *grew* all describe conditions.

Being

Edith *is* happy with the agreement.

They *are* home at last.

I *am* happy to welcome the new administrative assistants.

Ms. Russo *will be* a likely candidate for promotion.

Bob *was* very tired at the end of his run.

The verbs *is, are, am, will be,* and *was* do not describe actions or conditions in the sentences above, yet each is a verb. These verbs are "being" verbs.

Practise identifying verbs—that's the first step in using verbs correctly.

CHECKUP 1

Identify the verbs in the following sentences and label them as action, condition, or "being" verbs.

1. Anne invited Carlo Mendoza to the dinner meeting.
2. The Acme Glass Company wants this property for its new plant.
3. Warren and Tim are at our branch office right now.
4. Carlo has accepted the invitation.
5. The vice president seemed satisfied with the results of the campaign.
6. Frank was in Saskatoon when we discussed this proposal.

Regular Verbs

As we speak and write, the verbs we use indicate the time of the action, the condition, or the state of being. We select a verb form to indicate present time ("I learn," "I am learning"), past time ("I learned," "I have learned"), or future time ("I will learn," "I will be learning"). This time element for a verb is called its *tense*. Fortunately, most verbs in our language follow the same simple pattern to indicate time. These verbs are **regular verbs**.

Principal Parts of Regular Verbs

Knowing how to form the principal parts of verbs is necessary if you are to use verbs correctly. All verb tenses are formed from the principal parts of a verb. These parts are (1) the present tense form, (2) the past tense form, (3) the past participle, and (4) the present participle.

How can you distinguish between the *past tense* form and the *past participle*? Answer: You do so by seeing the word *in context.* A past tense form *never* has a helping verb; a past participle *always* has a helping verb.

Bette *called* us at 9 a.m. (Here, *called* is a past tense form; it has no helping verb.)

Matt came to tell us about the meeting, but Bette *had called* us at 9 a.m. (Here, *called* is a past participle.)

When *called* is used with the helping verb *had,* the combination forms a tense called the *past perfect.* Together, *had called* is a verb phrase or simple predicate and *called* is its main verb.

Verbs			
Present Tense Participle	**Past Tense**	**Past Participle**	**Present**
move	moved	moved	moving
prepare	prepared	prepared	preparing
hire	hired	hired	hiring
call	called	called	calling
enter	entered	entered	entering
listen	listened	listened	listening
study	studied	studied	studying

◀ **Figure 3.2**
Verbs
The table lists verbs in their present, past, past participle, and present participle forms.

Thinking Critically.
How does understanding a verb in context allow you to check your usage?

As you read the table in Figure 3.2, say to yourself "I move," "I prepare," and so on. Then notice that simply adding *d* to verbs that end in *e* forms the past tense. For verbs that do not end in *e*, add *ed: called, entered, listened*. For some verbs ending in *y*, change the *y* to *i* before adding *ed*.

Further simplifying this pattern is the fact that the past participle is the same form as the past tense, and the present participle is formed by adding *ing* to the present form. Note that for verbs ending in *e*, you must drop the *e* before adding *ing: moving, preparing, hiring*. Except for a limited list, all the verbs in English follow this pattern.

CHECKUP 2

Copy the following chart. Then fill in the missing parts for each entry.

Present Tense	Past Tense	Past Participle	Present Participle
1. talk	talked	talked	1. talking
2. elect	elected	elected	2 electing
3. order	ordered	ordered	3 ordering
4. indicate	indicated	indicated	4 indicating
5. remember	remembered	remembered	5 remembering
6. respond	responded	responded	6 responding
7. trust	trusted	trusted	7 trusting
8. use	used	used	8 using
9. marry	married	married	9 marr
10. answer	answered	answered	10 answering

Verb Phrases

As you read in Section 3.1, *a verb phrase consists of the main verb and any helping verbs used together to function as one verb.* A verb phrase may also contain an interrupting adverb. The main verb in the phrase is *always* the last verb. The other verbs are the **helping,** or **auxiliary verbs.** Some examples are:

can *move*   did *prepare*   will *hire*

The main verbs in the above three examples are *move, prepare,* and *hire.* The verbs *can, did,* and *will* are helping verbs. Note that *move, prepare,* and *hire* are the present tense forms listed in Figure 3.2.

has been *moved*   have *prepared*   will soon be *hired*

The main verbs are ***moved, prepared***, and ***hired***, which are the past participles listed in the third column in the table. The verbs ***has been, have***, and ***will be*** are helping verbs. The word *soon* is an interrupting adverb.

are *moving*   is *preparing*   will be *hiring*

Again, the last word in each phrase is the main verb: ***moving, preparing***, and ***hiring***, which are the present participles listed in Figure 3.2. The words ***are, is*** and ***will be*** are helping verbs.

Now note how verb phrases are used in sentences. Remember that the verb phrase can be interrupted by another word, most often an adverb. Some examples are:

Tomorrow Gene *will be moving* into his new office. (The verb phrase is *will be moving*. The main verb is the last verb, *moving*.)

Nadia *has* also *been preparing* her speech. (The verb phrase *has been preparing* is interrupted by the adverb *also*. The main verb is *preparing*.)

Zack's replacement *has* already *been hired*. (Hired is the main verb in the phrase *has been hired*. Already is an adverb.)

In questions, the verb phrase is often more difficult to identify because the sentence order is inverted. Finding the verb phrase in inverted sentences is easier if you change the sentence to normal order first.

When *did* Mr. Herzog *return* these cell phones? (The verb phrase is *did return*.)

Have Lynn and Robin already *been working* on this system? (The verb phrase *have been working* is tricky to identify because of the inverted order and the interrupting adverb *already*.)

CHECKUP 3

Identify the verb phrase or the verb in each of the following sentences. For each phrase, name the main verb.

1. Jonathan will be checking all these invoices tomorrow morning.
2. Anthony can complete this entire project by Friday.
3. The speaker will enter the auditorium by the rear door.
4. Have Alan and Ben already approved these diagrams?
5. Jason and Albert have been hoping for this news for many, many months.
6. Does Gregory really want another copy of this fax?

Verb Tenses

The verb tense is the form that tells when the action did or will occur.

Present Tense

The present tense is used to:

1. show action that is happening now ("Aziza is here");
2. describe an action that is repeated or habitual ("Fred jogs every day");
3. make a general statement of truth ("We all like ice cream").

In the following lists, there are only two present forms, *call* and *calls*. Use call to agree with I, you, we and they. Add *s* for the present tense form to agree with he, she, and it and with singular nouns.

I call	he calls
you call	she calls
we call	it calls
they call	Mary calls

We *call* every morning. (*Call* with the pronoun *we*.)

He *calls* every morning. Brad *calls* every morning. (*Calls* with the pronoun *he* and the singular noun *Brad*.)

They *enjoy* assembly work. (*Enjoy* with the pronoun *they*.)

She *enjoys* travelling. Alison *enjoys* travelling. (*Enjoys* with the pronoun *she* and the singular noun *Alison*.)

Past Tense

The past tense is used to indicate action that has already been completed. It is formed by adding *ed* to the present tense form, or *d* if the present tense form already ends in *e*.

I called	we called
you called	you called
he she } called	they called
it	

As you see, there is only one past tense form for a verb. The only exception is the verb *to be*, which will be discussed later.

Future Tense

This tense indicates action that is to take place in the future. To form the future tense of a verb, use *will* plus the infinitive form without the word *to*.

I will call	we will call
you will call	you will call
he she } will call	they will call
it	

The Perfect Tenses

Each of the present, past, and future tenses has a correlated "perfect" tense. Perfect tenses are commonly used in our everyday conversation and writing.

Present Perfect Tense. *The present perfect tense is used to show that an action or a state of being began in the past and may still be occurring.* This tense is formed by using the helping verbs *has* or *have* with a past participle. Some examples are:

Amelia *has redecorated* the first floor of the house. (Present perfect tense for an action that was begun in the past.)

Quincy and George *have debated* the pros and cons of this issue for years. (Present perfect tense for an action that began in the past and may be still continuing in the present.)

Past Perfect Tense. *The past perfect tense is used to show which of two past actions occurred first or that an action was completed before a specific time.* To form the past perfect tense, use *had* plus the past participle of a verb. Some examples are:

Rico *had mailed* his cheque before he received the cancellation notice. (The verbs *had mailed* and *received* show two past actions. The past perfect tense *had mailed* tells us that this action is the *first* past one. After this action was completed, a second action occurred—Rico *received* something. *Received* is in the past tense, to show that this action occurred second.)

Ana *had paid* her fees before July 5th. (Past perfect tense to show that an action was completed before a specific time)

Future Perfect Tense. *The future perfect tense shows that an action will be completed by some specific time in the future.* The action may have already begun, or it may begin in the future. The important point is that it will *end* by a specific future time, or before another action in the future. To form the future perfect tense, use the verb *will have* plus the past participle of a verb.

The architect *will have* completed his sketches for the new wing long before the deadline. (*Will have completed* is a future perfect tense verb describing an action that will end by some specific time—*long before the deadline*—in the future.)

The Progressive Tenses

Closely related to the six tenses just discussed are the progressive tenses, which depict actions that are still in progress.

Present Progressive Tense. *The present progressive tense describes an action that is in progress in the present.* To form this tense, use *am, is*, or *are* with a present participle. Some examples are:

I *am using* this software program to prepare my income tax return. (*Am using* shows action in progress now.)

Tom *is driving* his new truck. (*Is driving* shows action in progress now.)

Past Progressive Tense. *The past progressive tense describes an action that was in progress at a certain time in the past.* It is formed by using *was* or *were* with a present participle. An example is:

They *were reviewing* the field reports when Jenny Petroff arrived. (*Were reviewing* shows action that was in progress in the past.)

Future Progressive Tense. *The future progressive tense describes an action that will be in progress at a certain time in the future.* It is formed by using *will be* with a present participle. An example is:

Maria *will be* taking the first part of her CA examination next Thursday. (Is this action in progress now? No. In the past? Again, no. *Will be taking* shows an action that will be in progress in the future—specifically, "next Thursday.")

Conjugating Regular Verbs. The following table illustrates the three elements that determine verb forms: *person* (*I, you, he* or *she*, and so on), *number* (singular or plural), and *tense*. Every regular verb follows the same basic conjugation pattern shown here. When you are unsure about the correct form of a particular regular verb, check that verb against the table.

Verb Conjugation		
	Singular	**Plural**
Present Tense	I hope you hope he or she hopes	we hope you hope they hope
Past Tense	I hoped you hoped he or she hoped	we hoped you hoped they hoped
Future Tense	I will hope you will hope he or she will hope	we will hope you will hope they will hope
Present Perfect Tense	I have hoped you have hoped he or she has hoped	we have hoped you have hoped they have hoped
Past Perfect Tense	I had hoped you had hoped he or she had hoped	we had hoped you had hoped they had hoped
Future Perfect Tense	I will have hoped you will have hoped he or she will have hoped	we will have hoped you will have hoped they will have hoped
Present Progressive Tense	I am hoping you are hoping he or she is hoping	we are hoping you are hoping they are hoping
Past Progressive Tense	I was hoping you were hoping he or she was hoping	we were hoping you were hoping they were hoping
Future Progressive Tense	I will be hoping you will be hoping he or she will be hoping	we will be hoping you will be hoping they will be hoping

◀ **Figure 3.3**
Verb Conjugation
This table shows the conjugation of the infinitive verb *to hope.*

Thinking Critically.
How does reviewing such a chart enable you to improve your written and spoken communications?

Remember: you substitute singular nouns in place of the pronouns *he* or *she* and plural nouns in place of the pronoun *they!*

CHECKUP 4

Use each of the following regular verbs in a sentence.
1. have remembered   i have remembered, it was to let the dog out.
2. are listening   we are listening to our
3. will have noticed
4. will be   I will be there at 7:00
5. have asked
6. wanted
7. has rejected
8. reviews

Irregular Verbs

Most verbs follow the regular pattern shown in the preceding table for forming the present tense, the past tense, the past participle, and the present participle. However, more than 50 commonly used **irregular verbs** do *not* follow this pattern. The rest of this section discusses these irregular verbs.

Principal Parts of Irregular Verbs

Review Figure 3.4 in detail. We must memorize most of these forms, especially those that are used frequently.

CHECKUP 5

Correct any errors in verb tenses in the following sentences. Write *OK* if a sentence is correct.

1. Of course, Lynn known [*knew*] about the merger for several weeks.
2. Chris had began revising the merger papers before his supervisor asked him to do so. [*begun*]
3. In an effort to avoid a last-minute rush, Eric come [*came*] in early yesterday and today.
4. Ask Kim who has took [*taken*] the company name off the building.
5. Has the bell rung yet? [*OK*]
6. Our profits have grew [*grown*] steadily over the past three years. [*OK*]
7. Ask Dana if she seen [*has seen*] John's personnel folder.

"Being" Verbs

The "being" verbs are the forms of the verb to be. They show no action. Study first the present tense and the past tense forms.

Present Tense

I am	we are
you are	you are
he	
she } is	they are
it	

(There are three present tense forms: *am, is,* and *are.*)

Past Tense

I was	we were
you were	you were
he	
she } was	they were
it	

(There are two past tense forms, *was* and *were.*)

Verb Phrases with Forms of "To Be." As you saw earlier in this section, verb phrases are formed by using helping or auxiliary verbs with (1) the infinitive form *be,* (2) the past participle form *been,* and (3) the present participle form *being.* Some examples are:

Principal Parts of Irregular Verbs

Present Tense	Past Tense	Past Participle	Present Participle
am	was	been	being
begin	began	begun	beginning
bid (to command)	bade	bidden	bidding
bid (to offer to pay)	bid	bid	bidding
bite	bit	bitten	biting
blow	blew	blown	blowing
bring	brought	brought	bringing
burst	burst	burst	bursting
choose	chose	chosen	choosing
come	came	come	coming
do	did	done	doing
draw	drew	drawn	drawing
drive	drove	driven	driving
eat	ate	eaten	eating
fall	fell	fallen	falling
fight	fought	fought	fighting
flee	fled	fled	fleeing
fly	flew	flown	flying
forget	forgot	forgotten	forgetting
get	got	got or gotten	getting
go	went	gone	going
grow	grew	grown	growing
hang (to put to death)	hanged	hanged	hanging
hang (to suspend)	hung	hung	hanging
hide	hid	hidden	hiding
know	knew	known	knowing
leave	left	left	leaving
lie	lay	lain	lying
pay	paid	paid	paying
read	read	read	reading
ride	rode	ridden	riding
run	ran	run	running
send	sent	sent	sending
set	set	set	setting
shake	shook	shaken	shaking
sing	sang	sung	singing
speak	spoke	spoken	speaking
strike	struck	struck	striking
take	took	taken	taking
tear	tore	torn	tearing
throw	threw	thrown	throwing
wear	wore	worn	wearing
write	wrote	written	writing

◀ **Figure 3.4**
Principal Parts of Irregular Verbs
This table shows the principal parts of some irregular verbs.

Thinking Critically.
How does knowing these irregular verbs improve your communications with others?

1. the infinitive form *be* with a helping verb: *will be, shall be, may be, can be, would be, might be,* and so on;
2. the past participle *been* with a helping verb: *has been, have been, had been, will have been, could have been, might have been,* and so on;
3. the present participle *being* with a helping verb: *am being, is being, are being, was being,* and *were being.*

It is helpful to memorize the eight forms of the verb "to be": *am, is, are, was, were,* a helper plus *be,* a helper plus *been,* and a helper plus *being.*

Because "being" verbs are so often used as helping verbs, be careful to distinguish between "being" verbs that are helpers and "being" verbs that are main verbs in the phrase. Some examples are:

Pierrette *should have been* here by now. (The verb phrase is *should have been,* and the main verb is *been.* This verb phrase is a "being" verb.)

That contract *should have been signed.* (Now the verb phrase is *should have been signed. Should have been* is only a helping verb. The main verb is *signed.* Only the helping verb is a "being" verb.)

Arun Mehta *is* the vice president of telecommunications. He *was* formerly the director of technical services. (Both *is* and *was* are being verbs. There are no helping verbs.)

Do not use *of* instead of *have* in verb forms. The correct forms are *could have, would have, should have, might have, may have, must have, ought to have,* etc. For example, What Jason *should have* done is talk to his supervisor. (Not *should of done* …)

CHECKUP 6

Write the verbs and verb phrases in the following sentences. Identify each "being" verb that is a main verb by writing *B* next to the verb.

1. Of course, Judge Bancroft has been carefully evaluating the union demands.
2. Bill Vernon was the company's lawyer at one time.
3. Both Caroline Hahn and Emily DeLucca have been members of the arbitration board for two years.
4. Carter McGinn, our team leader, is on vacation this week.
5. Our company is proud of its active involvement in the community.
6. Nevertheless, the local media have been siding with the union.

Were Instead of Was. Good writing requires that we sometimes use *were* instead of *was* after *if, as if, as though,* and *wish.* Whenever such statements describe (1) something contrary to fact, or simply not true, or (2) something that is highly doubtful or impossible, use *were* instead of *was.*

If, on the other hand, the statement *is true or could be true* (as often happens after *if*), then do *not* substitute *were* for *was.* Some examples are:

We wish it *were* possible for us to predict future stock prices, but government regulations prohibit us from making such claims. (It is not possible. Therefore, *were* is correct.)

If I *were* you, I would purchase this stock while it is still selling at $22 per share. (Of course, I am *not you*—thus *were* is correct.)

Bill acts as if he *were* the only candidate for the position. (Bill is not the only candidate, so this statement is contrary to fact and takes the verb *were.*)

If Michelle *was* here earlier, she probably left a message with her assistant. (Michelle could indeed have already been here; thus this statement could be true. Do *not* substitute *were* for *was.*)

CHECKUP 7

Correct any verb errors in the following sentences. Write *OK* if a sentence is correct.

1. If I were Prime Minister, I would make some drastic changes.
2. At times Charles behaves as if he was the only travel agent in the country!
3. She has said that if she was younger, she would open her own travel agency.
4. Owen sometimes acts is if he was at a party instead of at work.
5. If Lou was at the airport, I certainly did not see him.

Lie, Lay; Sit, Set; Rise, Raise

Like the "being" verbs, the verbs *lie* and *lay, sit* and *set,* and *rise* and *raise* deserve extra attention. To use these verbs correctly, you must first understand the distinction between transitive and intransitive verbs.

Transitive Verbs. A **transitive verb** is a verb that requires an object to complete its meaning. A sentence may contain a direct object, or both a direct and indirect object. A **direct object** is a person or thing that directly receives the action of the verb. If there are both direct and indirect objects, the indirect object always appears before the direct object. The **indirect object** tells "to whom" or "for whom" something was done. An indirect object is usually a person or persons rather than a thing. Study these examples.

John *accepted* (accepted what? whom?)

John *accepted* the award. (*Award* is the direct object of the verb *accepted*—it tells what was accepted. Therefore, *accepted* is a transitive verb—it requires the object to complete its meaning.)

Ms. Milano *invited* (verb) (invited whom? invited what?)

Ms. Milano *invited* Nancy. (*Invited* is a transitive verb because it requires an object—in this case *Nancy*—to complete its meaning.)

The flight attendant *served* (transitive verb) a snack (direct object).

The flight attendant *served* (transitive verb) the passengers (indirect object) a snack (direct object). (*Passengers* is the indirect object—it tells "to whom" something was done.)

Adam *gave* his assistant the office key. (Adam gave (what?) the *key* (direct object) (to whom?) his *assistant* (indirect object). *Gave* is a transitive verb because it has an object, *key. Assistant* is the indirect object—it tells "to whom" something was done.)

Sometimes the subject rather than the object of the sentence serves as the receiver of the verb's action. You can identify transitive verbs that are used this way because they include a being verb helper and a past participle. Some examples are:

The award *should have been given* to Ahmed. (Do you have a being verb helper? Do you have a past participle? "Yes" to both questions. Therefore, this verb is transitive. What receives the action? the *award*.)

The concert *was cancelled,* according to Miriam. (Again, we have a being verb helper, *was,* and a past participle, *cancelled.* Thus we know that the subject, *concert,* receives the action of the verb. *What* was cancelled? the *concert. Was cancelled* is a transitive verb.)

Renzo has been nominated to the Executive Committee. (What is the verb in this sentence? Is it transitive? If so, explain why.)

Intransitive Verbs. *Verbs that do not have objects are* **intransitive verbs.** *Some examples are:*

Max Rosenthal *travels* frequently. (Travels *what*? Travels *whom*? No answer. *Travels* is an intransitive verb.)

Cindy Wolfe *will sail* at noon, according to this itinerary. (The verb *will sail* has no object; it is an intransitive verb.)

CHECKUP 8

Identify the verbs and verb phrases in the following sentences. Then label each verb or verb phrase as *B* for "being," *T* for "transitive," or *I* for "intransitive."

1. A new program manager had been appointed as of last week.
2. Sandra will be in the studio shortly.
3. Our next broadcast will be televised on Thursday, August 18.
4. Has Don told Lee Edwards about the proposed script changes?
5. Apparently, both of them have left.
6. As always, Bea has been very helpful with the United Way campaign.

Now that you have learned to distinguish between transitive and intransitive verbs, you will have an easier task of using *lie* and *lay, sit* and *set,* and *rise* and *raise.* The letter *i* is the key. Use the *i* in *intransitive* to remember that the *i* verbs—*lie, sit,* and *rise*—are intransitive and, therefore, do not have objects.

intransitive   l*i*e   s*i*t   r*i*se

The other three verbs, *lay, set,* and *raise,* are all transitive.

Now review carefully the principal parts of the following irregular verbs.

Present Tense	Past Tense	Past Participle	Present Participle	Infinitive
lie	lay	lain	lying	to lie
lay	laid	laid	laying	to lay
sit	sat	sat	sitting	to sit
set	set	set	setting	to set
rise	rose	risen	rising	to rise
raise	raised	raised	raising	to raise

One common mistake is confusing *lay* in its present tense form with *lay*, the past tense form of *lie*. How can you tell which is which? You can tell by remembering what you have learned about transitive verbs. Look at the following examples:

On Monday, Michael (*lay, laid*) the mail on the receptionist's desk.

After jogging, I usually (*lie, lay*) down for a short while.

Yesterday I (*lie, lay*) down for only five minutes.

Let's analyze these sentences. Does the first verb have an object? Yes, *mail*. Therefore, a transitive verb is needed. As you just learned, *laid* is the past tense form of the transitive verb *to lay*, so *laid* is correct.

In the second sentence, is there an object? No. *Down* is not an object; it is an adverb. Here you need a form of the verb *to lie*, so the answer is *lie*— I lie down.

In the third sentence, the word *yesterday* shows that the past tense is needed. Does the verb have a direct object? Answer: No. Thus the correct answer is *lay*, the past tense form of *lie*, an intransitive verb.

Some thinking and analysis are needed when choosing among the forms of *lie* and *lay*, so do not choose hastily.

Now let's apply the same principles to the transitive verbs *set* and *raise* and to the intransitive verbs *sit* and *rise*.

Neil and Lena (*sit, set*) the flowers on the windowsill before they left for lunch. (Is an object needed here? Yes. Which is the transitive verb? Answer: *set*. Set what? Set the *flowers*.)

As soon as the temperature (*rises, raises*), the air conditioner will automatically go on. (What is needed, a transitive verb or an intransitive verb? Answer: intransitive, because the verb has no object in this sentence. Which, then, is the intransitive verb? The *i* verb, *rises*.)

CHECKUP 9

Practise your ability to use the verbs *lie, lay, sit, set, rise,* and *raise.*

1. Les will (rise, raise) this subject at the meeting.

2. When she works on special writing projects, Danielle generally (sits, sets) in this office.

3. According to the new contract, our salaries have been (risen, raised) by about 5 per cent.

4. When you input the corrections on this report, please (sit, set) wider left and right margins.

5. Tell the messengers to (sit, set) the display racks in the lobby.

6. Because Alan felt ill, he (lay, laid) down for about an hour this morning.

7. The certificates that you were looking for had been (lain, laid) carelessly on a lunchroom table.

8. Please (rise, raise) for the national anthem.

Review of Key Terms

1. What is a *verb tense*? What are the six most commonly used verb tenses?
2. What is the difference between a *transitive verb* and an *intransitive verb*?

Practical Application

1. Identify the verb phrases in the following sentences. For the main verb in each phrase, tell where it would belong on a chart of principal parts—under *present, past participle,* or *present participle.*
   a. The deed should be signed by noon today.
   b. Betsy is being transferred to Moncton in January.
   c. Have they already hired a replacement for Sherry?
   d. Denise is requesting an assistant during the peak season.
   e. Joy and Heather had already arranged the documents.
   f. Kendra has visited our Montreal office three times.
   g. On July 1, Sue will be recognized for 20 years of service.
   h. Peggy easily finished the assignment by Friday.
   i. The travel agent is now preparing a revised itinerary for Dr. Gregg.
   j. We are ordering new equipment for our laboratory.

2. Practice your ability to form the principal parts of regular verbs by completing the following table. Use a separate sheet of paper.

Present Tense	Past Tense	Past Participle (Uses a helper)	Present Participle (Uses a helper)
a. explain			
b.	approved		
c.		selected	
d.			addressing
e.		stacked	
f.	insured		
g. bill			
h.	parked		
i.		argued	
j.			requiring

3. Identify the verb or the verb phrase in each of the following sentences. Label each choice *T* for "transitive," *I* for "intransitive," and *B* for "being."
   a. How safe are our airports?
   b. Our firm is studying this question.
   c. We have been very busy as a result of this project.
   d. Passengers at most airports are arriving more than two hours before flight time.

e. They need more time because of increased security checks.

f. Moreover, nearly all airports have been opening more luggage for inspection since the last terrorist attack.

g. As a result, of course, tempers are rising.

h. However, passenger safety has been improved.

i. We should be finishing our study in about a month.

j. Our findings will be published in *Travel & Leisure* magazine.

4. Correct any errors in the following sentences. Write *OK* if the sentence is correct.

a. Richard has already wrote to the Student Association about our concerns.

b. The memo that I was looking for was laying on my desk.

c. When Mrs. Merriwether arrived, we raised to greet her.

d. At this morning's meeting, Carl laid out a comprehensive plan for our project.

e. Has Karen ever flew to Europe before?

f. Mark has risen that same objection at every meeting on procedures.

g. If I was David, I'd enter the competition.

h. The builder promised us that the foundation will have been lain no later than July 8.

i. Please lay all those packages on the conference room table.

j. Sharon has lent us $75 to buy the materials that we need.

5. Write five sentences, each containing a direct and an indirect object.

Swap sentences with another team and identify each other's direct and indirect objects. Discuss the answers.

TEAMWORK

Editing Practice

Spelling Alert! Correct any spelling errors in the following sentences. Write *OK* if the sentence is correct.

1. At this morning's meeting with the manager of the personel department, we will discuss some specific problems concerning overtime pay.

2. Several of the comittee members offered suggestions that were acceptionally innovative.

3. We have also asked various enployees for ideas to solve these problems.

4. Opening this new store presents us with an excellent oportunity to expand our lines of merchandise.

5. This morning we recieved our first order from Glencoe Enterprises.

6. High-risk stocks are not apropriate invextments for Mr. Miller.

The Right Word. Select the correct word for each of the following sentences.

1. Rosemary suggested that we conduct a Canada-wide (pole, poll) of soft drink consumers.
2. According to Mr. DeFoe, the one-year freshness guarantee of Fruitfizz products is one of the (principle, principal) reasons for the company's success.
3. Fruitfizz has (its, it's) main plant in St. Catharines, Ontario.
4. Al and Rosemary are now planning (they're, their, there) trip to Niagara Falls.
5. The advertising cost cannot (exceed, accede) $10 000.

Discussion Points

1. How are the six verb tenses for regular verbs formed?
2. How do you know if you should use *were* or *was* after *if, as if, as though,* and *wish*?

Predicate Agreement

Be sure that your subject and predicate is [sic] in agreement.

—C.B. Camp, author

Popular songs, television shows, and movies do little to avoid subject-verb agreement errors such as "he don't" and "I been." As a result, listeners and viewers hear such errors so often that they may start to believe that "he don't" and "I been" are grammatically correct.

They are *not*. Pay special attention to the agreement rules to make sure you avoid such errors in your speaking and writing.

Predicate Agreement with Simple Subjects

In Section 3.1, you learned about predicates and simple subjects. Now let's review the way that these elements are related.

Basic Agreement Rule

A predicate must agree with its simple subject in number and in person. This statement is the basic rule of agreement for all sentences. A predicate always includes a verb, of course, and that verb must agree with the subject of the sentence in both number and person. In addition, if the predicate includes any pronouns that refer to the subject, those pronouns must also agree with the subject in both number and person.

Agreement of Subject and Verb. Note how the following *verbs* agree in number with their *subjects* in the following sentences.

Ray Singleton wants to shorten the manufacturing schedule. (The verb *wants* agrees with the subject, *Ray Singleton*—both are *singular*.)

Ray Singleton, our vice president, wants to shorten the manufacturing schedule. (Neither the subject nor the verb has changed. *Wants* agrees with *Ray Singleton*.)

Two vice presidents want to shorten the manufacturing schedule. (Now the subject is the *plural: vice presidents.* Therefore, the plural form *want*—not "wants"—is correct.)

Although plural nouns usually end in *s* or *es*, an *s* ending on a verb indicates that it is a singular verb.

Singular Noun and Verb	Plural Noun and Verb
the team wants	the teams want
one salesclerk has	all salesclerks have
Mrs. Salerno is	Mr. and Mrs. Salerno are

▶ Key Terms

▶ inverted sentences

▶ intervening phrases or clauses

▶ collective noun

▶ antecedent

MEMORY HOOK

Agreement of Pronoun with Subject. If the complete predicate includes a pronoun that refers to the subject, that pronoun must also agree with the subject in number. Some examples are:

The team wants to change *its* assignment in the company. The teams want to change *their* assignments in the company. (The pronoun *its* agrees with the singular subject *team.* The pronoun *their* agrees with the plural subject *teams.*)

Mrs. Salerno is eager to receive *her* dividends. Mr. and Mrs. Salerno are eager to receive *their* dividends. (*Her* agrees with the singular subject, *Mrs. Salerno.* In the second sentence, *their* agrees with the plural subject, *Mr. and Mrs. Salerno.*)

CHECKUP 1

Choose the correct verbs and pronouns in the following sentences.

1. The DeWitt Corporation (does? do?) not usually disclose (his? her? its? their?) acquisition plans.
2. All four managers (is? are?) going to bring (his? her? its? their?) reports with (him, her? it? them?).
3. Yolanda (wants? want?) to open (his? her? its? their?) third store in the Shady Hills Mall.
4. The union (has? have?) changed (its? their?) demands since our last meeting.
5. The design studio (is? are?) very well respected as a leader in (his? her? its? their?) field.
6. Mary Burroughs, one of the senior partners, (is? are?) planning to sell (his? her? its? their?) share of the company stock before (he? she? it? they?) retires next month.

Simple-Subject Agreement Problems

The most common problems concerning agreement of subjects and verbs are reviewed in the following discussion. Study them carefully.

Inverted Sentences. Agreement problems most often arise when the subject is difficult to identify, as in **inverted sentences**—where the verb comes before the subject.

Inverted Word Order. On your credenza (*is? are?*) the speakers. (At first glance, the subject and verb may appear to be "credenza *is,*" but a closer look shows that the subject of this inverted sentence is *speakers.* The correct verb is *are.*)

Other situations where sentences are in inverted order include questions and sentences beginning with *there.*

Questions. Are the files on the desk? (Here the subject, *files,* comes after the verb, *are,* because the sentence asks a question.)

Sentences Beginning with *There.* There (*is? are?*) still several vacancies. (Until you identify the subject, *vacancies,* you cannot choose the correct verb, *are.*)

Do you know whether there (*is? are?*) additional elevators in the hotel? (The simple subject of the dependent clause "whether there (*is? are?*) additional elevators in the hotel?" is *elevators.* Therefore, *are* is the correct verb.)

Other examples of sentences beginning with *there* include those beginning with *there has been* and *there have been*.

Intervening Phrases and Clauses. Another construction that may confuse the writer or speaker is one in which **intervening phrases or clauses** separate the subject from its verb. Again, the trick is to identify the simple subject. Some examples are:

The reason for the delays (is? are?) that half the department is away sick. (The subject is the singular noun *reason*. Therefore, the correct verb is *is*. Although the plural word *delays* immediately precedes the verb, *delays* is not the subject of the verb. *Delays* is part of the prepositional phrase *for the delays*.)

The treasurer, who must approve all expense forms signed by our sales managers, (has? have?) cut the travel budgets for all sales personnel. (The subject is *treasurer*, not *sales managers*. Therefore, the correct verb is *has*.)

CHECKUP 2

Correct any agreement errors in the following sentences. Write *OK* if a sentence is correct. Be sure to identify the subject of each sentence.

1. When we checked the directory, we found that there is only two stationery stores nearby.
2. Are you sure that there's no more than two stationery stores in the area?
3. The entire building, with all its offices, are to be painted during the summer.
4. The whole city, which consists of more than 800,000 people, are affected.
5. There is, as you already know, several reasons for the water shortage.
6. Did you know that there's a few individuals who water their lawns three times a week?

Pronoun Agreement with Common-Gender Nouns. When the gender of a noun is clearly masculine (*man, father, brother, son*) or clearly feminine (*woman, mother, sister, daughter*), choosing between the pronouns *he* or *she, or him* or *her*, is no problem. Common-gender nouns are those that can be either masculine or feminine, such as *employee, student, teacher, officer, owner, secretary*, and so on. The traditional rule has been to use masculine pronouns to represent common-gender nouns. However, good communicators today avoid using masculine pronouns to represent common-gender nouns. Instead, they use pronoun combinations such as *he or she, him or her*, and *his or her* to avoid suggesting either masculine or feminine gender. Some examples are:

Every employee knows his or her role in the upcoming fire drill. (*His or her* agrees with the common-gender noun *employee*.)

An executive must be sure that she or he is familiar with the fire regulations. (*She or he* agrees with the common gender noun *executive*.)

When such combinations are used too often, they make the message difficult to read. In such instances, consider using plurals to avoid the need for pronoun combinations.

Executives must be sure that *they* are familiar with the fire regulations. (*They* agrees with the plural *executives*.)

Indefinite-Pronoun Subject. The indefinite pronouns *each, either, every, everyone, everybody, every one, everything, someone, somebody, some one, something, anyone, anybody, neither, no one, nobody,* and *nothing* are always singular. When they are used as subjects, and when they modify other subjects, their predicates must be singular. Some examples are:

Each of the printers has a long cable that connects it to the computer. (The singular verb *has* and the pronoun *it* agree with the subject *each*.)

Each printer has a long cable that connects it to the computer. (Here *each* modifies the subject, *printer*. In this case, too, *each* is singular.)

Anyone in your district who wants to volunteer his or her time should be sure he or she registers. (*Wants, his or her, he or she,* and *registers* all agree with the singular indefinite pronoun anyone.)

Everybody is at the meeting. (*Is* agrees with the singular indefinite pronoun everybody.)

To remember the indefinite pronouns, memorize the phrase "**All** **e**mployees **n**eed **s**alaries." The indefinite pronouns are listed beneath the word in the phrase that shares the same first letter.

All	Employees	Need	Salaries
anybody	everybody	nobody	somebody
anyone	everyone	_____	someone
anything	everything	nothing	something
any one	every one	no one	some one
_____	either	neither	_____
_____	every	_____	_____
_____	each	_____	_____

CHECKUP 3

Correct the following sentences for any agreement errors in the use of indefinite pronouns. If a sentence is correct, write *OK*. For each sentence, identify the simple subject.

1. Nobody in these two departments have submitted his or her objectives for the next year.
2. Each of the administrative assistants want to attend the seminar.
3. Anyone who wants to participate in next week's training session must complete and return his or her form to the Personnel Department.
4. Every executive in this building is permitted to use these facilities if she shows her pass to the guard.
5. Neither of the service centres we visited have enough parking for their customers.
6. Every manager in this division is sure to want his senior staff members to take this course.

Predicate Agreement with Special Subjects

Remember the basic agreement rule: *A predicate must agree with its simple subject in number and in person.* As you review some especially troublesome agreement problems, keep this rule in mind.

Collective-Noun Simple Subjects

A **collective noun** is one that refers to a group or collection of persons or things. Esamples of collective nouns are: *class, jury, audience, department, company, committee,* and *association.* Because a collective noun may be either singular or plural, its correct number may not be easily recognized. Use the following Memory Hook to help you.

When the *class, jury,* and so on, *acts as one group,* treat the collective noun as *singular.* When the members of the collective noun *act as individuals,* treat the noun as *plural.* In other words, remember

One group is singular.
Individuals are plural.

- In a major case, the jury (does? do?) not give (its? their?) verdict quickly. (Is the jury acting *as one group,* or is the jury acting as *individuals*? Answer: *as one group.* Therefore, treat *jury* as a singular noun: "…the jury does not give *its* verdict quickly.")

- The jury (is? are?) arguing about the charges. (Is the jury acting *as one group,* or is the jury acting *as individuals*? In arguing, they would be acting *as individuals.* Treat *jury* as a plural noun: "The jury *are* arguing about the charges."

Foreign-Noun Subjects

Nouns of foreign origin do not form their plurals in the usual way. Review the list of foreign-origin nouns on pages 151 and 152. Always be careful to determine first whether the noun is singular or plural before deciding on the correct verb to agree with such nouns. Some examples are:

The basis for her statements (was? were?) unsound. (*Basis* is singular; therefore, the predicate must be singular. *Was* is correct.)

The bases for her statements (was? were?) unsound. (*Bases* is plural; therefore, *were* is correct.)

CHECKUP 4

Correct any errors in subject-verb agreement in the following sentences. Write *OK* if a sentence is correct.

1. The faculty was assigned to its new offices in the recently constructed building.
2. In this book, parentheses is used to enclose bibliographic references.
3. The economic stimulus that is being used by the federal government have been criticized by some experts.
4. The nutrition analysis for each menu item are printed in this pamphlet.
5. The media we prefer for our commercials is television and radio.
6. If you need more information, the criteria that we use to select meat for our restaurant chain is explained in detail in this report.
7. The marketing class are leaving for a field trip.
8. The group has reached its decision and will announce it shortly.

Part, Portion, or Amount Subjects

Other subjects that may be either singular or plural are those that refer to a part, a portion, or an amount of something. Thus *all, some, half, two-thirds (or any fraction)*, and *none* may be *either singular or plural* depending on the noun to which they refer. The noun may belong to an "of" phrase. To decide, find the answer to "Part of *what*?" "Portion of *what*?" "Amount of *what*?" Use the complete subject (not the simple subject) for your answer. If the complete subject is singular, then the verb is singular; if the complete subject is plural, then the verb is plural. Some examples are:

Some of the *house* (has? have?) been painted. (Part or some of what? Answer:part of the house. Therefore, "has been painted" is used to agree with the singular "house.")

Some of the houses (has? have?) been painted. (Part or some of what? Answer: some of the houses. Therefore, "have been painted" is used to agree with the plural "houses.")

Three-quarters of the *contestants* (is? are?) from Alberta. (What portion of the contestants? Answer: Three-quarters. Therefore, "are" is used to agree with "three-quarters" and "contestants.")

Two-thirds of the *chart* (is? are?) complete. (Part of what is complete? Part of the chart. Therefore, "is" is used to agree with the singular "chart.")

Note in the above examples that once you have located the complete subject, your decision concerning a singular or plural verb depends on the part of the subject other than "some," "three-quarters," and "two-thirds." Keeping this in mind, try the following examples:

All of the suitcases (was? were?) taken to the airport. ("All" can be singular or plural; "cases" is plural; therefore, use "were.")

Half of the workers (is? are?) on strike. ("Half" can be singular or plural; "workers" is plural; therefore, use "are.")

Half of the pie (has? have?) been eaten. ("Half" can be singular or plural"; "pie" is singular; therefore, "has been eaten" is correct.)

A Number, The Number

A number is always plural. *The number* is always singular. Some examples are:

A number of tenants have questioned the new rent increase. (*Have,* because *a number* is always plural.)

The number of tenants is declining. (*Is,* because *the number* is always singular.)

Note that an adjective before the word *number* has no effect on the choice. For example, "A *large* number of tenants have questioned the new rent increase." (Adding the adjective "large" has no effect on the choice of "have.") "The *total* number of tenants is declining." (Adding the adjective "total" has no effect on the choice of "is.")

Use the acronym APTS to remember the above principle.

A number
Plural
The Number
Singular

CHECKUP 5

Correct any agreement errors in the use of "a" number and "the" number. Write *OK* if a sentence is correct.

1. The number of volunteers have risen to ten.

2. Luckily, none of the boats were damaged by the storm.

3. Nearly two-thirds of the city was affected by the transit strike.

4. We know that a number of workers is unhappy about the changes in our medical coverage.

5. Some of the machines, Hank told me, was not adequately inspected before shipment.

6. Some of the tools, as you can see, has already begun to rust.

Predicate Agreement with Compound Subjects

To complete your study of predicate agreement, you will now work on predicate agreement with compound subjects—that is, two or more subjects joined by *and, or,* or *nor*—and on one other predicate agreement problem: agreement with the relative pronouns *who, that,* and *which*.

Subjects Joined by *And*

A compound subject joined by *and* is plural and must take a plural verb. Some examples are:

Greg *and* Howard *have* applied for a business loan. (The compound subject *Greg and Howard* is plural; the plural verb *have applied* is correct.)

A construction company *and* a plastics distributor have filed for bankruptcy. (The plural form *have filed* is correct because the compound subject is joined by *and.*)

Two exceptions to this rule are possible:

1. If the two nouns joined by *and* refer to *one* person, then that subject is really singular and takes a singular verb. Some examples are:

My business partner *and* investment advisor *is* my sister, Joanne Delilo. (Although the compound subject is joined by *and,* only one person is serving as *business partner and investment adviser.* The singular verb *is* is therefore correct.)

Strawberries and cream *is* going to be served for dessert. (One dessert, *strawberries and cream,* is the intended meaning.)

> Note that if two different people or two different desserts were intended, the verbs would then be plural. Some examples are:

My business partner *and* my investment adviser *are* not in agreement on this issue. (Two different people are intended.)

Strawberries *and* ice cream *are* among the desserts included in the fixed-price lunch. (Here, two different items on the menu are referred to.)

2. If two or more subjects joined by *and* are modified by *each, every,* or *many a,* then the predicate is singular. An example is:

Each secretary and assistant *has* been asked to return the completed questionnaire to the personnel department by May 15. *Every* supervisor and manager *is* supposed to check the questionnaires. Many a factory, office, and store throughout the country *is* now following this procedure.

(In each sentence, the predicate is singular because the subjects are modified by *each, every,* and *many a.* Members of the plural groups are being considered singly.)

CHECKUP 6

Correct any agreement errors in the use of subjects joined by *and* in the following sentences. Write *OK* if a sentence is correct.

1. Pizza and ice cream is at the top of most children's favourite-foods list.
2. Each returning patient and new patient are required to complete this form.
3. The letter and the envelope have two different addresses.
4. Many an auditor and business owner have complained about this new policy.
5. Ham and eggs are usually what I order for breakfast.
6. Every partner and associate in the accounting firms we contacted are writing to their Member of Parliament to show support for the legislation.

Subjects Joined by *Or* or *Nor*

For subjects joined by *or* or *nor*, simply match the predicate to the subject that follows *or* or *nor*. Some examples are:

The owner *or* her *assistants* (is? are?) going to discuss (her? their?) new winter clothing line at the sales meeting tomorrow. (Matching the predicate to the subject that follows *or*, the correct choices are *are* and *their*.)

The assistants *or* the *owner* (is? are?) going to discuss (her? their?) new winter clothing line at the sales meeting tomorrow. (Now the subject that follows *or* is the singular word *owner*. Therefore, the choices are *is* and *her*.)

Neither the owner *nor* her *assistants* (knows? know?) where the French designer went. (Which subject follows *nor*? The plural *assistants*. The choice is, therefore, *know*.)

Either the three Japanese couturiers *or* SmartShirt (is? are?) going to present (its? their?) collection this afternoon. (The subject that follows *or* is *SmartShirt*, singular; thus the choices are *is* and *its*.)

CHECKUP 7

Select the words in parentheses that match the compound subject.

1. Either the salesclerks or Mr. Lehman (like? likes?) to present (their? his?) customers' clothes in special garment bags.
2. Neither Mr. Lehman nor the district managers (has? have?) endorsed the suggestion.
3. Alicia Solomon or her store managers (has? have?) completed (her? their?) buying for the spring season.
4. My brother-in-law or his associates (is? are?) interested in purchasing sportswear for (his? their?) stores.
5. Either her buyers or Alicia herself (is? are?) going to coordinate the fashion show.

Predicate Agreement in Clauses Introduced by Relative Pronouns

The pronouns *who, that,* and *which* are called *relative pronouns* because they *relate* to other words (called **antecedents**). *The antecedent of the relative pronoun is a noun or a pronoun that is usually placed immediately before the relative pronoun.* Some examples are:

Grace Yancy is one *who* strives for perfection. (The relative pronoun is *who*, and its antecedent is *one*.)

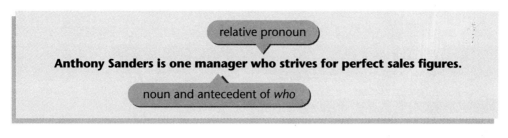

Grace Yancy is one of those *who* strive for perfection. (The relative pronoun is *who*, and its antecedent is *those*.)

Grace Yancy is one of those people *who* strive for perfection all the time. (The relative pronoun is *who*, and its antecedent is the noun immediately before it, *people*.)

The calculator *that* is on the shelf works accurately. (If *that* is a relative pronoun, what is its antecedent? Answer: *calculator*.)

This special offer is good until Saturday, *which* is the last day of our sale. (The relative pronoun *which* refers to *Saturday*, its antecedent.)

To help you choose the correct verb in clauses introduced by a relative pronoun, omit the relative pronoun and use the antecedent as the subject of the clause. For example, omitting the relative pronouns from the immediately preceding sentences would give:

one . . . strives	calculator . . . is
those . . . strive	Saturday . . . is
people . . . strive	

Let's look at some other examples:

Lisa prefers one of those microwaves that (has/have) rotating shelves inside (its/their) ovens. (By omitting the relative pronoun *that*, you can determine the agreement: microwaves . . . have . . . their.)

Cheryl Asuras is one of those sales representatives who (does/do) (her/their) best selling under pressure. (Omit *who*, and you have sales representatives . . . do . . . their.)

Note: An exception is a clause preceded by *the only one*. Such clauses must take singular predicates.

Nicole is the only one of the members who has cast her vote for the expansion. (*Has* and *her* are correct.)

Note that in each sentence the verb in the clause introduced by a relative pronoun agrees with the antecedent.

CHECKUP 8

Check the following sentences for any agreement errors in the use of clauses introduced by a relative pronoun. Write *OK* if a sentence is correct.

1. Barry is one of those stockbrokers who calls his clients once a month.
2. A.L. Landry and Co. is one of those dealerships which has shown an interest in leasing cars.
3. Management will soon close one of the several stores that is now operating at a loss.
4. Matthias is one of those proofreaders who always double-check their work carefully.
5. Isabel prefers one of those offices that has modern furniture in it.
6. Audrey is the only one of the council members who want to change the zoning.

◀ **Figure 3.5**
Subject Verb Agreement
Analyzing which word is the relative pronoun, which word is the verb, and which word is the antecedent can assist you in checking agreement.

Thinking Critically.
What is wrong with the use of the verb in the following sentence?

Tony submitted the reports that was due yesterday.

Review of Key Terms

1. What is the basic rule of *predicate agreement*?
2. How can a writer determine if a *collective noun* is singular or plural?

Practical Application

1. Correct any errors in the following sentences. Write *OK* if a sentence is correct.

   a. In the Emporium catalogue is many different kinds of interesting gifts.
   b. Don't Charles know how to use his voice mail?
   c. Don't you know how to move this equipment?
   d. Every medical doctor in the country have been surveyed to see which option they prefer.
   e. To exchange merchandise, each customer must show his or her receipt to the cashier.
   f. Either Fahad or Jamal are going to organize our annual picnic.
   g. Some of the shipments to Europe has been delayed by the winter storms.
   h. The number of managers in the Toronto office were higher than the number of line workers in Oshawa.
   i. Approximately three-fourths of her time, she says, are spent talking with customers about delays and errors.
   j. During the convention, the engineering association is staying at two hotels downtown.
   k. Because a number of people has complained about our billing policy, we are now reviewing it with our accounting department.
   l. Half of the area in this warehouse has been converted to office space.
   m. There's many a Tom, Dick, or Mary who wants just what you want.
   n. Every invoice and package that we send customers are carefully checked first.
   o. Neither Arnold nor Joanna plan to attend the national conference.
   p. Every glass and bottle on the truck were broken in the accident.
   q. The supervisor or the division managers was notified of the change in regulations.
   r. Each editor, proofreader, and designer were invited to a full-day conference on the magazine's future plans.
   s. As you probably already know, Mr. Mehta is one of those engineers who is always late in handling his paperwork.
   t. Neither the disks nor the manual is with the computer.

2. Correct any grammatical errors in the following sentences. Write *OK* if a sentence is correct.

a. Either Laura or Olivia should have corrected this data disk before they printed the files.
b. Congratulations, you deserve this promotion.
c. If I was you, I would accept their offer.
d. After Amy and Kami had spoke with Ms. Hamrick, we understood why Ms. Hamrick reassigned the project.
e. The jury was debating for two days about the guilt or innocence of the defendant.
f. Nearly three-fourths of the cars on the lot were damaged during the hailstorm.
g. Two forms of identification or a major credit card are required for cashing cheques.
h. Who has swam in the new pool?
i. Where's the monitor and the printer cable for this computer?
j. All the analysis that we received from our research and development department indicate that the new product is durable.
k. Please let me lay down before I fall down.
l. A number of boats was damaged in yesterday's storm.

3. Write a paragraph in which you recommend a colleague for a job. Use at least five of the following words as subjects: *everybody, most, nobody, some, a number, anybody, either, none, all, neither.*

TEAMWORK

Editing Practice

You typed the following copy quickly but didn't have time to proofread it. Do so now.

We appreciate your request for information about the Mountain Top Inn. To answer you questions about convention facilitys, we have enclosed our latest brochure.

As you will see in the broshure, the Mountain Top Inn can accomodate large groups of people as well as inimate getaways with the quality service that have made us famous for more than 40 years.

Discussion Points

1. What are some of the common problems concerning subject and verb agreement?
2. Compare the agreement rule with subjects joined by *and* with subjects joined by *or* or *nor.*

Chapter 3 Wrap-Up

SUMMARY

▶ To write and speak effectively, one must practice proper English grammar. Correct grammar usage requires knowing the rules governing the eight parts of speech: nouns, pronouns, verbs, adjectives, adverbs, prepositions, conjunctions, and interjections.

▶ A noun names a person, place, thing, or idea. Common nouns refer to general nouns while proper nouns refer to specific nouns. Pronouns are words that take the place of a noun. They may function as subjects, objects, appositives, or complements. A verb is a word that expresses action or a state of being. Adjectives are words that describe nouns and pronouns. Adverbs are words that describe adjectives, verbs, or other adverbs. Prepositions are connecting words that show the relationship between a noun or pronoun and other words in a sentence. A conjunction is a word that joins words, phrases, or clauses. An interjection is a word that expresses strong feeling.

▶ The parts of speech are used together to form sentences. Sentences must express a complete thought and contain a subject "what the sentence is about" and a predicate "what the subject is doing." A fragment does not express a complete thought.

▶ There are four principal parts of verbs—the present tense, the past tense, the past participle, and the present participle. Errors in verb tense can be avoided by learning how to form these verb patterns, especially with irregular verbs.

▶ Sentences may be simple or complex, depending on their use of dependent or independent clauses. Sentences must have subject-verb agreement. Errors in agreement can be avoided by knowing the difference between simple and compound subjects and by identifying phrases that may interrupt the subject from the predicate.

CASE 3.1

Craig Olson has been working with Ramseur Pharmaceuticals for almost two weeks now. He is administrative assistant to Helen Drexler, director of sales. Just before lunch, Ms. Drexler gave Craig a handwritten letter and asked him to type and send the letter to 25 of the company's best customers. Craig read the letter and found two grammatical errors in it.

During lunch, Craig pondered what action he should take. As a new employee, he wanted to be sure he approached the situation tactfully and that he did not offend Ms. Drexler.

What should Craig do? What is Craig's responsibility in this matter?

CASE 3.2

Pitney Bowes completed a study in August 2000 and found that the average worker managed more than 25 messages in an hour, including e-mails, voice mails, faxes, and hand written notes. Most workers use e-mail to keep others informed about progress on various projects. With all this writing, explain how important it is to use proper grammar. Do you think people are more careless with their grammar when writing an e-mail as opposed to writing a memo? Why?

Communicating in Your Career

People expect certain professionals to speak and write correctly. A teacher or college professor is expected to formulate impeccable sentences at every turn. Most commentators on television are also polished speakers of the English language. Compare and contrast the job of a teacher with that of a news reporter or sports commentator. Do you think that improper usage on the part of television commentators has a negative effect on the way their viewers speak?

On the Web

1. The name given to a part of speech tells how the word is used. For example, the word "noun" tells us that the word is a name for something. However, that same word could become a different part of speech in a different sentence.
   - Visit the following Web site belonging to the University of Ottawa **www.uottawa.ca/academic/arts/writcent/hypergrammar**.
   - Read the information that explains the above statements.
   - Give two of your own examples of the same word being used as a different part of speech.
2. The same site gives information about the parts of a sentence.
   - Choose one of the topics listed (e.g. Subject and Predicate) and compare the information with the information given in this chapter.
   - What similarities, and what differences, do you find?
   - What are two or three important points stated both on the Web site and in your textbook?

Key Terms

action verb	97	compound		direct object	125
adjective	98	subject	105	helping (auxiliary)	
adverb	98	conjunction	102	verbs	117
antecedent	138	coordinating		independent	
"being" verbs	122	conjunction	102	clause	108
collective noun	135	dependent clause	108	indirect object	125

Chapter 4

Mastering Nouns and Pronouns

Chapter Learning Outcomes

After successfully completing this chapter, you will have demonstrated the ability to:

▶ form the plurals of nouns;

▶ use the possessive forms of nouns and pronouns;

▶ give examples of nominative and objective pronoun forms.

Francis Laceese was recently hired by PR Plus in Regina to work in the Human Resources Department. Francis' supervisor, Kakali, asked him to draft a document outlining current procedures on vacations and leaves of absence. He felt honoured to receive this assignment as a new employee, especially when Kakali explained that the draft would be discussed at the next department meeting.

Francis did not know all the rules of English grammar but thought he could usually tell if something "sounded right." As he began drafting, he felt quite confident. However, as the work progressed, he had doubts about some of the sentences he wrote—were they grammatically correct?

Francis photocopied the draft for the meeting, and handed the work to Kakali. Kakali did not have time to read the draft before the meeting. It contained a number of grammatical errors. After the meeting, Kakali met with Francis and thanked him for drafting a document that contained all the important points. However, she also reviewed the grammatical errors, and explained that excellent writing skills would be needed to ensure promotion at PR Plus. She recommended that Francis take an evening class at the local college.

As you study Chapter 4, identify some of the grammar rules that would help Francis improve his writing.

▶ **Key Terms**

▶ proper nouns

▶ compound nouns

▶ courtesy title

▶ foreign nouns

Nouns: Plural Forms

If writing must be a precise form of communication, it should be treated like a precision instrument. It should be sharpened, and it should not be used carelessly.

—Theodore M. Bernstein, editor and author

As the above quotation points out, written communication needs to be precise to be effective. This is especially true when forming plurals. For example, when we say "several of our *customers*," or "this *customer's* opinion," or "all *customers'* orders," we do not ordinarily think of the differences in the written forms of *customers, customer's* and *customers'*. We pronounce all three words in the same way. In writing, however, these three words are not interchangeable. Each has its own distinct meaning and use.

Customers is a plural
Customer's is a singular possessive
Customers' is a plural possessive

In this section and the next, you will master the use of plurals and possessives.

Essential Principles for Forming Plurals of Nouns

Let's begin by reviewing the essential principles for forming plurals of most nouns.

Plurals of Common Nouns

Add "s" to most common nouns to form their plurals. Some examples are:

service	services	computer	computers
employee	employees	diskette	diskettes
avenue	avenues	valley	valleys

Add "es" to nouns that end in s, sh, ch, x, and z to form their plurals. Some examples are:

class	classes
dash	dashes
wrench	wrenches

tax   taxes

buzz   buzzes

Plurals of Proper Nouns

Add "s" to most **proper nouns** to form their plurals. Some examples are:

Professor Urbanski	the Urbanskis
Bob Keenan	the Keenans
Mrs. Bromberg	the Brombergs

Add "es" to proper nouns that end in *s, sh, ch, x,* and *z* to form their plurals. Some examples are:

Mrs. Ross	the Rosses
Mr. Walsh	the Walshes
Anita Karsch	the Karsches
Terry Fox	the Foxes
Ms. Herz	the Herzes

Plurals of Compound Nouns

A **compound noun** is a noun that consists of two or more words. Compound nouns may be written with a hyphen, with a space between them, or as one word. Make the main word (the most important word in the compound) plural. Some examples are:

bulletin board	bulletin boards
mother-in-law	mothers-in-law
general manager	general managers
major general	major generals
editor in chief	editors in chief
chief of staff	chiefs of staff

Plural Noun Exceptions

Endings	Noun Types	Plural Forms
Ends in *s, sh, ch, x, z*	Common Proper Compound	Add "es"
Ends in consonant + *y*	Common Compound	Change *y* to *i* and add "es"
Ends in consonant + *y*	Proper	Add "s"
All endings	Compound	Make MAIN word plural

◀ **Figure 4.1**
Nouns
Compound nouns made up of two or more words can have all types of endings.

Thinking Critically.
How can you decide which word is the main word in a compound noun?

Plurals of Common Nouns Ending in *Y*

1. Add *s* to form the plural if there is a *vowel* immediately before the *y*. Some examples are:

alloy   alloys

key   keys

valley   valleys

convoy   convoys

2. Change the *y* to *i* and add *es* if there is a *consonant* immediately before the *y*. Some examples are:

territory   territories

company   companies

faculty   faculties

Note that *proper nouns* ending in *y* do not follow these rules. For proper names ending in *y*, simply add *s* to form the plural. Some examples are:

Mrs. McCarthy   the McCarthys

Sally   two Sallys

John Langley   the Langleys

CHECKUP 1

Check the following sentences for the correct use of plurals. Write *OK* if a sentence is correct.

1. According to the article, one of the newly appointed editor in chiefs is Roxanne P. Chandler.
2. Mrs. Otabe and her two son-in-laws run the family business.
3. Two Marys—Mary Murphy and Mary Resnik—work on my team.
4. Please store the display materials and miscellaneous supplys in your office.
5. Several telephoto and wide-angle lenss are on sale at Ben's Cameras.
6. Most of the communitys in these two countys are popular because taxes are low.
7. Edward and Connie are the secretarys assigned to this project.
8. Both organizations have subsidiaries in Ottawa.
9. Two Crown attornies have been assigned to this case.
10. The last three majors general were from British Columbia.

Special Plurals

Certain plurals cause problems for writers because these forms follow no "regular" rules. For example, how would you form the plural of the courtesy titles *Mr.* and *Mrs.?*

Plurals of Titles with Names

The commonly used **courtesy titles** and their plurals are:

Singular	Plural
Mr.	Messrs.
Mrs.	Mmes.
Ms.	Mses.
Miss	Misses
Dr.	Drs.

Note the following:

1. *Messrs.* is derived from *Messieurs,* the French word for "Misters."
2. *Mmes.* is derived from *Mesdames,* the French word for "My ladies."

When forming the title of a name, make *either* the title or the name plural, *not both.* Some examples follow. Both plural forms are correct.

Singular	Plural Title	Plural Name
Ms. Toto	the Mses. Toto	the Ms. Totos
Mr. Werner	the Messrs. Werner	the Mr. Werners
Mrs. Ford	the Mmes. Ford	the Mrs. Fords
Miss Khan	the Misses Khan	the Miss Khans

Plurals with Apostrophes

In some situations the apostrophe is used to form the plural. Use an apostrophe plus "s" to form plurals of lowercase letters and lowercase abbreviations. Some examples are:

The *t's* and *f's* on this page are unclear.

The receptionist handles all *c.o.d.'s* for our office.

Add lowercase *s* alone to form plurals of capital letters and abbreviations ending with capital letters. For example, the plural of URL (uniform resource locator—e.g., www.CBC.ca) is URLs. Other examples of such abbreviations are VIPs (very important persons), CEOs (chief executive officers), CDs (compact discs), PCs (personal computers), DVDs (digital video discs), and SUVs (sport utility vehicles). These abbreviations have become commonly accepted words in our culture. They are written in all capitals to show they are abbreviations.

If simply adding an *s* to form a plural abbreviation would cause confusion, add an apostrophe before the *s.* Some examples are:

He got *A's, I's,* and *U's* on his report—not *As, Is,* and *Us.*

An apostrophe is *not* required to form plurals in phrases such as *ups and downs, temperatures in the 30s,* and *in the 1990s.*

Plurals with Special Changes

Some nouns form their plurals in an irregular manner. Some examples are:

Singular	Plural
man	men
woman	women
child	children
mouse	mice
goose	geese
shelf	shelves
oasis	oases
ox	oxen

CHECKUP 2

Check the following sentences for the correct use of plurals. Write *OK* if a sentence is correct.

1. Hugo asked us to send these letters to the Misses Smiths.
2. The summer temperature in the Niagara region is in the high 20s.
3. Because of her illness, she received two Is for her incomplete courses.
4. Yes, the Messrs. Martin are buying the property on Queen Street.
5. Many woman are senior managers in Canadian companys.
6. Carol and Mike Delos have managed our Halifax office since the 1960s.
7. Please take yesterday's bread off the shelfs.
8. Two men and two woman partners have joined the firm: Mr. Hill and Ryan and Ms. Kramer and Sung.

Plurals of Nouns Ending in *O*

Add *s* to form the plural of nouns ending in *o* preceded by a vowel. Some examples are:

studio	studios	video	videos
folio	folios	ratio	ratios

Add *es* to form the plural of nouns ending in *o* preceded by a consonant. Some examples are:

motto	mottoes	tomato	tomatoes
potato	potatoes	veto	vetoes
echo	echoes	cargo	cargoes

Note: There are exceptions to the rule. For example, *casino* becomes *casinos* and *disco* (short for discotheque) becomes *discos.* Consult your dictionary when you are unsure of a plural form.

Nouns ending in *o* that relate to music and art form their plurals by adding *s.* Some examples are:

Singular	Plural
piano	pianos
alto	altos
solo	solos
oratorio	oratorios

Plurals of Nouns Ending in *F* or *Fe*

To form plurals of some nouns ending in *f* or *fe,* simply add *s.* Some examples are:

Singular	Plural
plaintiff	plaintiffs
proof	proofs
roof	roofs
safe	safes
belief	beliefs
chief	chiefs

In other cases, change the *f* or *fe* to *v* and add *es.* Some examples are:

Singular	Plural
shelf	shelves
half	halves
life	lives
wife	wives
knife	knives
self	selves

CHECKUP 3

Write the correct plural forms of the following nouns. If necessary, consult a dictionary.

1. tomato, mosquito
2. logo, ditto
3. leaf, thief
4. loaf, knife
5. solo, video
6. wife, gulf
7. bailiff, handkerchief
8. volcano, concerto
9. radio, trio
10. watch, brush

Plurals of Foreign Nouns

There are many nouns in the English language that are of foreign origin, usually borrowed from Latin or ancient Greek. These **foreign nouns** have become part of our everyday communications. Plurals of these nouns are *not* formed according to the English rules. When unsure, consult your dictionary. Some examples are found in Figure 4.2.

Borrowed Plurals			
Singular	Plural	Singular	Plural
addendum	addenda	basis	bases
alumna (female)	alumnae	crisis	crises
alumnus (male)	alumni	criterion	criteria
analysis	analyses	datum	data
axis	axes	hypothesis	hypotheses
bacterium	bacteria	synthesis	syntheses

◀ **Figure 4.2**
Borrowed Plurals
Plurals of certain words borrowed from Latin and ancient Greek are formed as shown in this chart.

Thinking Critically.
What is the plural of maître d'?

Figure 4.3 ▶
English and Foreign Plurals

Some words borrowed from Latin and ancient Greek have two plural forms.

Thinking Critically.
Which would you probably use in informal writing?

	English and Foreign Plurals	
Singular	**Foreign Plural**	**English Plural**
appendix	appendices	appendixes*
curriculum	curricula	curriculums*
formula	formulae	formulas*
index	indices	indexes
medium	media	media or mediums
memorandum	memoranda	memorandums*
nucleus	nuclei*	nucleuses
stadium	stadia	stadiums*
vertebra	vertebrae*	vertebras
syllabus	syllabi	syllabuses

NOTE: *indicates the plural form that is generally preferred in English usage.

However, some words of foreign origin have two plural forms—the "original" plural form, and an English plural form (a plural formed by treating the singular noun as if it were an English word). Some examples can be found in Figure 4.3.

Nouns That Are Always Singular, or Always Plural

The following nouns are *always singular* even though they end in *s*. Use a singular verb to agree with a singular noun. Some examples are:

aerobics	aeronautics
civics	economics
genetics	mathematics
molasses	news
physics	statistics

The following nouns are *always plural*. Use a plural verb to agree with a plural noun. Some examples are:

auspices	antics	belongings
jeans	pants	proceeds
riches	series	scissors
slacks	statistics	thanks
tidings	tongs	tweezers
winnings		

Nouns with One Form

Some nouns have only one form. The noun may be used either as a singular or a plural, depending on the intended meaning. Some examples are:

aircraft	Chinese	corps	deer
French	moose	odds	politics
salmon	sheep	wheat	series

When another number modifies a noun, the following nouns usually have the same form to denote either a singular or a plural number. Some examples are:

four-*score* years   three *thousand* forms

two-*dozen* seniors   five *hundred* applicants

CHECKUP 4

Check the following sentences for the correct use of plurals. Write *OK* if a sentence is correct.

1. All three economists suggested the same stimuluses to help the construction industry.
2. To his surprise, Tom found the civic lesson very interesting.
3. The proceeds from our raffle were given to a local charity.
4. Many of the alumni are planning to attend the special celebration honouring Professor Janis Oleski.
5. We had almost five thousands hits on our Web site last month.
6. People are sick because the meat contained bacterias.
7. Salsa and merengue are popular dances in Puerto Rico's discoes.
8. Your analyses of the report is very helpful.

Review of Key Terms

1. What do the terms *compound noun* and *foreign noun* mean? Give two examples of each.
2. Give an example of a *courtesy title*. When would you use this title?

Practical Application

1. Select the correct or preferred plural noun for each item.
   a. Gordon bought over a hundred pounds of (potatos/potatoes) to bake for the banquet.
   b. His two (vetos/vetoes) were for significant decisions.
   c. The five stranded (deer/deers) were airlifted back to dry land.
   d. Jesse wrote one (memoranda/memorandum) this morning.
   e. Two new (formula/formulas) were developed to treat the weed problem.
2. Indicate whether each of the following nouns is always singular or always plural. Write *AS* to specify *Always Singular* and *AP* to specify *Always Plural*.
   a. news
   b. scissors
   c. economics
   d. aerobics
   e. slacks
3. For each noun, write the correct singular or plural form for those incorrectly used. Assume that the verbs in each sentence are correct. Write *OK* if a sentence is correct.
   a. What are the basis for your agreement?
   b. Mrs. Lewis has announced that her two daughter-in-laws will become partners in her catering business.
   c. As you suggested, we have already notified the two Mrs. Harrises of the good news.
   d. The cost of the new facilitys will exceed $3 million.
   e. A recent survey showed several hundreds new computer businesses.
   f. If we want the job done correctly, we'll have to do it ourselfs.
   g. We tried to call Mr. Kelly several times, but none of the Kellies answered the telephone.
   h. The local chamber of commerce prints a list of area church's.
   i. Who won—the yea's or the nay's?
   j. The Marxes are trying to buy the last residential lot on the lake.
   k. Only 5 CGA's have applied for the position in Germany.
   l. Brent traded his two used stereoes for a new CD player.
   m. Mr. Ananda said that the old benchs in the cafeteria will be replaced with comfortable chairs.

n. Send copies to Messrs. Stojko, Brandt, and Vance.

o. The goods delivered to both companys were damaged.

4. Supply the correct plurals in the following paragraph. (Hint: A *maid* of honour is an unmarried attendant, and a *matron* of honour is a married attendant.)

Katja and Jasna Bolinski, twin daughters of Al and Rita Bolinski, were married respectively to John Whitmire and Wade Randolph in a double ceremony. The brides chose one ceremony instead of two c_____. Because they have always had a close relationship, M_____ Natalie and Deidre Bolinski, the brides' sisters, served as m_____ of h_____.

After the wedding, the _____, parents of the brides, entertained at a reception. The couples will reside in adjoining duplex a_____. These adjoining d_____ are on the corner of King and Front S_____.

5. Correct any errors in the following sentences. Write *OK* if a sentence is correct. (Note: In Sections 4.1 through 4.4, the last Practical Application reviews some of the principles presented in earlier sections.)

a. Several woman applied for the transfer.

b. Mrs. Nagata suggested that we set the VCR on one of the shelf at the back of the room.

c. He completed the training course successful.

d. Jack has rised to the senior management level at Canada Paper Ltd.

e. Some of the students has registered for next semester.

f. Bert and Leslie have already spoke with Mr. Wexler about the shipping delays from his company.

g. Jean or Max is preparing the agenda for tomorrow's meeting.

h. The market price of our stock has risen almost 12 per cent in only two weeks.

i. Winnings of any kind are taxable.

j. We will offer expanded stock portfolioes for new investors.

Editing Practice

As a Matter of Fact…   In addition to checking for spelling and grammatical errors, you must check for inconsistencies and contradictions of facts within copy. Read the following statements to find any inconsistencies. Write *OK* if a statement has no error.

1. Mrs. O'Day wrote to say the toy top she ordered does not work, so I asked her to return the boy and promised to replace it.

2. Your total cost will be $100 less a 20 per cent discount plus a sales tax of 5 per cent. Thus we will send you an invoice for $94.

3. When Mrs. Reisling pointed out that we had overcharged her, we apologized for the error and told Mr. Riesling we would correct her next statement.

4. Anne Loomis is the supervisor of customer relations. We suggest that you call Anna to discuss this problem with her.
5. Although we are out of stock of model A199-2035, we have plenty of model A199-2035 stock.

Discussion Point

When Dan Quayle ran for Vice President of the United States, he was embarrassed in a nationally televised program because he could not spell the word *potato*. His confusion arose because of the spelling of the plural form, *potatoes*. Forming plurals of nouns that end in *o* can be difficult. Explain the rule that Mr. Quayle needed to know, and give some examples to illustrate your answer.

Nouns and Pronouns: Possessive Forms

Write with nouns and verbs, not with adjectives and adverbs. The adjective hasn't been built that can pull a weak or inaccurate noun out of a tight place.

—E.B. White, in *The Elements of Style*

▶ **Key Terms**

▶ possessive form of nouns

▶ gerund

Possessive Forms of Nouns

The possessive form of nouns and pronouns is used to show ownership. Errors in the use of the possessive form of nouns and pronouns are common, and very noticeable, in writing. This section will help you master the correct usage of possessive nouns and pronouns.

An apostrophe is *always* used with a noun to show possession. The following rules will help you place the apostrophe in the correct position to show possession.

Adding an Apostrophe Plus *s*

Add an *apostrophe plus s* for:

A Noun that Does Not End in *s*. An example is:

The man's portfolio and the woman's report are on my desk. (the portfolio of *the man,* or *belonging to the man,* and the report *of the woman,* or *belonging to the woman*)

A Singular Noun Ending in *s* (if the possessive form is pronounced with an added syllable). Some examples are:

One *witness's* comment was especially effective.

My *boss's* recommendation was helpful.

Adding Only an Apostrophe

Add only an apostrophe for:

A Plural Noun that Ends in *s*. Some examples are:

The *executives'* meeting has been rescheduled. (the meeting *of the executives*)

Approximately two *months'* time has been allotted for the project. (a time *of* approximately *two months*)

The *Browns'* new tractor arrived today. (the new tractor *of the Browns* or *belonging to the Browns*)

Figure 4.4 ▶
Singular and Plural
Possessives
In deciding which word
names the possessor and
which word is the object
of possession, ask your-
self the following ques-
tion: *Who or what owns
X?* This will help you decide which word is the
possessive.

Forming Possessives		
Noun Type	**Rule**	**Exceptions**
Singular	*Add apostrophe s*	Add 's to words ending in s if the extra syllable sounds awkward
Plural	*Add apostrophe*	Add 's if the plural does NOT end in s

A Singular Noun Ending in *s*. If the possessive form *is not* pronounced with an added syllable, then only add an apostrophe. An example is: Bruce Struthers' promotion will be announced tomorrow. (Note that if adding an apostrophe and an *s* would cause difficulty because people may attempt to pronounce the final *s*, then don't add the final *s*—For example, *Bruce Struthers's promotion will be announced tomorrow* is incorrect.)

The possessive word comes *before* the object of possession. By separating the ownership words from the objects of ownership, you will be able to apply the rules of possession more easily. Some examples are:

the *manager's* report (the report belonging to the manager)
the *students'* assignments (the assignments belonging to the students)
the *Browns'* newest store (the newest store of the Browns)

CHECKUP 1

Check the following sentences for any errors in the use of possessives. Rewrite the sentence if it contains errors.

1. John Rileys' investments have been successful in the last six months.
2. The actress' own account of Hollywood's history will appear in Sunday's newspaper.
3. Sam Canfield's goal is to rebuild his fathers business.
4. Elinor's latest article discusses womens' nutritional needs.
5. The applicants resumés are in the folder on your desk, Ms. Paoli.
6. No, we do not purchase our company cars; all our representatives vehicles are leased.
7. One man's report criticized the company's change in policy.
8. Our Travel Department makes all our supervisor's reservations for them.

Possessive Form of Nouns—Special Cases

Besides the basic rules of forming the possessives of nouns, there are a few special cases that need your attention.

Compound Nouns

To form the possessive of a compound noun, make the *last word* in the compound possessive. If the last word ends in *s*, add an apostrophe; otherwise, add an apostrophe plus *s*. Some examples are:

My *brother-in-law's* bid was accepted by the City Planning Department. The compound noun is *brother-in-law*. The last word, *law*, does not end in *s*, so add an apostrophe plus *s*.

Two *vice presidents'* recommendations are given in this report. The last word, *presidents*, ends in *s*. To form the possessive, add an apostrophe.)

Joint Ownership and Separate Ownership

To show joint ownership (that is, two or more people owning the same thing), add the apostrophe, or an apostrophe plus *s*, to the last part of the compound noun. Some examples are:

Susan and Randy's father is the one who started this restaurant in 1995. (The father of Susan and Randy. Note the singular noun *father* and the singular verb *is*.)

Isaac and Virginia's design studio is in Montreal. (one studio belonging to Isaac and Virginia)

To indicate separate ownership, add the apostrophe, or the apostrophe plus *s*, to each part of the compound noun. Some examples are:

Bradley's and Maria's mothers started this service in 1980. (Here, we are talking about two different people—in other words, Bradley's mother and Maria's mother.)

Irwin's and Vicki's agencies are in downtown Vancouver. (Irwin's agency and Vicki's agency—two agencies, each separately owned)

Nouns Used Before a Gerund

A **gerund** is a verb form that ends in *ing* and is used as a noun. A noun or pronoun used immediately before a gerund must be in the possessive. Some examples are:

Harry's proofreading was very helpful to us in meeting the deadline. *His* proofreading was very helpful to us. (The possessive form *Harry's* or *His*, is used before the gerund *proofreading*.)

We were unaware of *Nancy's* leaving early. We were unaware of *her* leaving early. (The possessives *Nancy's* and *her* are needed before the gerund *leaving*.)

The next section will provide examples of the possessive forms of personal pronouns such as *my, your, his,* and *her*.

CHECKUP 2

Check the following sentences for any errors in the use of possessives. Write *OK* if a sentence is correct.

1. Don and Sylvia's oldest daughter begins college next September.
2. Revising the e-mail policy was someone else idea, not Adrian's.
3. As you know, the two vice-president's reports contain confidential information.
4. Neil and Anne were engaged last week. Neil's and Anne's wedding is planned for next June.
5. My two sisters-in-law's parents live in Atlanta.
6. John's running is his favorite pastime.
7. My mother-in-laws' store is being renovated.
8. I find Anitas shouting very upsetting.

Possessive Forms of Personal Pronouns

Possessive forms of nouns *always* have apostrophes. However, personal pronouns (*I, you, he, she, it, we, you, they*) become possessive either by adding just an *s* (as in *its*), or by changing their spelling (as in *my, mine*.)

The possessive forms of personal pronouns are listed in Figure 4.5. Note that possessive forms of personal pronouns never have apostrophes.

Figure 4.5 ▶
Possessive Forms of Personal Pronouns
Personal pronouns take the place of people, places, or things. Their possessive forms have no apostrophe.

Thinking Critically.
What is the difference in meaning of your *and* you're?

Possessive Forms of Personal Pronouns	
Nominative Forms*	**Possessive Forms**
I	my mine
you	your yours
he	his his
she	her hers
it	its its
we	our ours
you	your yours
they	their theirs

*for more information on nominative forms, see Section 4.3.

Study the following examples that show the correct uses of these pronoun forms.

Valerie asked *her* assistant to revise the report.

The first car is *ours;* the second one is *theirs.*

Would you please lend me *your* calculator; *mine* is at home.

The college is holding *its* graduation ceremony next week.

Is this book *yours?*

Possessive Forms of Pronouns—Special Cases

The possessive pronouns *its, their, theirs, your,* and *whose,* are sometimes confused with words that sound similar, called *homophones.*

Its, It's

The possessive pronoun *its* means "belonging to it" or "of it." The contraction *it's* means "*it is.*" Some examples are:

This computer monitor is expensive but *its* screen has high resolution. (The screen belonging *to,* or *of,* the computer monitor; *its* is a possessive pronoun.)

I like this monitor because *it's* easier to read. (The contraction *it's* in place of "*it is.*")

Their, There, They're

Their, there, and *they're* are indeed pronounced alike. But *their* is the possessive pronoun meaning "belonging to them," and *there* identifies a place. *They're* is a contraction of "they are." Some examples are:

Sally and Mac have moved to *their* new house. (*Their* is a possessive pronoun. Whose new house? Sally and Mac's new house, or *their* new house.)

They're very happy *there.* (*They are* very happy *there*—in that place.)

Theirs, There's

The pronoun *theirs* and the contraction *there's* are pronounced the same way. However, the contraction *there's* means "*there is*," while *theirs* means "belonging to them."

Is this book *theirs*? (Does this book *belong to them*?)

There's the book we want. (*There is* the book…)

Your, You're

The possessive pronoun *your* means "belonging to you." The contraction *you're* means "you are." Some examples are:

Ron, when are you taking your driving test? (*Your* is a possessive pronoun. Whose driving test? Ron's.)

Ron, I heard that *you're* taking your driving test today. (*You're* is a contraction for you are.)

Whose, Who's

The possessive form of the relative pronoun *who* is *whose*. *Who's* is a contraction that means "*who is*" or "*who has*." Some examples are:

Do you know *whose* briefcase this is? (Do you know *to whom this briefcase belongs*?)

Do you know *who's* going to the meeting? (Do you know *who is* going to the meeting?)

Do you know *who's* applied for the position? (Do you know *who has* applied for the position?)

Possessive Pronouns and Homophones	
Possessive Pronouns	**Homophones**
its	it's
their	there, they're
theirs	there's
your	you're

◀ **Figure 4.6**
Possessive Pronouns and Homophones
Some possessive pronouns are easily confused with like-sounding words.

Thinking Critically. *How are the homophones in the table alike and different from their possessive pronouns?*

CHECKUP 3

Check the following sentences for any errors in the use of possessive personal pronouns. Write *OK* if a sentence is correct.

1. Whose at the shop this morning, Jerry or Daniel?
2. As Mr. Cellini clearly explained, theirs only one problem involved.
3. Most of our customers prefer to order by e-mail because its fast and convenient.
4. Please call me when your ready to discuss the report.
5. Our company is revising it's hiring procedures.
6. They're going to redecorate the office when there boss is on vacation.
7. Whose going with you to the concert?
8. Do you think theres a good reason for their decision?

Review of Key Terms

1. What is the function of the *possessive form of nouns* and pronouns? Use an example to illustrate your answer.
2. "A noun or pronoun used before a *gerund* must be in the possessive form." Please explain this statement.

Practical Application

1. Check the following sentences for any errors in the use of possessives. Write *OK* if a sentence is correct.
   a. Each managers' suggestion was discussed in detail.
   b. Did you know they're both from Australia?
   c. Louise Chretien, whose an excellent copywriter, has developed award-winning slogans for our products.
   d. We agreed that the womans' last complaint was completely justified.
   e. Although the Bass's have owned this property only since 2002, Bob and Donna Bass have decided to sell.
   f. Carole's and Diane's interior design business is very successful.
   g. Please let me know if your interested in receiving monthly reports.
   h. Does Ms. Gregoris know about him offering to complete this assignment on a freelance basis?
   i. After we compared the two models carefully, we realized that theirs very little difference between them.
   j. One of the most profitable departments in our Oakville store is the childrens' department.
   k. Denise and Chong's bosses are both at the weekly meeting.
   l. We're not sure if its possible to fix this network problem today.
   m. Everyone agreed that Mickeys presentation was excellent.
   n. I agreed with him rejecting the offer.
   o. Despite the fact that our competitor's product is expensive, its unique design attracts many buyers.

2. Form a group of four or five class members. Have each member of the group write a sentence containing the possessive form of a noun or pronoun. Then share your sentences, explaining the use of the possessive form, and making any corrections.

   TEAMWORK

3. Correct any errors in the following sentences. Write *OK* if a sentence is correct.
   a. Please check in someone elses office for a blank diskette.
   b. The report must be finished before tomorrows board meeting.
   c. Jill Carters credentials are impressive.
   d. Claudia requested about two dozens more parking passes for the Olympic trials.

e. Both Mr. Cleavers will receive a special award at the banquet.

f. There's several talented people writing musicals today.

g. Carol's rewriting the e-mail saved us from an embarrassing situation.

h. I was surprised to find so many messages from the presidents assistant when I returned from vacation.

i. After the alarm had rang, we went to the fire exit.

j. We studied all the analysis that our department managers submitted.

Editing Practice

Spelling Alert! Correct the spelling errors in the following paragraphs.

As we explained, we are intrested in learning more about government securitys. According to the materiel we recieved from our broker, a minimum investment of $5000 is requirred. The yield on primary issues is currantly aproximately 9.5 per cent.

Call an Editor! Correct the errors in the following paragraph.

Mike and I had spoken with Dr. Merriam about computor training for staffs. Dr. Merriam and her husband are noted experts in information processing and have written many articles on this topic. Copys of some of there articles are enclosed. We are planing to begin the new training program next month if its possible to get space. Theres severel dates available for these classes. Both Merriam's will be present.

Discussion Point

Look up the meaning of *ownership* and *possess* in your dictionary. Using this information, explain the concept of ownership. How does this concept relate to the possessive forms studied in Section 4.2?

Pronouns: Nominative and Objective Forms

▶ **Key Terms**

▶ case
▶ object
▶ compound subject
▶ compound object
▶ antecedent

A pronoun is a noun that lost its amateur status.

—Bill Watterson, cartoonist and creator of *Calvin and Hobbes*

Without pronouns, most of our sentences would be repetitive and cumbersome. Therefore, understanding the function of pronouns, and using them correctly, is an essential communication skill. To communicate well in writing, you must be able to use the correct forms of nominative and objective pronouns, and the pronouns ending in *self,* in a number of different contexts.

Case Forms

The term **case** refers to the form of a pronoun. The case of a pronoun shows how it relates to other words in a sentence. There are three cases, or forms of pronouns—possessive, nominative, and objective. In the previous section you studied the possessive forms of pronouns. This section covers the other two forms of pronouns—the *nominative* and the *objective* cases—and pronouns ending with *self.*

Nominative Case Pronouns

Follow these three rules for using nominative pronouns correctly in writing.

Rule 1: Subject of a Verb. If a pronoun is the subject of a verb, that pronoun must be nominative. Some examples are:

Figure 4.7 ▶
Singular and Plural Pronouns
Figure 4.7 details singular and plural pronouns.

Thinking Critically. How does a pronoun's position in a sentence affect its case?

Singular and Plural Pronouns

Nominative Case		Objective Case	
Singular	**Plural**	**Singular**	**Plural**
I	we	me	us
you	you	you	you
he	they	him	them
she	they	her	them
it	they	it	them
who	who	whom	whom
whoever	whoever	whomever	whomever

I have reviewed the income statement. ("*I* [nominative case, singular] have reviewed," not "*me* [objective case, singular] have reviewed.")

She and Ricardo will speak at the luncheon. (*She*, [nominative case, singular] not *her* [objective case, singular].)

Who is the director of customer service? (*Who* [relative pronoun, nominative case] is the subject of the verb *is*.)

Rule 2: Complement of a "Being" Verb.
The "being" verbs are *am, is, are, was,* and *were* and *be, being,* and *been* used with helping verbs. If a pronoun follows and completes the meaning of a "being" verb, that pronoun must be nominative.

Perhaps it was (they? them?) who sent us these samples. (*Was* is a "being" verb. The pronoun that follows was must complement the "being" verb. Therefore, the pronoun must be the nominative *they.*)

It must have been (he? him?) in the convertible. (The nominative *he* correctly complements the "being" verb phrase *must have been.*)

Rule 3: Pronoun Completes the Infinitive.
If a pronoun follows and completes the meaning of the infinitive verb "to be" when "to be" has no subject, that pronoun must be nominative. An example is:

The patients appear to be (they? them?) There is no noun or pronoun immediately before the infinitive verb "to be." Therefore, use the nominative form "they".)

To help you remember the exception rule about the infinitive verb *to be,* make this connection:

No subject—*No*minative case
Let the *no* in the word *nominative* remind you to choose the nominative pronoun when there is *no* subject before the infinitive verb *to be.*

CHECKUP 1
Check the following sentences for any errors in the use of pronouns. Write *OK* if a sentence is correct.

1. Do you think it was them who complained about the new schedule?
2. When a caller asks for you by name, you should reply, "This is she."
3. Sam, if you were me, would you have called the police?
4. All of us agree that the winner should be she.
5. Some drivers had suggested that the union delegate should be him.

Objective Case Pronouns
The **object** is a person or thing that receives the action of the verb.

Rule 1: Pronouns as Objects of Verbs, Prepositions, or Infinitives.
Use the objective case pronoun forms *me, him, her, them,* and *whom,* when the pronouns are objects of verbs, prepositions, or infinitives. Some examples are:

Mr. Pappas promoted *me* to executive assistant. (The verb is *promoted.* The object of the verb is *me* [objective form], not *I.*)

Mei-Yu had already given a copy to *us,* so we bought an extra copy for *him.* (*Us* is the object of the preposition *to,* and *him* is the object of the preposition *for.*)

To *whom* did Elmer send a package on Monday? (*Whom* is the object of the preposition *to.*)

Ms. Rosenberg plans to visit *them* next week. (*Them* is the object of the infinitive verb *to visit.*)

Rule 2: Subjects of Infinitives. Use the objective case pronoun forms for subjects of infinitives. An example is:

Ken wants *us* to travel to England in June or July. (*Us* is the subject of the infinitive verb *to travel.*)

Rule 3: A Noun or Pronoun Precedes "To Be." Use the objective case pronoun following the infinitive verb *to be* when a noun or pronoun immediately precedes *to be.* An example is:

When she first answered the telephone, Eva thought Robert to be *me.* (The noun *Robert* immediately precedes the infinitive verb *to be;* therefore, the objective form *me* is correct.)

Who and Whom	Whoever and Whomever
Nominative Pronouns Who Whoever	**Objective Pronouns** Whom Whomever

In deciding which form to use, apply the nominative case rules; if you can not justify a nominative case pronoun, use the objective form.

The consultant (who? whom?) Jay recommended is Peter Chung.

("whom Jay recommended"—objective case. When the nominative rules are applied, the use of a nominative pronoun can not be justified.)

CHECKUP 2

From the choices in parentheses, select the correct pronoun for each of the following sentences.

1. Perhaps the person (who? whom?) you saw during the press conference was Jean McDonald.
2. Eleanor is the publicist (who? whom?) should be assigned to this campaign.
3. The election committee can fine (whoever? whomever?) does not observe the rules.
4. Mitch Chaffee, (who? whom?) we consider the best organizer in our company, will head the committee.
5. (Whoever? Whomever?) wrote this manual did an excellent job.
6. We asked Peter, (who? whom?) has campaign experience, for his advice.

Case Forms—Special Situations

There are writing situations where it is more difficult to select the nominative or objective form. These situations follow.

Pronouns in Compound Subjects or Compound Objects

he = who
him = whom.

Compound subjects or compound objects are nouns and pronouns joined by the coordinating conjunctions *or, and,* or *nor.* When the pronoun is part of a subject, use the nominative case. When the pronoun is part of an object, use the objective case. Some examples are:

Nominative in Subjects	Objective in Objects
Kevin and *I* want…	…for Kevin and *me*
Ms. Royce and *he* asked…	…asked Ms. Royce and *him*
She and *I* will write…	…written by *her* and *me*
They and *we* agree…	…agree with *them* and *us*

To choose the right pronoun in compounds, remove the other parts of the compound and test the pronoun choices with the rest of the sentence. Some examples are:

Judy Sinclair and (I/ me?) leave for Mexico City on Monday. (When you omit the words *Judy Sinclair and,* the answer becomes: "*I* leave…," not " *me* leave.")

Sylvia sent copies to Mr. Chernof and (I? me?). (Omit the words *Mr. Chernof and,* and the answer becomes: "Sylvia sent copies to…*me.*")

Pronoun Phrases. When faced with a pronoun choice in phrases such as *we supervisors* or *us supervisors,* remove the noun following the pronoun and test the sentence with the pronoun choices. An example is:

(We? Us?) supervisors met with the union delegates: (Remove the noun *supervisors,* then say "*We* met with…" and "*Us* met with…" Which pronoun would you choose? It becomes clear that the nominative pronoun *we* is correct.)

Pronouns with *Than* or *As*. Another pronoun problem may arise in sentences that contain the conjunctions *than* or *as.* Some examples are:

"Roxanne has more vacation time than (I? me?)." "This problem affects Aaron as much as (I? me?)."

When the word *than* or *as* is used in such comparisons, it usually represents an incomplete clause. By completing the clause, the correct pronoun becomes clear. Some examples are:

Roxanne has more vacation time than I (have vacation time). (By completing the clause, it is clear that the clause is "*I* have vacation time," not "*me* have…")

This problem affects Aaron as much as (this problem affects) me. (The missing words *this problem affects,* are understood and therefore not repeated. However, by using them to complete the clause, your pronoun choice becomes clear.)

CHECKUP 3

Check the following sentences for any errors in the use of pronouns. Write *OK* if a sentence is correct.

1. The voting information was sent only to ~~we~~ three union stewards.
2. The procedure is to ask Dr. Humphreys or I for an advance.
3. The majority of the committee members voted for Tanya and he.
4. Do you agree that most of the speakers were not as well prepared as her?
5. Peter is certainly a more effective speaker than me.
6. The college president asked we students for our comments on the new registration system.
7. As you can see, Paul keyboards more quickly and accurately than she.
8. Only Radmila or him has the authority to approve changes in the shift schedule.
9. She quickly learned that none of we nurses wants to change the schedule.
10. Between you and me, I think that Elizabeth Garcia will become regional manager when Mr. Seeley retires.

Pronouns Ending in *Self*

Pronouns ending *self,* such as *myself, yourself, himself, herself, itself, ourselves, yourselves,* and *themselves,* serve two functions. (1) They emphasize or intensify the use of a noun or another pronoun (intensive use). (2) They refer to a noun or pronoun that has already been named in a sentence (reflexive use).

Intensive Use. Pronouns ending in *self* provide emphasis. Some examples are:

Suzane *herself* announced the competition results. (This is more emphatic than, "Suzanne announced the competition results.")

We requested Howard to write the ad copy *himself.* (This is more emphatic than "We requested Howard to write the ad copy.")

Reflexive Use. Pronouns that end in *self* refer to a noun or another pronoun that has already been used in the sentence. Some examples are:

The owners paid *themselves* a cash bonus. (*Themselves* clearly refers to *owners.* This saves us from saying, "The owners paid the owners a cash bonus.")

Angela distributed all the copies but forgot to keep one for *herself.* (*Herself* clearly refers to *Angela,* and saves us from saying, "Angela distributed the copies but forgot to keep one for Angela.")

Common Errors

Lack of Clear Antecedent. A pronoun that ends in *self* must have a clear antecedent within the sentence. An **antecedent** is a noun or noun phrase that is referred to by the pronoun. An example is:

Gordon Taada and *myself* developed the strategy. (To whom does *myself* refer? It has no antecedent in this sentence. Instead, the sentence should read, "Gordon Taada and *I* developed...")

Misplacing the Pronoun. A pronoun must be place correctly in the sentence. An example is:

When we asked the painter for his advice, he said that he prefers spray-painting *himself*. (Obviously, the person does not want to spray-paint *himself*! Change the position of the pronoun in the sentence to correct this error."…he said that he *himself* prefers spray-painting."

CHECKUP 4

Check the following sentences for any errors in the use of pronouns. Write *OK* if a sentence is correct.

1. The prisoner himself pleaded for mercy. oK

2. When Elaine and myself suggested the idea, we did not realize the project would be so complex.

3. After seeing the sports club, Ms. Romero specifically said that she wants to join her~ self. *herself* *herself*

4. The president herself will talk to the staff about the child care centre. oK

5. As Bobbi and himself said, "It's too late now." *himself said*

6. Sean and myself will call the applicants today.

Review of Key Terms

What does the term *case* mean in reference to pronouns, and what are these cases? Use examples to illustrate your answer.

Practical Application

1. Check the following sentences for any errors in the use of pronouns. Write *OK* if a sentence is correct.
    a. Parveena has better keyboarding skills than I.
    b. We were delighted when Jess said, "I invited Danielle and him to the parade."
    c. Last summer Jean and me went to our first training session.
    d. Whom in your opinion is the most deserving contender?
    e. The Sullivans are the only ones whom I believe do not rent their beach house.
    f. Us police officers were all suffering because of the mistakes of a few.
    g. Do you really think that Sebastian is more reliable than her?
    h. Two of my best friends, Armande and him, asked to be excused from the negotiations because of a conflict of interest.
    i. He signed the letters and mailed them to the Joneses and her.
    j. If the price is right, Davy and myself will certainly sell our concession stand on the boardwalk.
    k. Douglas himself will be in charge of filing the complaints.
    l. When we asked our manager which of the two methods he preferred, he said he liked photocopying himself.
    m. The president thinks that Ralph is more productive than her.
    n. Sam, if I were you, I would certainly join the company's pension plan and begin making voluntary contributions like Jurij and me.
    o. Jack and myself will organize the company Christmas party.
2. Correct any errors in the following sentences. Write *OK* if a sentence is correct.
    a. Yesterday Ms. Singh invited Joan and I for lunch.
    b. Ask Mr. Freeman if he knows whose working this weekend.
    c. Luke Stevens, whom I know is a registered nurse, can help you.
    d. He and me studied nursing together at the community college.
    e. The two Marylou's were our supervisors at Memorial Medical Centre.
    f. One of Andreas first patients was a well-known news broadcaster.
    g. In fact, he gave her a couple of autographed photoes.
    h. With governments reductions to health care funding, a serious crisis in health care is imminent.
    i. I myself think its time we found a way to help the homeless.
    j. Theirs nothing you can do but work harder.

3. Rewrite the following paragraphs, correcting errors in plurals, possessives, and pronoun usage.

As I am sure you know, our competitors are eager to compete with us for the Wolfe account. John and myself have begun the proposal process by reviewing the video's of there most recent advertising campaign. Here's the three areas of emphasis for selling their playroom equipment: safety, exercise, and cost.

This six month's project should incorporate your most creative thoughts. The president has issued herself a special incentive. If we get the Wolfe account, us, the advertising campaign staff, will get an extra weeks' vacation with pay.

Kaitlyn and Scot Wolfe want to work with our company. However, the Wolfes' are looking for the best advertising campaign available. Obviously, they will be spending much money on the campaign selected. You and me must give this project our best efforts.

Editing Practice

Using Your Computer. You keyed the following on your computer yesterday but did not proofread it or do a spellcheck. Please do so now.

Pleas review the enclosed cost estamate for the equipmant we are planning to purchase in February. As you will see, the contract for maintenence is $500 a year, and instalation alone will cost nearly $2000. Let's review this financail data carefully before we proceed.

Discussion Point

The concept of possession is a vital one in Canadian law and in many facets of our daily lives. Discuss the concept of possession as it relates to the Canadian Charter of Rights and Freedoms; that is, what are some of the rights and freedoms "possessed" by Canadian citizens? (Note: If you need information on the Charter of Rights and Freedoms, visit **http:/laws.justice.gc.ca/en/charter.**)

SUMMARY

▶ Many plurals of English nouns are formed by following certain principles. For example, most common nouns and proper nouns add *s* to form their plurals; nouns that end in *s, sh, ch, x,* or *z* add *es* to form their plurals; plurals of compound nouns are formed by making the main word plural; and common and compound nouns ending in a consonant and then *y* form their plurals by changing the *y* to *i* and adding *es.*

▶ Other nouns, such as some proper nouns, titles with names, or those of a foreign origin, have their own special rules for forming plurals. Additional types of nouns have special changes to become plural, are always singular or always plural, or have one form for both singular and plural.

▶ Nouns and pronouns have possessive forms that are used to show ownership. An apostrophe is always used with a noun to show possession. For some nouns you add an apostrophe plus *s,* and for others an apostrophe only to show possession.

▶ Form the possessive of a compound noun by making the last word in the compound possessive. To show joint ownership, add an apostrophe, or an apostrophe plus *s,* to the last part of the compound noun. To show separate ownership, add the apostrophe, or the apostrophe plus *s,* to each part of the compound noun.

▶ The possessive forms of personal pronouns do not use apostrophes. Personal pronouns become possessive either by adding just an *s* (as in *its*) or by changing their spelling, as in *my* becoming *mine.*

▶ There are three cases, or forms, of pronouns—possessive, nominative, and objective. The relationship between the pronoun and certain other words in a sentence determines whether you use the nominative form or the objective form of a pronoun. For example, if a pronoun follows and completes the meaning of a "being" verb, that pronoun must be nominative.

Communicating in Your Career

The ability to communicate effectively is often cited by employers as a major factor in selecting people for jobs. For example, a job ad for a Help Desk/Network Administration position listed "excellent verbal and written communication" as necessary qualifications. Another ad from Tricon Global Restaurants Inc., the operating company of Taco Bell, Pizza Hut, and KFC, for a Manager in Training stated that applicants required "good oral and written communication skills." York University in Toronto advertised for a Head Football Coach, stating that this person should be "a motivating communicator."

Research one of these positions and give examples of the ways in which written communication skills would be used in the job.

CASE 4.1

Acela works as a Customer Service Representative in the call centre of NorthCon, a large Canadian telecommunications company. She recently applied for the position of Team Leader. She submitted her resumé and completed a written test given by the Human Relations department.

Acela is disappointed and surprised when she does not get an interview. She asks her friend Michael to look at her resumé. He notices the following errors — "Assisted with review of the companys telephone system," and "Objective: Assist a team to reach it's full potential."

How will Michael explain the necessary corrections to Acela?

Why do you think the applicants for the team leader position were given a written test?

CASE 4.2

The first awards for on-line journalism were announced in November, 2000. This annual, international competition is sponsored by the Online News Association and the Columbia Graduate School of Journalism. For more information, you can visit **http://www.onlinejournalismawards.org/**.

What particular writing skills do you think the judges look for? Why?

On the Web

The University of Calgary Web site gives information on count nouns, mass nouns, and collective nouns. Review this information and take the on-line test. **www.ucalgary.ca/UofC/eduweb/grammar/course/speech/1_1b.htm** Review plural and possessive nouns on this same Web site and take the on-line test.
www.ucalgary.ca/UofC/eduweb/grammar/course/speech/1_1c.htm

Key Terms

Chapter 5

Expanding Language Skills

Chapter Learning Outcomes

After successfully completing this chapter, you will have demonstrated the ability to:

▶ identify and correctly use descriptive, possessive, limiting, proper, compound, demonstrative, and predicate adjectives;

▶ identify and correctly use adverbs, and avoid adjective and adverb confusions;

▶ identify and correctly use prepositions;

▶ identify and correctly use coordinating, correlative, and subordinating conjunctions.

Asad is a first-year journalism student at Lakehead University in Ontario. Like all students in this program, Asad is aware excellent writing skills are a key requirement for success in the program and for subsequent employment.

In today's Language Structure class, the professor asked Asad what he understood about the importance of parallelism in writing. Asad knew that parallelism was something to do with making sentences balanced, but was unable to give any details. After several other students had similar difficulty providing a clear explanation of parallelism, the professor wrote the following items on the board:

"To err is human, to forgive divine." (Alexander Pope)

The Canadian Charter of Rights and Freedoms guarantees freedom of religion, freedom of expression, and freedom of association.

The students were asked to write an explanation of the use of parallelism in these two examples.

As you study Chapter 5, look for information that would help Asad explain the principle of parallelism in general, and its use in the two examples in particular.

Adjectives

The adjective is the banana peel of the parts of speech.

—Clifton Fadiman, American writer and editor

Without adjectives, our speech and writing would be dull and lifeless. Used wisely, adjectives make nouns and pronouns interesting, vivid, and specific. This section will introduce you to the many kinds of adjectives and discuss the ways that we commonly misuse them. A mastery of the use of adjectives will help make your speech and writing better tools of communication.

Identifying Adjectives

Any word that modifies or describes a noun or a pronoun is an **adjective.** *An adjective usually precedes the noun it modifies.* It tells "what kind," "how many," "how much," "which one," and "in what order." Some of the most commonly used kinds of adjectives are described below.

Articles

The words *a, an,* and *the* are called **articles.** Note how these special adjectives are commonly used:

The sailboat captain pointed out *a* beautiful sunset.

The gelatin salad recipe includes *a* banana and *an* apple.

Descriptive Adjectives

The most commonly used adjectives are **descriptive adjectives**—the *adjectives that describe or tell "what kind of."*

In a *strong, clear* voice, Andrea rejected the *irresponsible* policies that some *real estate* companies use to lure *unsuspecting* consumers into buying *overpriced* and sometimes *worthless* property. (*Strong, clear, irresponsible, real estate, unsuspecting, overpriced,* and *worthless* are descriptive adjectives.)

Possessive Adjectives

Possessive personal pronouns, such as *my, your, his, her, its, our,* and *their,* and possessive nouns, such as *Ben's, Inge's, Gary's,* and so on, are **possessive adjectives** that modify nouns.

Your partner reviewed *our* prospectus and submitted it to *Taylor's* manager.

Limiting Adjectives

Adjectives that tell "how many," "how much," or "in what order" are called **limiting adjectives**. Some examples are:

The top *five* seniors will receive *at least three* full scholarships. (*Top* tells "in what order," *five* tells "how many seniors," and *at least three* tells "how many scholarships.")

Each senior had won *many* awards. (*Each* modifies *senior; many* modifies *awards*.)

Proper Adjectives

Proper nouns are very often used as proper adjectives.

Used as a Noun	Used as an Adjective
in *Winnipeg* near *Montreal* in *Manitoba*	a *Winnipeg* hotel a *Montreal* firm *Manitoba* residents

Proper adjectives include words derived from proper nouns, such as *Mexican, British,* and *Israeli.*

Compound Adjectives

Two or more words joined to modify one noun or pronoun form a **compound adjective.**

Murray wanted a *long-term* agreement but signed a *one-year* contract instead. (*Long-term* modifies agreement and *one-year* modifies contract.)

She is a *well-known* author of *time-management* books. (*Well-known* modifies author, and *time-management* modifies books.)

My sister works as a *real estate* agent. (*Real estate* modifies agent.)

Demonstrative Adjectives

The pronouns *this, that, these,* and *those* are demonstrative pronouns that can function as adjectives (**demonstrative adjectives**).

As Pronoun	As Adjective	As Pronoun	As Adjective
this is *that* has been	*this* property *that* building	*these* are *those* might be	*these* keys *those* tenants

Note that *these* is the plural of *this;* both *these* and *this* indicate nearness to the speaker. *Those* is the plural of *that,* and *those* and *that* indicate distance from the speaker. Never use the pronoun *them* as a substitute for *these* or *those.* Some examples are:

Please return *those* books to the library. (Not *them* books.)

These kinds of problems occur early in the semester. (*These* kinds, not *them* kinds or "*these kind.*")

CHECKUP 1

Identify the adjectives in the following sentences and label each possessive (*P*), limiting (*L*), proper (*PR*), compound (*C*), descriptive (*D*), or demonstrative (*DM*). Disregard the articles *a, an,* and *the.* (Note: Some adjectives may fit in more than one category.)

1. The first realty office we opened has been a major success for our company.
2. A special seminar is being scheduled for new agents to learn these important procedures.
3. Two well-known firms bid on this large building, which was formerly owned by Brian's mother.
4. In two weeks her older brother will join this company and will work out of the Regina office.
5. In Harry's opinion, our two-year forecast is an accurate one.
6. The Vancouver lawyer who represents that company asked our office for additional information on the Hendersons' property.
7. One of Kelly's crucial accounts is a new client who represents a Vancouver broker.
8. These bonds are tax-free investments, according to their new prospectus.

Comparison of Adjectives

Descriptive adjectives can be compared. For example, *strong* and *clear* can be compared to show degrees of strength and clarity: *strong, stronger,* and *strongest; clear, clearer,* and *clearest.* These three forms of comparison are called the *positive,* the *comparative,* and the *superlative* degrees.

1. The **positive degree** expresses the quality of *one* person or thing. Some examples are:

a *strong* foundation

a *clear* message

2. The **comparative degree** allows us to compare that quality in *two* persons or things. Some examples are:

a *stronger* foundation

a *clearer* message

3. The **superlative degree** enables us to compare that quality in *three or more* persons or things. Some examples are:

the *strongest* foundation

the *clearest* message

   Now that we know how the three degrees are used, we need to know how they are formed.

Forming the Comparative and Superlative Degrees

The comparative degree is formed by adding *er* to the positive form or by inserting the word *more* or *less* before it. The superlative is formed by adding *est* to the positive form or by inserting the word *most* or *least* before it.

The comedian was the most funniest person we had ever heard.

Funniest instead of *most funniest*

Positive	Comparative	Superlative
quick	quicker	quickest
funny	funnier	funniest
poor	poorer	poorest
decisive	more decisive	most decisive
	less decisive	least decisive

In addition, some commonly used adjectives form their comparative and superlative degrees by changing the form to another word completely. Memorize these for quick reference.

Positive	Comparative	Superlative
good	better	best
bad	worse	worst
little	less	least
much	more	most
many	more	most

Selecting the Correct Forms

For adjectives of only one syllable, form the comparative and superlative by adding *er* or *est* to the end of the adjective. For adjectives of three or more syllables, add the words *more* or *less* or *most* or *least* before the adjective. Adjectives of two syllables vary: some add *er* or *est;* others add *more* or *less* or *most* or *least.* Sometimes an error may be obvious: *more useful,* not *usefuler; most useful,* not *usefulest; happier,* not *more happy; happiest,* not *most happy.*

Avoiding Comparison Errors

The following discussion highlights two of the most common comparison errors in using adjectives: making double comparisons and comparing absolute adjectives.

Making Double Comparisons. Do not mix the different ways in which adjectives can be compared—use only one comparative form at a time.

greatest, not *most greatest*

better, not *more better*

Comparing Absolute Adjectives. Adjectives whose qualities cannot be compared are called **absolute adjectives.** For example, a glass of water cannot be *fuller* or *fullest.* Full is already the maximum!

Here are some other adjectives that cannot be compared:

accurate	empty	round	true
complete	immaculate	square	ultimate
correct	perfect	straight	unanimous
dead	perpendicular	supreme	unique

Although they cannot be compared, the qualities of these adjectives can be approached, as indicated by the following:

more/nearly accurate   *most/nearly* correct

less/nearly complete   *least/nearly* perfect

You may hear (especially in advertisements) of products that are *most unique*, but *unique* really says it all. Remember that absolute adjectives cannot logically be compared.

CHECKUP 2

Check the following sentences for any errors in the use of adjectives. Write *OK* if a sentence is correct.

1. Allen said that we had enough water, but the container was very empty.
2. Which refrigerator uses the most electricity, Model K123 or Model K987?
3. As you can see, Sasha is more happier now that he is working with the homeless.
4. Which is the largest shelter, Hill House or Mercy Centre?
5. All of us agree that Dirk's suggestion is very unique.
6. The yellow container is obviously fuller than the blue container.
7. These offices are preferable to the offices on Maple Street because they are more quiet and more big.
8. Bob is definitely a better tennis player than Eric. In fact, he is probably the best tennis player in our club.

Selecting Adjectives for Clarity

Use the following guidelines to make your prose expressive and precise.

More Than Any Other, More Than Anyone Else. In "more than" comparisons, include the word *other* or *else* if the person or thing is being compared with *other* members of the same group. Some examples are:

Lou is *more* ambitious *than anyone else* in the Research Department. (With the word *else*, the sentence clearly says that Lou is a member of the Research Department. Without the word *else*, the sentence would indicate that Lou is *not* part of the Research Department but is being compared with people who are in this department.)

Andrej is *more* creative *than any other manager* in my company. (Andrej is a manager "in my company." Without the word *other*, this sentence would indicate that Andrej is *not* a manager "in my company.")

Repeated Modifier. In the following examples, repeating the modifier *a* (or *an*), *the*, or *my* indicates that *two* different people are intended.

The accountant and *the* financial analyst (was? were?) formerly with the municipal government. (Repeating *the* shows that *two* people are referred to. *Were* is the correct verb.)

The accountant and financial analyst (was? were?) formerly with the municipal government. (One person who is both an accountant and a financial analyst is referred to. *Was* is correct.)

Selecting Adjectives For Added Polish

The following short discussions will help you make correct choices when referring to two, or more than two, persons or things.

Each Other, One Another. Use *each other* when referring to two in number; use *one another* when referring to three or more. Some examples are:

Emily and Fred work very effectively with *each other*. (two people)

Several students commented to *one another* about the professor's announcement. (three or more students)

Either, Neither; Any, Any One, No One, Not Any, None. Use *either* or *neither* when referring to one of two persons or things. When referring to three or more, use *any, any one, no one, not any,* or *none.* Some examples are:

Either of the professors should be able to answer your questions. (There are only two professors, therefore, *either* is correct.)

Any one of the ticket agents in Union Station will give you a train schedule. (There are more than two agents; *any one* is correct.)

Neither of us has finished reading Chapter 12. (*Neither* refers to two of us.)

None of us has finished reading Chapter 12. (*None* refers to more than two people.)

Compound Adjectives

Two or more words joined to modify one noun or pronoun form a compound adjective.

Hyphenate most compound adjectives that appear before a noun. Some examples are:

first-quality merchandise	*two-kilometre* trail	*fund-raising* committees
no-fault insurance	*air-conditioned* rooms	a *three-year* contract
tax-free bonds	*up-to-date* figures	

When they appear after the noun, compound adjectives such as *air-conditioned* and *tax-free* retain the hyphen. Most other compounds do not.

Some compound adjectives that almost always take hyphens before or after nouns include the following:

adjective + noun + *ed*	open-ended; single-spaced
adjective + participle	high-ranking; soft-spoken
noun + adjective	toll-free; year-round
noun + participle	computer-aided; decision-making

Before the Noun	After the Noun
air-conditioned buses	buses that are *air-conditioned*
tax-free bonds	bonds that are *tax-free*
a *well-known* artist	an artist who is *well known*

Long-time use has made the following compounds so familiar that they are no longer written with hyphens:

high school teachers	a *life insurance* policy	*real estate* services

When the adverb *well* is used with a participle as a compound adjective, it is usually hyphenated before and after the noun. An example is:

The well-known speaker gave us some advice that was well-timed. (*Well-known* and *well-timed* are compound adjectives.)

Confusion may result when *well* and a participle appear after the noun and the participle is part of the verb. An example is:

The speaker is *well known*. (In this sentence, *well* is an adverb and *known* is part of the verb. The two words do not form a compound adjective.)

CHECKUP 3

Apply the rules just presented by correcting the following sentences. Write *OK* if a sentence is correct.

1. Benjamin Lee is a three time winner of the press writers' annual award.
2. Dana's proposal is better than any proposal that we have evaluated so far.
3. Mr. Jefferson's court appointed lawyer will probably be named this afternoon.
4. The Kaiser automatic coffeemaker is guaranteed to last longer than any electric coffeemaker on the market.
5. My supervisor, Sandra Weinstein, handles more contracts than any one in our department.
6. Tom scheduled a 15 minute question and answer session after each presentation.
7. Marketing research has shown that word of mouth advertising is our best form of sales promotion.
8. My tax consultant and investment adviser is well known in financial circles.
9. Ask Sally or Stavros—any one of them should have a sample.
10. Pat is a well known public speaker on environmental issues.

Predicate Adjectives

In Section 3.3 we discussed *being* verbs—verbs that express a state of being. Linking verbs include all forms of the verb *to be* (such as *am, was, will be, should have been*) and verbs like *feel, seem,* and *appear.* A **predicate adjective** follows a *linking* verb and modifies or describes the subject of the sentence. Some examples are:

His voice seems hoarse. (*Hoarse* follows a being verb and modifies the subject *voice.*)

The nurse has been helpful. (*Helpful* follows a being verb and modifies the subject *nurse.*)

Predicate nominatives also follow a being verb, but they rename—not modify—the subject. Some examples are:

Max was the most successful graduate. (*Graduate* follows a being verb and renames the subject *Max.*)

Dina will be my first choice for the award. (*Choice* follows a being verb and renames the subject *Dina.*)

Pronouns can also be predicate nominatives. An example is:

The candidate is he. (*He* follows a being verb and renames the subject *candidate.*)

CHECKUP 4

Identify the words in parentheses as either predicate adjectives (*PA*) or predicate nominatives (*PN*).

1. Spring semester seems (short).
2. Phyllis is the (newscaster) on Saturday nights.
3. Ms. McKibben is (capable) and (well-suited) for the position.
4. Juan is (president) of the local Rotary Club.
5. My preference for the trip is (Cancun).

Review of Key Terms

1. How do *adjectives* make writing and speaking more meaningful? Provide several examples.
2. What is a *compound adjective*? What is the rule about using a hyphen in compound adjectives?

Practical Application

1. Correct the errors involving adjectives. Write *OK* if a sentence is correct.
   a. Passengers may purchase last minute gifts at the duty free shops at the airport.
   b. Every board member will give a ten minute summary of his or her views on the issue.
   c. For security reasons, door to door soliciting is prohibited throughout the building.
   d. Although the price is substantially higher, this television set is no more better than that one.
   e. Most of them desks are too high for computer use.
   f. This particular model has a heavy duty motor that was especially designed for professional use.
   g. Unless otherwise specified, each machine is equipped with a 120-volt, 10-ampere motor.
   h. Of all our branch offices across the country, the Edmonton branch receives more orders than any office.
   i. We evaluated both copiers carefully, and we decided to order the one that was least expensive.
   j. Because they cooperated with one another so well, Rachel and Tony were able to complete their report two days ahead of schedule.
   k. The new president of our company has expanded our overseas activities more than any president of this company.
   l. Ollie and Myra have been with Warner Pharmaceuticals for several years, but I believe that Myra has been there longest.
   m. No, these type of damages are not covered by your insurance.
   n. Our three project managers always work closely with one another to meet their deadlines.
   o. The room has no windows, but it is well-ventilated.
2. Correct any grammatical errors in the following sentences. Write *OK* if a sentence is correct.
   a. There <u>has been</u> several promising applicants for the job.
   b. Because of his seniority, Jesse receives a higher commission on net sales than anyone in our division.

else

   c. The Sherman Stationery Company reported revenues of $2 million last year—<u>their</u> best year ever.

   d. Whom has Harry selected to help him work on the landscaping, Bernie or her?   oK

   e. Ms. Van Cleef wants we assistants to handle the details.

   f. As of yesterday afternoon, we had received several dozens responses to the classified ad.

   g. Has Hamid or Peggy flew to Florida before?

   h. Although I am not sure, the person who called this morning could indeed have <u>been</u> him.

   i. One managers' recommendation was to replace the company cars every three years.

   j. Several of the analysis that were submitted were rather startling.

   k. Please find out who's analysis this is.

   l. Scot and me both enjoy working with the advertising agency on special promotions.

   m. After you have met with Mr. Takeda and she, prepare a summary report of your discussion.

   n. Simone said that the Willis's were invited to the grand opening.

   o. Next month we will begin <u>lying</u> our <u>plans</u> for the fall collection.

   p. Two designers, Emily Sung and her, have been asked to prepare preliminary sketches.

   q. Shauna and me are hoping that we will be promoted this year.

   r. At the moment, the candidate who Ricardo likes best of all is Joe Paiva.

   s. Dimitra has been working in the human resources department ever since she graduated from college.

   t. If the Messrs. Kennedys are available, please confirm both the date and the time of our luncheon.

3. It is often easy to use adjectives to describe a person or place. It is more difficult to use descriptive language with mundane objects.

Choose a product, such as ceiling fans, office chairs, or mufflers, and write a paragraph using at least seven adjectives. Share your paragraph with the group and ask them to identify the adjectives. Discuss how the adjectives add to the description of the product.

TEAMWORK

Editing Practice

Plurals and Possessives. Correct any errors in the use of plurals and possessives. Write *OK* if a sentence is correct.

1. My editor in chief's comment was, "Send a copy to the legal department for approval."

2. Roger's and Jane's newest yogurt stand will open on May 24 at the Westfield Mall.

3.   The Norton's are certainly worth the high fee they charge.
4.   Did you know that its Louise's birthday?
5.   Elizabeth and I enjoyed Terry working with us on the colour scheme.
6.   As soon as you receive there tickets, please send them to the district managers.
7.   Our accountants' brother is a well-respected builder in this community.
8.   The striker's finally voted to accept the contract offer.
9.   Shoji managing the office has helped us to work more efficiently.
10. If the Smith's accept our company's offer, we will become the largest property owner on Queen Street.

Proofreading. The following is an excerpt from a printout. Please proofread it.

A three day delay will cause us trucker's to take coast to coast action. Furthermore, let me assure you that we will be well-organized.

Homonyms, Anyone? Correct any errors in the use of homonyms—words that look or sound alike but have different meanings.

Let's take a brake before we get to tired. When we get tired, we may loose our patients. We no that we should consider the situation carefully.

Discussion Points

1.   Explain how to form the comparative and superlative forms of adjectives. Provide several examples for single, double, and multi-syllable adjectives.
2.   Besides descriptive adjectives, what other types of adjectives are there? Provide an example of each.

Adverbs

Speaking and writing correctly isn't the icing on the cake; it is the cake.

—Anonymous

The above quote talks about the importance of speaking and writing correctly. As you continue your study of each of the parts of speech, this section will show you how to use adverbs correctly to enhance your communications.

▶ **Key Terms**

▶ **adverb**
▶ **comparative**
▶ **superlative**
▶ **conjunctive adverb**
▶ **adverbial clause**
▶ **double negative**

Identifying Adverbs

An **adverb** is a word that modifies an adjective, a verb, or another adverb. Adverbs answer questions such as "Why?" "When?" "Where?" "How?" "In what manner?" and "To what extent?" Many adverbs are formed simply by adding *ly* to an adjective. Adverbs that end in *y* change their *y* to *i* before adding *ly*. Some examples are:

Adjective	Adverb
adequate	adequately
clear	clearly
happy	happily
immediate	immediately
perfect	perfectly

Most words that end in *ly* are adverbs, but not all adverbs end in *ly,* as the following list of common adverbs shows:

also	never	soon
always	now	then
hard	often	there
here	quite	too
much	right	very

Note how adverbs are used in the following sentences.

Jack Alonzo arrived *late.* (Arrived when? Answer: *late.* The adverb *late* modifies the verb *arrived.*)

That is a *very good* spreadsheet program. (How good? *Very good.* The adverb *very* modifies the adjective *good.*)

She worked *quite well* under the pressure of the tight deadlines. (How well? *Quite well.* The adverb *quite* modifies another adverb, *well.*)

Some words can be used either as adjectives or as adverbs, depending on their position in the sentence. Some examples are:

He swallowed *hard* and then started to speak. (Here *hard* is an adverb that modifies the verb *swallowed.*)

Henry complained that painting the garage was *hard* work. (Here *hard* is an adjective that modifies the noun *work.*)

Comparison of Adverbs

Adverbs can be compared in much the same way as adjectives. To indicate the **comparative** and **superlative** forms of a one-syllable adverb, add *er* or *est* to the positive form. Some examples are:

Positive	Comparative	Superlative
fast	faster	fastest
late	later	latest
soon	sooner	soonest

For adverbs ending in *ly,* use *more* or *most* or *less* or *least.* Some examples are:

Positive	Comparative	Superlative
quickly	more quickly	most quickly
quickly	less quickly	least quickly
confidently	more confidently	most confidently
skilfully	less skilfully	least skilfully

Certain adverbs form their comparative and superlative degrees by completely changing their forms. Some examples are:

Positive	Comparative	Superlative
well	better	best
badly	worse	worst
much	more	most

Some examples of their usage are:

John did well in this class. Mary did better than John in this class.

Huda did the best work in this class.

My project is badly done. Harry's project is worse than mine.

Michael's project is the worst in the class.

Zora has much to learn. Bjorn has more to learn than Zora. In our group, Tim has the most to learn.

CHECKUP 1

Identify the adverb or adverbs in each of the following sentences.

1. Johann walked quickly down the hallway.
2. Judy swallowed hard before starting her presentation.
3. The new printer works quietly and efficiently.

4. Boris has been very busy organizing his wife's birthday party.
5. Mary and Richard will soon move to their new house.
6. Our team did quite well in the customer service competition.
7. Jack always works diligently on the end-of-year inventory, and he usually completes the inventory report early.
8. Toshi stayed late yesterday to finish the report.
9. The client specifically indicated that she wanted Ms. Estevan to represent her.
10. My test mark is very good, but yours is better.

Conjunctive Adverbs

Conjunctive adverbs are adverbs that serve as conjunctions—words that join. These adverbs are also known as transitional words. Some examples are:

accordingly	likewise	still	whereas
consequently	moreover	then	yet
furthermore	nevertheless	therefore	
however	otherwise	thus	

These adverbs join two independent clauses, as shown in the following sentences:

Insurance premiums are a big expense; *moreover,* the premiums will go up again at the end of the year.

Our expenses through June 30 are about 15 per cent over budget; *however,* we expect the expenses to decrease as our quality increases.

Note, again, that each sentence consists of two independent clauses joined by a conjunctive adverb.

Adverbial Clauses

Subordinating conjunctions introduce dependent clauses that serve as adverbs modifying an adjective, verb, or adverb in the main clause (an **adverbial clause**). Here are some commonly used subordinating conjunctions:

after	before	unless
although	for	until
as	if	when
because	since	while

Note the following examples of adverbial clauses introduced by subordinating conjunctions. In identifying an adverbial clause, remember that the adverbial clause will tell you things such as *how, when, where, why, how much,* or *to what extent.*

Paula Stacy will become our chief executive officer when George Johnson retires. (The adverbial clause *when George Johnson retires* modifies the verb *will become* in the main clause. It answers the question *When?*)

Our new line of decorator items will be profitable if we market it properly. (The adverbial clause *if we market it properly* modifies the adjective *profitable.* It answers the question *How?*)

CHECKUP 2

Identify the italicized words in the following sentences by labelling each as simple adverb (*SA*), conjunctive adverb (*CA*), or subordinating conjunction (*SC*).

1. Jody has been *unduly* busy *since* her assistant has been away from work with a knee surgery.

2. *Because* Dillon was behind in his work, he stayed *here late* two nights this week.

3. Joel *specifically* stated that he wanted an exercise room; *accordingly,* his architect designed a *very* modern room that was later furnished with top-of-the line equipment.

4. *Since* Donald opened his computer repair service, he has been *extremely* busy.

5. Murphy and Alicia have requested assistance *when* Mr. Ramsey returns from Québec.

6. The deadline for completion of the computer files conversion is next Friday; our vice president, *therefore,* has approved our working overtime.

7. *If* you would like information regarding the cost and availability of our electric scooter, please e-mail me at toysonwheels@yahoo.com.

8. The new copier works *quickly* and *quietly;* it does, *however,* have more paper jams than our last copier did.

Principles of Adverb Use

In speaking and writing, be sure to conform to the following five principles of adverb use.

1. **Position of the Adverb.** Place an adverb as close as possible to the word that it modifies. The meaning of a sentence changes depending on the position of the adverb. Some examples are:

Only Miss Berenson has a printer in her office. (No one else has one.)

Miss Berenson has only a printer in her office. (She has nothing else in her office, only a printer.)

Miss Berenson has a printer only in her office. (She has one nowhere else but in her office.)

2. **Double Negative.** Adverbs that have negative meanings, such as *scarcely, hardly, only, never,* and *but,* should not be used with other negatives. Such a construction is called a **double negative**. Some examples are:

Gregory *has scarcely* any money left for his holiday shopping. (*Not:* Gregory *hasn't scarcely…*)

With three copiers working, Pamela *could hardly* hear Frank. (*Not:* Pamela *couldn't hardly…*)

Olivia *couldn't help sliding* on the icy pavement. (*Not:* Olivia *couldn't help but slide…*)

3. ***Never* or *Not*.** *Never* and *not* are both adverbs, and both have negative meanings. *Not* expresses simple negation, but never means "not ever". Note the word *ever.* Use *never* only when an appropriately long time is intended. Some examples are:

Huyen has *not* sent me an e-mail this week. (*Never* would be incorrect because the meaning "not ever…this week" would be wrong.)

Wesley has *never* been married. (Even though *not* could be substituted for *never, never* is a better choice because it indicates a longer period of time.)

4. ***Where* for *That*.** The subordinating conjunction *that,* not the conjunctive adverb *where,* should be used in expressions such as the following:

I read in the newspaper *that* the Mellow Record Company is bankrupt. (Not: I read in the newspaper *where*…)

We heard on the radio *that* the mayor has resigned. (Not: We heard on the radio *where*… But: We saw the house *where* the famous writer once lived.)

5. **Badly** or **Worst Way** for **Very Much.** Too often, we hear people say *badly* or *in the worst way* when they really mean *very much.* An example is:

Janice said that she wanted a vacation *very much.* (Not: "wanted a vacation *badly*" or "wanted a vacation in the *worst way.*")

The teacher ordered the students to sit down angrily.

(The teacher angrily ordered…)

Adjective and Adverb Confusions

Remember that adjectives, not adverbs, must following linking verbs. The "being" verbs, such as *am, is, are, was, were, be, been,* and *being,* are all non-action, or "linking," verbs. In addition to these "being" verbs, the sense verbs such as *feel, appear, seem, look, sound, taste,* and *smell* can be used as non-action verbs. Some examples are:

Mr. Gunning was (angry? angrily?) when he heard about the delay. (The being verb *was* links the subject *Mr. Gunning* to the adjective *angry.* The verb *was* shows no action.)

Mr. Gunning appeared (angry? angrily?) when he heard about the delay. (The linking verb *appeared* shows no action; thus the adjective *angry* is correct.)

The refugees were (patient? patiently?). (Because the verb *were* indicates no action, the adjective *patient* is correct.)

The refugees seemed (patient? patiently?). (Like the non-action verb *were, seemed* links the noun *refugees* to the adjective *patient;* thus *patient* modifies *refugees.*)

Keep in mind that some of these verbs can also be used as action verbs. An example is:

Dr. Giordano felt carefully for a possible fracture. (Here, *felt* is an action verb; thus the adverb *carefully* modifies the verb *felt.*)

Frequently Confused Pairs

Several adjective–adverb pairs cause special problems for writers and speakers. Learning the differences between the words will help you express your ideas clearly. In the following pairs, the adjective is listed first.

Bad, Badly. *Bad* is an adjective; *badly* is an adverb.

Sera performs *badly* under pressure. (Performs how? *Badly.* The adverb *badly* modifies the action verb *performs.*)

The problem in selecting between *bad* and *badly* arises following non-action verbs.

Margaret felt (bad? badly?) when she heard about the layoffs. (Here, *felt* is a linking verb, not an action verb. The answer here will not modify the verb *felt* but the noun *Margaret.* Thus an adjective is required because an adverb cannot modify a noun. Margaret felt *bad.*)

Real, Really; Sure, Surely. *Real* and *sure* are adjectives. Use the *ly* endings to remind you that *really* and *surely* are adverbs. In the following examples, note that you can substitute the adverb *very* or *certainly* whenever *really* or *surely* is correct.

Suzanne and Manny were (real? really?) dedicated to helping seniors ("*Very* dedicated" makes sense. The adverb *really* is correct.)

Kolette (sure? surely?) was smart to have the house checked for termites. ("*Certainly* was" makes sense. The adverb *surely* is correct.)

Good, Well. *Good* is an adjective, and *well* is an adverb. The adjective *good* can modify nouns and pronouns; the adverb *well* can modify adjectives and verbs. Some examples are:

Van always prepares *good* presentations. (The adjective *good* modifies the noun *presentations*.)

Van generally prepares presentations *well*. (The adverb *well* modifies the verb *prepares*. Prepares presentations how? Prepares *well*.)

Exception: *Well* can also be an adjective, *but only when referring to personal health.*

Because Amanda did not feel *well*, she went home early. (Here, *well* is an adjective referring to a person's health.)

Remember the term *well-being* and you'll be sure to recall that *well* is an adjective only when it refers to health.

Some, Somewhat. *Some* is an adjective; *somewhat* is an adverb. To use *somewhat* correctly, test to be sure that you can substitute the phrase *a little bit*. Some examples are:

As we anticipated, Ms. Feingold was (some? somewhat?) surprised when she received the award. (Does "a little bit surprised" make sense? Yes—thus *somewhat* is correct.)

As you requested, we have listed (some? somewhat?) suggestions for the consultant. (Does "a little bit suggestions" make sense? No. Thus, the adjective *some* is correct.)

Most, Almost. *Most* is an adjective, the superlative of *much* or *many*, as in *much, more, most*. *Almost* is an adverb meaning "not quite" or "very nearly." Some examples are:

(Most? Almost?) administrative assistants hope to become administrators. (Because "very nearly administrative assistants" makes no sense, *almost* cannot be correct. "*Most* administrative assistants" is correct.)

Jaclyn brought (most? almost?) enough hard hats for everyone at the work site. ("Very nearly enough hard hats" *does* make sense. *Almost* is correct.)

CHECKUP 3

Check the following sentences for any errors in the use of adverbs. Write *OK* if a sentence is correct.

1. Cynthia was some surprised by the news of her promotion.
2. Most of us in the real estate sales community found the reports real distressing.
3. After almost two years, the development plan has worked out very well.
4. Of course, she was sure justified in her request for equal salary.
5. Because you don't feel good, James, we suggest that you stay at home tomorrow.

6. Maria appeared angrily at the idea of closing the clinic.

7. Because of the recent problems, we were somewhat hesitant to discuss this sensitive issue.

8. During the January sale, you can get a real good deal on this notebook computer.

9. Needless to say, she and I felt badly when we heard that Mrs. Jordan was retiring.

10. Because she was rushed, Shula treated the customer badly.

Review of Key Terms

1. How do *adverbs* differ from *adjectives*?
2. What is the role of a *conjunctive adverb*? Write a sentence using a conjunctive adverb and punctuate it correctly.

Practical Application

1. Correct any adverb errors in the following sentences. Write *OK* if a sentence is correct.
    a. We read in the newspaper where the proposed tax increases had been defeated.
    b. Although this dinner special does smell deliciously, I really am not very hungry right now.
    c. Harris and I only know about the planned expansion; no one else knows about it yet.
    d. Retaining our present retail prices should sure work very well during the holiday sales.
    e. Because Tim has been late so frequent, Ms. Gordon has spoken with him about the importance of arriving on time.
    f. No, Mr. Ghan never told me that John left early this morning.
    g. We immediately noticed that Louis had fallen and that he needed help in the worst way.
    h. Elizabeth appeared very confident as she accepted the award.
    i. As you know, our sales decreased some during the summer months.
    j. Did you notice that this water tastes very bitterly?
    k. Because our offices are so close to the harbour, we can clear hear the tugboats.
    l. Needless to say, we felt very badly when we heard of your misfortune.
    m. Follow these guidelines to make sure that you prepare your speech good.
    n. This proposal hasn't scarcely one new idea for our convention exhibit.
    o. "We have," Bruno said, "a real good chance of winning the contract."
    p. According to Jackie, Mr. Lombardi wants to buy her award-winning photograph in the worst way.
    q. Yes, I do believe that his suggestion will work out very good.
    r. Vic never received the samples from our Saskatoon office, although the package was mailed more than a week ago.
    s. As we expected, all the brokers are real concerned about the possible change in the commission schedule.
    t. The credit for preparing the annual report so good must go to Marion.

2. Correct any errors in the following sentences. Write *OK* if a sentence is correct.

   a. Gabriella's estimates were due last Monday but she never completed them.

   b. According to Peter's supervisor, Peter works more quick than Eleanor.

   c. Last year, Sareena had three assistants in her department; since the budget cutbacks, however, she hasn't but one assistant.

   d. Here is all the nuts and bolts that you asked for, Ms. Hammond.

   e. Of course, Barry and myself will be happy to help if you get extremely busy.

   f. As you can well imagine, the Bradleys' were really pleased to learn of the tax free interest on their investments.

   g. Mr. Flax sent Jeffrey to the infirmary because he wasn't feeling very good.

   h. Neither the two managers nor the four assistants has the time to devote to this extra work.

   i. Because Toula been dedicating all her time to the upcoming annual sales meeting, she has hired part-time help.

   j. Seth and Donna will help you process all them invoices if you fall behind, Martin.

   k. Where's the keys to the storeroom and the supply closet?

   l. Sabrina has been doing very good since she was transferred to the accounting department.

   m. Be sure to focus careful so that you get a crisp, sharp picture.

   n. Carla sure does a superb job of handling customer complaints.

   o. Are these kind of disks available through our purchasing department?

   p. Perhaps the two best adjusters in our office are Zora and him.

   q. Of course, if Dana and me are selected to attend the convention, we will be really delighted.

   r. There's about three or four ways to set up this trust fund.

   s. The babys in the new formula advertisement must look healthy and happy.

   t. Only the Walsh's have requested specific changes in the standard contract.

3. People often read reviews of restaurants before deciding if they will eat

TEAMWORK

   there. Choose two restaurants and write a one-page review comparing the two. Review the quality of the food, the service, and the expense. Underline all comparative adverbs.

Editing Practice

Proofreading for Accuracy. Proofreading accurately requires more than spelling and grammar expertise—it requires accuracy in every detail. Check the following excerpt carefully. Does it have any errors?

The following discount schedule on purchases will become effective on April 31:

Over	Discount
$ 500	0.5%
1,000	0.75%
1,500	1.0%
2,000	1.25%
5,000	1.5%
10,000	1.75%
20,000	20.%

Proofread the following paragraph and correct any errors.

Ms. Lindsey called the managers office yesterday to request additional funds for her research project. She reported that she hasn't scarcely any money remaining in her budget. She had read in a newsletter where more funds would be available in may. Ms. Lindsey believes that she is working on a real good project, and she would like to complete it.

Discussion Points

1. Explain how to form the comparative and superlative forms of adverbs. Provide several examples for single, double, and multi-syllable adverbs

2. The use of "good" instead of "well" in everyday speech is a frequently heard mistake. What are some examples of this mistake that you hear? How would you explain the correct use of "good" and "well"?

Prepositions

Words are one of our chief means of adjusting to all situations of life. The better control we have over words, the more successful our adjustment is likely to be.

—Bergen Evans, American author

▶ Key Terms

▶ preposition

▶ prepositional phrase

▶ object of the preposition

▶ idiomatic usage

Such prepositions as *for, in, of, on,* and *to* are used so often that native speakers generally pay no attention to them. To avoid some common preposition errors, however, everyone must pay attention to the rules presented in this section.

Identifying Prepositions

A **preposition** is a connecting word. It connects a noun or a pronoun to the rest of the sentence. The preposition combined with that noun or pronoun makes up a **prepositional phrase.** Examine the following commonly used prepositions and some sample prepositional phrases. Note: *But* is a preposition only when it means "except." In other cases, *but* is a conjunction.

Prepositions			Prepositional Phrases
about	but (except)	off	*off* the shelf
above	by	on	*above* the sink
after	except	over	*after* the meeting
among	for	to	*to* the new restaurant
at	from	under	*from* Gary and Feisal
before	in	until	*before* your first lesson
below	into	up	*into* the fray
beside	like	upon	*like* that newspaper
between	of	with	*with* my partner

The noun or pronoun that follows the preposition in a phrase is the **object of the preposition.** The phrase may include modifiers—for example, *new* in *to the new restaurant* modifies *restaurant,* which is the object of the preposition *to.* Also, a phrase may have compound objects, as in *from Gary and Feisal.*

Because prepositional phrases often interrupt the subject and the verb in a sentence, your ability to make subjects and verbs agree will sometimes depend on your ability to identify prepositional phrases. Examine the following examples:

The managers *in this department* are reviewing the new budget carefully. (The prepositional phrase *in this department* separates the subject *managers* from the verb *are.* A careless speaker, therefore, may incorrectly say "department *is,*" which is wrong.)

One employee from both teams has volunteered for the pilot project. (The prepositional phrase *from both teams* separates the subject *employee* from the verb *has volunteered.*)

CHECKUP 1

Identify the prepositions and the prepositional phrases in the following sentences.

1. The main reason for the delay is that Jill is still doing research.
2. All of the invoices that Laura put on my desk have been approved and sent to the Accounting Department.
3. Only one of our members indicated that she was dissatisfied with the new meeting schedule.
4. Because Mr. Sanders was in a rush, Stephan drove him to the airport.
5. You will need the instructions that were put in my file cabinet.
6. Between you and me, I do not believe that dropping out of college was a smart idea.
7. Natalie went into the conference room, I think, with her guest.
8. The final decision on the site of the new mall will be made by the planning board.

Words Requiring Specific Prepositions

Through years of use, certain expressions are now considered "correct," even though there may be no rule or logical reason to make them correct. Such usage, called **idiomatic usage**, governs many expressions in our language. The use of certain prepositions with certain words is *idiomatic.* Long-accepted use has made it correct to use these prepositions. Examples are given in the list in Figure 5.1.

The idiomatic expressions that are used, and misused, most often are given special attention below. Be sure to learn to use these expressions correctly.

I cannot agree to this decision.

(agree with)

Agree With, Agree To

Use *agree with* when the object of the preposition is a person or idea; use *agree to* when the object is not a person or an idea. Some examples are:

Does the president *agree with* Mr. Kyowski on the need to improve security in the parking lot? (Because the object of the preposition is a person, the preposition *with* is correct.)

Yes, the president *agrees to* the recommendation to improve security in the parking lot. (Here, the object of the preposition is *recommendation;* because the object is not a person or idea, *agree to* is correct.)

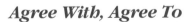

Angry With, Angry At

Use *angry with* when the object of the preposition is a person; use *angry at* or *about* when the object is not a person. Some examples are:

Glenn appeared to be *angry with* Jacob because of the delay in shipment. (*With* is correct because its object is a person, *Jacob.*)

Idiomatic Expressions with Prepositions

abhorrence of
abhorrent to
abide by a decision
abide with a person
abound in *or* with
accompanied by a person
accompanied with an item
acquit of
adapted for (made over for)
adapted from a work
adapted to (adjusted to)
affinity between
agree to a proposal
agree with someone
agreeable to (with is permissible)
angry at *or* about a thing *or* condition
angry with a person
attend to (listen)
attend upon (wait on)
beneficial to
bestow upon
buy from
compare to the mirror image (assert a
   likeness)
compare with the reverse side (analyze
   for similarities or differences)
compliance with
comply with
confer on *or* upon (give to)
confer with (talk to)
confide in (place confidence in)
confide to (entrust to)
conform to
in conformity to *or* with
consist in (exist in)
consist of (be made up of)
convenient for (suitable for, easy for)
convenient to (near)
conversant with
correspond to *or* with (match; agree
   with)

correspond with (exchange letters)
credit for
deal in goods *or* services
deal with someone
depend *or* dependent on (but independent of)
different from (not than or to)
disappointed in *or* with
discrepancy between two things
discrepancy in one thing
dispense with
employ for a purpose
employed at a stipulated salary
employed in, on, *or* upon a work *or*
   business
enter at a given point
enter in a record
enter into (become a party to)
enter into *or* upon (start)
exception to a statement
familiarize with
foreign to (preferred to from)
identical with
independent of (not from)
inferior *or* superior to
need of *or* for
part from (take leave of)
part with (relinquish)
plan *or* planning to (not on)
profit by
in regard to
with regard to
as regards
retroactive to (not from)
speak to (tell something to a person)
speak with (discuss with)
wait for a person, a train, an event
wait on a customer, a guest

◀ **Figure 5.1**
Idiomatic Expressions
Speakers of English
in countries such as
Australia and Britain
differ in their idiomatic
usage compared to
speakers of English in
Canada.

Thinking Critically. *How
can misunderstandings in
idiomatic usage hinder
communication?*

Glenn appeared to be *angry at* the delay in shipment. (Now the object of the preposition is not a person; thus *angry at* or *about* is correct.)

Part From, Part With

Part from means "to take leave of"; *part with* means "to relinquish" or "to give up." Part from is generally used when the object of the preposition is a person. Part with is generally used when the object is not a person. Some examples are:

As soon as we *part from* Yusuf Habib at the conference, we will return to the hotel. (*Part from* a person.)

Although we certainly appreciate the features of the new telephone, we hate to *part with* our old ones. (*Part with*, meaning "to relinquish" or "to give up.")

Discrepancy In, Discrepancy Between, Discrepancy Among

Use *discrepancy in* when the object of the preposition is singular. Use *discrepancy between* when the object specifically denotes two in number. Use *discrepancy among* when the object denotes three or more persons or things. Some examples are:

I checked this chart carefully and found no *discrepancy in* it. (One chart is mentioned.)

Compare these two graphs carefully; then let me know if you find any *discrepancy between* the two. (Two graphs are mentioned.)

There were many *discrepancies among* the ten charts. (More than two charts are mentioned.)

In Regard To, With Regard To, As Regards

The three terms *in regard to, with regard to,* and *as regards* are equally correct, but only the word *regard*, not *regards*, can be used in the phrases *in regard to* and *with regard to*. Some examples are:

Mark has already consulted Mr. Johanson (in? with? as?) *regard to* the changes in the agenda. (Either *in* or *with* is correct.)

(In? With? As?) *regards* the changes in the agenda, please be sure to consult Mr. Johanson. (Only *as* is correct—*as regards*.)

Note: In many cases, you can simplify and improve your sentence by substituting the word *about* for *in regard to, with regard to,* or *as regards*. An example is:

Mark has already consulted Mr. Johanson *about* the changes in the agenda.

Different From, Identical With, Plan To, Retroactive To

Memorize the correct prepositions that go with these phrases so that you will use them properly.

different *from* (not different *than*)

identical *with* (not identical *to*)

plan *to* (not plan *on*) (For example: We plan *to design* a new student centre; not We plan *on designing* a new student centre.)

retroactive *to* (not retroactive *from*)

CHECKUP 2

Check the following sentences for any errors in the use of prepositions. Write *OK* if a sentence is correct.

1. When she discovered that the negatives had been carelessly handled, Ms. Cutter was angry at the messenger.
2. Rosemary plans on opening her own salon next year.
3. The jury members were surprised to find several discrepancies in the testimony.
4. The company wrote to me in regards to the invoice that was lost in the mail.

5. Sharon said that the most difficult aspect of transferring to our Montreal office was parting from all her good friends.

6. Dagmar explained how the new fax machine is different than the old one.

7. Sue and I proofread both draft copies of the wedding invitation; fortunately, we found no discrepancy in the two of them.

8. No, I frankly do not agree with Louis concerning the need to upgrade our graphics software.

9. According to the union leader, the new pay scale will be retroactive from October 1.

10. Although this year's model looks different, it is really identical to last year's copier.

Commonly Confused Prepositions

Deciding when to use *between* and when to use *among* is one preposition choice that traps many writers and speakers. Other pitfalls concern adding unnecessary prepositions and omitting necessary prepositions. Study the following to avoid the most common preposition pitfalls.

Between, Among

Use *between* when referring to two persons, places, or things, and use *among* when referring to *three or more.* Some examples are:

The contest for top sales agent was tied *between* Marjorie and Horton. (between *two* people)

The prize was divided *among* our three best students. (among *three* students)

   Between may also be used to express a relationship of one thing to each of several other things on a one-to-one-basis. An example is:

A separate agreement was signed *between* the parent company and each of the franchises.

Beside, Besides

Beside means "by the side of;" *besides* means "in addition to." Some examples are:

Yes, the man seated *beside* Ms. McMann is Vito Pirelli, our guest speaker. ("by the side of" Ms. McMann)

Do you know who is scheduled to speak *besides* Mr. Pirelli? ("in addition to" Mr. Pirelli)

Inside, Outside

Do not use the preposition *of* after inside or outside. When referring to time, use *within*, not *inside of.* Some examples are:

The elevator is on the left just *inside* the main entrance. (not *inside of*)

We expect to have both houses painted *within* the week. (not *inside of*)

All, Both

Use *of* after *all* or *both* only when *all* or *both* refers to a pronoun. Omit *of* if either word refers to a noun. Some examples are:

All the protesters blocked the clinic entrance. (*of* is not needed.)

All of them were eventually arrested. (*of* is required here with the pronoun them.)

Among Laurel and Hardy existed disharmony; between the Three Stooges existed harm.

(Between Laurel and Hardy...among the Three Stooges)

—Adapted from *The Writer's Block Calendar.*

At, To; In, Into

At and *in* denote position; *to* and *into* signify motion. Some examples are:

Khrystyna arrived *at* the stockholders' meeting and immediately went *to* the podium. (*at* for position; *to* for motion.)

They went *into* the hotel and set up the display *in* the main ballroom. (*into* for motion; *in* for position.)

Note: When either *at* or *in* refers to a place, use *in* for larger places and *at* for smaller places.

Edgar lives *in* Essex County and teaches *at* the local community college. (*in* Essex County, the larger place; *at* the local community college, the smaller place.)

Behind, Not *In Back Of*

Use *behind,* not *in back of. In front of,* however, is correct. An example is:

Until the audience arrives, place the microphones *behind,* not *in front of,* the curtain.

From, Off

From is generally used with persons; *off* is used with things. *Off* is used with persons only when something on the person is physically being lifted away. Never use *of* or *from* after *off.* Some examples are:

Get some extra binders *from* Barbara. (not *off* Barbara)

After five minutes, take the ice pack *off* your leg. (Something is physically being lifted away.)

Let's take these coffee cups *off* the conference room table. (not *off of* the conference room table)

Where, Not *Where…At* or *Where…To*

Adding *at* or *to* to *where* is a glaring error. Some examples are:

I do not know *where* Dr. Torres is. (not *is at*)

Where did John go? (not *go to*)

Help, Not *Help From*

Do not use the word *from* after the verb *help.* An example is:

The lecture was so interesting that we could not *help* asking Mr. Bart some questions. (not *help from* asking)

Opposite, Not *Opposite To*

Do not use the word *to* after *opposite.* An example is:

The bus stop is directly *opposite* the college entrance. (not *opposite to*)

Like, Not *Like For*

Omit the word *for* after *like.* An example is:

We told the mayor that we would *like* her to visit the housing project. (not *like for*)

CHECKUP 3

Check the following sentences for any errors in the use of prepositions. Write *OK* if a sentence is correct.

1. I'm sure that Sally knows where the two of them are at.
2. We know that Melanie cannot help from talking about her vacation.
3. Do you know where the doctor has gone to.
4. The new computer store is opposite the bus station.
5. Perhaps you should go in the new hotel to inspect its conference facilities.
6. We may get our free flu shots inside of working hours.
7. The reward was divided between Fred, Rosemary, and Vincent.
8. When we arrived at the resort, we immediately pulled in the garage.
9. Is the man seated besides Andrew the visitor from France you spoke of?
10. Let's leave all of these chairs in the storage room.
11. Both of the police officers received awards for their part in organizing the Young Athletes program.
12. Peter's mother would like for him to be more ambitious.

Review of Key Terms

1. What is a *prepositional phrase*? What is its role in a sentence?
2. What is *idiomatic usage*? Provide examples of some idiomatic expressions with prepositions.

Practical Application

1. Correct any errors in the following sentences. Write *OK* if a sentence is correct.
   a. What does Mr. Dexter plan to do in regards to the insurance claims relating to the warehouse fire?
   b. The directions for assembling the workstation were inside of the package.
   c. Beside all the department heads, the regional managers should receive a courtesy copy.
   d. Have you asked Nancy where Roberta went to?
   e. Please tell the visitors to park their cars in back of the building.
   f. Leo will take all of these schedules off of the noticeboard.
   g. Both of the tennis courts are being resurfaced.
   h. We would very much like for Mrs. Russo to be our guest at the banquet.
   i. Effie arrived in the meeting without her agenda.
   j. Unfortunately, Mr. Smyth, your name was taken off of our mailing list in error.
   k. T.J. was angry at the vice president until he realized the reason for the transfer.
   l. Marcia carefully proofread the statistical report to ensure that there was no discrepancy in it.
   m. The restaurant that you mentioned is opposite to the library on Queen Street.
   n. Helen dislikes parting from the special pieces in her collection.
   o. Who beside Raoul will be transferred to the Regina office?
   p. Most of us could not help from wondering why the advertising manager was so enthusiastic about the Fruitfizz campaign.
   q. If we ship the cars Tuesday, you should receive them inside of two weeks.
   r. As all the invoices are received, they are divided among the three accounting clerks for processing.
   s. With regards to the possibility of staff cutbacks, I have been asked to make no comments to the press.
   t. In terms of strength, this new plastic is no different than this metal.
2. Correct any errors in the following sentences. Write *OK* if a sentence is correct.
   a. A number of complaints about this new model has been received by our product manager.

b. Yes, Jodie generally works longer hours than me.

c. Do you know whose in charge of the Maintenance Department?

d. Jean Bouchard, who you met at the luncheon last Thursday, has been named head of the new division.

e. Each of our many branch offices have their own conference room.

f. Don't Phyllis want to attend the first session on Monday morning?

g. Don't Bernice and Alan want you and I to help them with their house renovation?

h. Among the stores that we manage are The Computer Wizard in the Edmonton Mall.

i. I think that you should order more of them sizes, because they're very popular.

j. Do these specifications conform with international standards?

k. Did you ask if there's tickets available for the concert?

l. If you were the head of this department, who would you select to be your assistant?

m. Do the Ferraro's plan to vacation in Hawaii again this year?

n. In your opinion, who is the best sales representative in our company, Denise or he?

o. Teresa always does a real good job on the inventory reports.

p. Perhaps the reason Albert doesn't feel good is that he has poor eating habits.

q. Janet thinks that Lance writes better copy than her.

r. Every executive in the company will surely improve their management skills by reading Paul Drinker's informative new book.

s. Professor Stoddard said that you and me will receive a high mark because of our excellent work all semester.

t. No, I certainly was not angry at Mark for his remarks about yesterday's meeting.

3. Using too many prepositional phrases in one sentence can lead to a

 confusing sentence. Without losing the meaning, each member of the group is to rewrite the following sentences by eliminating some prepositional phrases. Then compare the answers within the group. If the solutions are different, which sentence does the group like best as a replacement for 3a, and which for 3b? Why?

TEAMWORK

a. There will be a negotiation of a settlement by the lawyers that is agreeable to both parties by tomorrow.

b. There will be an evaluation of the training program by personnel to assure quality training within our company.

Editing Practice

Using Business Vocabulary. From the list below, select the word that best completes each of the sentences. Write the corresponding letter of the correct word for each sentence.

a. beneficiary ✓   f. irreparable ✓
b. quorum   g. collusion
c. enumerate ✓   h. monopolize ✓
d. hesitant   i. negligible ✓
e. inexhaustible   j. unscrupulous

g **1.** In his opening argument, the plaintiff's lawyer hinted at _____ between the defendant and the insurance company.

f **2.** The insurance company will pay our claim because the damage is _____.

d **3.** Michelle appeared somewhat _____ to discuss her plans to reorganize the warehouse space.

i **4.** Fortunately, the amount of damage to the books was _____.

h **5.** The chairperson should not allow any one team member to _____ the discussion.

c **6.** To make this agenda clearer, _____ the topics in table form.

b **7.** Were there enough members at the meeting to form a _____?

a **8.** Joe was named as a _____ in his uncle's will.

9. She wrote a best-selling exposé of excessive profiteering by _____ companies during the oil shortage.

e **10.** Our supply of this metal is virtually _____, but mining it is very expensive.

Writing Sentences. Each of the following words is a "must" for your vocabulary and your spelling lists. Do you know the meaning of each word? Can you spell each one correctly?

Write a sentence using each word correctly.

1. accommodate
2. cancellation
3. chief executive officer (CEO)
4. comparable
5. essential
6. guarantee
7. necessary
8. omission
9. potential
10. questionnaire
11. survey
12. recommendation
13. strategic planning

Discussion Points

1. How does one know when to use *between* and when to use *among*?

2. How can writers avoid agreement errors when using prepositional phrases?

Conjunctions

▶ **Key Terms**

> *With* but *and* or, *the compound sentence becomes more thoughtful. The mind is at work, turning its thought first one way then another, meeting the reader's objections by stating them.*
>
> —Sheridan Baker, author of *The Practical Stylist*

As you will recall from Section 3.1, a *conjunction* is a word that is used to *connect* words, phrases, or clauses within a sentence. Some examples are:

The printer *and* the software are included in this price. (In this sentence, the conjunction *and* joins the words *printer* and *software.*)

You may get a copy from my office *or* from the library. (The conjunction *or* joins two phrases, *from my office* and *from the library.*)

Wanda wants to buy this printer, *but* she is waiting for a sale. (The conjunction *but* joins the two independent clauses.)

Writing varied sentences and punctuating them correctly becomes much simpler once you have mastered the uses of conjunctions. This section presents three different kinds of conjunctions, discusses the most common pitfalls in using conjunctions, and then considers parallel structure—an important topic that is closely related to conjunction use.

Types of Conjunctions

There are three types of conjunctions: coordinating, correlative, and subordinating conjunctions. Coordinating and correlative conjunctions connect two or more items of equal grammatical rank. Subordinating conjunctions, however, connect a subordinate clause to a main clause.

Coordinating Conjunctions

The seven **coordinating conjunctions**—*for, and, nor, but, or, yet,* and *so*—are very commonly used. Note that they connect only *like* elements of grammar: two or more words, two or more phrases, or two or more clauses. Some examples are:

Breakfast *and* dinner are included in the total price. (The conjunction *and* connects two words, *breakfast* and *dinner.*)

Breakfast, lunch, *and* dinner are included in the total price. (Here the conjunction *and* joins three words.)

Karen has been with clients *or* in meetings most of the day. (The conjunction *or* joins two prepositional phrases, *with clients* and *in meetings.*)

Mr. Stuyvesant planned to spend the week at the ski resort *but* he couldn't get a hotel room. (The conjunction *but* connects two independent, or main, clauses.)

Use the mnemonic "fanboys" to remember the seven coordinating conjunctions.

For

And

Nor

But

Or

Yet

So

Correlative Conjunctions

Correlative conjunctions are *pairs* of conjunctions that are regularly used together to connect *like* elements. Note, again, that both coordinating and correlative conjunctions connect *like* elements only. The most commonly used correlative conjunctions are these:

both…and

either…or

neither…nor

not only…but also

whether…or

Like coordinating conjunctions, correlative conjunctions connect words, phrases, or clauses of equal grammatical rank. Some examples are:

Both Bob *and* Martha will take part in the ribbon-cutting ceremony next Wednesday. (Here the correlatives *both…and* connect two words, *Bob* and *Martha.*)

Antonio has been working on his MBA thesis *not only* in the evening *but also* on weekends. (Two phrases, *in the evening* and *on weekends,* are joined.)

Not only does Yusuf intend to finish his report, *but* he *also* plans to publish it. (Here two clauses are connected.)

Subordinating Conjunctions

Subordinating conjunctions join clauses of *un*equal rank. A subordinating conjunction introduces a subordinate, or dependent, clause and connects it to a main, or independent, clause. Some examples are:

Although we lowered the price, sales failed to show a significant increase for the quarter. (*Although* is a subordinating conjunction that introduces the subordinate clause *although we lowered the price.* Further, *although* connects this subordinate clause to the main clause.)

Ask Ms. DePalma for a registration form *if* you plan to enrol in this course. (The subordinating conjunction *if* introduces the subordinate clause *if you plan to enrol in this course* and connects this clause to the main clause.)

Subordinate Conjunctions			
after	before	provided that	when
although	even if	since	whenever
as	for	so that	where
as if	how	than	wherever
as soon as	if	that	whether
as though	in case that	unless	while
because	in order that	until	why

◀ **Figure 5.2**
Subordinate
Conjunctions
Subordinate conjunctions
form subordinate clauses
that indicate ideas of
unequal rank.

Thinking Critically. *How
can identifying subordi-
nate clauses improve your
comprehension?*

Study the above list of commonly used subordinating conjunctions so that you will be able to identify subordinate clauses.

CHECKUP 1

Write the conjunctions used in the following sentences. Label each conjunction "coordinating," "correlative," or "subordinating."

1. Barry will discuss his findings as soon as he returns from Halifax.
2. While Ms. Beauchamp was at lunch, we planned her surprise birthday celebration.
3. Have you submitted both the completed registration form and your references?
4. Our lawyer and the president of Canadian Steel carefully reviewed the price-fixing allegations.
5. Order today if you would like to receive this handsome ornament in time for the holidays.
6. Unless you find your wallet immediately, you must cancel your credit cards.
7. Frances, do you know whether Sergio or Larry has called this client yet?
8. Yes, I'm sure that Larry called him already.
9. Please ask either Armin or Karla to investigate the cause of the accident.
10. You may pay 12 monthly instalments, or you may save $100 by paying the entire amount before January 31.

Pitfalls of Using Conjunctions

The following discussion focuses on two major conjunction pitfalls: (1) choosing a conjunction that does not accurately convey the meaning intended; and (2) choosing a preposition when a conjunction is needed.

Choosing the Correct Conjunction

***But* or *And*?** The conjunction *but* provides a contrast while *and* simply joins two elements. Use *but* when a contrast is intended. Some examples are:

The difference in price between the two models is minimal, *but* only one model is energy-efficient. (*but* for contrast)

The two models are similar in price and both are on sale. (*and* to join two items)

Who, Which, or That? Use who to refer to persons and which to refer to objects. Never use and who or and which. Some examples are:

Send an invitation to Harry Pierson, *who* is the new research director. (*Who* refers to a person.)

We were instructed to send our recommendations to the board, *which* is responsible for all major decisions. (*Which* refers to an object.)

That is used to refer to persons, objects, or animals. Some examples are:

The speaker *that* you heard is Edith Tobin, a well-known architect. (*That* refers to a person. Note that *whom* could also have been used.)

One process *that* you will find interesting is four-colour separation. (Here, *that* refers to an object.)

The dog *that* Hilary adopted is a Dalmatian. (*That* refers to an animal.)

***Since* or *Because*, Not *Being That*.** There is no such conjunction as *being that*. Use *since* or *because* instead. An example is:

Because I could not leave the office all day, I missed the exercise class. (*Because*, not *Being that*)

***The Reason Is That; Pretend That*.** Do not say or write "the reason is *because*" and "pretend *like*." Instead, say "the reason is *that*" and "pretend *that*." Some examples are:

The reason for the sudden strike, according to informed sources, *is that* the company has threatened to lay off 1000 workers. (not *reason…is because*)

Of course, we cannot *pretend that* sales are healthy. (not *pretend like*)

***Unless*, Not *Without* or *Except*.** *Without* and *except* are prepositions. A preposition always introduces a prepositional phrase. A preposition is not a substitute for the subordinating conjunction *unless*. (Remember: A prepositional phrase consists of a preposition plus its noun or pronoun object and any modifiers.) Some examples are:

You cannot return this application *without* Ms. Ford's approval. (This sentence is correct. *Without Ms. Ford's approval* is a prepositional phrase: *approval* is the object of the preposition *without*, and *Ms. Ford's* is a modifier.)

You cannot return this merchandise *unless* Ms. Ford approves it. (The subordinating conjunction *unless* introduces a clause. An error occurs when people incorrectly say or write *without Ms. Ford approves it*. The preposition *without* cannot introduce a clause.)

***As, As If, As Though*, Not *Like*.** Remember that *like* is a preposition as in "a car *like* mine," or a verb as in "I *like* this model." It is *not* a conjunction. Therefore, do not use *like* when *as, as if*, or *as though* is intended. An example is:

Celine acted as *if* she wanted to go home. (as *if*, not *like*)

CHECKUP 2

Check the following sentences for any errors in the use of conjunctions. Write *OK* if a sentence is correct.

1. She told Bill not to sit around like he has no work to do.

2. Toula can't come to the meeting, being that she's taking her daughter to the doctor.

3. Ella's new job is not very glamorous, and she is really enjoying the challenge it presents.

4. According to the newspaper reports, the main reason for the sudden increase in oil prices is because OPEC has curtailed production.

5. Ann recommended several musicians which would be appropriate for the reception.

6. Charles said, "It seems like artists have surrounded us."

7. Do not send this sample to Mr. Martin without you get official authorization from your supervisor.

8. Arlene was told not to send the sample unless she receives official authorization.

9. It seems like almost every home has at least one computer.

10. Todd, please do not use any of these mailing labels except I specifically ask you to do so.

Parallel Structure

Observing the rules of parallel structure will provide balance to your writing. "The ability to write a good parallel sentence is invaluable in essay work. Faulty parallelism, on the other hand, produces an effect in your reader similar to changing gears without using the clutch. A successful parallel sentence reads smoothly, while a faulty parallel sentence lurches awkwardly." (University of Victoria, *The UVic Writer's Guide*) When a sentence has **parallel structure**, the same part of speech is used to express similar thoughts. This means that the grammatical elements of parallel clauses must match. Some examples are:

This printer works *quietly and quickly.* (The conjunction *and* joins two parallel elements—two adverbs, *quietly* and *quickly.*)

This printer works *quietly and with speed.* (The same ideas are expressed here but not in parallel form. Now we have an adverb, *quietly,* joined to a prepositional phrase, *with speed.* These two grammatical elements are not alike; they are not parallel.)

The rule about matching grammatical elements applies not only to adverbs, but to verbs, nouns, adjectives, and other parts of speech. The remainder of this section deals with parallel structure with coordinating and correlative conjunctions.

With Coordinating Conjunctions

Coordinating conjunctions connect *like* elements: an adjective with an adjective, a prepositional phrase with a prepositional phrase, and so on. Therefore, make sure that the elements before and after a coordinating conjunction match. Some examples are:

Our fire alarm system is checked carefully and (regularly? with regularity?). (An adverb, *carefully,* appears before the coordinating conjunction *and;* therefore, the adverb *regularly* should follow *and.* Together, *carefully* and *regularly* achieve parallel structure.)

Running the first mile is relatively easy, but (finishing? to finish?) the marathon is quite challenging. (Which choice matches running? Answer: *finishing.* Both *running* and *finishing* are gerunds.)

CHECKUP 3

Balance the following sentences to make them parallel.

1. Completing this course will help you understand the basics of finance and applying these basics to your job.

Tammy speaks quietly and with confidence.

(confidently)

2. The fitness expert said, "Eating the proper foods is important, but to exercise is also important."

3. In my opinion, both applicants seem to be personable and have courtesy.

4. You may submit your application by fax, by e-mail, or you can apply in person.

5. Cathy enjoys reading, hiking, and to study French.

6. The receptionist we are seeking should be gracious in manner, a person who helps everyone, and loyal to the company.

With Correlative Conjunctions

Pairs of correlative conjunctions such as *either …or* and *both …and* introduce clauses that must be parallel. Make sure that the element that follows the first conjunction is the same part of speech as the element that follows the second conjunction. Some examples are:

Minh wants *either* Jacques *or* me to work overtime. (The elements that follow *either…or* are a noun (*Jacques*) and a pronoun (*me*). Nouns and pronouns are considered like elements because pronouns are substitutes for nouns. Thus the phrase *either Jacques or me* is parallel.)

Not only … but also can be a little more difficult because of the placement of *only* and *also*, but the same rule applies. An example is:

The colour green is predominant *not only* in the reception area's furnishings *but also* in its carpet. (Notice the parallelism of two prepositional phrases, one after each of the correlatives.)

Not only did the volunteers do all the painting, *but* they *also* hung the wallpaper. (*Not only* is followed by an independent clause, and *but also* is followed by an independent clause and may be interrupted by *they.* The sentence is parallel. Do not be misled by the inverted order of the first clause.)

Misplaced Conjunctions

Be sure that the placement of the correlative conjunction is correct. A misplaced conjunction can change the meaning of a sentence. Some examples are:

She likes *either* to eat pizza *or* to eat spaghetti. (Correct.)

She likes to eat *either* pizza *or* spaghetti. (Correct.)

She likes to eat either pizza or to eat spaghetti. (Wrong.)

CHECKUP 4

Balance the elements joined by correlative conjunctions so that they are parallel.

1. In an effort to save fuel, we are trying to either form car pools or to use public transportation.

2. For 50 years the shop has been opened either by Mr. Forcini or his father.

3. Among the activities I like best are reading mystery novels and to surf the Internet.

4. Maude neither went to the hospital nor to the clinic.

5. Higher discounts are generally given to either our best customers or to our employees.

6. This book is both well written and has colourful illustrations.

Review of Key Terms

1. What are the three types of *conjunctions*? Describe the function of each one.
2. What is *parallel structure*?

Practical Application

1. Check the following sentences for any errors in the use of conjunctions. Write *OK* if a sentence is correct.
   a. Store policy states that discounts are not given without a manager's approval.
   b. Store policy states that discounts are not given unless a manager approves them.
   c. Our manager neither feels that overtime work nor part-time help will solve the problem.
   d. Vanessa seems to give away free samples of merchandise like they cost the company nothing.
   e. Micheline is neither happy with her job nor with her salary.
   f. The reason I am is buying these clothes is because I just got a new job.
   g. They not only agreed to thank Jason but also to give him a bonus.
   h. The small model sells very well, and the larger model is probably the better value.
   i. The man which you saw in my office is the manager of our Dorval plant.
   j. Because you looked like you were tired, we decided not to bother you.
   k. Please do not mail this contract without the client signs it first.
   l. We agreed to cancel the meeting, being that several people were absent.
   m. The members of the arbitration board seem objective and to be impartial.
   n. Your duties will include screening applicants and to interview candidates.
   o. Being that you like Mexican food, we thought we'd treat you to tacos on your birthday.
   p. The deadline is only a few hours away, and we will be able to file the forms on schedule.
   q. The reason total sales increased in the fourth quarter is because each regional office sponsored a sales contest.
   r. You must test applicants for their skills in keyboarding, writing e-mail, and to handle numbers.
   s. When you make your speech, pretend like you are talking to a few close friends.
   t. Please do not throw out these tapes except I ask you to do so.

2. Correct any errors in the following sentences. Write *OK* if a sentence is correct.

   a. A large number of customers, according to Rory, was interested in our new cellular phones.

   b. Rory says that the Stockton's are very eager to buy another cellular phone.

   c. We are looking for one of those printers that sells for under $500.

   d. Last week Jesse invited Cora and I to see her new apartment.

   e. Our Lake Scugog property is neither for sale or for rent.

   f. Today we have no baguettes and not any bagels.

   g. Yes, there's been a few problems with the new payment system, but we are confident that it will work out well.

   h. Carolyn does not plan on ordering any new printers this year.

   i. Have you received any more information in regards to the changes in our medical and dental coverage?

   j. "When talking with your clients," our sales manager suggested, "pretend like our humidifiers are the only ones on the market."

   k. We decided to purchase all our equipment from Super Computers Inc., being that SCI has such a great reputation for service.

   l. Did you read in our company newsletter where we may open a new office in Quebec?

   m. Sam, don't Norma know about the four o'clock deadline?

   n. Nicole left a message for Dr. Hamid this morning, but Dr. Hamid never called back.

   o. If you and me complete this layout today, we can take tomorrow off.

   p. Jeanne neither completed the forms correctly nor mailed them on time.

   q. We received many excellent suggestions; Kenneth's recommendation, however, was the most unique.

   r. On the bulletin board in the main hallway is the announcements in regard to the upcoming staff meeting and the company picnic.

   s. If your looking for value, quality, and durability, we honestly believe that the SCI notebook computer should be your choice.

   t. It's too cold to go for a walk; moreover, there's ice on the sidewalks.

3. Revise the following paragraph so that (1) short, choppy sentences are combined, and (2) each sentence has parallel structure.

   TEAMWORK

   Mr. Mendoza is going to tour our plant this month. Mr. Cassio is going to tour our plant this month. They are concerned about recent problems in understocking, shipping, and returned goods. The warehouse is not the only place they will check. They also will visit customer relations.

Editing Practice

Proofreading. Proofread the following excerpts from a memorandum.

Begining March 15, account executives must sign each new-account form before sending the form to the sales department. Each account executive should proofread the form carefully to make sure that the client's name and address (as well as the details of the transaction, of course) is correct in every detail.

Remember that an error in the new-account form can delay shipments of merchandise to your client and cause errors in billing, both of which will contribute to poor customer relations. Lets strive to get it right the first time!

Thank you for you're assistance with the new procedures.

Plurals and Possessives. Correct any errors in the following sentences. Write *OK* if a sentence is correct.

1. Among the people that were not able to attend were the Ross's, who have been in Nova Scotia since April.
2. One of the foremost childrens' clothing stores is Kids' Stuff, a Canada-wide chain with headquarters in Vancouver.
3. According to the newspaper, his three brothers are all majors general in the Canadian Forces.
4. Most of the designs that we reviewed showed creativity and flair; however, we all agreed that her's was the best.
5. Correct this column of numbers, making sure that the zeroes and the decimals align properly.
6. I believe that some of the ratioes given in this table are incorrect; please check them carefully.
7. Julie and Mike's new apartment is only about ten minutes away.
8. Tonights' guest speakers, the Messrs. Klein, will surely entertain the audience.
9. Thank goodness my calculations do agree with your's.
10. No, I was not aware of Adnan leaving early, but apparently the boss gave him permission to do so.

Discussion Points

1. How can writers verify that their sentences are parallel when using coordinating and correlative conjunctions?
2. In the anecdote at the beginning of this chapter, the students in Asad's class were given two items that demonstrated parallelism. How is the principle of parallel structure used in these two examples?
3. Look at the quote by Sheridan Baker at the beginning of Section 5.4. Explain how the conjunctions *but* and *or* can make writing "more thoughtful."

Chapter 5 Wrap-Up

SUMMARY

▶ Writers use adjectives to make their writing more lively and concise. Adjectives are usually placed before the nouns they modify. Adjectives answer the questions *what kind, how many, how much, which one,* and *in what order.* Some adjectives, such as possessive and proper adjectives, have their own special punctuation rules.

▶ Descriptive adjectives are often used to compare. Adjectives used in the comparative degree are usually formed by adding *er* or using the word *more* or *less* before the adjective. The superlative is formed by adding *est* or inserting the word *most* or *least* before the adjective. Other comparative and superlative adjectives are formed by changing the word completely.

▶ Adverbs are also descriptive words. They modify adjectives, verbs, and other adverbs. Like adjectives, they also have comparative and superlative forms that are indicated by adding *er* or *est* to the adverb. In some cases, the comparative and superlative is formed by adding *more/less* or *most/least* before the adverb.

▶ Prepositions are words that point out a relationship in time or space. Prepositions introduce the prepositional phrase that connects a noun with the rest of the sentence. The ability to recognize prepositions is a key skill in making sound grammatical decisions.

▶ Conjunctions are connecting words. There are three types of conjunctions—coordinating, correlative, and subordinating. The relationship between the two parts of the sentence that are joined determines the type of conjunction that is necessary.

CASE 5.1

Teresa is an intern at *The Yukon Trader,* a local newspaper. She is studying creative writing at college and hopes to get a part-time position writing for the newspaper in the summer. She was asked to write a sample article about tourist attractions in the area.

When Teresa received the edited copy of her article, she was surprised at some of the comments. Her writing was not descriptive and left the reader thinking, "Why would I go there?"

What can Teresa learn from this experience as an intern?

How can Teresa improve her article without making it read like fiction?

CASE 5.2

EDS, a North-American company, has set up offices in Antwerp. At the Antwerp offices, language experts handle calls to and from customers worldwide. The language operators answer software-troubleshooting questions from clients.

What kind of verbal skills are important for those who work in call centers? What kinds of problems do you think occur? What are the advantages and disadvantages with talking to someone on the phone rather than face-to-face?

Communicating in Your Career

People often have a vision of what they want their dream house to look like. How can they make that vision into a reality? Most people begin with hiring an architect. They present their ideas and the architect offers advice. Once the architect completes a design, the house plans are passed on to a contractor who begins to build the new house.

Give examples of how verbal and written communication skills assist an architect in his or her work with contractors and clients.

On the Web

Writing creatively is not an easy task. For some, using modifiers and placing them correctly in a long sentence can prove troublesome. Visit **http://www.uottawa.ca/academic/arts/writcent/hypergrammar/modifier.html** and answer the following questions.
1. Click on "Using the Comparative and Superlative." What is a double comparison? Next complete the review for Adverbs and Adjectives.
2. Click on "Misplaced and Dangling Modifiers." What is a misplaced modifier? Complete the review for Fixing Misplaced Modifiers.

Key Terms

Chapter 6

Applying the Mechanics of Style

Chapter Learning Outcomes

After successfully completing this chapter, you will have demonstrated the ability to:
▶ use punctuation correctly;
▶ apply capitalization rules to business writing;
▶ use abbreviations appropriately;
▶ apply number expression rules in business writing.

Renata, born in Germany, was the head teller of a branch bank in Winnipeg. Her native language was German, but she spoke English quite well. Her problem areas were capitalization and punctuation. She knew that if she were promoted to assistant branch manager, she would have to write many more memos, letters, and reports and would need to be a polished writer. She decided to speak with Allison in the human resources department about her desire to improve her writing skills.

Allison was impressed that Renata had diagnosed her own difficulty and that she wanted to overcome it. Allison ordered several books that Renata could work through on her own and also recommended an evening course at the local community college.

As a result of her efforts, Renata made rapid progress. She had recognized her own difficulty and had sought assistance in dealing with it. What role will improving her skills play in Renata's chances for promotion?

As you read Chapter 6, follow Renata's example and identify areas of punctuation, capitalization, and numbers use in which you need to improve. What strategies will you use to help you improve your skills?

▶ **Key Terms**

▶ periods
▶ declarative
sentences
▶ imperative
sentences
▶ indirect questions
▶ fragments
▶ period faults
▶ comma splices
▶ question marks
▶ direct questions
▶ exclamation
points

End-of-Sentence Punctuation

One who uses many periods is a philosopher; many interrogations, a student; many exclamations, a fanatic.

—J. L. Basford, author

Punctuation marks do for writing what pauses, changes in pitch, and gestures do for speaking: They provide the necessary road signs to help readers and listeners understand our messages correctly. As you saw in the case study at the beginning of this chapter, Renata realized that her proficiency in using capitalization and punctuation directly affected her chances of promotion. The three punctuation marks discussed in this section—periods, question marks, and exclamation points—are used to end sentences. In addition, these marks have some other uses, which are also discussed in this section.

Periods

It's important to learn when to use **periods** and when not to use periods, as well as how to avoid some common pitfalls in using them.

When to Use Periods

Use periods (1) to end declarative or imperative sentences, (2) to end requests that are phrased as questions simply for the sake of courtesy, and (3) to end indirect questions.

After Declarative and Imperative Sentences. **Declarative sentences** make statements, and **imperative sentences** order someone to act. Two examples are:

All these contracts must be proofread carefully. (declarative sentence)

Proofread all these contracts carefully. (imperative sentence)

After Requests Phrased as Questions. In an effort to soften commands and orders, speakers and writers often phrase such orders as questions (requests phrased as questions). Because such statements are not really questions, use periods to end these sentences.

Will you please send us your completed forms immediately. (This is not a question—no answer is required.)

May we please have the entire order shipped by the fastest method. (This is a polite way of saying, "Send the order as quickly as possible." It is not really a question.)

Will you be able to ship the order by the fastest method? (This is a definite question which requires an answer and, therefore, requires a question mark rather than a period.)

After Indirect Questions.
An indirect question is a question restated as a declarative sentence. Some examples are:

She asked me whether I had already sent a confirmation copy to Mr. Ortiz. (Stated as a declarative sentence, this sentence requires a period.)

Mark, have you sent a confirmation copy to Mr. Ortiz? (Stated as a question, the sentence requires a question mark.)

CHECKUP 1

Select either a period or a question mark to end the following sentences.

1. May we schedule the meeting for Tuesday
2. Karen asked Ms. Eng whether she plans to cancel the appointment
3. Can I have your completed questionnaire by Monday
4. Jonathan, would you stop by my office this afternoon
5. Dave asked permission to attend the grand opening
6. Will you please send the remainder of the merchandise before the end of the month
7. Submit your suggestions to your supervisor before December 31
8. Did Mr. Russo say that the deadline is December 31

When Not to Use Periods

Do *not* use periods in the following instances.

After Sentences Ending in Abbreviations.
Do *not* use two periods for sentences that end with abbreviations that use periods. If a sentence-ending abbreviation requires a period, let that period serve both functions. Some examples are:

As you know, the reception will begin at 8 p.m. (not *8 p.m..*)

May I ask you a question about this assignment? (not *assignment?.*)

After Headings or Titles or After Roman Numerals.
A heading that is set on a separate line (for example, see the headings in this textbook) should not be followed by a period. Also, Roman numerals used with names or titles should not be followed by periods. Some examples are:

Please read Chapter IV and make notes on the important points before our next class. (not *Chapter IV.* and make...)

John L. Jackson III has been appointed to lead the trade commission. (not *III.*)

After Numbers or Letters in Parentheses.
Do not use periods after numbers or letters enclosed in parentheses that precede enumerated items in a sentence. An example is:

Their portfolio consists mainly of (1) government bonds, (2) insurance bonds, and (3) utilities stocks.

When numbers or letters are not in parentheses and are displayed on separate lines and grammatically complete the introductory sentence, use a comma (or semicolon) after each and a period after the last item. In the following example, each item is the object of the preposition *of* in the introductory statement. Therefore each item ends with a comma and the entire list ends with a period.

Their portfolio consists mainly of

1. government bonds,

2. insurance bonds,

3. utilities stocks.

Note: If the items do not grammatically complete the introductory statement, no punctuation would be needed.

If the introductory statement for a numbered list is grammatically complete, do not use periods after the items in the list. For example:

Their portfolio includes all of the following investments:

1. government bonds

2. insurance bonds

3. utilities stocks

In addition, if each item in a list is a complete sentence or a long phrase, use a period.

After Even Amounts of Dollars. Except in tables (when it is important to align numbers), do not use periods or unnecessary zeros in even-dollar amounts. An example is:

Thank you for sending us your $75 deposit so quickly. (not $75. and not $75.00)

CHECKUP 2

Check the following sentences for any errors in the use of periods. Write *OK* if a sentence is correct.

1. Until April 1, you can join the new health club for $600. a year.

2. The best presentation was given by the sales manager of Argosy Computers, Inc..

3. Have you heard that Simon Frazer II. has been elected to our board of governors?

4. The enclosed materials include (1) a booklet describing the medical benefits program, (2) an application form, and (3) a postage-paid envelope.

5. By renewing your subscription now, you can save $39.00 over the newsstand price.

6. The survey polled the following employees:

    a. commission sales representatives

    b. executives

    c. support personnel

Period Pitfalls

Using a period at the end of an incomplete thought, or **fragment**, is a **period fault.** Using a comma when a period is needed is a **comma splice.** Avoid these errors in your writing.

The Period Fault. An incomplete thought, or fragment, is not a sentence and therefore cannot stand alone. It should not end with a period. Generally, joining the incomplete thought to a main clause will solve the problem.

Brent is taking a computer applications course. Because he believes it will help him get a promotion. (The second group of words cannot stand alone. This dependent clause should be joined to the preceding independent clause as shown in the following example.)

Brent is taking a computer applications course because he believes it will help him get a promotion. (Now the dependent clause does not stand alone but is joined correctly to an independent clause.)

The Comma Splice. A comma by itself should not be used to join two independent clauses. A period is needed. Comma splices may also be remedied by using a semicolon or a conjunctive adverb.

Your seeds and bulbs are enclosed, a planting guide for your location will be mailed within ten days. (Put a period after *enclosed* to separate these two independent clauses.)

Jedd is recruiting students to tour Israel, he said that the reservation deadline is May 15. (Again, these two independent clauses should be separated by a period.)

CHECKUP 3

Check the following sentences for any period faults or comma splices. Write *OK* if a sentence is correct.

1. Tomas was at a conference last week, but he called the office each day to check on his clients.
2. The flight was delayed for almost four hours. When a severe thunderstorm developed near the airport.
3. As we discussed at a recent committee meeting. We must continually update our technology.
4. Requests for specific software should be made by Tuesday noon, we get a discount on software ordered when we order our computers.
5. Since he came to work here a year ago. Rafael has not missed a day of work.
6. Dr. Ramirez is being honoured at a reception on Monday, he is retiring at the end of the year.
7. The cashier stamped the cheques for deposit, he immediately placed them in the safe.
8. Even though Hagar exercises daily at the spa for about an hour. She jogs two miles each evening.

Question Marks

Use **question marks** after direct questions and in a series of questions.

After Direct Questions

Direct questions always end with question marks. Some examples are:

Have you prepared your resumé?

Mr. Abdul, have you received your airline tickets yet?

Should we stamp these cartons "Fragile"?

Gwen asked, "What time is your training session?"

Sentences that begin as statements but end as questions are considered questions. Use question marks at the end of such sentences. Two examples are:

Jehann shipped all the software updates to the Calgary office, didn't she? (The question at the end of the statement—*didn't she?*—requires a question mark at the end of the sentence.)

Nicolas is planning to take the accounting course after work, isn't he? (Again, the question following the statement makes this an interrogative sentence. Use a question mark at the end of the sentence.)

In a Series of Questions

When a sentence contains a series of questions, the series may be joined by commas and a conjunction (like other series) and end with one question mark. Alternatively, each question may be separated from the main sentence and may have its own question mark. Examine the following examples.

Have you sent this confidential report to the president, the executive vice president, and the treasurer? (The items in the series are joined by commas and the conjunction *and.* The sentence ends with a question mark.)

Have you sent this confidential report to the president? the executive vice president? the treasurer? (Each item in the series is separated from the main sentence, and each ends with its own question mark. Note that a lowercase letter begins each item to show that it is connected to the main sentence.)

Question Mark Pitfall

So many questions include the word *why, ask,* or *how* that some writers automatically use a question mark at the end of any sentence with one of these words. However, many sentences with *why, ask,* or *how* are simply *indirect questions*—that is, declarative sentences. Two examples are:

Ramon did not ask why the meeting had been postponed. (This statement is an indirect question. Use a period.)

Ms. Mazur asked how we intended to decrease expenses. (This is a statement, not a question.)

CHECKUP 4

Check the following sentences for any errors in the use of periods and question marks. Write *OK* if a sentence is correct.

1. Ask Jordan why the proposal is not ready?
2. When will Kareem complete his training at the Police Academy?
3. Henry knows how to use this spreadsheet program, doesn't he.
4. Pat asked Nazir how she completed the assignment so quickly?
5. The cassettes that she is looking for are in that cabinet, aren't they.
6. Doesn't Robin know that the seminar has been cancelled?
7. The manager asked how charts could be used to enhance the report?
8. Has Ms. Annau already met with the branch managers? the regional directors? the vice president of personnel?

Exclamation Points

We see many exclamation points as we read signs and advertisements: "Special Sale!" "Limited-Time Offer!" "Hurry! Place Your Order Today!" The **exclamation point** is used to show strong emotion or feeling. An exclamation point can be used after a single word or at the end of a sentence. Do *not* overuse the exclamation point! Some inexperienced writers incorrectly use two or three exclamation points at the end of a sentence for extra emphasis. One exclamation point is sufficient. Some examples are:

Congratulations! You have been named employee of the month.

We were awarded the construction contract. What great news!

Sandy, you exceeded your sales goal by 45 per cent!

Sometimes the exclamation point may replace a question mark when a question is really just a strong statement.

What happened to the fax machine! (This is worded like a question but really is an exclamation.)

Review of Key Terms

1.   What kind of sentences should end with a *period*?
2.   What is a *comma splice*? Provide an example.

Practical Application

1.   Correct any errors in the use of periods, question marks, or exclamation points. Write *OK* if a sentence is correct.
   a.   The lease must be signed by March 31, we should send it to our lawyer no later than tomorrow.
   b.   Jane is now comparing colour copiers from various manufacturers. So that she will be able to make a wise choice.
   c.   This cellular phone is not very expensive. Although it is obviously not the top-of-the-line model.
   d.   When you write to Midway Construction, be sure to ask for (1.) an itemized estimate, (2.) a breakdown of costs for parts and labour, and (3.) a schedule for completing the entire project.
   e.   Do you agree that the best suppliers are Ames Chemicals, Berg Industries, and Paulison Supply Company.
   f.   Did you ask Carla whether she has drafted the space ad that is due to the printer next week.
   g.   Brian asked Carla whether she has drafted the copy for the space ad.
   h.   Do you know whether we can obtain a grant for this project under Title II.?
   i.   Hyung is scheduled to return from Windsor on the 4:30 p.m. flight, isn't he.
   j.   The original purchase price was $13,500.00, but strong competition has resulted in a lower price of only $11,750.00.
   k.   Should we submit bids for the Blue Hills Shopping Centre? the West Street Mall? the Fairview Mall?
   l.   Selwyn can sign vouchers for up to $500, Mohamed can sign vouchers for up to $750.
   m.   Our financial adviser suggested the following alternatives. For investing in a conservative manner:
      a.   Canada Savings Bonds
      b.   Guaranteed Investment Certificates
      c.   Long-term bank deposits
   n.   Collette is going to Halifax next week, isn't she.
   o.   Steven wants to know whether the database has been updated?
2.   Correct any errors in the following sentences. Write *OK* if a sentence is correct.
   a.   Are you certain that these expenses will be approved.
   b.   Esther appreciated us helping her with her annual report.

c. Many customers asked whether these are also on sale?

d. There's only two or three original windows left in the building.

e. With the 10 per cent discount, this copier will sell for $950.00.

f. Please ask the Purchasing Department to send new forms to Gail and I.

g. Tabulating all these responses was more hard than we expected.

h. To make sure that we would be finished by the deadline, we divided all the invoices between Marie, Jason, and me.

i. Sometimes Sheldon acts like he were the president of this company instead of an assistant manager.

j. Patrice, do not place these orders without your supervisor approves them.

k. We discontinued the sale. When we depleted our inventory.

l. You should sign up for this seminar now, only eight people will be accepted.

m. We predict that this advertisement will be more effective than any advertisement we ever placed.

n. Usually, Celeste don't like to take an early lunch hour.

o. Jessica is confident that she and her staff will exceed their sales goals, her group is only about $100 000 short of its target.

p. As you can see, each customers' account is carefully checked before a monthly statement is mailed.

q. Advance copys of the annual report will be delivered today.

r. Have you called suppliers in Montreal, in Quebec City, in Ottawa?

s. Jeanne or Greta are going to organize the meeting.

t. Only one of the supervisors were against the idea of reducing our total production for the next month.

3. Find and read an article with information about the stock market. Then, write a group response that summarizes the article and includes the following end marks—period, question mark, and exclamation point.

TEAMWORK

Editing Practice

Are We in Agreement?   Correct any agreement errors in the following sentences.

1. As you know, every consumer has the right to request a copy of his credit history.

2. On the shelf in Ms. Herzig's office is the latest studies on industrial pollution.

3. One of the studies contains an analysis of the environmental impact of the proposed factory.

4. All tax records prepared before 1985 has been discarded, according to Ms. Yamoto.

5. The number of customers who asked for more information on the new credit accounts are surprisingly high.

6. The newspaper article said that some of the land have already been purchased by a major real estate developer.

7. Bill, here is the VCR and the remote-control device that you requested.

8. Every executive in the company will be able to increase their productivity after reading this helpful study.

9. Pauline said that either Marisa or Raymond have been assigned to the mailroom.

10. Dependability and initiative is important for advancement to executive positions.

Spelling Alert! Correct any misspelled words in the following excerpt.

As a valued customer of Swiss Chalet Restaurant, you are invited to take advantage of the atached coupon that allows you to bring a guest for lunch at a reduce price. Your meal will be at the regular price; your guest's meal will be at half price. Lunch is served from 11 a.m. to 2 p.m. daily. This coupon offer is good on any Monday, Tuseday, or Wednesday during Septeber.

Thank you for your continued patronage.

Discussion Points

1. What is the difference between an *indirect question* and a *direct question*?

2. Why would some sentences end with an *exclamation point* instead of a *question mark*?

Commas

Commas are not a recent creation. Their use was described in the eighth century by an English monk named Alcuin who set down certain laws of grammar: "Let them (writers) distinguish the proper sense by colons and commas...and let them see the points, each one in its due place..."

—John Tierney, *The New York Times*

Effective writers use **commas** to connect thoughts and to separate elements within sentences. This helps readers make sense of the information.

A thorough discussion of the many uses of the comma follows. Study these applications so that you will be able to use commas correctly in all forms of business writing.

In Compound Sentences

To use commas correctly in compound sentences, you need to be able to distinguish a compound sentence from a simple sentence with a compound predicate. To accomplish this, review the distinction between simple and compound sentences.

A **simple sentence** contains a subject and a verb. The subject or the verb may be compound. A simple sentence with a **compound predicate** has only one subject and a compound verb. Do *not* use a comma to separate a compound predicate. Some examples are:

Zadene moved to Charlottetown last week and started her new job with Breyer Real Estate today. (*Zadene* is the only subject for the two verbs in the compound predicate—*moved* and *started.* No comma is needed.)

The Reynolds & Sturgis Company originally planned to build a mall on the vacant lot but later decided to sell the land instead. (*Company* is the subject for the compound predicate verbs *planned* and *decided.* No comma is needed.)

A **compound sentence** has two or more independent clauses, each with a subject and a predicate. Note in the following sentences how commas are used with the coordinating conjunctions *and, but, or,* and *nor* to join two

▆ Key Terms

▶ comma

▶ simple sentence

▶ compound predicate

▶ compound sentence

▶ series

▶ semicolon

▶ introductory words

▶ introductory phrases

▶ infinitive phrases

▶ participial phrases

Key Terms

- prepositional phrases
- introductory clauses
- dependent clause
- main clause
- interrupting elements
- parenthetical elements
- explanatory elements
- appositives
- consecutive adjectives
- direct address

independent clauses. (The "fanboys" mnemonic introduced in Chapter 5 will help you remember the co-ordinating conjunctions—*for, and, nor, but, or, yet,* and *so.*)

Zadene moved to Charlottetown last week, *and* she started her new job with Breyer Real Estate today. (The comma and the conjunction *and* join two independent clauses.)

The Reynolds and Sturgis Company originally planned to build a mall on the vacant lot, *but* it later decided to sell the land instead. (The comma and the conjunction *but* join two independent clauses.)

Erin will take a refresher course in spreadsheets this semester, *or* she will take a course in database management. (The comma and the conjunction *or* join two independent clauses.)

Hans does not plan to apply for the position, *nor* does he plan to transfer to another office. (The comma and the conjunction *nor* join two independent clauses.)

To help distinguish between a simple sentence with a compound predicate and a compound sentence, use the following:

Simple sentence with compound predicate

> subject + verb + verb

> *Tim finished* the analysis on time but *forgot* to report his results.

Compound sentence

> subject + verb + (comma and connecting word) + subject + verb

> *Tim finished* the analysis on time, *but he forgot* to report his results.

A discussion of exceptions to the use of commas in compound sentences follows.

No Comma Between Very Short Clauses

When the independent clauses are very short, the comma is usually omitted. Read the following examples aloud; as you do so, note that each sentence sounds "natural" without a pause before the conjunction.

Shirley wrote the memo and Leo revised it. (The two independent clauses are short; the comma may be omitted.)

Jeff Belden attended the conference and Larry joined him there. (Again, two short independent clauses do not require a comma.)

Semicolon to Avoid Possible Misreading

If either clause of a compound sentence already contains one or more commas, a misreading may result. To avoid misreadings, use a semicolon, not a comma, to separate the clauses. An example is:

This next benefits meeting will cover changing dental plans, submitting claims for reimbursement, and establishing flexible working hours; and a company-sponsored child-care centre will be the topic of next month's meeting. (The semicolon provides a stronger break and prevents misreading a company-sponsored child-care centre as part of the preceding series.)

When the two independent clauses in a compound sentence are very long, the brief pause of a comma to separate them may not be strong enough. It may be better to rewrite very long clauses as separate sentences. An example is:

The findings of our research staff clearly point to the possible effectiveness of polyvinyl chloride (PVC) as a replacement for the more expensive materials we are now using, and we fully support the need to fund further research to explore the uses of PVC for our entire line of products. (The items are long clauses. An alternative is to write these long clauses as independent sentences.)

CHECKUP 1

Correct these sentences. Write *OK* it a sentence is correct.

1. Mike declined the job offer, but Gail accepted it.
2. Curtis recommended Yvette, Ivan, and Samantha, and Sean recommended Sharon, Theresa, and Vince.
3. Bonnie does not plan to join the company softball team, nor does she plan to rejoin the bowling league this year.
4. Jennifer will be promoted to district manager next month but her successor has not yet been chosen.
5. Wendy will retire in December, but will work part-time next year.
6. I received the customer's e-mail this morning, and immediately sent a response.
7. We should revise these estimates, or we should request up-to-date bids.
8. Henri drove, and Paulette slept.

In a Series

A **series** consists of three or more items in a sequence. As you will see in the following examples, the items may be words, phrases, or clauses.

Michelle took additional courses in accounting, statistics, economics, and public administration. (In a series of words, a comma is used between the words and *before* the conjunction.)

Many of our employees do volunteer work in hospitals, at homeless shelters, and for various charitable organizations. (In a series of phrases, a comma is used between the phrases and before the conjunction.)

Gregory will be moving to our Edmonton Office, Anne will take his place at head-quarters, and Rhonda will become Anne's assistant. (In a series of independent clauses, a comma is used between the clauses and before the conjunction.)

When Etc. Ends a Series

Etc. means "and so forth." Never write *and etc.* because that would mean "*and and* so forth"!

When *etc.* ends a series, use a comma before and after it unless *etc.* ends the sentence. Some examples are:

According to the agenda, we will meet the visitors, take them to lunch, show them the plant, *etc.* (Use a comma before *etc.* No comma is used after *etc.* because *etc.* ends the sentence.)

We will meet the visitors, take them to lunch, show them the plant, *etc.,* according to the agenda. (When *etc.* ends a series part way through a sentence, use a comma before and after *etc.*)

Semicolons Instead of Commas in a Series

When the items in a series are long clauses or if the items already contain commas, use a **semicolon** to provide a stronger break between items.

We should like you to do the following: arrange our goods into shipping units; transport them to the place where they are to be consumed; store them there if storage is necessary; and obtain a signed receipt showing the time of delivery and the condition of the goods. (A long pause between items is helpful to the reader.)

During the first six months of this year, Jack Shapiro attended sales meetings in Kamloops, British Columbia; Red Deer, Alberta; Moose Jaw, Saskatchewan; and Portage la Prairie, Manitoba. (Using semicolons to separate the parts of the series enables the reader to grasp the meaning immediately.)

When Not to Use Commas

Do not use commas in the following situations.

At the End of a Series. Do not use a comma after the last item in a series, that is, the item following the conjunction, unless the sentence structure requires a comma. Only the items preceding the conjunction are separated by commas. Some examples are:

Luigi, Lisa, and Carl will coordinate the orientation sessions for new employees. (There is no comma after *Carl,* the last item in the series.)

Luigi, Lisa, and Carl, who are trainers in our home office, will coordinate the orientation sessions. (The comma after *Carl* is required because of the interrupting clause beginning with *who.*)

With Repeated Conjunctions. When the conjunction is repeated between each item in the series, no commas are needed. An example is:

You may send us the contract by Priority Post or private courier or fax. (Because the conjunction *or* is repeated between each item in the series, no commas are needed.)

In Certain Company Names. Write a company's name exactly as it is printed on the company's letterhead. Some companies write their names *without* a comma before *and*; others use a comma. Follow the company preference. In all cases, no comma is used before an ampersand (&). Some examples are:

Balbach, McIntyre and Bridgeman bid on the contract. (Follows the official company name precisely.)

D'Amato, Weisel & Wilkes is an excellent consulting firm. (Do not use a comma before an ampersand.)

CHECKUP 2

Check the following sentences for any errors in the use of commas. Write *OK* if a sentence is correct.

1. Every morning Ralph arrives early to make coffee, turn the copier on, water the plants, and etc.

2. Bartlett, Starr, & Haney received the BranFoods national advertising account.

3. Appliances, furniture, hardware, etc. will be on sale next week at all our outlet stores.

4. Paolo will order all the supplies, Carmen will print and mail the agendas and Barbara will handle registration.

5. You can send us the report by fax, modem, or messenger or if you prefer, you can send it by overnight express.

6. Please tell Seth, Andrea and Maurice to submit their reports by Friday, and ask them to send copies to Ms. Dodaro.

7. Excellence Press prints all our brochures, pamphlets, and direct-mail advertising; catalogues, however, are printed by the Zippy Printing Company.

8. You can use this bag as a purse, a backpack or an overnight bag.

Following Introductory Words, Phrases, and Clauses

Commas follow introductory words, phrases, and clauses to provide a needed pause and thereby prevent possible misreading or confusion.

Introductory Words

Commas follow **introductory words** at the beginning of sentences or clauses. Some of the most commonly used introductory words are listed in Figure 6.1.

Note how commas are used after introductory words in the following sentences.

Naturally, we were disappointed with the results of the survey. (The introductory word *naturally* is at the beginning of the sentence. A comma follows the word.)

The survey showed that our product was the least favoured by consumers; naturally, we were disappointed with the results. (Here, the word *naturally* introduces the second clause in the sentence. Again, it is followed by a comma.)

Introductory Phrases

Commas are often needed after **introductory phrases** such as infinitive phrases, participial phrases, and prepositional phrases.

After Infinitive Phrases. An **infinitive phrase** that begins a sentence or a clause is followed by a comma unless the phrase is the subject of the sentence or clause. Some examples are:

Common Introductory Words		
consequently	moreover	obviously
finally	namely	originally
first	naturally	therefore
however	no	yes
meanwhile	now	

◀ **Figure 6.1**
Common Introductory Words
Figure 6.1 lists common introductory words.

Thinking Critically.
What is another introductory word that you commonly use in business communications?

To finish calling these clients, Jeannette will have to work overtime. (The infinitive phrase *to finish calling these clients* introduces the sentence. It modifies the subject *Jeannette.*)

To finish calling these clients is Jeannette's priority for today. (Here, the infinitive phrase is the subject of the sentence.)

After Participial Phrases. A participial phrase is always followed by a comma. Some examples are:

Waiting for the meeting to start, Joe reviewed his schedule for the week. (Use a comma after a participial phrase.)

Delayed by the heavy fog, Fiona's flight was two hours late. (Use a comma after a participial phrase.)

Do not confuse participial phrases with gerund phrases. A gerund phrase at the beginning of a sentence is always a subject while a participial phrase is always an adjective. Study the following examples and note the difference.

Controlling costs carefully is every manager's responsibility. (*Controlling* is a gerund. The gerund phrase *Controlling costs carefully* is the subject of the sentence.)

Controlling costs carefully, Claire was able to make the shop profitable in a very short time. (Here, *Controlling* is a participle—an adjective that modifies the subject, *Claire.*)

After Prepositional Phrases. Use commas after long **prepositional phrases** and prepositional phrases that contain verb forms such as gerunds. Some examples are:

For more detailed installation instructions, please call our toll-free number. (long prepositional phrase)

After securing the lucrative account, Genevieve received a promotion as well as praise from the CEO. (Note the gerund *securing* in the prepositional phrase.)

Do not use a comma if the prepositional phrase is short or if it flows directly into the main thought of the sentence. Some examples are:

By next week the new telephone system will be installed and operational. (The prepositional phrase *By next week* is short and flows directly into the sentence; therefore, no comma is required.)

On Monday I would like to leave work early. (The prepositional phrase *On Monday* is very short; therefore, no comma is required.)

Introductory Clauses

A comma is needed after an **introductory clause**, that is, a dependent clause that precedes a main clause. Note how the comma provides a necessary pause in the following example.

When Tori Amos returned from his vacation, he met with the lawyers and discussed the terms of the contract. (Use a comma after a dependent clause that precedes the main clause.)

To apply this comma rule, you must be able to identify the words and phrases that commonly begin introductory clauses. You will remember the list in Figure 6.2 better if you try using each word or phrase to introduce a clause.

Words that Begin Introductory Clauses		
after	how	though
although	if	till
as	inasmuch as	unless
as if	in case	when
as soon as	in order that	whenever
as though	otherwise	where
because	provided	whereas
before	since	wherever
even if	so that	whether
for	then	while

◀ **Figure 6.2**
Introductory Clauses
Figure 6.2 lists words that introduce clauses.

Thinking Critically.
Which word would best finish the following sentence?
If at first you don't succeed, _____ try again.

CHECKUP 3

Correct any comma errors. Write *OK* if a sentence is correct.

1. Between the close of business today and the start of business tomorrow we will have finished taking inventory.

2. As soon as orders are received they are entered into the computer and processed immediately.

3. Installing the new software, took Tom and Connie all day. omit

4. Installing the new software, Tom and Connie worked diligently all day. OK

5. We should be able to leave Regina Friday afternoon; therefore, we should arrive home by 9 p.m.

6. Unless Sherri disapproves of our plan, we will be able to begin next Monday.

7. To have lunch in the company cafeteria visitors must present a pass.

8. Unless you file a claim within 30 days you will not get your money back.

9. To succeed in this business, requires persistence, determination, and drive. omit

10. Mr. Andersen gave his consent to the restructuring plan; he approved moreover hiring two more people for our team.

With a Dependent Clause Following a Main Clause

We have already seen that a **dependent clause** preceding a main clause is always followed by a comma. An example is:

As we agreed at our last directors' meeting, we will review the commission rates for full-time and part-time sales representatives. (Place a comma after a dependent clause preceding a main clause.)

But when the dependent clause *follows* the **main clause**, use a comma only if the dependent clause offers *non*essential information—information not needed to complete the meaning. As you read the following examples, note how the dependent clauses differ.

We will review the commission rates for full-time and part-time sales representatives, as we agreed at our last directors' meeting. (The words *as we agreed at our last directors' meeting* are certainly not critical to understanding the meaning of the sentence. They merely provide extra information. A comma separates nonessential words.)

Ms. Stavas will meet with each department manager after she has made her final decision regarding staffing. (No comma here because the clause *after she has made her final decision regarding staffing* is important to the meaning of the sentence. It provides *essential* information, *not* additional information. It tells precisely when *Ms. Stavas will meet with each department manager.*)

When writing such sentences, you will know the meaning you intend and will have an easier job of deciding whether a comma is needed or not.

With Interrupting, Parenthetical, and Explanatory Elements

Interrupting Elements

Interrupting elements do not provide essential information. Use commas to set off interrupters.

The company's sales performance, naturally, has delighted the stockholders. (Commas set off the interrupting word *naturally.*)

Each department's proposed budget, consequently, can be increased because of the significant increase in profits during the last fiscal year. (Again, commas set off the interrupter *consequently.*)

Parenthetical Elements

As we speak and write, we add words, phrases, and clauses within sentences to emphasize a contrast, express an opinion, soften a harsh statement, qualify or amend the meaning, and so on. These **parenthetical elements** should be set off by commas. Some examples are:

Any change in these schedules, as I see it, must be approved by the staff committee. (The parenthetic expression *as I see it* is not essential to the meaning of the sentence and is set off by commas.)

The text of the annual report, but not the appendices, has been approved by the executive committee. (The parenthetic statement separated by commas emphasizes the contrast.)

Explanatory Elements

Additional information that is not essential to the meaning of the sentence is set off by commas. To determine if information is nonessential, read the sentence without the **explanatory element**. If the sentence makes sense, use commas to set off the additional information.

The systems analyst, suspecting a virus in the computer network, issued an advisory memo to all network users. (Read this sentence aloud. As you do so, note how you would pause at the beginning and at the end of the participial phrase *suspecting a virus in the computer network.* Use commas to set off such explanatory elements. Also note that the sentence makes sense if you omit the information between the commas.)

Dr. Hoverman, who developed this vaccine, works at Pharma Research. (The clause *who developed this vaccine* is set off by commas. Again, read this sentence aloud to note how you would pause before and after the explanatory element.)

Clauses that are essential are not set off by commas. An example is:

Our firm has four senior researchers. The one who developed this vaccine is Dr.

Hoverman. (In this sentence, the clause *who developed this vaccine* does not provide extra information; it specifies one of the "four senior researchers." Note that in reading this sentence aloud, you would not pause before and after the clause.)

CHECKUP 4

Are commas used correctly in the following sentences? Make any necessary corrections. Write *OK* if a sentence is correct.

1. The recruiter, who is interviewing applicants for this position is Jason Bloom.
2. Anna waiting for the call from our Kelowna office did not go out for lunch.
3. One possible alternative as we discussed yesterday is to delay this shipment until Trent & Fitch has paid its bills.
4. Cynthia Crain, who designs our brochures, met with the marketing director today.
5. The litigation lawyer, whom you should consult, is Pat Reilly.
6. The interest received but not the principal returned is subject to taxation.
7. The only person on our staff, who is a CA, is Arnold Rudolf.
8. Please order additional supplies, if the special discount is still in effect.
9. An effective alternative Jin and I think will be to postpone the production of these items until after the summer rush.
10. The department managers, but not the staff supervisors, must attend the hearing.

With Appositives and Related Constructions

The use of commas with appositives, degrees and titles, calendar dates, and province names is explained in the following discussion.

Appositives

An **appositive** is a word or a group of words that gives more information about a preceding word or phrase. When an appositive is not essential to the meaning of a sentence, the appositive is set off by comma, as shown in the following examples.

The director of corporate communications, Indira Baghwandi, is giving a seminar on desktop publishing. (The appositive, *Indira Baghwandi,* offers additional information and is set off by commas.)

The president of our company, a previous Member of Parliament, is a well-known public speaker. (The appositive, *a previous Member of Parliament,* offers additional information and is set off by commas.)

When the appositive is very closely connected with the noun that precedes it, no commas are used to set off the appositive. This occurs most often with one- or two-word appositives such as names, which are read as a unit.

My son Donald will graduate in June. (The appositive *Donald* is read as part of the unit *My son Donald,* so no commas are used. Strictly speaking, if the speaker has only one son, *Donald* could be set off by commas, since the name would not be needed to indicate *which* son, but in expressions like this, the name is considered part of the unit.)

The motivational speaker Elizabeth Thomas will open our annual meeting. (The appositive *Elizabeth Thomas* is closely connected to the noun preceding it; therefore, no commas are needed.)

The year 2005 will mark the 100th anniversary of our firm. (Here, *2005* is essential to the meaning of the sentence. It is not set off by commas.)

Degrees, Titles, and Similar Terms

Several commonly used abbreviations offer additional information about the names that precede them. For example, *M.D.* following a person's name tells that he or she is a doctor of medicine, and *Inc.* following a company name tells that the firm has been incorporated.

Abbreviations such as *M.D.*, *Ph.D.*, and *D.D.S.* are always set off by commas when they follow a person's name. Some examples are:

Allen Chang, D.D.S., is a consultant to the Acme Dental Company.

Alice O. Bruno, Ph.D., is the director of research and development at Sterling Products.

The abbreviations *Inc.* and *Ltd.* may or may not be preceded by a comma, depending on the preference of each company. Always follow the style shown on a company's letterhead. Two examples are:

Singh Enterprises, Inc. has moved to Brampton, Ontario. (*Singh Enterprises, Inc.* is the official company name.)

Ms. MacGrath works for Ross Inc. in Burnaby. (*Ross Inc.* is the official company name.)

The abbreviations *Jr.* and *Sr.* may or may not be set off with commas. Follow the preference of each individual when writing *Jr.* and *Sr.* or roman numerals after a person's name. Two examples are:

William D. Achison Jr. has been named to the Board of Directors. (Mr. Achison prefers no commas setting off *Jr.*)

Andrew Matthews, III, is the chief executive officer of Pinnacle Development. (Mr. Matthews prefers commas setting off *III* following his name.)

Note that when commas are used to set off such abbreviations as *M.D.* and *Jr.*, they are used in pairs. Do not use a single comma to set off such abbreviations unless the abbreviation appears at the end of a sentence. If the person's preference is not known, do not use commas to set off *Jr.*, *Sr.*, or roman numerals after the name.

Calendar Dates

In month-day-year dates, the year is set off with two commas. In month-year dates, the commas are omitted. Some examples are:

On February 9, 1990, we purchased the land for this office building.

In February 1990 we purchased this land.

When the day is included, it is also set off with a comma. An example is:

We purchased the land on Thursday, February 9, 1990.

Province Names

A comma is used to separate the city or town from the province and the province from the rest of the sentence. An example is:

We are opening an office in Red Deer, Alberta, next April.

CHECKUP 5

Check the following sentences for any errors in the use of commas. Write *OK* if a sentence is correct.

1. A recruiter in the Personnel Department, Martha Salinger will represent the company at the job fair tomorrow.
2. Theresa Edwards, one of our engineers, lived in Gander Newfoundland for many years.
3. During July 2000 a hurricane damaged our property in Florida.
4. Jane L. Davis, M.D., works for Doctors Without Borders.
5. Two new staff writers, Elyse Dvorak and Rick Davidovitch were recently hired by the *North Country Gazette.*
6. On December 31, 2001 our lease will expire.
7. One of our divisions Simco Chemicals has been very active in the field of pollution control.
8. Winnie Ackerman is going to London, England to visit her aunt.
9. I need a flight to Rome on Friday June 20.
10. His wife Patricia is a senior partner in a prominent law firm.

Which and *That* Clauses

Clauses that are not necessary to the meaning of a sentence should be introduced by *which* and set off by commas. Clauses that are necessary to the meaning of a sentence are introduced by *that.* They are not set off by commas. Some examples are:

Only the inventory that is damaged will be sold at a 50 per cent discount. (No commas separate a "that" clause.)

The damaged inventory, which includes VCRs and stereos, will be sold at a 50 per cent discount. (The "which" clause gives additional information and is correctly set off by commas.)

Comma Pitfalls

Here are two more comma pitfalls that trap many writers: (1) using a comma to separate a subject from its predicate, (2) using a comma to separate a verb or an infinitive from its object or complement, and (3) using a comma to separate co-ordinate adjectives.

Comma Separating Subject from Predicate

Never separate a subject from its predicate by a comma. Two examples are:

All invoices from outside vendors, must be initialed by both the supervisor and the department head. (Incorrect. No comma should separate the subject, *invoices,* from its verb, *must be initialed.*)

All invoices from outside vendors, according to the accounting manager, must be initialled by the supervisor and the department head. (Correct. Commas separate a phrase that gives additional information.)

Comma Separating Verb from Object

Never separate a verb from its object or complement with a comma. Likewise, never separate an infinitive from its complement with a comma. Two examples are:

Since 1995 Lido has been, one of the hospital's most dedicated volunteers. (Incorrect. A comma should never separate a verb from its complement.)

Most of the staff were surprised to learn, that Frank resigned yesterday. (Incorrect. A comma should never separate an infinitive from its complement.)

Comma Separating Co-ordinate Adjectives

Do not separate coordinating adjectives with a comma. An example is:

We saw two large, gray whales off the coast of Newfoundland. (Incorrect. A comma should not separate *large gray*.)

However, note that commas *are* used between consecutive adjectives. An example is:

Ralf's new car is fast, sleek, and sporty.

CHECKUP 6

Check the following sentences for any errors in the use of commas. Write *OK* if a sentence is correct.

1. Our Canada News outlet which is one of the largest in the West is our company's most profitable revenue division.
2. Environmentalists have urged customers to boycott products, that have excess packaging.
3. All cleaning products, that are listed on our Web site, may also be purchased in our retail stores.
4. This magazine which describes the work of the Humane Society is published four times a year.
5. Several employees in our Burlington office, are interested in moving to our headquarters in Oakville.
6. We are busy preparing for the annual stockholders' meeting, which is to be held at the Royal York Hotel.

With Consecutive Adjectives

When two or more adjectives come together but separately modify a noun, use a comma to separate the adjectives. To test whether the two adjectives separately modify the noun, use the word *and* between the adjectives, as shown in the following examples.

Deidre voiced her opinion in a forceful, logical way. (A comma is placed between the adjectives *forceful* and *logical.* Note that the word *and* can be used between the modifiers: in a way that is forceful *and* logical.)

Jill and Gary are the most creative, most experienced, most versatile players on our squad. (Commas are placed between the adjectives that *separately* modify the noun *players:* most creative *and* most experienced *and* most versatile.)

Note that no comma follows the last adjective in a series—that is, no comma separates the last adjective from the noun. Some examples are:

The new outpatient clinic is staffed by skilled, experienced personnel. (No comma is used to separate the last adjective, *experienced,* from the noun *personnel.*)

Olivia Baxter's unique negotiation style is her greatest attribute. (Using the word and between the modifiers *unique* and *negotiation* makes no sense. These adjectives do not separately modify the noun.)

We discussed conservative financial investments with our adviser. (You would not say "investments that are conservative and financial." Here, the adjective *financial* modifies *investments*. But the adjective *conservative* modifies the unit *financial investments*. In other words, "financial investments that are conservative.")

CHECKUP 7

Insert commas as needed between adjectives in the following sentences. Test by using the word *and* between adjectives. Write *OK* if a sentence is correct.

1. Hugh is considered a brilliant reliable ambitious Bay Street analyst.
2. Guy and Rachel received an industry award for their fascinating documentary film on toxic wastes.
3. The latest marketing research reports are available in Mr. Luciano's office.
4. Their portfolio contains solid high-yielding investments.
5. Jonas & Westerly produces lightweight thermal blankets.
6. Ms. Kane has developed a creative dedicated staff of advertising professionals.

For Omissions, with Repeated Expressions, and in Direct Address

The comma is also used to save time and words, to emphasize an important thought, and to set off names and terms in **direct address.**

Omissions

Sometimes writers can use the comma to avoid repeating words that have already been stated in the sentence. The comma makes the reader pause long enough to mentally supply the omitted words.

Effective June 15, Mr. Hard *will be in charge of* the Bennett account; Ms. Dirkins, the Hastings & Ames account; Ms. Ellison, the Barker Fertilizer account; and Mr. Donnely, the Henderson Trucking account. (Rather than repeat the words *will be in charge of* three times, the writer uses a comma after each name to indicate the omission and cause the reader to pause long enough to supply these words.)

Repeated Expressions

Repetition is one of the most effective ways to emphasize an important point. Repetitions, of course, must be planned if they are to be effective, and the repeated words must be separated by a comma.

The manual says, "Never, never guess the answer to a customer's question." (Note the comma that separates the repetition *Never, never.*)

Direct Address

In writing, when we address people directly, we set off their names (or similar terms) with commas.

As you may know, Mrs. Boudreau, this software program offers you direct on-line support.

Without your encouragement and support, Professor Ryan, I would not have graduated.

CHECKUP 8

Check the following sentences for any errors in the use of commas. Write *OK* if a sentence is correct.

1. Ms. Doyle we unanimously endorse your proposal.
2. To complete the project on time, we will have to work long long hours.
3. The Amherst office is scheduled to be audited on August 3; the Dartmouth office August 10; and the Summerside office August 17.
4. Investing in that stock is a risky risky venture!
5. We are pleased to announce that Brett & Umberto has donated $1000 to United Way; Red Deer Industries, $5000; and Northern Logging, $10 000.
6. We are glad to hear, Larry that you are revovering quickly.

In Numbers and Between Unrelated Numbers

In SI metric, do *not* use a comma to separate thousands, hundred thousands, millions, and so on, in numbers of five or more digits. Use spaces to separate long lines of digits into readable blocks of three digits. With a four-digit number, the space is unnecessary except when it appears in a column with other numbers that require spaces.

1312	12 121	2 312 100	25 000
			1 312
			26 312

When unrelated numbers are written together, use a comma to separate them.

On May 10, 847 students will graduate from our MBA program. (The comma slows down the reader and makes each number distinct.)

More Comma Pitfalls

Now that you know all the important uses of the comma with numbers, be sure to master the following principles for when *not* to use a comma with numbers.

In Numbers. Never use commas in the following numbers, regardless of the number of digits: years, page numbers, house and telephone numbers, postal code numbers, serial numbers, and decimals.

in 1991 (years)
page 1318 (page number)
RD 14315789 (serial number)
A4L 3W4 (postal code)

2718 Mountain Street (house number)
(416) 555-2184 (telephone numbers)
12.75325 (decimal)

In Weights, Capacities, and Measurements. Never use a comma to separate the parts of one weight, one capacity, or one measurement.

The videotaped presentation runs for exactly 1 hour 18 minutes 20 seconds. (No commas to separate the parts of one time measurement.)

The package weighs 2 kilograms 86 grams. (No comma to separate the parts of one weight.)

The exact distance is 4 kilometres 28 metres. (No comma to separate the parts of one distance measurement.)

CHECKUP 9

Check the following sentences for any errors in the use of commas. Write *OK* if a sentence is correct.

1. By 2007 700 new franchises will have opened across Canada.

2. Surprisingly, the question-and-answer period lasted 2 hours, 45 minutes.

3. Refer to pages 1,232 through 1,336 for a detailed explanation of how to apply for federal grants.

4. The medical supply company moved to 4,840 Crescent Avenue.

5. As you will see on Invoice 17-19853, 14 items were shipped, not 15.

6. My copy of Policy 80,876 is in my safety deposit box.

7. My cousin Mika's address is 66 Ryan Road, Toronto Ontario M4E,2E6.

8. This package weighs 2 kilograms, 25 grams.

Review of Key Terms

1. How is a *simple sentence* different from a *compound sentence*?
2. When are commas used with *appositives*?

Practical Application

1. Correct the following sentences. Write *OK* if a sentence is correct.
   a. To be well groomed and dressed appropriately, helps an applicant make a good first impression.
   b. The contract was originally to be signed on March 15; last-minute revisions however have delayed the date until March 31.
   c. When Mr. Marshall arrives we will begin the festivities.
   d. To produce a professional-looking report you may wish to include charts and other graphics.
   e. See the enclosed catalogue for our line of modern-looking, ergonomic office furniture.
   f. The budget was originally set at $9,000; actual expenses, however, totalled $12000.
   g. Without your assistance Kelly we would never have completed this project on schedule.
   h. Katherine Quinn, Ph.D. is the director of the Pharmaceutical Division.
   i. The new computer system, which Mr. Jerome ordered last week, was installed today.
   j. We were surprised to see the typographical error, that appeared in our competitor's latest brochure.
   k. This article describes the advantages of conservative investments such as government bonds, long-term deposits and managed portfolios.
   l. One of the most interesting analyses of the topic, appears in this economics journal.
   m. Charlie will send you our annual report, as soon as we receive copies from the printer.
   n. Her husband Raoul is an investment banker in Montreal.
   o. I suggest that you ask Schmidt, Davidson, & Associates to prepare an estimate.
   p. The order can be shipped by truck, or by air freight.
   q. For an incredibly low price, you can purchase a vacation package that includes airfare, accommodation, meals, and entertainment.
   r. The company's goal is to add to, not detract from the advantages it enjoys in the marketplace.
   s. The announcement, that the rival companies were merging, shocked the industry.

t. Buying Bio Tek stock according to my broker is not a sound investment.

2. Correct any errors in the following sentences. Write *OK* if a sentence is correct.

   a. Our new showroom in Westmount, Quebec is scheduled to open in September.

   b. Heat, electricity, water, and etc., are included in these utility estimates.

   c. The SuperSpeed copier is neither inexpensive, nor easy to service.

   d. Whenever an error message appears on your screen, set down and consult your software manual.

   e. By subscribing now, you can save $30 for two full years or $45 for three full years.

   f. This proposals' opening paragraph is very confusing.

   g. Is Susan Chan one of the consultants who we met in Winnipeg?

   h. Since the prices of laser printers have fell, we decided to purchaser several for our publications department.

   i. A job freeze, obviously, would hamper us from hiring the two Max's.

   j. Deborah asked us to set up a meeting for next Wednesday to discuss the different bids?

   k. Either Lisa or Raj are planning to visit the branch office in Richmond.

   l. On March 20, 1992, the cornerstone was lain for the new convention centre.

   m. Harrison P. Smith Jr., is laying in the middle of the corridor.

   n. You and her will have to decide how to share the workload.

   o. A disagreement arose between Alec, Tracy, Don, and Jerry.

   p. Several bids, as he knows, was considered, but only one matched our budget.

   q. Maeka claims that their are hidden costs that no one has considered.

   r. Isn't it apparent that their plan is not cost-effective.

   s. In my opinion, you should ask for help with this assignment.

   t. If I was in Florida, Bermuda, or Jamaica, I wouldn't be shovelling snow now.

3. Write the directions on how to operate an office machine, such as a personal computer, a copying machine, or a security system. In your directions, include sentences that use the following: a series, introductory words or phrases, an explanatory element, and an introductory clause.

Editing Practice

Test Your Skills.   You are applying for a position in a major corporation. Assume you have been asked to take an editing test. The test involves reading the following excerpt from a letter addressed to shareholders and making any necessary corrections.

Most of you have already seen the article in the January issue of *Consumer Facts* naming our software as the number one comunications software in Canada. Obviously I am exceptionally proud of this accomplishment, I congratulate our research and development staff, our marketing team and our office staff for all their hard work.

How did we accomplish this goal. We had competent, energetic dedicated people whom worked as a team. All of you should share in this recognition. Your the reason for our success. Thank you.

Discussion Points

1. How are commas like road signs?
2. If you are unsure about using a comma with interrupting, parenthetical, or explanatory elements, what could you do?

Semicolons, Colons, and Dashes

▶ **Key Terms**

▶ semicolons

▶ enumerating words

▶ explanatory words

▶ colons

▶ dashes

The dash says aloud what the parenthesis whispers. The dash is the more useful—since whispering tends to annoy—and will remain useful only if not overused.

—Sheridan Baker, *The Practical Stylist*

This section discusses three marks of punctuation that are used *within* sentences—semicolons, colons, and dashes. These punctuation marks enable the writer to guide the reader through the message. At the same time, they enable the writer to add variety and interest to the message. Each mark has its own specific function.

Semicolons

Semicolons are intended to make the reader pause; by providing timing cues, they guide the reader in understanding the message clearly. **Semicolons** are used (1) in place of a co-ordinating conjunction to join independent clauses, (2) before an introductory word that begins the second independent clause in a sentence, and (3) before explanatory or enumerating words.

In Place of a Conjunction to Join Independent Clauses

In a compound sentence two or more independent clauses are usually connected by a comma or commas and one or more co-ordinating conjunctions.

Thea competed her degree in pyhsical therapy in April, and she began working at Hamilton Medical Centre in May. (This sentence is a compound sentence; it has two independent clauses connected by a comma and the conjunction *and*.)

The conjunction and comma in a compound sentence may be omitted, and a semicolon may be used to replace them.

Thea completed her degree in physical therapy in April; she began working at Hamilton Medical Centre in May. (Here, a semicolon joins the two independent clauses, replacing the comma and the conjunction.)

Figure 6.3 ▶
Introductory Linking Words

Introductory Linking Words	
accordingly	however
again	indeed
also	moreover
besides	nevertheless
consequently	otherwise
furthermore	therefore

Before a Second Clause Starting with an Introductory Word

In some compound sentences, the second independent clause starts with an introductory word such as in Figure 6.3.

Our company has announced a significant profit; consequently, our shares have risen in value. (The second clause begins with the introductory word *consequently.*)

In such sentences, use a semicolon before the introductory word that introduces the second independent clause. The semicolon provides the necessary pause between the independent clauses, and the introductory word provides a connection between the two clauses.

Many of our guest made reservations before the special offer was introduced; nevertheless, we will give them the discount. (The semicolon separates the two independent clauses, and the introductory word *nevertheless* signals the reader to contrast the two clauses.)

This bond offers a 7 per cent after-tax return; consequently, we are increasing our total investment. (Again, the semicolon separates the two independent clauses and tells the reader to pause. The introductory word *consequently* establishes a specific relationship between the two clauses; it shows that the second statement is a result of the first statement.)

Note that the introductory word is not always the *first* word in the second clause. Remember that the semicolon belongs between two independent thoughts, regardless of where the introductory word is placed.

Many of our guest made reservations before the special offer was introduced; we are willing, *nevertheless,* to give them the discount.

This bond offers a 7 per cent after-tax return; we are, *consequently,* increasing our total investment.

Before Explanatory or Enumerating Words

Use a semicolon before such terms as *for example, for instance,* and *that is* when they introduce an independent clause, an enumeration (**enumerating words**), or an explanation that is incidental to the meaning of the rest of the sentence (**explanatory words**). What is an incidental explanation? This means that the independent clause expands on the previous clause which comes before the semicolon, but the first independent clause does not lead us to anticipate this additional information. Therefore, the explanation in the second clause is incidental information.

Elena is seeking to advance her career; for example, she has registered for two economics courses at the university. (*for example* introduces an independent clause)

Raymond is now looking at possible ways to cut expenses; for instance, leasing rather than buying delivery vans, using less expensive cartons and packing materials, and buying in larger quantities. (*for instance* introduces an enumeration)

List units of measurement as abbreviations; that is, 12 m, 8 cm, and 15 mm. (*that is* introduces an explanation)

CHECKUP 1

Check the following sentences for any errors in the use of semicolons. Write *OK* if a sentence is correct.

1. I will be attending a conference next week, however, I will be answering my voice mail.

2. In the summer, we manufacture our winter line, in the winter, we manufacture our summer apparel.

3. The new policy states that we must request at least three estimates for such projects, accordingly, we have asked four contractors to bid on this job.

4. The company reimburses employees for job-related courses; all employees are eligible.

5. Ms. Atwood's lecture on Canadian writers was interesting and informative, indeed, the local newspapers called it "fascinating"!

6. The board of directors has decided to open another factory, the new one may be located in Moncton.

7. Vanessa will be promoted to office manager next month, we expect, therefore, to see many changes in procedures in the future.

8. We cancelled the order because we have not been happy with the service from Premier Printers, besides, we already have an oversupply of brochures and posters.

Colons

Colons make readers pause and take note of what follows.

Colons Before Listed Items

When an expression such as *the following, as follows, this, these,* or *thus* is used to introduce a list of items, it is often followed by a colon. The list may follow on the same line as the colon, or it may start on a new line.

Our meeting next Wednesday will cover these topics: (1) marketing strategies for next year, (2) the advertising and promotion budget, and (3) expansion of our client base.

Our meeting next Wednesday will cover these topics:

1. marketing strategies for next year

2. the advertising and promotion budget

3. expansion of our client base

Sometimes the words *the following, as follows,* and so on, do not directly lead into the list; for example, an "interrupting" sentence appears between the lead-in sentence and the list. In such cases, use a period, not a colon.

We have amended the course requirements. The new requirements are as follows. They may be completed in any order.

1. Submit Form 470A.

2. Meet with your supervisor.

3. Request an examination date.

(A period, not a colon, is used after *as follows* because the actual list does not follow directly. A sentence separates the lead-in *as follows* and the actual list.)

If a list of items is preceded by an introductory clause that does not express a complete thought, do not use a colon to separate the clause from the list.

Our computers always contain internal modems, CD-ROM drives, and built-in Internet access. (No colon is needed before the list of items since the clause *Our computers always contain* is not a complete thought.)

Colons Instead of Semicolons

You already have learned that semicolons are used before such expressions as *for example* and *that is* when these expressions introduce independent clauses, enumerations, and explanations that are incidental to the rest of the sentence. However, when you are led to anticipate or expect an explanation or enumeration, a colon is used instead of a semicolon.

Karl gave two good reasons for postponing our decision: namely, a new CEO will be appointed next month, and the budget has not been finalized. (The statement *Karl gave two good reasons for postponing our decision* leads us to anticipate the two reasons to be given next.)

Colons to Emphasize

Writers use colons most often to emphasize important thoughts or words.

Marianne quickly pointed out the most important factor: convenience. (The colon provides special emphasis to *convenience.*)

Remember: Beginning Monday, all employees must use photo ID badges to enter the laboratory. (More emphatic than "Please try to remember that beginning Monday…")

Capitalizing After Colons

Capitalize the first word following a colon if (1) it begins a complete sentence requiring special emphasis or (2) it begins a sentence stating a formal rule.

The salary adjustment applies to two groups of employees: part-time employees and commission employees. (not a sentence; the first word is not capitalized)

Peter stated a good reason for accepting the proposal: It will increase profits. (The first word is capitalized because the sentence requires special emphasis.)

The first step is the most important: Create an outline for your report. (The first word is capitalized because the sentence states a formal rule.)

CHECKUP 2

Check the following sentences for any errors in the use of colons. Write *OK* if a sentence is correct.

1. The changes in benefits affect these areas, medical insurance, dental coverage, and maternity leave.

2. When you submit your assignment, follow this procedure. Sign and date the attached form.

3. We finally discovered why the messenger had not arrived: He went to the wrong address.

4. Claudia gave three reasons for hiring Matthias. Namely, experience, enthusiasm, and communication skills.

5. Only two people in our division were invited to the board meeting: My supervisor and Mannon Vennat.

6. Check your document for spelling errors: use the spellcheck feature.

Dashes

Dashes share some of the features of semicolons and of colons: All three make the reader pause—but dashes do so more forcefully. Compare, for example, the differences in impact of the punctuation in each of the following examples. Notice how the dash provides greater impact than either the semicolon or the colon.

Your Internet advertising will bring you the greatest return if you post ads on UniversalNet; this Internet service is the one most used by consumers worldwide. (This is a good sentence, but not a forceful one.)

For the best return on your advertising dollar, do this: Buy ads on UniversalNet, the most widely used Internet provider in the world. (This is a better sentence. It is more forceful.)

Your Internet ads will bring you the greatest return if you post them on Universal-Net—the Internet service most used by consumers worldwide. (The dash snaps off the main thought and thereby adds power to the rest of the message. This is the most forceful of the three sentences.)

The semicolon provides the needed pause between clauses. The colon provides more than a pause: It promises that something important will follow. The dash goes even further by drawing special attention to what follows the dash. Therefore, the dash makes the third example the strongest of the three.

For Forceful Summarizing and Forceful Repetition

In your writing you may wish to summarize the main points of your message to make sure that your readers remember these key points. Repeating a key point is another technique that you can use to make a stronger impression on your readers. The same is true when you are speaking. When you are summarizing or repeating main points, use a dash to separate the summary or the repetition from the rest of the sentence.

Challenging games, helpful business programs, educational software—all are available at the CompuCentre nearest you. (The dash provides forceful summarizing.)

Remember to get all your computer needs from CompuCentre—CompuCentre, where we keep you and your computer needs in mind. (Forceful repetition. Here, the writer deliberately repeats the most important part of the message—the store's name.)

With Afterthoughts

To add variety to their writing, to arouse the reader's curiosity, to soften a statement that might otherwise offend, to provide special emphasis—for all these reasons, good writers *plan* their afterthoughts.

Our Labour Day sale will surely save you money—and offer you some exciting *un*advertised specials! (to provide variety in writing style and to arouse the reader's curiosity)

Of course, we wish that we could send you a free copy of our latest software as you requested—but company policy limits free copies to educational institutions. (to soften a refusal)

This catalogue is sent only to our preferred customers—no one else receives one! (to reemphasize a statement)

CHECKUP 3

Add dashes where needed. Write *OK* if a sentence is correct.

1. Fine restaurants, department stores, art galleries these are among the many places where you will enjoy using your new SuperCard.
2. Our company is unable to take advantage of your discount offer at least for now.
3. Complete and mail the enclosed card for your free sample—but don't delay.
4. Our reorganization plans seem to be taking shape but more about this later.
5. The complete set of CDs, the CD player, the instruction booklet all are yours if you order before May 31.

Punctuating Words Set Off by Dashes

Use dashes to set off words at the end of a sentence or within a sentence.

At the End of a Sentence.   When you want to set off words at the end of a sentence, use one dash before the words to be set off; a period, question mark, or exclamation point then ends the sentence.

This office chair has several features not usually found at this low price—arm rest, castors, and backrest adjustment. (The dash precedes the words to be set off; then a period ends this declarative sentence.)

Note that no punctuation is used with the dash unless an abbreviation or quotation precedes the dash. No punctuation ever follows the dash.

The contract was awarded to Motion Inc.—Ms. Forman approved the bid. (The period before the dash belongs with the abbreviation.)

Within a Sentence.   To set off words within a sentence, two dashes are needed. Again, no punctuation is used with the first dash unless an abbreviation or quotation precedes the dash. The second dash may have a question mark or an exclamation point *before* it, but only if the words set off require a question mark or an exclamation point.

Our new Director of Personnel—have you met her?—will join us for lunch. (The dashes set off a question; thus a question mark precedes only the second dash.)

Fatima Vahed won—for the third consecutive year!—the company golf trophy. (The words set off by dashes require an exclamation point.)

Many sales representatives in our district—Ted Kyowski, Harry Cheng, and Lisa Zebrowski are among them—have suggested changes in the incentive compensation plan. (no period before the second dash)

Note also that the first word after an opening dash is not capitalized even if the words between the dashes constitute a sentence.

CHECKUP 4

Check the following sentences for any erros in the use of dashes. Write *OK* if a sentence is correct.

1. Please send these files to Ms. Rosario—she's still in Vancouver, isn't she—before she leaves for Calgary.

2. The doors will open on Monday at precisely 9 a.m.—but I suggest that you arrive no later than 8:45 a.m.

3. It will probably be Glen and Danny—do you know them?—who will build the new facility.

4. Service, dependability, fair prices,—these are the reasons for dealing with O'Connell Business Systems.

5. After she won last year's award—there was a $5,000 cash prize.—she travelled in Europe for two weeks.

6. Friendly people, reasonable prices, expert skiing facilities—these are some of the reasons the Mountainview Inn is so popular.

Review of Key Terms

1. Why might a *semicolon* be preferred over other punctuation in a compound sentence?
2. When is it appropriate to use a *dash*?

Practical Application

1. Correct any errors in the following sentences. Write *OK* if a sentence is correct.

   a. In long-term international trade transactions, these are the three major problem areas for exporters (1) losses, (2) delayed payments, and (3) political risks.

   b. Here is the new policy: accept no credit cards for purchases under $25.

   c. The manager of our Sydney office is Rosie De Manno, the manager of our Charlottetown office is John Theme.

   d. A number of the employees polled were in favour of the four-day workweek, however, the majority favoured keeping our present system.

   e. Clothing from Milan, leather goods from Florence, foods from Naples,—these were among the items imported this week.

   f. The rule is clear: smoking is prohibited on the airplane.

   g. The following changes in the insurance plan will become effective January 1: Note that employees will not pay extra for the additional coverage.

   h. The aluminum screens were due from the manufacturer on June 12, however, the recent strike delayed the delivery.

   i. Our newest model is temporarily out of stock—all other models are in inventory.—but we will have more after Friday.

   j. Three specialty stores—a cheese shop, an art supply store, and a bookstore—have signed leases for space in the new mall.

   k. Rita Zekas is a dynamic speaker,—dynamic and very informative.

   l. Subscribe today to make sure that you hear the latest news on: interest rates, the bond market, stock prices, and much more.

   m. The Fitness Centre—have you ever visited it—has the most up-to-date equipment.

   n. The original bylaws were approved on November 11, however, they were later amended.

   o. The original bylaws were approved on November 11, they were, however, later amended.

   p. Remember: employees entering the restricted area must have security clearance.

   q. At first the bank offered us a low interest rate—wasn't it under 4 per cent—before we negotiated better terms.

r. The Newtech Company has a virtual monopoly on these lower-priced projectors; the Somoto Company has a virtual monopoly on the higher-priced projectors.

s. Unfortunately, tickets are no longer available for the May 3 performance, more tickets may become available, however, if there are cancellations.

t. When we heard the rumour, both Maxine and I had the same reaction, no comment!

2. Correct any errors in the following sentences. Write *OK* if a sentence is correct.

a. The final copy of the long-term lease will be ready, according to Ms. Sanford, within one weeks' time.

b. Do you know whether the person who you spoke with is Maria Chu, the head of the department?

c. Within the next six months or so, there should be opportunities for May and I to transfer to the Halifax office.

d. Mr. D'Ambois, here is the revised statistics that you requested this morning.

e. Kathy said that we'll call a taxi whenever your ready to leave for the airport.

f. Any employee who wants to apply for a job listed on the bulletin board should leave their name with Ms. Chen in the Personnel Department.

g. As you probably know, Romulo Fernandez is one of those accountants who insists on meticulous record-keeping.

h. Most of the investment analysts in this department prefer this new computer system.

i. Kenneth reminded us not to mail them cheques until Ms. Dhalival has approved each one.

j. Beside her small condominium in Victoria, Dorothy owns a home in Arizona.

k. It was obvious that Pamela couldn't hardly wait to return home after her three-week tour of our overseas offices.

l. Did Dominic say that he plans on beginning his draft of the proposal this weekend?

m. Yes, Winston already seen Mrs. Keto about the revisions in the advertising copy.

n. Why don't James or Hilda head the committee meeting in Sylvia's absence?

o. We returned all the damaged merchandise to the manufacturer, the rest of the order was sent to our warehouse.

p. There's still extra catalogues in the supply room if you should need them, Carlotta.

q. We do not accept credit cards for purchases under $15. Because it is not profitable for us to do so.

r. The estimate, in our opinion, was certainly reasonable, in fact, it was only 5 per cent over the price we paid two years ago.

s. We will lease cars from O'Connell Industry—the monthly cost is only $175 a vehicle.—as soon as we get official approval from our corporate headquarters.

t. Vito will sure be happier in his new position.

3. Find an article in a professional journal of your choice. Look for use of the semicolon, colon, and dash. For each mark, discuss which rule is being implemented. Are the punctuation marks used correctly? If not, state what changes should be made, and why. Do you find an overuse of these punctuation marks? Do they aid in reading difficult material?

TEAMWORK

Editing Practice

Using Business Vocabulary.   Fill in each missing word with the correct word from the list below.

a. allocated
b. productivity
c. eliminate
d. foreign
e. debit
f. grievance
g. itemize
h. permissible
i. persuasive
j. resources
k. outsourcing

1. Together, the union and management representatives established a (?) committee to hear employees' complaints.

2. A credit card charges purchases to your account; a (?) card takes money from your account.

3. According to tax regulations, it is not (?) to deduct commuting expenses.

4. Because we do not have the (?) to complete this complex assignment in such a short time, we are (?) the work.

5. Be sure to (?) the cost of each computer before sending the order to the Purchasing Department.

6. Our vice president is now exploring opportunities to expand our (?) trade.

7. Everyone who works with Bob Kline knows how (?) he can be!

8. The total expense dollars were carefully (?) by the committee.

9. To process orders faster, we are now studying ways to (?) unnecessary, time-consuming steps in the handling of the telephone and mail orders.

10. Clearly, the analysis shows that the new workstations will increase our overall (?).

Using Your Computer.   As a business writer, you are asked to supply a synonym for each of the italicized words below. Use a thesaurus (hard copy or software) to help select these synonyms.

1. The board is *aware,* of course, of our consolidation strategies.
2. Bernice was *truthful* in describing the problems we are now facing.
3. A business worker cannot *shirk* his or her responsibilities.
4. Wilfred was indeed *generous* in sharing the credit with his staff.
5. Ted Sylvester has had *intermittent* problems in getting along with the research staff.
6. Several of these concessions will *mitigate* the present strain between management and labour.

Discussion Points

1. How do colons prepare a reader for enumerations?
2. Colons are used in other situations than those listed in the text. What are they?

Quotation Marks, Parentheses, and Apostrophes

Every quotation contributes something to the stability or enlargement of the language.

—Samuel Johnson, *Dictionary of the English Language*

Quotation marks serve primarily to tell the reader the exact words written or spoken by someone, but they also have other important uses. Parentheses share some (but not all) of the uses of commas and dashes. Apostrophes have one common use besides indicating ownership.

Knowing how to correctly use these three marks of punctuation will add to your written communication skills.

Quotation Marks

The common uses of quotation marks are described and illustrated in the following discussion.

For Direct Quotations

To indicate the *exact* words—a **direct quotation**—that someone has written or spoken, use quotation marks. In the following examples, note how commas, semicolons, colons, and periods are used together with quotation marks.

Ms. Ornette said, "Sam and I are taking a class in money management." (A comma precedes the direct quotation.)

"Sam and I are taking a class in money management," Ms. Ornette said. (A comma ends the quotation, separating it from the explanatory words that follow the quotation.)

"Sam and I," Ms. Ornette said, "are taking a class in money management." (Note how *two* commas are used to separate the interruption, *Ms. Ornette said.* The quotation marks still enclose the speaker's *exact* words.)

Ms. Ornette said: "Sam and I are taking a class in money management. We feel that we are not saving and investing enough of our salaries. In looking at our future, we saw that we will need to send two children to college and to finish paying for our home. Without planning and executing the plan, we will not be able to achieve our goals." (Use a colon before a long quotation, including a quotation of more than one sentence.)

"Sam and I are taking a class in money management," Ms. Ornett said. "We feel that we are…" (Note that the interrupting expression is separated from the exact words of the speaker by a comma and a period.)

Remember that *indirect* quotations (restatements of a person's exact words) are not enclosed in quotation marks. Indirect quotations are often introduced by the word *that.*

She said that they were taking a course in money management. (This example is an *indirect* quotation.)

For Quotations Within Quotations

Use single quotation marks for words quoted within other quoted material.

Mr. Chung asked, "Did she say '16 days' or '60 days'?" (Note the position of the question mark: It is *outside the single quotation mark* but *inside* the double quotation mark because the question mark belongs to the entire sentence.)

"In my opinion, this spreadsheet program is certainly not 'user-friendly,'" said Martina. (A final comma is placed inside both the single and the double quotation marks.)

Martina said, "In my opinion, this spreadsheet is certainly not 'user-friendly.'" (A period that ends a quotation is also placed inside both the single and the double quotation marks.)

For Definitions, Special Expressions, Unfamiliar Terms, Translations, and Slang

Use quotation marks to enclose definitions and special expressions following such phrases as *known as, marked,* and *signed.*

In computer terminology, GUI means "graphical user interface." (Use quotation marks for definitions.)

Boxes marked "Handle With Care" usually contain breakable objects. (Use quotation marks for special expressions following the word "marked.")

Note: Words introduced by *so-called* do not require quotation marks since *so-called* itself provides them with sufficient emphasis.

Also, use quotation marks for unfamiliar terms and for translations.

The illustration below shows a "light pen," which is used to read bar codes. (quotation marks for unfamiliar terms)

Par avion is simply the French term for "by airmail." (quotation marks for translations)

Slang may be deliberately used to add punch to a message, to attract attention, or to make a point. Such uses should be limited. Use quotation marks to enclose a slang expression, a funny comment, or a grammatical error. Note that instead of quotation marks, italics or underlining is now commonly used with definitions and special expressions.

There are only two selling days left in the month, but Tony Rella says the sales contest "ain't over yet!" (quotation marks for intentional use of a grammatical error)

The city editor said to "kill" the investigative report on contract fixing. (quotation marks for a slang expression)

CHECKUP 1

Check the following sentences for any errors in the use of quotation marks and /or associated punctuation. Write *OK* if a sentence is correct.

1. "The new catalogue will be distributed to customers by April 11," said Victor.
2. "The new catalogue, said Victor, will be distributed to customers by April 11."
3. "Magda will attend only the morning session, announced Mr. Caruso, because she must meet an important client in the afternoon."
4. Mr. Caruso announced, "Magda will attend only the morning session because she must meet an important client in the afternoon."
5. We concluded that the so-called "window of opportunity" is not open after all.
6. We marked all the cartons "Fragile," of course.
7. Graham said, "Mark all the cartons 'Handle With Care.'"
8. The cheque was signed Barbara Myers, but the teller said that the signature did not match with the signature on file.

For Certain Titles

Use quotation marks for the titles that represent only part of a complete published work—for example, parts of a book such as titles of chapters, sections, or topics; titles of articles in a magazine or newspaper; and titles of conference themes, essays, and short poems. (The titles of complete published works are italicized.) An example is:

She wrote "The Electronic Message," which appeared in October's issue of *Modern Workplace.* (quotation marks for article title)

In the preceding example, note that while the article title is in quotation marks, the title of the magazine is in italics. In addition, book titles, titles of newspapers, booklets, long poems, plays, operas, and movies are also printed in italics.

His new book, *Customer Relationships,* was favourably reviewed in *The Globe and Mail.* (Italics are used for book title and for newspaper name.)

This book, *Securing a Sound Financial Future,* contains a chapter entitled "Bonds: Safe Investments for Unstable Times," which I highly recommend. (Use quotation marks for chapter title; use italics for book title.)

Note that while chapter titles are enclosed in quotation marks, other book parts are not. Words such as *preface, index, glossary, introduction,* and *appendix* are not enclosed in quotation marks. They are capitalized only when they refer to a specific part within the same book.

Dr. Nagi, our economics professor, wrote the preface to the enclosed volume as well as Chapter 7, "Analyzing Trends." (chapter title enclosed in quotation marks)

Refer to the Glossary for these definitions. (The sentence appears in the same book as the glossary.)

Quotation marks are used around the titles of complete but unpublished works, such as reports and manuscripts. An example is:

Can we get a copy of Avril's report, "Improving Supply Chain Management?"

Punctuation at the End of Quotations

For a summary of how to use periods, commas, colons, semicolons, question marks, and exclamation points with quotation marks, study the following.

1. Periods and commas are *always* placed *inside* the closing quotation mark.

"Before each meeting," said Joan, "your team leader will distribute a draft agenda."

2. Colons and semicolons are *always* placed *outside* the closing quotation mark.

Barbara disagrees that these stocks are "blue chips": Canadian Metals, Inc.; Paige Industries; Clemson Rubber Company; and Verona Plastics.

Mr. Somer thinks that all the estimates are "outside the ballpark"; for this reason, he is reconsidering the project.

3. Question marks and exclamation points may be placed *either inside or outside* the closing quotation mark depending on whether or not the question mark or exclamation point is part of the quotation. Follow these rules to decide.

   a. If the quoted words are a question, then the question mark belongs with those quoted words. Place the question mark *inside* the closing quotation mark.

Ahmed asked, "Do you think this amount is realistic?" (Only the quoted words make up the question; thus the question mark belongs with the quoted words—*inside* the closing quotation mark.)

   Treat exclamations the same way.

Karen said, "I can't believe that we have run out of copier paper again!" (Only the words in quotations make up the exclamation; thus the exclamation point belongs with those words—*inside* the closing quotation mark.)

   b. If the quoted words do not make up a question (that is, if the quotation is part of a longer question), then the question mark belongs to the entire sentence. Place the question mark outside the closing quotation mark.

Do you agree with Mr. DuPont that their responses to the new schedule were "flagrantly excessive"? (The entire sentence is a question; the quotation is only part of the question. The question mark belongs *outside* the closing quotation mark.)

   Treat exclamations the same way.

Imagine calling these stocks "blue chips"! (The entire sentence is an exclamation; the quoted words are only part of the exclamation. The exclamation point belongs *outside* the closing quotation mark.)

Punctuation with quotation marks:

Periods and commas . . . . always inside
Colons and semicolons . . . . always outside
Exclamation points and question marks . . . . where they belong

CHECKUP 2

Check the following sentences for any errors in the use of quotation marks. Write *OK* if a sentence is correct.

1. Jerry said that the costs were "ridiculously overstated;" moreover, he said that he would prove his charges.

2. Did Ms. Burzese specifically say "50 per cent discount on all discontinued models?"

3. During her speech she quoted a few lines from Robert Frost's well-known poem "The Road Not Taken".

4. Waste not, want not is an apt slogan for our cost-cutting campaign.

5. This book, *Designing a Career,* has a bibliography that I found very helpful.

6. She included these people in her list of "top performers:" Bernard Quin, Zaira Lupp, and Tofi Mussivand.

7. Impatiently waiting for the documents to arrive, Robert exclaimed, "Where is that courier"!

8. Did you hear that one of the major shareholders say he was "selling half his stock"?

Parentheses

Although commas, dashes, and parentheses share certain common uses, they should not be used interchangeably. Just as words that have similar meanings still have subtle distinctions, so, too, do commas, dashes, and parentheses. The careful business writer is aware of these distinctions. Study the following information on the use of **parentheses.**

For Words That Give Additional Information

Commas, dashes, and parentheses may be used to set off words that give additional information. The words set off by commas may be omitted, but they generally add something to the main thought. The words set off by dashes are often given additional emphasis by the dashes. The words set off by parentheses, however, are clearly de-emphasized; they may be omitted.

Sandy Evanson, after forty years of service, has finally retired. (The words set off by commas may be omitted, but they do add something to the main thought.)

Ms. Fredericks personally selected four new employees—including Jim Kendall from our department—for the executive training program. (The words set off by dashes may be omitted; however, the writer deliberately uses dashes to draw attention to these words.)

In the past year, we lost only one account (Benson Plastics, which had small billings for the past three years). (The words in parentheses are extraneous; they contribute little to the main thought.)

For References

Parentheses are used to enclose references and directions. Some examples are:

When I first wrote to you (see my letter of June 8 attached), I enclosed a copy of the mortgage terms.

Include your credit card details (type of card, number, and expiry date) on the order form.

With Dates

Use parentheses to set off dates that refer to a person, a publication, or an event. Some examples are:

Sir John A. MacDonald (1815–1891), Canada's first prime minister, was knighted for his efforts in bringing about Confederation.

The Basics (1996) is a writer's handbook that includes a guide for ESL students.

Punctuation with Words in Parentheses

Parentheses may be used to enclose some of the words within a sentence, or they may be used to enclose an entire sentence.

Parentheses Within a Sentence.   No punctuation mark goes *before* the opening parenthesis within a sentence. Whatever punctuation would normally be used at this point is placed *after* the closing parenthesis.

When we meet next Monday (at the weekly planning session), we will discuss the fire drill procedures. (The comma that is needed after the clause *When we meet next Monday* is placed *after* the closing parenthesis, not *before* the *opening* parenthesis.)

Mr. Bellini suggested that we limit the number of overtime hours each week (to 5 hours for every employee), and a long discussion followed. (The comma needed to separate the two independent clauses is placed *after* the *closing* parenthesis, not *before* the *opening* parenthesis.)

Kilgore Electronics estimated a unit cost of $1.26 (see the itemized statement enclosed); however, this cost applies only to manufacturing 100 000 units or more. (The semicolon is placed *after* the *closing* parenthesis.)

Note that these rules do not affect any punctuation needed *within* the parentheses. Study the following examples:

As soon as we decide where we will hold our next product information meeting (probably Kingston, Ontario or Hull, Quebec), we must immediately reserve 100 rooms.

I would like to revise the last paragraph of the report I wrote (is it on this disk?) and ask Sal to comment on it.

If an independent clause in parentheses within a sentence is a question or exclamation, the question mark or exclamation mark is included within the parentheses. If the independent clause is a declaration, however, no period is used within the parentheses. Note, too, that when parentheses are included within a sentence, the first word in parentheses is not capitalized (unless, of course, the first word is a proper noun) even if the words in parentheses are an independent clause.

Paula Steig (she's the manager of contracts) is the person whom you should consult.

Parentheses for Complete Sentences.   When the words enclosed in parentheses are entirely independent (that is, they are not part of another sentence), the first word in parentheses is capitalized and normal end punctuation is used before the closing parenthesis.

As you requested, we have amortized the loan over a 15-year period. (Please see Appendix A, page 105.)

Please be advised that payments received after the due date will result in extra charges. (A late fee of $10 will be added to your next bill.)

CHECKUP 3

Are parentheses used correctly in the following sentences? Correct any errors. Write *OK* if a sentence is correct.

1. According to these new safety guidelines (see the attached memorandum,) we will have to revise our product specifications.

2. Abercrombie Industries, (formerly known as "Abercrombie Travel Services"), is expanding at a very rapid pace.

3. Take advantage of this exciting offer to trade in your printer on a new model. (This special offer ends July 15). Call us today!

4. Do you think Kent will accept the transfer to the Vancouver office (after all, it is a lateral move?)

5. Ms. Phelps insists that all these invoices (every one of them!) be processed by the end of the day.

6. If S & D merges with Renco Developers (We think they will do so), the new company will be the largest construction firm in Canada.

7. Several incorrect prices were printed in our new catalogue (see the attached photocopies) and these must be corrected without delay.

8. The plan is to introduce the earphones at a special low price (say, $19.95); then, in three or four months, we can test the feasibility of raising the price.

Apostrophes

As you learned in Section 4.2, the primary use of the **apostrophe** is to form possessives of nouns (*John's* office, several *technicians'* recommendations, and so on). A second common use of the apostrophe is to form contractions—shortened forms of one or more words. (Note the difference between a contraction such as *cont'd* and an abbreviation, such as *cont.* A contraction uses an apostrophe, and an abbreviation ends with a period.)

Another use of the apostrophe is to show that the first two figures have been omitted from a year date; for example, '02 is a shortened form of 2002.

Figure 6.4 ▶
Contractions

Thinking Critically.
What is the difference between a contraction and an abbreviation? Name a possessive and a contraction that can be homonyms.

Contractions	
Contraction	**Full Form**
I'm	I am
you're, we're, they're	you are, we are, they are
she's, he's, it's	she is, she has; he is, he has; it is, it has
I've, you've, we've, they've	I have, you have, we have, they have
I'd, you'd, he'd, she'd	I had, I would; you had, you would; he had, he would; she had, she would
we'd, they'd	we had, we would; they had, they would
I'll, you'll, he'll, she'll, we'll, they'll	I will, you will, he will, she will, we will, they will
there's, where's	there is, there has; where is, where has
don't, doesn't	do not, does not
didn't, can't, couldn't, won't, wouldn't	did not, cannot, could not, will not, would not

Review of Key Terms

1. Why are words set off by *parentheses*?
2. What does an *apostrophe* indicate to the reader?

Practical Application

1. Correct any errors in the use of quotation marks, parentheses, or apostrophes and/or associated punctuation in the following sentences. Write *OK* if a sentence is correct.

   a. Dont Joel and Celeste realize that the fax machine is not for personal use?

   b. Nicole asked, "What is a *non sequitur*?" Sharon replied, "A *non sequitur* is a 'statement that does not follow."

   c. While adding a column of figures, Arthur exclaimed, "These numbers are wrong"!

   d. The new billing system (its already operational) will save us time and will help us serve our customers better.

   e. Maureen asked, "Which representative handles the Clifford Textiles account"?

   f. "Perhaps," said Mrs. Vreeland, we should include a clause that gives us the right to renew this lease."

   g. Check with Amanda (shes the supervisor of computer services) to find out whether the market research survey is ready yet.

   h. Nearly 90 per cent of our employees have signed up for the additional coverage. (Our survey had shown that the majority of them were very interested in expanding their life insurance).

   i. When Martin graduated in '99, he worked at the CBC.

   j. "We believe we have produced the healthiest breakfast cereal on the market" said Lane Allen, "consequently, we should let people know its benefits."

   k. Mr. D'Souza said "that candy canes will be distributed on December 15."

   l. We will place signs in all the windows (each sign will read "Special Sale"!) and will advertise in the local papers.

   m. After viewing my slides, Lee said, "Well done—just splendid!"

   n. Jackie Howell, the consumer advocate on WFIT 83.8 on the FM dial enthusiastically endorsed our new car seat for children.

   o. Stephen said, "Their so-called experts could not even read the schematic diagrams"!

   p. Please take all these specification sheets to Ms. Mueller (is she still on the second floor) before you leave for lunch, Clyde.

   q. One client asked whether all the bonds in the portfolio were rated "AAA."

r. Randall couldn't communicate the message to Ms. Hentgen because she was in transit between Ottawa and Sarnia.

s. Please make sure that the envelope is stamped "Private and Confidential".

t. According to the company handbook (see the attached photocopy of page 34,) our dental plan has significantly improved.

2. Correct any errors in the following sentences. Write *OK* if a sentence is correct.

a. A brief explanation of the new system is included (see pages 10 through 15.).

b. After skimming the "introduction," I decided to buy the book.

c. Francis' idea for modifying the design is brilliant, I think.

d. Beth suggested that, the fonts be changed to give the report a more professional look.

e. Although the list price of this laser printer is $1,200.00, it sells for $999 in many discount computer stores.

f. Mr. Mijikowski said, "Kenneth been with our firm for more than 15 years, we will certainly miss him when he moves to Yellowknife."

g. Eleni's article on job-hunting tips, Planning Your Career Moves, will soon be reprinted in several magazines.

h. The seminar will cover (1.) time-management techniques, (2.) interpersonal relations, and (3.) decision making.

i. "Without question, we have assembled the best possible team," said Benjamin Gan, "consequently, our product will be the best on the world market."

j. The Appendix lists several excellent sources for more information (see page 1,265).

k. Graham requisitioned printer cartridges, form-feed paper, file folders, and etc., for the department staff.

l. Pirasanthy asked, "What did John think of our report?" Syreeta replied, "He said, "You've done an excellent piece of work. Congratulations!"

m. Joseph McKeachie is the new director of marketing (he has been recruited from a rival company.)

n. If you read the book *Success Without Stress,* pay special attention to Chapter 5, "The Importance of Communication Skills".

3. Write a dialogue between an employee and an interviewee. Then, rewrite the dialogue in paragraph form, deleting all quotation marks. Exchange dialogues with another team and insert the proper punctuation.

TEAMWORK

Editing Practice

Correct any errors in the following paragraph.

Once a month the children's Hospital allows volunteers to come, and join the children for lunch. These lunchons usually have a theme, such as Valentines Day or Canada day. However, they all have one thing in common they make the children forget about their illnesses', even if it is only for a short while. Wont you become a volunteer?

Discussion Points

1. What is the difference between a direct quotation and an indirect quotation? How are they punctuated?
2. What are the rules regarding the use of end punctuation (periods, commas, colons, semicolons, exclamation points, and question marks) with quotation marks?

Capitalization

Don't use capital letters without good REASON.

—William Safire, in *Fumblerules*

The rules of **capitalization** help writers make words distinctive, emphasize words, and show that certain words are especially important. Some of the rules for capitalization are easy to remember because they are well known and long established. These rules are reviewed briefly in this section. Other capitalization rules may cause writers problems, however, and these pitfalls are fully discussed here.

First Words

Always capitalize the first letter of the first word of the following:

1.   A sentence or a group of words used as a sentence.

That report must be finished by tomorrow morning. (complete sentence)

Yes, *tomorrow* morning. (a group of words used as a sentence)

2.   Each line of poetry (unless the original work shows otherwise).

What they are doing is turning

The earth

In ordered furrows.

   —Ken Belford, "Turn"

3.   A sentence in a direct quotation.

The lawyer specifically said, "Be sure to get permission from the copyright holder to reprint this excerpt."

4.   A complete sentence after a colon when that sentence is a formal rule or needs special emphasis.

The store's rule is: Refund the customer's money if there is a receipt. (rule)

Computer experts stress this point: Always check your disks for viruses. (for emphasis)

5.   The first word after a colon when the material that follows consists of two or more sentences.

She described in detail the two main reasons for changing delivery services: First, lower rates will substantially decrease shipping costs. Second, expanded access to global markets will make it easier to reach overseas customers.

6.   A salutation. (All words begin with a capital letter except *and*.)

Dear Dr. Jackson

Ladies and Gentlemen

Dear Mr. and Mrs. Brown

7. A complimentary closing. (The first word begins with a capital letter.)

Sincerely

Sincerely yours

Yours truly

Main Words in Titles

Always capitalize the main words of headings and titles of publications. Do not capitalize articles (*a/an/the*), conjunctions, and short prepositions unless they are the first word or the last word in the heading or title.

In this morning's edition of *Canada Today,* under the headline "The Science of Age and Health," Myra Sikorsky commended the Canadian Medical Association for its research on aging. (*The* is capitalized in the title of the article because it is the first word. The preposition *of* and the conjunction *and* are not capitalized in the article title.)

You should read "What Olympic Athletes Strive For," a well-written, perceptive article by Jonathan Millard that appears in the current issue of *Sports Today* magazine. (Here, *for* is capitalized because it is the last word in the title.)

Hyphenated titles follow the same rules:

In "Out-of-Work Blues," Anne Replano tells job seekers how to retain their self-esteem and their sense of humour.

Capitalize the first word that follows a colon or dash in a title.

Denzel Morris wrote the book *The Space Race: A Look Back.*

CHECKUP 1

Check the following sentences for any errors in the use of capitalization. Write *OK* if a sentence is correct.

1. I use the closing "Sincerely," in all my business correspondence.
2. Is this bid much lower than the other bids we received? Substantially lower.
3. Remember: Always keep receipts of all expenses.
4. Did you read the article "Labour-Management Problems And How To Avoid Them"?
5. We are pleased to give you the good news: Sales and profits are up. OK
6. We are now reviewing our needs for the following hardware: 1. Servers 2. Printers 3. Notebook computers
7. Has the copier been repaired? No, it hasn't.
8. He is now writing "Tips For Business And Pleasure Travelling" for *Business And Industry* magazine.
9. As Harriet closed the door, she said casually, "All's fair in love and war."
10. Tonight's meeting includes the following: A report by the treasurer, the minutes of the last meeting, and speeches by the candidates for city council.

Names of Persons

The problems surrounding the capitalization of names concern the use of prefixes such as the following:

D', Da, De, Di. *D'Amato, d'Amato; Da Puzzo, daPuzzo, DeLorenzo, De Lorenzo, deLorenzo; DiFabio, Di Fabio, diFabio.* Spell each name precisely as the person spells it.

L', La, Las, Le. *L'Engle, LaRosa, Las Varca, LeMaster.* Follow the capitalization, spelling, and spacing used by the person.

Mc, Mac. *McMillan, Macmillan, MacMillan.* The prefix *Mc* is followed by a capital letter and no spacing. The prefix *Mac* may or may not be followed by a capital.

O'. *O'Brien, O'Toole, O'Malley.* The prefix *O'* is followed by a capital letter and no spacing.

Van, Von. *Van Fossen, van Fossen; van Hoffman; Von Huffman; von der Lieth, Von der Lieth, Von Der Lieth.* Follow the capitalization, spelling, and spacing used by each person.

In all cases, be sure to write each person's name precisely the way he or she writes it—this rule refers not only to capitalization but also to the spelling of and the spacing in names. Note, however, that even prefixes that begin with lowercase letters are capitalized when the surname is used without the first name.

Donald received a letter from Marie la Salle today. (She writes her name *la*.)

He thinks La Salle's comments about the proposal are valid. (When her first name is not used, capitalize *la* to avoid misreading.)

Names of Places

Capitalize names of geographical localities, streets, parks, rivers, buildings, and so on, such as *South America, King Street, Bryant Park, Humber River, Medical Arts Building.*

Capitalize the word *city* only when it is a part of the city's name: *Quebec City,* but the *city of Montreal.*

Capitalize the word *province* only when it is used to denote a particular area: the *Maritime Provinces,* but the *province of Nova Scotia* (unless used in a heading or legal document).

Capitalize the word *the* in names of places only when *the* is part of the official name: *The Hague,* but *the Maritime Provinces.*

Capitalize the words *north, south, east,* and *west* whenever they refer to specific sections of the country and, of course, when they are part of proper names. They are not capitalized when they refer merely to direction.

We need a warehouse in the West in order to lower our shipping costs. (*West* is a specific part of the country.)

We are going to North Carolina for our vacation. (*North* is part of a proper name.)

An industrial park is under construction 20 kilometres east of the city. (Here, *east* simply indicates direction.)

Names of Things

Capital letters identify official names of companies, departments, divisions, associations, committees, bureaus, buildings, schools, course titles, clubs, government bodies, historical events, documents, and so on.

Jill and Bruce are taking Statistics for Business at Metropolitan College. (*Statistics for Business* is the official course title; *Metropolitan College* is the official name of the school.)

Jill and Bruce are taking a statistics course at a nearby college. (No capitals. The actual title of the course has not been used.)

Ms. Dimitrios is a consultant for the Hamilton Investment Company, which has offices here in the Frobisher Building. (Capitalize the official name of the company and the building.)

She is a consultant for a public relations company in this building. (No capitals. The name of the company has not been used.)

The Direct Mail Department has leased two entire floors in the Exchange Building. (Official department name; official building name.)

Capitalize the names of the days of the week, the months of the year, religious days and holidays, and the names of years and periods: Tuesday, Wednesday; March, June; Easter, Passover, the Roaring Twenties, the Middle Ages. Do not capitalize the seasons of the year: summer, fall, winter, spring.

Capitalize **proper adjectives**, which are adjectives formed from proper nouns; for example, Canadian, American, Puerto Rican, and so on. (Note: Certain adjectives [venetian blind, india ink, turkish towel, and panama hat, for example] are no longer capitalized, because through many years of use, they have lost their identification as proper adjectives. Consult a dictionary when in doubt.

CHECKUP 2

Are capitals used correctly in the following sentences? Write *OK* if a sentence is correct.

1. There is an interesting article on mexican exports in today's newspaper.
2. The Decorative Textile Company has a showroom in Quebec city.
3. My associate von Spielmann owns and manages the Serenity inn on lake George.
4. Miriam's speech, "Women In Business: a Guide For Today's Executives," was both amusing and informative.
5. The association of canadian community colleges is exploring the possibility of moving its headquarters into the Toronto-Dominion centre.
6. Our last Victoria day picnic was a great success, Hans von hoffman tells me.
7. Read "Doing Business In Japan—an Up-to-date Approach."
8. On the first monday in october we will meet to plan our Spring catalogue.

Capitalization Pitfalls

The following discussion presents some useful solutions to several typical problems writers face in using capitals correctly.

Short Forms

Writers often substitute one word for the complete name of a person, place, or thing. Such substitutions are usually capitalized to give special distinction or emphasis, as when they indicate a specific person, place, or thing. Some short forms are capitalized if they are personal titles of high rank, organizational names, or governmental bodies.

The most recent biography of the Admiral is entitled *Nimitz in the Pacific.* (Here, *Admiral* is a personal title of a specific person.)

She has written a biography about an admiral who was famous in World War II. (Because *admiral* does not refer to a particular person, it is not capitalized.)

After the civil engineers completed their inspection of the Lakeview Bridge, they issued a report stating that the bridge needed routine repairs. (Lowercase the second use of *bridge* because it is a common noun.)

The words *company, department, association, school, college,* and so on, are not usually capitalized when they stand alone, even though they may substitute for the official name of a specific organization. The word *company* may be capitalized when it carries special emphasis, as in legal documents and minutes of meetings.

Her company is considering a merger with Ace Personnel.

Rita visited the museum during a recent trip to Ottawa.

Two staff assistants in our department were promoted.

The terms *government* and *federal government* are not capitalized. Federal is capitalized, of course, when it is part of an official name, such as *Federal Business Development Bank.*

Personal and Official Titles

Always capitalize a title written before a name.

Among the directors are Colonel Sanders, former Senator Elias, and Professor Mona Majid.

A title written after a name or without a name is capitalized when (1) it is a very high-ranking national or international title or (2) it is part of an address.

Kofi Annan, Secretary General of the United Nations, championed the development of a relief fund. (Always capitalize this internationally known title.)

In yesterday's editorial, she discussed the Prime Minister's economic policies. (*Prime Minister*—referring to the Prime Minister of Canada—is always capitalized.)

Magdalan Chan, president of Vanguard Enterprises, Inc., plans to retire in June. (Do not capitalize *president* in such situations.)

Capitalize a title that is part of an address.

Ms. Erica Godfrey, President
Godfrey Electronics, Inc.
1500 College Street
Toronto, ON M5J 2E7

When joined to titles, *ex-* and *-elect* are not capitalized. Also, *former* and *late* are not capitalized.

Among the dignitaries invited to the dinner was former Mayor Holland.

The late Senator John Heinz will be remembered for his strong stand on environmental issues.

Mayor-elect Olins said that she would balance the city's budget without raising property taxes.

Next semester, ex-Premier Peterson will teach a course in political science.

Commercial Products

Distinguish carefully between a proper noun that is part of the official name of a product and a common noun that names the *general* class of the commercial product. For example, you would write *Arch Saver shoes,* not *Arch Saver Shoes,* because the official brand name is *Arch Saver.* Note the following:

Kleenex tissues   Xerox machine

Coke (Coca-Cola) Hoover vacuum cleaner

Scotch tape   Yellow Pages directory

CHECKUP 3

Correct any errors in the use of capitalization in the following sentences. Write *OK* if a sentence is correct.

1. The employees in the information systems department collected contributions for the Children's aid Society.

2. Laser Recordings is building a new plant and warehouse 15 kilometres West of London, Ontario.

3. Langille Electronics will announce the appointment of a new President at Monday's press conference.

4. Throughout the country we lease as many as 10 000 General Motors Cars.

5. The federal Court of Canada has an office on University Avenue.

6. When your Supervisor returns, Homer, please ask her to meet with us in the Auditorium.

7. Send the original copy to the Manufacturing Division at our headquarters office. OK

8. Esther Goodwin, President of Creative Plastics, has announced a major agreement with Liu Industries in Taiwan.

9. These Nabisco Crackers are low in sodium and high in fibre.

10. Which Agency currently has the Folger account?

Review of Key Terms

1. What is a *proper adjective*? How can one be sure if a proper adjective should be capitalized?
2. What types of words are not *capitalized* in titles?

Practical Application

1. Correct any capitalization errors in the following sentences. Write *OK* if a sentence is correct.
   a. Our Company now has exclusive distribution rights to these products anywhere on the East Coast.
   b. According to reliable sources, the Prime Minister will not seek re-election.
   c. Marla Volpe, Vice President of Kline & Volpe Inc., purchased the property last week.
   d. She suggests that we use "yours truly" rather than "sincerely yours" for business letter closings.
   e. "Stocks And Bonds: an Investor's Guide" is the title of her recent article.
   f. Severe winds delayed our Flight from Pearson International airport yesterday.
   g. When we were staying in Ottawa, we visited the National gallery and the Parliament buildings.
   h. Before she was named Manager of the Niagara Falls regional office, Melita was a supervisor in one of our District offices.
   i. The Majestic restaurant will be closed on New Year's day.
   j. For years the policy has been the same: plan your work and work your plan.
   k. The company's distribution centre is in the west, but its main office is located in the City of Montreal.
   l. Trusty Truck Rentals is relocating to the Northern part of the city next Summer.
   m. For two weeks we will call on clients in the Provinces of Quebec, Nova Scotia, and New Brunswick.
   n. Rowena hopes to find a position with a newspaper on the west coast.
   o. Because of the success of our Fall fashions, we have exceeded our revenue goals for the year.

2. Correct any errors in the following sentences. Write *OK* if a sentence is correct.
   a. Joan, the security guard, sometimes acts like she was the chief of police!
   b. The new communications system, according to the operations manager, will be completely installed inside of one week.

c. The travel agent sent our itinerary, airline tickets and hotel confirmations to the wrong address.

d. I installed a new hard drive in your personal computer, and it should work as good as any new PC you could purchase.

e. Do you know whether there is a Federal Government Department that helps small businesses?

f. Yes, the official name of the department is Counselling Assistance to Small Enterprises.

g. The maps that you're looking for are in back of those cabinets.

h. Don't Maureen know the way to the cafeteria yet?

i. When she saw the logo, Caryl could not help but tell the designers why it was inappropriate.

j. Where's the paper and crayons I requested this morning?

k. Is that young man standing besides Althea Watson the new receptionist?

l. Alex, do you know where Fernanda and Bissoondaye are at?

m. No, I do not know where they went to, Harold.

n. Do you have a purchase order form like this one in your file folder?

o. Merilee asked, "Why did you delete these files from the current directory, Stuart"?

p. One of the new teachers who you met at this morning's orientation is Wilma's brother.

q. Ivera Fasano, former president of the Retail Jewellers Association, has been named to premier Laurent's Task Force on business development.

r. The only one of the regional managers who was aware of the merger, was Andrew Abbate.

s. Each department heads status report must be submitted no later than August 31.

t. Because Cynthia has been training our new staff for the last two weeks her assistant publisher has been handling these negotiations.

3. Choose two or three newspaper advertisements and note the use of capitalization. Is this done effectively? Why or why not? Is capitalization used according to the rules discussed in Section 6.5? If there are differences, what are they and why do you think they occur? Share your findings with the class.

TEAMWORK

Editing Practice

Proofreading. Edit the following sentences to correct any errors they may contain. Write *OK* if a sentence is correct.

1. Being that we did not pay the bill within ten days, we cannot deduct the 2 per cent discount.

2. Please do not schedule the meeting for next Friday without you make sure that Tass Karakola is free to attend it.

3. One of the reporters asked her several questions in regards to the proposed legislation.

4. This stack of new insurance claims will be divided between the three most experienced adjusters.

5. According to the announcement, the increases are retroactive from last January.

6. No one noticed that the inventory control number written on this form was different from the number on this computer printout.

7. We read in the company newspaper where Elliot has been on sabbatical.

8. As you can well imagine, Joy Obuchi was real happy when she heard that the contract had been cancelled.

Using Business Vocabulary. Fill in the missing words with the correct words from the list below.

a. approximate	f. freight
b. bankruptcy	g. irrelevant
c. chronological	h. mandatory
d. exhaustive	i. negotiate
e. extension	j. valuable

1. Stocks, bonds, and all other (?) securities must be locked in a fire-proof vault overnight.

2. At tomorrow's meeting we will try to (?) a 15-year loan at 10 per cent interest per year.

3. The other committee members thought that Evan's remarks were (?) and insensitive.

4. Because Norton Industries has been unprofitable for three years, (?) proceedings will begin early next month.

5. Please take these memos from Chairman Reo and arrange them in (?) order, beginning with January memos.

6. The (?) cost for the entire system is $10 000.

7. According to the contract, the shipper pays the (?) charges.

8. Because they could not meet the payment deadline, we have agreed to a 30-day (?) for the total balance.

9. The utility company announced that the (?) round of talks with the government has ended and that a rate increase of 3 per cent has been approved.

10. Our company no longer has any (?) retirement age.

Discussion Point

When should words such as *north, south, east,* and *west* be capitalized? When should they remain lowercase?

Abbreviations

▶ **Key Terms**

▶ abbreviations

▶ business abbrevi-
   ations

▶ units of measure

▶ expressions of
   time

---

*It may help to think of abbrevia-
tions as belonging to the same
class of objects as instant coffee,
powdered eggs, and TV dinners.
They don't take up much space
and they're great when you're in a
hurry, but they never have the
taste of the real thing.*

—William A. Sabin, *The Gregg Reference Manual*

Abbreviations provide writers with shortcuts, and shortcuts are certainly
appropriate at times. As a business writer, you must know when abbreviations
are acceptable—and when they are not. In addition, you must know the correct
forms of those abbreviations.

Periods and Abbreviations

Throughout Section 6.6 you will find information on when to use a period
with an abbreviation. In addition to this information, two general guidelines
are as follows:

An abbreviation of a single word requires a period at the end. Some
examples are:

Jr. (for Junior), *Wed.* (for Wednesday), and *approx.* (for approximately)

Abbreviations for units of measurement are now commonly written without
periods and the abbreviation is the same for the singular as for the plural (e.g.,
1 cm (one centimetre); *55 cm* (centimetres)).

Lower-case abbreviations made up of single initials require a period after
each initial, but all-capital abbreviations made up of single initials normally
require no periods. Some examples are:

c.o.d. (cash on delivery); *6 a.m.*

CAA (Canadian Automobile Association); CBC (Canadian Broadcasting Corporation)

Personal Names

Study the following rules for using abbreviations before and after personal
names.

Before Personal Names

Most of the titles used before personal names such as *Mr., Mrs.,* and *Dr.,* are abbreviations.

Singular	Plural
Mr.	Messrs. (from the French word messieurs)
Mrs.	Mmes. or Mesdames
Ms.	Mses. or Mss.
Miss	Misses
Dr.	Drs.

Other titles used before personal names are spelled out whether the full name or only the last name is given: *Premier* Billington, *Senator* Kuris, the *Honourable* Jane W. Cleary, the *Reverend* Arthur Franks, *General* MacKenzie, and so on.

After Personal Names

Academic Degrees and Similar Abbreviations.
Abbreviations of academic degrees, religious orders, and similar abbreviations generally have internal periods: *M.D., D.D.S., Ph.D., D.V.M., Ed.D.; S.J., D.D.* Check your dictionary whenever you are not sure of the abbreviation.

Do not use *Mr., Ms., Mrs., Miss,* or *Dr.* before a person's name that is followed by an abbreviation of an academic degree or religious order.

Jane T. Prentiss, M.D. *or* Dr. Jane T. Prentiss (Not: *Dr.* Jane T. Prentiss, *M.D.*)

Phillip S. Raymond, Ph.D. *or* Dr. Phillip S. Raymond (Not: *Dr.* Phillip S. Raymond, *Ph.D.*)

Other titles before the person's name may sometimes be appropriate:

Reverend Mark Seany, S.J.

Professor Katelin Marsh, Litt.D.

Note that in a sentence, any such abbreviation following a name must be set off with *two* commas, unless the abbreviation ends the sentence.

Jane T. Prentiss, M.D., is the subject of today's "Pediatric Medicine" column.

Jr. and Sr.
Omit the comma before *Jr.* and *Sr.* when either follows a person's name unless the person specifically uses a comma, as some people still do.

Mr. Sloan P. Renwick Jr.

Dr. A. Phillip Carlton, Sr. (Dr. Carlton *does* use a comma before Sr.)

Do not use *Jr.* and *Sr.* with a person's last name only.

Ms. Owens faxed the summary to Charles J. Smith Sr., and Mr. Smith responded immediately. (Mr. Smith not Smith Sr.)

Initials

Initials are abbreviations of names; in some cases, initials stand for given names but, through common usage, have come to take on the status of a name. Two initials can be written with or without a space between them (e.g., T. J. or T.J.).

Will T. J. handle the arbitration case?

Get approval from T.J. Forsythe before we leave today.

Note: Reference initials written at the end of memos and letters are ususaly written with no periods and no spaces (see Section 7.3).

CHECKUP 1

Are abbreviations used correctly in the following sentences? Write *OK* if a sentence is correct.

1. Ms. Oliva wrote a letter to Paul C. W. Bradley Jr., but Mr. Bradley ~~Jr.~~ has not responded yet.
2. Her students were pleased when *Proffessor* Prof. Laughton announced that she would discuss the assignment.
3. The property has been owned by the Messrs. Fleming since the 1970s. OK
4. Dr. Lucretia T. Harper, M.D., will be director of the new Fraser Clinic in Ottawa.
5. While *Mr.* Mister Kinsky is on vacation, his associate will oversee the project.
6. I read in the news that Ms. Jessica W. Taft, Ph.D., has resigned her university position.

Companies and Organizations

Always write the name of a company or an organization precisely as its *official* name is written on its letterhead stationery.

Perkins & Burke Limited	Wing-on Funeral Homes Ltd.
Olsten and Jonas, Inc.	Landry Bros.
Bits 'n' Bytes Co.	L. T. Marquette & Sons
Magnolia Construction Company	The Abbas/Al-Sama Development Group

Inc. and *Ltd.*

Omit the comma before *Inc.* and *Ltd.* unless the official company name is written with a comma.

Pam works for Games & Toys Ltd. in Moncton. (The official company name does *not* include a comma.)

Write to HiTech Wares, Inc. for more information. (The official company name has a comma before Inc.)

All-Capital Abbreviations

Many names of organizations, associations, government agencies, and so on, are abbreviated in all-capital letters with no periods or spaces between the letters.

CAA	Canadian Automobile Association
CBA	Canadian Bankers Association
CNIB	Canadian National Institute for the Blind
TSE	Toronto Stock Exchange
UPS	United Parcel Service
NHL	National Hockey League
YWCA	Young Women's Christian Association
UN	United Nations
ACCC	Association of Canadian Community Colleges

An acronym is a shortened form of a name. An acronym is formed from the initial letters of the words in the full name. Pronounce an acronym as you would a word.

OPEC   Organization of Petroleum Exporting Countries

PIN   personal identification number

NAFTA   North American Free Trade Agreement

The call letters of broadcasting stations are always written in all-capital letters without periods.

WPAT-FM   WNBC-TV   CFHI   CBC

When *United States* is abbreviated (before the name of a government agency, for example), periods are used.

the U.S. Department of Commerce

Business Abbreviations

In addition to their use with personal names and in the names of companies and organizations, abbreviations are used in many other instances in business correspondence (business abbreviations).

Address Abbreviations

Street Names.   On envelope labels, space restrictions sometimes make the use of *St.* and *Ave.* necessary. In letters, however (and on envelopes whenever possible), avoid abbreviating the words *Street, Avenue,* and so on. When abbreviations such as *NW, SW,* and *NE* appear after street names, usual practice has been to use a comma to separate the street name from the abbreviation. However, Canada Post prefers no punctuation. For full details of Canada Post addressing preferences, please visit **www.canadapost.ca**.

405 West Ninth Street

28 Kingston Boulevard

317 Mountain Avenue, NW

Post Office Box Numbers.   The words *Post Office* may or may not be abbreviated with box numbers.

Post Office Box 605 or P.O. Box 605

City Names.   Except for the abbreviation *St.* for Saint in such city names as *St. John's,* do not abbreviate city names.

Province and Territory Names.   With addresses on envelopes and inside addresses, use either (1) the two-letter abbreviations of province and territory names or (2) the spelled-out name. In both cases, always use a postal code.

Dr. Francine P. Snowden
1301 Westerly Avenue
Markham, ON L2K 1W9 or Markham, Ontario L2K 1W9

When province names are used elsewhere, that is, not on envelopes or with inside addresses, spell them out.

Do not be surprised to see mail with computer-printed labels in all-capital letters with no punctuation and nearly everything abbreviated. Many companies that send large mailings use this style.

Province or Territory	Canada Post Abbreviation	Province or Territory	Canada Post Abbreviation
Alberta	AB	Nunavut	NU
British Columbia	BC	Ontario	ON
Manitoba	MB	Prince Edward Island	PE
New Brunswick	NB	Quebec	QC
Newfoundland	NF	Saskatchewan	SK
Northwest Territories	NT	Yukon Territory	YT
Nova Scotia	NS		

DR F P SNOWDEN
MARKHAM DISTRICT HOSP
2500 CLARK ST
MARKHAM ON L2K 1W9

Units of Measure

General Use. In routine correspondence, **units of measure** are spelled out: *kilograms, degrees, metres, hectares, centimetres,* and so on. Use numerals with units of measures.

Each piece is about 3 metres by 4 metres.

We will need at least 8 two-litre containers.

The sample that we tested contained about 3 grams of zinc.

Technical Use. In technical work and on invoices, units of length, mass, area, volume, temperature, and time are usually abbreviated. Among the commonly used terms are those in Figure 6.5:

Abbreviations for Units of Measure			
cm	centimetre, centimetres	L	litre, litres
ft	foot, feet	lb	pound, pounds
g	gram, grams	m	metre, metres
gal	gallon, gallons	mm	millimetre, millimetres
in	inch, inches	oz	ounce, ounces
kg	kilogram, kilograms	pt	pint, pints
km	kilometre, kilometres	yd	yard, yards
ha	hectare, hectares	min	minute, minutes
h	hour, hours	s	second, seconds

◀ **Figure 6.5 Abbreviations for Units of Measure**

Thinking Critically.
Why are units of measure abbreviated in charts and diagrams?

Abbreviations for Days and Months	
Days of the Week	**Months of the Year**
Sun., Mon., Tues. (or Tue.), Wed., Thurs. (or Thu.), Fri., Sat.	Jan., Feb., Mar., Apr., May, June (or Jun.), July (or Jul.), Aug., Sept., Oct., Nov., Dec.

Expressions of Time

Write *a.m.* and *p.m.* in lowercase letters with periods but with no spacing with **expressions of time**. Always use numerals with these abbreviations, and do not use *o'clock* with *a.m.* or *p.m.* Remember: *a.m.* means "before noon" and *p.m.* means "after noon."

The bus will leave at 8:30 a.m. on Thursday. (not 8:30 o'clock a.m.)

Days and Months

The days of the week and the months of the year should be abbreviated only when space forces the writer to do so, as in tables and lists. In such cases, use the abbreviations in Figure 6.6. Note that *May, June,* and *July* are not usually abbreviated.

No. for Number

The abbreviation *No.* is used only before a figure: *License No. 465-75E, Patent No. 769,878,* and so on. Note that *number* is spelled out when it is the first word in a sentence and that it may be omitted after such words as *Room, Invoice,* and *Cheque.*

Have you found copies of the following purchase orders: Nos. 125–76, 125–89, and 126–13? When you do, please bring them to Room 1272.

Number 5632 is the only outstanding cheque, Ms. Tobias.

Note: The symbol # may be used on forms or in technical copy.

Miscellaneous Abbreviations

In addition to the abbreviations discussed so far, there are many more that are used in business, including those shown in Figure 6.7. Check a dictionary or another reference book for a complete list of terms and their acceptable abbreviations.

Other Abbreviations			
ASAP	as soon as possible	PE	price-earnings (ratio)
atty.	attorney	RAM	random-access memory
CAD	computer-assisted design		
CEO	chief executive officer	reg.	registered
ETA	estimated time of arrival	ROM	read-only memory
OTC	over the counter		

CHECKUP 2

Are abbreviations used correctly in these sentences? Write *OK* if a sentence is correct.

1. Mr. John Trevette, a U.A.W. official from Oakville, is the guest speaker at the rally tonight. *UAW*

2. According to the agenda, the second session will begin at 10:15 AM. *a.m.*

3. Please arrange for a news conference on Tues., Mar. 7, at 3:00 p.m. *Tuesday March*

4. The chip is about two inches long, which is equal to slightly more than 5 CM. *centimeters 5 cm*

5. Johanna moved to St. John, NB, after she retired from IBM. *Saint New Brunswick*

6. Since the carton weighs more than 10 kg, we cannot send it by Speedy Courier. *kilograms*

7. After she speaks in Alberta, Karen will travel to B.C. and Manitoba. *British Columbia*

8. No. 686 is the last item on my list. *Number*

Review of Key Terms

1. When should *abbreviations* be used in business communications?
2. What are rules concerning the use of abbreviations in *units of measure*?

Practical Application

1. Correct any errors in abbreviation use in the following sentences. Write *OK* if a sentence is correct.
    a. Barbara Henry, a senior accountant at the Port Albernie office, will audit our accounts.
    b. One of our research chemists, Dr. Morris Anthony, Ph.D., holds Patent No. 987,789.
    c. A reporter for W.A.B.C. interviewed two VPs of our firm.
    d. Most of Lauren's territory is in the SW part of the province, isn't it?
    e. Next semester Prof. Weinburg will teach Labour Relations at the Calgary campus of the Univ. of Alberta.
    f. To save gas, just add 16 mL of Magic Oil to every 5 L of gasoline.
    g. No. 456-654 is the only file that is missing.
    h. The committee members agreed to meet again on Fri. a.m.
    i. Our guest speaker for the charity drive will be the Rev. Barbara Williams.
    j. Has Mister Rosselini had an opportunity to respond to this letter from the Canadian parks service?
    k. This C.A.A. booklet offers helpful tips on car insurance.
    l. Station WZXY-FM has almost 30 per cent of the morning "drive time" audience.
    m. Charlene once worked for the NHL in Edmonton, AB.
    n. Alfred, please check the files for License Number 393-576.
    o. We renewed our lease on Feb. 1, 2001.
    p. Packages weighing over two kg. will be shipped at book rate.
    q. Monica now works for C.M.H.C. in Ottawa, doesn't she?
    r. Steve reserved Room 2914 for the conference next Tuesday.
    s. Louisa T. Clarkson, M.D. is the head of the Research Dept.
    t. Please call Sen. Bedard's office to confirm our appointment.
2. Correct any errors in the following sentences. Write *OK* if a sentence is correct.
    a. Traffic circles in the U.K. are called roundabouts.
    b. Yes, either Christina or José are going to supervise the completion of the project.
    c. Mr. Hunter asked, "why did our lawyer cross out this clause in the contract"?
    d. Naturally, we're confident that our Fall list of trade books will sell extremely well.

e. On her desk is the sales report for the first quarter and the performance evaluation for each staff member.

f. As a result of our campaign, we raised more than $5,000 for U.N.I.C.E.F.

g. Don't Priscilla need these graphs ad charts for her presentation tomorrow morning?

h. When you finish, please call Ms. Blakes assistant to change our meeting to Friday afternoon.

i. Do you know where Sean has gone to Louie?

j. Since we don't need to check these envelopes now, we can just let them lay there until tomorrow.

k. Whom has been named to head the Finance Committee?

l. All these terminals are connected to our mainframe computers in the B.C. office.

m. Kim is indispensable because he is such a hard-working dependable experienced underwriter.

n. Our current inventory will last only until June or July, you should plan, therefore, to reorder in time for the summer rush.

o. AMC Plastics sent a deposit in September, the rest of the payment is due in November.

p. Send all purchase orders to the centre on Third Ave. unless Mr. Banderas instructs you to do otherwise.

q. One co. on the West Coast has estimated the total cost to be under $10,000.

r. The total payment was $2,000, our current balance is approximately $450.

s. In my opinion, we should seek our accountants advice before the new fiscal year.

t. Although the union has not yet ratified the new contract. Management is conducting business as usual.

3. Browse through a magazine, newspaper, or manual. Look for use of abbreviations. Discuss how often abbreviations are used and which format uses them the most.

TEAMWORK

Editing Practice

Spelling Alert! Correct any spelling errors in the following sentences. Write OK if a sentence is correct.

1. Our decision to make the salary increases retractive to May has been approved by the Executive Committee.

2. The secretarys both took minutes at the committee meeting.

3. The newspaper reports were clearly eroneous; there is no truth to the allegations.
4. We are now equiping each store with its own computerized inventory-control system.
5. Mrs. Lerner coroborated Bob's statement concerning the sale of the LaSalle Street property.
6. In our opinion, the value of the building and the property is overated by as much as 30 per cent.
7. To no one's surprise, the Widget Manufacturing Company has exagerated its share of the marketplace.
8. In carefully controled experiments, we proved that our product removes stains better than any other product on the market.
9. Abigail is not only a compatent systems analyst, but she is also a congenial and diligent co-worker.
10. Correct pronounciation is necessary for clear communication.

Discussion Points

1. What is the difference between an *abbreviation* and an *acronym*?
2. Should all abbreviations be capitalized? Support your answer with examples.

1

Numbers

When you can measure what you are speaking about, and express it in numbers, you know something about it.

—William Thomson, Lord Kelvin, British mathematician

▶ **Key Terms**

▶ numbers
▶ ordinal numbers
▶ consecutive numbers

Numbers are commonly used in business to express sums of money, order quantities, discounts, time, measurements, percentages, addresses, dates, sales statistics, versions of computer programs, and so on. Business writers know that the correct use of numbers is often critical to clear, accurate communication. Errors in number use can cause more than simple confusion; they can be expensive, time-consuming, and exceptionally disruptive. Be sure to master the following principles of number usage, and make it a habit to proofread numbers carefully whenever you write business messages.

Using Words to Express Numbers

Why is it important to know when to express numbers in numerals and when to express them in words? One reason is that long-established use dictates certain rules. Another reason is that numerals and words have different effects on different readers. The use of numerals, for example, tends to emphasize a number, while the use of words tends to de-emphasize a number: *$100* is more emphatic than *a hundred dollars*. Thus we use numerals when the number is a significant statistic or deserves special emphasis, while we use words for numbers in a formal message and for numbers that are not significant and need no special attention.

The business writer must know the general rules for expressing numbers in words and for expressing them in numerals and must be able to manipulate the rules when it is necessary to achieve a greater degree of formality or to provide greater emphasis.

First, we will discuss when the writer should use words to express numbers. Then, we will discuss when the writer should use numerals to express numbers.

At the Beginning of a Sentence

To express a number at the beginning of a sentence use a spelled-out word, not a numeral. If writing the word seems awkward, reword the sentence so that the number does not occur first.

Ninety-two per cent of the students we surveyed said that they prefer the new registration process. (not *92 per cent…*)

Of the students we surveyed, 92 per cent said that they prefer the new registration process. (better than *ninety-two per cent...*)

Numbers from One Through Ten

In business correspondence, the numbers from one through ten are generally spelled out. Numbers greater than ten appear as numerals, unless they begin a sentence.

Last month our representatives acquired nine new accounts.

Ms. Wrigley began as a junior manager ten years ago.

John has been working here for 20 years.

Their store was formerly on Fifth Avenue. (Note that numbered streets from *first* through *tenth* are also spelled out.)

Note: Within a sentence or paragraph, it is important to be consistent in the expression of numbers. For example: There are 3 printers and 15 computers in our office.

Ordinal numbers, *first* through *tenth,* are spelled out.

This is the third time I have visited New York.

Fractions

Fractions are expressed in words in general business correspondence.

About one-third of the people surveyed said that they were dissatisfied with our banking services.

Only one-third of our members were at the annual meeting.

However, a mixed number (a whole number plus a fraction) is expressed as a figure by using a decimal or a fraction.

Our corporate headquarters is located on 8.5 hectares of land near the Rocky Mountains.

Indefinite Numbers

Spell out indefinite numbers and amounts, as shown in these phrases:

a few million dollars

hundreds of telephone calls

several thousand people

Ages and Anniversaries

Ages are spelled out—unless they are significant statistics.

Winona Ames, who is in her late fifties, is our technology expert.

Angela Russo, 27, has been appointed director of marketing. (a significant statistic)

When ordinal numbers (*1st, 2nd, 3rd, 4th,* and so on) are used for ages and anniversaries, they are generally spelled out.

his twenty-first birthday

our seventeenth anniversary

But when more than two words are needed to spell the number, or when special emphasis is desired, express the numbers in numerals.

our town's 125th anniversary (not *one hundred and twenty-fifth*)

A 10th Anniversary Sale! (for emphasis)

Centuries and Decades

Centuries are generally expressed in words.

the nineteen hundreds (but for emphasis, the 1900s)

the twenty-first century

nineteenth-century factories

Decades, however, may be expressed in several ways. Note: Do not use an apostrophe to make the plural.

the nineteen-nineties *or* the 1990s *or* the nineties *or* the '90s

CHECKUP 1

Check the following sentences for any errors in the use of numbers. Write *OK* if a sentence is correct.

1. The auditor's report, which should be about 8 [*eight*] pages long, will be printed and distributed tomorrow.
2. Bertell & Company bought this property in the late 1970's [*1970s*], when it cost less than $100 000.
3. Last year, less than 1/3 [*one-third*] of our budget was spent on advertising.
4. 47 [*forty-seven*] per cent of the customers we interviewed valued quality over discounts.
5. Employees between the ages of 19 and 40 will pay only $18 a month for dental insurance; employees over 40 will pay slightly higher premiums. *OK*.
6. Our Victoria office is responsible for three and a half [*3.5*] times more revenue than our next highest producer.
7. 16 [*sixteen*] people have already called this morning about renting the ski chalet. *(or Reword)*
8. Cyril, I think that we should reprint a few 1,000 [*thousand*] more of these.
9. We received hundreds of resumés in response to our advertisement. *OK*.
10. The museum curator thought the painting might be the work of a 17th-century [*seventeenth-*] Dutch artist.

Using Numerals to Express Numbers

For Numbers Higher than Ten

As you know, numbers from *one* through *ten* are spelled out. Numbers higher than *ten* are expressed in numerals.

Last month 14 condominiums were sold at an auction.

This 16-page brochure describes our complete list of member services.

However, express related numbers in the same way. If any of the numbers are above *ten*, express all the numbers as numerals.

In Conference Room B we will need 4 tables, 24 chairs, and 2 easel stands. (Because one of the related numbers is above *ten*, all are expressed in figures.)

Note: Numerals are more emphatic than words because numerals stand out clearly, especially when they are surrounded by words. Therefore, when greater emphasis is required for a number from one to ten, use a numeral to express that number. For example:

for 10 minutes (more emphatic than *ten minutes*)

a 3-year loan (more emphatic than a *three-year loan*)

For Sums of Money

Sums of money are written in figures.

Clement's travel expenses totalled $536.75.

We have already exceeded the budget of $500. (Not $500.00. The extra zeros are unnecessary.)

We spent between $4000 and $5000. The unit cost is estimated to be 55 cents. (Not *$.55*. Use the symbol ¢ in tables and in technical copy only.)

Note, however, the following usage for related numbers in the same sentence.

The unit cost will be $.65 for the small vase and $1.12 for the large vase.

Note that words and numerals are often used to express amounts of a million or more.

$9 million or 9 million dollars

$12.5 million or 12.5 million dollars

To avoid misreading, be sure to repeat the word *million* in expressions such as this:

between $2 million and $3 million (not *between $2 and $3 million*)

Also be sure to treat related numbers in the same way.

between $500 000 and $1 000 000 (not *between $500 000 and $1 million*)

Remember that indefinite amounts are spelled out.

William's tax refund amounted to a few hundred dollars.

They bought about a thousand dollars' worth of antique china and crystal at the auction.

In legal documents amounts of money are usually expressed first in words and then in numbers within parentheses. For example:

One thousand dollars ($1000) *or* One thousand (1000) dollars (Note that One thousand ($1000) is *not* correct.)

In Addresses

Use numerals for house numbers except for *One*. For streets named by numbers, spell out the ordinal numbers *first* through *tenth*. Numerals are generally used for all other street numbers.

The post office is located at One Maple Street. (Spell out *One* when it is a house number.)

The bookstore that was at 121 West 12 Street is now located at 94 West 14 Street.

When the house number and the street number are not separated by East, West, or a similar word, use the ordinals *st, rd,* and *th* with the street number; it is also a good idea to separate the numbers with a dash.

2131 96th Street

or

2131—96th Street (The ordinal *96th* and the *dash* help to prevent possible confusion.)

Canadian postal codes contain both letters and numbers and follow a set pattern (letter-number-letter one space number-letter-number).

Toronto, Ontario M4L 3S4

Note that *no punctuation* is used in a postal code.

ZIP code numbers for the United States of America are always given in numerals.

New York, New York 10020 (Note that *no comma* precedes the ZIP code number.)

New York, NY 10020-1221 (ZIP plus four numbers)

CHECKUP 2

Check the following sentences for any errors in the use of numbers. Write *OK* if a sentence is correct.

1. Please note that the term of the loan is 2 years, not 4 years, as had originally been *OK* requested.
2. Commercial paper is an unsecured note that has a maximum maturity of two hundred seventy days. *270*
3. To meet the project deadline, fourteen staff members volunteered to work on Saturday. *14*
4. All these securities must be delivered by messenger to Ms. Catherine Reilly, 190-12 *th.* Avenue, by 2 p.m. today.
5. The potential market for this product, according to our preliminary estimates, is between $4 and $5 million.
6. The new software program has a list price of $495.00, but a local computer store is *million* selling it at a 20 per cent discount.
7. If you subscribe now, you will pay only 75 cents a day for your paper. *OK.*
8. Our fleet of vehicles includes five vans, seven trucks, and 15 cars. *5* *7*

With Units of Measure and Percentages

Use numerals, even for numbers less than ten, with units of measure and with percentages, as shown in the following examples. Also note that metric symbols are used to accompany numerals in technical work.

Each office measures 4 m by 5 m.

This television screen measures 30 cm diagonally.

Each vial contains exactly 5 cm of the serum.

We are offering a 20 per cent discount on all refrigerators and freezers.

Note: Use the symbol % only in tables and forms. In other cases, spell out *per cent.*

With Decimals

Decimal numbers are always expressed as numerals:

Mix this compound with water in a ratio of 4.5 parts compound to 1 part water. (A ratio may also be expressed as follows: 4.5:1 ratio of compound to water.)

When no number appears before the decimal, add a zero to help the reader understand the number quickly.

A very slight increase—0.5 per cent—was reported for the month of March. (Without the zero, the reader might read *.5 per cent* as *5 per cent* instead of *5 tenths of a per cent.*)

With *a.m.* and *p.m.*

As you already learned, always use numerals with *a.m.* and *p.m.*

at 9 a.m.

between 11:45 a.m. and 12:30 p.m.

With *O'Clock*

With the word *o'clock,* either numerals or words may be used. For greater emphasis and less formality, use numerals. when stating the time. For more formality but less emphasis, use words.

You are cordially invited to join us at eight o'clock on Friday, the first of June, to celebrate the one hundredth anniversary of the founding of Marsh Enterprises. (*Eight o'clock* is more formal than *8 o'clock.*)

All regional booksellers are invited to a brunch and book-signing party to be held at the Warwick Inn on Saturday, September 14, at 11 o'clock.

In Dates

Use numerals to express the day of the month and the year in dates.

March 19, 1993 (not *March 19th, 1993*)

When the day is written before the month, use an ordinal figure or spell out the ordinal number.

the 4th of June *or* the fourth of June

the 21st of April *or* the twenty-first of April

Note: The ordinal figures are 1st, 2nd, 3rd, 4th, and so on.

With Consecutive Numbers

Consecutive numbers should be separated by a comma when both numbers are in numerals or when both are in words.

In 1992, 121 employees were promoted.

Of the original seven, two employees remain in the Yukon office.

But if one word is in figures and the other is in words, no comma is needed.

On May 12 two executives retired from Piedmont Industries Inc.

When one of the numbers is part of a compound adjective, write the first number in words and the second number in numerals (unless the second number, when spelled out, would be a significantly shorter word). Do not separate the numbers with a comma.

two 9-page booklets (but 200 nine-page booklets)

fifty $10 bills (but 100 ten-dollar bills)

CHECKUP 3

Correct any errors in the use of numbers. Write *OK* if a sentence is correct.

1. The maturity date for this bond is July 1st, 2010.
2. If the meeting is rescheduled for three o'clock tomorrow, all the committee members will be able to attend.
3. On March 15, 76 shareholders will meet with the president in the auditorium.
4. For best results, mix five and a half parts of Kleenall to two parts water.
5. The interest on this money market account is 6.5 per cent.
6. The annual company picnic has been scheduled for the fifth of June.
7. The meeting will begin at 11:30 a.m. and will end by 12:45 p.m.
8. Although this room is small (it measures only two metres by four metres), it will serve well as a storeroom.

Review of Key Terms

1. Why is it important for business writers to accurately express *numbers*?

2. What are *ordinal numbers,* and when should they be spelled out?

Practical Application

1. Correct any errors in number use in the following sentences. Write *OK* if a sentence is correct.

   a. According to the agreement, the monthly interest charge will be one and a half per cent higher than the prime rate.

   b. The new office building on 1st Avenue is fully leased.

   c. During the first quarter, our net operating profit was 12.5% higher than for the same period last year.

   d. Mr. Southerby approved overtime for the 7 people working on the Blake & Graydon account.

   e. The first day of the sales conference is the 6 of June, isn't it?

   f. The federal government has allocated a total of $40,000,000 to the mass-transit improvement program.

   g. The unit cost for printing these brochures is $0.19 in quantities of 10,000 but only $0.16 for 25,000 or more.

   h. Each lifelike reproduction stands 40 cm high and weighs about 4 kg.

   i. Ms. Teague said, "I am pleased to announce that all 5 divisions showed a profit for the 3rd consecutive year."

   j. According to our records, we have distributed about two thousand five hundred samples so far this month.

   k. The sixty-seven cars that are now in our fleet will be replaced within the next six months or so.

   l. We have three estimates for the cost of repaving six and a half spaces in the parking lot.

   m. The difference between the estimated cost and the actual cost was minimal (only .7 per cent).

   n. Please buy 100 fifty cent stamps at the post office today.

   o. As many as 2/3 of our employees have indicated an interest in our evening training courses.

   p. Ms. Steinbach said, "We expect to begin 1995 as a billion-dollar corporation thanks to the success of all 4 of our divisions."

   q. A few 1,000 people are expected to attend the Trade Expo in the InternationalCentre.

   r. If you order now, you may pay four monthly installments of $25.00 each.

   s. Because we must follow the schedule closely, please start your session at 11:45 a.m. and end it no later than 12:30 p.m.

t. We have forecast an increase of 12.5 per cent in gross sales and 14.5 per cent in net income.

2. On a sheet of paper, correct any errors in the following sentences. Write *OK* if a sentence is correct.

a. Do you subscribe to "Business Week" magazine?

b. For the past several years, Ms. Rulinsky's commissions have averaged $15,000.00.

c. The premier has appointed one of our executive vice presidents to the new task force on the environment.

d. Between you and I, Derrick, I doubt that this line of products will compete effectively.

e. Victor's older sister Dr. Rona Mendoza works for our Genetic Research Division in Ottawa.

f. Next Tuesday morning we will meet with Francis J. Smith, President of Tyko Toys Inc.

g. Because the cost of printing these full-colour brochures is so expensive. We decided to spend the money on other forms of sales promotion.

h. We plan, for example, to run two page ads in major magazines.

i. The bonds that we discussed are rated "AAA"; therefore they are very safe investments.

j. The new procedure for obtaining approvals for cost overruns are detailed in this operations manual.

k. The deadline for the March issue is January 5, for the April issue February 4.

l. As many as 60% of our employees wish to attend the computer training sessions.

m. Moshe don't your supervisor want you to attend the training session next month?

n. It's major subsidiary, the AmCo Supply company, is responsible for nearly thirty per cent of the parent corporation's profits.

o. When Kathleen returns from Norway on June 15 we will discuss our new export agreement.

p. It may be too late Ying to run this ad in the July issue.

q. If your planning to sell this product for less than $10, you should explore less expensive packaging.

r. Janet Ko is the only one of the regional managers who like the idea of merging both smaller plants into one large plant.

s. Nicola and I reviewed the production schedules for the next two months but we were not able to find any easy way to expedite the product-completion date.

t. Send this draft to the district managers; ask each to respond by April 15th.

3. Collect examples of appliance manuals or bank brochures. Find examples of the rules covered in Section 6.7. Are there any rules that were not followed?

Editing Practice

Correcting a Letter. Proofread the following excerpt from a letter and correct any errors.

September 10 20—

Ms. Renee Nadeau
15 Oak Drive
Calgary, Alberta
T2L 3S4

dear Ms. Nadeau

Welcome to the Sunset family! As the proud owner of a new Sunset sedan, you has our best wishes.

To help us meet your needs please take a few minutes to complete the enclosed questionnaire. The information you provide will help us customize the maintenance schedule for your new sedan. All you will need to do is drive to your local service centre we will handle the rest.

Our records show that you choose the 2-year or 20000-mile warranty. If you would like to extend your coverage, keep our 3-year and 5-year warrantys in mind.

Discussion Points

1. When are numbers spelled out in business correspondence?
2. Why are units of measurement, percentages, and decimals expressed in numerals?

Chapter 6 Wrap-Up

▶ The mechanics of style—punctuation and capitalization—are writing signals for readers. They let readers know when one thought ends, how ideas are connected, and when to pause. Periods, question marks, and exclamation points indicate the end of a sentence. Commas, semicolons, colons, and dashes indicate pauses and clarify how groups of words should be read. Quotation marks, parentheses, and apostrophes also point out how readers should interpret words.

▶ Capital letters provide important information to readers. Besides indicating the beginning of a sentence, they indicate proper names, business names, titles, and essential words.

▶ It is not always appropriate to use abbreviations in formal writing. When using abbreviations in business writing, follow the company name. Writers should consult a business reference book when in doubt about correct abbreviations.

▶ When writing numbers, writers must know when to use words or numerals. Whether one is expressing sums of money, quantities for orders, addresses, or statistics, errors in number use can be expensive and time-consuming. Typically, numerals are used when the number is a significant statistic. Words for numbers are generally used in formal messages. Employees should know and follow company guidelines.

CASE 6.1

Marina Lourdes works at Centennial Travel Agency. One of her responsibilities is to revise, edit, and format a monthly newsletter that is sent to all business customers. Andrea Jeager, a travel agent, writes the draft of the newsletter and then submits the draft to Marina.

Andrea was busy and submitted her newsletter to Marina without checking it. Because the newsletter was also late, Marina had only one day to work on her revision.

Marina found several inconsistencies in punctuation. She also noticed that Andrea used both numerals and words for the same types of numbers.

Marina is working on a tight deadline. Should she format the newsletter first and then check the content for errors? What resources could Marina use to help her check the use of punctuation and numbers?

CASE 6.2

Khalida emigrated to Canada from Afghanistan. She is eager to learn about Canada and recently heard a talk in which someone quoted a section on fundamental freedoms from the Canadian Charter of Rights and Freedoms.

Khalida is taking a grammar and punctuation course at the local community college. For a current assignment on punctuation, she decides to find out how the section she heard from the Charter is punctuated. On the Government of Canada Web site at **http://laws.justice.gc.ca/ en/charter,** Khalida locates and prints the following section.

"Everyone has the following fundamental freedoms:

a. freedom of conscience and religion;

b. freedom of thought, belief, opinion and expression, including freedom of the press and other media of communication;

c. freedom of peaceful assembly; and

d. freedom of association."

Assuming that Khalida gives a correct explanation of the use of the colon, semicolon, comma, and period in this quotation, what will she say?

Communicating in Your Career

A lot of personal information is discussed in a company's human resource department. Assistants, administrators, managers, and counselors are privy to confidential material. Although this information should remain within the office, there are always people who want to know everything—curious employees who want to be in the know. If they encounter such an inquiring person, how should human resource employees handle questions about revealing information that may affect their jobs or that of other employees?

On the Web

Need some help in using punctuation correctly? Then explore the Paradigm® Online Writing Assistant Web site. You'll find how to use commas, periods, question marks, exclamation marks, semicolons, apostrophes, colons, parentheses, dashes, quotation marks, brackets, and ellipses. Go to **http://www.powa.org/punctuat.htm**. (Please note that if you decide to do some of the activities, solutions are not provided. You will need to bring your answers to class to check them.)

Key Terms

Chapter 7

Sharpening Writing Skills

Chapter Learning Outcomes

After successfully completing this chapter you will have demonstrated the ability to:

▶ revise, edit, and proofread documents;

▶ recognize and correct errors in thought units;

▶ write effective sentences and paragraphs;

▶ use a dictionary and thesaurus to select the correct word;

▶ improve your spelling.

Loi will graduate from his community college in two weeks. Loi excelled in accounting courses, getting mostly A's. In other courses, such as communications, Loi averaged a C.

Ms. Arendas, Loi's accounting instructor, told him about an excellent accounting position that would become available at a nearby hospital in about two weeks. Loi applied and an interview was arranged with Mr. Tallenega, the human resources manager. There would also be a test after the interview.

Loi went for the interview, which he felt went quite well. Then, Mr. Tallenega took Loi to the hospital library to give him the test. Loi was surprised to see that the test was a writing test.

"Mr. Tallenega," Loi commented, "I applied for an accounting position, and this test is asking me to write a memo and to correct the grammar and punctuation in a letter."

"You have the right test, Loi. We know that you can do accounting, because you have excellent grades in all of your accounting courses. In this position, you will have contact with hospital board members and local business executives. You will be asked to write reports about your accounting work and to present the reports to board members. We must have someone who can speak and write well," Mr. Tallenega said.

After completing the interview and the test, Loi drove back to the college to talk with Ms. Arendas. "Do most accounting jobs require writing skills?" he asked.

"Well, many of them do, especially those which are more challenging. If you wish to move ahead in your career and eventually achieve a supervisory or management position, your communication skills will be vitally important."

As you read Chapter 7, identify strategies that Loi could use to develop his writing skills.

Revising, Editing, and Proofreading

▶ **Key Terms**

▶ revising

▶ tone

▶ grammar checker

▶ editing

▶ proofreading

Revise, edit, and proofread because [sic] pobody is nerfect.

—S. C. Camp, author

After writing the initial draft of a document, writers go through these three steps—revising, editing, and proofreading.

Revising improves the content and organization of writing; *editing* refines the revised draft and adds polish; *proofreading* spots typographical and grammatical errors.

Using Proofreaders' Marks

When revising, editing, and proofreading documents, use proofreaders' marks as a quick, simple way to indicate changes or corrections in handwritten or keyed copy.

The proofreaders' marks shown in Figure 7.1 are standard marks used to indicate corrections in handwritten or keyed copy. Study the marks and become familiar with their use.

Some of the proofreaders' marks are particularly useful in reorganizing the content of a memo, letter, or report. For example, you can easily see from the illustration how to use these marks to indicate the relocation of small and large segments of text. Simply identify the material to be moved by marking the beginning and the end of the segment with a vertical line and labelling the block with a letter of the alphabet. You can also use this block identification to mark material that should be checked for accuracy before the final document is printed or keyed. Place a question mark in the margin next to the block. Include marginal notes as needed for clarification.

Once you have marked changes and corrections on the hard copy, it is a simple process to make the changes on the computer. Remember to proofread the document after it has been printed to make sure all the indicated changes have been made correctly and no further errors have been introduced.

What Is Revising?

Revising is the process of "seeing again." In other words, when you revise, you have to stand back from your work and read it with fresh eyes in order to improve the writing. To do that, you need to allow some time to put your writing

Proofreaders' Marks

Capitalization

Capitalize a letter	toronto	Toronto
Lowercase a letter	This	this
Capitalize all letters	Cobol	COBOL
Lower case a word	PROGRAM	program
Use initial capital only	PROGRAM	Program

Changes and Transpositions

Change a word	price is only $10.98 ($12.99)	price is only $12.99
Change a letter	deductable	deductible
Stet (do not make the change)	price is only $10.98	price is only $10.98
Spell out	(2) cars on Washburn (Rd.)	two cars on Washburn Road
Move as shown	on May 1 (write to him)	write to him on May 1
Transpose letters or words	hte time (the of) meeting	the time of the meeting

Deletions

Delete a letter and close up	strooke or strooke	stroke or stroke
Delete a word	wrote two two cheques	wrote two cheques
Delete punctuation	report was up-to-date.	report was up to date
Delete one space*	good/day	good day
Delete space	see ing	seeing

Insertions

Insert a word or letter	in ^the office buildng^	in the office building
Insert a comma	may leave early^...	may leave early,...
Insert a period	Dr⊙Maria Rodriguez	Dr. Maria Rodriguez
Insert an apostrophe	all the boys' hats	all the boys' hats
Insert quotation marks	Move on, she said.	"Move on," she said.
Insert hyphens	up to date report	up-to-date report
Insert a dash	They were surprised --even shocked!	They were surprised —even shocked!
Insert parentheses	pay fifty dollars $50	pay fifty dollars ($50)
Insert one space	may leave	may leave
Insert two spaces	1.The new machine	1. The new machine

*Use marginal notes for clarification.

◀ **Figure 7.1**
Proofreaders' Marks
Proofreaders' marks provide a standard set of symbols for marking corrections.

Thinking Critically.
Who are proofreaders' marks written for?

Proofreaders' Marks (continued)

Format Symbols: Boldface and Underscore

Print boldface	Bulletin
Remove boldface	Bulletin
Underscore	<u>Title</u>
Remove underscore	Title

Format Symbols: Centring

Centre line horizontally	] TITLE [

Format Symbols: Page and Paragraph

Begin a new page	*pg* ...order was delivered today by common carrier. We have all the...
Begin a new paragraph	...order was delivered today by common carrier. We have all the...
Do not begin new paragraph (run in)	...order was delivered today by common carrier. *No ¶* We have all the materials...
Indent five space	*5* We have the raw materials in our warehouse. Production will...

Format Symbols: Spacing

Single space	ss XXXXXXXXXX XXXXXXXXXX
Double-space	ds XXXXXXXXXX XXXXXXXXXX
Triple-space	ts XXXXXXXXXX XXXXXXXXXX

aside for a few hours or even for a day. Then you should be able to read what you have written more objectively—as your potential audience will read it.

Checking Purpose, Audience, and Tone

Revising is not a hit-or-miss procedure. You need to ask yourself specific questions when revising any piece of writing. To begin the revision process, you should always ask questions about the purpose, audience, and tone of your message.

Is the Purpose of the Document Clear?   If your purpose, for example, is to persuade your reader to take a certain action, does that message come across clearly, without possibility of being misunderstood? If your purpose is to inform, have you included all pertinent information? If your purpose is to promote goodwill, have you used appropriate wording?

Is the Writing Tailored to the Audience?   To tailor the writing to the audience, consider your audience's familiarity with the subject. Suppose you must write a memo to new employees about company copying and mailing procedures. Did you consider that your audience—the new employees—know very little about the company, its policies, or other procedures? Did you use any terms, abbreviations, or references that might not be understood by the new employees?

Is the Tone Appropriate for the Audience?   Tone usually refers to the general effect created by a piece of writing. For example, the tone of your writing could be formal or informal, serious or humorous, positive or negative.

   Although seldom stated directly, the tone is inferred by the reader through the choice of words and other elements of style. For example, if you were writing a memorandum to a supervisor, you would avoid a negative, critical tone—even if you were reporting on some aspects of company procedures that needed improvement. To keep the attention of your audience, you should establish a positive, upbeat tone that offers constructive suggestions for dealing with problems and challenges.

Reviewing the Organization

After answering the basic questions about purpose, audience, and tone, you should examine the organization of your message.

Is the Organization Logical?   Begin the message with a strong opening paragraph or introduction that states the main idea or purpose of the message. The middle paragraphs should sufficiently support or explain your stated purpose, and the conclusion should summarize your ideas or arguments.

   One way to make sure that your writing has a logical organization is to prepare an outline. Then follow that outline carefully as you write.

Do All Sentences Stick to the Point?   As you review the organization of your message, pay particular attention to any sentences that seem to stray from the main idea of each paragraph. Such sentences usually contain unnecessary information that should be deleted because it detracts from the message and create confusion. For example, if you were making the point in a report that good math skills are necessary for all entry-level jobs in your company, you would be wandering off the subject if you described your own math training.

Are Transitions Used to Connect Ideas?   If your paragraphs are complete and if you have presented them in a clear, logical order, you should then make sure that you have included effective bridges, or transitions, between ideas, sentences, and paragraphs. Refer to the list of transitional words and phrases in Figure 7.6 on page 313.

Use Revision Checklist 1 in Figure 7.2 to check the purpose, audience, tone, and organization of your messages.

"Police union to seek blinking arbitration."

(binding)

Figure 7.2 ▶
Revision Checklist 1

Thinking Critically.
*What effect does an
inappropriate tone have
upon readers?*

Revision Checklist 1

Purpose, Audience, and Tone

- Is the purpose clear?
- Is the wording suited to the audience?
- Is the tone appropriate?

Organization

- Is the content complete?
- Is the organization of the message logical?
- Does the message have a strong introduction, middle, and conclusion?
- Do all sentences relate to the main idea of each paragraph?
- Are appropriate transitions used to connect sentences and paragraphs?

Reviewing the Language

Once you are confident that you have included all the necessary information, take a close look at the words that comprise the sentences and paragraphs.

Are Words Used Correctly?   First, make sure that you have used each word correctly. If you are unsure of the meaning of a word, either look it up in a dictionary to make sure the word is appropriate or find an alternative word that expresses your exact meaning.

Are the Words Vivid and Specific?   Now determine whether the words you have chosen will have the effect you intend. The purpose of all writing is to transfer your thoughts and ideas—as completely and as forcefully as possible—to someone else. Colourful, vivid, and specific words help accomplish that purpose. Refer to Section 7.5 for additional discussion of descriptive words.

Are Any Words Overused or Unnecessary?   Check to see whether you have used the same words or expressions over and over. Readers sometimes become annoyed at such unnecessary repetition. For example, if you find that you have repeatedly used the word *told* throughout a report, consult a thesaurus for alternative words, such as *related, announced, declared, asserted, directed,* or *replied.* You will avoid repetition and at the same time describe more clearly the various ways people speak or make statements.

Is the Sentence Structure Varied?   Most people write exactly as they speak, and most people begin sentences with the subject. The monotony of this sentence structure is much more noticeable in a letter or report than it is in conversation. You can reduce reader boredom by adding some variety. For example, occasionally begin a sentence with an adverb or an adverbial phrase, a participial phrase, or a prepositional phrase.

Subject: *Employees* often have to wait in line for 15 minutes in the cafeteria.

Adverb: *Often* employees have to wait in line for 15 minutes in the cafeteria.

Prepositional Phrase: *In the cafeteria,* employees often have to wait in line for 15 minutes.

Revision Checklist 2

Language Use

- Do the meanings of the words used fit the content of the message?
- Are there any dull or overused nouns, adjectives, or verbs that could be replaced with more colourful, specific words?
- Are there any repeated words or expressions that could be deleted or replaced?
- Should synonyms be used to make the message clearer and more forceful?
- Are the sentence beginnings varied?
- Are sentences written in the active voice whenever possible?

Thinking Critically.
How does overusing words hinder your communications with others?

Is the Message Written in Active Voice?   Another important step is to see if verbs are in the active voice wherever possible. In the active voice, the subject is the doer of the action; in the passive voice, the subject is the receiver of the action. Your writing will be much livelier if you use the active voice. Refer to Section 7.3 for more information. Compare the following sentences.

Passive: The long-awaited announcement was read by the Defence Minister.

Active: The Defence Minister read the long-awaited announcement.

Use Revision Checklist 2 in Figure 7.3 to improve the language use in your messages.

When revising and editing, remember to apply the KISS philosophy:

Keep It Short and Simple!

MEMORY HOOK

Revising with Grammar Checkers

A **grammar checker** is software that evaluates grammar and suggests ways to improve the grammar and wording of a document. Grammar checkers identify certain weaknesses such as errors in subject-verb agreement, overuse of the passive voice, lack of variety in sentence structure, and wordiness.

Some grammar checkers estimate the reading level of a text segment. You can revise your document if the reading level is too high or too low. For example, if your company is inviting employees' children to attend a summer day camp, you could use a grammar checker to make sure the invitation is written so children can understand it.

Most grammar checkers highlight "potential" errors. You, as the writer, must decide if the highlighted text contains an actual error. You must also determine how to correct the error. You must ask yourself these questions: Is what I keyed correct? Should I make a change? What is the correct change? Although grammar checkers can be very helpful, they should not replace detailed revising and editing.

What Is Editing?

Editing is the process of checking a revised draft to make sure it meets the criteria of the six Cs of communication. That is, you make sure the document

Figure 7.4 ▶
Editing Checklist

Thinking Critically.
What else can you add to
this editing checklist?

Editing Checklist

- Is the message clear?
- Is the message complete?
- Is the wording concise?
- Is the wording consistent?
- Is the wording correct?
- Is the message courteous?

is clear, complete, concise, consistent, correct, and courteous. Editing not only helps improve the quality of your document but also helps improve your skill as a writer.

Developing an editing skill is important for anyone involved with written communication. The purpose of editing is to make the document as effective as possible. You can improve a document by using the questions posed in the Editing Checklist in Figure 7.4.

The Six Cs of Editing

Is It Clear? Business communications are written to get action—not to entertain or increase the vocabulary of the reader. Good business writers use simple words and proper English. They also make every effort to avoid clichés. Documents should be coherent: that is, they should flow appropriately. Using transitional words and phrases contributes to clarity.

Is It Complete? A complete message includes all necessary information. Because the writer is so familiar with the message, omitted details are not always obvious to the writer. These missing details may, however, be obvious to the reader. Imagine receiving a brochure for a business seminar that gives only the hour, place, and topic of the seminar. The message is incomplete without the date. Further communication would be needed to clarify the information.

Is It Concise? Unnecessary words, phrases, clauses, sentences, and paragraphs are a barrier to effective communication. Needless repetition of words decreases the effectiveness of your message because the reader must read a lot of words to get a little information. To make your writing concise, include only necessary words, and avoid repeating the same words several times in a message.

Is It Consistent? Business messages should be consistent in fact, treatment, and sequence. A message is consistent in fact if it does not contradict itself, an established fact, or a source document.

Treating similar items the same way results in consistency in treatment.

- When listing both men's and women's names, use courtesy titles for all or none of the names: *Mr. Lawrence, Ms. Ruiz, Mrs. Thomas.*
- Use a consistent style in writing numbers and amounts. For example, *$1000* and *$10 000, 36 customers* and *67 customers.*
- Use the same formatting, such as indenting paragraphs, throughout a document.

- Use such special formatting techniques as underlining and italics consistently for names of books and titles of articles.
- Use a consistent sequence (alphabetical, chronological, or numerical) to improve the flow of a message. For example, list names in alphabetical order to avoid conveying unintentional bias by listing one person's name before another's.

Note: Many companies use an established style guide. Be sure to refer to the preferred style guide used in your place of business.

Is It Correct? Accuracy in content and mechanics (capitalization, grammar, spelling, punctuation, and so on) makes the message more effective. Proofread the document to eliminate these kinds of errors.

Is It Courteous? Courtesy in a business communication means that it is pleasing to the eye, reader-centred, and positive. In addition to using the you-attitude and positive words, follow these suggestions for achieving courtesy:

- Select fonts that are easy to read. Cursive type fonts (Cursive) and solid-capital fonts (ALL CAPITALS) are more difficult to read than the more traditional fonts, such as Times, or Times New Roman, in both upper- and lowercase-letters. Also, use a standard font size, such as 12 point. Very small fonts are difficult to read.
- Create an eye-pleasing communication by using several short paragraphs instead of one long paragraph.
- Position your document attractively on the page, including enough white space (blank space) to make the page appear uncluttered.
- Use a table format or a bulleted or numbered list for appropriate information to add visual variety and to make reading easier.

What Is Proofreading?

Proofreading is the process of examining a document to find errors that should be corrected. Sometimes proofreading is a verification process, such as checking a letter keyed from a handwritten rough draft. When you are proofreading your own work, however, you may not have a document to compare the final draft against. In either case, you should look carefully for errors in capitalization, content, format, grammar, word usage, number usage, punctuation, spelling, typing, and word division.

To be a good proofreader—to be able to identify errors—you must be familiar with all these types of errors. If you are unsure of a spelling, a usage, and so on, rely on reference sources. You may, for example, see the word *accomodation* and wonder whether it is spelled correctly. After checking a dictionary, you change the word to *accommodation*.

The proofreading process should begin in the early stages of document preparation and continue throughout each stage, including the final copy. In other words, check the document for errors before keyboarding from notes, a handwritten draft, or a keyed draft. Today, with the use of electronic communication such as e-mail, some documents are not printed before transmission. However, for important documents, when errors could be extremely devastating, proofreading a printed document is a necessity.

The farmer bought 200 cows for his diary.

(dairy)

"And now, the Superstore—unequaled in size, unmatched in variety, unrivaled inconvenience." (From Pet Market section of Classified Ads)

(in convenience)

Proofreading for Yourself and for Others

Proofreading is an essential step in the writing process, whether you are proofreading your own work or someone else's. As a student or as an office professional, you must get into the proofreading habit. Grades will suffer if errors are found on a research paper, and a potential salary increase or promotion may be lost if errors are found in a sales report you prepared. Habitual proofreading problems may even result in a loss of one's position.

In a business situation, you may be responsible for writing memos or reports. Consequently, you would need to proofread your own work. A coworker, realizing the importance of an error-free document, may ask you to check his or her work for errors. Occasionally, you might ask others to proofread your work, but you do not want to convey to them that you lack proofreading skills. If you keyboard business letters, reports, or other correspondence, you must proofread as an important step in document preparation.

Proofreading your own writing is usually considered more difficult than proofreading the work of others for two reasons. First, you, as the writer, may tend to be overconfident, believing that you corrected all errors. Second, you may be overly familiar with the document, which may cause you to "read" what you intended to key instead of reading what you *actually* keyed.

Proofreading and Technology

Technology offers some assistance in proofreading for spelling and keyboarding errors. Most word processing programs have spell checkers that will locate words not recognized by their built-in dictionaries. However, spell checkers will not locate a missing word or a misused word if it is correctly spelled. For example, the errors in the following sentences would be undetected if you relied on a spell checker alone.

Incorrect: We submitted the completed form *bye* March 2.

Hour company *if* the number *won* manufacturer of plastic containers in *their* country.

Correct: We submitted the completed form *by* March 2.

Our company *is* the number *one* manufacturer of plastic containers in *the* country.

Some spell checkers will find repetition errors like this one:

He gave me *the the* calendar.

Technology streamlines the process of making identical changes, called *global changes,* throughout a document. Suppose, for example, you mentioned the name *Steven Smathers* five times in a document. After keyboarding, you learn that the correct spelling is *Stephen Smathers.* Using the global function, you would have to make the correction only once; the other four changes would be made automatically.

Proofreading on the computer screen is similar in many ways to proofreading a printed page. However, you must condition your eyes and mind to this different medium. Note the techniques in Figure 7.5 that are useful for finding errors on the computer screen.

You should do your first proofreading on the screen, make the necessary changes and corrections, and then print a copy. You should also proofread the printed copy to make sure that your changes were entered correctly. Experience will help you build confidence and skill in proofreading on the computer screen.

Proofreading Checklist

- Use a bright-coloured pen to make changes easier to spot.

- Quickly scan for problems such as format errors. Are the date and other standard parts included in letters and memos? Do all headings in a report follow the same format?

- Check typeface styles and sizes. Is the same font style and size used for similar headings?

- Turn the document upside down to check for spacing and placement errors.

- Superimpose subsequent drafts over previous drafts and hold the drafts up to a light to detect possible errors.

- Read carefully for correct content, making sure there are no factual errors and that no words, sentences, paragraphs, and other portions of text were omitted.

- Make sure that text that has been moved electronically does not appear in both the original position and the new location.

- Read for correct capitalization, grammar, word usage, number usage, punctuation, spelling, typing, and word division. Spell check and grammar check the entire document.

- Read the document backward to help detect spelling and punctuation errors by concentrating on each word separately.

- Give special attention to locations where errors frequently occur: (a) at the end and the top of the next page, (b) in line endings and line beginnings, (c) in numerical and alphabetized lists, and (d) in cross-references to items.

- Check all numbers and technical terms for accuracy. Use a calculator to add columns of figures to verify that totals are correct.

- Ask a co-worker to proofread the document.

- Read the document aloud. Reading aloud increases concentration and thus helps you identify awkward sentences.

- Use the print preview feature of your software to proofread your document.

- Temporarily enlarge the font to ensure you are seeing everything clearly, including punctuation.

◀ **Figure 7.5**
Proofreading Checklist

Thinking Critically.
What else can you add to this proofreading checklist?

Importance of Proofreading

Uncorrected errors create a bad impression. They also can cost your company money and cause other problems. Consider these two examples.

Suppose, in a handwritten draft, you quote a price of $32 453 for a new minivan. When the final copy is keyed, the price is incorrectly listed as $23 453. If not detected, this simple transposition of numbers could cost your company $9000. Correcting the error after the customer receives the incorrect quotation would cause ill will, the loss of a sale, and possibly legal action.

Suppose, on a travel itinerary, the train departure time is erroneously listed as 10:50 a.m. instead of the correct time of 10:05 a.m. This simple transposition could cause the recipient to miss the train.

In both examples, efficient proofreading would result in the error being caught. For this reason, executives encourage the detection and correction of errors to prevent problems. Therefore, it is essential that you approach proofreading in a systematic way.

After using the electronic tools available to you, such as grammar checkers and spell checkers, use the Proofreading Checklist both to proofread onscreen and later when you proofread printed documents. You need not use *all* these techniques for every document.

Review of Key Terms

1. How does the audience of a document affect its *tone*?
2. What are some advantages and disadvantages of using a *grammar checker*?

Practical Application

1. Write or key each sentence, making the indicated changes.
   a. Dr. Sam Martinez autographed copies of his latest book, <u>Healthy Eating for Busy Executives</u>.
   b. His letter was mis interpreted by the ~~the~~ newspaper editor.
   c. Phils Sandwich Shop opens dialy at 10:30 a.m.
   d. The camera were shipped February 10 and the film.
   e. Mrs. ~~Anderson~~ I apprecciate your willingness to help our organize annual fund-raising dinner. *Lagros*
   f. The shipment will arrive in ③ days. *three*
   g. Many business expenses are tax deductable. *change letter*
   h. Tom and Mariel are looking forward to Their Summer Vacation. *lowercase*
   i. Alexandra went to Mexico and to south America. *Delete punctuation capitalize south*
   j. We need a new POSTAL Code Directory. *Postal*

2. Key one screen of information by copying from this textbook. Then use the Proofreading Checklist in this section to determine which of these proofreading techniques are effective when proofreading from the computer screen.

3. Edit the following sentences to eliminate unnecessary words and to use clearer wording.
   a. We found the new computers to be adequate ~~enough~~.
   b. ~~Kindly~~ return your completed form by August 4. *please*
   c. All committee members need to cooperate together.
   d. Almost all of the ~~gratis~~ samples have been given away. *free*
   e. Our ~~past~~ experience with this supplier has been positive.

4. Edit the following sentences to eliminate inconsistencies.
   a. Mark Rummel and Ms. Se Ri Pak conducted the training session. *Mr. Rummel*
   b. Over 70 per cent of our clients travel in April, June, and May. *April, May, and June*
   c. Of the 7 applicants, only three have programming experience. *3 or seven.*
   d. We ordered the books *Legal Procedures* and <u>NOT LIABLE</u> for the law library.
   e. Doctors <u>Klein</u>, <u>Desjardins</u>, and <u>Diniz</u> are opening a new office. *alphabet order. Desjardins Diniz Klein*

5. Edit the following sentences to make them positive and to achieve the you-attitude.
   a. If you are unable to understand the operating instructions for your computer, please call our toll-free number for assistance.
   b. Your delay in completing the report put us behind schedule. *A*

c. We are sorry we cannot ship your complete order at this time.

d. I need you to process the patients' insurance forms by this afternoon.

6. Rewrite the following paragraph, making any necessary changes and corrections. Assume that Monday is July 1.

Nancy Threlkeld will assume the position of Director of Employee Activities on Monday, July 1. In this position, she will be in charge of and responsible for athletic teams, organizations, trips, and all other social events sponsored by our company. On Wednesday, July 3, she will attend a conference to learn about activities offered by other companies. She will hold a meeting Tuesday, July 3, at 2:30 p.m., in the Recreation Hall, to get your suggestions for August and September activities.

7. Make a list of words used incorrectly in the following paragraph. Beside each incorrect word, write the correct word that should have been used.

In the passed ate weaks, my assistance have placed twenty adds in you're newspaper. As you may no, their was some confusion about the invoice. Your paper accidentally build us twice for the same advertisements. Will you please make an appropriate adjustment to our account. Advertising with you has been affective in increasing our sales, and we plan to buy more advertising space soon.

8. Interview someone you know who writes daily. Consider interviewing

TEAMWORK

a campus or local newspaper reporter or editor. Then, write a brief summary of how that person manages the writing process. What is the most difficult part of the process? The easiest?

Editing Practice

Proofread and correct the following memo.

On Tuesday January 30, Dr Sam Martinez will be at Tonys Book Shop for a book signing from 10:30 a.m. to noon. His newest Book, *Healthy Eating for Busy Execturives,* will be availabel at a 20% discount while supplies last.

Discussion Points

1. Compare the role of revising with the role of editing.

2. Why is it important to proofread documents throughout the entire writing process?

Building Effective Paragraphs

To write simply is as difficult as to be good.

—W. Somerset Maugham, English novelist

Writing effective paragraphs requires writing good sentences and connecting the sentences to get the message across to the reader. Each sentence should support the main idea of the paragraph. If sentence structure is faulty, or if paragraph organization is poor, the whole communication will fail.

Message Structure

To be effective, each written message should have one purpose. Each paragraph in the message should have one main idea. Each sentence in a paragraph should have one main thought that supports the main idea of the paragraph.

Message → One purpose

Paragraph → One main idea

Sentence → One main thought

A written communication, such as a letter or a memorandum, should be limited to one main purpose. Two or more main purposes within a communication can cause confusion or can make one idea seem more or less important than another. In the following examples, note how the first message covers more than one purpose, while the second message focuses on one purpose.

More Than One Purpose

Thank you for inquiring about our automobile loans. Enclosed is a loan application form for your review.

You may also be interested in our certificates of deposit. We offer variable interest rates for three-month, six-month, and nine-month certificates.

One Purpose

Thank you for inquiring about our automobile loans. Enclosed is a loan application form for your review.

We offer flexible payment schedules for all automobile loans so that you can select a monthly payment that fits your budget.

Paragraph Control

To achieve paragraph control, the writer should relate all sentences to the main idea of the paragraph and keep paragraphs a reasonable length. In addition, the writer should use transitions and make sound decisions about where to separate paragraphs.

Paragraph Unity

The main idea of a paragraph is usually stated in a topic sentence. This topic sentence is often the first sentence in the paragraph. All other sentences in the paragraph should support the main idea, creating **paragraph unity**. For example, in the following paragraph, note how all the sentences relate to the main idea about techniques for improving your memory.

There are several techniques for improving your memory. One technique is to use certain images to remember the names of people and things. For example, to remember the name of an important client, Ms. Flowers, you could remember her picking flowers. Another technique is to use a word or an acronym to remember a concept. For example, use the word *homes* to remember the names of the Great Lakes: *Huron, Ontario, Michigan, Erie,* and *Superior.* Still another memory technique is to associate a list of items with travelling a particular route. Each item becomes a part of your walk along this route. For instance, to remember an item on a grocery list, you might picture yourself putting a litre of milk in the mailbox as you walk to your neighbour's house.

Before writing the first sentence of a paragraph, the writer should have the main idea of the paragraph clearly in mind. The writer must know where the paragraph is going before attempting to guide the reader there. The writer who does not know the purpose of that paragraph should stop writing and start thinking.

Transitional Words and Phrases

Transitional words and phrases provide connections between sentences and between paragraphs. Skilful use of transitional words and phrases can move the reader through the communication—from one idea to another—without a break in continuity that could detract from the message.

Figure 7.6 lists some common transitions you could use to show how items, ideas, or events are related to one another.

Note the transitions used in the following examples.

Sequence: *After* he receives the spreadsheets, Ned will compile the final report.

Location: *Below* is a list of specifications.

Emphasis: *Again,* this new insurance policy will be available to all employees.

Conclusion: *Therefore,* in recognition of Michelle Wellington's outstanding sales record, we are naming her Employee of the Year.

As you read the following message, note the length of the paragraph and the lack of transitions.

We were surprised to hear that you did not enjoy your tour of Jasper National Park in Alberta last month. We feel that our literature gave you an accurate impression of what to expect. Our literature states that "Explorer Nature Tours are not for the faint of heart. Our naturalist guides take you to remote and pristine areas where you will see scenic landscapes and encounter native wildlife." Our tour literature does

Transitional Words and Phrases

Indicate Sequence

after	during	later
as soon as	finally	meanwhile
at present	first (second, third,	next
at the same time	fourth)	soon
before	immediately	then

Show Location

above	below	outside
ahead	higher	
behind	inside	

Compare or Contrast

also	however	on the other hand
although	instead	rather
both	likewise	similarly
but	neither	still
by contrast	nevertheless	yet
even though	on the contrary	

Add Information

also	despite	moreover
and	equally important	next
another	further	one reason
as well	furthermore	
besides	in addition	

Provide an Example

for example	namely	that is
for instance	specifically	
in particular	such as	

Add Emphasis

after all	even more	in fact
again	for this purpose	more important
especially	indeed	

Indicate a Result or Conclusion

as a result	consequently	therefore
because of	finally	thus

◄ **Figure 7.6**
Common Transitions
Figure 7.6 lists common transitions.

Thinking Critically.
When explaining a new project to colleagues, how might transitions assist in determining objectives and responsibilities for each member of the group?

not explicitly say that you will wake up to find a bear outside your tent, as you did. We do indicate that such encounters are a remote possibility. Our experienced guides handled the situation quickly so that no harm resulted. We regret that you did not enjoy your tour. We must remind you that our policy, as stated in the tour literature, does not permit us to give you a complete refund. In your situation, we are willing to make an exception to our no-refund policy.

Let's look at how the preceding paragraph could be improved by making several shorter paragraphs and adding the transitions shown in italics.

We were surprised to hear that you did not enjoy your Explorer Nature Tour of Jasper National Park in Alberta last month. We feel that our literature gave you an accurate impression of what to expect. *For instance,* our literature states that "Explorer Nature Tours are not for the faint of heart. Our naturalist guides take you to remote and pristine areas where you will see scenic landscapes and encounter native wildlife."

Although our tour literature does not explicitly say that you will wake up as you did, to find a bear outside your tent, we do indicate that such encounters are a remote possibility.

Fortunately, our experienced guides handled the situation quickly so that no harm resulted. *Nevertheless,* we regret that you did not enjoy your tour.

We must remind you that our policy, as stated in the tour literature, does not permit us to give you a complete refund. *However,* in your situation, we are willing to make an exception to our no-refund policy.

Paragraphing Decisions

Paragraphing decisions can create an attractive, uncluttered format that makes business documents easier to read and understand. Ideally, content determines paragraph length. However, when it is practical, adjust paragraphs to fit the guidelines below. *Remember:* These are guidelines, not hard-and-fast rules.

Paragraphing Guidelines

Adopt the following paragraphing suggestions to improve the appearance and readability of a document.

- Keep the first and last paragraphs short, usually two to five lines each.
- Keep middle paragraphs an average of four to eight lines in length, and make them longer than the first and last paragraphs.
- Combine several short paragraphs to avoid a choppy appearance.
- Avoid writing several long paragraphs.
- Avoid a top-heavy appearance (beginning paragraphs too long); avoid a bottom-heavy appearance (ending paragraphs too long).
- Use an odd number of paragraphs. Three paragraphs look better than two, and five paragraphs look better than four.

Sentence Control

Maintaining sentence control is one way to improve the readability of a document. **Readability** refers to the ease with which something can be read. Sentence length and sentence structure are two factors that affect readability.

Variety in Sentence Length

Long sentences tend to be harder to understand than short ones. Yet, short sentences can seem choppy and boring. What is the solution to the sentence-length problem? Variety. Most sentences should range in length from 10 to 20 words. This range is a guide. To provide variety, some sentences will have fewer than 10 words; others will have more than 20 words.

Extremely long sentences seem to bury the main thought. Beyond a certain length, sentences often grow weaker with each added word. Overly long sentences may be grammatically correct, but often they are wordy. Compare the following examples.

Wordy: Thank you for informing us in your letter of May 30 that you still have not received the illustrated *Complete Guide to Organic Gardening* that we shipped to you by parcel post on or about last May 1, but there's no need for you to worry, because we are going to send you another copy of this excellent handbook on the techniques of successful gardening without chemicals.

The reader has to swallow far too many words merely to learn that another copy of the book will be sent.

Better: Thank you for letting us know that your copy of the *Complete Guide to Organic Gardening* has not reached you. We are mailing you a new copy at once.

On the other hand, a succession of short sentences weakens writing, because the reader is jerked along from thought to thought.

Choppy: I received your proposal yesterday. Your approach to tracking inventory in our distribution centre is interesting. We have a manufacturing committee meeting next week. I will present your proposal at that time.

Instead, the writer should smooth out the bumps, as in this revision.

Better: Your proposal arrived by messenger yesterday morning. In my opinion, your approach to tracking inventory in our distribution centre is promising. I will present your proposal to the other members of the manufacturing committee when we meet next week.

In some situations, the planned use of short sentences can be very effective. Short sentences are useful to bring out a series of important facts, to emphasize a point, and to break up a series of longer sentences. Note the short sentences in the following example.

The Fast-Action camera is made especially for quick-moving action photography. Its autofocus feature prepares you for your next shot a fraction of a second after you press the shutter. You just point and shoot—there's no need to focus! Its easy-open back permits you to insert a new roll of film faster than you can in any other camera. You can reload in 15 seconds! Best of all, the Fast-Action camera is equipped with a built-in computerized flash that works on a rechargeable battery. The camera provides a flash only when it's needed! See your dealer for complete details.

Variety in Sentence Structure

A communication that lacks variety lacks interest. One sure way to produce a dull communication is to use only simple sentences. Equally dull is a communication with all compound sentences or one with all complex sentences. Your goal should be to vary the sentence structure of a message.

In the following example, note how too many compound sentences and too many *ands* make the paragraph dull.

Dull: Your new Metro Spirit coupe costs more, *and* it offers a variety of convenient standard features. The fuel-injected engine is durable, *and* you will enjoy its trouble-free operation. The engine uses less fuel while idling, *and* it uses less fuel on the road. Our coupes stand up to years of wear *and* have a high resale value. You chose the right car, *and* you will find this out in the coming years.

In the following revision, note how variety in sentence structure improves the paragraph.

Better: Your new Metro Spirit coupe costs more, *but it* offers convenient standard features. *Because* the fuel-injected engine is durable, you will enjoy years of trouble-free operation. You will use less fuel *both* when idling and when moving. *Finally,* because Spirit coupes stand up to years of wear, they have high resale value. The years will prove that you chose the right car.

Review of Key Terms

1. How can a writer achieve *paragraph unity*?
2. How do *transitional words* and *phrases* provide connections between ideas? Provide an example.

Practical Application

1. Edit the following paragraph. Make sure that each sentence has one main thought and that each sentence supports the main idea of the paragraph. If the paragraph contains more than one main idea, break it into two or more paragraphs. Omit sentences that do not support the main idea of the paragraph.

   The computer operator's body should be erect; he or she should sit well back in the chair and lean forward slightly from the waist. Feet should be placed firmly on the floor. The body should be about a handspan from the front of the keyboard. Sitting too close to the computer can cause bottom-row errors, just as sitting too far away can cause top-row errors. Most printers offer several font sizes. Likewise, sitting too far to the left or right causes errors of the opposite hand. Keyboarding speed increases only through practice.

2. Rewrite the paragraph, varying the sentence structure. Some sentences should be combined. Omit the sentence that does not support the main idea.

   There will be a reception on Wednesday, September 26. It will honour Graham C. Dobbs. He has been the purchasing director for 30 years. He is retiring on September 30. The reception time is 5:30 p.m. to 7:30 p.m. It will be held in the corporate dining room. Everyone is invited.

3. Each of the following paragraphs contains one sentence that does not relate to the main idea of the paragraph. The sentence, however, does relate to the main idea of another paragraph. Rewrite the letter, putting the misplaced sentences in the correct paragraphs.

   Dear Mr. Morris:

   Thank you for requesting information about Lakeview Family Campground. Baby-sitting services are available ($4 per hour) through the local Teen Club.

   Free activities include morning aerobic workouts, afternoon water games, and nightly movies. Shuttle bus service to the village, panoramic boat tours, and water skiing—all reasonably priced—are offered daily.

   You may select various optional services, which are available at very low rates. Cable television, water connections, and electrical hookups are the most popular selections. Each Saturday night, the camp recreation director arranges such free entertainment as puppet shows, folk singing, and short plays.

The enclosed brochure lists our rates. Our grounds, arranged to provide privacy, can comfortably accommodate tents, camping vehicles, and mobile homes. Please phone us soon to make sure that you get the reservations you want.

Sincerely yours,

4. Rewrite the following paragraphs. Add transitional words and phrases to connect the ideas.

Thank you for telling us about your experience with our products. We have strict quality control procedures. Some defective products may be getting by our inspectors.

Of course, comments like yours help us improve. We have already initiated actions that may be helpful. We respect your opinion. We plan to try your suggestions for a while and monitor the results. We may explore other options for quality control.

Your special order is ready and will be shipped some time later today. Thank you for your feedback. We sincerely appreciate your business.

5. Write a three-paragraph document that is informative. You may want 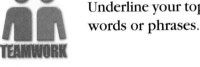 to inform your readers about a current news event. Underline your topic sentences and circle any transition words or phrases.

Editing Practice

Rewrite each sentence that has a grammatical error. Write *OK* if a sentence is correct.

1. Where was the cases shipped?
2. Ellie Topp and myself will give the presentation on Monday afternoon.
3. Before being considered, each applicant must send their resumé.
4. The committee on civil rights meet tomorrow at 7 p.m.
5. The supervisor spoke sharply to Giancarlo and I.
6. Bill Hovanic and me were invited to attend the ceremony at which the Technical Innovation award will be presented.

Discussion Points

1. How does variety in sentence length and sentence structure improve the readability of a document?
2. In what ways does the appearance of a document affect readability?

Writing Effective Sentences

▶ **Key Terms**

▶ you-attitude
▶ voice

Long sentences in a short composition are like large rooms in a little house.

—William Shenstone, English poet

A well-written business communication flows smoothly. The reader is more aware of the flow of ideas than of individual sentences, clauses, and phrases. Nothing should interrupt the reader's concentration—no awkward phrases, vague references, or unbalanced constructions.

Because a well-written document flows so easily, the reader may feel that the words flowed as easily from the writer's mind. In reality, however, the first draft was probably full of awkward phrases, vague references, choppy sentences, and unbalanced constructions. After completing the draft, the writer took the time to look for problems and to apply good writing techniques.

Word Usage

Writers combine words to make sentences and sentences to make paragraphs. You cannot write effective sentences without using the right words. Here are some suggestions for writing effective sentences.

1. Use the you-attitude and positive words.
2. Use planned repetition of words to emphasize important points.
3. Use pleasant-sounding words instead of harsh or awkward sounds.

Use the You-Attitude and Positive Words

Sentences that use the **you-attitude** emphasize the reader instead of the writer. By focusing on the reader, you are more likely to gain his or her acceptance or cooperation. Compare the following sentences.

I-Attitude: I would like to thank you for your interest in Fiber-Tec, Inc.

You-Attitude: Thank you for your interest in Fiber-Tec, Inc.

I-Attitude: We need to receive your reply to this offer no later than Thursday, April 5.

You-Attitude: Please send us your reply to this offer no later than Thursday, April 5.

One way to achieve the you-attitude in business writing is to use *you* with positive words. Such words create a receptive, pleasant impression in the mind of a reader. Compare the positive words and the negative words in Figure 7.7.

Figure 7.7 ▶
Positive or Negative?

Thinking Critically.
*How can the following
sentence become more
positive?*
It is not difficult to fill
your order by 4/1/03.

Positive or Negative?			
Positive Words		**Negative Words**	
advancement	happy	anxious	failure
agreeable	integrity	apologize	incapable
capable	pleasure	blame	loss
cheerful	profit	cannot	not
courage	success	complaint	problem
eager	warmth	damage	sad
easy	welcome	difficult	sorry
fun		dishonest	wrong

Note how using a negative word with *you* can result in a negative sentence. Such sentences should be reworded to make them more positive.

Negative: We cannot fix your computer until next Tuesday.

Positive: We can fix your computer by next Tuesday.

Use Planned Repetition of Words

Although careless repetition of words shows a lack of imagination, *planned* repetition can sometimes achieve striking emphasis of an important idea. Repeating the words *too* and *flexible* in the following examples helps to emphasize each point.

She arrived *too* late *too* often to keep her job.

Take advantage of our *flexible* hours to keep your schedule *flexible*.

Repetition is often used in advertisements where the major goal is to make readers remember the name and purpose of the product. Sometimes this goal is accomplished by simple repetition of the name. Clever writers manage to vary the order of the repeated words to prevent monotony, as in the following sentence.

Flexicise Workouts will add muscles to your body, and Flexicise Workouts will add body to your muscles.

Use Pleasant-Sounding Words

Excessive repetition of certain vowel or consonant sounds can create tongue twisters that detract from the message. Even when reading silently, the reader cannot ignore a sentence like the following.

Sylvie sold seven synthetic slipcovers on Saturday.

Sound repetition can cause problems other than tongue twisters. Although easy to say, the following sentence is hardly a pleasure to hear.

Steer your weary, dreary body to O'Leary's Health Club.

Avoid words with unpleasant sounds, and do not attempt to write business letters that sound musical or poetic. A business document should be courteous and concise.

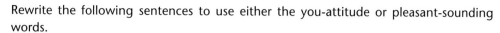

CHECKUP 1

Rewrite the following sentences to use either the you-attitude or pleasant-sounding words.

1. I have enclosed the samples requested in your April 5 letter.
2. The Thornton account takes up three thick files.
3. Include your payment with the completed order form.
4. Give me a response by Friday.
5. To avoid being a failure, you should try harder.

Proper Subordination of Ideas

Proper subordination of ideas depends on the ability to determine the difference between an important idea and a lesser idea. The important thought is expressed as a main clause, and the lesser idea is properly written as a subordinate clause. The principle can be remembered as follows: "Main idea—main clause; subordinate idea—subordinate clause." Subordinate clauses begin with subordinate conjunctions such as *because, since, when,* and *although.* Consider the following sentence.

Weak: Your proposal is interesting, although it does not meet our specifications.

Which statement is more important—*your proposal is interesting* or that *it does not meet our specifications*? That the proposal does not meet the specifications is the more important idea; therefore, it should be expressed as the main clause, as in the following example.

Better: Unfortunately, your proposal does not meet our specifications, although we did find it interesting.

Coordinate and Subordinate Ideas

When a sentence contains two ideas of equal importance, divide the sentence into two main clauses. Use a coordinating conjunction (*and, but, or, nor*) to join the ideas, as in the following sentence.

The work is difficult, but the rewards are great.

On the other hand, writing power is diminished when the writer fails to see that the thoughts belong not in two main clauses but in a main clause and a subordinate clause.

Weak: Other candidates were equally qualified, but the research director chose Herbert as her new assistant.

This sentence places equal stress on what the writer considers to be two main ideas. The emphasis should properly be placed on the director's choosing Herbert even though others were qualified. For force, as well as for clarity, the sentence should be rewritten.

Better: Although other candidates were equally qualified, the research director chose Herbert as her new assistant.

Eliminate Interrupting Expressions

Some writers unwittingly destroy the forcefulness of proper subordination by writing the lesser idea as an interrupting expression. For instance, read the following sentence.

Weak: You are, considering the risks involved in such an investment, very fortunate.

The main thought, *you are very fortunate,* is interrupted by the lesser idea, *considering the risks involved.* This interruption breaks the flow of the main thought and detracts from the force of the statement. If a short interrupting expression is used, it will have less impact; the longer the interrupting expression, the more it will detract from the main thought. Properly written, the sentence reads as follows.

Better: Considering the risks involved in such an investment, you are very fortunate.

Stronger: You are very fortunate, considering the risks involved in such an investment.

Correcting the *So* and *And So* Faults

Whenever you read a sentence that uses *so* or *and so* to introduce a clause, you can improve the sentence by substituting a more meaningful conjunction. Notice how weak the connection is between the two clauses in the following sentence.

Weak: Elena has been a dedicated literacy volunteer for ten years, so we gave her a special tribute at last night's fund-raising dinner.

The first clause gives the reason for the second clause. *Because* is a better choice for joining clauses that give causes and results. The following sentence is stronger, clearer, and more polished than the previous version.

Better: We gave Elena a special tribute at last night's fund-raising dinner because she has been a dedicated literacy volunteer for ten years.

And so is not a two-word conjunction. These words are two separate conjunctions used to form a vague connection between two clauses. Consider the following sentence.

Weak: Mr. Velez is a talented graphic designer, and so we recommend that you hire him.

The first clause is the reason for the second. The relationship is easier to detect in the following revision.

Better: We recommend that you hire Mr. Velez because he is a talented graphic designer.

CHECKUP 2

In the following sentences make the corrections indicated in parentheses.

1. Some additional options were presented, but the manager decided to go with Susan's proposal. (Subordinate an idea.)
2. The report is due March 4, and Jeff has been working all week on the calculations. (Subordinate an idea.)
3. We are, despite the costs involved, committed to expanding our markets overseas. (Eliminate an interrupting expression.)
4. Our accounting department is understaffed, and so we propose hiring three additional accountants. (Correct the *and so* fault.)
5. Save the computer files in a new directory. Print a copy of each file. (Coordinate ideas.)

Active Versus Passive Voice

Voice is that property of a transitive verb that shows whether the subject acts or is acted upon. When the *active voice* is used, the subject of the sentence is doing the action or being acted upon. The *active verb* directs the action towards an object. An example is:

John *finished* the assignment. (The subject of the sentence, *John,* does the action; the verb is *finished.* The verb, *finished,* directs the action towards an object, *assignment.*)

When the *passive voice* is used, the subject of the sentence is being acted upon. The *passive verb* directs the action towards the subject of the sentence. An example is:

The assignment *was finished* by John. (The subject of the sentence, the *assignment,* receives the action of the verb, *was finished.*)

Note that the passive voice uses a *two-part verb.* This consists of some part of the *auxiliary (helping) verb "to be"* and the *past participle of the main verb.* In the above example, *was* is the auxiliary verb and *finished* is the main verb.

If you want to emphasize the receiver of the action, use the passive voice. By making the receiver of the action the subject, it is emphasized. Note in the above example that *the assignment* becomes the subject and focus of the sentence when you use the passive voice, while *John* is emphasized when the information is conveyed in the active voice. Therefore, if the doer of the action is not important, or is deliberately not mentioned, use the passive voice. Consider these examples:

I was upset as a result of your actions. (This emphasizes *I,* the receiver of the action. Using the active voice—*Your actions upset me*—would emphasize the doer of the action *You.*)

This project is based on careful research. (Here the doer of the action is not important and is not mentioned.)

The passive voice is useful in business writing when you want to soften the impact of negative views. In the following sentences, note how the sentence using the passive voice is the more diplomatic of the two.

Active: Because the college *did not send us* a copy of your transcript, we *cannot consider* your application to our program at this time.

Passive: Your application to our program *will be considered* when a copy of your transcript *is sent* to us by the college.

The active voice expresses thoughts in a stronger, livelier way than does the passive voice. Compare the following sentences.

Passive: Your order *will be shipped* on Monday, July 8.

Active: We *will ship* your order on Monday, July 8.

Both sentences state the same information, but the active voice sentence is more direct. In the following pair of sentences, note that the sentence using the active voice makes a stronger point than the weak, passive voice does.

Passive: Last year our telecommunications systems *were sold to* three out of every four new businesses in the city.

Active: Last year, we *sold* our telecommunications systems to three out of every four new businesses in the city.

Parallel Structure

Parallel structure is a must for similar parts of a sentence. A noun should be parallel with a noun, an adjective with an adjective, and a phrase with a phrase. For example, look at this sentence.

Unparallel: The new staff assistant is eager, diligent, and has much knowledge.

Lack of parallel structure causes the sentence to lose momentum. The writer erroneously coordinated two adjectives and a clause. The following revision coordinates the three adjectives, making the sentence grammatically parallel and effective.

Parallel: The new staff assistant is eager, diligent, and knowledgeable.

In the paragraphs that follow, you will study techniques for balancing comparisons, modifiers, verbs, prepositions, conjunctions, and clauses.

Balance Comparisons

Comparisons are balanced only if they are complete. They can be complete only if they include all the necessary words. The omission of one necessary word can throw a comparison out of balance, as in the following sentence.

Unbalanced: Recent studies show that women spend more money on eating in restaurants than men.

As written, the sentence could mean that women spend more money on eating in restaurants than they spend on men. The comparison lacks balance, as well as sense, because an essential word is omitted. One word, properly placed, can make the meaning of the sentence clear.

Balanced: Recent studies show that women spend more money on eating in restaurants than men *spend.*

Or the sentence could be rearranged.

Balanced: Recent studies show that women spend more money than men *do* on eating in restaurants.

Here is another unbalanced comparison.

Unbalanced: Ms. Ridgeway's role in the corporation is more than a financial analyst.

This sentence lacks sense because essential words have been omitted. The following revision improves the clarity.

Balanced: Ms. Ridgeway's role in the corporation is more than *that of* a financial analyst.

An unbalanced comparison like the one that follows provides a chance for skilful revision.

Unbalanced: Celia can program just as well, if not better, than George.

Disregarding the words set off by commas, the sentence reads as follows: *Celia can program just as well than George.* However, no one would say *as well than.* The first revision below is acceptable, but the second one is a much better sentence.

Balanced: Celia can program just as well *as,* if not better than, George.

Balanced: Celia can program just as well *as* George, if not better.

Balance Modifiers

Omission of single-word modifiers can destroy the balance of a sentence in several ways. Such an omission can produce, for example, an illogical message.

Incorrect: The company is hiring a receptionist and field engineer.

Failure to write "*a* field engineer" makes "a receptionist and field engineer" refer to one person. It is unlikely that one person could serve in this dual capacity.

Correct: The company is hiring a receptionist and *a* field engineer.

Balance Verbs

Structural balance demands that whenever the parts of verbs in compound constructions are not exactly alike in form, no verb part should be omitted. The following sentence breaks this rule.

Incorrect: Rhonda always has, and always will, do a good job.

The word *do* cannot act as the main verb for the auxiliary verb *has. Has* requires the past participle *done.* Without the word *done,* the sentence seems to read "Rhonda always has *do* and always will do a good job." The verbs required in this compound construction are not exactly alike in form; therefore, all verb parts should be included.

Correct: Rhonda always *has done* and always *will do* a good job.

The following sentence shows the same kind of error.

Incorrect: Your revised report was received today and copies sent to the members of the advisory committee for their comments.

The omission of the auxiliary verb after *copies* structures the sentence to read "Your revised report was received today, and copies *was* sent to the members of the advisory committee for their comments." The plural noun *copies* requires a plural verb; therefore, the sentence should be revised.

Correct: Your revised report was received today, and copies *were* sent to the members of the advisory committee for their comments.

Balance Prepositions

The omission of a preposition can also throw a sentence off balance. Usage requires that some words be followed by specific prepositions. (See Section 5.3 for words that require specific prepositions.)

When two prepositional constructions have the same object, use the preposition that is correct for each construction.

Incorrect: Senior documentation writers must demonstrate expertise and knowledge of software programming.

In this illustration *expertise* and *knowledge* both are modified by the prepositional phrase *of software programming.* However, it is incorrect to say "expertise of software programming." The correct preposition to use with *expertise* is *in.* To be balanced the sentence should read as follows.

Correct: Senior documentation writers must demonstrate *expertise in* and *knowledge of* software programming.

Balance Conjunctions

In speech, subordinating conjunctions, particularly *that* and *when,* can often be omitted without causing any confusion. In writing, however, such omissions may destroy the balance of the thought units of a sentence and confuse the reader. Read the following example aloud.

Weak: Marc often talks about the time he had neither money nor position.

If this were an oral communication, the speaker could make the meaning clear by pausing slightly after the word *time*. The reader, however, might see the thought unit as *Marc often talks about the time he had,* with the result that the words following *had* would not make sense. The reader would have to reread the sentence to understand the meaning. In business communication, you want the reader to get the message the first time. The sentence should read as follows.

Better: Marc often talks about the time *when* he had neither money nor position.

The following sentence may also be misread.

Weak: I searched and discovered the contract folder was missing.

The reader may see *I searched and discovered the contract folder* as one thought unit. The subordinating conjunction *that* adds clarity.

Better: I searched and discovered that the contract folder was missing.

Balance Clauses

Another mark of writing distinction is to avoid incomplete, or elliptical, clauses. In the sentence "You are a faster typist than I," the meaning "than I am" is clear. But note the following sentence.

Unbalanced: Did Mr. Norville pay the bill or his accountant?

This sentence could be interpreted as follows: "Did Mr. Norville pay the bill, or did he pay his accountant?" It could also be interpreted this way: "Did Mr. Norville pay his bill, or did his accountant pay the bill?" The following sentence clarifies the intended meaning.

Balanced: Did Mr. Norville pay the bill, or did his accountant pay it?

CHECKUP 3

1. Jack can read just as well, if not better than, Jill.
2. My uncle's job at Nortel is more than an engineer.
3. Bombardier is hiring an office manager and an assistant to the CEO.
4. Your memo was received today, and copies sent to the Budget Committee.
5. Did you e-mail the president or her assistant?

Review of Key Terms

1. How does using the *you-attitude* improve business writing?
2. When is it appropriate to use the passive *voice* in business writing?

Practical Application

1. The sentences below repeat similar sounds too often. Rewrite the sentences to make them less distracting to the reader.
   a. The lawyer summarized some of his comments.
   b. The cashier's cheque, of course, cleared up the confusion.
   c. Miss Pellettieri missed Miss Carr's call.
   d. The board became bored by noon.
   e. A pair of paralegals perused the law publications in the library.
2. Rewrite each sentence, using positive words.
   a. I failed to finish the report by noon, but I will finish it by 5 p.m.
   b. Your qualifications and lack of experience do not match our hiring needs.
   c. Discuss any complaints about your cable TV service with our 24-hour customer-service representatives.
   d. Installation instructions should not be difficult to understand.
   e. Cashiers should not be dishonest.
3. Rewrite these compound sentences, subordinating the less important ideas.
   a. The copier was broken, and we could not distribute the report that was prepared yesterday.
   b. My train was late, and I missed my first appointment.
   c. You did a superb job on the project, and you will get a bonus.
   d. The sales figures were not accurate, and we underestimated our losses.
   e. You are the most qualified applicant, and we are going to employ you.
4. Rewrite each sentence, correcting the *so* and *and so* faults.
   a. The contractor was concerned about the rising cost of raw materials, so he added 5 per cent to his estimated price.
   b. He injured his foot while operating the forklift, and so he has applied for Worker's Compensation benefits.
   c. My flight to Saskatoon was cancelled, so I spent an extra night in Mississauga.
   d. Dolores has been promoted, so we wonder who will be named to fill her position.
   e. The shipment was damaged in transit, and so I refused to accept it.
5. Rewrite each sentence to change the voice of the verb, following the directions in parentheses.

a. Gary was praised by Mrs. Bonney when his design was accepted by the committee. (Change to the active voice.)

b. We cannot accept your credit application because of your short employment history. (Change to the passive voice.)

c. The new vacation policy was discussed by the department managers. (Change to the active voice.)

d. The new procedures were outlined by Susan Sokolvsky, and the details were filled in by Jim Conte. (Change to the active voice.)

e. The provincial parliament passed the proposed health legislation. (Change to the passive voice.)

6. The following sentences need changes to balance the elements. Assign two or three sentences to each person in your group. Share and discuss your answers.

TEAMWORK

a. Her business acumen is equal, if not sharper than, theirs.

b. Did Jeanne call the client or her assistant? (Who called the client?)

c. I have, and will continue to try, to contact her.

d. The latest survey shows that women own more shares in our company than men.

e. In his briefcase were a calculator, pen, file folder, and umbrella.

f. Sarah reminded me about the time she had neither money nor employment.

g. I have much respect and confidence in Ms. Nelson's decisions.

h. Armstrong Investment Specialists advertised for a mailroom assistant and account executive.

i. We need temporary personnel to keyboard documents, to proofread correspondence, and answering the phone.

j. Daria's communication skills are as good, if not better than, those of her co-workers.

Editing Practice

Choosing the Right Word. Choose the word that correctly completes each sentence.

1. The board of directors plans to (adapt, adopt) its first policy manual.
2. Most employees can (access, excess) the computer files by telephone.
3. Elisabeth gave me some helpful (advice, advise) when I graduated from college.
4. Please order some letterhead (stationary, stationery).
5. Much planning (preceded, proceeded) the warehouse expansion.
6. Komala (lead, led) the trainees in sales last quarter.
7. The report (cited, sighted) several studies that support our position.
8. Brendan Sullivan, (formally, formerly) a director, chairs the board.

9. The customers are completely satisfied with (their, there) purchases.
10. Sofia is more qualified (than, then) Gwen.

Discussion Points

1. Look at the quote by William Shenstone at the beginning of Section 7.3. What does he mean by this analogy? What strategies discussed in this section could you use that apply to this analogy?

2. Why are subordination and coordination of ideas essential in effective writing?

Structuring Phrases and Clauses

▶ **Key Terms**

▶ thought unit

▶ dangling modifier

▶ pronoun

▶ antecedent

The surest way to arouse and hold the attention of the reader is by being specific, definite, and concrete. The greatest writers—Homer, Dante, Shakespeare—are effective largely because they deal in particulars and report the details that matter. Their words call up pictures.

—William Strunk, Jr. and E. B. White, writing in *The Elements of Style*

Thought Units

A combination of words that properly belong together is called a **thought unit.** One example of a thought unit is a noun or pronoun and its modifiers; another example is a verb and its complement. When the words of a thought unit are placed correctly, the reader can understand the meaning quickly and easily. When the writer incorrectly places the words of a thought unit, however, the reader may get a mistaken idea of the writer's meaning. Sometimes the mistaken idea is laughable, but in business communications such mistakes are more likely to cause problems or confusion, as in the following example.

Incorrect: Calling the meeting to order, the new Palm Pilot drew the praise of the vice-president of sales.

Introductory phrases and clauses logically lead the reader to the words that directly follow. In the preceding example, however, a Palm Pilot cannot really call a meeting to order. To avoid a confusing statement such as this one, the writer should group together words whose meanings belong together.

Correct: When the meeting was called to order, the new Palm Pilot drew the praise of the vice-president of sales.

Words in Thought Units

Sometimes a confusing, laughable, or simply false meaning is conveyed because a single word is not connected with its proper thought unit. The following advertisement is an example of a misplaced adjective.

Incorrect: Gigantic men's clothing sale begins today!

The modifier gignatic has been misplace—it seems to indicate that *gigantic men's* is a thought unit. The correct thought unit is *gigantic sale.*

Correct: Gigantic sale of men's clothing begins today!

Misplaced adverbs can lead to confusion also.

Incorrect: The idea for changing our sales emphasis came to me after I had opened the meeting suddenly.

What happened suddenly—the opening of the meeting or the idea for the sales emphasis?

Correct: The idea for changing our sales emphasis suddenly came to me after I had opened the meeting.

Yesterday a car sprayed him with mud while helping a stranded motorist.

(while he was helping)

CHECKUP 1

Rearrange the following words so that they reflect appropriate thought units.

1. Our bargain children's Christmas sale will be held on Saturday.
2. The conference topics were selected after we met several times carefully.
3. Sally and Anne discussed their plans as they rode in the elevator hurriedly.
4. The rotating men's and women's tennis schedule is posted on the club notice board.

Phrases in Thought Units

Incorrectly placed phrases, as well as incorrectly placed words, can completely change the meaning of a message. Careful writers edit their work to see that they have placed phrases correctly.

Incorrect: This Zip drive can be installed by anyone who has studied the computer manual in ten minutes.

No computer manual could be studied in ten minutes, but someone who had studied the computer manual for a reasonable length of time could probably install a Zip drive in ten minutes.

Correct: This Zip drive can be installed in ten minutes by anyone who has studied the computer manual.

Now read the following classified advertisement and see the confusion that results from an incorrectly placed thought unit.

Incorrect: Three-room apartment for rent. Ideal for professional person with balcony.

Correct: Three-room apartment with balcony for rent. Ideal for professional person.

Two misplaced phrases can be even worse than one. Imagine receiving a direct-mail advertisement that contained the following sentence.

Incorrect: Our interactive, multi-media games are guaranteed to give you hours of entertainment without qualification for your home computer.

The correct thought units are *games for your home computer* and *guaranteed without qualification.* The following revision would be more likely to encourage you to order a game or two.

Correct: Our interactive, multi-media games for your home computer are guaranteed without qualification to give you hours of entertainment.

CHECKUP 2

Rearrange the following sentences so that they reflect appropriate phrase thought units.

1. This photocopier can be operated by anyone who has read the instructions in a few minutes.
2. Marla picked up the fax machine during her lunch hour at the repair shop.
3. This software program will help you produce professional assignments for your personal computer.
4. Roseanne studied the travel advertisement while on coffee break in the local newspaper.

Clauses in Thought Units

A misplaced clause can have even more devastating consequences than a misplaced word or phrase. How would the public react if the president of your company made the following announcement?

Incorrect: Our goal in marketing is to encourage the public to try our products until our health foods become better known.

The sentence sounds as if once the products are better known, no one will want to buy them. Moving the *until* clause clears up the matter.

Correct: Until our health foods become better known, our goal in marketing is to encourage the public to try our products.

Because clauses pose a special hazard, since they often are used to explain people's motives. Consider the following statement.

Unclear: The clerk hardly listened to the customer's complaint because she was concentrating so intensely on completing the form.

Was the clerk or the customer completing the form? While the original sentence is not wrong, the following sentence better describes the situation.

Clear: Because she was concentrating so intensely on completing the form, the clerk hardly listened to the customer's complaint.

Ambiguous *Which* Clauses

The word *which* is a pronoun that refers to another word in the sentence. If the *which* clause is misplaced, the word being referred to is unclear, and confusion will result.

Unclear: Our gallery has a book on important nineteenth-century Canadian paintings which you can purchase for a special price of $19.95 plus postage.

Placing *which* immediately after *paintings* alters the meaning of the sentence. Can the paintings be purchased for only $19.95? The writer of the sentence above actually intended to say that the book could be purchased for $19.95.

Clear: Our gallery has a book, which you can purchase for a special price of $19.95 plus postage, on important nineteenth-century Canadian paintings.

While clear and a definite improvement, the rewritten sentence would gain force and polish if the *which* clause were removed as in this revision:

For a special price of $19.95 plus postage, you can purchase our gallery's book on important nineteenth-century Canadian paintings.

Although it is acceptable for *which* to refer to a general idea rather than to a

"She died in the home in which she was born at the age of 88"

—*Boston Globe*

(She died at the age of 88 in ...)

single noun, the writer must take extra care to see that the reference is clear. In the following sentence, the pronoun reference is ambiguous.

Unclear: Further resistance to the board of directors will only jeopardize your job, which neither of us wants.

The problem here is that the *which* clause may refer either to the general idea *will only jeopardize your job* or to the single noun *job. Which* seems at first to belong to the thought unit *your job.* If neither of the persons referred to wants the job, why should either one care whether the job is jeopardized? A revision would clear up the confusion.

Clear: Further resistance to the board of directors will only jeopardize your job, and we do not want that.

Here is an example of a *which* clause making clear reference to a general idea.

Ms. Bergen predicted that an out-of-court settlement would be reached, which is precisely what happened.

Used with care, *which* clauses achieve a degree of clarity that would be difficult to equal in as few words. Note the following sentence.

Read Section 5, which contains the salary schedule under the new contract.

CHECKUP 3

Correct the following sentences to reflect proper use of clauses as thought units.

1. Our company's aim is to increase our range of products until our annual profits are satisfactory.
2. Did you see the green sweater on the counter which is on sale for $35.99?
3. Meghan did not read the report submitted by her students because she misplaced her glasses.
4. Hugo barely read the newspaper article which his secretary pointed out because he was worried about the board meeting.

Who Did What?

In written business communications, the writer must make it absolutely clear *who* has done or will do a specific action. Sometimes, however, the writer confuses the thought by connecting the wrong person, place, or thing with an action. As a result, the intended meaning is not conveyed to the reader. Such a violation of the thought-unit principle can cause doubt or uncertainty as to *who* did *what.*

Faulty: If not satisfied, we will refund your money.

The thought unit is *If not satisfied, we.* The meaning here is that *we* (the manufacturer) are the ones who might not be satisfied. If a customer returned the goods and asked for a full refund, could the manufacturer refuse on the grounds that the manufacturer was well satisfied with the customer's money? The correct meaning is immediately apparent to the reader when the sentence is revised.

Correct: If you are not satisfied, we will refund your money.

Occasionally, if the who-did-what principle is violated, the sentence becomes ridiculous, because an object, not a person, seems to be performing an action.

Faulty: Receiving the customer's urgent request, the order was immediately processed by Jerry.

The thought unit *Receiving the customer's urgent request, the order* suggests that the order was receiving the request. This kind of phrasing shows a serious lack of communication know-how. In this revision, Jerry performs the action.

Correct: Receiving the customer's urgent request, Jerry immediately processed the order.

Here is another illustration of this type of error.

Faulty: After climbing to the top of the tower, the whole city lay spread before us.

What does the thought unit *After climbing to the top of the tower, the whole city* mean? How could a city climb to the top of the tower? In a revision, the people would perform the action.

Correct: After climbing to the top of the tower, we saw the whole city spread before us.

A who-did-what violation, sometimes called a **dangling modifier**, does not necessarily occur at the beginning of a sentence. For example, note the error in the following sentence.

Faulty: Ms. Pak saw the prospective customer leaving the stockroom.

As written, the thought unit is *customer leaving the stockroom.* Where was Ms. Pak when she saw the customer, and why was the customer in the stockroom? Most likely it was Ms. Pak who was leaving the stockroom. To eliminate the confusion, the writer should revise the sentence.

Correct: Leaving the stockroom, Ms. Pak saw the prospective customer.

Now read the following sentence, which is another example of unclear word reference.

Faulty: Rolanda Wilson was promoted to branch manager, thus confirming everyone's opinion that she is the most qualified person for the position.

Thus, as used here, is ambiguous. The thought could have been expressed more clearly and more directly by eliminating *thus.*

Correct: Rolanda Wilson's promotion to branch manager confirms everyone's opinion that she is the most qualified person for the position.

Confusing Pronoun References

Each **pronoun** borrows its meaning from a noun. It must be clear which noun is referred to by a pronoun. One vague or mistaken pronoun reference can garble an entire message. The careful writer checks each pronoun used to make certain that its reference is clear.

Confusing *He* or *She*

When you use either the pronoun *he* or *she,* you must make certain that the **antecedent**—the noun to which the pronoun refers—is clear. If more than one man or more than one woman is mentioned in the sentence, place the pronoun as near as possible to the person to whom you refer. The following sentence leaves the reader wondering "Who returned from the meeting?"

Unclear: Mr. DeSouza asked Richard to write a report immediately after he returned from the regional sales meeting.

Amanda said to call them for a copy of the health plan.

(call someone in Human Resources)

Does the *he* in this sentence refer to Richard or to Mr. DeSouza? If the reference is to Mr. DeSouza, then the sentence should be revised as follows.

Correct: Immediately after he returned from the regional sales meeting, Mr. DeSouza asked Richard to write a report.

If, on the other hand, Richard is the one who attended the meeting, then the correct way to write the sentence is:

Immediately after Richard returned from the regional sales meeting, Mr. DeSouza asked him to write a report.

Confusing *It*

Using the pronoun *it* to refer to something that is not immediately clear is a common mistake.

Unclear: I will place the football in the kicking tee, and when I nod my head, kick it.

Kick what? This indefinite *it* could result in a painful injury. The word *it* must be replaced by the noun to which it should refer.

Correct: I will place the football in the kicking tee, and when I nod my head, kick the ball.

Other Indefinite Pronoun References

Speakers who are uncertain of their sources frequently use the vague "they say" as a reference. Writing that uses the same vague "they" reference is considered amateurish; in written communication, references must be definite and exact.

Vague: They say that the joint venture between Eastern Transport Inc. and the Maritime provinces will be launched early next year.

Who is meant by *they* in this sentence? A precise writer would replace "they say" with a more exact reference.

Clear: *International Market News* reports that the joint venture between Eastern Transport Inc. and the Maritime provinces will be launched early next year.

Another type of indefinite reference that is puzzling and annoying to a reader is an unclear pronoun reference.

Faulty: Although I dictated all Tuesday morning, the secretary input only two of them.

The thought unit *two of them* is vague. Two of what? stories? letters? reports? news releases? A clear and explicit thought could be communicated by revising the sentence.

Correct: Although I dictated all Tuesday morning, the secretary input only two of the letters.

Correcting *This* Faults

A common writing fault is the use of *this* to refer to an entire preceding thought. This lack of precision sometimes forces a reader to read a sentence several times to understand the writer's meaning.

Faulty: Employees can't find parking spaces. This has existed since we hired 50 new employees.

To what does the *this* refer? This refers to *the shortage of parking spaces.* Stating the point specifically makes the meaning clear.

Correct: Employees can't find parking spaces. This shortage of parking spaces has existed since we hired 50 new employees.

Review of Key Terms

1. How can one avoid writing a confusing *thought unit*?
2. When using a pronoun, why must a writer use a clearly stated *antecedent*?

Practical Application

1. Rewrite each sentence, making sure all thought units are clear.
   a. Marcel put the video in the VCR, which everyone had been waiting to see.
   b. After breaking for lunch, the meeting reconvened.
   c. Because of design defects, the manufacturer recalled the Model Zoom lawnmowers.
   d. Exotic-looking men's ties are fashionable this season.
   e. Hold the two pieces in place with your fingers and glue them together.
   f. Walking on crutches, stairs were difficult to climb for Rick.
   g. The veterinarian was unable to complete the exam for the cat's owner because she was nervous.
   h. Sitting close to the window, the skyscrapers were clearly visible.
   i. People often buy things with credit cards that they don't need.
   j. The new computers, with little or no training, can be operated by skilled technicians.
   k. Cooking in the microwave oven, Ned finds that he spends less time in the kitchen.
   l. Your rental agreement says that you may not have animals or children unless caged.
   m. After doing much planning, the budget finally balanced.
   n. The mixer truck was wrecked by a substitute driver only half full of cement.
   o. We have a brochure of our diverse financial services, which we will give you upon request.
   p. The acerbic theatre critic's review hurt ticket sales.
   q. When walking through the office, the printer noise was distracting to the visitors.
   r. Covered with proofreading marks, Ms. Kantor sent the draft back for corrections.
   s. The company's top designer was not able to work with us because she was on vacation when we launched the project. This has affected the quality of our project.
   t. To remove paint without scraping, you should plan on a two-hour soak in solvent.
2. These sentences have confusing pronoun references. Rewrite them, making the specified corrections.
   a. Alice saw Mia when she was in Ottawa last week. (Alice was in Ottawa.)

b. Len and Adan researched the topic, but he did the actual writing of the report. (Adan wrote the report.)

c. Dan told Charlie that his explanation was not clear. (Dan's explanation was not clear.)

d. They think that more test trials are needed for the new arthritis treatment. *(They* refers to Dr. Anne McCurry and Dr. David Ramsaroop.)

e. Although we interviewed 30 applicants, we hired only 3 of them. (*Them* refers to laboratory technicians.)

f. It is a positive attitude that can make the difference between success and failure. (Remove the *It*.)

g. The computer terminal is on my desk. Don't move it for any reason. (*It* refers to the computer terminal.)

h. It may be a good idea to rearrange the desks in this office. (Remove the *It*.)

i. Ms. Nichols was offered a five-year lease or a ten-year lease. She will probably sign it next week. (It refers to the longer lease.)

j. Martha asked Ryle to review the contract as soon as she received it. (Martha received the contract.)

3. As a team, look in newspapers to find examples of inexact pronoun references and *this* faults. Sports articles or articles involving several participants are good starting places. Rewrite the sentences to clarify any unclear references.

TEAMWORK

Editing Practice

Pronoun Practice.   Correct the pronoun errors in the following sentences.

1. Our company holds it's annual picnic in August.
2. Warren, Elizabeth, and him volunteered to work overtime for two weeks.
3. When can you and me meet to plan Jo's party?
4. Who's request should be granted?
5. Will you give your recommendations to Damon or I?
6. What one of the account representatives will be transferred?
7. Whom is going to the meeting in Halifax next week?
8. The article was written by she last summer.
9. The fee will be divided between you and I.
10. John and her will finish the training program tomorrow.

Discussion Points

1. It is often difficult for writers to find confusing thought units in their own writing. Suggest ways in which writers could revise their own work.
2. How do misplaced words, phrases, or clauses interfere with a writer's message?

Using Words Effectively

▶ **Key Terms**

▶ phonetic spelling

▶ inflectional forms

▶ synonyms

▶ thesaurus

▶ homonyms

▶ pseudo-homonyms

▶ denotation

▶ connotation

▶ clichés

▶ antonyms

on Test

Never use a foreign phrase, a scientific word, or jargon word if you can think of an everyday English equivalent.

—George Orwell, "Politics and the English Language"

The Dictionary and the Thesaurus

Words are the building blocks of sentences, and sentences form our communciation. To be accurate and effective in your written communication, you must use words effectively. This section will enhance your word skill through two tools—the dictionary and the thesaurus.

The Dictionary

The dictionary is the most useful reference book for business writers. You should always keep a dictionary nearby and know how to use it.

As a writer, you can use the dictionary to find information on the spelling, definition, and capitalization of words, as well as synonyms and other information that will help you use words effectively. As an example of the detailed information provided by a dictionary entry, review the entries for the words *complement* and *compliment* in Figure 7.8.

Spelling.   The dictionary entries in Figure 7.8 show in bold type how the words *complement* and *compliment* are spelled. Keep in mind that many words have more than one spelling. Spellings that are equally correct are joined by *or,* as in "adviser *or* advisor." When one spelling is less commonly used, the dictionary joins the spelling by *also,* as in "lovable *also* loveable."

Definition.   A good dictionary lists all of a word's definitions, usually in the order of comparative familiarity and importance. Often the dictionary gives examples of the word's use in more than one sense.

Capitalization.   The dictionary may show whether a word is to be capitalized when it is not the first word of a sentence. For example, the word *west* is usually not capitalized, but when it refers to a specific region, as in *the West*, it is capitalized.

Hyphenation.   Dictionary entries sometimes use centred periods to indicate the correct places for hyphenating words: *com•mu•ni•cate; con•trol; ap•pre•ci•ate,* but *ap•pre•cia•tive.*

◀ Figure 7.8
Dictionary Entries for Compliment and Complement

Dictionary entries showing the spelling, pronunciation, meanings, and origin of a word.

compliment • noun /kompliment/ **1** an expression of praise or admiration, either in words or by an action. **2** (**compliments**) formal greetings.
• verb /kompliment/ politely congratulate or praise.
– PHRASES **return the compliment** retaliate or respond in kind. **with the compliments of someone** given without charge.
– USAGE On the confusion of **compliment** and **complement**, see the note at COMPLEMENT.
– ORIGIN Italian *complimento* 'fulfilment of the requirements of courtesy', from Latin *complementum* 'completion, fulfilment'.

complement • noun /kompliment/ **1** a thing that contributes extra features to something else so as to enhance or improve it. **2** the number or quantity that makes something complete. **3** a word or words used with a verb to complete the meaning of the predicate (e.g. *happy* in the sentence *we are happy*). **4** Geometry the amount by which a given angle is less than 90º. • verb /kompliment/ serve as a complement to.
– USAGE **Complement** and **compliment** are frequently confused. As a verb, **complement** means 'add to in a way that enhances or improves', while **compliment** means 'politely congratulate or praise'.
– ORIGIN Latin *complementum*, from *complere* 'fill up'.

Thinking Critically.
When you tell a person that you admire his or her work, are you giving the person a complement or a compliment?

From *The Oxford Dictionary, Thesaurus, and Wordpower Guide,* 2001, Oxford University Press.

Sometimes a word must be divided at the end of a line of writing. Unless the word is divided correctly, the reader may be confused. Here is an example of this kind of problem:

Please sign and return the enclosed statement promptly if you want a refund.

To use the dictionary effectively, follow these guidelines for verifying the spelling of a word:

- Place the letters in their correct order; for example, *neither*, not *niether*.
- Avoid inserting extra letters in a word, as in the incorrect *athaletic* (instead of *athletic*).
- Include all the letters that are in the word; for example, mortgage, not morgage, and business, not busness.
- Verify that the word is not some other word with a similar spelling. Read the definition. For example, would you give someone complementary tickets or complimentary tickets?
- Pay close attention to compound words to determine whether they are written as one word (checkpoint), two words (check mark), or a hyphenated word (drip-dry).
- Include any accent marks that are part of a word. For example, exposé is a noun that means "the revelation of something discreditable"; but expose is a verb that means "to cause to be visible."

Pronunciation and Division into Syllables. Immediately after the regular spelling of a word, the dictionary shows the word's **phonetic spelling.** Depending on the dictionary, this feature can indicate how the word should be broken into syllables, how each syllable should be pronounced, and which syllable or syllables should be accented. Figures 7.8 and 7.9 show different methods of presenting this information. If phonetic symbols are new to you, refer to the section of the dictionary that explains them.

Look again at the sample dictionary entries for *complement* and *compliment* in Figure 7.8 on page 339. The entries show the pronunciation of both words is '**kom**plimənt. The boldface indicates the syllable that should be stressed when pronouncing the word.

Inflectional Forms and Derivatives.   **Inflectional forms** are forms of a word that show tense, number, and other meanings. For example, *goes* is an inflectional form of *go*. A *derivative* is a word formed from another word. For example, *affirmation* is a derivative of *affirm*.

The dictionary shows the irregular plural of nouns, the past tense and participial forms of irregular verbs, and the comparative and superlative forms of irregular adjectives and adverbs. After the definition of the noun *contract,* for example, are its derivative noun *contractibility* and its derivative adjective *contractible.* The entry for the irregular verb *fall* gives its past tense, *fell,* its past participle, *fallen,* and its present participle, *falling.*

Synonyms.   For many entries the dictionary also lists **synonyms**—words that have almost the same meaning as the entry. For example, the entry for *complete* in Figure 7.9 gives the synonym "entire" for the adjective "complete." Note that although synonyms have what the dictionary calls a "shared meaning element," each has its own distinct shades of meaning. For example, "with all the parts; lacking nothing; whole; full," has a different shade of meaning than "thorough; total; utter." (Note that synonyms are not given in Figure 7.8 because those entries are from a book that contains both a dictionary and a thesaurus.)

Other Information   In addition to word information, a good abridged dictionary contains the following special sections that a writer may find helpful.

- Signs and Symbols. This section consists of signs and symbols frequently used in such fields as astronomy, biology, business, chemistry, data processing, mathematics, medicine, physics, and weather. This section could be helpful in verifying the correct use of symbols in technical documents.
- Biographical Names. The names of famous people, each with the proper spelling and pronunciation, are listed. Biographical data such as dates of birth and death, nationality, and occupation are also given. Use this mate-

Figure 7.9 ▶
This entry explains the meaning and derivation of *complete*, gives illustrations of its use, and provides synonyms.

Thinking Critically.
What synonym could be used in place of "complete" in the following sentence:
Is it completely necessary to revise my assignment?

From Gage Canadian Dictionary, 1997, Gage Educational Publishing Company.

com•plete [kəm'plit] *adj., v.* **-plet•ed, -plet•ing.**—*adj.* **1** with all the parts; lacking nothing; whole; full: *a complete set of Dickens' novels.* **2** thorough; total; utter: *complete surprise, complete confidence.* **3** ended; finished; done: *My homework is complete.* **4** consummate; proficient; expert: *She is the complete recorder player.*
—*v* **1** make up all the parts of; make whole or entire: *She completed her set of dishes by buying a sugar bowl.* **2** make perfect or thorough: *The good news completed by happiness.* **3** get done; end; finish: *She completed her homework early in the evening.* ⟨ME < OF *complet* < L *completus,* pp. of *complere* < *com-* (intensive) + *plere* fill⟩—**com'plete•ly** *adv.* —**com'plet•ness,** *n.*
☛ *Syn. adj.* **1.** Complete, ENTIRE = with all the parts. **Complete** = with all the parts needed to make something whole or full: *I have the complete story now.* **Entire** = with no parts taken away: *He gave the entire day to his work, not even taking time for lunch.*

rial for checking the pronunciation of names or for identifying unfamiliar names encountered in reading or conversation.

- Geographical Names. This section provides information about places—name, pronunciation, location, population, and so on. Therefore, it can be helpful when you are checking the spelling of place names in correspondence.
- Handbook of Style. Included in this very useful section are rules on punctuation, italicization, capitalization, and plurals; citation of sources; and forms of address.

The Thesaurus

If you know a word, the dictionary will give you its meaning. The **thesaurus** works the other way around: If you have a general idea of the meaning you want to convey, the thesaurus will give you a choice of specific words to express it. Look up the general idea, then choose the word or expression that best fits your meaning. If unfamiliar words are given when you search in a thesaurus, check these words in a dictionary to make sure that their meaning accurately matches your intended meaning.

Roget's International Thesaurus and *Webster's Collegiate Thesaurus,* two popular references, are arranged differently. Roget's has two parts: the main section, which lists synonyms and associated words, and the index to the main section. For example, to find a synonym for the adjective *careful* in the *Concise Edition* of *Roget's Thesaurus,* look up *careful* in the alphabetic index. There you will find these three entries, each followed by a key number:

careful

careful 457 adj.

economical 814 adj.

parsimonious 816 adj.

The key numbers refer to numbered paragraphs in the main section. Thus, if *economical* is closest to the idea you wish to convey, turn to entry number 814 in the main section for a listing of synonyms.

Webster's Collegiate Thesaurus is organized like a dictionary, with one list of entries arranged in alphabetic order. To find synonyms for *careful,* just turn to the entry *careful.* Within this entry the capital letters for the word *CAUTIOUS* indicate that more information can be found at that entry, which is also in alphabetic order.

---

creative *adj syn* INVENTIVE, demiurgic
deviceful, ingenious, innovational, innovative, innovatory, original, originative
rel causal, institutive, occasional; Promethean
and uncreative

inventive *adj* adept or prolific at producing new things and ideas
<had a very *inventive* turn of mind>
<she was an *inventive* genius>
syn creative, demiurgic, deviceful, ingenious, innovational, innovative, innovatory, original, originative
rel fertile, fruitful, productive, teeming; causative, constructive, formative
con sterile, uncreative, unproductive
ant uninventive

◀ **Figure 7.10
Thesaurus Entries**

Thinking Critcally.
What does the entry "con" contain? What is the full word represented by the contraction "con"?

By permission. From Merriam-Webster's Collegiate® Thesaurus © 1994 by Merriam-Webster Incorporated.

Whichever thesaurus you select, learn to use it properly. A thesaurus can be useful when you want to (1) find the most suitable word for a given idea, (2) avoid overusing a word by finding a suitable synonym, (3) find the most specific word, (4) replace an abstract term, or (5) find slang or colloquial terms.

To Find the Most Suitable Word. Imagine that you write advertising copy, and you are working on an advertisement about new fall fashions. One aspect you wish to emphasize is the smartness of the clothes. Using your thesaurus, you can find that smart may be expressed as chic, fashionable, dapper, well-groomed, dressed up, and dressy, among a number of other words and expressions.

To Avoid Overusing a Word. Suppose you have written a letter in which you use the word great several times. Consulting the index of your thesaurus, you find a list of other adjectives, such as grand, chief, important, large, and famous. When you check these references, you discover additional words and expressions that are synonyms of great. You now have at your disposal a wide choice of words that you can use in place of great.

To Find the Most Specific Word. Sometimes you have a general word for an object or idea in mind, but you want to use a more specific word. For example, you may be discussing the possibility of taking a *trial* vote, but that is not the specific word you are seeking. You look up the word *vote* in your thesaurus. Among the many choices shown is the expression *straw vote,* which is precisely the expression you are seeking.

To Replace an Abstract Term. Imagine that you are writing a memo and that you wish to replace the word *precipitous* in the phrase *a precipitous decision.* Among the substitutes that you would find in your thesaurus are *hasty, abrupt, hurried,* and *sudden.*

Electronic Dictionary and Thesaurus

Most word processing programs have an electronic dictionary and a thesaurus you can use to verify the spelling of a word or to find suitable synonyms. An electronic dictionary will highlight misspelled words, such as *apreciate* for *appreciate.* An electronic thesaurus will suggest possible synonyms for a word. If, for example, you have used the word *extravagant* three times in a report, you could check your thesaurus to find appropriate synonyms to substitute for one or two of them. Synonyms listed would include *abundant, excessive,* and *lavish.*

Improving Word Choice

The words that you use can either earn the respect and admiration of those with whom you communicate or mark you as unimaginative and even uneducated. The words you use might brand you as insensitive. To be an effective communicator, you must use the appropriate word at the right time. You must use words correctly, avoid overusing words, and predict how readers will interpret the words you use.

The Correct Word

Careful writers know the difference between correct and non-standard usage. Usages that are unacceptable in standard English must be avoided in business writing.

Some non-standard usages result from errors; for example, a speaker might use *irregardless,* which is not a word, for *regardless.* Some are correct words used incorrectly; for example, a writer might use *accept* for *except.* Others are glaring grammatical errors.

When you make errors such as these, readers may know what you mean, but they will probably not have a positive view of your competency and expertise.

Homonyms

Homonyms are words that look or sound alike but have different meanings. Choosing the incorrect word, although it may sound or even look correct, is one of the most frequently committed errors in word usage.

For example, the tenants of a large apartment building receive a letter urging "all the *residence* to protest the proposed rent increase." This important message might be ignored simply because the writer cannot distinguish people, *residents,* from place, *residence.* Another letter writer might place an order for a ream of *stationary,* instead of *stationery.*

Figure 7.11 lists some homonyms that every business writer should know and should use correctly.

Pseudo-Homonyms

Pseudo-homonyms are words that sound somewhat alike but have different meanings. When pronounced correctly, these words do not sound exactly alike. For example, the statement "Smathers, Delgado, and Hull placed orders for $800, $1000, and $1300, *respectfully,*" is incorrect. The communicator has confused the word *respectfully,* meaning "courteously" with *respectively* meaning "in the order given." The pseudo-homonyms that give the most trouble are listed in Figure 7.11.

CHECKUP 1

In the following sentences, the underlined words have been used incorrectly. Replace these words to correct each sentence.

1. Their prices acceded the usual market price.
2. Raymond's favourite desert is cheesecake.
3. Mr. Hanniken is adverse to changing the work schedule.
4. Wanda's suggestion for rearranging our vacation schedule is ingenuous.
5. Which addition of the book did you use?

Spelling

If you were a business executive, would you hire an engineer whose resumé listed a degree in *compewter* science? Would you hire someone who had taken courses in *acounting?* Poor spelling would make you doubt that these people could do the jobs they were seeking. Avoid being a poor speller by using a dictionary either in printed or electronic form.

Thinking Critically.
What is the difference between a homonym and a pseudo-homonym?

Homonyms and Pseudo-Homonyms

Homonyms

ad, add	dual, duel	plain, plane
aisle, isle	foreword, forward	presence, presents
allowed, aloud	forth, fourth	principal, principle
altar, alter	foul, fowl	raise, raze
ascent, assent	gorilla, guerrilla	rap, wrap
assistance, assistants	grate, great	residence, residents
attendance, attendants	hear, here	right, write
aural, oral	hire, higher	roe, row
bail, bale	hole, whole	so, sow, sew
base, bass	idle, idol	sole, soul
berth, birth	instance, instants	some, sum
born, borne	intense, intents	stake, steak
brake, break	lean, lien	stationary, stationery
canvas, canvass	leased, least	straight, strait
capital, capitol	lessen, lesson	taught, taut
cereal, serial	lesser, lessor	their, there, they're
cite, sight, site	loan, lone	threw, through
coarse, course	mail, male	to, too, two
complement, compliment	medal, meddle	vain, vane, vein
core, corps	miner, minor	waist, waste
correspondence, correspondents	overdo, overdue	wait, weight
council, counsel	pain, pane	waive, wave
dependence, dependents	passed, past	weak, week
discreet, discrete	patience, patients	weather, whether
dew, do, due	peace, piece	
	pedal, peddle	

Pseudo-Homonyms

accede, exceed	deceased, diseased	later, latter
accept, except	decent, descent, dissent	liable, libel
adapt, adopt	deference, difference	loose, lose, loss
addition, edition	desert, dessert	moral, morale
adverse, averse	detract, distract	our, are
advice, advise	device, devise	persecute, prosecute
affect, effect	disburse, disperse	personal, personnel
allusion, illusion	disprove, disapprove	precede, proceed
anecdote, antidote	elicit, illicit	quiet, quit, quite
appraise, apprise	eligible, illegible	reality, realty
carton, cartoon	emigrate, immigrate	recent, resent
casual, causal	eminent, imminent	respectfully, respectively
clothes, cloths	expand, expend	statue, statute
choose, chose	facilitate, felicitate	suit, suite
conscience, conscious	fiscal, physical	than, then
cooperation, corporation	formally, formerly	
dairy, diary	ingenious, ingenuous	

You can improve your spelling by paying careful attention to the similarities and differences between homonyms, or pseudo-homonyms, and the suggestions in Section 7.6. The most important step to improved spelling, however, is developing the dictionary habit.

Look up and remember the difference between prefixes that have similar meanings. Such words can be confusing.

*bi*weekly—occurring every two weeks
*semi*weekly—occurring twice a week
*dis*interested—impartial

*un*interested—bored; unconcerned
*inter*provincial—between provinces
*intra*provincial—within one province

Graduates were amused to find that they had graduated from the Navel Academy instead of the *Naval* Academy. The company that printed the diplomas apologized for the error and agreed to replace them.

Words Suited to the Audience

In a letter to a customer, a computer specialist would lose the attention of the reader if, in discussing how a computer could be useful to everyone, he or she used such technical terms as *backups, checkdisk,* and *batch file.* By using nontechnical terms, the writer could better hold the attention of the reader. Using a specialized vocabulary that is unfamiliar to an audience is as serious a mistake as speaking in a language an audience doesn't know. Communication takes place only when a writer chooses words geared to the interests and knowledge of that audience.

Words with Varying Connotations

The dictionary meaning of a word, the **denotation**, is often different from its **connotation**, which is the meaning readers associate with the word based on their experiences and emotions. For example, a solitary person might be called a *wallflower,* a *recluse,* or a *rugged individualist.* The wrong choice of terms can distort the speaker's or writer's meaning and perhaps even offend someone.

Look at the shades of meaning in the two words *cheap* and *inexpensive.* Certainly no salesperson would mistake the two. *Cheap* means "worthless or shoddy"; *inexpensive* refers only to cost, not to quality. Sometimes an *inexpensive* suit is a bargain; a *cheap* suit never is.

Whenever you are in doubt about a word's meaning, check the dictionary before using the word. If there is no time to look up the unknown word, then phrase your idea in a way that avoids it.

Words to Avoid

Building a successful business or career requires building goodwill. Because words play a vital part in establishing goodwill, a skilled communicator chooses words and phrases that the listener and reader can both understand and appreciate. In general, this means choosing positive rather than negative terms, presenting information directly and without repetition, and using fresh and current expressions rather than outdated and overused ones.

Avoid Negative Words. Which of the following statements is more likely to build or retain customer goodwill?

You neglected to specify the sizes and colours of the dress shirts you ordered. We cannot ship the order with such incomplete information.

The four dozen dress shirts you ordered will be shipped as soon as you tell us what sizes and colours you prefer.

The second statement is the better selection, although both statements try to convey the same idea. The second statement is positively worded and avoids such unpleasant expressions as *you neglected* and *cannot ship with such incomplete information.* Negative words are almost sure to evoke a negative response. The customer reading these negative words may cancel the order or may choose a different supplier for future orders.

Words result in negative responses when the reader feels blamed or accused. Most expert business writers consider words such as *failed, careless, delay,* and *inexcusable* to be negative words. They are unpleasant primarily when they are accompanied by *you (you failed)* or *your (your delay). Your oversight, your error, your claim* signal the reader to react negatively.

The following words sound negative when used with *you* or *your:*

blunder	damage	inability	regret
careless	defective	inadequate	trouble
claim	delay	inferior	unfavourable
complaint	error	mistake	unfortunate
criticism	failure	neglected	unsatisfactory

Eliminate Unnecessary Words. Words that are repetitious are a waste of the reader's time. Such words clutter the message and can distract, delay understanding, and reduce emotional impact. The italicized words in the expressions in Figure 7.12 are unnecessary and should be omitted.

Avoid Out-of-Date Words. Words that are out of date suggest that the writer is behind the times. Imagine the reaction to a sign that said "Eschew Smoking"! In certain uses, the words in Figure 7.13 have a similar effect.

Avoid Overused Words. Replacing overused words with more exact and colourful terms can make your writing lively and interesting. The adjective *good* is overused and weak: a *good* manoeuvre, a *good* negotiator, a *good* speech, a *good* applicant. Instead, for greater interest, say: a *clever, smart,* or *skilful* manoeuvre; a *patient, forceful,* or *persuasive* negotiator; an *eloquent, informative,* or *engrossing* speech; a *qualified, intelligent,* or *competent* applicant.

Adjectives such as *awful, bad, fine, great,* and *interesting* are also overused. The following sentences show how meaningless these words can be.

Figure 7.12 ▶
Redundant Phrases
Figure 7.12 lists groups of unnecessary words.

Thinking Critically.
Why is the pair cooperate together *redundant?*

Redundant Phrases

adequate *enough*	connect *up*
as yet	continue *on*
at above	*and* etc.
up above	*as to* whether
both alike	*past* experience
new beginner	*free* gratis or *for* free
cooperate *together*	inside *of*
same identical	my *personal* opinion
lose *out*	rarely (seldom) *ever*
meet *up* with	repeat *back* or *again*
modern methods *of today*	refer *back*
over *with*	*exact* same
customary practice	*true* facts

Outdated Language	
advise or state (for *say, tell*)	kindly (for *please*)
beg (as in *beg to advise*)	party (for *person*, except in legal work)
duly (as in *comments are duly noted*)	same (as in *we will send for same*)
esteemed (as in *my esteemed colleague*)	trust (for *hope, know, believe*)
herewith (except in legal work)	via (for *by*)

◀ Figure 7.13
Outdated Language

Thinking Critically.
Imagine using some of the out-of-date words in Figure 7.13 in a sales pitch for a new digital camera. *How would the words you chose affect your sales pitch?*

Avoid: The new guidelines on hiring workers will result in a *bad* situation.

Use: The new guidelines on hiring workers will result in a (*difficult, painful,* or *troublesome*) situation.

Avoid: Kari Michaels gave an *interesting* sales presentation.

Use: Kari Michaels gave an (*informative, enlightening,* or *educational*) sales presentation.

Avoid: We have an *awful* backlog of orders.

Use: We have (*an enormous, a huge,* or *an overwhelming*) backlog of orders.

CHECKUP 2

Delete any unnecessary words and replace any out-of-date words in the following sentences.

1. We are in receipt of your cheque in the amount of $120.
2. Jack has past experience handling customer complaints.
3. In my personal opinion, Joan and Fred have always co-operated together well.
4. It is our customary practice to reply to e-mail the exact same business day.
5. Up to this writing, we believe the true facts have not been stated.

Avoid Clichés.   Clichés are overworked expressions such as *crystal clear, needs no introduction,* and *at a loss for words* that lost their strength long ago. Out-dated expressions such as *attached hereto, attached herewith please find,* and *under separate cover* still find their way into business documents, creating the perception of a stale, backward organization.

The use of clichés exposes a lack of imagination—the tendency to repeat the familiar, even when the familiar is not worth repeating. Clichés waste time, obscure ideas, and bore readers and listeners.

Some commonly overused words and expressions, together with suggested substitutions for them, are listed in Figure 7.14.

Using Creativity to Achieve Variety

Although there are reference books to help you achieve variety in expression, you won't find ready-made phrases to express every idea. Achieving variety in word usage requires creativity.

Select Suitable Synonyms.   Choosing suitable synonyms is the most direct means of achieving variety in your vocabulary. Although synonyms have the same basic meaning, each synonym has a different shade of meaning. To select

Figure 7.14 ▶
Clichés

Thinking Critically.
Marketing pitches
sometimes use clichés
to describe a product's
benefits to the consumer.
*How might using clichés
weaken your sales pitch?*

Clichés

Cliché	Substitute
along the lines of	like
asset	advantage, gain, possession, resource
at all times	always
by the name of	named
deal	agreement, arrangement, transaction, contract
each and every	each *or* every
face up to	face
factor	event, occurrence, part
field	branch, department, domain, point, question, range, realm, region, scene, scope, sphere, subject, theme
fix	adjust, arrange, attach, bind, mend, confirm, define, establish, limit, place, prepare, repair
inasmuch as	since, as
input	comment, information, recommendation
in the near future	soon (or state the exact time)
line	business, goods, merchandise, stock
matter	point, question, situation, subject, (or mention what is specifically referred to)
our Mr. Smith	our representative, Mr. Smith
proposition	affair, idea, offer, plan, proposal, recommendation, undertaking
reaction	attitude, impression, opinion
recent communication	letter of (give exact date)
say	articulate, assert, declare, exclaim, express, mention, relate, remark

the best synonym, you must go beyond the basic idea and learn the distinctions.

A dictionary can help you create a phrase to achieve varity. Under the word *explore,* for example, a dictionary may list no synonyms, but give the following definition: "to investigate, study, or analyze; to look into; to examine minutely; to make or conduct a systematic search." Thus, instead of using *explore,* you can make a phrase to fit: "*study* the options," "*examine* the records *minutely,*" or "*systematically search* the files."

Use Appropriate Antonyms. An antonym is a word that means *exactly* the opposite of another word. For example, *light* is an antonym of *dark.* Antonyms are also formed by using such prefixes as *il-, in-, ir-, non-,* and *un-* before a word. For instance, *legible* becomes *illegible; credible, incredible; abrasive, nonabrasive;* and *acceptable, unacceptable.*

Skill in the use of antonyms opens broad possibilities to the communicator. To *upset* someone seems harsh, to *unnerve* someone seems less critical. It is sad when the dead are *forgotten,* but sadder still when they are *unmourned.*

CHECKUP 3

In each of the following items, three words are synonyms and one word is an antonymn. Select the antonym in each item.

1. ancient   modern   archaic   antique
2. liberate   rescue   release   capture
3. soothe   pacify   aggravate   appease
4. relevant   unrelated   pertinent   applicable
5. ample   plentiful   meagre   abundant

Choose Descriptive Words. Descriptive words make readers "see" what is being described. Notice how the first sentence uses abstract words and the second sentence uses specific words to call an image to mind.

Vague: Our new building is well located and the apartments are comfortable.

Descriptive: Our new high-rise building is located on a quiet, tree-lined street near the centre of town. The apartments are spacious and equipped with all the latest modern conveniences.

Using descriptive words will improve your written messages. To develop this skill, visualize a complete picture of what you want to describe, then consult the thesaurus until you find the most specific descriptive terms that apply. Use this technique to compose messages that hold the attention of your readers.

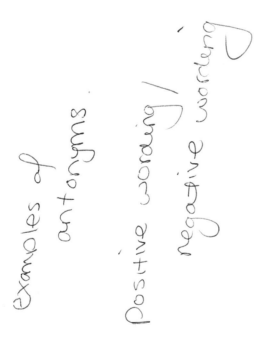

examples of antonyms

Positive wording / negative wording

Review of Key Terms

1. How is a *thesaurus* different from a *dictionary*?
2. What is the difference between a word's *denotation* and a word's *connotation*?

Practical Application

1. Using a thesaurus, list three words that can be used to replace the italicized word in each of the following phrases:
   a. A *dynamic* presentation
   b. A *beautiful* view
   c. A *good* person
   d. A *good* book
   e. A *good* employee
2. In each of the following sentences the writer confused two similar words. Replace the incorrect word with the correct one. Define both the correct and the incorrect words.
   a. The spreadsheet should give the some of all our invoices.
   b. Jacques Villeneuve asked that the breaks on his company car be inspected.
   c. Your property is being considered as a cite for the new manufacturing plant.
   d. Jan and Seana called to say that there flight will be late.
   e. Joyce Brown submitted the logo for our new stationary.
3. In each of the following sentences, select the word in parentheses that correctly completes the thought intended.
   a. The police chief's reassuring speech (disbursed, dispersed) the crowd.
   b. Because he did not sign the contract, he is not (a disinterested, an uninterested) party to the negotiations.
   c. Being caught in a traffic jam for hours had no apparent (affect, effect) on her mood.
   d. All the (fiscal, physical) assets of the restaurant are to be sold at auction.
   e. He was appointed (council, counsel) in the company's legal section.
   f. The report was prepared with the (assistance, assistants) of the research staff.
   g. Bill Dubois was asked to prepare a (bibliographical, biographical) description for his employer to use in introducing the speaker to the audience.
   h. He waited (awhile, a while) before calling his lawyer.
   i. Your account is long (passed, past) due.
   j. The designer made a (sleight, slight) change in the pattern.

4. The following sentences are negative. Rewrite them in positive terms.
   a. Not until today did your letter reach us, too late for our special offer, which ended last week.
   b. There is no excuse for misunderstanding my clear instructions, even if you were interrupted while I was talking.
   c. Since you failed to state whether you want legal- or letter-size, we cannot send the filing cabinets that you ordered.
   d. I will not be in the office on Tuesday, so I will be unable to help you then.
   e. Do not use a box number address when sending a letter by an overnight delivery service because the letter cannot be delivered without a street address.
   f. We are not able to send you the stationery you requested, because your order form did not give complete details.
   g. The courier was unable to deliver the documents because you did not give us your apartment number.
   h. It is unfortunate that you did not bring the problem to our attention as soon as you received the shipment.
   i. It is now too late for you to receive our special sales discount.
   j. We asked you for the original document but you sent us a photocopy.

5. Substitute more precise words for the overworked words in the following phrases.
   a. a great book
   b. a good meeting
   c. a fine program
   d. fix the letter
   e. a bad presentation
   f. a fine supervisor
   g. a good secretary
   h. a great film
   i. a fine building
   j. a lovely sunset
   k. an awful test
   l. a little house
   m. an awful shock
   n. an interesting report
   o. a nice smile
   p. a lovely surprise
   q. a bad mark
   r. a great TV commercial
   s. a lovely ring
   t. a great car

6. Find original replacements for the clichés italicized below.
   a. a worker who never *leaves you in the lurch* — someone you can count on (dependable)
   b. must stop *passing the buck* — passing the blame
   c. get it done *somehow or other* — in some way
   d. *ironing out the bugs* in our procedure — fixing minor problems
   e. thought about *calling it quits* — quitting
   f. he *gets on his high horse* — indignant
   g. she *racked her brains* — thought carefully
   h. he *sets no store by* — doesn't pay any attention
   i. she *made short work of it* — she did it quickly
   j. she likes to *blow her own horn* — conceited / brags.

7. Write an antonym for each of the following words.
   a. reliable
   b. implausible
   c. exorbitant
   d. lengthen
   e. sensitive
   f. fascinating
   g. trivial
   h. synthetic
   i. openly
   j. encourage

8. Collect several travel brochures from a local travel agency. Then, identify words or phrases in the brochure that are used to attract potential guests. Are there any overused or trite expressions? Next, create a new brochure using your own descriptive words. You may want to consult a thesaurus.

TEAMWORK

Editing Practice

Descriptive Words.   Rewrite these sentences, substituting exact, descriptive words for the italicized words.

1. The high waves *hit* the side of the ship.
2. The manager made a *bad* decision.
3. When he lit the cigar despite their objections, they all *looked* at him through the smoke.
4. When the bus finally arrived, they were all *very cold.*
5. His words *set off* the crowd, which *moved* in a body toward the barricades.

Hidden Pairs.   From each group of words below, two of the words are synonyms. Find each pair. On a separate sheet of paper, write the letters that indicate the pairs.

Example: (a) practice (b) proscribe (c) placate (d) preempt (e) appease
Answer: c and e

1. (a) compensation (b) consideration (c) pay (d) compensatory (e) satisfaction
2. (a) hearing (b) audit (c) examine (d) listening (e) seeing
3. (a) suspense (b) procure (c) dispense (d) distort (e) obtain
4. (a) circumstance (b) sanitation (c) deduction (d) situation (e) accident
5. (a) dispense (b) depreciate (c) spend (d) disburse (e) disperse
6. (a) dispatch (b) keep (c) retain (d) locate (e) indicate
7. (a) unlawful (b) illegible (c) ineligible (d) unreadable (e) uncouth
8. (a) ease (b) alleviate (c) deny (d) impound (e) obfuscate
9. (a) wretched (b) depicted (c) obsolete (d) fastidious (e) meticulous
10. (a) neutral (b) innovative (c) despicable (d) positive (e) new

Discussion Points

1. How can a misspelled word or a pseudo-homonym affect the credibility of a business writer?
2. How do negative words and overused words interfere with establishing goodwill?

What effect does the drug have on the nervous system?
N

One of the patients was adversely affected by the medicare.

Mastering Spelling Techniques

A word is not a crystal, transparent, and unchanged; it is the skin of a living thought and may vary greatly in color and content according to the circumstances and time in which it is used.

—Oliver Wendell Holmes, Jr., American jurist

Misspelling a word in a document makes both the writer and the organization look unprofessional. To increase your chances for employment and advancement, make every effort to improve your spelling.

Guides to Correct Spelling

Although there are many variations in the spelling of English words, some spelling principles always hold true. Every writer must know and be able to apply these principles—the basic guides to correct spelling.

Final *Y*

Many common nouns end in *y*: *company, industry, entry, territory, warranty, supply, day, secretary, survey.* The spelling of the plurals of these common nouns depends on whether the *y* is preceded by a **consonant** or a **vowel.**

- If *y* is preceded by a consonant, change *y* to *i* and add *es: company, companies; industry, industries; entry, entries; territory, territories; warranty, warranties; supply, supplies; secretary, secretaries.*
- If *y* is preceded by a vowel, leave the *y* and add *s: day, days; survey, surveys.*

Ei and *Ie* Words

Among the most frequently misspelled words are these: *believe, belief, conceive, conceit, deceive, deceit, perceive, receive, receipt, relieve,* and *relief.* Use the following Memory Hook to help you remember when to use *ie* and *ei.*

To help you spell ie and ei words correctly, remember this saying:

Use *i* before *e*
Except after *c*
Or when sounded like *ay*
As in *neigh*bour or *weigh*.

Exceptions:

Words in which *ei* makes a long *e* sound (*either*, *caffeine*, and *seize*)

- For*ei*gn
- H*ei*ght
- Forf*ei*t.

Endings *Ful, Ous, Ally, Ily*

To spell the endings *ful, ous, ally,* and *ily* correctly, remember the following:
The suffix ful has only one *l*: *careful, skilful, masterful, beautiful, meaningful.*
An adjective ending with the sound "us" is spelled *ous: previous, various, miscellaneous, humorous, obvious.*
The ending *ally* has two *l*'s: *financially, originally, incidentally, basically, finally.*
The ending *ily* has one *l*: *necessarily, hastily, busily, gloomily.*

Doubling a Final Consonant

Knowing when to double a final consonant before adding an ending to a word is a matter of distinguishing between vowel sounds.

Words of One Syllable.   If you can hear the difference between long and short vowel sounds, you can tell whether or not to double the final consonant of a one-syllable word. If the vowel sound is long, do not double; if the vowel sound is short, double the final consonant. See Figure 7.15 for some examples. Exception: Do *not* double the final consonant of words ending in *w* (saw) or *x* (fix).

(Note also that a final silent "e," such as in "hope," is dropped when "ing" is added.)

Words of More Than One Syllable.   The only rule needed is this one: Double the final consonant if the last syllable of the base word is accented, if the vowel sound in the last syllable is *short,* and if the suffix to be added begins with a vowel. Some examples are listed in Figure 7.16.

When to Double Consonants—One-Syllable Words

hope	hoping (*long vowel*)	hop	hopping (*short vowel*)
mope	moping (*long*)	mop	mopping (*short*)
plane	planing (*long*)	plan	planning (*short*)
scare	scaring (*long*)	scar	scarring (*short*)
stripe	striping (*long*)	strip	stripping (*short*)
tape	taping (*long*)	tap	tapping (*short*)
weed	weeding (*long*)	wed	wedding (*short*)
mix	mixing (*ends in x*)		

◀ **Figure 7.15**
When To Double Consonants
Figure 7.15 lists words of one syllable that do and do not double the final consonant.

Thinking Critically. *How does reading your writing out loud assist you in making doubling decisions?*

Figure 7.16 ▶
Multi-Syllabic Words

Figure 7.16 shows how
the final consonant is
doubled in words of
more than one syllable.

Thinking Critically.
*What resources can
you use to assist you in
doubling words of more
than one syllable?*

Doubling Consonants—Multi-Syllabic Words

commit	committed	committing
equip	equipped	equipping
occur	occurred	occurring
omit	omitted	omitting
prefer	preferred	preferring
regret	regretted	regretting
transmit	transmitted	transmitting

To remember the correct spelling of *accommodation,* think of two cots (*c*'s) and two mattresses (*m*'s).

CHECKUP 1

Correct any misspelled words in the following sentences. Write *OK* if a sentence is correct.

1. First, she tried scrapping the ice off her windshield.
2. Are you referring to Gene Davis in accounting or Jean Davis in marketing?
3. The sales manager assigned the two new sales territorys to Paul and Rona.
4. The day we won the marketing competition was truly momentus.
5. Jasper wandered around in the zoo looking for the monkies.
6. I beleive the Burnside file is in the green filing cabinet.
7. Judge Beauvais believed that the testimony was not necessarilly accurate.
8. All our competitors are envius of our rapid sales increase.
9. Dr. Mallory, the surgeon, said that scaring would be minimal.
10. We transmited the document by attaching it to an e-mail message.

Dictionary Alerts

Even the best spellers need to use a dictionary. However, no one has time to look up every word. Therefore, you should learn how to recognize your own spelling pitfalls—words that you are most likely to misspell. These pitfalls alert careful spellers to consult the dictionary.

The most common spelling pitfalls are presented here. In addition, you may have your own list of problematic words. *Remember:* Use the dictionary whenever in doubt, but especially if the word in question contains one of the following prefixes or suffixes.

Word Beginnings

These pairs of prefixes—*per, pur* and *ser, sur*—present a spelling difficulty because the words in each pair sound like they could be spelled with the same prefix. Study the following words:

permanent	purchase	serpent	surplus
personal	purpose	serenity	surprise
persuade	pursuit	service	surtax

Word Endings

The following groups of word endings are tricky because they have similar sounds or because they may be mispronounced. The spellings of these endings differ. Do not try to guess at spellings of words with the following ending sounds.

Sounds "unt," and "uns."   The endings *ant, ance, ent,* and *ence* are all usually sounded "unt" and "uns." Because there are so many words with these endings, they are spelling danger spots. They must be spelled by eye, not by ear. Here are some common words with these endings.

accountant	compliance	dependent	existence
defendant	maintenance	incompetent	independence
descendant	perseverance	permanent	interference
tenant	remittance	silent	violence

Sounds "uhble," and "uhbility."   The sound "uhble," which might be spelled *able* or *ible,* is another trap. The alert writer consults a dictionary to avoid misspelling words that end in *able, ible, ability,* or *ibility.* Some common "uhble" and "uhbility" words are the following:

changeable	availability	collectible	credibility
movable	capability	deductible	flexibility
payable	predictability	illegible	possibility
receivable	probability	reversible	visibility

CHECKUP 2

Correct any misspelled words in the following sentences. Write *OK* if a sentence is correct.

1. Mitch, do you realize that your perpose is to persuade members to renew their subscriptions?
2. The judge asked the defendent to rise.
3. Ask Pedro to take the returnible bottles to the market on his way to work.
4. Sue is responsible for the maintenence of all our office equipment.
5. This handwriting is completely illegible.
6. Is Mr. Ibrahim's transfer to Moncton permanant?

Sounds "shun," and "shus."   Words ending with the sound "shun" might be spelled *tion, sion,* or even *cian, tian, sian, cion* or *xion.* The ending sound "shus" might be spelled *cious, tious,* or *xious.* Learn the spelling of the words listed here.

ambition	ignition	anxious	malicious
collision	profession	conscientious	pretentious
complexion	suspicion	conscious	superstitious
dietitian	technician	fictitious	suspicious

Sounds "shul," and "shent."   The ending that sounds like "shul" is sometimes spelled *cial* and sometimes *tial.* A "shent" ending might be spelled *cient* or *tient.* Study the following words and learn how they are spelled.

artificial	essential	omniscient	impatient
beneficial	partial	deficient	proficient
judicial	substantial	efficient	quotient

CHECKUP 3

Correct any misspelled words in the following sentences. Write *OK* if a sentence is correct.

1. Charlotte needs a capable and consciencious counselor.
2. Although I was conscious of his presence in the doorway, I did not turn around until he spoke.
3. Keizo found the orientation session very benefitial.
4. Mike made a substantial donation to the United Way.
5. Our new assistant is both efficient and ambicious.
6. Peter's supervisor explained that the questions were just part of routine office procedure, but Peter was still ankcious.

Sounds "ize," and "kul." The ending "*ize*" might be spelled *ize, ise,* or even *yze* (*analyze*). A "kul" ending could be spelled *cal* or *cle*. A careful writer, therefore, consults a dictionary for words with these endings. Study the following "ize" and "kul" words.

apologize	advertise	identical	obstacle
criticize	enterprise	mechanical	particle
realize	improvise	statistical	spectacle
temporize	merchandise	technical	vehicle

Words Ending in *ar, ary, er, ery, or,* and *ory*. Words that end in *ar, ary, er, ery, or,* and *ory* should be recognized as spelling hazards; you should always verify each spelling. For example, *stationary* and *stationery* end with the same sound. Memorize the spellings of the following words:

calendar	temporary	advertiser	debtor
customary	adviser	laboratory	inventory
grammar	advisory	customer	realtor

Do you get stationery and stationary confused? There's an easy memory hook to remember. Simply put, think of *paper,* which ends in *er,* and you'll never confuse it with *stationary*—to stay in one place.

The Sound "seed." Although only a few words end with the sound "seed," they are often written incorrectly because the ending has three different spellings. As shown in the following table, only one word ends in *sede* and only three words end in *ceed*. All other "seed" words are spelled *cede.*

sede	ceed	cede	
supersede	exceed proceed (*but* procedure) succeed	accede cede concede intercede	precede recede secede

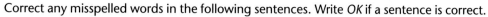

CHECKUP 4

Correct any misspelled words in the following sentences. Write *OK* if a sentence is correct.

1. Nancy proceeded to circle the date on her calander.

2. The realter is supposed to come by tomorrow afternoon to look at our house.

3. Please explain the grammar lesson preceeding Figure B.

4. Particals of dust cause an allergic reaction in some people.

5. Since our inventory is low, this would be a logical time to design new letterhead stationary.

6. We need someone with a technicle background to help us with statisticle data.

Your Spelling Vocabulary

Business writers cannot take the time to verify the spelling of every word. Therefore, they must take the time to learn the correct spellings of the words used most often in their communications. Knowing how to spell troublesome words requires more than memorization. You must analyze each word and fix its peculiarities in your mind. Use strategies like the one shown in the following Memory Hook.

Remember the spellings of troublesome words by using tips such as these:

accommodate (two *c*'s, two *m*'s)
aggressive (two *g*'s, two *s*'s)
convenient (*ven, ient*)
definite (*ni*)
develop (no final *e*)
embarrass (two *r*'s, two *s*'s)
forty, fortieth (the only *four* words without a *u*)

ninth (the only *nine* word without an *e*)
occasion (two *c*'s, one *s*)
privilege (*vile*)
recommend (one *c*, two *m*'s)
repetition (*pe*)
separate (*par*)
until (only one *l*)

Review of Key Terms

1. When should you double a final *consonant* before adding an ending to a word? Provide an example.

Practical Application

1. Without using a dictionary, write the correct forms of the words enclosed in parentheses. Then check your answers in a dictionary.
    a. The wheat sale proved (advantage) to both Canada and Russia.
    b. According to the warranty, the manufacturer is responsible for the (maintain) of the computer.
    c. It was (presume) of the customer to go to the head of the line.
    d. We are (scrap) the ineffective procedures.
    e. Aaron had (plan) to go by plane but ended up taking a bus.
    f. Tina made it (abundant) clear that she preferred to remain in Calgary.
    g. What are the (eligible) requirements for entering the contest?
    h. It would be (waste) to dispose of the contents too (hasty).
    i. Herman is the one in the blue (stripe) suit.
    j. Is Gabe Hart on the (advise) board?

2. Make any spelling corrections needed in these sentences. Write *OK* if a sentence is correct.
    a. Raoul has been faxxing the information to me as soon as he receives it.
    b. If you can't print this report by noon tomorrow, the order must be cancelled.
    c. Joan siezed the opportunity and is now president.
    d. May knew Keith was in a good mood when she heard him huming.
    e. Ms. Cousto retired from the business after bakking about a million cookies.
    f. Archibald Crane could never be called a lovible boss.
    g. From Glen's comment, Emily infered that the company was in financial trouble.
    h. She drew up a list of the uncollectable accounts yesterday.
    i. Apparently, sales have been declining steadely.
    j. Employee morale is still noticebly high, however.
    k. With firmness of purpose, the firm will sermount its present crisis.
    l. After such a late lunch Asha won't be dinning early tonight.
    m. The union rebeled when management called for employee salary reductions.
    n. Now the two sides are confering, thank goodness.
    o. The first day of the electronics show is Wensday.
    p. Mr. Chilelli was very embarassed that he could not remember the name of the new vice president.

3. Correct any words that are misspelled in the following letter.

Dear Ms. Chan:

We would like to take this occassion to reccommend our newest hotel, Casa Grande. Your reservation at Casa Grande guarantees first-class accomodations and all the priviledges that go with them. You may apply now for seperate personal and business rates far below those of other deluxe hotels. You will find inclosed a broshure describing the new Casa Grande.

If you have any questions, please notefy us.

Very truely yours,

4. Make a list of words that you find difficult to spell. Each member of the group should contribute at least one word. Make sure the words are spelled correctly and then brainstorm ways of remembering the correct spelling of each word on your list.

Editing Practice

Using Business Vocabulary. Choose the correct word from the following list to complete each sentence.

a. delinquent   e. principal   i. retrieval
b. perplexed   f. principle   j. visualize
c. personal   g. secede
d. personnel   h. supersede

1. Several nations are threatening to (?) from the international trade alliance because they feel it is too restrictive.
2. Matt Turner suggests that we turn over all (?) accounts to a collection agency.
3. Isabel was (?) by Sandeep's contradictory phone messages.
4. The slides helped us (?) the components that Theresa was describing.
5. We have a sophisticated (?) system for all our stored files.
6. Granting them exclusive rights to market our products will (?) all earlier licensing agreements.
7. Mr. Kowalski wrote a (?) note to Ms. Bordon to congratulate her on her promotion.
8. The lecturer stressed that economic recovery was her (?) concern.
9. The (?) in our laboratory are well-trained, experienced researchers.
10. Although we stand to gain little from the lawsuit, we believe winning is a matter of (?).

Discussion Point

Discuss ways in which you can improve your spelling. Compile a class list of suggestions.

Chapter 7 Wrap-Up

SUMMARY

▶ After a draft is written, the revision process begins. Writers should be mindful of their audience in regard to tone and language. The organization of the document should be logical. All sentences should be complete and grammatically correct. Once the editing has been incorporated, the writer should proofread the document to make sure it is error free.

▶ Effective paragraphs have one main idea. Transition words and phrases show readers how ideas are related to one another. Paragraphs should contain a variety of sentence structures. Writers should make use of white space to improve a document's appearance and readability.

▶ A well-written document is understood the first time it is read. To create effective messages, phrases and clauses should be placed correctly in each sentence. Although an incorrectly placed phrase or clause can be humorous, it usually leads to misunderstanding and confusion. Incorrect and vague pronoun placement can also lead to misinterpretation.

▶ Good writing should be clear, concise, and complete. To achieve this goal, writers should use precise language. Effective words chosen carefully create precise sentences, which in turn lead to effective paragraphs that focus on one main idea.

▶ Writers should use reference tools, such as dictionaries, thesauruses, and style manuals. These tools are essential for accurate and vivid communication.

▶ Business documents should be free of spelling errors. Although electronic spell checkers are helpful, writers should not rely on them to catch every spelling mistake. Proofreading is essential to catch words spelled correctly but used incorrectly. Always use a dictionary when in doubt about how a word is spelled.

CASE 7.1

Martin Reeves works as the administrative assistant to Amy Pataki, the human resources director of a large manufacturing company. Amy relies on Martin to edit and proofread all her correspondence.

Amy has drafted a memo to be distributed to all employees and has asked Martin to finalize the memo.

Read the following paragraph from the memo, which is the first notice regarding the abuse of coffee breaks. If you were Martin, what changes would you make to improve the memo? Keep in mind that your revision should be tactful in order to foster cooperation.

Employees are spending too much time in the coffee room. They are spending their time drinking coffee, rather than doing their work. The coffee room was first opened five years ago. The room temperature is always uncomfortable. It might be stopped by the senior officers if people don't stop misusing the privilege of using it. I would be very sorry to see that happen.

CASE 7.2

Megan has been a computer services technician with CanGlobal Associates for two years. She has worked hard to prove her worth as an employee, completing her work on time. She looks for creative solutions and accepts additional responsibilities. Megan wishes to advance to a supervisory position within the company. She has decided to write a memo to her supervisor in which she will analyze her strengths and weaknesses, identify her reason for seeking a promotion, and list her qualifications for promotion.

Adopt the role of Megan. Write the body paragraphs of the memo that you would send to your supervisor. Keep the guidelines for writing effective sentences and paragraphs in mind as you compose your message.

Communicating in Your Career

On the job, people read a great variety of documents—memos, letters, requests, orders, briefs, and reports. Not all the words in these documents are familiar. In addition, other memos, letters, briefs, and reports need to be written. The language needs to be fresh and exact.

Visit **http://www.yourdictionary.com** and suggest how this site can help make your writing fresh and exact. How can improving your vocabulary help you improve your communication skills?

On the Web

Purdue University's Online Writing Laboratory (OWL) covers a wide range of topics for writers, including planning/starting to write, effective writing, and tips on revising, editing, and proofreading. Go **http://owl.english.purdue. edu,** choose "Handouts and Materials" and then "General Writing Concerns."

Key Terms

Chapter 8

Writing Business Correspondence—Pt. 1

Section 8.1
Planning Business Correspondence

Section 8.2
Writing E-Mails and Memos

Chapter Learning Outcomes

After successfully completing this chapter, you will have demonstrated the ability to:

▶ plan business correspondence;

▶ correctly format e-mails and memos;

▶ list and use several guidelines for effective e-mails and memos.

Vanessa, a graduate of the Wellness and Lifestyle Program at Centennial College, had recently been promoted to a supervisory position at the Canadian Special Olympics Association. Vanessa believed that communication was one of her strong points and that additional communication at the association would improve both operations and employee morale.

Vanessa started putting all her observations, suggestions, and ideas in e-mails. She spent very little time planning and organizing them and they were quite lengthy and wordy. In addition, Vanessa always sent copies to anyone who ranked above her.

To make matters worse, most of the messages contained errors—spelling, grammar, punctuation, and so on. The other employees began to resent receiving a lengthy e-mail about every little thing when they were accustomed to receiving most of their communication through a brief conversation or phone call. Vanessa's supervisors were tired of the proliferation of e-mails about details in which they had no interest.

Fausto Reyes, Vanessa's immediate supervisor, had received several verbal complaints from other employees about Vanessa's memos. Behind Vanessa's back, other employees were referring to Vanessa as the "E-mail Queen."

Although Fausto realized that Vanessa needed to learn more about the basics of communication—communicating to one's supervisors, as well as to people being supervised—he thought that a good first step might be to point out the spelling, punctuation, and formatting errors in Vanessa's messages. He asked Vanessa to meet with him to discuss her e-mail writing

As you read Chapter 8, identify some strategies Vanessa could use to write more effective e-mails.

▶ **Key Terms**

▶ direct approach

▶ indirect approach

▶ persuasive approach

Planning Business Correspondence

Planning is a prerequisite to getting things done.

—Rulon G. Craven, author

In business writing, careful planning and proper formatting are key to producing e-mails, memos, and letters that reflect positively on you and your organization.

Determining Your Reader's Reaction

The first step in planning a business message is to determine what your reader's reaction will be to your message. Recipients generally react one of these four ways: pleased, neutral, displeased, or little or no interest. Depending on what you expect your reader's reaction will be, you will use one of three approaches for planning a message: direct, indirect, or persuasive (see Figure 8.1).

Figure 8.1 ▶
Message Approaches
Here are direct, indirect, and persuasive approaches to writing messages.

Thinking Critically.
When is each approach most useful?

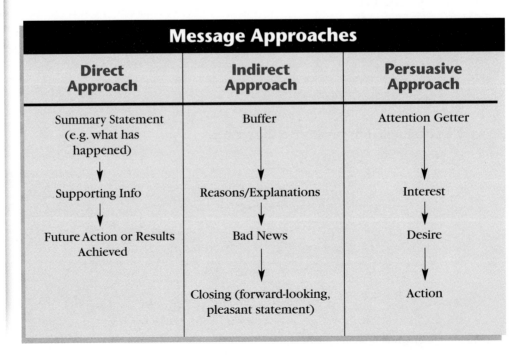

Message Approaches		
Direct Approach	**Indirect Approach**	**Persuasive Approach**
Summary Statement (e.g. what has happened)	Buffer	Attention Getter
↓	↓	↓
Supporting Info	Reasons/Explanations	Interest
↓	↓	↓
Future Action or Results Achieved	Bad News	Desire
	↓	↓
	Closing (forward-looking, pleasant statement)	Action

Pleased or Neutral Reaction

If your reader will be pleased to get your message, or at least have a neutral reaction, you can get right to the point: the good news or the information. Use the **direct approach**, in which you state the main point of the message in the opening sentence. Follow the opening statement with supporting information. Close with an upbeat ending. In a memo, you might close by stating what action to take or by requesting information. In a letter, you should close by reselling your service and/or product and building goodwill.

Displeased Reaction

When you expect the reader to be displeased, unwilling, or even hostile to your message, use the **indirect approach**, in which you begin the message with a "buffer" that presents background information. Never start a message with bad news. This puts the reader in a negative frame of mind. Instead, place the bad news in the middle of the message between neutral "buffers" and an explanation for the bad news.

Little-or-No-Interest Reaction

If your recipient will have little interest in your message, you must sell the recipient on the message you are sending. This type of message calls for the **persuasive approach** in which you begin by getting the reader's attention in the opening sentence. This "hook" is crucial in encouraging the reader to continue reading. Follow the hook by presenting benefits that generate the reader's interest. Then provide additional information that creates a desire on the reader's part for the plan, product, or service. Close the message by asking for the desired action on the part of the reader.

To remember components of the persuasive approach for messages, think of the name "Aida."

MEMORY HOOK

Attention
Interest
Desire
Action

Improving Message Content and Presentation

Once you determine your reader's reaction and the approach to use in organizing the message, plan the special formatting techniques you will use to make a favourable impression on the reader.

Use the Six Cs of Communication

By using the six Cs of communication, you can write messages that are tailored to the reader's needs. Your writing should be:

- **Clear.** Use specific information, direct wording, and transitions. Replace specialized terms and jargon with words familiar to readers.
- **Complete.** Include all pertinent details so the reader has all the information needed to make a decision.
- **Concise.** Get to the point quickly without being abrupt, curt, or rude. Cut irrelevant words, sentences, or paragraphs. You will save your reader time and improve your message.

- **Consistent.** Use the same treatment for similar items, such as using courtesy titles with names and using two-letter province abbreviations in addresses. Also, use formatting techniques such as indenting, numbering, and single- or double-spacing consistently throughout a document.
- **Correct.** Verify that the information is accurate and check the document for correct grammar, usage, spelling, and punctuation.
- **Courteous.** Write your message with the reader's viewpoint in mind.

Use Special Formatting and Mechanical Techniques

Formatting and mechanical techniques can simplify the overall organization of business correspondence to encourage further reading. Some suggestions for using special formatting techniques follow.

1. *Enumerate lists of important items.*

   Please complete the following tasks before tomorrow morning:

   1. Make 20 copies of the inventory report and the sales report.

   2. Collate and staple the reports and put a copy in each manager's folder.

   3. Call the managers to remind them of the meeting.

2. *Use bullets to emphasize several points* when the sequence of the items is not important.

   Here are some topics we will discuss at next week's staff meeting:

   - Orientation program for new employees

   - Stock purchases by employees

   - Employee training programs

   - Education benefit program

   - Severance plan

3. *Use bold, underline, italics, solid capitals,* or *centering* to emphasize important details.

   Tomorrow at 9 a.m. Leo Coleman will be here to discuss

   MANAGING CHANGE IN OUR ORGANIZATION

4. *Use columns with headings* to make reading and understanding easier.

   Below are the inventory figures for March:

Number	Product	Cases
Y-3346	Wallpaper	1300
Z-4384	Cushions	2856
M-8729	Curtains	1438
L-4778	Comforters	1143

5. *Use underlining or bold and side headings* to show natural breaks in a message.

   Our new vacation policy rewards continued employment.

   Service—6 Months or Less

   Employees who have been with the company 6 months or less will receive one-half day of paid vacation for each month of full-time employment.

Dear Ms. Lee:

Thank you for the opportunity to interview your students last week.

Offers of Employment
We wish to offer field placement to the following students:
* Jonathan Riley
* Monique Allard
* Ursula Friedman

Reporting Information
Would you please pass on the following information to these students:
* Starting Date and Time: January 6, 200x, at 8:30 a.m.
* Location: 86 Bay Street, Toronto (Corner of Bay and King Streets; King subway station).
* Contact Person: Mr. Bill Mayfield—416-909-3403

We look forward to welcoming your students to Highland Credit.

Angela Fernandes
HR Specialist, *HIGHLAND Credit Company*
416 277-3455

◀ **Figure 8.2**
Formatting Techniques
Note the use of headings and bullets to help the reader quickly absorb the information in this e-mail message.

Thinking Critically.
What would be a suitable subject line for this message? Why?

Service—7 to 11 Months

Employees who have been with the company 7 to 11 months will receive three-fourths of one day of paid vacation for each month of employment.

Service—1 to 2 Years

Employees who have been with the company 1 to 2 years will receive 14 days of paid vacation.

6. *Use colour coding* to attract attention. For example, use yellow paper for all messages from the accounting department. Or use a coloured highlighting pen to attract attention. The colour used can have a special meaning: For example, blue could be used for general announcements (Our profits are up); red could signify needed information (All expense reports must be submitted by June 6).

Exercise caution in using these special techniques—overuse reduces their effectiveness.

Review of Key Terms

1. Explain the process of using a *direct approach*.
2. When would you use the *persuasive approach*? What are the steps in this approach?

Practical Application

1. Discuss how you could use some special formatting techniques to write the body of a memo using the following information. Present your suggestions to the class.

TEAMWORK

In her memo of July 15, your supervisor, Rosa Hernandez, asked you to give her a list of sales by region for April, May, and June. The sales figures are, respectively, Region 1—$23,494, $22,577, $19,482; Region 2—$33,458, $32,332, $25,854; Region 3—$21,589, $21,887, $20,492.

Editing Practice

1. Revise the following underlined expressions to use clearer, more up-to-date wording.
   a. In regard to your letter of the 27th of June, ...
   b. At the present writing, we still have not received ...
   c. Please be advised that your dividend will be $6000, not $600.
   d. In the event that August 14 is an inconvenient date, kindly let us know when you would like to have the speakers delivered.
   e. Due to the fact that property sales are down because of ...
2. Revise the following sentences to make them more concise.
   a. Prior foresight would have saved us these cost overruns.
   b. The same identical error message appeared the last time I used this word processing command.
   c. Unless the whole staff cooperates together, we won't finish the manuscript in time for spring publication.
   d. Their management styles are both alike.
   e. The heating system has been converted over from gas to solar power.

3. Make the following sentences clearer and more forceful by using simple words.
    a. From the expression on Michael's face, we knew that he was engaged in deep ratiocination.
    b. The managing partner discommended the proposal.
    c. Juana was the cynosure of the labour negotiations.
    d. His dark blue suit was in every way comme il faut.
    e. Her remarks precipitated a veritable brouhaha.

Discussion Point

Why should writers be careful when using special formatting techniques in business correspondence?

Writing E-Mails and Memos

▶ **Key Terms**

▶ electronic mail
▶ 24/7
▶ memos
▶ emoticons
▶ spamming
▶ virus
▶ guidewords

*"The horror of that moment," the
King went on, "I shall never, never
forget!"
"You will, though," the Queen said,
"if you don't make a memorandum
of it."*

—Lewis Carroll, *Through the Looking Glass*

Electronic mail, more commonly referred to as e-mail, is written communication just like memos and letters. The primary difference is the method of transmitting the message. E-mail messages are sent instantly through the Internet. E-mail can be sent 24/7, that is, "24 hours a day, 7 days a week," to any e-mail address worldwide.

Memos are printed and sent to people within your organization through an interoffice mail delivery system. Memos may be sent within a department, among departments, and among company branches at different geographic locations. E-mail messages are sent to people both outside and inside your organization. E-mail can be stored on your computer, or a copy can be printed, for later reference. The printed copy automatically includes the date and time the message was sent.

E-mails and memos, like letters, are essential to business communications because they put important or complicated matters in writing. They provide a written record for both the reader and the writer. They can, for example, clarify and confirm instructions or information given orally and can be referred to many times if necessary.

Purposes of E-Mails and Memos

Memos and e-mails are used for a variety of purposes. The main purposes are to request, to inform, to report, to remind, to transmit, and to promote goodwill.

To Request

Use memos or e-mails to request information, action, or reactions. Messages written for this purpose take the direct approach, as in the following examples.

We need revised sales figures from you before the cost estimates for the Bryant project can be completed.

A confidential memo giving specifics about a new product was accidentally faxed to a competitor.

Please make arrangements for a one-day seminar for all trainees.

Please review this proposal and give me your opinion.

To Inform

Use memos or e-mails to communicate procedures, company policies, and instructions. If the message contains good news, use the direct approach; if the message contains bad news, use the indirect approach.

Our safety procedures require a 15-minute rest period for every four hours of work.

Company policy permits escorted visitors sixteen years old and older to tour our plant.

Use your key card to enter the King Street gate.

To Report

Use memos or e-mails to convey organized data such as schedules, sales figures, and names of clients or patients, as in these two examples.

Below is our schedule for the completion of McMaster Hall.

Here is a list of the supplies we will need.

To Remind

Use memos or e-mails as reminders about deadlines, important meetings, and so on. Such reminders should be brief and use the direct approach.

Please send me your travel itinerary by Friday, May 22.

Our appointment with the Northern Telecom representatives is on Monday, April 3, at 2 p.m. in the conference room.

To Transmit

Use memos or e-mails to tell readers about an accompanying message. The memo could describe, explain, or simply identify the attachment or enclosure. The direct approach works best for such messages.

Attached are the time sheets to be distributed to all hourly employees.

Enclosed is a printout listing the names and home addresses of all regional managers.

To Promote Goodwill

Use memos or e-mails to establish, improve, and maintain goodwill. These messages could congratulate, welcome, or convey appreciation.

Congratulations on your promotion.

Welcome to Huntle Industries.

Your advertising designs got us the Wright order. Thanks for doing a great job!

Message Structure

A memo or e-mail is more likely to achieve the writer's goal if it is brief and to the point without seeming abrupt or incomplete.

The organization of the message should be based on these three elements: (1) a statement of purpose, (2) a message, and (3) a statement of future action (see Figure 8.3).

**Figure 8.3 ▶
Organizational
Elements**
This memo is printed
on plain paper using
standard memo format.

Thinking Critically. Why
does the writer use three
paragraphs rather than
one or two?

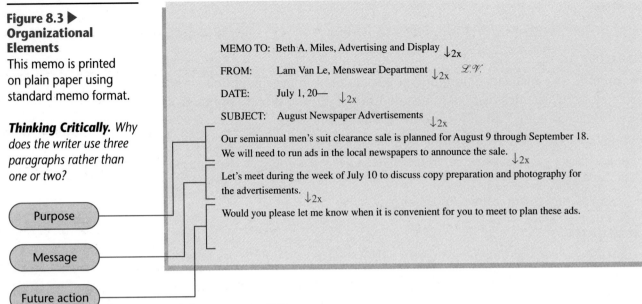

Purpose

Message

Future action

MEMO TO: Beth A. Miles, Advertising and Display ↓2x

FROM: Lam Van Le, Menswear Department ↓2x *L.V.*

DATE: July 1, 20— ↓2x

SUBJECT: August Newspaper Advertisements ↓2x

Our semiannual men's suit clearance sale is planned for August 9 through September 18.
We will need to run ads in the local newspapers to announce the sale. ↓2x

Let's meet during the week of July 10 to discuss copy preparation and photography for
the advertisements. ↓2x

Would you please let me know when it is convenient for you to meet to plan these ads.

Statement of Purpose

The subject line tells the reader what the message is about but does not usually
state the writer's reason for writing. Often the writer can make the purpose
clear simply by referring to an earlier memo or to a previous meeting or
telephone conversation. Here are two examples of how a writer can state the
purpose of a memo or e-mail in the first paragraph.

At the Advertising Department's meeting on October 5, you asked me to investigate and report on the comparative costs of print and broadcast advertisements.
Here is a summary of what I found.

Attached is the independent review of our admissions procedures from Dr. O'Hara.
We will meet on April 5 from 9 to 11 a.m. in Conference Room A to discuss his recommendations.

Message

After making the statement of purpose, the writer should go directly to the
main points of the message. The object is to help the reader grasp the main
points as easily as possible, as in these two examples.

We could admit patients more quickly and efficiently if we gave them a checklist to
complete. The checklist would take the place of the long-answer forms now being
used.

A new form has been designed to simplify taking telephone orders. A copy of the
new form is attached.

Statement of Future Action

The body of the message should usually end with a statement of future action
to be taken or with a request for further instructions, as illustrated in the
following examples. Note that the time frames for future action are specific.

I will send further details about our advertisement for the catalogue by November 15.

Please notify me of your decision by February 15 so that I can either put this procedure into effect or develop a new plan.

Message Tone

The tone of a memo or e-mail depends largely on the position of, and the writer's relation to, the recipient. In general, use a more formal tone when addressing top management than when writing to a peer or a subordinate, unless you know that the addressee prefers an informal tone.

If you're not certain which tone to use in a memo or e-mail, choose a balanced one—neither too formal nor too casual. Avoid using contractions like you'll and here's, but do not use stilted language either. Stick to business. Note the balanced tone in the following example:

Attached (or enclosed) is the report on last month's video camera sales, with the changes you requested yesterday. The figures on Model A26 are now broken down to show the number of these video cameras sold in each sales region. In addition, the appropriate tables now have an added line showing Model A26 sales by region for the same period last year.

Subject matter also determines the choice of tone for a memo or e-mail. A message announcing the schedule of the company's bowling team would obviously have a lighter tone than a message justifying costs that ran over budget. The more serious the topic, the more serious the tone should be. Here are some words that convey a positive tone.

able	great	outstanding
absolutely	guarantee	particular
advantage	happy	perfect
appreciation	helpful	permanent
approval	honest	pleasure
assist	important	productive
assure	initiative	progress
benefit	kind	promise
complimentary	lasting	recommended
comprehensive	long-lasting	recognition
congratulations	major	revolutionary
delighted	markedly	reward
determine	marvelous	save
easy	modern	security
effective	monumental	superior
efficient	motivation	thank you
enhanced	notable	timely
enriched	offer	unique
favourable	opportunity	valued
grateful	original	wonderful

E-Mails—Format and Guidelines

E-mail is so quick, easy, and inexpensive that its use is increasing at a phenomenal rate. Because e-mail messages are so easy to send, some people become careless about the content and formatting. Use the following formatting information and guidelines to ensure that your e-mail messages will convey a professional image of you and your company.

E-Mails—Format

1. Address Line. Always check the accuracy of an e-mail address. One typographical error in the address means your e-mail message will not be delivered. E-mail addresses have a username followed by the @ symbol and the host's domain name. For example, the e-mail addresses *yourname@eiu.edu* and *tsmith@aol.com* follow this pattern. Use the address book feature of your e-mail software to record frequently used addresses.

2. Subject Line. E-mail messages with nothing in the subject line or something vague, such as "message" or "information," are read last, if at all. Subject lines should be concise phrases that clearly identify the content of the message. If your message is urgent, use the word *URGENT* in all caps as the first word in your subject line, followed by the topic. If your message is a request, use the word *REQUEST* in all caps as the first word in the subject line. If your message is an announcement or information that requires no response, use the abbreviation *FYI*, (which stands for *for your information*), in all caps as the first word in the subject line.

Subject: URGENT: Need Safety Mask

Subject: REQUEST: Return First Aid Kit by Noon

Subject: FYI: Free Ticket to Tonight's Hockey Game

Don't mark a message urgent unless it really is. You wouldn't call 911 if a colleague had a paper cut on his or her finger. No one likes to be tricked into reading an e-mail message.

Also, don't assume the recipient read your message just because you marked it urgent. The recipient may be away and unable to read e-mail for several hours or days. If you do not get a reply quickly to an urgent e-mail, follow up with a phone call.

3. Greeting. When you meet someone or call them on the phone, you greet that person with "Good morning," "Hello," or something similar. For some e-mails, such as those written to customers, you can use the same type of greeting you would use in a letter; for example, *Dear Ms. Jones.* For e-mail to colleagues you know well and with whom you are on a first-name basis, use their first name; for example, *Dear Susie,* or simply, *Susie,* as a greeting.

4. Body. Leave one blank line after the greeting, between paragraphs, and between the end of the last paragraph and the closing.

Don't use all-capital letters in your e-mail because it is hard to read, and it is considered the same as shouting at your reader. Also, do not use very small type. This is not only difficult to read but is also interpreted as speaking so softly that people have trouble hearing you.

5. Closing. Type your name at the end of your message. Some e-mail addresses do not use the name of the sender, so the signature may be the only clue as to who the sender is. A complimentary closing is not necessary—just your first, or first and last, name. Many e-mail programs have an auto signature feature which can include your name, e-mail address, phone number, and

To: Wayne Johnson

Subject: Marketing Opportunity

Wayne,

Several community colleges and high schools have asked us about stocking videotapes in the following areas: contemporary Canadian plays, Canadian literature, customer service, and communication skills.

I believe this is an opportunity to significantly increase sales, as no other video company is carrying a rental inventory of educational materials.

Would you please check the availability and cost of tapes in these topic areas and provide me with a list by July 15.

Joyce Mercado
VP Marketing VideoClassics

◄ **Figure 8.4**
E-Mail Message
Note that the subject line will immediately capture the interest of the recipient and that the message is clear and concise.

Thinking Critically.
From the content of the message, it is obvious that the sender works in the same company as the recipient. Why is the closing so detailed? What other closing could Joyce Mercado have used on this e-mail?

mailing address in case the recipient needs to get in touch with you some way other than e-mail.

6. Attachments. A document prepared in a word processing, spreadsheet, or graphics software program can be attached to an e-mail so it can be saved and printed by the recipient in its original form. Because of the increase in computer viruses, it is best to let your recipient know in your e-mail message that you are attaching a file to an e-mail and what the attachment is. It is also common courtesy to ask permission before sending a large attachment.

E-Mail—Guidelines

1. Limit the Length, Topics, and Recipients. Limit your e-mail message to one topic, which makes writing a subject line much easier. E-mail messages are supposed to be brief and should be a maximum of about 25 lines of text. Use the default single-spacing with word wrap and keep the paragraphs short for easier reading.

Send the e-mail only to those who need the information. Information overload and e-mail overload have a negative effect on productivity.

2. Be Careful with Humour and Emoticons. When you talk with someone in person, you have additional means of communicating besides words. Because there is no body language or tone of voice to help convey your meaning in an e-mail, you should be very careful about using humour. Your e-mail recipient may have trouble telling if you are joking or serious.

Emoticons, or smileys, are a way of visually expressing your emotions in e-mail. Some common examples are:

:-) to send a smile

:- (to send a frown

;-) a wink and a smile

Only use these symbols when you are sure the recipient will understand them and that they will be displayed correctly. Not all e-mail software, especially in other countries, can display special characters, so your recipient may not see the emoticon as you sent it. What you see on your screen may be different from what your recipient sees on his or her screen.

3. Check Content, Spelling, and Grammar. Always read and proofread your e-mail before you send it to ensure that it is correct and that all details have been included. A message with errors or omissions is unprofessional and creates a poor image of you and your organization.

Some e-mail programs will automatically check your spelling or grammar before sending the e-mail. This feature does *not* take the place of proofreading. Automatic spelling and grammar checks will not detect a variety of errors, including using a word in the wrong context.

4. Do Not Send Confidential Information. E-mail is not private or confidential. A good rule to follow is: Do not send anything by e-mail that you wouldn't be willing to have posted on the company noticeboard. Think of your e-mail as a postcard. Many people have the opportunity to read a postcard after it is sent and before it gets into the hands of the recipient. Once you send an e-mail you have lost control of it because the recipient can easily forward it to others.

5. Know Your Company Policy. Study your company's policy on e-mail and follow it. If you violate the policy, you could be fired. Some companies are very strict about not allowing employees to use the Internet or e-mail for personal use—either during or after working hours. Your company owns the e-mail system, and courts have subpoenaed e-mail messages as evidence. Even though you deleted the e-mail, it is probably still on the server's backup system and can be retrieved.

6. Spamming. **Spamming** is sending unsolicited e-mail, particularly advertisements, to others. It is the electronic version of junk mail. Spammers get your e-mail address the same way companies get your mailing address for junk mail—they buy lists. Send unsolicited e-mail only when you believe the recipient will want to receive it.

7. Reply Promptly to E-Mails. Check your e-mail at least twice a day. Respond to urgent e-mails as soon as you read them, and respond to non-urgent e-mails that require an answer by the end of the day. It is common courtesy to respond to, and unprofessional to ignore, an e-mail that asks for a response.

When you reply to an e-mail, key your answer above the original message. This saves the recipient from having to scroll through the original message to see your reply. You may wish to delete parts of the original message and leave only the question(s) you are answering. If you choose to compose a new message for your reply, be sure to include enough information that your recipient will know *which* e-mail message you are answering and what you are talking about.

Avoid: "I will attend."

Instead: "I will attend the seminar this Friday in the Copper Penny Room."

8. Viruses. A **virus** is a self-replicating code planted illegally in a computer program for the purpose of damaging or shutting down a system or network. Unfortunately, it is through attachments to e-mail that many computer viruses are spread to other computers. If you do not know the sender or you are not expecting an attachment, be cautious about opening it.

Memos—Format and Content

Memos provide a method of communicating within an organization. Although e-mail can also be used for this purpose, memos are required when you want everyone to have a hard copy of information, or when the content is not suitable for an e-mail. Information on formatting and writing memos follows. However, as a new employee, find out if your organization has a preferred style or standard format for memos.

A memo has two main parts, the heading and the body. The body may be followed by ending information in the form of notations at the left margin.

Memo Heading

The heading of a memo contains the **guidewords** *MEMO TO, FROM, DATE,* and *SUBJECT.* Guide words may be keyed in all-capital letters or with initial-capital letters. Never mix these two formats within the same memo.

1. **The MEMO TO or TO Line.** The *MEMO TO* or *TO* line contains the first and last name of the person or persons who are to receive the original copy of the memo. Courtesy titles are usually omitted on memos.

MEMO TO: Carl Martin

Kam-Lin Ng

Olaf Trunzer

The writer should include an addressee's job title in the following situations:

a. When the writer wishes to show deference:

MEMO TO: Rodolpho Gonzalez, Chief Executive Officer

b. When the addressee has more than one job title, but the writer's message concerns the duties that pertain to only one of the titles.

TO: Mary O'Malley, Chair, Committee on Community Relations

(Ms. O'Malley is also the human resources director.)

c. When the addressee has the same name as another employee, or a very similar name, so that the writer must clarify which person should receive the memo.

TO: Mike Boose, Assistant Chief Engineer

(Another employee, also named Mike Boose, is the production manager.)

Dana asked Ellen, her new office assistant, to type and send a memo to Terry Israel, director of marketing. Ellen included a courtesy title on the memo and sent it to Mr. Terry Israel. Terry was upset because she did not appreciate being addressed as a man.

In large companies, it helps to include address information in the *MEMO TO* or *TO* line of an interoffice memo. For example:

MEMO TO: Antonio Pappas, Room 3301, Benefits Office

TO: Michelle Gold, Laboratory 3, Research Department

If the memo is being sent to more than a few people, type *See Distribution* or *Distribution Below* on the *TO* line and place the list of recipients at the end of the memo under the heading *Distribution.* Type *Distribution* on the third line below the reference initials, file notation, or enclosure notation, whichever appears last. List the names of recipients in alphabetical order; this is an objective way to determine the order of names. The memo in Figure 8.5 shows a distribution list for individuals who are all branch managers.

2. The *FROM* Line. The writer may include a job title, department affiliation, room number, and telephone extension in the *FROM* line.

FROM: Edith L. Fitzpatrick, Researcher, Investment Department, Room 2403, Ext. 988

3. The *DATE* Line. Write the date in full rather than using abbreviations or all numerals.

Business Style	December 19, 20—
European Style	19 December 20—

Figure 8.5 ▶
Distribution List
This memo is a template from a word processing program and shows how a distribution list is typed.

Thinking Critically.
How are the names on the distribution list ordered? Why?

TO: Branch Managers—Distribution Below ↓2x

FROM: Michael Ireland, General Manager ↓2x 𝓜.𝓵.

DATE: August 18, 20— ↓2x

SUBJECT: Meeting for Branch Managers ↓2x

The Human Resource Department has announced improvements in the employee benefits plan. ↓2x

A meeting to explain our new benefits package will be held on Tuesday, August 28, at 9 a.m., in Conference Room A adjoining my office. ↓2x

Please read the enclosed booklet about the package before the meeting and let me know if you have any questions about it. ↓2x

dk emp-benf
Enclosure ↓3x

Distribution:
Carlos Alvarado
Joe Danford
Sally Dillon
Carroll Henderson
Tyler Jones
Paulette Meyers √
Harry Potter
Camille Weise

4. The *SUBJECT* Line. State the subject of a memo clearly and briefly. Choose a subject line that accurately sums up the contents of the memo. This is important not only to immediately tell the reader what the memo is about, but also because the subject line will usually determine how the memo is filed and how easily it can be retrieved. To give a memo a more professional appearance, do not abbreviate the word *SUBJECT.* Only in exceptional cases should the subject line require more than a single line. The following examples say all that is necessary; the rest should be left to the body of the memo.

SUBJECT: Request for Additional Personnel

SUBJECT: Submitting Time Sheets

The Body

A memo does not contain a salutation (e.g. Dear Ms. Smith). Instead, it begins with the first paragraph of the message. Leave one or two blank lines between the last line of the heading and the body of the memo, or divide the heading and the body with a solid line. Single-space the body of the memo with a blank line between paragraphs. Use blocked paragraphs with no indenting. Remember to begin the first paragraph of the memo with a statement of purpose.

If the memo continues on to a second page, include a header at the top of page two stating the name of the recipient, the page number, and the date. For example:

Sujhkinder Atwal 2.   February 6, 20—

or

Sujhkinder Atwal
Page 2
February 6, 2004

Notations

Two lines below the body of the memo at the left margin, include any notations—for example, attachment notations and copy notations—that may be needed. If the writer is the person who typed the memo, no reference initials are needed. For ease of reference, add the document name and disk location. For example, notations could be added as follows:

Attachment
c: John W. Palmer
mfd/Apex/MemoFeb02.doc

The Signature

The writer should sign each memo with a blue or black pen by writing his or her initials after the name on the *FROM* line. Typing or signing your full name at the end of a memo is unnecessary because the full name appears after the guideword *FROM.*

Review of Key Terms

1. Compare the use of *guidewords* in memos and e-mails.
2. Explain the term *24/7* as it relates to *electronic mail.*

Practical Application

1. Memos have the following purposes:
   a. To request   d.   To remind
   b. To inform   e.   To transmit
   c. To report   f.   To promote goodwill

   For each item below, write the purpose that best describes a memo that accomplishes the following:
   a. Identifies an attached prospectus
   b. Asks about the servicing of company vehicles
   c. Announces a new employee dental plan
   d. Congratulates someone who has been promoted and transferred to London, England
   e. Lists sales figures by division for the last three months
   f. Asks about a production schedule that was due last Friday
   g. Explains the company bonus policy
   h. Welcomes a new employee
   i. Asks your opinion on a specific matter
   j. Gives instructions for ordering new computers

2. Write the body of a memo, using information from the following paragraphs. Include a statement of purpose, a message, and a statement of future action.

   After six months' full-time employment, employees are eligible for tuition reimbursement for evening and Saturday courses taken at a college or university. Employees must have the course approved by George Earl, human resources manager. Mr. Earl requires each applicant to write a memo requesting approval. The memo must list the course title, the dates of the course, the college, the cost, and how successful completion of the course will help the employee perform his or her job.

   You want to take Computer Concepts 101 at Cranbury Community College. The course begins the first Monday of next month and meets each Monday for 12 weeks. The cost is $185 for this three-credit course. Taking this course will help you improve your productivity in processing customer requests. Include your telephone extension and the deadline for enrolment.

3. Write an interoffice memo notifying staff that new insurance coverage will take effect at the beginning of next month. Representatives from Prudential, the new company, will be in Conference Room A to

provide information and to answer any questions regarding the new policy. Remember to include the time and date of the meeting. Follow the formatting guidelines for memos given in this section. Key and print your memo.

4. You are the manager of your department. You have just hired a student on co-op placement. Write an e-mail to your staff introducing the new team member. Create any necessary background that you think your staff would find helpful.

5. Your company has recently hired eight customer service representatives. They will be answering phone calls and e-mails from customers. Because you write a lot of e-mails to customers, your supervisor has asked you for suggestions on e-mail training for the new employees. What main principles should be covered? Write a memo or an e-mail to your instructor giving your suggestions.

6. Contact companies in your town or city to collect information on their e-mail policies, and/or research any law cases related to the use of e-mail. Prepare a short presentation for the class.

TEAMWORK

Editing Practice

Possessives, Plurals, and Contractions. Rewrite each incorrect item by adding, moving, or deleting apostrophes to make the sentences correct. Write *OK* if a sentence is correct.

1. Lets walk over to Lisas office.
2. Two trainees are working in the mens sportswear department.
3. Its almost time for our annual safety inspection.
4. Most manager's agree with the Art Departments new procedures.
5. Until Gwynn's car is repaired, she is driving her daughter-in-laws car.
6. Damien and Sergei's faces were sunburned during the softball game.
7. One witnesses' statement agreed with Johns.
8. Two employees must check the lock on the bank vaults' door.
9. His sisters-in-law's store was designed by both of them.
10. This is Ted Wilson, our companies computer consultant.

Discussion Points

1. Describe three specific situations in which you would use e-mail on the job. Is it appropriate to use e-mail for personal use on the job? Why or why not?
2. What adjustments should you make in style and tone when writing a business e-mail to someone you have never met?

SUMMARY

▶ A business message, whether a memo or an e-mail, should be carefully written and properly formatted. In preparing the message, the writer should be aware of the reader's reaction, which will dictate the approach the writer should take—direct, indirect, or persuasive. Business messages are easier to read when the writer uses formatting techniques; for example, listing items, using bullets, and emphasizing important details by using features such as bold, italics, and underlining.

▶ Business memos and e-mails are essential to business communications because they put important information in writing. Memos are used within an organization, while e-mails are used for correspondence within and outside an organization. E-mails and memos are used to request, inform, report, remind, transmit attached information, and promote goodwill.

▶ Messages usually begin with a statement of purpose, followed by the body of the message, and then a statement of future action. The tone of the message should correspond to its audience and content.

▶ Employees must follow their organization's e-mail policy. Follow the formatting and content guidelines for e-mails to ensure that your messages create a professional image of you and your organization. For example, use a brief, specific subject line; check the content, spelling, and grammar; limit the length, topics, and recipients; and include appropriate closing information.

▶ Memos are divided into a heading and body, plus any notations. The heading includes the guidewords *MEMO TO, FROM, DATE,* and *SUBJECT.* The body is typically keyed in single spacing with a blank line between paragraphs. Notations and distribution lists appear at the bottom left-hand margin, two lines below the final paragraph.

Communicating in Your Career

On the job you will be using e-mail. To help prepare for this responsibility, conduct a brief interview with someone who uses e-mail at work. How do they manage their e-mail? What suggestions do they have for efficient e-mail use? What do they like, or not like, about e-mail as a method of communication? Report your findings by writing a memo to your instructor.

On the Web

Most companies have a written e-mail policy. To learn about the reasons for these policies and their contents, visit *http://www.emailreplies.com.* Choose Policy and read the information on "What Should Be Included in an E-Mail Policy." Then download and print the sample policy. Review it, and bring it to class for discussion.

CASE 8.1

Shakell Sa'eed has been working as an insurance representative at Canadian Assurance Company for one month. Shakell uses e-mail to correspond with company colleagues and to respond to e-mails from clients. When his manager, Elaine Pelligreni, reviewed several items from Shakell's correspondence she discovered that Shakell was not using tactful language. He frequently used expressions such as *your error, your claim,* and *you failed.* The messages also contained spelling, punctuation, and grammatical errors.

If you were Elaine, how would you approach Shakell about the negative tone and errors in his correspondence?

What steps could you and Shakell take to ensure that his future correspondence is acceptable?

CASE 8.2

People in Japan are using keypads to communicate. The clunky keyboard and large American home computer do not impress the Japanese. Instead, they are using i-mode, technology that can be accessed on their cell phones.

I-mode is more than just e-mail; you can listen to music, make reservations, find out about restaurants, get stock quotes, and find medical help—all with a keypad.

How do technological advances, such as the i-mode, improve business communications? Do you think there are any disadvantages in using these methods of communication? Why or why not?

Key Terms

24/7	372	guidewords	379	spamming	378
direct approach	367	indirect approach	367	virus	379
electronic mail	372	memos	372		
emoticons	378	persuasive approach	367		

Chapter 9

Writing Business Correspondence—Pt. 2

Chapter Learning Outcomes

After successfully completing this chapter, you will have demonstrated the ability to:

▶ correctly format letters;
▶ write instructions, directions, requests, and claims;
▶ grant and reject requests while keeping recipient's goodwill;
▶ explain the objectives of sales letters;
▶ write claim letters and adjustment letters;
▶ write public relations and social-business letters;
▶ describe the process of constructing form letters and write form paragraphs.

Chris Gagnon had worked at Metro Hospital for four years as an orderly. In the *Medical Notes* weekly newsletter, the president of the hospital asked for volunteers to serve on a team to plan some special events and activities to recognize the hospital's 100 years of service to the community. Chris volunteered and was chosen as a member of the Centennial Celebration Team.

The team decided on several events and activities. One was to be a formal gala for approximately 500 people who were contributors to the Metro Hospital Foundation. The committee decided to hold a silent auction during the gala. Chris agreed to draft a letter that would be sent to local businesses asking for donated items for the auction.

Chris was able to write the body of the letter but realized he didn't know how to set it out properly. He also realized that each business would get basically the same letter, with a few variations to customize it a little to the particular type of business. To get a favourable response, the letter would have to look attractive, be error-free, and be complete. Thinking through the task, Chris saw that it was more complex than he had anticipated.

As you study Chapter 9, identify the information that would help Chris prepare this letter.

Business Letters— Parts and Format

A handsome appearance is a silent recommendation.

—Aristotle, Greek philosopher, 384–322 B.C.

Two style factors—*appearance* and *content*—can be used to describe a business letter. How does the letter *look*, and what does the letter *say*? The appearance and the content of a business letter make up the **style** of a letter, just as a person's manner of dress and the content of his or her conversation contribute to that person's style.

The style of a business letter contributes as much to that letter's success as a person's style contributes to his or her success. If your business letters are to achieve their goals, you must first learn how to control the appearance of a letter, which will be discussed in this section.

A writer conveys a professional appearance by using standard letter parts and arranging these parts according to accepted letter formats, thus ensuring that the letter is arranged attractively on the page.

Business Letter Parts

Business letters often contain many parts. All the standard letter parts, plus some optional ones, are shown in Figure 9.1.

1. *Letterhead.* The term **letterhead** refers to either (1) the printed information on business stationery or (2) the actual sheet of paper used for the first page of a business letter. Figures 9.1 and 9.3 show two examples of company letterhead. This printed information usually appears at the top of the page, but may be in the left margin area, or at the bottom of the page.

2. *Date Line.* Most companies use a business-style date line with the month spelled in full, the day of the month written in numerals and followed by a comma, and all four digits of the year. The European or military style date line starts with the day of the month followed by the month, no comma, and all four digits of the year. Here are examples of each:

   Business style: July 10, 20—

   European style: 10 July 20—

3. *Inside Address.* The **inside address** contains the information that will be shown on the envelope; for example:

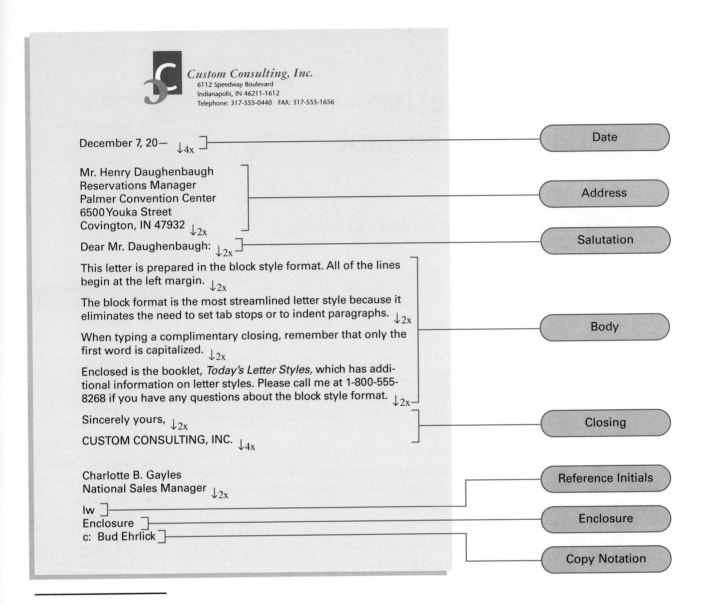

Figure 9.1
Block Letter Format
The block format is very streamlined. This letter shows all the standard parts, as well as some optional ones.

Thinking Critically.
What is the advantage of this format?

Ms. Camille R. Barry
General Manager
Northern Outfitters Inc.
85 East Road
Winnipeg, Manitoba R4C 2B5

Mr. Louis Massue
President
Massue Consulting
Suite 27, 1376 Yonge Street
Toronto, ON M5A 2W6

An address in the United States of America is set out with the ZIP code on the same line as the city and state names.

Mr. Detlef Bauer
Personnel Director
Electronic Designs Inc.
575 Harbourview Drive
Chelsea, Massachusetts 02150
U.S.A.

Mr. Mohamed Al-Sabah
Director
Habitat for Humanity
85 Perth Road
Conway, AR 72032
U.S.A.

For an international address, type the name of the country in all-capital letters on a separate line at the end of the address. Do not abbreviate the name of the country.

Mr. Ferdinand Villa	Ms. Akiko Kagami
Camino de San Rafael	The Togin Building
Málaga 29010	4-1-20 Toranomon
SPAIN	Chuo-Ku, Tokyo, 105
	JAPAN

4. *Attention Line.* The attention line is an optional part of a letter. When used, it appears as part of the inside address or on the second line below the inside address. Type the attention line in all-capital letters or capital and lowercase letters. Use a colon after the word *Attention:* or the abbreviation *ATTN:*.

Butler, Richards & Meighen, LLP	The Equity Group
Barristers and Solicitors	99 Mountain Road
ATTN: MS. ANGELA ROSSINI	Victoria, BC V7B 3E3
45 King Street West, Suite 800	
Toronto, Ontario M5E 2J6	ATTN: Office Manager

Use an attention line when you want to stress that the letter is technically intended for the *company*, not the *person*. Also use an attention line when you do not know and cannot find out the name of the person to whom your letter should be directed. In this situation, the attention line should indicate the person's job title, such as *Sales Manager* or *Customer Service Representative*.

5. *Salutation.* The **salutation,** or greeting, immediately precedes the body of the letter. Include a courtesy title such as *Mr.* or *Ms.* If the letter is intended to be less formal and more friendly, then the salutation will contain the addressee's first name.

Dear Ms. Grant:	Dear Sir or Madam:
Dear Jim: Ladies and Gentlemen:	

(Note the colon in each of the above examples. Traditionally, the salutation ends with a colon and there is a comma after the complimentary close. This is known as the **standard** or **mixed punctuation** style. However, you may omit both the colon after the salutation and the comma after the complimentary closing. This is called an **open punctuation** style.)

6. *Subject Line.* A subject line is optional. It is used to quickly identify the topic of a letter.

7. *Body.* The body, the main part of the letter, is keyed single-spaced with one blank line between paragraphs.

8. *Complimentary Closing.* The "good-bye" of the letter, the complimentary closing, is an ending such as the following:

Regards,	Yours truly,
Sincerely,	Sincerely yours,

Capitalize only the first word and place a comma at the end if you are using standard punctuation. If you are using open punctuation, omit the comma.

9. *Company Name (Optional).* Some writers, and companies, prefer including a company name after the complimentary closing; others do not. If using this, leave one blank line after the complimentary closing and type the company name in capital letters.

10. *Writer's Identification.* The writer's identification consists of the writer's typed name and job title.

11. *Reference Initials.* **Reference initials** are the *keyboarder's* initials. Key the reference initials in lowercase letters on the second line below the writer's identification. If the writer's initials are also used, they should appear before the keyboarder's initials, e.g. BM:CD; bm/cd; or BM/cd. If the writer typed the letter, no reference initials are used.

12. *File Name Notation (Optional).* A growing trend with business letters is to include the file name of a document to aid retrieval of the document from disk.

proposal.131   csmith.let

Type the file name notation on the same line as or on the line below the reference initials.

13. *Enclosure Notation.* When an item or items are enclosed with the letter, the word *Enclosure* (or *Enclosures*) is keyed on the line below the reference initials or the file name notation, whichever is last. If there are a number of different documents enclosed, state exactly how many; for example, *Enclosures (6).*

14. *Transmittal Notation (Optional).* A transmittal notation is used to indicate that a letter and enclosure(s) are to be sent by some means other than first-class mail. Type the transmittal notation on the line below the enclosure notation, reference initials, or file name notation, whichever is last.

By Certified Mail   By Courier   By Fax

15. *Copy Notation (Optional).* When a copy of a letter is to be sent to a person or persons other than the addressee, the writer includes a **copy notation**; for example, *c: David Fischer* on the line below the reference initials, the enclosure notation, or transmittal notation, whichever is last. The abbreviation *c:* or *c* means "copy to."

c: Jerry Habaneroc Mischa Schneider

Leroy Vaughn

16. *Postscript (Optional).* The postscript is positioned at the *end* of a letter—deliberately or as an afterthought. Because it is part of the body of the letter, it is keyed in the same way as the paragraphs in the body of the letter. Key the postscript on the second line below the last notation in the letter. Postscripts may be indicated by keying *PS:* or *PS.* before the message:

PS: Be sure to bring a copy of your report with you.

Standard punctuation	Open punctuation
Colon after salutation	No punctuation after salutation
Comma after complimentary closing	No punctuation after complimentary closing

Business Letter Formats

There are various acceptable formats for letters. Note that the *sequence* of the letter parts, including the optional parts, does not vary from one letter format to another. The differences in formats are primarily concerned with whether or not a particular part is aligned left, indented, or centred.

Block Format (Also Called Full Block Format)

In the **block letter format**, all letter parts begin at the left margin except tables and other offset material. Because there are no indentions, the block style is easy to set up and, therefore, very popular. See Figure 9.1 for an example of a letter in block format.

Modified Block Format

The **modified block format** differs somewhat from the basic block style—namely, the date line, the complimentary closing, and the writer's identification line start at the centre of the page. See Figure 9.2 for an example.

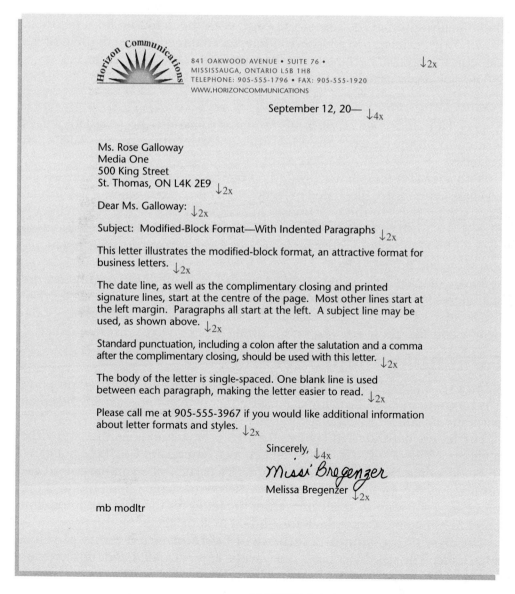

**◄ Figure 9.2
Modified Block Letter
Format**
The modified-block format begins the date and closing at the centre of the page.

Thinking Critically.
What are the advantages and disadvantages of this format?

Simplified Format

In an effort to simplify letter writing, the Administrative Management Society (AMS) developed what it calls the *simplified letter style*. See Figure 9.3 for an example. The **simplified format**.

1. Begins each part at the left margin (except unnumbered lists, which are indented five spaces).
2. Omits the salutation and the complimentary closing. As a substitute for the salutation, the first paragraph always includes the addressee's name.
3. Has an all-capital subject line.
4. Has an all-capital writer's identification line, which includes both the writer's name and the writer's title.

Personal-Business Letter Format

A **personal-business letter** is one written by a private individual for business purposes. For example, you may wish to write to a software company requesting information about your home computer, or you may be sending a letter of application for a job advertised in your local newspaper. Personal-business letters are not typed on letterhead stationery unless you have printed your own personal letterhead. In place of a letterhead, a *return address* was traditionally keyed at the top of the page, with the date two lines below it. Now, however, the return address is often placed directly beneath the writer's name, at the bottom of the letter, and positioned at the left margin.

The personal-business letter format is illustrated in Figure 9.4.

Social-Business Letter Format

A special format, the *social-business* format, is sometimes preferred for letters written to business associates when the subject matter is more social than business.

For a social-business letter printed on company letterhead, use the social-business letter format illustrated in Figure 9.5. This social-business letter format has its letter parts in the usual position *except the inside address*, which is placed last, positioned at the bottom of the page. In addition, the salutation ends with a comma rather than with a colon. Reference initials, copy notations, and so on, are not included.

Some companies provide special letterhead (called *monarch* and *baronial* stationery) for social-business and other letters. This stationery is smaller than the regular letter-size page and usually printed on high-quality paper. Some people consider these sizes especially fitting for executive correspondence.

Formatting Guidelines

Whichever letter style is used, the letter must be typed and formatted properly. The top, bottom, and side margins must be adequate, and the spacing between parts should adhere to certain standards.

The letters illustrated in Figures 9.1 to 9.5 have notations that show the number of lines of space generally left between letter parts. Use these notations to guide you in the vertical spacing of letter parts. Once you have used the proper spacing for all letter parts, use the centre page command in word processing software to vertically centre the letter on the page. An important point to remember is that the letter should look balanced on the page.

The first impression of a letter will be determined by its physical appearance. The stationery used, the way the letter is folded, and the envelope used all influence that impression.

FINANCE WEEKLY PUBLICATIONS, INC.

One South Street   A Global Industries Company
Saskatoon, SK S4N 1N5   www.financeweekly.com (306) 555-2000

November 28, 20--   ↓5

Mr. Jerome P. Kirsch
840 Woodland Avenue
Thompson, Manitoba R8N 0K1
                    ↓2
SUBSCRIPTION DELAY
                    ↓2
Thank you, Mr. Kirsch, for calling to tell us that you have not been receiving
your issues of FINANCE WEEKLY since you moved to your new home. We have
corrected our oversight so that normal service can now resume.
                                                            ↓2
As you suspected, your change-of-address notice had not been processed.
Your new address has now been included in our weekly subscriber mailing list. You
should receive the first December issue about the same time you receive
this letter.
                                                            ↓2
I have enclosed the two issues of FINANCE WEEKLY that you missed. If you should
have any future concerns, please call me toll-free at 1-800-925-1212.

                                                            ↓5

Marcia Alcott

MARCIA ALCOTT
CIRCULATION MANAGER
                    ↓2
jpc
Enclosures
                    ↓2
PS. To apologize for being late with two issues of FINANCE WEEKLY, I will send you
the new FINANCE WEEKLY ALMANAC as soon as it is available. I hope
that you will enjoy using this popular reference book, which sells for $9.95 at
newsstands Canada-wide.

◄ **Figure 9.3
Simplified Letter
Format**
Figure 9.3 shows the
simplified letter format.

Thinking Critically. *How
does this format differ
from the block letter
format?*

Figure 9.4 ▶
Personal-Business Letter
Figure 9.4 shows the personal-business letter format.

Thinking Critically.
What format is best for a personal-business letter? Why?

August 3, 20— ↓4x

DCS Electronics Company
Buena Vista Way
Suite 38
Vancouver, BC V3W 2E9 ↓2x

Dear Sales Manager: ↓2x

On July 15 I purchased your new book, *Business Letter Formats for the Twenty-First Century.* I've enclosed a copy of your Invoice 254 for $21.99, which I paid in full. ↓2x

When I received the book this morning, I discovered that the cover was badly damaged and the corners bent. ↓2x

Please send me a new book to replace the damaged one. If you would like me to return the damaged book, please call me at 250-555-9748. ↓2x

Sincerely, ↓4x

Tyler Swider
Tyler Swider
378 Westwood Avenue
Kamloops, BC V8B 1J9 ↓2x

Enclosure
By Certified Mail

Stationery

The paper used for letterhead contributes to the tone of the letter. Paper is available in many different weights and finishes. Better-quality paper also contains a **watermark**, which is the "signature" of the paper manufacturer. You can see the watermark by holding the stationery up to the light. If you can read the watermark from left to right, you are looking at the front side of the paper.

Most organizations have a letterhead designed to create the image and impression they wish to convey. All letterheads should include the name of the company, the mailing address, telephone and fax numbers, and possibly an e-mail address. Most letterheads also include a company logo.

The first page of a letter is prepared on letterhead. Continuation pages are prepared on plain paper or paper printed with information such as a company name or logo. This paper is of the same color, weight, and finish as the letterhead. The continuation page should have a heading that includes the following information: name of recipient, page number, and the same date that appears on the first page of the letter, as shown in the following examples:

Molly Sullivan
Page 2
June 1, 20—

Molly Sullivan   2   June 1, 20—

◀ **Figure 9.5**
Social-Business Letter
Figure 9.5 shows the
social-business letter
format.

Thinking Critically.
*Why does the salutation
in this letter differ from the
salutation in Figure 9.4?*

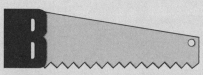

BARTLETT CONSTRUCTION, INC.
The Jerry Building 1200 Western Highway
Hamilton, Canada L8L 4R3
Tel: 800-269-7730 / 905-720-3000
Fax: 905-720-3220
www.bartlettcon.com

March 13, 20-- ↓**5**

Dear Ms. Jung,

↓**2**

Please allow me to express my congratulations on your promotion to Senior Vice
President. All of us at Bartlett Construction offer you our best wishes in your new
position.

↓**2**

In the two years since you joined Hillside Building Supplies, you have been
instrumental in making your firm the number one source for materials for all
major construction projects in this area. As a result, contractors have come to
expect fair prices, high-quality materials, and reliable, on-time deliveries from
Hillside. With your help, we can now estimate project costs accurately and
develop schedules precisely. As you can imagine, we genuinely appreciate
the pleasure of working with you.

↓**2**

Ms. Jung, we hope that your promotion will not reduce the opportunities we will
have to work together. In any case, we wish you success in your new position.

↓**2**

Sincerely,

↓**4**

Pierre T. Laurier
Manager
Purchasing Department

↓**5**

Ms. Courtney Jung
Senior Vice President
Hillside Building Supplies
50 Excelsior Avenue
Hamilton, Ontario L1W 2E9

Review of Key Terms

1. What is the difference between *block format* and *modified block format*?
2. What is a *salutation*? Give two examples. Is a salutation used in other business correspondence?

Practical Application

1. Write this list of letter parts in the order in which they would appear in a letter:

   writer's identification
   enclosure notation
   date line
   attention line
   file name notation
   complimentary closing
   reference initials
   copy notation
   inside address
   salutation
   body

2. Explain when you would use the following letter formats and state any special features of these formats:
   a. personal-business letter format
   b. social-business letter format

3. Collect examples of business letters from correspondence received at your residence. Each member of the group should bring at least one business letter to class. Examine these letters and note the differences in format. Prepare a short presentation by:

   a. Listing the features that create both favourable and unfavourable reactions.
   b. Choosing one letter, copying it onto an overhead transparency, and critiquing the format.

Editing Practice

Updating Vocabulary. Rewrite these excerpts from business letters, eliminating or replacing all outdated words and expressions.

1. I would like to make an appointment at your earliest convenience.
2. Hoping to hear from you soon, I remain, Sincerely yours,
3. Kindly advise us of your decision in the very near future.
4. At the present writing, we are revising the production schedule.
5. Due to the fact that manufacturing costs are rising, we must increase prices accordingly.

6. Thank you in advance for your assistance in this matter.
7. We have received your order for a scanner and are shipping it at the present time.
8. Enclosed please find our remittance.
9. In the event that you have a better suggestion, please advise me of it as soon as possible.
10. Research was not part of the director's purview.

Spelling Alert! Correct the spelling errors in the following paragraph:

Because we specialize in the needs of the legal profesion, our building is uniquely equipped to serve lawyers. Each suite already has a large room furnished with shelfs and tables—ideal for a legal liberry. In addition, there are rooms suitible for large and small meetings and, of course, sevral private offices.

Discussion Points

1. How does the appearance and content of a business letter affect the reader?
2. What are some of the standard parts used in a business letter that improve its appearance?

Informing and Requesting

▶ **Key Terms**

▶ informative
   messages
▶ procedures book
▶ claim letter

I only ask for information.

—Charles Dickens, *David Copperfield*

As a business communicator you will often be called upon to write messages to give information to others. **Informative messages** include giving instructions; giving directions; and making announcements about things such as events, people, meetings, and procedures.

Giving Instructions

As a business writer, you will have opportunities to provide written instructions on how to complete a task or how to carry out a procedure. Follow these guidelines when writing step-by-step instructions:

1. Number the steps to make them easier to follow, and use phrases rather than complete sentences.
2. Include only necessary information. Avoid giving all the "what-ifs" so that your instructions won't seem too complex.
3. List the steps in the order they are to be completed.
4. Write the instructions with the user in mind—define unfamiliar terms, and explain complicated items.
5. Avoid unnecessary cross-references to information in another document. Instead, provide all the necessary information in the set of instructions.
6. Use white space, headings, and indentions to make the instructions visually clear. Start each new instruction on a separate line.
7. Test your instructions by having someone try them as written to see if they are clear and complete. The best test is to have someone who does not know the procedure try your instructions.

The ability to write clear step-by-step instructions is a vital skill for people who write manuals. To start looking at some resources in this area, visit Web sites that specialize in writing manuals.

Giving Directions

When giving directions for getting from one location to another—whether it is to a different location in the building or to a different city—remember that some people learn visually and others learn verbally. Keep these guidelines in mind:

- For visual learners, draw a map from the point of departure to the point of destination or, if possible, photocopy a map and use a light-coloured highlighter to mark the route.
- For verbal learners, write the directions so that each part of the directions appears on a separate line.
- Differentiate between stop signs and stoplights, indicate turns as right or left, and give specific compass directions as in "Drive north for 5 kilometres."

Making Announcements

A great deal of information is communicated through various forms of announcements. Announcements are made through news releases, flyers, and formal cards as well as by memos and letters. Every announcement should be checked against the completeness test. Does the announcement include answers to the questions "Who?" "What?" "Where?" "When?" "Why?" and "How?" or "How much?" Anticipate the questions your receiver may have, and answer them in the announcement.

Events

Events such as open houses, anniversary celebrations, special programs, commemorative events, holiday celebrations, and ribbon-cutting ceremonies for new buildings, are frequently communicated through announcements.

People

Occasions for announcements about people include when a new employee is hired, when someone is promoted, when a person retires, when someone is elected or appointed to a position, and when a person receives an award or another recognition. An announcement about someone's accomplishments is an excellent way to recognize the person and to let others know about the person's achievements.

Meetings

When meetings are needed, a meeting notice is the most efficient way to get the information to everyone, whether it is sent as a memo, an e-mail, or a flyer. When meetings are scheduled weeks in advance, a reminder notice close to the date of the actual meeting will ensure better attendance.

Procedures

When a new procedure is implemented (for example, a new procedure for ordering supplies), a written, step-by-step guide makes it easier for everyone to follow the new procedure. Many organizations have a **procedures book** that contains copies of all procedures that have been developed. It is important to date each procedure, including revision dates, so employees can easily identify the most recent version. These procedures may also be posted on an organization's Web site for easy access by users who have been given passwords.

Writing Requests

Some of the most routine business tasks you will perform involve making requests of some kind—for example, asking for appointments, reserving conference rooms, obtaining price lists and catalogues, asking for copies of reports and studies, seeking technical information about goods and services, and asking favours.

Although most requests are routine, they are not to be treated routinely. What is more, extraordinary requests require extraordinary planning and writing skills! Whether you are simply asking an office supply company for a copy of its catalogue or asking a busy, important executive to go out of his or her way to speak at your conference, your requests should be:

- Complete
- Precise
- Reasonable
- Courteous

Be Complete

When writing a request, ask yourself, "What can I provide the reader to make sure that she or he has *all* the information needed to grant the request?" Also, "Will any more information be helpful for some reason?" Consider the following two situations:

You are requesting information from Data-X Company about CD-RW systems for a report that you are preparing. Tell the reader at Data-X the purpose of your request. He or she might have additional materials to share with you or might grant the request solely to get publicity for his or her company.

You send a letter to a company asking them to send you the office supplies that you discussed yesterday during your telephone conversation. You are assuming the reader will remember facts from your last letter or your last conversation. Don't assume! Repeat the model or type, the catalogue number, the price, the preferred shipping method, and any other facts that will help your reader.

Put yourself in the reader's place so that you can better understand how the reader might feel and what information he or she might need to know. Note how the request in Figure 9.6 successfully answers the questions "Who?" "What?" "Where?" "When?" "Why?" and "How?" or "How Much?"

In your effort to be complete, however, do not give the reader an excessively detailed description or needless information. For example, decide whether it will help the reader to know that you are planning to write a detailed report. If it will help, include this fact in your request; if this information is not relevant to the reader, omit it. Likewise, decide whether you must include the model or type, the catalogue number, and so on. If all this information is already included in the enclosed purchase order, then there may be no need to repeat it in the letter.

Apply the five Ws and one H to test the completeness of requests—"Who?" "What?" "Where?" "When?" "Why?" and "How?" or "How Much?"

Be Precise

To ensure that your written requests are precise, you should present material in a format that makes it easy to comprehend. Using a table is a precise way to present facts and figures. Proofreading carefully is another way to make your written requests precise. This helps you eliminate errors that may be embarrassing, costly, and time-consuming.

SHESKEY INSURANCE AGENCY
617 Crossroad Square Suite 21 Saskatoon, SK S4N 1N5
Telephone: 306-555-9300 FAX: 306-555-9337
www.sheskeyinsurance

September 23, 20—

Ms. Jerry Gasche
Training Director
MetLife Financial Services
38 Alexandria Drive
Calgary, AB T2W 1E6

Dear Ms. Gasche:

One of your insurance representatives, Ivan Chansuvan, told me that
MetLife has produced a research report about the frequency and types
of claims filed by policyholders. I would like to obtain this report.

Our company is interested in receiving information for claims relating
to both homes and automobiles. We would like to incorporate this
information into update sessions for our agents and to disseminate it
to agents we may hire in the future.

Ivan did not know the answers to these questions:
• Is the report free, or would there be a charge?
• What would the charge be?
• Would I need to buy multiple copies, or could I duplicate portions for
our employees?

We want to make applicable portions of the research report immediately
available to our personnel. Please give me a call at 501-555-6245 so I
can clarify the order, costs, and duplication issues. We are certainly
willing to pay duplication costs and costs for mailing the materials by
Federal Express two-day delivery service.

Sincerely yours,

Lance Sheskey

Lance Sheskey
President

tr

Thinking Critically.
*What kinds of questions
should a request letter
answer?*

Be Reasonable

Even people who are usually reasonable will sometimes make unreasonable
requests when they are faced with job pressures or do not fully understand that
their requests are exceptionally difficult, time-consuming, or complicated.

Consider your request *from the reader's perspective.* Are you asking for too
much of someone's time? Are you asking for a character reference from
someone who hardly knows you? Can you reasonably expect this person to
expend such effort on your request? Consider these factors before making
a request.

Be Courteous

Courtesy is a must in business communications. Whether you are requesting
something that is legally or morally owed to you, something that you ha̶
paid or will pay for, something that is yours and should be ret̶
something that the reader should be delighted to send to y̶
always be courteous in writing your request.

Although few people intentionally write discourteous requests, in their rush to complete a job people *do* sometimes write impolite requests. For example, read this request for a free videotape describing vacation time-shares.

I saw your ad in *Leisure Days* magazine about a free videotape describing vacation time-shares at Morning Glory Resorts. Send one to me at the address in the letterhead.

The recipient *did* advertise free videotapes, obviously in the hope of selling vacation time-shares. Does this mean, however, that the reader of the request letter does not deserve common courtesy? Of course not! The writer would have shown more thoughtfulness, more respect for the reader, by writing the request along these lines:

Please send me the free videotape advertised in *Leisure Days* magazine that describes vacation time-shares at Morning Glory Resorts. My husband and I enjoy golf and tennis, and your resort sounds like an ideal place to spend our two-week summer vacation each year.

We are also interested in buying a two-week time-share at a ski resort during the month of January. We would also appreciate receiving information about time-shares at winter resorts.

Please mail the video and the other information to us at the address in the letter-head. We look forward to hearing from you.

The writer might have reaped additional benefits from this revised, more courteous request. The recipient will gladly send not only the free videotape advertised in the magazine but also any information about vacation time-shares at winter resorts, because the writer took the time to state specific needs and did so *courteously.*

Writing Claim Letters

A **claim letter** is a type of request letter written when there is a problem with a product or service. The person who writes a claim letter believes, of course, that he or she has been wronged. Indeed, the claim is justified if, for example, the writer:

1. Ordered Model R-75 but received Model R-57.
2. Requested 150 booklets but received only 100.
3. Requested size 10 but received size 14.
4. Enclosed full payment but was billed anyway.
5. ~~Sp~~ecified brand Q but received brand T.

~~Sometim~~es, however, the writer *intended* to order brand Q but forgot to ~~specify a~~ particular brand. Or the writer neglected to proofread the order ~~and the purc~~hase order and did not correct the "100" booklets to "150." Or ~~the writer wrote~~ the cheque for the full amount but did not enclose it. The ~~first step in making~~ a claim, therefore, is to get the facts—*before* you write

~~A good way to start is to~~ find out what happened and why.

~~Was~~ there a packing slip that clearly says the ~~items would be sent sep~~arately? Check your original order to ~~confirm exactly what~~ *was* ordered.

- If merchandise was damaged, should you write your claim to the supplier or should you write it to the shipping company? You will be embarrassed if you write a strong letter to the supplier and later discover that the shipping company was at fault.
- If the wrong merchandise was delivered, check the original order first. Before you write your claim letter, try to find out if anyone phoned in a change in the order.
- When you write a claim letter, you should rely on facts as the basis of your claim. Until you have sufficient facts, do not write the letter. When you do have all the facts, use them to describe the claim completely and accurately. Enclosing copies of pertinent documents such as invoices, bills, receipts, and warranties will support your claim and assist the reader in understanding your request.

Describe the Claim Completely and Accurately

It is especially important to be complete and accurate when you are writing a claim letter because, in effect, you are making an accusation. To make a convincing argument and to be fair to the reader, you should present all the facts, and you should do so accurately.

Read the following letter. Note how the writer cites all the necessary details such as size, quantities, times, and descriptions.

Dear Mr. Congdon:

We have received your invoice for 25 200-kilogram bags of polypropylene resins of injection-moulding concrete. When we placed this order 17 days ago, we stressed the need for speedy delivery of the resins and were promised delivery within 10 days. Your invoice for 25 bags arrived on the tenth day, but we received none of the resins until the fifteenth day, when we received only 5 bags.

Would you please check your records to make sure that all the resins have been shipped. If so, please check with the shipping company at once. Our customer desperately needs the items to be made from these resins and is understandably upset that we have not delivered them as promised. We are counting on you to help us make up for lost time.

Please telephone me at 416-289-7200 to let us know the status of this vital shipment. We will hold your invoice until we receive all 25 bags of resins. Then of course we will be happy to send payment.

Sincerely,

The writer not only tells the reader *everything* that happened concerning the materials that were ordered but does so in chronological order. By giving complete information and delivering it accurately, the writer makes an honest, believable claim.

Let's look at another example of a claim letter that is both complete and accurate.

Dear Ms. Draper:

I was distressed to receive your notice of March 1 indicating that you have cancelled my home owner's insurance policy No. AZ1843687 due to failure to pay the premium of $350 due on January 15.

On January 4, I mailed cheque 186 for $350. On January 17, the cheque, endorsed by your company and stamped "Paid," was returned to me. I reported this information to you on the back of a notice of cancellation mailed to me January 30. Since I received no further word from you, I assumed that the matter had been resolved.

I am enclosing a photocopy of the front and back of my cancelled cheque. Would you please send me a notice of the reinstatement of my insurance.

Very truly yours,

The letters gives *all* the details—completely and accurately—so that the insurance company can quickly correct its error. Note, however, that even though the above letter is filled with facts, it does not accuse, threaten, or demand.

Avoid Accusations, Threats, and Demands

The goal of the claim letter is to get the missing merchandise, to correct the billing error, to return the damaged goods—in other words, to get results, not to accuse, or lay blame, to threaten, or to demand. For example, assume that the above letter to the insurance company was not answered in a reasonable time. What would you do? Write a threatening letter? Demand that the company send you a formal apology? These are reactions, not solutions. Writing a letter saying "You know very well that I paid my premium," or "You failed to reply," or "I will sue you," would be a waste of time.

Instead, write a reasonable letter, this time addressed to someone with more authority. For example, a letter to the president of the agency that handles your insurance, would probably get results.

Dear Mr. Kovacs:

I am enclosing a photocopy of a letter I wrote to your main office on March 5. My letter has not yet been acknowledged, and I am concerned about whether my homeowner's insurance is in force.

I would appreciate your investigating this matter and providing written notification regarding the status of my insurance policy.

Yours truly,

Without threatening, demanding, or accusing, the letter will get results. After all, if you were the president of the agency, would you overlook this letter? The president would understand that the company is in danger of losing a client.

Suggest Reasonable Solutions

The opposite of accusing, demanding, or threatening is suggesting reasonable solutions. Remember: Except in rare circumstances, you are dealing with honest business people who have made a mistake *and realize it*. By suggesting reasonable solutions, you strengthen your chance of getting a just settlement quickly. For example, if you placed an order and received only part of it, one solution might be to indicate that you will accept the missing portion if it arrives by a specific date, as shown by the following statement:

We will gladly accept the 25 camping tents if they reach us by May 15, the first day of our Great Outdoors Savings Spectacular.

Or suppose that you were charged $100 too much on an order. In this case, you might say:

We were billed $650 for the merchandise on our purchase order 3290, dated July 7. The figure should have been $550. Therefore, please credit our account for $100 and send us a credit memorandum for this amount.

It is usually best to suggest the kind of solution that you consider acceptable. If you received defective merchandise, for example, you might request replacement of the merchandise, cancellation of the order, a credit of the amount to your account, or substitution of a similar item. Suggesting a solution tells the company what kind of action you want taken. When your suggestion is reasonable, there is a good chance that the company will follow it.

Review of Key Terms

1. What types of *informative messages* are used in business?
2. What guidelines should a writer follow when writing a *claim letter*?

Practical Application

1. Write a letter to Canadian Office Furniture, 1199 Mountain Boulevard, Edmonton, Alberta T2G 1A4, to order a desk. Before writing the letter, jot down answers to each of the following questions:

   Why are you writing?
   What kind of desk are you ordering?
   How do you want to pay for and receive the desk?
   When do you want the desk?
   Who should the desk be shipped to?
   Where do you want the desk delivered?

2. Find in magazines or newspapers two advertisements that invite you to write for additional information about goods and services. Write a letter to each company to ask for a catalogue, sample, brochure, or other descriptive information.

3. Write a letter to the president of your college, asking her/him to visit your class as a guest speaker.

4. The City-Wide Newspaper Delivery Service, 322 Oxford Street, Cobourg, Ontario P1A 2E1, has billed you for a month's delivery of both daily (Monday to Saturday) and Sunday newspapers. You ordered only the daily newspaper, however, and that is all you received. The delivery service has charged you $32 for 65 issues of the daily newspaper and $22.75 for 13 issues of the Sunday newspaper. For an adjustment to your bill, write to Benjamin Davis, the customer service representative for the City-Wide Newspaper Delivery Service.

5. Write a letter for Louis Roland, the manager of Le Crépuscule, a French restaurant located at 665 Darien Street, Montreal, Quebec H2T 2E6. Today Mr. Roland has received a new, heavy-duty commercial food processor, but his chef shows him that it does not slice foods as precisely as advertised. Write to the manufacturer, Whirling Wonder Kitchen Co., One Niagara Parkway, St. Catharines, Ontario L3E 1K4, requesting replacement of the food processor.

6. You ordered a CD player from Orion Inc. on December 5 as a gift. Orion promised shipment by December 20. However, the CD player arrived December 27 without the necessary hardware to connect it to an amplifier. The catalogue stated that all necessary hardware would be included.

TEAMWORK

Each member of the group should draft the body of a claim letter explaining what happened and suggesting a solution. Then compare your drafts and compile one letter that combines the best features of the individual efforts.

Editing Practice

Proofreading. Edit and rewrite the following paragraph, correcting all errors.

Please send me the compleat two-volume set of *Marketing and Distribution.* I understand that for the price of $53.99 I will also recieve a one-year subscription to *Canadian Business Today,* along with a callendar for business executives. Please refrane however from placing my name on any mailing lists.

Updating Correspondence. Rewrite these excerpts from letters, replacing any dated expressions.

1. The information in your application has been duly noted.
2. We wish to extend our thanks to you for taking the time to complete the questionnaire.
3. I have before me your letter of October 10.
4. Up to the present writing, we have not received your payment for last month.
5. We will be sending the CDs to you under separate cover.
6. I am enclosing an invoice in the amount of $210.98.
7. In the event you will be unable to accept the offer, please advise.
8. I am sending herewith the prospectus for Oakgrove Condominiums, Ltd.

Discussion Points

1. Discuss ways in which a writer can present clear written instructions or directions.
2. Why is it essential that business requests be precise, reasonable, and courteous?

Responding to Requests

▶ **Key Terms**

▶ tickler file

▶ indirect selling methods

▶ adjustment

You comply with a request more willingly than with an order.

—Anonymous

If writing requests is a common business task, then answering requests is equally common. In this section you will learn how to effectively answer requests and how to use techniques for both granting and denying requests. You will also learn how to respond to claim letters by sending an adjustment letter granting or denying a claim.

Answering Requests

Common courtesy dictates that a *prompt reply* be sent to request letters. Whether the response is an easy-to-write, positive reply or a more difficult rejection, the reader should not be kept in suspense. Also, the writer should try to *help* the reader as much as possible, even if the request must be refused. In either case, the letter should be written in *positive* language.

Writing a response—whether the reply is positive or negative—presents an opportunity to promote goodwill and to make a sale. Thus the response should be *sales-minded*. In addition, the response (like the request) should be *specific* and *complete*.

As you can see, then, answering requests requires the writer to be:

- Prompt
- Helpful
- Sales-minded
- Specific
- Complete
- Positive

Let's take a closer look at each of these six rules for answering requests.

Be Prompt

Many companies have policies requiring their employees to respond to letters within 48 hours—some, within 24 hours. Why? Because the companies realize that being prompt in replying is simply good business.

Even when an inquiry cannot be answered in detail, common business courtesy demands that a reply—at least an acknowledgement of the request—be sent *promptly*.

Dear Mr. Miller:

Your recent request for a price quotation for two cases of glossy photo paper (HP C6039A) is being handled by Beverly Jenrette. The manufacturer now has this paper on back order. Ms. Jenrette is checking to determine how soon your paper will be available and what the price change, if any, will be.

She expects to have this information for you by October 15. In any case, she will write to you before then to give you an update on your request.

Sincerely,

This prompt response (1) acknowledges the request, (2) tells the potential customer specifically who is taking care of his request, and (3) tells when the customer can expect an answer. The writer in this situation would send a copy to Ms. Jenrette and place another copy in a **tickler file**—a reminder file—for October 15.

Because promptness is both a courtesy and a sign of good business, your reader will always be impressed by your promptness. Therefore, take advantage of situations in which your promptness will be a plus. Note how one writer capitalized on a quick response:

When I received your request by fax this morning, I checked immediately to make sure that we could process the colour slides you requested for your March 19 meeting. I am pleased to tell you that we can process and deliver the slides by...

Another short cut that helps a writer achieve promptness when faced with a large volume of responses is to write a brief message on a printed reply card or letter. The card or letter may have blanks that the writer can quickly fill in, or it may simply give a printed message with no blanks. Despite their lack of personalization, printed responses allow a company to respond to hundreds or thousands of requests *promptly*. Printed "Dear Subscriber:" responses, such as the one in Figure 9.7, facilitate prompt replies.

Dear Subscriber:

MANY THANKS . . .

for renewing your subscription to *Canadian News and World Report*. Your cheque for $23—half our usual subscription price—indicates that this publication meets your high standards and expectations because you chose to invest your money in this product.

We believe *Canadian News and World Report* presents a variety of issues and perspectives in a different way from any other media. Our magazine attempts to bring the facts to you with many points of view and in an objective, rational way. Our short, easily readable stories allow you to have current information.

By renewing *Canadian News and World Report*, you have indicated that we are doing our job in providing the information you need about national and international politics. However, we know it is always possible to improve a product. Therefore, please take a few moments to jot us a note and tell us how we can improve any aspect of your magazine. Simply return your comments in the enclosed, postage-paid envelope.

Sincerely,

◀ **Figure 9.7
Preprinted Response**

Thinking Critically.
What does this printed form letter aim to achieve?

Be Helpful

A customer or a potential customer who asks for information expects to receive assistance, whether the customer is asking in person, on the telephone, or in writing.

When responding to a request, try to understand why the person is asking for help, and remember why your company wants you to help. Whether or not you can grant the request, consider whether there is something additional you can do to help the person. Do you know of a store where the person can find the product he or she needs? Do you know of a company that makes the product he or she is looking for? Do you know of a book or a Web site that covers the very topic the person wants to research? Do you know of a service organization that can help the person?

Note how the writer of the following letter did more than fill the request—the writer anticipated Ms. Dhalival's interest in a closely related product. Good sales expertise? Good business? *Both!*

Dear Ms. Dhalival:

It's good to know that you are considering ImageMaker, our telephone facsimile-transmitting system. One of our most popular items, the ImageMaker will enable you to send any graphic design 60 cm by 60 cm or smaller to any office in the world equipped with an ImageMaker and a telephone. The ImageMaker should be particularly valuable to you and your architects in other cities. Now you won't have to wait days to react to one another's latest sketches.

A wonderful complement to ImageMaker is our reducing, high-resolution photocopier, the ImageReducer. With no discernible loss in precision, the ImageReducer will reduce graphic designs as large as 120 cm by 120 cm to 60 cm by 60 cm—small enough to transmit by the ImageMaker. The combination of ImageMaker and ImageReducer will save not only the transit time of mailing or of shipping by airfreight but also the cost.

We very much appreciate your interest in our products and would be happy to demonstrate them for you soon.

Sincerely,

Although it is rather easy to be helpful when you are granting a request, you can also be helpful in many situations when you cannot grant the request, as the writer of the following letter proves.

Dear Mrs. Gonzales:

Thank you for your recent order for the 15-mm, f/2.8 Canon underwater antifogging lens. Although we generally carry this superb lens, we are currently out of stock, and Canon will not be shipping more until September or October.

Because you mentioned that you wanted the lens for your upcoming scuba-diving trip, I called another supplier to find this lens. Good news: The Shutter Shop, a photography specialty store, has the lens that you want. You may call the Shutter Shop toll-free at 800-555-1800.

Good luck! And please be sure to try us again next time.

Sincerely,

This letter has certainly won a friend for the writer's company—just by being helpful.

Be Sales-Minded

Whenever you respond to a request letter, you should look for possible ways to make a sale. Whether you work in the sales department or not, your company depends on sales of goods or services to make a profit and to pay your salary.

The hard-sell approach is rarely effective; you will not make much progress by bluntly saying "Buy this product!" Yet you can help sell your company's products or services by responding promptly to requests and by being helpful. Both responses will make your readers appreciate the quality customer service that your company provides and will convince them to deal with your firm.

In addition to these indirect sales techniques, there are several direct ways to help sell your company's goods and services when you are responding to requests. For example, if you are sending a potential customer a catalogue, include both an order blank and an addressed envelope to make it easy to place an order. If a customer complains about having had to wait a long time to receive a previous order, take a few minutes to write an apology and an explanation. Better yet, tell the customer to write directly to you next time so that you may personally help track the order. Such extras are selling techniques.

Can you uncover the **indirect selling methods** used by the writer of this letter?

Dear Mr. Neumann:

Thank you for asking about the service contract for Gorden's Model-X camcorder. We are pleased to share some information with you.

The enclosed booklet includes a list of all the specific items that are covered by our service contract. In fact, Mr. Neumann, it also lists, in equally large print, the few items that are not covered in the contract, so that there will be no surprises if something should happen to the product; you will know exactly what is covered. By doing so, we avoid the unfortunate experience that you described in your letter.

Because service is such an important factor in your buying decision, I recommend that you ask your local Gorden dealers how they rate the service of two or three of the brand names that they sell. (A list of dealers in your area is enclosed.) Further, I invite you to visit Peter Cleary of Cleary & Sons in Woodmere, which I believe is near you. Mr. Cleary has operated an authorized Gorden service centre for more than twenty years. Not only will visiting Peter be informative, but also this will give you a chance to meet the person who would service any Gorden product that you own.

Please review the enclosed booklet; then let me know of any way that we can help. You may call me toll-free at 800-555-9250 whenever you have any questions for us. We would be delighted to be of service.

Sincerely,

As you respond to requests, look for ways in which you can help sell your company's goods or services.

Be Specific

The need to *be specific* is a general rule; it applies to any letter or memo, whether the message is a request, a response to someone's request, or any other type of communication.

When acknowledging receipt of money, cite the exact amount, form of payment, and purpose of the payment.

We appreciate receiving your cheque for $1250 in payment of invoice 17290.

When discussing dates, times, airline flight numbers, or other specific statistics, cite them clearly.

I am delighted to accept your invitation to discuss my career in graphic design with your students. It has been a long time since I visited the Design Institute, and I look forward to our discussion on April 28 at 3 p.m. As you suggested, I will bring samples of my newest designs to share with your students.

My Air Canada flight 741 arrives at Pearson International Airport at 2:30 p.m. on Monday, April 28...

When you receive something of value, acknowledge its receipt, including any specific information that is appropriate. Remember that your letter will become part of the reader's files—proof that you received the important mailing.

Your portfolio of industrial photographs arrived this morning. When Carrie Foster, our art director, returns from vacation next week, she will call you to discuss the prints she has selected for the September issue of *Modern Manufacturing*.

When acknowledging receipt of an order, include the date of the order and the purchase number. Although the reader already knows this information, it is repeated because the letter will be filed for future reference. In addition, mention how the materials will be shipped, when the reader can expect to receive the merchandise, and so on.

We are delighted that you are taking advantage of our annual stock-reduction sale. Your order No. 575, dated June 20, will be shipped by Federal Express this afternoon. As you requested, the merchandise will be delivered to your Queen Street store.

Be Complete

Although many writers try to be complete, important information is often omitted because of carelessness.

One way to make sure that your responses are complete is to underline the specific points in the request letter. Another way is to note in the margin each answer to a specific point in the request letter. The underlined points or the marginal notes serve as an outline in writing the reply. For example, when Judy Anderson received the letter of inquiry illustrated in Figure 9.8, she made marginal notes to make sure that her response, shown in Figure 9.9, would be *complete*.

One technique that fosters completeness is listing major points in your response, using either numbers or bullets. Note how the writer of the follow-up letter in Figure 9.9 lists the major points the customer mentioned in his letter, as illustrated in Figure 9.8.

Be Positive

The need to *be positive* is especially important when handling problem requests. Saying no to people who have applied for credit, who do not qualify for discounts, whose warranties have expired, who have asked for confidential information, who have requested contributions that must be turned down—these situations require extra tact and diplomacy from the writer. Never start your message with bad news; use the indirect approach. Remember: Whatever the cause of the problem, the writer's goal is to keep the reader's goodwill.

October 27, 20—

Ms. Judy Anderson
Sales Manager
Majestic Fireplaces
4929 Kingston Road
Etobicoke, ON M8Y 2Y9

Dear Ms. Anderson:

I am interested in installing a gas log in my fireplace. I have studied your brochure but have some additional questions before deciding whether to invest in this product.

1. How would the unit be mounted in the fireplace? *Middle of fireplace on floor*
2. What special electrical hookup would be required? *None*
3. How much installation time would be required by your technicians? *2 hours*
4. How would a gas log affect my gas consumption? *Minimally*
5. What would be the total cost of the unit, including installation? *$259*
6. What type of warranty exists for this product? *Full 10-year*

I am thinking about having the gas log installed before December 25. Please answer these questions in time for me to make my decision.

Very truly yours,

Daniel Lutje

Daniel Lutje
245 South Hill Street
Parry Sound, ON P2A 1B1

To begin, consider the contrast between the statements listed below. Notice how the "positive" statements say no without greatly hurting the reader's ego.

Negative	Positive
Your product does not meet our specifications.	Our engineers believe that the brand we selected is closest to our specifications.
You do not meet our standards for this particular job.	Although your qualifications are excellent, we feel that we must continue to search for someone who meets all the unique requirements of this job.
In view of your poor payment record, we are unable to grant you credit.	We shall be glad to evaluate your credit record after you have settled some of your financial obligations.
We must say no.	Unfortunately, we are unable to grant your request at this time.
Your prices are too high.	While the quality of your product is indeed excellent, we cannot afford a purchase at this price.

Figure 9.9 ▶
Response to a Request

Thinking Critically.
*How should a writer reply
effectively when answering
a reader's questions?*

Majestic Fireplaces

4929 KINGSTON ROAD
ETOBICOKE, ONTARIO M8Y 2Y9
TELEPHONE: 416-555-6419
FAX: 416-555-6500   WWW.MAJESTICFIREPLACES.COM

November 1, 20—

Daniel Lutje
245 South Hill Street
Parry Sound, ON P2A 1B1

Dear Mr. Lutje:

Thank you for inquiring about our fireplace gas logs. I'll be glad to answer the questions you asked in your October 27 letter.

1. The gas log would be mounted in the middle of the fireplace on the floor.
2. The catalytic igniter does not require electricity so no special electrical hookup would be required.
3. Assuming no complicating factors, our technicians can install the gas log in about two hours.
4. Your gas log has three settings of flame; the lowest setting would use as much gas as a gas stove burner.
5. The total cost of the gas log and the installation would be $259.
6. Our gas log units carry a full, 10-year warranty.

Enclosed is a brochure that describes the gas log in which you are interested. I am sure you will find that this unit is an outstanding product for the money.

Please call me at 1-800-555-4793 if you have further questions and to set up an installation date.

Sincerely,

Judy Anderson

Judy Anderson
Sales Manager

lam
Enclosure

Note how the negative comments stress *you* while the positive comments stress *we*. Always avoid saying "Because of your mistake…" or "You failed to…" Placing blame on the reader will accomplish nothing. Remember, preserving goodwill toward your company should be your goal in all business writing.

Although it is important to phrase your comments in a positive manner and to avoid placing blame, you should not make false statements in refusing a request. If possible, share with the reader some of the genuine reasons why the request is being rejected.

Layoffs this year have reduced our staff; as a result, our remaining employees' workloads have increased.

As much as we would like to help you with your research project, gathering the information you requested is beyond our present resources. As you can imagine,

Ms. Granger, we simply cannot take that much time away from our usual duties. However, we enclose a list of reference sources that we think will be useful.

Perhaps the most positive aspect of such refusals is to offer the possibility of future cooperation.

Perhaps next year we will be able to …

Of course, we will keep your application on file so that …

Once again, remember to put yourself in the reader's place. When you consider your reply from your reader's perspective, you will seek creative ways to be positive.

Fairly Evaluating Claims and Making Adjustments

Whether a business is a multinational corporation or a small family store, it will have customers who claim that they received fewer items than they ordered; damaged goods; the incorrect size, colour, or model; unsatisfactory merchandise; and so on. Each customer's claim must be answered, and each situation must be studied. The business must (1) determine whether the claim has any merit and (2) examine how the merchandise was damaged or why the wrong item was shipped to ensure that the same mistake does not happen again.

In many cases an **adjustment** will be made—the customer will receive a full or a partial credit, will be allowed to exchange the merchandise, or will be granted a refund.

Several qualities are required to evaluate a claim, determine a fair adjustment, and approve the adjustment: (1) business experience; (2) company authority; (3) familiarity with company policy, industry standards, and consumer laws; and (4) common sense. You are essentially playing the role of judge; but since you have a vested interest in the case, being impartial is difficult. Yet an equitable adjustment requires you to be reasonable, fair, honest, and impartial in making your decision.

Making the right decision, therefore, is a difficult task. The sources of evidence that you must weigh are the company; the claimant, that is, the person making the claim; the transaction; and, in some cases, the law. Let's look at each source to see how it influences or affects the final decision.

The Company

As an ethical business, your company will want to examine its responsibilities in light of a claim. Ask yourself the following questions to determine the extent of your company's responsibility in causing the situation.

- Do you know, without a doubt, that the company is not at fault?
- Could anyone in the company have made a misleading statement?
- Could the advertising be misinterpreted?
- Could your records be at fault?
- Is it possible that someone in the company made a mistake?

If such questioning reveals an element of blame on the part of the company, you, the adjuster, will probably decide to honour the claim, at least in part.

The Claimant

To help you evaluate the claimant's share in causing the claim, ask questions such as:

- Could the claimant be mistaken?
- Is the claim, if true, a reasonable one to make?
- Has the claimant provided all the information you need to check the claim and place responsibility for it?
- Does the claimant have a record of fair dealings with your company?

Even if you find that the claimant is wrong beyond any doubt, good business sense may tell you that perhaps the claim should be honoured anyway.

The Transaction

The answers to the following questions will help you arrive at an equitable decision about the transaction.

- Did your company carry out all its obligations—both explicit and implied—to the customer?
- Has your company made any claims with reference to this product, such as, "Double your money back if you are not absolutely satisfied"?
- Were any misleading statements made to the customer by your sales personnel?
- Is there evidence of faulty materials or workmanship in the product?
- Were the instructions for use of the product clear and complete?

If you find a defect, either in the product or in the handling of the transaction, you should decide in favour of the claimant. This correction is just one more application of the business rule of trying to please the customer.

Sometimes you will have to seek further information before you can answer the above questions. You may need to question some of your co-workers or to write to the claimant before you have all the facts. The following letter is an example of an inquiry addressed to a claimant.

Dear Mrs. Zima:

Thank you for your October 17 letter about your StairTrainer treadmill. We are sorry that you are having problems with the treadmill, a product that is usually very reliable.

We cannot locate a copy of your warranty agreement, which should be on file here. The period of the warranty is normally one year. If you could send us the transaction number from the top right corner of your receipt, we could confirm the purchase. If you do not have the receipt, then please give us the name of the dealer from whom you made the purchase and the approximate date of purchase.

As soon as we receive the information, we will be happy to make an adjustment.

Sincerely yours,

When you receive the necessary information, you will be able to make an equitable decision on the claim.

The Law

In some cases, laws will affect your decision regarding a claim. Laws intended to protect consumers, for cxample, allow a consumer to cancel certain contracts within a specified number of days "without penalty or obligation." Provincial laws or local by-laws may apply in special situations in your industry.

In any case, you should realize that there are potential legal problems in some situations. Although you now know that you should not threaten when making a claim, many writers will threaten you with legal action in their first claim letters just because they believe that making such threats will get results. Does your company have a policy that requires all employees to notify the legal department any time there is a possibility of a lawsuit? Whether it has such a policy or not, you *should* notify someone in authority, perhaps your supervisor *and* the legal department, whenever legal action is even remotely possible.

Writing Adjustment Letters

After probing all the sources of evidence and reviewing all the facts in a claim, you may determine that (1) the claim is indeed allowable, (2) the claim is partially allowable, or (3) the claim is not allowable. Now comes the task of using your writing skill to respond to a claim letter with an adjustment letter.

◀ **Figure 9.10**
Letter Granting an Adjustment

Thinking Critically. *Why should a letter granting an adjustment start with the good news?*

Turbak Instruments

9376 West Century Boulevard
Brandon, Manitoba R4H 2L4
204-555-4678 • FAX: 204-555-4699
www.turbakinstruments.com

November 5, 20—

Dr. Carlos A. Gotardo
Anderson Manufacturing Corporation
3976 State Street
Medicine Hat, ABT2L 3E9

Dear Dr. Gotardo:

A new barometer has been shipped to you by airfreight.

From your description in your November 2 letter, we believe that your aneroid barometer was mistakenly calibrated for use as an altimeter. We manufacture altimeters and aneroid barometers using the same mechanism—only the calibrations are different.

Somehow the wrong model number and nameplate were placed on the barometer you received. Please accept our sincere apology. We are reviewing our procedures in an effort to prevent this kind of mix-up from happening again.

When we can be of further assistance to you, Dr. Gotardo, please write or call.

Sincerely yours,

Art Dale

Art Dale, Supervisor
Customer Service Department

yr

An Allowable Claim

Mistakes occur in every business. What separates a well-run business from a poorly run business is not whether the company makes mistakes but *how it handles its mistakes.*

Question: What do you do when the error is yours? Answer: Admit that it was your fault, without quibbling or trying to avoid responsibility. Note how effectively this is done in Figure 9.10.

The writer grants the adjustment in the opening sentence and admits the error without hedging. The writer also strives to keep the customer's goodwill. In an effort to maintain goodwill, some companies will even grant doubtful claims if the costs are not excessive. In this way they develop an excellent reputation among their customers and gain new business.

A Partially Allowable Claim

Granting part of a customer's request means reaching a compromise with a claimant. For instance, if the transaction involves a heavy piece of equipment worth $10,000, the manufacturer will probably be reluctant to exchange the equipment and pay for double shipping charges besides. Yet that may be what the claimant asks for.

Suppose, for example, that a recent purchaser of a commercial automatic film processor wants to exchange the processor. The customer states that the processor is unsatisfactory because the developed film comes out wet instead of dry. You feel certain that the problem is caused by failure of the small fan under the drying hood. Replacement of the fan will take one of your technicians an hour and cost you only $100. Exchanging the entire processor, which weighs 90 kilograms and is valued at $9,000, will be expensive because of shipping costs. Moreover, the customer will have to wait at least three weeks for a new processor. You decide to seek a compromise adjustment.

How much of an adjustment a company makes in a case like this depends on company policy. You believe that the customer will be satisfied with the processor after the fan is replaced. You are also willing to offer the customer a $100 discount toward the purchase price as compensation for the inconvenience caused by the failure of the fan. Your letter describing this proposed adjustment might read as follows:

Dear Ms. Younglai:

Thank you for your letter about the problem you are having with your new SuperSpool Rapid Film Processor. Replacing the fan under the drying hood is the solution.

Exchanging your processor for a new one would leave you without a processor for at least three weeks. We seriously question the wisdom of exchanging the entire unit when only one small component is the cause of the trouble.

Ms. Younglai, we want you to be satisfied with our products and service. We realize that the fan's failure has inconvenienced you. We can send a service technician to your plant with a new drying fan. Replacement of the defective fan should take only one hour, and you can test the processor immediately to make sure that everything is working properly. Please call our service centre at 800-555-2243 to make an appointment for our service technician to visit your plant.

In addition, we have enclosed a $100 discount certificate.

We are confident that your SuperSpool Rapid Film Processor will provide good service for years to come.

Sincerely yours,

The writer is trying to reach a fair settlement with the customer. Nonetheless, Ms. Younglai may reply by asking to be compensated for all the film wasted as a result of the fan's failure.

A Nonallowable Claim

Although a business may strive to satisfy its customers and may have the most lenient claim policy in its industry, it will encounter situations in which claims simply cannot be allowed. For example, a customer may try to return a perfectly good lamp that he ordered simply because he no longer wants that style. Another customer may wrongly insist that she ordered merchandise before a price increase. If the business granted such claims once, of course, it would set a dangerous precedent. Besides, it would be poor business to do so. Whatever the reason, the company is faced with the uncomfortable but necessary task of saying no to a customer.

Assume, for example, that you are employed by Essex Distribution Company, a computer products wholesaler. Last month you featured a special offer on the complete Epic Model KL computer system. In your mailer to dealers, you specifically stated that you are discounting your current inventory of the KL model by 30 per cent "to make room for new inventory." Many dealers took advantage of the superb discount offer. You specifically stated in the mailer that this sale was a "clearance sale" and that no returns would be permitted.

Frances Itani, manager of the Metropolitan Computer Centre, purchased 50 of the Epic KL systems, sold 20, and then asked permission to return the remaining 30 systems. Because Metropolitan is a good customer, in the past you have "bent the rules" to allow Ms. Itani special return privileges for unsold merchandise. This time, however, you simply cannot accept the 30 Model KL systems. You must write to Ms. Itani to tell her this, but you must also try to retain her goodwill—and her future business. To do so, perhaps you would send the following letter:

Dear Ms. Itani:

Thank you for complimenting us on our special offers on the top brand names in computers. We at Essex pride ourselves on being the number-one computer distributor in the province, and we sincerely appreciate having the opportunity to do business with the number-one computer store in the province, Metropolitan Computer Centre.

As you know, Ms. Itani, no other distributor has offered such a drastic discount on Epic computers as our recent 30 per cent discount. We did so, frankly, because we were forced to make room for new inventory. We simply had to clear our stock at the time of the special sale. That's why we specifically stated that the sale was on a no-return basis. I'm sure that you, too, have been faced with similar situations.

As much as we would like to help you, we really cannot accept a return of 30 Epic KL systems. For one reason, we now have on order more than 500 of the new Epic XP system. As you can imagine, these 500 systems will take up much warehouse space as well as inventory dollars. We are also increasing our inventory of other major brands so that we can continue to deliver to dealers like Metropolitan all computer merchandise in the minimum amount of time. By serving you better, of course, we help you to serve your customers better.

May I make a suggestion? A few days ago Raj Bawa of Computer World, located in the Warren Mall, was eager to get more Epic Model KL systems. Perhaps you can arrange to sell your stock to Mr. Bawa. Of course, if I should hear of any other dealers who are looking for Epic KLs, I will be sure to call you.

By the way, let me give you some "advance notice" of a special sale we are planning for next month. We will be offering the popular Speedex zip disk drive for only $75 and the Lark DSL 2400 modem for only $95!

Sincerely yours,

Although the reply is clearly "no," the letter has a positive tone and maintains the customer's goodwill. The writer used the indirect approach, which gives the reasons before the refusal. The letter begins with a positive tone by thanking the customer. The reasons for not granting the request are clearly stated. The writer then suggests an alternate plan of action to solve the customer's situation, and ends with news of a special offer.

Review of Key Terms

1. What kind of claim *adjustments* do customers receive from businesses? How does a business determine how to make an equitable adjustment?

2. Explain how responding promptly to requests and being helpful are *indirect sales techniques*.

Practical Application

1. Write a letter answering each of the following requests.

   a. Sonya Gervais, 23 Lachine Drive, Lachute, QC H3T 1W9 requested from your company, Allword Publishing Inc., a copy of your new magazine, *Video Visions.* Demand has exceeded expectations, and the first issue has sold out. Write an appropriate response to Ms. Gervais.

   b. Gladys Panofsky, sales manager for Bermuda Beauty Lawn Products, 1132 South Avenue, Niagara Falls, ON L3W 1J9 received an order from the Howard House and Garden Shop, 853 Wallace Street, Guelph, Ontario N1H 5H4. The order, dated March 1, is large and is the first received from Howard House and Garden Shop. John Rosetti, the manager of Howard, wants to know the terms of payment and how and when the merchandise is to be shipped. Write Ms. Panofsky's reply to Mr. Rosetti.

   c. Rosa Copetti, director of public relations for Advantage Office Systems and Networks, 332 Pacific Avenue, Victoria, BC V2J 3B9, has telephoned Craig Curtis, chief advertising consultant for Best Business Consulting, 212 Lenore Street, Winnipeg, Manitoba R3B 2C3, and asked him to make a presentation on "Advertising in the Electronic Age" at the convention of the Western Advertising League. The presentation is to take place on June 24 at the Renaissance Hotel in Victoria, starting at 4:30 p.m. Mr. Curtis is to make a 40-minute presentation and then participate in a 20-minute discussion period. The meeting will be held in the Peerless Ballroom and will be followed by dinner at 5:30. Mr. Curtis is invited to the dinner as a guest of the Advertising League. Write the letter that Ms. Copetti should send to Mr. Curtis to confirm all the details of his participation in the convention.

2. Write a letter expressing each of the following claim or adjustment messages.

   a. You work in the Claims and Adjustments Department of Whirling Wonder Kitchen Co. You receive a letter from the manager of Le Crépuscule requesting replacement of a food processor that is not slicing evenly. You know from experience that uneven slices usually result from a damaged slicing disk. Write to Mr. Roland, the manager of Le Crépuscule. First, ask whether the food processor performs correctly with other attachments, such as the two-bladed knife and the shredding disk. Explain that if the machine does correctly dice, chop, grate, grind, and shred, the problem is definitely the damaged slicing disk. Offer to replace the slicing disk at no cost if this is the problem.

b. Review the letter of adjustment addressed to Ms. Younglai concerning the problem film processor. Assume that Ms. Younglai is not satisfied with your offer to replace the fan and to give her a $100 discount. Ms. Younglai also wants full compensation for all film wasted as a result of the defective fan. You decide not to commit yourself at this point to pay for all film wasted. Write Ms. Younglai offering to send a claims adjuster to her photography business to examine the wasted film and determine its value.

3. Review the letter to Mr. Neumann on page 411. Identify the indirect selling techniques used by the writer. How effective do you think each of these methods would be, and why? Prepare a short report or presentation on your team's findings.

TEAMWORK

Editing Practice

Applied Psychology.   Rewrite the following sentences so that each promotes goodwill.

1. There is no chance that we can deliver your order on time because many smarter consumers placed their orders before you.
2. Because you were careless and forgot to write your taxpayer's identification number on the form, we are returning it to you.
3. You must be too lazy to open your mail, because we have already written to you once about this matter.
4. Your October 3 letter fails to explain satisfactorily your delay in paying.
5. Your inability to operate computer equipment means that we will have to send a technician to your office.
6. We will repair the cabinet that you claim was damaged in transit.
7. You are the only person who ever found our sunscreen product unsatisfactory.
8. You neglected to send us the sales receipt for your stolen watch when you filed your claim.
9. You complained that order 977 did not arrive on time.
10. You made a mistake of $27 on our March 15 invoice.

Discussion Points

1. If you have just received a request letter, what steps would you take to answer the request?
2. How do the company, the claimant, the transaction, and the law determine the outcome of a claim? Provide current examples.

Persuasive Communications

Would you persuade, speak of interest, not of reason.

—Ben Franklin, writing in *Poor Richard's Almanac*

Sales and other persuasive letters represent an effective, direct contact with the customer. You should know the guidelines for writing sales letters because most business letters are really sales letters written to promote the sale of goods or services.

Writing Sales Letters

Businesses spend millions of dollars on sales letters every year because letters have two major advantages over radio and television advertisements. First, letters give recipients something they can put their hands on and see or read more than once. Second, letters sent to a carefully selected audience can be more direct and personal than commercials, which are produced for a mass audience.

Targeting Audiences

Think about the sales letters you receive. They range from magazines to insurance offers to invitations to join a CD or DVD club. Do you think that everyone on your street or in your town gets the same sales letters that you do? You might be surprised to learn that marketing specialists make a living by choosing very select target audiences for different products and services. A **target audience** is a group of potential customers chosen on the basis of certain characteristics such as age, geographic location, income, or lifestyle.

If the new product, for example, is exercise equipment, the target audience will be fitness trainers or athletes who might be able to use such equipment. If the product is a new line of children's clothing, the target audience will be families with young children. Of course, finding the target audience is not always as easy as in the two preceding examples. Companies that want to sell a new product such as a colour laser printer to prospective business customers may have to do extensive research to determine the best target audience.

When the target audience for a product is the general public, the challenge facing the writers of sales letters is to determine which of the following buying motives are most likely to appeal to the readers.

Understanding Buying Motives

Identifying buyers' needs and wants and then satisfying those needs and wants is the key to understanding buying motives.

Identifying Needs and Wants. In general, people buy products and services to satisfy specific needs and wants. **People's needs** are vital but relatively few: food, shelter, clothing, and perhaps transportation. **People's wants,** by contrast, are endless. People want not just any food, but delicious food; not just any shelter, but a comfortable apartment or house; not just any clothes, but the latest fashions. Most people also want security, status, the approval of others, health, personal attractiveness, conveniences—microwave ovens, remote controls, home security systems, and garage door openers, for example—and various forms of recreation and entertainment.

While people are usually aware of their wants in a general way, they may not know how a new product or service would fulfil any of those wants. The aim of your sales letter, therefore, is to convince people that a specific product or service will satisfy one or more of their wants.

Satisfying Needs and Wants. To make readers interested in a product or service, you must show how purchasing the item will provide your readers with prestige, good health, fun, beauty, savings, romance, freedom from drudgery, and so on. For example, the following list indicates the kinds of personal wants and needs that can be satisfied by the products and services shown.

Product or Service	Need or Want
Pillow-top mattress	Comfort
Ready-to-serve salad in a bag	Convenience
Toothpaste	Health and attractiveness
Home swimming pool	Recreation, status, or prestige
Outdoor lighting	Security
Charitable contribution	Self-esteem

Objectives of Sales Letters

After identifying the target audience's motives for buying a particular product or service, the writer will proceed to write the sales letter. Keep in mind, however, that there is no standard formula for all sales letters. They can vary in length, organization, and content. However, an effective sales letter will generally follow the persuasive approach discussed in Chapter 8—AIDA—Attention, Interest, Desire, Action.

1. Attract the reader's **attention.**
2. Create **interest** in your product or service.
3. Create a **desire** to buy.
4. Prompt the reader to take **action**.

Attracting *Attention*

A sales letter must immediately attract favourable attention. The appearance of a sales letter often determines whether it is read or tossed into the wastebasket. Because appearance starts with the envelope, sales letters often come in envelopes that promise big prizes, valuable certificates, and great savings inside. Creative advertisement writers have taken advantage of computers to add personalized attention-getting questions to envelopes. "Where would you take your FREE vacation, Mrs. Martin?" Many readers would react by opening the envelope to see what they have to do to get a free vacation.

Once a reader opens the envelope, other factors come into play. For example, heavy-stock stationery and an engraved letterhead give an appearance of importance, and an attractively displayed letter and clear printing give an impression of careful preparation of the correspondence. An enclosed free sample can also be used to get a reader's attention.

Creating Interest in Your Product or Service

One way to create interest is to start the letter with a question that will result in a *yes* answer. For example:

Isn't it time you took a really good photograph?

Do you dream of a vacation in the sun?

The following techniques can also be used in the opening: (1) using imperative sentences; (2) using informal punctuation such as dashes, exclamation points, underscores, ellipses, and parentheses; (3) using short, informal sentences; and (4) repeating the reader's name in the letter. The sentences that follow are additional opening lines that illustrate these techniques.

Opening	Product or Service
Protect your family with Burglar Beware.	Security system
Do it now! Don't wait a minute longer. Heath—happiness—fitness: they're all yours at Exercise World!	Fitness club
Mr. and Mrs. Engles, don't you want your child to get better-than-average grades?	Tutoring service

Creating a Desire to Buy

Take advantage of market research and other knowledge about the target audience of your sales letter. Make a connection between the features of the product or service and the presumed buying motives of the reader. The goal is to induce the reader to buy. Incentives to buy are called **sales appeals**, and they are the main act of the sales letter. Keep in mind, therefore, that the envelope, the stationery, and the opening line only set the stage. Notice how the following excerpts use sales appeals to stimulate the reader's desire to buy.

Sales Appeal	Buying Motive
Your family will ask for more each time you serve Barilla pasta.	Family approval
You can get twice the work done in half the time if your employees use Dell computers.	Convenience and economy
You can relive all your happy moments time and time again if you catch them with a Sony camcorder.	Enjoyment; nostalgia
Don't drive just any car. Drive a car that people will notice. Drive an elegant Mercedes!	Personal status

The sales appeal brings your reader to the point of wanting to buy a product. You must then nudge the reader just a little further by persuading that person to act on his or her desire to buy.

Prompting the Reader to Take *Action*

To increase the pressure on the reader to say "Yes, I want to buy this!" the writer often uses techniques that help develop a close relationship between writer and reader.

The most effective of these techniques is the rhetorical question. A **rhetorical question** is a question that is posed solely for effect, with no expectation of a reply or a clear yes or no. Rhetorical questions are asked to stimulate thought about a specific topic. Although a sales letter may contain several rhetorical questions at various points, a question can be used most effectively after the sales appeal. For example, after the virtues of the product have been described and the sales appeal has been made, questions such as the following could be effective.

Do pressures, deadlines, and difficult people leave you feeling frazzled?

Are your fuel bills too high?

Would you like to be free from back pain?

After reading rhetorical questions like these, readers are as ready to act as they will ever be. The writer's job is still not over, however.

What happens if the reader has no opportunity to act on an urge to buy? Writers of sales letters should include at least one of the following opportunities for immediate reaction:

1. A postage-paid reply card
2. An order form
3. Coupons
4. A toll-free, 24-hour telephone number
5. A Web site address

The sample letter in Figure 9.11 gives the reader straightforward instructions for action.

Writing Credit and Collection Letters

Another type of persuasive letter is the **collection letter,** a letter in which a company reminds certain customers that they have not paid their bill. Collecting an overdue account is not an easy task because no one likes to ask for money. Yet businesses must ask—or they lose money. The goal, therefore, is to get customers to pay without losing their goodwill.

Making Sure Customers Understand Credit Terms

The terms of credit must be explained to the customer at the time credit is granted. In commercial credit, that is between wholesaler and retailer, it is also advisable to review credit terms pleasantly, but firmly, when acknowledging a customer's first order. If the terms are 30 days net, expect your money in 30 days and do not hedge with weak statements like, "We hope you will send your cheque within 30 days." Instead, say, "Our terms are 2 per cent discount if you pay within 10 days; the net amount is due in 30 days."

Figure 9.11 Sales Letter with a Return Card

Thinking Critically. *How does the return card make it easier for the reader to respond?*

Skinner & Kennedy COMPANY INC.

August 11, 2002

Mr. Bill Brandenberger
531 Clark Avenue
London, ON N6G 3R5

Dear Mr. Brandenberger:

Studies show that . . .

. . . the successful people in business control time and do not let time control them.
. . . remembering important events strengthens friendships and relationships.
. . . being organized and getting things done result in advancement opportunities.

We know these statements describe you, Mr. Brandenberger, because you purchased one of our convenient Day Planners last year for just $102. You and the many other individuals who use our day planning products are better organized and get more accomplished than those who do not use them.

Now we offer you a special, three-year subscription to calendar refills for 2003, 2004, and 2005 for an incredible $72.86. The price includes shipping and handling for all three years. Your 2003 calendar will be sent immediately.

To reserve your Day Planner fillers and have them shipped at the appropriate times, just check the "Yes" option on our enclosed postage-paid return card, and mail it to us. We will bill you later.

Your time is valuable, Mr. Brandenberger. Let our Day Planner continue to help you make the most of it by acting now on this special offer.

Sincerely,

Mason Hicks

Mason Hicks
President

Enclosure

Assuming Customers Will Pay

When a customer first fails to pay a bill on time, it is wise to assume that this failure is an oversight. Therefore, if the usual monthly statement does not produce results, companies often send the customer a second statement a week or ten days later. Sometimes this second statement is stamped "First Reminder" or "Please Remit." Some credit departments use printed reminder forms such as the one shown in Figure 9.12.

Most customers will respond to gentle hints that their accounts are overdue. Remember, therefore, that the first reminder should never be an attack. Rather, it should be a highly impersonal nudge.

Sending Additional Reminders and Follow-Up Letters

If there is no payment after a second statement and a reminder, most companies will send a series of three to five follow-up letters before turning the account over to a lawyer or a collection agency.

Figure 9.12 ▶
Overdue Reminder Form
An impersonal printed form provides a gentle reminder that an account is overdue.

Thinking Critically. *Why is it important to have an impersonal approach to overdue collections?*

Moser's Fine Footwear

Market Place Shopping Centre
2000 North Neil Street
Fredericton, NB E3B 2L4
506-455-9328
www.mosers.com

January 15, 20—

Have you forgotten . . . ?

Because of the holidays, you may have overlooked mailing your December payment for your charge account at Moser's Fine Footwear.

Sending your payment for the amount due will be appreciated. In case you have already mailed the payment, please disregard this reminder.

Credit Account:	FF376-829-50
Amount Due for December 20—	
Charges:	$240.57
Minimum Payment Due:	$24.57

Thank you for shopping at Moser's Fine Footwear, and Happy New Year!

   If a five-letter **follow-up series** is used, the following procedure will be used.

1. *The first follow-up letter*, though clear and firm, should still give the customer the benefit of the doubt.

   Dear Mr. Dooley:

   The balance owing on your account is $547.53. To date you have not responded to two statements mailed to you.

   Could you please send payment immediately to clear this balance and to maintain your present credit rating with our company.

   Thank you for your prompt attention to this matter.

   Yours truly,

2. *The second follow-up letter*, which should be mailed no later than 15 days after the first letter, should remain friendly and courteous but should be firmer and more insistent than the first.

   Dear Mr. Dooley:

   We still have not received the $547.53 balance owing on your account, or any word of explanation for the delay in payment.

   In reviewing our records, we note that:

- The net amount was due on April 20.
- A second statement was mailed on May 4.
- We wrote to you on May 25 requesting payment.
- As of today, June 5, we have had no response from you.

Please let us hear from you by return mail.

Yours truly,

3. *The third letter* should be even more insistent and forceful.

Dear Mr. Dooley:

Help us save your credit reputation.

Your account is now 75 days overdue. Two statements and two previous letters have been ignored. You will owe us $547.53

You received the merchandise. You knew our credit terms. At this point your credit standing is in doubt.

Please send us your cheque today for $547.53.

Yours truly.

4. *The fourth letter* should demand payment.

Dear Mr. Dooley:

This letter is the 6th reminder that you owe us $547.53. Your account is now 90 days overdue!

We believe that these 6 reminders represent a maximum of patience on our part. We must insist that you send us a cheque within the next 7 days. Failure to do so will mean a change in your current credit privileges with our company.

Yours truly,

5. *The fifth letter* should state what legal action will be taken if the delinquent customer fails to take advantage of this last opportunity to pay. The goal of this last letter, of course, is to get the reader to pay the bill in order to avoid legal action.

Dear Mr. Dooley:

Unless we receive your cheque for $547.53 within 10 days, we shall have to turn your account over to our lawyer for collection. This action will also mean the cancelling of future credit privileges with our company.

We regret the need for this action. However, this letter is the 7th reminder of the amount you owe, which is now 100 days overdue.

Please send us your cheque immediately so that we may avoid taking further action.

Yours truly,

Review of Key Terms

1. What advantages do *sales letters* have over radio or television commercials?
2. What is a *rhetorical question*? How could you use a rhetorical question in a sales letter?

Practical Application

1. Explain: (1) when an organization would use the first follow-up letter for an unpaid account; (2) the difference in tone between first, second, third, and fourth follow-up letters.
2. After looking through magazines, newspapers, catalogues, and sales letters that you have received, list at least ten different types of sales appeals you find. Prepare your list under these three headings: (1) Type of Product, (2) Trade Name, and (3) Sales Appeal.
3. Draft a sales letter—including an attention-getting envelope—that asks young people to buy a home in a new housing development in your town or city. Assign one section of the AIDA (Attention, Interest, Desire, Action) guidelines to each group member and have him or her suggest ideas for using this particular section of the AIDA guidelines. Discuss the ideas and draft a letter.

TEAMWORK

Editing Practice

Promoting Good Public Relations. Rewrite the following excerpts so that they will be more diplomatic.

1. You claim that your VCR was not tested after it was repaired.
2. Why would we deliver the furniture free if you have never bought anything from us before and may never buy anything from us again?
3. Because you didn't include your warranty number, we won't repair your CD player.
4. Don't expect a discount if you don't remember to include your coupons.
5. If you don't pay your bill immediately, you'll be sorry.

Discussion Points

1. How do businesses find their target audience?
2. What is the goal of a sales letter? Discuss examples of sales letters you have received in the mail. Did they satisfy the five objectives of sales letters discussed in this section?

Public Relations Letters

Modern businesses and persons and organizations that seek publicity must recognize their obligations to the public and to the press.

—Henry F. Woods, Jr., author of *How to Become Well Known* (1947)

▶ **Key Terms**

▶ public relations campaign

▶ public relations

▶ public relations specialist

Major corporations have public relations departments that specialize in creating favourable images of their firms and minimizing the negative impact when their firms get unfavourable news coverage in the media through **public relations campaigns**. Although you may not work in the public relations department, as an employee you will certainly affect your company's public image.

Public relations is the business of influencing the public's feeling or attitude toward a company or an organization.

Whenever you communicate with the public as a representative of your organization—when you talk with or write to anyone outside the business—you have an opportunity to affect the public's attitude toward your firm. Your communication skills, therefore, can contribute to your firm's favourable public image.

Special Public Relations Opportunities

You have seen advertisements that say, for example, "Working Hard to Keep You and Your Family Safe…SAFE-TEE SMOKE DETECTORS." This sign is not designed specifically to sell Safe-Tee's Model 121-E smoke detector or to sell Safe-Tee's line of products, but to promote the Safe-Tee Company in general. The ad is designed to convince you that the Safe-Tee Company has your safety in mind. Why? So that when you *do* shop for smoke detectors, you will—either subconsciously or otherwise—select Safe-Tee—a name you can trust.

The **public relations specialist** looks for opportunities to show the company in the best possible light. When an employee receives a commendation from his or her community for civic work, the company might send a press release to various newspapers to share this good news with the public. The good civic work of one of its employees helps to enhance the firm's image. On the other hand, the public relations specialist tries to minimize anything the public could interpret in a negative way.

Unfavourable public opinion can ruin a firm. For example, if a newspaper report states or implies that the All-Natural Bread Company uses chemical preservatives and artificial colouring despite claims that their bread contains only natural ingredients, public opinion of that company will certainly drop—even if the report is later proved false. Consumers who remember the negative report may start buying another brand if they doubt the integrity of the company.

Knowing the benefits of good public relations, all businesses strive to create—and to keep—a favourable image in the eyes of the public. An oil company may televise a short film showing the public that the company strives to protect the environment wherever it drills for oil. A well-known, reputable person may narrate the film to lend it additional credibility. At no time does the narrator say "Buy your oil and gas from Enviro-Go." Instead, the narrator points out all the benefits the company offers the public.

The public relations specialist tries to win friends and customers when faced with the opportunity to:

- Promote a new business.
- Announce a special privilege or service to preferred customers.
- Offer special incentives to encourage charge customers to use their credit cards.
- Welcome new residents—who are new *potential customers*—to the community.
- Congratulate someone for a special achievement.
- Invite someone to a lecture, art show, demonstration, or film.
- Thank someone for his or her business.

Let's take a closer look at some of these special public relations opportunities.

Promoting a New Business

To promote a new business, the first step toward establishing good public opinion is to announce the grand opening—for example, in a letter such as this one:

May we introduce you to—

        Piérre Maigrette

chef and managing partner of Niagara's newest and most exciting restaurant:

        ENTRE NOUS

Chef Maigrette, a graduate of the Canadian Culinary Arts Institute and author of two best-selling cookbooks, has practised his culinary magic in several fine restaurants in Vancouver and Montreal. *Good Food Magazine* has hailed Piérre Maigrette as "one of Canada's most creative young chefs."

Dining at Entre Nous is the ultimate dining experience. Surrounded by understated elegance, you and your guests will be attended by a well-trained staff who will describe in detail the tempting appetizers, entrées, and desserts that Chef Maigrette and his staff will prepare for you.

Reservations are necessary, and all major credit cards are accepted.

Join us at Entre Nous for a relaxed evening of fine dining.

Cordially,

This letter alone is simply one step in a public relations campaign. To effectively promote this grand opening requires newspaper ads, spot announcements on local radio stations, circulars, and news releases, all focused on the general theme and tone of this letter. Together, these messages make up a public relations campaign that will reach the potential diners in the Niagara area.

Handling Special Opportunities

The sharp businessperson has an eye for opportunities to improve public relations—and takes every advantage of those opportunities. For an example of how to create letters for special occasions, see the letter in Figure 9.13.

Everyday Public Relations Opportunities

Unless your job is in the public relations department, you may not have all the special public relations opportunities that have been discussed so far. But the techniques will be useful because you *will* have everyday opportunities to improve public relations for your company.

Canadian General Finance
302 N.E. Third Avenue ❖ Charlottetown, PE C1A 2E4
Telephone: 800-555-8835 ❖ www.cgf.net

October 8, 20—

Mrs. Lynn Dubea
9376 Valley View Parkway
Charlottetown, PE C1D 4R3

Dear Mrs. Dubea:

Congratulations! You now own the big screen television you purchased one year ago. Our enclosed cancelled note is your record that all payments have been made on this product.

We hope you will consider us again to finance your purchase of additional major household items.

The enclosed certificate entitles you to our lowest possible finance rates when you seek loans from us for indoor and outdoor household items as well as new vehicles. Present the certificate to a representative at any one of our conveniently located offices for service on your loan requests. We will be most pleased to work with you again.

Cordially yours,

Sofia Martinez
Sofia Martinez
Vice President

ms/note3689
Enclosure

◀ **Figure 9.13**
Public Relations Letter
The writer makes an opportunity to contact a former customer.

Thinking Critically.
What are the objectives of this public relations letter?

Note in the following letter that the writer sells the company. In other words, the writer employs good public relations techniques in replying to a routine request for information.

Dear Mr. Gould:

Thank you for thinking of the Banff Inn as the place to hold your annual sales convention.

For several years now, you have used our facilities to host your special dinners, to demonstrate products to customers, to train your new representatives, and to lodge your employees and guests whenever they are in our area. We do, indeed, make special efforts to make all your meetings successful, because your appreciation of our efforts always shows.

Mr. Gould, we sincerely enjoy serving you, your employees, and your customers. Thank you for doing business with us.

Yours sincerely,

As you see, then, public relations is part of every letter you write for your company. When you write your letters, even *routine* letters, look for ways to incorporate good public relations techniques.

Review of Key Terms

1. Why are *public relations* important to business?
2. How can a *public relations campaign* promote a business?

Practical Application

1. Suppose that you are a college graduate with five years of business experience as (1) an administrative assistant in a law firm, or doctor's office, or large company; (2) a travel agent in a large agency; or (3) a tax accountant in a public accounting firm.

   You decide to set up your own (1) office services agency, (2) travel agency, or (3) tax accounting business. You choose to begin promoting your new business by writing a letter and sending it to 100 businesses in the community. You wish to emphasize both your business experience and your excellent college education. Write a letter that includes all the details that will improve your chances of succeeding in your new business.

2. You are manager of Lindemann's Hardware Store, an established business on the outskirts of a large city. Traditionally, your customers have come from the city. New towns and neighbourhoods are springing up beyond city limits, however, and you are looking for a way to develop business with the residents of these new areas. You decide to write a letter, enclosing a discount coupon worth $5, that invites each resident of the new areas to visit your store. Write an appealing invitation addressed to new residents.

3. You work for Newlook Decorators. You want to encourage prior customers with good credit to make another purchase on your new line of furniture. Each member of your team drafts a letter that invites your charge customers to a special preview showing of the new line. Admission will be by ticket only, and you are enclosing a ticket with each invitation. The general public will not see the new line until after the special showing. Then, compare your efforts and compile a letter that includes the best features from the drafts. Key and print your letter and present it to the class.

TEAMWORK

Editing Practice

Editing to Improve Writing Techniques.   Edit the following sentences to improve any poor writing techniques.

1. Arriving to pick up the package, I asked the messenger to wait while the cover letter was signed by Ms. Drake.
2. Employees must now submit their health insurance claim to Robert Bergman in the personnel office.
3. Ellen borrowed the dictionary which was on my desk.

4. Anezka said she couldn't find any stamps for the letters after looking in the desk drawers.
5. You can use either of these four spreadsheets as a model for your training course.
6. In order to prepare the inventory report, all the figures will be needed by you.
7. Within two days after I sent my request to Ms. Medina, a reply was received from her.
8. There is no future for the business communicator who is careless or indifferent to the techniques of writing.
9. The mail would remain in the out-basket for hours and sometimes days.
10. Our engineers have made many improvements in design, and so we shall be able to produce a better product.
11. The committee must complete the research, assembling of facts, and writing the report.
12. In his writing, Simon consistently used unnecessarily big words, thus making his communications ineffective.
13. Perry always has and always will be a team player.
14. Andre is one of the brightest if not the brightest summer interns in the program.
15. He felt the furniture was too expensive.

Discussion Points

1. What effect can one negative incident have on public opinion? Discuss some examples of unfavourable public opinion and its effect.
2. How do companies promote public relations through their business letters?

Social-Business Communications

▶ **Key Term**

▶ social-business communications

"Kind words can be short and easy to speak, but their echoes are truly endless."

— Mother Teresa, Nobel Peace Prize recipient

Common courtesy and tradition demand that business workers send **social-business communications** to congratulate someone on a special occasion, express condolence when a business associate suffers the loss of a loved one, reply properly to a formal invitation, thank someone for a special favour or gift, and so on. Just as you would appreciate hearing from your co-workers and business associates in these situations, you should let them hear from you whenever appropriate.

Congratulations Letters

Special honours and special events provide ideal public-relations opportunities. They present you with an appropriate occasion to say "Congratulations!" Your reader will appreciate your thoughtfulness, and you will certainly win favour both for yourself and for your company. Remember: Everyone wants to be respected and admired, and a congratulatory message shows your respect and admiration for someone's accomplishment or recognition.

For Promotions

The degree of friendliness or informality of your congratulatory note will depend on the specific relationship you have with the reader.

Congratulatory letters often are written to employees of the same company. In fact, it is virtually *mandatory* for executives to acknowledge promotions of employees in their company. The following letter is written to a valued employee:

Dear Louis,

Congratulations on your promotion to District Manager. You certainly are "the right person for the right job."

Catherine Terranova has been talking about promoting you to this position since she became Marketing Manager six months ago. All of us in management are equally convinced that you will be able to continue to turn in the high sales volume for which the Western District is well known.

In any case, Louis, I am very pleased to welcome you to the sales management team for our Consumer Division, and I wish you success in your new position.

Sincerely,

For Anniversaries

A co-worker's anniversary also calls for written congratulations. Note the friendliness and informality—and the sincerity—of this letter:

Dear Gene,

Congratulations on your tenth year with Vector Products Inc. I remember your first day with the company, when Len Denaro introduced you to me and my staff. When Len retired one year later, I knew that you were the right person to replace him—and you've continued to prove that for the last nine years.

Gene, I think you know just how pleased I've been to have the opportunity to work with you. Thanks to your manufacturing expertise and management leadership, our production department is the best in the industry. My staff and I appreciate your fine work. You certainly help make things easier for the rest of us!

Cordially yours,

For Retirements

The retirement of a co-worker or of a business associate also deserves recognition. Retirement letters deserve extra care; if you are not sure that the person welcomes retiring, be especially sensitive in writing the note.

Dear Veronica,

What will Clarion Advertising be like without you? Our clients, our suppliers, and of course, all our co-workers have come to depend on that smiling face, that cheerful voice, and that friendly attitude whenever we approach the Graphic Arts department. It seemed as if you were always there to help a lost visitor, to reroute a messenger, and to answer the phone when no one else was around. I know that you were always there to assist me.

Thank you, Veronica, for all you have done to help me since the first day I joined the company. All my best wishes to you in your retirement. I hope that you will enjoy many years of health and happiness with your family and your friends. I hope, too, that you will visit us from time to time.

Sincerely,

Thank-You Letters

During our daily interaction with people, we always have many opportunities to say "Thank you." A special occasion, however, requires a *written* thank-you—for example, when we receive a gift, hospitality, or special courtesy from a business associate.

For Gifts

Business executives may receive gifts from suppliers and vendors. When they do, courtesy demands that they write a thank-you note to the giver.

Dear Matthew,

Thank you for your thoughtfulness in sending me such a beautifully bound edition of *Modern Art in Canada*. You certainly selected a book of very special interest to me.

Since I received your package late Friday afternoon, I have done little else but read, read, read. Admittedly, I spent lots of time on the photographs too!

Matthew, my sincere appreciation to you for your kindness. You may be sure that I will enjoy this book again and again.

Cordially yours,

Some companies have policies prohibiting employees from accepting such gifts under any circumstances. If your firm has such a policy, you will of course adhere to it. Your thank-you letter, then, will obviously require a different approach.

Dear Matthew,

Thank you for your thoughtfulness in sending me such a beautifully bound edition of *Modern Art in Canada*. You certainly selected a book of very special interest to me.

I wish that the company permitted me to keep this thoughtful gift, but we have a specific policy that prohibits my doing so. Therefore, when I have completed reading the book, I will give it to the company library with this inscription: "Donated to the Canco Library by West Hill Printers Inc."

Matthew, please accept my sincere appreciation for your kindness. You may be sure that I will borrow this book from the library often; when I do, I will remember your thoughtfulness.

Cordially yours,

For Hospitality

A business associate's hospitality is not to be taken for granted. Even if the person is also an employee of your company, he or she still deserves a thank-you letter for special hospitality.

Dear Rona,

Thank you for the many courtesies extended to me on my recent visit to Edmonton. My stay was certainly much more pleasant because of your thoughtfulness in arranging for my comfort.

The high spot of the entire visit was the evening spent in your beautiful home. You and Alistair are most gracious hosts. The food was excellent; the conversation, stimulating; the people, delightful. The time passed so quickly that I was embarrassed to find that I had stayed so long; I was so engrossed and comfortable being part of such good company.

Enclosed is a small token of my appreciation for the many kindnesses shown me. I will remember my visit to Edmonton with pleasure.

Sincerely yours,

For Recommendations

Many businesses flourish almost solely on the basis of the recommendations of clients, friends, suppliers, and other business associates. When someone recommends you or your firm, she or he is doing you a special favour—a favour that certainly deserves a thank-you letter.

Dear Ms. Boyle:

This morning we visited Bruce Stargell of Stargell's Sports Centre Inc. Mr. Stargell mentioned your recommendation when he placed an order for display and storage equipment for the chain of new stores that he will open this fall.

We thank you, Ms. Boyle, for recommending us to Mr. Stargell. We appreciate the order and your confidence in us. Please accept our thanks for this favour.

Cordially yours,

Condolence Letters

When business associates and friends suffer tragedies or misfortunes, common courtesy requires you to communicate your sympathy with a condolence letter. Depending on your specific relationship, you may send a printed sympathy card.

Condolence letters are difficult to write simply because it is difficult to console and comfort someone who has recently suffered a tragic loss. For the same reason, however, condolence letters are always very much appreciated. You may type a condolence letter, but if you really wish to give your letter a personal touch, send a handwritten note.

Dear Larissa,

The news of your brother's untimely death yesterday has stunned and saddened me. I know that you have suffered a great loss. Please accept my sincere sympathy.

When my mother died last year, a friend sent me a copy of Dylan Thomas's poem "And Death Shall Have No Dominion." I found the poem a source of consolation again and again. I am enclosing a copy and hope it will serve you as well as it did me. My heart goes out to you and your family in your time of grief.

Sincerely yours,

Formal Invitations and Replies

From time to time, businesspeople receive formal invitations to such events as an open house, a special reception to honour a distinguished person, a special anniversary, or a formal social gathering. Such invitations are usually engraved or printed and are written in the third person.

The illustration in Figure 9.14 shows a formal printed invitation. Handwritten invitations and replies are written on personal stationery, special note-sized stationery, or plain white notepaper. Historically, an acceptance or a refusal was handwritten; today, if a phone number is provided on the invitation, a telephone response is acceptable.

Figure 9.14 ▶
Printed Formal Invitation

Thinking Critically.
Which voice is a formal invitation written in: first, second, or third? What kind of stock is it printed on?

The Vermilion Fitness Centre

requests the pleasure of your company
at its presentation of expanded health facilities
Friday, the sixth of February
at six o'clock in the evening
3170 South Hamilton Road in Victoria.

Our health bar will be serving refreshments.

R.S.V.P.

250-555-6786

Review of Key Term

How does *social-business communication* improve a company's public relations?

Practical Application

1. You are the president of a medium-sized company, Meridien Decorative Fabrics. When informed that one of the company's oldest employees, bookkeeper Albert Wickford, is retiring after thirty years with Meridien, you genuinely want to thank him for such long service. You decide to write a letter thanking Mr. Wickford for his years with the company and to enclose a cheque for $500. Write the letter.

2. Annette Rossi was a classmate of yours in college. You read in the newspaper that Annette, after only three years at Harvest Investing, has been chosen Outstanding Financial Analyst. Annette's reward is twofold: a promotion to Assistant Director of Financial Analysis and an expense-paid business tour of the Far East. Write a letter of congratulation to Annette on her achievements.

3. You have just learned of the illness and death of Mrs. Frederick Olson, the wife of one of your company's suppliers who has become a friend of yours. In addition to Mr. Olson, Mrs. Olson (Helga) leaves a married daughter (Anne) and three young grandchildren (Tom, Alex, and Inga). Write a letter of condolence to Frederick Olson, Director of Marketing for Ludlow Manufacturing, 668 Bay Road, Charlottetown, Prince Edward Island C1A 8LA.

4. Your team just returned from a business trip to Calgary. During your three-day stay, employees from your sister company, Brandon Inc., personally drove you to business appointments, took you to restaurants, and planned a night at the Stampede. Write a note of thanks to the team at Brandon Inc.

Editing Practice

Editing for Redundancies.   Eliminate all unnecessary repetitions in the sentences below.

1. We are planning to revert back to personal contact as our main sales strategy.
2. These forms confuse me because they are both alike.
3. With every new subscription, a utilities disk is sent free, gratis.
4. By the time I arrived, the festivities were over with.
5. Please repeat the instructions again so that everyone understands them.
6. Do you know what files are stored inside of this cabinet?
7. Past experience shows that Michael is reliable.

8. The manufacturer suggests that you clean the heads of the videocassette recorder on a regular basis, as otherwise you will not get a satisfactory recording.

Electronic Mail. Rewrite the following wordy E-mail, making it concise.

One of Canada's outstanding experts on stress is Dr. Maria Cotsaftis of Halifax. We are fortunate to be able to have Dr. Cotsaftis as a speaker for two presentations that she will give here in our company auditorium next month. Actually, she will repeat the same presentation on two consecutive days.

The title of her talk is "Stress on the Job." The first presentation will be at 10 a.m. on April 18; the second presentation will be at the same time on the next day, April 19. Each speech will be one hour long, and each will be followed by a session during which Dr. Cotsaftis will answer questions from the audience.

If you are interested in hearing this noted author and lecturer, you are welcome to attend either one of the scheduled sessions. Because seats are limited, of course, we ask you to notify the Training Department if you are interested in hearing Dr. Cotsaftis.

Discussion Points

1. Discuss the appropriate business situations that call for congratulation letters, thank-you letters, and condolence letters.
2. How should you reply to a formal business invitation?

Form Paragraphs, Form Letters, and Templates

Written communications should act as goodwill ambassadors for you and your organization.

—The Canadian Office

▶ **Key Terms**

▶ form letters
▶ variables
▶ boilerplate
▶ data file
▶ form file
▶ template

You have learned that writing quality business communications takes much time and effort. Because time and effort cost money, many companies look for acceptable ways to reduce the amount spent. One very good way to reduce writing costs is to use form letters. **Form letters** are letters in which the same message is sent to many addressees. Sometimes details of the message, called **variables**, change from letter to letter. Sometimes form letters are composed by combining various prewritten paragraphs, called **boilerplate**, into a particular communication.

Advantages of Using Form Letters

Here are the major advantages of using form letters.

1. Using form letters saves time in planning, dictating, and transcribing.
2. Company representatives can respond more quickly to routine writing situations, and thus the receiver gets an answer sooner.
3. The content quality will be better. Much time and thought can go into writing form letters.
4. Fewer errors will result because the spelling, punctuation, and grammar have to be approved only once.
5. Form letters and paragraphs do not have to be rekeyed. They are simply selected and printed.

Disadvantages of Using Form Letters

As with most good ideas, there are some disadvantages of using form letters. Here are three.

1. Some of the "personal touch" can be lost in mass-producing letters. Attempts should be made to make letters more personal. You could, for example, include the person's name within a sentence. "I look forward to seeing you, Ms. Tate, on Friday, at 2 p.m."

2. If readers find out that they have received a form letter, they may feel somewhat disappointed. A manager, for example, wrote you a congratulatory message when your son finished college. You felt good about the letter until your co-worker showed you one exactly like it he received when his daughter graduated from college. The purpose of the letter was goodwill, but the goodwill was lost. For this reason, form letters should be revised and updated on a regular basis.

3. The use of form letters and boilerplate can be abused. Some business writers use them when they do not quite fit the situation and are thus inappropriate.

Types of Form Letters

Executives often find that they are repeatedly writing the same content in response to frequently occurring—almost identical—writing situations. When this happens, they should invest some time and effort in developing general responses that can be used and reused. These general responses fall into three main categories.

- Form letters
- Form letters with variables
- Letters with form paragraphs

Form Letters

Form letters are used to respond to identical situations. The letter shown in Figure 9.15 would be used to respond to any general inquiries about cruises to Alaska. The entire body of the letter remains the same; the date, inside address, and salutation are the only changes. These letter parts are highlighted in the sample.

Form Letters with Variables

Form letters with variables are used when similar, but not identical, responses are needed. In addition to the date, inside address, and salutation, other details are changed throughout the body of the letter. These changes are called *variables*. Figure 9.16 shows the form letter with the variables added and highlighted.

Letters with Form Paragraphs

For similar writing situations that occur frequently but vary in content, experienced business communicators use form, or boilerplate, paragraphs. Paragraphs dealing with the most common situations are written. Each paragraph has a number. Instead of dictating the body of each letter, the executive gives the assistant a list of paragraphs by number. Sample boilerplate paragraphs and a resulting letter are shown in Figure 9.17.

Boilerplate paragraphs and complete letters can be stored on disk and retrieved and altered as necessary. Only the variables have to be keyed. As a result, routine letters can be prepared quickly and efficiently.

Merged Letters

Merged letters save time when you need to send the same letter to a group

Current Date

Name
Address
City, Province Postal Code

Salutation:

Thank you for inquiring about our fantastic cruises to Alaska. For the past several years, our six cruise packages to this spectacular area have continued to become increasingly popular.

I am enclosing a brochure that summarizes the dates and costs of the various cruise packages. You can readily see the differences among the packages and determine the one that best fits your preferences.

When you are ready, please complete our enclosed reservation form and return it to me at your earliest possible convenience. Since these cruises are so popular, they tend to fill up quickly.

If you have other questions, please call me at my number shown above. Let me help you make the details for your memorable vacation.

Sincerely,

DESTINATIONS UNLIMITED

Lisa Miller
Manager

??
Enclosure

of people. Merging requires a **data file**, which contains the names and addresses of people on your mailing list, and a **form file**, which contains the form letter and the codes to merge the information with the data file. Merging the two files allows you to print letters that appear to be individually typed and addressed. The next time you wish to send a letter to the same group of people, you need only to change the body of the letter.

Templates

Many word processing programs today come with templates of letters. A **template** contains the format for a letter and can include the letterhead in addition to the skeleton of a letter. To use a template, you insert the template into your blank document or you open a copy of the template, add the text in the places indicated, and print. This saves time and helps the user who is unsure of the correct letter format.

Figure 9.16 ▶
**Form Letter with
Variables Filled In**

Thinking Critically. *If
you were sending this
letter, would you highlight
the variable information?
Why or why not?*

Travel Design Agency
449 North Boulevard, Markham, ON L4P 2J9
Phone: 905-555-8728, Fax: 905-555-8728
E-mail: traveldesign@cactusnet.com
www.traveldesign.com

August 15, 20—

Mr. Rick Rotramel
247 Magnolia Drive
Victoria, BC V8E 7A4

Dear Mr. Rotramel:

Your reservations for two tickets to see "The Sound of Music"
have been made, and your tickets are enclosed. You should
be pleased with the seats you have been assigned. Two
individuals will sit in Row 4, centre.

A total amount of $160, including taxes and service fees, has
been charged to your MasterCard credit card. These tickets
cannot be exchanged, and no refunds can be given.

We thank you for ordering tickets from us, and we know you
will enjoy this fabulous musical. Seeing this show will certainly enhance your trip to Toronto.

Sincerely,

Nanette Mellon

Nanette Mellon
Reservation Agent

Thinking Critically.
If you are not currently hiring, what paragraphs would you select to respond to an application for employment?

March 1, 20--

Ms. Ellen DePaula
24 San Remo Blvd.
Hamilton, Ontario L9C 5T9

Dear Ms. DePaula:

1   Thank you for expressing an interest in employment with our firm. We are pleased that you want to discuss your career plans with us.

4   Before we can consider you for a position, your application file must be complete. Please send us the name, address, and references.

5   As soon as we we will call you to a

6   Thank you for y forward to hearing f

dk

EMPLOYMENT APPLICATION BOILERPLATE

1   Thank you for expressing an interest in employment with our firm. We are pleased that you want to discuss your career plans with us.

2   Business trends will not permit us to hire additional employees at this time. However, we anticipate position openings in several specialized areas within the next three to six months.

3   The qualifications shown on the application you recently completed impressed us. Would you please submit a résumé, and include details of your experience with various types of office equipment, your office skills, and three references.

4   Before we can consider you for a position, your application file must be complete. Please send us the name, address, and telephone number of three references.

5   As soon as we receive the requested information, we will call you to arrange an interview.

6   Thank you for your interest in our company. We look forward to hearing from you.

7   We will keep your application on file and notify you if a suitable position becomes available in the future.

Review of Key Terms

1. Why do businesses use *form letters*?
2. What are *boilerplate* paragraphs? Why are they used in business letters?

Practical Application

1. Use the form letter in Figure 9.15 to model a letter to Denis Prior, P.O. Box 2849, your town/city. You made reservations for Mr. Prior for four tickets in row 8, centre, to see *Bells Are Ringing*. The total came to $400, which has been charged to Mr. Prior's Visa credit card.
2. You own a motel in a very popular coastal or lake area. Write a form letter to respond to general inquiries. In the letter, mention that you are enclosing a brochure listing the various kinds of accommodations and the rates.
3. You work for a restaurant supply company. You need to create three boilerplate paragraphs: one to list and describe some of the products you sell; a second to reply to restaurants that request a catalogue; and a third to thank potential customers for their interest in your company.

TEAMWORK

Editing Practice

Missing Words.   A word has been left out of each of the following sentences. Select a word that will correctly complete each sentence.

1. A helpful highway gave us directions to your plant.
2. We were late for the ceremony, because we trouble with our car.
3. Most of the employees have decided participate in the dental insurance program.
4. Our sales representative in your area Catherine Vanderzwan.
5. Newspaper advertisements radio advertisements aroused our interest.

Missing Letters.   A letter has been incorrectly omitted from some of the words in the following sentences. Write the correct word. Write *OK* if a sentence is correct.

1. On which disk did you store the thre documents?
2. Inside the large manila envelop is a photocopy of the stock certificates.
3. Janine Daoust overses the modular furniture installations for our corprate clients.
4. The camping trailer is equiped with a gas stove.
5. Alex Magruder is the agent who makes all the travel arangements for our company's executives.

Discussion Points

1. What are some of the advantages and disadvantages of using form letters?
2. Explain how variables in form letters provide a personal touch.

Chapter 9 Wrap-Up

SUMMARY

▶ A business letter is a critical element in business writing. Letters must look professional, as they are judged on their appearance as much as their content. Business letters should be typed on high-quality stationery. The acceptable formats of letters include the block format, the modified-block format, and the simplified format.

▶ The content of a business letter is to inform, make requests, respond to requests, and to deliver social-business messages. Writers should provide complete information in giving directions, making announcements, or informing the public about events. Effective requests should also be complete and reasonable. Writers should maintain a courteous tone in their letters.

▶ When responding to a customer request, business correspondence should be prompt, sales-minded, and promote a positive image of the company.

▶ Whether you are persuading a customer to act, or sending a collection letter, a claim letter, a letter of adjustment, a form letter, or social-business communications, each message should be written with the audience in mind. When composing a message for a specific communication situation, accuracy and completeness of facts, knowledge of company policy, and selection of an appropriate tone are all necessary for the ultimate effectiveness of the letter, card, or note.

▶ Public relations specialists use persuasive appeals to promote new business by offering specialty services and incentives, welcoming new residents, and using social-business communications. Social-business communications are a thoughtful way to extend congratulations, condolences, or formal invitations.

▶ Overall, business professionals should always consider the audience to whom they are writing and target their message with the specific communication situation in mind.

▶ Form letters can be used when the same message is sent to many addressees. Each letter can be customized by including variables. Form letters can also be composed by combining a selection of pre-written paragraphs.

CASE 9.1

Gavin O'Malley is the communications specialist at Columbia Advertising in downtown Vancouver with branches in Kelowna and Victoria. Columbia is a fairly new company that seeks to project a sleek, modern image. The president of the company told Gavin that he wishes to adopt a standard format for all company letters. Gavin must make a presentation to the president and the marketing vice president recommending a letter style and letterhead design.

Outline the presentation that you think Gavin should make, including recommendations and reasons for the choice of letter style and letterhead design.

CASE 9.2

Jewel Pinkerton works in the public relations department at East Multimedia, a Web development company. Jewel has been asked to assist the Web development team in updating the Web site for their client Godiva chocolatier, **http://www.godiva.com/**.

Jewel's boss has asked her to add a Web page to the business-gift-giving category by including a sales letter from the Godiva marketing department.

You are the representative from Godiva's marketing department who has been assigned to draft that sales letter for Jewel. Using the recommendations for sales letters explained in Chapter 9, write a sales letter for Godiva's Web site.

Communicating in Your Career

You are being interviewed for a job. The job posting had stated that applicants should have "superior communication skills" and you know that the position also requires writing a lot of e-mail messages and letters. How will you answer the following questions in the interview?

- What do you believe are your main strengths as a communicator?
- What would you do in your written correspondence to foster a positive image of our company?

On the Web

The art of acknowledging people is extremely important in social-business communications. Everyone—be they employer or employee, business associate or friend or acquaintance—appreciates this type of communication.

Jackie Lakeview is a senior accountant with Roadway Trucking. You got to know Jackie during the 10 years you drove trucks for Roadway. You left the company to return to school and earn a degree in accounting. Now you want to send Jackie a thank-you note because, based on her letter of recommendation, you were hired for an entry-level accounting position with H&R Block. Given your long history with Jackie, it would be awkward to send her a formal thank-you note. You decide to e-mail her a personalized thank-you note instead. Locate a card on the Internet and write a thank-you note that communicates your sincere thanks.

Key Terms

adjustment	415	modified block		salutation	389
block letter		format	391	simplified format	392
format	391	open punctuation	389	social-business	
boilerplate	443	people's needs	424	communica-	
claim letter	402	people's wants	424	tions	437
collection letter	426	personal-business		standard (or	
copy notation	390	letter	392	mixed)	
data file	445	procedures book	399	punctuation	389
follow-up series	428	public relations	431	style	387
form file	445	public relations		target audience	423
form letters	443	campaign	431	template	445
indirect selling		public relations		tickler file	409
methods	411	specialist	431	variables	443
informative		reference initials	390	watermark	394
messages	398	rhetorical			
inside address	387	question	426		
letterhead	387	sales appeals	425		

Chapter 10

Writing Reports, Minutes, and News Releases

Chapter Learning Outcomes

After successfully completing this chapter, you will have demonstrated the ability to:

▶ describe the different types of reports and their purposes;

▶ gather information for a report and document your sources;

▶ write informal or formal reports;

▶ prepare minutes of a meeting;

▶ write a news release.

Dave Quilt was the public relations officer at the Simcoe Chamber of Commerce. He received a phone call from Dr. Dave Ehman, the career dean at Canadore Community College, requesting information on job opportunities for graduates in northern Ontario. Dr. Ehman needed the survey information to prepare a report for the college board on revising and updating programs.

Ms. Shirleen Hackman, executive director of the chamber, agreed that Dave should conduct a survey of local and regional employers. The survey would focus on gathering information regarding job openings and the skills and training needed by entry-level employees.

Dave decided to use the chamber of commerce's Web site to reach these businesses. He knew that Simcoe's Web site was linked to the Web sites for other cities in the province and with other provinces. With feedback from his inquiry on the chamber of commerce's Web site, Dave identified 300 employers to receive the survey. He prepared and distributed the report, sending most of the copies by e-mail.

By the reply date, Dave had received responses from over 50 per cent of the recipients. He was ready to compile the report.

As you read Chapter 10, identify some tasks that Dave needs to complete to compile and submit his report.

Report Types and Information Sources

Progress lives from the exchange of knowledge.

—Albert Einstein, American physicist

Types and Purposes of Reports

Before writing a report, you need to determine its purpose and analyze your audience. This will determine the type of report you prepare. The two basic kinds of reports are informative reports and analytical reports.

Informative Report

An **informative report** gives facts and other information on some aspect of an organization's operations. Examples of informative reports include reports on company policies and procedures; sales reports of company's products or services; and reports on patient admissions, clients served, cases processed, bids submitted, customer service requests, and so on. An informative report usually identifies a problem or gives background information but does not make recommendations or persuade. Informative reports are divided into three report types: periodic, progress, and unsolicited.

Periodic Report. A **periodic report** is prepared at regular intervals, for example, weekly, monthly, or quarterly. Any report prepared at specified intervals is considered a periodic report. A quarterly sales report is an example. It is prepared four times per year at the end of each business quarter. If a business uses the beginning of the calendar year as its fiscal start, the end of the first quarter is March 31.

Progress Report. A **progress report** gives the current status of a project, tells what has been completed since the last progress report, and states when the project will be completed. Progress reports usually are done for projects that require an extended period of time, such as three months or more. They are often presented informally in memorandum format, but can include details of the progress in separate documents created in project-management software. Progress reports may also include supporting documents to show the progress of the entire project or specific parts of the project.

Unsolicited Report. An **unsolicited report** is one that you make on your own initiative. In business, any idea for increasing efficiency, saving money,

▶ Key Terms

- ▶ informative report
- ▶ periodic report
- ▶ progress report
- ▶ unsolicited report
- ▶ analytical report
- ▶ justification report
- ▶ feasibility study
- ▶ proposal
- ▶ secondary source
- ▶ primary source
- ▶ pilot test
- ▶ CD-ROM
- ▶ Internet
- ▶ World Wide Web
- ▶ on-line services
- ▶ browsers
- ▶ working bibliography
- ▶ plagiarism
- ▶ paraphrasing
- ▶ footnotes
- ▶ endnotes
- ▶ bibliography
- ▶ textnotes

increasing productivity, or increasing profits will usually be welcome. It's advisable to put your idea in writing so that you can present it in the most complete, logical, and generally effective manner. Unsolicited reports can be done formally or informally and include specific intended results, proposed new products, or proposed new procedures to accomplish an existing task.

Analytical Report

An **analytical report** examines a situation or problem, draws conclusions, and makes recommendations, in addition to providing information and data. This type of report may explore the feasibility of taking possible action by looking at several alternatives, systematically analyzing each alternative, and then making recommendations.

Examples of analytical reports are justification reports, feasibility studies, and proposals. These three types of reports are somewhat similar.

Justification Reports. A **justification report** is usually prepared for someone at a higher level of management; it gives the rationale for a recommendation or a decision. Sample subjects would include making a major expenditure for new equipment, expanding facilities, and hiring additional personnel. Justification reports are often unsolicited reports prepared by someone who has a problem or concern.

Feasibility Studies. A **feasibility study** describes the pros and cons of proceeding with a project, in addition to giving the costs and a time frame for the project. This type of report would include recommendations on whether or not to go ahead with the project.

Proposals. A **proposal** is a report that may be prepared for someone inside or outside your company. It is designed to persuade the reader to purchase your products or services, to adopt your idea or plan, or to provide or donate money or services for a worthwhile project. The proposal may offer a solution to a problem and usually gives the cost of the plan. Proposals usually include a plan of action which outlines the initial step or set of steps to be taken to get the proposed result.

Gathering Information

The value of any report depends on the quality of the material on which it is based. With reliable, relevant facts behind it, a reliable report can be written; with questionable data, only a questionable report can result.

Information for reports can be obtained through two types of sources—*primary sources* of data and *secondary sources* of data. Your first step should be to see what secondary data already exist to save yourself the time and trouble of gathering data that may already be available. Also, you want to include in your report information that is common knowledge.

Secondary Sources of Information

A **secondary source** is a document or other material that contains information gathered by someone else. This information is usually published in books and periodicals, or it may be found in company records and reports. Secondary information is also widely available through electronic sources such as CD-ROM databases and World Wide Web sites. In gathering secondary information, you should be familiar with the authoritative references in your field. There are, in addition, many general references that are invaluable helps to every writer, some of which are listed here.

Indexes. An index includes a list of the titles of articles appearing in a variety of periodicals. *Periodicals* include journals, magazines, pamphlets, and newsletters that are published on a regular basis. Such indexes include the *Readers' Guide to Periodical Literature* and the *Business Periodicals Index*.

Almanacs and Yearbooks. These sources contain concise information on important events that occurred during a given year. Examples include *The World Almanac and Book of Facts, Information Please Almanac,* and *Facts on File*.

Databases. In library usage, *database* is usually an electronic version of a print index. Most of these allow for a computerized search for your topic. Information on databases accessed via the Internet is discussed later in this section.

Periodicals. Periodicals that are of general interest to report writers include magazines such as *Maclean's* and *Business Week*. Newspapers such as *The Globe and Mail* and *The National Post* are reliable secondary sources of information. Many professional journals are published in every field, and the applicable ones should also be reviewed frequently by report writers.

Using Technology for Research

Computerized Library Listings. Today most libraries have automated card catalogues that tell you not only what books are in the library but also what books are in other library systems. The automated card catalogues are frequently on-line, which enables researchers in remote locations, as well as those physically located in the library, to have access to the library's list of holdings. Many college, university, and municipal libraries offer intra-library loan opportunities, giving researchers access to books and publications housed in different locations.

SEARCHING LIBRARY LISTINGS. Computerized card catalogues can be searched in the same manner as the hard copy card catalogue files: by author, by title, and by subject. You can also search for key words and get a listing of all the books that may have information about the key words.

USING CD-ROMs. Much of the information that is available in traditional hard copy format is now available on **CD-ROM** (*CD-ROM* is an acronym for compact *disc—read-only memory*).

Search a CD-ROM using key words for the subject you are interested in to get the most references. Print the list of references, choose the relevant ones, and then review those sources.

The Internet. The **Internet** is the fastest-growing electronic source of information. People from all over the world and in all professions, including governments and educational institutions, can exchange and retrieve information through the Internet. Internet tools that can be used to find information include the World Wide Web, on-line services, Usenet newsgroups, chat services, and listservs. The way to access this information is through the use of Internet software, including Web browsers, e-mail software, and chat tools.

WORLD WIDE WEB. The **World Wide Web** (WWW) is a segment of the Internet that contains electronic documents. Information on the Web is in the form of *Web pages* that contain text, graphics, video, and hypertext to link pages. Hypertext appears as highlighted words on a Web page. Clicking with your mouse on a highlighted word leads you to another Web page that contains related information. Graphics can also include hypertext links to other graphics or text.

ON-LINE SERVICES. **On-line services** are self-contained, fee-based services that provide extensive resources to their members. Examples of these resources are discussion groups, e-mail, on-line banking, news, and software. Many on-line services also provide a gateway to the Internet. Popular on-line services include America Online, CompuServe, Prodigy, and Microsoft Network. Business-oriented on-line services include Nexis and Lexis. These services are highly reliable; businesses pay fees to access them. Additionally, some groups of educational institutions pool their resources to provide research databases as a service to their respective campus communities. Some of these databases offer article abstracts, while others provide full text.

Internet service providers, also called Internet access providers, offer access only to the Internet and the World Wide Web—not to any other services.

INTERNET SOFTWARE. To access resources on the Internet, you must use special Internet software. Software you need includes the following:

- Dial-in software connects your computer to an Internet Service Provider (ISP) or on-line service.
- A Web **browser** enables you to navigate on the World Wide Web and displays Web pages. Popular browsers include Microsoft Internet Explorer and Netscape Navigator.
- E-mail software allows you to create, send, receive, and read electronic mail messages and listserv messages. Listservs are automated services that send out electronic messages on a given topic to a list of recipients.
- Chat tools are used to allow real-time communication between two or more users on the Internet. Most chat tools enable you to type text to another person or group of people, send that message immediately, and receive responses back from them immediately.

SEARCHING THE INTERNET FOR INFORMATION FOR A REPORT. When you are ready to start your search on the Internet, you must visit special Web sites that provide searching capabilities. These sites provide search tools called search engines. Some of the popular search engines are Yahoo!, Alta Vista, Infoseek, Google, Lycos, and Ask Jeeves.

You must give some thought to how you will approach your search on the Internet. Develop a plan to make the best use of the search tools. Such a plan might include the steps in the following chart:

Tips for an Internet Search

1. Identify the topic you want to research.
2. Determine keywords to use for your search. For example, if you are searching for job listings, you might use keywords such as *job listings, employment opportunities,* and *job postings.*
3. Choose a search engine or set of search engines to assist in your search. If necessary, do some research on the search engine and how it works to identify the appropriate Web pages for your search.
4. Be certain that the information is the quality that you need. Not every article on the Internet is research based; it may just be someone's opinion.
5. Develop a plan for using the keywords and the search engines to search for the information you need.
6. Begin searching using your first keyword and first choice for a search engine.
7. Examine the information you receive initially and adjust your plan, perhaps using a different search engine as necessary to obtain the information you seek.
8. Repeat the procedure in step 7 for each keyword that you have identified.

Of Primary Importance

You should include both primarily and secondary sources in your report.

(primary is the correct word, not *primarily*)

The sample screens shown in Figure 10.1 and Figure 10.2 illustrate some steps in a keyword search on the Internet.

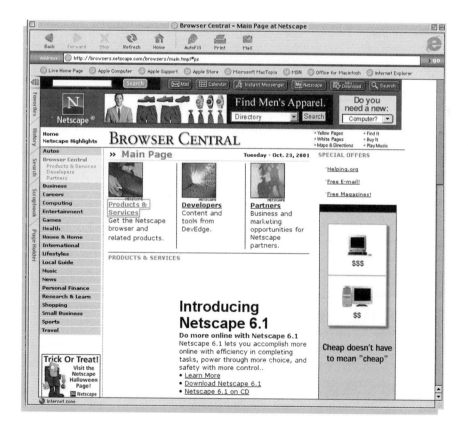

◀ **Figure 10.1 Internet Browser Search Engine**

Thinking Critically.
Explain how a browser allows you to search for information.

Figure 10.2 ▶
**Internet Browser
Keyword Search**

Thinking Critically.
*Where are the results of a
keyword search displayed
within the browser?*

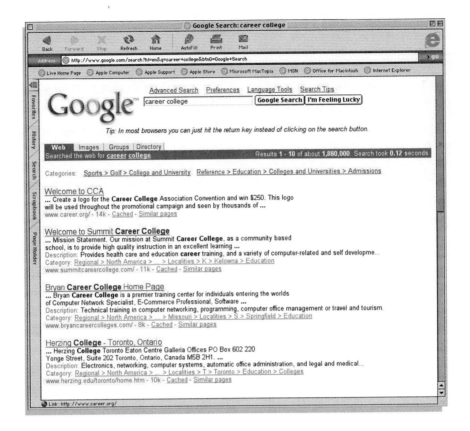

Naturally, anyone doing research must first learn how to find and use books, periodicals, card catalogues, databases, and various indexes, as well as the many sources available through the Internet.

After you know the topic of your report, make a list of key words and key phrases that might give you information on your topic. Also make a list of the sources (books, periodicals, magazines, and so on) that you plan to search for additional information on your topic.

A word of caution about secondary data—always check the date of publication and the source. You don't want to use outdated information, and you want it to be from a credible (reputable and unbiased) source. For example, an article on the benefits of certain medication for allergies published by a drug company that manufactures and sells the medicine may present a slanted view. Remember, just because information appears in print or on the Internet doesn't necessarily make it true.

Use the following checklist to help you determine the reliability of a secondary source of information:

- Does the source provide current information on the topic?
- Is the source reliable?
- Is the information pertinent to your topic?
- Is the author an authority on the subject?
- Does the author identify his or her opinions?

When the information you need is not available from secondary sources, you have to gather the information and collect the data for your report from primary sources.

Primary Sources of Information

A **primary source** is a source from which information or data are obtained firsthand for your particular need. Primary source data may be obtained through surveys (such as questionnaires), personal interviews, or telephone interviews as well as through observation or experimentation. Eyewitness accounts, given by people who experienced the event firsthand, are also considered primary sources.

One problem with many primary sources is the accuracy of the information you receive. For example, many people will not bother to complete and return a questionnaire, so you may not get a representative sampling. Other people may not answer the questions truthfully so your results will not be accurate. Eyewitness accounts also can lead to unpredictable or even inaccurate data. Be sure, when possible, to interview multiple eyewitnesses to corroborate the data provided by each of them.

Surveys are done to identify customer likes and dislikes or needs and wants, to poll patients on the care they received, to learn the level of customer satisfaction, to determine public opinion on a controversial topic or project, and so on. Well-constructed surveys require much time and effort. Always conduct a **pilot test** of a survey. This means that you survey a small group to check the quality of your survey. Analyzing the results from this test group will help you find survey questions that could be misunderstood, are incomplete, or confusing. It can also point out problems if you are performing some statistical analyses on the responses.

Surveys can be conducted by several methods. These may include telephone surveys, questionnaires, interviews, and observations.

Telephone Surveys. To conduct an effective telephone survey, identify yourself and your organization, and state the purpose of the survey at the beginning of each telephone interview. Ask questions that provide data that can be compared or measured. For example, if conducting a survey about the quality of service during a recent visit to a hospital, ask each person to rank the service using a scale from 1 to 10, with 1 being the worst, and 10 being the best. Keep the number of questions manageable so as not to bore or anger the person surveyed. Including an open-ended question near the end of the questionnaire will often provide you with valuable information, as this question gives the participant an opportunity to freely express ideas, observations, and opinions. Record the responses accurately and thank the person at the end of the survey.

Questionnaires. As with any kind of survey, you should determine what types of questions will yield the most helpful answers to get the data you are seeking. The most effective types of questions to yield measurable data include yes-or-no questions, multiple choice questions, ranking according to preference, and rating in order of importance. For example, a questionnaire on a new product line to be sent to current and potential customers might ask the respondent to rank the new products in the order in which they might be purchased.

Interviews. To gather information by interviewing, you should first familiarize yourself with the topic and terminology of your subject and then create a survey using this information. Schedule an appointment for each interview and give an estimate of how much time you need. Begin the interview by explaining its purpose. If you wish to tape record the interview, you must get permission. Ask your questions in an objective manner. At the end of the interview, ask if the interviewee has anything he or she would like to add; there may be relevant information that you did not ask about in your interview. Be sure to take copious notes and ask if the interviewee can be quoted and identified in your report. For example, to gather information about starting a child-care facility at your company, you might interview human resources managers at companies that have these facilities. Your questions could cover topics such as how in-house child-care facilities affect hiring policies, employee absenteeism, turnover rates, and employee morale. Thank the person for his or her time and follow-up with a thank-you letter.

Observations. Objectively observing a practice or procedure can help you determine if the procedure and policy could be improved. Use facts and statistics, not opinions, to present your observations. For example, you might record the number of telephone calls received in a doctor's office during the lunch hour. Your observations may be used to change the policy of closing the office between noon and 1 p.m. for lunch. Your recommendation may be to use staggered lunch hours to better serve the patients.

Documenting Sources

Once you have identified the sources of information for your report, you need to read and review the articles and take notes.

Working Bibliography

As you consult the various reference works pertinent to the topic of your report, you should make a list of the books, periodicals, reports, and other sources to be used as references in the report. This preliminary list of sources is called the **working bibliography**. If you make each entry of the working bibliography on a separate card, the final bibliography of sources actually used will be easier to assemble because you can simply arrange the cards in the appropriate order. You will also find the bibliography cards useful when footnoting material in the report.

Some researchers prefer taking a notebook computer with them to the library and saving the bibliographic information electronically. You can use a word processing program to automatically sequence the bibliography entries each time you input a new one. Set up your working bibliography the same way as you would on index cards. List each resource on a separate page of your document, or in a table, so that you can quickly locate the resource when you put your report together.

A bibliography or source card for a book or reference should contain all the information shown in Figure 10.3. In addition, it is helpful to include for your own use the library's call number for the reference.

When consulting a magazine, newspaper, or other periodical, prepare a bibliography card or entry like the one illustrated in Figure 10.4.

Highlighting. Many times you will have a photocopy of the article or a printout from the computer. Start by reading the article. As you read, underline or highlight the information you might need. This practice will make note taking easier.

Note Taking. Taking notes from your sources helps you pick out the information you can use, organize the information, and retain the information. You should use note cards for taking notes because they are sturdy and can be sorted and re-sorted easily. Alternatively, take notes on a computer, creating separate documents for each source or for each topic.

When you take notes from your reading, follow these tips:

- Identify each source, including the name of the writer, the title of the work, resource name (such as the periodical name), the name of the publisher, and the date published.

- Use a new card for each new source or topic. Normally, summary statements or phrases with page references are sufficient for note cards.

- Copy quotations word for word, exactly as they appear in the source. Enclose each quotation in quotation marks, and list the number of the page from which the quotation was taken.

Cormier, Robin A.

Error-Free Writing: A Lifetime Guide to Flawless Business Writing, Prentice-Hall, Inc., Englewood Cliffs, NJ, 1996

◀ **Figure 10.3 Book Bibliography Card**

Thinking Critically. *What are the elements listed on this bibliography card?*

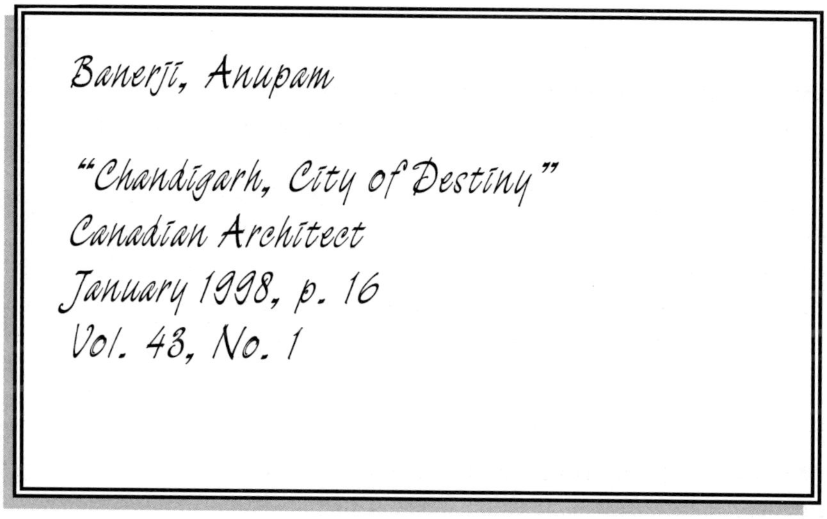

Banerji, Anupam

"Chandigarh, City of Destiny"
Canadian Architect
January 1998, p. 16
Vol. 43, No. 1

◀ **Figure 10.4 Article Bibliography Card**

Thinking Critically. *How do the elements differ on a bibliography card for an article versus a book?*

Citing Electronic Sources

Source	Citation Information
E-mail	Author's name, e-mail address, subject line, date the message was posted
Mailing list	Author's name, e-mail address, subject line, date the message was posted, mailing list address, date the material was accessed
Web site	Author's name, title of the document, last date updated or revised, the address of the Web site, date you accessed the site

As you organize your research, include a brief subject reference at the top of each note card or computer document page; for example, if you are tracing the development of a product, you might identify each card by subject references like "year," "developer," or "site of development."

Documenting Electronic Sources

When you cite material taken from an electronic source, such as an on-line database or a Web page on the Internet, you need to provide enough information so that someone reading your report can access the source. With electronic sources, this means identifying information such as that described in the chart entitled "Citing Electronic Sources."

Plagiarism

Careful note taking will help you guard against plagiarizing material. **Plagiarism** is using someone else's words—exact or paraphrased—or ideas as your own; that is, without giving credit to the original author. **Paraphrasing** is taking someone else's idea and stating it in your own words. When you paraphrase, give credit to the original author.

Credit for exact written words (quotes) and paraphrases can be given to the originator by doing the following:

- Using quotation marks for direct quotes.
- Mentioning the source in your text.
- Documenting the source in a footnote, endnote, or textnote.

Plagiarism can occur in a number of ways. These include the following situations.

- Submitting someone else's work as your own. This is the most blatant type of plagiarism.
- Copying portions of a text without crediting the author.
- Taking ideas, phrases, sentences, or paragraphs from a variety of sources, putting them together and representing them as your own.
- Using footnotes or material quoted in other sources as if they are the results of your own research.

To avoid plagiarism, use the following guidelines.

- Keep accurate and complete notes of all sources.
- Clearly distinguish between your own words and ideas and the words and ideas of others. When writing your report, use quotation marks around

any material that you copy word for word, acknowledge the source of other people's ideas and words, whether these ideas and words are quoted or paraphrased.

- Remember that if you have to ask yourself, "How many words do I have to change to avoid plagiarism?", you are about to plagiarize. Original work comes from original thought, not copied material.

Plagiarism is a serious offence in both the academic and working worlds and can result in legal action. Consult your school's code of conduct for information on how plagiarism is handled at your institution.

Documentation Formats

Several methods of documenting sources are used in the business world. Some organizations have even adopted their own format for documentation. Three of the more widely-used formats appear in *The Chicago Manual of Style, The Publication Manual of the American Psychological Association,* and *The MLA Style Manual* from the Modern Language Association.

Chicago Style. This documentation form is preferred in the humanities, and has been used for years. This style uses consecutive raised (superscript) numbers to identify quoted or paraphrased material throughout the report. (e.g. ...most recent information.[1]) Complete information on the source for each number is either given as a footnote at the bottom of the page or on an endnote page, usually titled "Notes," at the end of the report.

As well as giving source information, footnotes and endnotes can be used to explain part of the report text, or to make cross-references to other parts of the report.

FOOTNOTES. The traditional method of acknowledging sources is to use **footnotes**. Footnotes appear at the bottom of the relevant page and are linked to the text body by using the same superscript number in the text and at the beginning of the footnote. They are numbered consecutively throughout a report, or if the report is long, the numbering may begin again with each chapter or section. Footnotes are single spaced and are divided from the report text by a line 5 centimetres (2 inches) long.

ENDNOTES. The use of superscript numbers and the layout of **endnotes** is the same as for footnotes, except that the endnotes are grouped together at the end of the report. (See Figure 10.5 for a sample Endnotes page.)

In addition to footnotes or a notes page, a **bibliography** is required after the body of the report. The bibliography is an alphabetical listing by author's last name of all the sources used in your report. If a source has no author, it is alphabetized by the first important word in the title of the work. A hanging indentation style (first line of each entry located at the left margin with the second and succeeding lines indented one-half inch), with a blank line between each entry, makes it easier to quickly locate a particular reference.

BIBLIOGRAPHY GUIDELINES. Begin the bibliography on a new page, centre the heading on line 13, and leave two blank lines before the first entry. The left and right margins should be the same as for the rest of the report. Start each entry at the left margin and indent other lines within an entry five or ten spaces.

Figure 10.5 ▶
Sample Endnotes Page

Thinking Critically.
Why does the order of the entries in these endnotes differ from the order of the same entries in the bibliography in Figure 10.6? In what other ways does the set up differ?

Notes	
1. Graham Fraser, "Commissioner Still Waiting for Federal Plan on Language Policy," *The Toronto Star,* 4 October, 2002, A8.	Newspaper article
2. Norma Acoose and Timothy Greyeyes, *First Nations of Canada.* (Vancouver: Whitefeather Press, 2000), 187.	Book, two authors
3. Jack Mintz, "Smoke, Mirrors and Kyoto," 14 October 2002 [on-line Web site]; available from www.canadianbusiness.com/index.asp.	Web site
4. Citizenship & Immigration Canada, *Notes on the Immigration and Refugee Protection Act* (Ottawa: Department of Citizenship & Immigration, 2002), 3.	Government publication
5. "Do Less Harm," *The Globe and Mail,* 4 October, 2002, A16.	Newspaper article, editorial
6. Walter Crinnion, "Environmental Medicine," *Alternative Medicine Review* 5, no. 3 (2002): 790-812.	Journal article
7. Anthony Wilson-Smith, "500 Days to Remake Canadian Politics," *Macleans Magazine,* 7 October, 2002, 4-6.	Magazine article
8. RBC Financial Group, *2003 Annual Report* (Toronto: RBC Financial Group, 2002), 4–5.	Annual report

Single-space the entries with a blank line between entries.

Use the following guidelines to key the bibliography entries.

- List entries in alphabetical order by the author's last name.
- If there are two or more authors, only change the order of the name for the first author. For example,

  Guffey, Mary Ellen, and Brendan Nagle, *Essentials of Business Communication,* Nelson Thomson Learning, Toronto, 2000.

- If there is no author name, alphabetize by title. Disregard "A" or "The" at the beginning of a title in deciding the alphabetic sequence. See Figure 10.6 for an example.
- If there is more than one work by the same author, replace the author's name with a long dash in the second and subsequent entries. List the works alphabetically by title.

  Ondaatje, Michael, *Anil's Ghost,* McClelland & Stewart Ltd., Toronto, 2000.

  ——, In the Skin of a Lion, McClelland & Stewart Ltd., Toronto, 1987.

Content and Punctuation for Footnotes and Endnotes	
Source	**Citation Information**
Book	Superscript number Author's name. *Book Title.* ed. if applicable (Place of publication, Publisher, year) page reference. **[1]Ron Cameron. *Acting Skills for Life.* 2nd ed. (Toronto: Simon & Pierre, 1991) 202.**
Book with editor/s	**[5]Carol Shields and Marjorie Anderson, eds. *Dropped Threads.* (Toronto: Vintage Canada, 2001) 199–122.**
Newspaper article	Superscript number Author's name (or, if no author's name is given, title of the article), "Article title," *Newspaper name,* date: page number. **[9]Graham Fraser, "Commissioner Still Waiting for Federal Plan on Language Policy," *The Toronto Star,* 4 October 2002: A8.**
Cross-reference	Superscript number Cross-reference information with page number. **[12]See Names of Pan-Canadian Significance on page 4.**

- Do not include page numbers in bibliographic entries unless the material cited is part of a larger work. When this occurs, indicate the range of pages on which the material appears. For example,

Buscemi, Santi V., Albert H. Nicolai, Richard Strugala, and Richard Monaghan, *The Basics—A Rhetoric and Handbook,* McGraw-Hill Ryerson Limited, Toronto, 1996, pp. 315–319.

See Figure 10.6 for a sample bibliography.

APA Style. The American Psychological Association (APA) style gives reference information using **textnotes**—that is, the notes immediately follow the quote or paraphrased material in the body of your report. APA style is heavily used in social science and education fields. This style emphasizes the date of publication because in these fields it is important that the information be current. The author's name, the year of publication, and the page numbers are separated by commas and given in parentheses in the text. (e.g. ...most recent information (Masters, 2000, p. 148)). If the author's name is given as part of the quote or paraphrased material, it does not need to be included again in the parentheses. To find a referenced work, the reader would consult the References section at the back of the report and look for the author's name.

A *References* section is the same as the bibliography in *The Chicago Manual of Style.* The entries are arranged in alphabetical order by author's last name, and a hanging indentation style is used for ease of locating information quickly.

For additional information on APA style, see the most recent edition of the *Publication Manual of the American Psychological Association.* Find more information on the APA's Web site: **http://www.apastyle.org/**.

Figure 10.6 ▶
Sample Bibliography

Thinking Critically.
Bibliography entries are listed in alphabetical order. Is the entry for The Globe and Mail *out of order? If not, why not?*

Bibliography	
Acoose, Norma and Timothy Greyeyes. *First Nations of Canada.* 2000. Vancouver: Whitefeather Press.	Book, two authors
Crinnion, Walter J. 2002. "Environmental Medicine." *Alternative Medicine Review* 5, 3:790–812.	Journal article, with volume and issue numbers
Fraser, Graham. 2002. "Commissioner Still Waiting for Federal Plan on Language Policy." *The Toronto Star,* 4 October, A8.	Newspaper article
The Globe and Mail. 2002. "Do Less Harm." 4 October 2002, A16.	Newspaper article, editorial
Mintz, Jack. 2002. "Smoke, Mirrors and Kyoto," 14 October. [on-line Web site]. Available from www.canadianbusiness.com/index.asp.	Web site
Notes on the Immigration and Refugee Protection Act. 2002. Citizenship and Immigration Canada. Ottawa: Department of Citizenship & Immigration, 3.	Government publication
RBC Financial Group. 2004. *2003 Annual Report.* Toronto: RBC Financial Group.	Annual report
Wilson-Smith, Anthony. 2002. "500 Days to Remake Canadian Politics." *Macleans Magazine,* 7 October, 4–6.	Magazine article

MLA Style. The MLA style was developed by the Modern Language Association and is heavily used in the humanities area. MLA style also uses a "*textnotes. number*" format to facilitate locating the exact information. It is similar to APA style in many ways, but here the textnotes emphasize the page number to facilitate finding the exact information. The author's last name and the page number appear in parentheses immediately following the quoted or

Documentation Overview		
Format	**Type of Notes and Inclusion Method in Report Body**	**Title for List of Referenced Material**
Chicago	Footnotes or Endnotes Raised (superscript) numbers Footnotes at bottom of relevant page Endnotes at end of the report	Bibliography
APA	Textnotes In text of the report with (Name, year, page number)	References
MLA	Textnotes In text of the report with (Name page number)	Works Cited

paraphrased material. (e.g. ... most recent information (Masters 148)). One difference is that no comma is used to separate the author's name and the page number.

The complete list of sources used in an MLA paper is given at the end of the paper. This list is titled Works Cited and is similar to the bibliography used in *The Chicago Manual of Style*. The entries are double-spaced and arranged in alphabetical order by the author's last name. A hanging indentation style makes it easy to locate a specific source quickly.

For detailed information on the MLA style, see the most recent edition of the *MLA Handbook for Writers of Research Papers*. Find more information on the MLA's Web site: **http://www.mla.org/.**

Protecting Your Report

Technology has made keyboarding reports much easier and faster. However, some caution should be exercised to prevent loss of text, especially when working with long documents. Most students know someone who has worked hours on a report only to lose it because of technical difficulties or sudden power outages. Losing an entire document, however, is preventable. Here are some tips that will help you protect your document.

Protecting Your Document

1. Save your document frequently. In addition to manually saving your work, most word processing software includes a feature that automatically backs up or saves your document at regular intervals. Make sure that this feature is operating and that the time set between automatic backups is reasonable.

2. Save your document in at least two places—on the hard drive and on a separate backup disk.

3. Print your document at intervals. It is much easier to re-enter information from a printout than to compose it again.

4. Complete and print out your document at least one day before the deadline to allow for delays caused by technical difficulties such as printer problems.

Review of Key Terms

1. Explain how an *informative report* differs from an *analytical report*, giving examples of each type.
2. Why is a *working bibliography* an important part of a report? What information should be included in a bibliographic entry?

Practical Application

1. Identify the primary and secondary sources you would use to gather information on the following topics:
    a. electronic banking
    b. business ethics
    c. cross-cultural communication
    d. electronic resumés
2. Choose a topic that interests you, and find three different sources of information on your topic, for example, a book, a periodical, and an Internet source. Photocopy or print the articles or pertinent pages, and make source cards for each one. Then, take notes on what you read, paraphrasing the information you might use in a report.
3. Your team will conduct an Internet search on purchasing new computers for your company. Begin by making a list of keywords you might use. Print several articles. Highlight important information. Once your team has read the articles and discussed the merits of each computer, write a memo to your instructor, proposing which computer would better serve the needs of the company. Consider the computer's capability, its performance record, and cost. Turn in all notes, keywords used, and highlighted articles along with your memo.

TEAMWORK

Editing Practice

Editors' Alert. Find the incorrect word or words in each sentence and write the correct substitution.

1. Marcy told the members that she wood not except any additional orders after the deadline.
2. Please let me no weather their is a carrying case four the projection devise.
3. The presentor asked the staff to complete there vacation request forms buy too o'clock tomorrow.
4. Since there payment is now for months passed due, a penalty will be imposed.
5. The fifth addition of the book will be published early next year.

Discussion Points

1. What is the difference between primary and secondary sources? What are some methods to use for gathering primary data? How can you be sure a secondary source is reliable?

2. If you incorporated someone else's ideas into your report, are you required to provide the source of that information? What are the consequences of plagiarizing information in business? How can you avoid plagiarism?

▶ **Key Terms**

▶ memorandum report

▶ paragraph format

▶ outline format

▶ table format

Writing Informal Reports

Information is the oxygen of the modern age. It seeps through the walls topped by barbed wire, it wafts across the electrified borders.

—Ronald Reagan, 40th President of the United States of America

In the business world, the report is probably the primary method for providing information. This information is intended to help executives, supervisors, managers, department heads, and others to understand their roles and perform their duties more effectively. Report information is vital in improving the effectiveness of decision making. Therefore, anyone who wishes to succeed in today's business world must be able to gather information and prepare reports.

A report may be given orally, in writing, or both. Important information in an oral report may be quickly forgotten, especially statistical data. Even a forceful oral report will grow weaker with each passing day, whereas a written report can be referred to again and again. Each reading of the report reinforces the message conveyed in the report and the report provides a precise and permanent record. A written report that is also delivered orally will have increased impact.

Writing Principles

Before you can write informal reports of the highest quality, you need to study, think about, and apply the following principles.

Be Clear, Complete, Correct, and Concise

As you know, concise writing should still be complete writing. To be concise, you must say everything that needs to be said, but you must say it in the fewest possible words.

You are also well aware that your writing must be clear and complete. You would not write a "fuzzy" sentence like this:

Tom Bennett told Mr. Delgado about the construction delays at the industrial park, and he said he would have the report on his desk by Wednesday.

Instead, you would write a clear, complete message, such as this one:

Tom Bennet told Mr. Delgado that he would have the report on the construction delays at the industrial park on Mr. Delgado's desk on Wednesday, October 20, 20—.

All reports must be correct in every detail. Perhaps we should use the stronger term *accurate*, because any information important enough to be reported must be more than substantially correct; it must be completely accurate. For example, if you are asked to report the number of free-sample requests that come in on a given day, you must be sure that you give an exact, not an approximate, count.

Wording

The wording of reports differs from that of letters. A letter is designed to do more than convey a message, for its accompanying purpose is often to win new customers or clients for the company and to retain old ones. Therefore, the tone of a letter is warm and friendly. A report, on the other hand, is a straightforward, factual presentation—and it should be worded as such.

As an illustration, read the following opening paragraph of a letter answering a request for information about your company's free tuition program for employees.

In response to your April 10 request, we are pleased to tell you that we do provide free tuition for employees taking work-related courses at local schools under the following circumstances: [At this point, you would itemize and explain the circumstances under which your company pays the tuition for its employees.]

Now, note how the wording changes when the same information is given in a report.

Employees taking work-related courses at local schools will be reimbursed for tuition when the following requirements have been met:

1. The course has been approved in advance by the employee's supervisor.
2. The employee earns a grade of B or better.
3. The employee has been with the company for one year or more.

Style of Informal Reports

In Chapter 8 you learned how to use a memorandum as a means of corresponding with other employees within an organization. The same memorandum form is used for writing informal reports, hence the name **memorandum report**.

The memorandum report begins with the same information contained in the memorandum format that you learned to use for interoffice correspondence.

MEMO TO:

FROM:

DATE:

SUBJECT:

Whether you use this format exactly as it is or adapt it will depend upon the report style preferred by the company where you work.

File Copies

When you write an informal report, be sure to make a copy for your own files. At least keep a copy on disk. Anything important enough to be put in writing is important enough to be retained. You or someone else may need some of the information in the report at some time in the future.

Presentation Formats

How brief or how detailed should your informal report be? Should you give the requested information in a single paragraph? Should you present the information in outline form? Should you tabulate the information?

Because you are preparing the report, you are the one who must answer these questions. Only you are close enough to the situation to know why the report was requested, to project the probable uses of the information, and so on. In order to make a wise decision about the form your report should take, you must be familiar with the different presentation formats and their uses.

Paragraph Format

If the report is quite short, you may decide to simply write your information in **paragraph format**. Using headings as well as paragraphs, especially if your report discusses several points, can be an effective way of presenting material and making it easier for the reader to immediately grasp the main points. See Figure 10.7 for an illustration of a report which uses paragraphs and headings.

Outline (List) Format

If, for example, you are reporting on overtime statistics, set out the information in **outline format** as follows.

Information regarding overtime in the Accounting Department during March, 20— is as follows:

1. Total employees in department: 35
2. Total hours of overtime: 15
3. Employees working overtime: 7 (20 per cent)

   Mark Petrone, 2 hours
   Cynthia Rogers, 2 hours
   Ruth Stein, 2 hours
   Kenneth Ulrich, 1 hour
   Alicia Velez, 3 hours
   Robert Williams, 4 hours
   Steven Wimmer, 1 hour

Table Format

In some cases, a table is the most effective way to present information. The advantage of a tabulated presentation is that the reader can more easily see the total situation at a glance without wading through a great many words. Obviously, the decision to tabulate should be influenced by the amount and the kind of information to be included and also by the writer's projection regarding the likely uses of the information. In **table format**, the above overtime information would be presented in the following way.

PRAIRIE COLLEGE

M E M O R A N D U M

To: Mohamed Al-Sabah
          Chair, Board of Governors
From: Carlyle Thomas
          Team Leader, Curriculum Development
Date: July 18, 2001
Re: **Progress Report—Customer Service Curriculum**

TERMS OF REFERENCE

On May 1, 2003, you requested that our Curriculum Development Team
investigate the possibility of including customer service training in the Prairie
College curriculum. Our team was asked to make recommendations concerning the appropriate content and placement of this training in all programs
which deal with customer contact, and in particular those which have a service
orientation.

PLAN OF ACTION

The following is our action list, with time lines for completion:
*   Visits to local employers (August 31, 2003)
*   Review of customer service curriculum from Northern Lights College
     and the Maritimes Institute (August 31, 2003)
*   Review of Prairie College curriculum (August 31, 2003)
*   Drafting recommendations (October 15, 2003)

ACHIEVEMENTS TO DATE

We have visited six local employers of graduates from service-oriented
programs, and three local employers of graduates from general business
programs.

Review of curriculum from Northern Lights College is under way. We are
awaiting receipt of curriculum from Maritimes Institute.

Meetings have been held with representatives from the School of Business
and the School of Applied Arts to review their curriculum and discuss the
inclusion of customer service content. These two Schools will be finalizing
their recommendations for us by the end of this month. A meeting with the
School of Health Sciences is scheduled for July 24.

FUTURE ACTION

We anticipate completing our report by October 30 and requesting permission
to present it at the Board's November meeting.

Thinking Critically. Why
did the writer use bullets
under "Plan of Action"?

Accounting Department Overtime
Month of March, 20–

Employee	Hours	Reason
Petrone, Mark	2	To complete January billing
Rogers, Cynthia	2	To prepare for business trip
Stein, Ruth	2	To prepare expense statement
Ulrich, Kenneth	1	To complete checking cost estimates
Velez, Alicia	3	To prepare cost analysis
Williams, Robert	4	To analyze travel expenses
Wimmer, Steven	1	To complete January billing

Total employees: 35
Overtime hours: 15
Total employees working overtime: 7
Per cent of employees working overtime: 20

Review of Key Terms

1. How is a *memorandum report* similar to a standard memo? How is it different?

2. Briefly describe *paragraph format, outline format,* and *table format* for a report.

Practical Application

1. Your supervisor, Ms. Hamida Ghafour, wants to purchase a two-drawer, metal filing cabinet for her office. She asks you to check the prices and features of the cabinets available at your local Business World store. You obtain the following information. The Economy File has a lock, accommodates letter-size files, and costs $69.95. There is no warranty and it only comes in black. The Professional Filer is available in either legal or letter size, a lock is optional, and the cabinet comes in sand, grey, or black. It has a 10-year parts warranty. It costs $129 for the letter size and $139 for the legal size. The Versatile Cabinet accepts both letter- and legal-size files, comes in black or dark green, and has a lock. There is no warranty and it costs $99.95. The General File Cabinet costs $89.95, has a lock, comes in black or sand, and accommodates letter-size files. There is no warranty.

   Organize this information into a concise, easy-to-read memorandum to submit to Ms. Ghafour.

2. Select two stocks or bonds that are listed in the stock market report of your local newspaper. From the information that is provided in the newspaper, write an informal report about the status of these two securities during the past five days. Address the report to your instructor.

3. Prepare a report in table format. The table will be a report of students in your team. List the names of your team members and choose four other categories of information on each team member.

TEAMWORK

Editing Practice

Spelling Alert! Can you find any spelling or homonym errors in the following excerpt from a magazine's circulation department report? If possible, use the spell-check and thesaurus features on a word processing program to assist you.

Newsstand sales plus subscription sales of the magazine acceded 1.5 million copies in the month of December. Clearly, the principle reasons for this sharp increase in sales is that our radio television advertising in November and December was well planned. In fact, we expect sales of our February addition to reach 1.6 million copies; sales should than level off in the months of March and April and, as usual, decrease over the summer months.

Discussion Point

The Student Association at George Brown College in Toronto wishes to build a student centre. The association executive has conducted a survey with students at each campus of the college concerning a possible location for this centre and the main functions the students wish it to perform. What type of report should the Student Association prepare for the Board of Governors of the college? Other than examining the situation, what should this report do?

Writing Formal Reports

Knowledge is the most democratic source of power.

—Alvin Toffler, author

▶ **Key Terms**

▶ formal business reports
▶ purpose
▶ scope
▶ title page
▶ table of contents
▶ introduction
▶ statement of purpose
▶ procedures
▶ summary
▶ body of the report
▶ conclusions
▶ recommendations
▶ supplementary material
▶ illustrations
▶ appendix
▶ bibliography
▶ letter or memo of transmittal

Formal business reports, in addition to being longer than informal memorandum reports, are usually concerned with more complex problems or questions necessitating more investigation, analysis, research, and documentation. Some typical formal report subjects might be an analysis of the methods of marketing a company's products; a study to determine how to modernize a particular aspect of a business, such as a study to determine which type of computer accounting and billing system to install; or an experiment to determine how to improve the quality control of a product.

Writing a formal business report may require weeks or even months of extensive research related to the report topic. The completed report could contain anywhere from several pages to more than a hundred pages. Regardless of its length, however, a formal report must be accurately documented and well written, because often the report is the basis upon which a company makes vital decisions.

Preparing to Write a Formal Report

Not all reports look alike. There are some variations in the style and form used in formal reports. These variations are usually determined by the nature of the subject being investigated. For example, a technical report that specifies the requirements for manufacturing computer components may be organized in outline form with very little text. Similarly, the reports of chemists, engineers, and other scientists are likely to include many tables, charts, and graphs, with a relatively small amount of narrative interpretation. On the other hand, many business reports are mainly narrative, possibly with some tabular material. Despite this variation in the style and form, most formal reports include these main sections:

Title Page
Table of Contents
Introduction
Summary (often called an Executive Summary in business reports)
Body of the Report
Conclusions and Recommendations
Supplementary Material

Before beginning to write a formal report, you must first determine the purpose and the scope of the report. To make this determination, you must gather reliable facts, assemble and analyze those facts, draw conclusions from the analysis, and make recommendations that are reasonable in view of company needs.

Defining Purpose and Scope

The **purpose** of the report is the reason it is being written. Why is the report being written? The answer to this question should appear in the introduction of the report. For example, in a study to determine whether a company should buy notebook computers for each sales representative to submit orders from the field, to communicate with head office, and to maintain current inventory figures and prices, the purpose of the report might be stated as follows:

1. To determine the benefits of providing notebook computers to sales representatives.

2. To determine the cost of providing notebook computers to sales representatives.

3. To determine if the benefits will justify the costs.

The **scope** of a report determines the extensiveness of the research; that is, the scope specifies boundaries that keep the research within reason.

A report writer must avoid selecting a topic that is too large in scope to be handled effectively. The experienced report writer, therefore, clearly defines the scope of the report and sets reasonable boundaries. For example, think how difficult it would be to do research involving "Computer Uses by Office Personnel." This topic is much too broad in scope to be treated in one report, if it could be treated at all. The topic needs to be limited to a more specific group. A revised title that would be more practical might read "Computer Uses by Accountants at Royal Sales and Service."

Organizing the Report

After all the material related to the topic has been collected and studied, you can begin to organize the report. At this time, your notes should be revised, sorted by topic, and tentatively organized into a logical sequence for the report.

Outline

Using organized notes as a guide, create an outline to serve as the structure, or framework, of the report. The outline should be kept as simple as possible. While determining the outline, keep in mind the kinds of topic headings the report requires. If outline entries are carefully thought out, many of them can be used as topic headings in the final report.

Headings

Most books, articles, and business reports use headings to indicate the organization of the material. Headings of equivalent weight should be formatted alike. For example, the main divisions of an article, a report, or a chapter in a book may be centred, and the subdivisions of each main heading may be typed as paragraph headings. When there are more than two divisions, however, the following arrangement of headings (excluding the report title) can be used:

CENTRED FIRST-ORDER HEADING

Side Second-Order Heading

Run-In Third-Order Heading. Text follows on the same line...

If the report writer is consistent in the use of headings, the reader will better understand the report's organization and content. Consistency should be observed in the wording as well as in the style of the headings. In general, a topic form is preferred to a sentence form. For example, "How to Write Reports" is preferable to "This Is How to Write Reports." For detailed suggestions on headings, consult a reference such as *The Gregg Reference Manual.*

Writing the Report

There are considerable differences between the informal writing style of business letters and memorandums and the writing style commonly found in formal reports. These differences are examined in the following discussion.

Writing Style

Long business reports are important documents upon which management bases many of its high-level decisions. Consequently, such reports tend to be written in a serious, formal style, usually in the third person. The impersonal style helps the writer avoid interjecting a personal tone that might weaken a report by making it seem merely a statement of one person's opinions and beliefs. The more the writer can de-emphasize the *I* and cite facts to support the evaluation, the more objective and more persuasive the report will be.

In the following example the writer carefully avoids any expressions that may imply that the evaluations are based on personal opinions instead of sound reasons and facts.

The evidence revealed by this survey indicates that the modified block style of letter takes 10 per cent more keyboarding time than the block style.

Use of the block letter style would be appropriate for New Visions Entertainment, Ltd., because the style has the modern look of simplicity and is also faster and easier to type.

Three of the five departments studied use mixed punctuation; however, adoption of open punctuation would have the following advantages: [Explanation of those advantages would follow.]

The same impersonal writing style illustrated above should characterize every section of the report. Remember: Making it possible for the reader to reason from the facts presented is an important factor in the success of any business report.

Title Page

The **title page** usually includes the complete title of the report, the name and title of the author, the name and title of the person for whom the report is prepared, and the date the report is submitted. These items should be attractively arranged on the page. A typical title page is shown in Figure 10.8.

Table of Contents

The **table of contents** is prepared after the report has been completed. It should start at the top of a new page and list in sequence each separate part of the report. See Figure 10.9 for an example.

Figure 10.8 ▶
Title Page of a Report

Thinking Critically.
What are the elements listed on this title page?

THE FEASIBILITY OF ESTABLISHING AN
INTERNATIONAL BUSINESS CENTRE
AT
EASTERN UNIVERSITY

Prepared by

Douglas Ling
Director of Administrative Services

Submitted to

Lynn Vernon
President

June 10, 20—

◀ **Figure 10.9** ▶
**Table of Contents
Page of a Report**

Thinking Critically.
Name the elements on this table of contents. Why are leader dots used?

CONTENTS

Introduction

The **introduction** tells the reader why the report was written, what the scope of the report is, and how the data were gathered.

Suppose that Lynn Vernon, president of Easter University, has assigned Douglas Ling, the director of administrative services, to investigate the feasibility of establishing an international business centre as a way to improve the university's service to the corporate business world. In the introduction to the report, Mr. Ling would include the purpose and scope of the report, as well as a description of the procedures followed to collect and analyze the data presented in the report.

Statement of Purpose. In a **statement of purpose** the writer should first state the issue that the report addresses—the need to improve the handling of correspondence as well as to cut costs. Next, the writer should list the objectives of the report as in the following example:

This report was prepared at the request of Ms. Lynn Vernon, president of Eastern University. The report addresses the need to improve service to the corporate business world. The purposes of the report are to determine:

1. the need for an international business centre;
2. the functions of an international business centre;
3. the resources involved in the initial start-up of the centre;
4. the proposed budget of the centre;
5. a potential list of corporations that would benefit from the services provided.

Scope or Limitations. A brief statement of the scope of the investigation may be included in the introduction. The scope may include limitations.

This investigation is limited to the corporate community within the Province of Nova Scotia.

Procedures. The introductory section of the report should describe the research procedures. **Procedures** are the methods that were used to collect and analyze the data. Here is an example:

Information for this report was collected through telephone interviews with corporate chief executive officers of companies in Nova Scotia. The interview questions are in Appendix B of this report.

A survey was mailed to each Chamber of Commerce in Nova Scotia. The survey instrument appears in the report as Appendix C.

The consulting firm of Fraser & McKenzie prepared a budget that includes start-up costs.

Summary

The **summary**, often called an *executive summary* in business reports, is a brief review of the report.

It is placed early in the report, usually following the introduction. The summary may range from one paragraph to several pages, depending on the amount of material covered. The following example is the opening paragraph of the summary of the study to determine the feasibility of establishing an international business centre as a way to improve the university's service to the corporate business world.

This study recommends that an international business centre be established at Halifax Campus of Eastern University, and demonstrates that such a centre would serve the corporate community in Nova Scotia. The specific data gathered during this investigation resulted in the following conclusions that led to the above recommendation:

- A distinctive need for an international business centre exists in Nova Scotia.
- Three major functions of an international business centre were determined.
- The major resources involved in the initial start-up of the centre were identified.
- A proposed budget for the centre has been projected for a five-year time period.
- A potential list of corporations that would benefit from the services provided has been identified.

Body

The **body of the report** is the actual text of the report. In this section the writer tells what research was done, how it was done, and what the writer found. For example, in the report on the international business center at Eastern University, the body of the report would include the following:

- An analysis of responses to the telephone interviews with corporate officers.
- The results of the surveys mailed to each Chamber of Commerce.
- A list of the major resources involved in the start-up of the centre.
- A justification for the proposed five-year budget.
- A discussion of the categories of businesses that would benefit from the services provided.

Writing the body of the report should present few difficulties if the writer follows a carefully prepared outline and has detailed notes. The writer should use accurate, verifiable facts and present them in a clear, concise manner. The suggestions given in Chapter 7 for forceful, clear writing apply also to writing reports.

Figure 10.10 shows the first page of the body of the report investigating the feasibility of an international business centre at Eastern University.

Conclusions and Recommendations

This section can easily be the most important one in any report, for it is here that the real results of the report appear. The writer's conclusions tell the busy executive, on the basis of the most reliable data available, "Here is what the report tells us."

Personal observations should be kept to a minimum—**conclusions** should be drawn only from the facts. In the light of the conclusions and from experience with the company, the writer can make **recommendations**. As a guide to making worthwhile recommendations, the writer should refer back to the listed purposes of the report. As a rule, there should be at least one recommendation for each stated purpose.

By referring to the purposes stated in the introduction of the report on the feasibility of an international business center at Eastern University, the writer might include the following conclusions and recommendations.

From the analysis of the data gathered in this study, the following conclusions are drawn:

◀ Figure 10.10
Report Body, Sample
Page 1

Thinking Critically. Why
is there an indent at the
beginning of each para-
graph?

THE FEASIBILITY OF ESTABLISHING AN
INTERNATIONAL BUSINESS CENTRE AT EASTERN
UNIVERSITY
(*Report Heading*)

INTRODUCTION
(*Section Heading*)

This report was prepared at the request of Lynn Vernon, president of Eastern University. The report addresses the need to improve the service to the corporate business world.

Statement of Purpose (*Side Heading*)

The purposes of the report are:

1. To determine the need for an international business centre.
2. To determine the functions of an international business centre.
3. To determine the resources involved in the initial start-up of the centre.
4. To determine the proposed budget of the centre.
5. To determine a potential list of corporations that would benefit from the services provided.

Scope

The investigation is limited to the corporate community within a 200-km radius of Eastern University's main campus in

---

1. An international business centre would be an asset to the Nova Scotia business community.

2. The major function would be to facilitate business transactions between the Nova Scotia business community and international markets.

3. The resources involved in the initial start-up include office space with utilities, computer equipment with Internet access, typical office expenses, and a three-person staff.

4. The proposed budget is accurate and comprehensive.

5. Corporate personnel in Nova Scotia are eager to use the international business centre.

With these conclusions in mind, the following actions are recommended:

1. Eastern University to establish an international business centre to be operational by January 1, which will require approval of the university's Board of Trustees.

2. Staff members to be employed as soon as feasible to begin establishing contacts with the corporations and contacts in the international markets.

3. Expenditure approvals to be initiated to acquire and equip an office for the international business centre.

4. Adopt the proposed budget and establish financial liaisons and the necessary bank accounts.

5. Establish an Advisory Committee for the International Business Centre with representatives from the corporate community.

Figure 10.11 illustrates how the conclusions could be formatted.

Figure 10.11 ▶
Report Body,
Conclusion Page

Thinking Critically. *Why has the writer numbered the conclusions? Why do the numbers begin at 1. again for the Recommendations?*

10.

other business communities across Canada could benefit from this initiative, those in the specified area in eastern Canada would be the main partners.

CONCLUSIONS AND RECOMMENDATIONS

From an analysis of the data gathered in this study, the following conclusions are drawn:

1. An international business centre would be an asset to the specified business community in Eastern Canada.

2. The major function would be to facilitate business transactions between this business community and international markets.

3. The resources involved in the initial start-up include office space with utilites, computer equipment with Internet access, typical office expenses, and a three-person staff.

4. The proposed budget is accurate and comprehensive.

5. Corporate personnel in the identified geographic area are eager to use the international business centre.

With these conclusions in mind, the following actions are recommended:

1. Eastern University to establish an international business centre to be operational by January 1, 20xx, which will require approval of the university's Board of Governors.

Supplementary Material

Supplementary material, which is given after the conclusions and recommendations, provides substantiating data for the report. One or all of the features discussed below may be included.

Illustrations. A formal report can often be enhanced by including graphics or **illustrations.** When should graphic displays be used to supplement the material in your report? Consider using graphics when any or all of the following situations occur:

1. The information—ideas, facts, or figures—being presented is complex, and illustrations will help simplify it.
2. Visuals will reinforce the logic of your conclusions and recommendations.
3. You are comparing or contrasting two sets of data, or you are analyzing trends.
4. Statements need to be documented, and tables and other displays will provide the necessary information.

What kinds of graphic or visual displays should be included? Your selection depends on the information you are presenting and your purpose in presenting this information. The possibilities include:

1. Tables—to provide a visible comparison of two or more sets of data and ready access to information.
2. Bar Graphs—to depict relationships between fixed groups of data or to compare or contrast two sets of data.
3. Line Graphs—to illustrate trends or how sets of data have changed over a period of time.
4. Pie Charts—to show the relationships between parts and a whole.
5. Diagrams, Flowcharts, Organizational Charts—to simplify complex relationships or operations.
6. Photographs—to document information or statements.

Refer to Figure 10.12 for some examples of illustrations used to present data in a report. How graphic displays are prepared varies from company to company. Use of graphics software is now the most common method of producing this material. Several excellent programs that produce sophisticated, professional-looking graphic displays are available. In a large organization, you may have specialists on staff to do this work, or an agency may be employed if the report is extremely important.

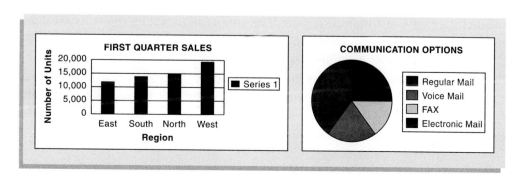

◀ **Figure 10.12
Bar Graph and Pie
Chart**

Thinking Critically.
*What function do bar
graphs and pie charts
serve in a report?*

When illustrations are included in the body of the report, leave a generous amount of white space around them. This will increase the impact of your illustrations and make them easier to view.

Appendix.   The **appendix** consists mainly of supporting information to back up the material in the body of the report. Long tables, charts, photographs, questionnaires, letters, and drawings are usually placed in this section. By including such material at the end of the report, you keep the body of the report free of the kind of detail that makes reading difficult.

Bibliography.   The **bibliography** is an alphabetic listing of all the references used in the report. Bibliographic entries are listed in alphabetic order by author. Forms for book and periodical entries are shown in the following examples.

Books

Brown, Frieda F., *International Markets,* Bear Publishing Company, Toronto, 20—.

Lane, S.C., *Exporting for Profit,* Hanley Book Company, Vancouver, 20—.

Periodicals

Stevens, Zachary, "International Banking and Exporting," *Export Entrepreneur* Vol. 5, No. 2 (20—), pp. 69–84.

Wong, A.K., "Cutting International Red Tape," *The Exporter* Vol. 4, No. 2 (20—), pp. 24–38.

Refer to Section 10.1 for more information on bibliographic entries.

Letter or Memo of Transmittal

A short **letter or memo of transmittal** is composed after the report has been completed. It accompanies the report and documents that you have completed the report and are submitting it to the person or persons addressed in the letter or memo. A memorandum is usually used when the report is directed to a person within the organization (see Figure 10.13), and a letter is used when the report is prepared for someone outside the organization. The transmittal memo or letter usually contains such information as:

- A reference to the person who authorized the report.
- A brief statement of the general purpose of the report.
- Appropriate statements of appreciation or acknowledgment.

Mechanics of Report Writing

An immaculate physical appearance, expert placement, and careful attention to the mechanics of English, spelling, and punctuation emphasize the importance of the finished report. For this reason, mechanics, as well as organization and writing style, are important in preparing the report.

All the mechanics of English, spelling, and punctuation discussed in earlier chapters apply to report writing. In addition, you should apply the six Cs of editing and the revision, proof-reading, and editing skills learned in Chapter 7. Some suggestions for setting up a report are also necessary, and they are presented in the following paragraphs.

◀ Figure 10.13
Transmittal Memo

Thinking Critically. Why
is a transmittal memo
used here, rather than a
letter?

EASTERN UNIVERSITY

To: Ms. Lynn Vernon, President

From: Douglas Ling, Director of Administrative Services

Date: June 10, 20--

Re: **Attached Report on the Feasibility of Establishing an
             International Business Centre**

On April 30, 20--, you authorized a feasibility study concerning the possible
establishment of an international business centre. This study is now complete.
The results of the study, together with my conclusions and recommendations,
are contained in the attached report.

Valuable assistance was provided by Monica Alvarez, especially in carrying out
the surveys and interviews.

I would be pleased to discuss the report with you at your convenience.

                              DL

mee
Attachment

Paragraphing

Use common sense and show variety in paragraphing; try to avoid too many
long and too many short paragraphs. Keep in mind that the topic sentence,
telling what the paragraph is about, frequently comes first. Also, the closing
sentence is often used to summarize the meaning of the paragraph.

Nonparallel	Parallel
Writing the Introduction	Writing the Introduction
The Body	Writing the Body
How to Write the Closing	Writing the Closing

Headings

Be generous in using headings. Take care to leave plenty of white space around major headings, tables, and other display elements. Be sure that all headings of the same value within a section are parallel in wording. For example:

Notes

Use footnotes or endnotes to give credit when citing the ideas of others, either verbatim or modified. A footnote is placed at the bottom of the page carrying the footnoted item; endnotes are grouped together and listed at the end of the report. Number notes consecutively, whether they appear at the bottom of each footnoted page or are grouped at the end of the report. Since notes vary in style, it is advisable to consult the company's reference manual or a standard reference manual. Refer to Section 10.1 for further information on footnotes and endnotes.

Graphics

Select carefully any tables, charts, diagrams, photographs, drawings, and other illustrated materials used to supplement the writing. To promote better understanding of the contents, choose the items that contribute most to the report. Eliminate items that are not pertinent.

Format

Observe these rules of good manuscript form:

1. Print reports on standard letter-size paper. Whether you print on one side of the sheet only, or on both sides, will depend on company policy.

2. Use double spacing except for long quotations (usually three or more lines), for which single spacing is preferred.

3. Leave ample margins. Depending on how the report will be bound, leave extra space in that particular margin. For example, most reports are bound at the left, so the left margin should be generous. Commonly accepted margins are:

    Left margin: 1 1/2 inches to provide for side binding.

    Other margins: 1 inch.

    First page only: 2-inch top margin when the page contains the title.

4. Traditionally, the first page is not numbered when it contains the title. All other pages, beginning with page 2, should be numbered.

5. Always prepare at least one file copy.

6. Follow this pattern for any material presented in outline form:

    I.
        A.
            1.
                a.
                    (1)
                        (a)

Binding

Bind the report attractively. Many types of binding, from the single staple to an elaborate sewn binding, can be used. Reports that are subject to frequent, rigorous use should be placed inside a special hardback report folder for protection.

Review of Key Terms

1. How do you determine the *purpose* and *scope* of a formal report?
2. What kind of information goes in an *appendix* of a formal report?
3. What would you put in a *bibliography* of a formal report?

Practical Application

1. Your company, Canadian Business Writing Consultants, is producing a formal report on Current Practices in Report Presentation. The report is for the Association of Business Professionals. Prepare a title page for this report.
2. The above report contains an Introduction with sub-headings entitled Statement of Purpose and Procedures; Executive Summary; Presenting Reports—Techniques for Maximum Effect (with sub-headings Getting the Most From Technology, Charts and Graphics, Style Guidelines, and Achieving a Professional Look); Conclusions and Recommendations; and a Bibliography. Prepare the Table of Contents.
3. Name the report part indicated by each of the following descriptions.
   a. Tells what research was done, how it was done, and what the writer found
   b. Contains a Statement of Purpose
   c. Shows for whom the report was prepared
   d. Provides substantiating data (such as an Appendix) for the report
   e. An alphabetic listing of all the references used in the report
   f. Is in memo or letter format and accompanies the report
4. The appearance of a formal report must be impeccable. Prepare notes on each of the following features of a formal report. Be prepared to use these notes as the basis for an oral presentation or class discussion.
   - Essential issues in report appearance
   - Mechanics
   - Use of graphics
5. Have each member of your team interview someone who is in business or works for the government. Ask what kinds of reports they read or write. Ask for a copy, if possible, and bring it to class. Compare the formats of the samples your team has obtained with the format presented in this section. Prepare a short oral report to give to the class.

Editing Practice

Editing for Writing Power. Edit and rewrite these sentences to improve clarity and conciseness.

1. Ms. Mueller is the new administrative assistant, and she is very proficient in computer graphics.
2. Spend an afternoon at the job fair, and there you can learn about job opportunities for recent college graduates.

3. I liked the graphics in your report. They were readable. They contained accurate and complete information.
4. Although wanting information for his report, because he felt he had invested enough time, Johar began the writing without it.
5. The report to the executives about the new billing system that was started for the Calgary branch, was long and complicated so then the credit manager had to call a special meeting to explain it.

Discussion Points

1. What kind of writing tone and style is appropriate for a formal report?
2. How would you use an outline in report writing?

Writing Minutes and News Releases

● TOPICS

▶ Recording Minutes

▶ Writing a News Release

Many ideas grow better when transplanted into another mind than in the one where they sprang up.

—Oliver Wendell Holmes, Jr., American jurist

▶ **Key Terms**

▶ minutes
▶ agenda
▶ quorum
▶ verbatim
▶ news release

Every organization, business or social, has meetings and must keep a record of what happens at these meetings. These records of the proceedings of meetings, called **minutes**, are another type of report used in business. The minutes serve as a permanent record of the decisions reached and the actions that are to be taken. The minutes can also be used to inform those who were not at the meeting of what took place. At one time or another, many business employees serve as recorder in a group or committee and are responsible for keeping an accurate set of minutes.

Recording Minutes

Preparing accurate minutes is an important function, because the minutes usually serve as the only historical record of a meeting. Minutes are taken, prepared in an acceptable format, and distributed to meeting participants and others who have reason to see them.

There is probably no one best way to record what happens at a meeting. If an agenda of the meeting has been prepared beforehand, the recorder (the person taking the minutes) should receive a copy. The **agenda** lists briefly the business to be transacted and acts as a guide to the person presiding at the meeting. The agenda also helps the recorder check that all scheduled items are accounted for in the minutes. Any person preparing to record the proceedings of a meeting should find the following general guidelines helpful:

1. List the name of the group, committee, or team and whether the meeting is a regular or special one.
2. Record the day, time, and place of the meeting.
3. With a small group, list the persons attending and those absent. In a large group, either state the number of people present, such as "Forty-five members were present," or list the names of the absentees only. Some minutes simply note that the committee chair determined that a quorum was present. A **quorum** is the number of group members required by the group's bylaws (or other document) to conduct business.

4. In the opening section of the minutes, mention that the minutes for the previous meeting were read and approved, amended, approved as printed, or not approved.

5. Record the important points in the discussion of each item on the agenda. Presenting supporting facts helps those who were present recall the discussion and informs those who were not present. Reports and papers read during the meeting are often attached to the minutes.

6. Record **verbatim** (exact quotation) all resolutions and motions, as well as the names of the persons who introduced and seconded the motions. If this information is not recorded when the motion is made, the recorder should request that the motion be repeated or even put in writing so that the exact motion is recorded.

7. Keyboard, edit, and prepare the minutes in final form. Sometimes, the recorder may want to get another person's approval before issuing the minutes in final form. The recorder signs the minutes, thus certifying their accuracy according to his or her notes. Sometimes the presiding officer countersigns them.

8. File one copy of the minutes in the folder, notebook, or binder used for this purpose. Usually minutes are duplicated and sent to each member of the group and to designated officers who would be interested in the business of the meeting.

Format of Minutes

Various formats are used for minutes. Regardless of the format used, all essential information should appear in a neat, well-arranged form. Some organizations prefer to emphasize the main points on the agenda by using a standardized format.

The minutes shown in Figure 10.14 illustrate one acceptable format. Notice the standard pattern and the topical headings that are used for all meetings of this group and the way in which the motions and the discussion are summarized.

Writing a News Release

Public relations specialists use a particular type of report called a **news release** to inform the media of newsworthy events. They hope that the media will prepare a story for publication or broadcast, based on the news release. Knowing how to prepare news releases is another way of making yourself valuable to your employer.

The Function of the News Release

An important means of getting the planned publicity of a business into the hands of the public is the news release. Whenever a business plans an announcement or an event that it considers newsworthy or capable of enhancing its public image, its public relations personnel prepare and submit a news release to various news outlets for publication or broadcast. Such a news announcement may publicize the introduction of a new line or new product or highlight the awarding of some honour to a member of the organization. Any item that will interest the public and create goodwill for the organization is an appropriate subject for a news release.

◀ **Figure 10.14**
Minutes of a Meeting

Thinking Critically.
*What kind of information
is contained within the
column headings?*

ASSOCIATION OF BEST COMPANY EMPLOYEES

MINUTES OF MEETING OF April 19, 20--

TIME, PLACE, ATTENDANCE	The monthly meeting of the Association of Best Company Employees was held in the Blue Room at 5:30 p.m. The president, Jan Dixon, presided. All members and officers were present.
MINUTES	The minutes of the last meeting, March 15, 20--, were read and approved.
OFFICERS' REPORTS	Treasurer: The treasurer reported receipts of $650, disbursements of $150, and a balance of $967 as of April 1, 20--. Tony Valenti moved the acceptance of the report. Ann Terry seconded the motion. Motion carried.
COMMITTEE REPORTS	Chairperson William Ferris presented the report of the **nominating committee.** The nominees were:

President: Indira Mistry
Vice President: Larisa Yudina
Secretary: Antonio Valdez
Treasurer: Garth Kimberly

	Rosa Sanchez moved that nominations be closed and that a unanimous ballot be cast for the slate of officers presented by the committee. The motion was seconded by Yamen Abdulah. Motion carried.
UNFINISHED BUSINESS	Plans for the **Annual Retirement Dinner** to be held June 30 were discussed. Tory's Inn and Edwin's were suggested for this event. The president will report to the group at the next meeting about these restaurants.
NEW BUSINESS	The president reported that the Board of Directors is considering a policy change regarding **tuition reimbursement** for college courses taken. The change would involve getting approval for each course in advance. The group agreed that the words "unless prior approval is not feasible" be added to this change in policy.
ADJOURNMENT	The meeting adjourned at 6:30 p.m.

Respectfully submitted,

Ivy Lewis

Ivy Lewis

Any news story sent by a company must be approved for release. In large companies, the director of public relations would have this responsibility. In small companies, individual department heads might handle their own news and distribute it in keeping with company policy, or releases might be issued from the office of the president or of one particular executive.

To be printed or broadcast and thereby serve its purpose, the release must be newsworthy; that is, the contents of the release must be of interest to the public. Naturally, the writing style of the news release, as well as the form in which it appears, will have a strong effect on the news editor who decides whether the story is worth printing or broadcasting.

News Release Format

With hundreds of releases coming to their desks each week, news editors will select for publication or broadcast the items that require the least amount of rewriting, everything else being equal. Therefore, the news release must give complete, accurate information in a news style of writing that presents the facts in a clear and interesting way.

Many organizations use a special form for issuing news releases. These forms are arranged so that editors can get to the heart of the story without wasting time. Like a letterhead, a news release form usually contains the name and address of the company or organization and the name, address, and telephone number of the person responsible for issuing the release to the public, as shown in Figure 10.15.

The following information lists some standards for preparing news releases:

1. Double-space the news release and leave space in the margins for editing by the news editor.

2. Include a headline in all-capital letters to identify the story. An editor may change this title to fit the space requirements and style of the publication or broadcast.

3. Indicate the time when a story may be published. In the example in Figure 10.15, note the prominence of the phrase *FOR: Immediate Release*. A release may be sent to the media before an event occurs so that news will reach the public at almost the same time the event takes place. For example, if a company plans to announce a million-dollar gift to a local hospital at a banquet on Saturday, June 25, the release might read *For release after 6 p.m., Saturday, June 25*.

4. In a long release, insert subheads between parts of the release to guide the editor who wants to scan the story.

5. If there is more than one page to the release, type the word MORE in parentheses at the end of each page but the last one. At the end of the last page, key the symbols -XXX-, o0o, -30-, or type END to indicate the end of the release.

The Paragraphs

However good the format of a written communication, the subject and the words determine whether the release will be read and used. In writing a news release—just as in writing letters, memorandums, and reports—certain guides will help the writer develop an effective writing style and will improve the chances of getting the release printed. The arrangement of paragraphs is especially important.

The opening paragraph of a news release should summarize the entire story and present the most newsworthy information first. In this opening section, the writer should give the *who, what, why, how, when* and *where* of the news story in such a form that this paragraph can stand by itself, as in the following example.

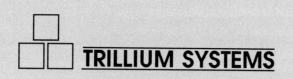

TRILLIUM SYSTEMS

To: All news media   FOR: Immediate Release

                                CONTACT: Isaac Stern
                                              Public Relations
                                              Trillium Systems Inc.
                                              150 Lesmill Road
                                              Don Mills, Canada
                                              M5J 2B6
                                              (416) 555-7300
                                              Fax: (416) 555-7099

Toronto, July 6, 20--

TRILLIUM SYSTEMS FINALIZES ACQUISITION OF U.K. FIRM

    Toronto-based Trillium Systems Inc. has completed its acquisition of
a British manufacturing company, Telesystem Products Limited.
    Telesystem, based in Reading, England, was established in 1990 to
manufacture telecommunications components. Its system has been on
the market since 1996, with sales increasing 100 per cent each year
since that time.
    Garth Binsky, CEO of Trillium, said, "This acquisition will provide
Trillium with a strong presence in the international marketplace, particularly in the European sector." Trillium, a fast-growing telecommunications
company, has assets approaching $100 million and approximately
150,000 shareholders.
The company's common stock is listed on the Toronto, Montreal and
London stock exchanges under the symbol "TRI."

                            -xxx-

Thinking Critically.
*What kind of information
is contained within a news
release?*

Mr. Philip Browning has been named international marketing director of New Millennium
Electronics, Ltd., by its president, Angela Omerto.

Each succeeding paragraph should supply background facts in the order
of decreasing importance. In this way, editors who need to shorten the
release because of space or time limitations can easily cut the story from the
bottom up. For example, notice that the first two paragraphs in the news
release illustrated in Figure 10.15 make a complete news story by themselves. The remainder of the copy provides additional details. A common
practice is to include quotations from an official or an other important person commenting on the news in the release.

Review of Key Terms

1. Why are *minutes* an important part of business communication?
2. What is the purpose of an *agenda*?
3. What is the purpose of a *news release*?

Practical Application

1. Assume that you are the assistant of the Millstone Employees' Association. From the following information, prepare in a concise format the minutes of the latest meeting:

   a. The regular meeting, held in Room 5A, Tyler Building, was called to order by President Karl Swensen at 5:30 p.m., March 15, 20—.

   b. Minutes of preceding meeting (February 15) approved, with the following correction: Ina Singer, not Rita Singer, was appointed chairperson of the Welfare Committee.

   c. Karen Bjorn reviewed employee suggestions for January. Awards of $100 each for two accepted suggestions were approved. Bjorn to make arrangements for presenting the awards at the spring banquet.

   d. Revised written procedure for handling employee suggestions presented by Jack Stuhlman. Accepted with editorial revision to be made by a committee appointed by the president.

   e. Meeting adjourned at 5:15 p.m., with the understanding that the next meeting would be a dinner meeting at Jackson's Restaurant, April 21, to begin at 6:30 p.m.

   f. The following members were absent: W. Holden, R. Yates, B. Witmer.

2. Research how meetings are conducted in your local government. Find out what rules and guidelines apply to the meeting. Is there a quorum requirement? How are the minutes taken? Is the meeting recorded on tape? Do participants receive an agenda beforehand? Write a brief summary for your instructor.

3. The AEP (Association for Environmental Protection) held its first organizational meeting in your community yesterday evening. Margot Hayden was elected president, and you were elected secretary-treasurer. The technical adviser is Professor Abdul Khan, chairperson of the Science Department at Lakehead College. The group plans to meet on the first Wednesday of each month. Its aims are to publicize instances of local pollution and toxic waste dumping, to investigate possible conservation measures in the community, and to recommend publicity to make the community more conservation-oriented. Write a news release about the organization—its officers, aims, and plans—for your local newspaper. Supply any additional facts that you feel are needed.

4. Your supervisor, Georgina Theodorakis, vice president of Northwest Paper Company of your town/city, requests that you write a news

release announcing the retirement of the company president, Philip Alvarez. Mr. Alvarez has been with the company for 25 years, serving as president for the last 10 years. Following his retirement, Mr. Alvarez will serve as chairperson of the board of directors. Supply any additional information that you think should be included, using the news release in this section as a model.

5. Attend a meeting, such as a homeowners association meeting, a club meeting, or a student association or board of governors meeting at your college or university. Take minutes of the first half-hour of the meeting. Remember to include the name of the organization, the date, and place. Use your notes to prepare minutes in an acceptable format.

6. 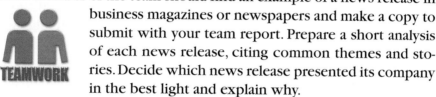 Each member of the team should find an example of a news release in business magazines or newspapers and make a copy to submit with your team report. Prepare a short analysis of each news release, citing common themes and stories. Decide which news release presented its company in the best light and explain why.

7. 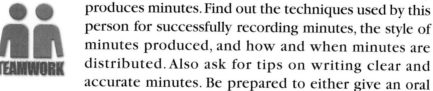 Interview a person at your college or in business who frequently produces minutes. Find out the techniques used by this person for successfully recording minutes, the style of minutes produced, and how and when minutes are distributed. Also ask for tips on writing clear and accurate minutes. Be prepared to either give an oral report to the class, or a written report in memorandum format to your instructor.

Editing Practice

Spelling Check.   Correct any spelling errors in the following paragraph.

Harrison, who dislikcs meetings, thought the comittee meeting was a waist of time. Everyone else, of corse, disagreed. Alice Croft chaired the meeting and encouraged the members to participat fully. Clark recorded the minuets—a task that he enjoys and takes seriusly. Accept for Harrison, we all left the meeting convinced that a productive meeting had been adjorned.

Discussion Points

1. Discuss how listening skills and note-taking skills are important for the person recording minutes at a meeting.
2. If you were asked to record minutes at a meeting, what steps would you take to prepare yourself?
3. What effect does a business-related news release have on the public?
4. Can a news release ever provide information that may interfere with a company's business? Explain.

Chapter 10 Wrap-Up

SUMMARY

▶ In today's information age, the success of an employee depends on his or her ability to compile and write informational reports (for example, periodic, progress, or unsolicited), analytical reports (for example, justification, feasibility studies, or proposals), formal business reports, and informal memorandums.

▶ Meetings are held for a variety of reasons including discussing reports and their recommendations. Accurate minutes of a meeting ensure an exact record of decisions, and assist in achieving goals by noting the assignment of tasks and their associated timelines. Meeting notes should appear in a neat, well-arranged form.

▶ A news release is used to inform the media of an event that is capable of enhancing a company's public image. The writer should give the who, what, where, when, and how in the news story.

Communicating in Your Career

If you were the recorder for a meeting to determine the benefits of providing palm computers to delivery representatives of Speedy Parcel Delivery, how would you organize the agenda of the meeting? Compose an agenda that would easily allow you to take minutes.

CASE 10.1

Anya Mueller works as lead financial analyst at General Electric in Peterborough, Ontario. Anya has been asked by senior management to present her proposal on the establishment of a GE plant in Vancouver, British Columbia. Being a part of Anya's team, you have been asked to provide a rationale for why GE should expand to Vancouver. This will require gathering secondary sources on population statistics, skilled labour potential, and possible competition. Anya has asked you to put together a report so she can submit her initial ideas in a formal report to the board of directors.

- What type of informal report would be best to send to Anya explaining the rationale for expanding GE to Vancouver? Why?

- Using the Internet, look up three sources on Vancouver population statistics, skilled labour statistics, and possible competition. Provide a two-paragraph rationale for expansion citing the three sources; use one of the three documentation styles discussed in Chapter 10.

CASE 10.2

Press Release Network is a global electronic press release distribution service and on-line media monitoring service. These services help clients promote their business on the Internet. Carry out the following activities and write a report for your instructor.

- Visit its Web site at **http://www.pressreleasenetwork.com**.
- Look at one of its press releases on-line. Print out the press release; highlight the most important content and critique it based on the guidelines suggested in Chapter 10 on composing a press release.
- Find out how much the company would charge you to write a press release.
- Click on "Frequently Asked Questions" (FAQs). Find out how often they update their media database.

On the Web

University Web sites commonly give information about research. Visit the following Web site of the Scarborough Campus of the University of Toronto— **http://www.library.scar.utoronto.ca**.

- Choose "Research 101, the Basics." Under "Getting Started" choose "The Five Stages of Research." What are the five stages?
- Go back to "Getting Started" and choose "What are Primary and Secondary Sources?" and study the information provided. What are some of the examples of primary and secondary sources?

Key Terms

Chapter 11

Improving Communication with Customers

Section 11.1
The Importance of Customer Service

Section 11.2
Communicating Effectively with Customers

Chapter Learning Outcomes

After successfully completing this chapter, you will have demonstrated the ability to:

▶ define customer service and explain the importance of building customer loyalty;

▶ distinguish between internal and external customers;

▶ discuss ways of meeting customers' needs for speedy, convenient communications;

▶ discuss techniques for communicating respect to customers;

▶ explain how to use communication skills to resolve customers' issues and keep communications positive.

atrice wanted to buy virus protection software. She decided to visit a business that had recently advertised a sale.

When she entered the store, Patrice received a blank stare from two employees who stood near the entrance and continued with their conversation. Patrice found the Computer Software section but couldn't find what she wanted. An employee walked by, and Patrice asked for assistance. "Sorry, I don't work in this section," was the response. Patrice went to the Service Department at the back of the store. Four other customers were waiting in line. Finally, it was Patrice's turn. She was about the say what she wanted when a telephone on the desk rang and the sales associate spent several minutes talking to the caller. When she stated what she needed, the sales associate said, "You'll have to ask in Customer Service."

Feeling frustrated and very annoyed, Patrice asked to see the store manager. The manager listened carefully to Patrice's complaint, apologized for the inconvenience, asked a staff member to help her and to also make sure that Patrice received a 10 per cent discount. After searching the shelves, the employee told Patrice, "Someone forgot to restock this area. I'll have to look in the storage room." After waiting another ten minutes, Patrice finally got the software she wanted.

As you study Chapter 11, identify policies this business should implement to improve its communication with customers.

The Importance of Customer Service

It is not the employer who pays the wages. Employers only handle the money. It is the customer who pays the wages.

—Henry Ford, automobile maker

▶ **Key Terms**

▶ customer service
▶ referrals
▶ external customer
▶ internal customer

Customer service is a complex function that has many facets. Many people have a simplistic view of customer service, thinking that it is only involves being friendly and helpful to customers. In the chapter opening case, although the store manager was friendly and helpful, Patrice's experience was far from satisfactory because of all the other negative moments that occurred.

Customer service is often viewed as a reactive, problem-solving function that comes into play only when there has been a complaint. Effective customer service involves more than reacting to customers. It also requires an organization and its employees to be proactive. This means establishing a culture of excellent customer care in an organization, anticipating customers' needs, seeking customer feedback, and using this feedback to improve customer service.

What Is Customer Service?

Customer service is the consistent performance of activities or services for the purpose of ensuring customer satisfaction. Customer satisfaction occurs when the customer's needs and wants are met and when the customer feels valued by the company. Goods and services must be provided to the customer when and where they are needed and at a competitive price. Making customers feel valued instills the feeling that their business is appreciated, that they will be treated with respect, and that their business will receive prompt and competent attention.

The requirement that customer service procedures be implemented throughout an organization must come from top management. Top management's support and specific directives to key employees are necessary to establish a culture of customer service in an organization.

Customer Loyalty

Customer relationship management has become a key term in the business world. Businesses realize that, to be successful, they must establish and maintain successful relationships with their customers. In other words, they must build a solid base of loyal customers. Achieving this requires employees with excellent customer service skills who can communicate effectively with customers both orally and in writing. These employees must have instant access to comprehensive customer profiles stored in a database. A customer profile will provide not only the customer's name and contact information, but also a history of the account, buying patterns, etc. This information is used by employees to make customers feel recognized and important, to solve issues more efficiently, and to identify opportunities for selling additional products.

Why is building customer loyalty such an important issue? Outstanding customer service helps you retain your current customers and attract new ones. Customers who receive excellent service will tell others. This enhances a company's reputation and results in additional business. Many businesses derive much of their new business through referrals. **Referrals** are recommendations from satisfied customers. In addition, delighted customers will be repeat customers; they will continue to use your product or service, will be open to trying other products or services from your company, and will be much less likely to be lured away by your competitors.

External and Internal Customers

The discussion of "customers" in this chapter is intended to include anyone who buys goods or services or requests assistance or information. The traditional definition of a customer is someone who buys goods or services, while a client is regarded as someone who engages the professional services of another person or business. For example, if you buy a computer at Future Shop, you are a customer; when you go to the dentist, you are a client. However, with the increasing focus on customer service, the word customer is often more widely used to encompass both customers and clients. In addition, a customer should be thought of as someone who requires service from a non-profit organization or government department. A taxpayer who calls, for example, the Canada Customs and Revenue Agency to inquire about the goods and services tax on a particular item is a customer of that agency. A person who phones a food bank asking for assistance is a customer of that not-for-profit organization.

The definition of customer can be furthered widened to include internal customers, as well as external customers. Too often we think of customers as only being from outside the business or organization where we work. **External customers** are people outside of a business who purchase its goods or services. A company may work with external customers in person, through its Web site, or by mail, telephone, fax, or e-mail.

Only a small proportion of the employees at any organization may work directly with the external customer. To serve external customers effectively, these front-line employees require support from everyone else in the organization. Some examples of types of support are information; supplies; well-stocked shelves; a clean, pleasant environment; clear labelling of products and prices; attractive display of items; and technical support for computers, networks, e-mail, fax machines, photocopiers, and telephones.

This situation creates the internal customer. An **internal customer** is a co-worker or supervisor—anyone within the organization who depends on products, supplies, or services from another person in the same organization to properly serve the external customer. Even when front-line workers give each other information or help, the person receiving the information or help is the customer. Customer service should be thought of as a chain, with all the employees forming links in that chain. When one link breaks, the person in the front-line does not receive the needed support, and service to the external customer suffers. Suppose, for example, you work in the marketing department. Before you can determine the selling price for an item, you need cost figures from the company's budget office. You are the internal customer of the budget office. Without being promptly and accurately supplied with the information, you are unable to complete a task that directly affects the external customer. Similarly, if you are directly serving a customer, and ask a colleague for a customer's credit rating, you become the internal customer of your co-worker. Once again, without prompt and correct information, your service to the external customer will be unsatisfactory.

Employees who understand the concept of internal customers will also understand the importance of working as a team. They know that all employees are involved in customer service, whether or not they interact directly with the external customers. For example, in the chapter opening case, the person who failed to stock the shelves on time did not realize the impact this would have on other members of the team and on the customer's experience.

Good communication skills, a positive attitude, and product and company knowledge allow the internal team to work together to create customer satisfaction. For a business, this customer satisfaction has a direct effect on the "bottom line"—the profit earned by the business. Satisfied customers will tell others of their experience, will return to buy again, and will be less likely to be lured away by competitors. For a non-profit organization or government department, customer satisfaction has a direct effect on meeting goals and budget targets. In all cases, pleasant, efficient service for customers in both the public and private sectors means fewer call backs on the same issues, and less time in handling complaints, which translates into saving time and money. In addition, when customers visit or call again for different business or assistance, they already have a positive attitude towards the service provider, which assists communication.

Customer Communication Methods

External and internal customers use a variety of contact methods. You may be involved in face-to-face interactions, telephone conversations, or written correspondence via e-mail, text chat messages, or letters. In addition, customers will visit your organization's Web site to seek information or use the site's self-serve features for conducting transactions. Excellent verbal, nonverbal, and written communication skills are required to deal with this range of customer activities.

Whatever contact method is used, customers are looking for satisfaction of the same major wants and needs, which will be discussed later in this chapter. Customers not only want a choice of contact methods, they also want their inquiries and concerns dealt with accurately, promptly, and with respect. In the next section, you will look at how to use your communication skills to satisfy these major customer service requirements.

Review of Key Terms

1. Explain the difference between *internal customers* and *external customers*. Include examples from a place where you have worked, or from an organization at which you are a customer.

2. What is *customer service*?

Practical Application

1. Research a business in your community to determine the ways in which it can be contacted by customers. List the contact information, such as the telephone number and e-mail and Web site addresses. Use one of these contact methods and make notes about your experience. How user-friendly was the contact method? What impression did you form of this company's customer service, and why? Write a brief report to present to your instructor or to the class.

2. Develop a short role-play involving a customer-service situation such as a face-to-face conversation or telephone call from a customer. Team members will write scenarios to show both the "wrong" way and the "right" way to handle a particular situation. Role-play the scenes for the class.

TEAMWORK

Editing Practice

Correct any spelling errors in the following paragraph.

Chris, a disatisfied customer, wanted to speak with the store manager. He said if the manager did not speak with him immediatly, he would make a scine. The manager spoke with Chris, who critecized the quality of work he recently had done on his car. Their were oil stains on the upholstery and cigarette butts left in the ashtray. The condition of the car was not acceptible. Chris announced he would go elsewhere if the car was not restored satisfactorly.

Discussion Points

1. Why is customer loyalty a key issue for a business?

2. What types of communication skills do you need to deliver excellent customer service, and why?

Communicating Effectively with Customers

Goodwill is the one and only asset that competition cannot undersell nor destroy.

—Marshall Field, founder of Marshall Field department stores

What Do Customers Want?

Firstly, customers want an organization to be accessible; that is, they want to interact with a business at a place and time when it is convenient for them, and to have a choice of ways to contact that business. Secondly, when they make contact, they want to be treated with respect, to be acknowledged, to have their concerns treated seriously, and to receive courteous service. Thirdly, they want to deal with someone who will provide knowledgeable answers to their questions and prompt resolution of their problems.

Providing Convenient, Speedy Communications

Customers associate telephone, e-mail, and Internet communications with speed and expect a prompt response.

Responding Promptly

Respond promptly to customers' letters, e-mail, and telephone communications so that customers feel valued and know that communication is important to your organization. Follow the guidelines given in Chapter 2 for responding promptly and appropriately to telephone calls and for leaving an appropriate voice-mail greeting in case you are not immediately available.

If you deal with customers by e-mail and cannot respond quickly, send a brief acknowledgment that you received the message and stating when a full reply will be sent. Some employees use their e-mail's auto-responder function when they receive messages and are unavailable to answer them. The **auto responder** is a message-response system that automatically replies to e-mails in the employee's absence. A sample auto-responder message follows: "Gordon Lang is attending an engineering show and will be back in his office Monday, May 5. Please e-mail his assistant, Robert Baker at rbaker@city.com if you need immediate help with your computer system." Such a message conveys that Gordon Lang is not simply ignoring the message and that he will be available on May 5 to reply to the e-mail. The e-mail also tells the reader who to contact for assistance in Mr. Lang's absence.

Accessibility

Customers determine how convenient it is to deal with a business depending on its **accessibility**. For example, if they wish to visit the business in person, is the location convenient? If they wish to contact the business by telephone, e-mail, or Internet, is the system user-friendly?

Here are some examples of services that provide convenient access for customers:

- Web sites allow customers to conduct business anytime from a computer.
- Banks provide automated teller machines (ATMs), and 24-hour self-serve banking via telephone or the Internet.
- Many companies have toll-free telephone numbers that are answered 24 hours per day, seven days per week.
- A catalogue-sales company installed a telephone device for the deaf (a *TDD*), to communicate with deaf customers by telephone.
- Hotels that cater to business travelers have rooms wired for Internet and fax connections.
- Customers can contact businesses through e-mail, and many businesses also offer the option of text chat, which provides an immediate response to written messages.
- Major airlines provide telephones for passengers to use in flight.
- Some dentists schedule evening and Saturday appointments.

In addition, the following are some common Web site features that provide convenience and accessibility for customers.

- A *Frequently Asked Questions (FAQs)* section. Clicking on this section takes you to a list of common questions and their answers.
- A section called *Contact Us.* Clicking on this section takes you to a screen with a preaddressed e-mail. This makes e-mailing the company easier.
- An *order confirmation function.* When you place the order electronically, you will have an e-mail confirmation within about 15 minutes. This confirmation assures the customer that the products have been purchased. The confirmation also lists the tracking number, which enables you to follow your shipment as it makes its way to your office.

Communicating with Respect

Showing respect for another person means showing consideration for that person; that is, giving careful thought to what they say and how they feel, and treating them with kindness. The following guidelines will help you show respect in your communications with customers.

- *Acknowledge customers promptly.* In a face-to-face situation, recognize a visitor's presence immediately. Even if you are busy, interrupt your work for a moment to smile and say to the new arrival, "I'll be with you in a moment. Would you like to sit down?" On the telephone, the smile should be expressed through a pleasant, friendly tone of voice. Use an appropriate greeting such as "Good morning" and then ask how you can help.

Ignoring a customer who is waiting for assistance will cause the customer to react to you and your firm in a negative way.

- *Use the customer's name* in your conversation or correspondence. Unless you know the customer well and have been asked to use his/her first name, always show respect by using the title and last name (e.g. "Good morning, Mrs. Jones.") Using the customer's name adds a personal touch and makes the customer feel that they are being treated as an individual.
- *Give customers your full attention.* Never treat a customer as an interruption, even if you are extremely busy. Remember, without customers the business and therefore your job would not exist. Focus totally on the customer and use active listening techniques.
- *Communicate with courtesy.* Courtesy is a key ingredient of respect. As well as using a pleasant, friendly tone of voice and giving the customer your full attention, courtesy involves treating the customer's question or problem seriously. For example, even though an issue may be very straightforward to you, if the customer has taken the time to contact you, the concern is serious for them. Put yourself in the customer's place and see things from their viewpoint. Remember to use "please" and "thank you" in both verbal and written communications.

Sending a fax addressed "To Whom It May Concern" will certainly reduce the likelihood of a positive response—or of any response.

Resolving Customers' Issues

Customers want their questions and concerns handled efficiently and effectively. This means that employees should be knowledgeable about their organization's products and services, as well as its policies.

Providing Knowledgeable Responses

When customers ask questions, give them an accurate, complete answer. Ask questions to make sure you fully understand the issues and that you have all the information you need to assist the customer. If you don't know the answer, find a colleague who can help the customer. If this isn't possible, tell the customer that you will call back with the information and give a timeframe. Make sure that you will be able to deliver on your promises. Never give a customer false expectations; for example, don't promise to call back by 3:00 p.m. unless you are sure this will be possible. Should something happen to prevent you getting the information by the promised time, contact the customer and give a progress report. Similarly, if you ask a customer if he or she is satisfied, make sure you are prepared to handle a "No" response.

Here are some ways you can give knowledgeable responses to customers.

1. Familiarize yourself with the products and services your company offers.
2. Know the functions of key departments and personnel and to whom you can refer a customer or client.
3. Have copies of pertinent company information, such as brochures, fliers, and catalogues available for your reference.
4. Provide the customer with specific information, such as dates and costs.

Dealing with Customers' Complaints

If a customer is upset or angry, listen carefully and let the customer vent his/her feelings. Do not interrupt. When you respond, show that you have listened by empathizing with the concern. **Empathy** means recognizing, and appropriately responding to, another person's feelings. These feelings will be communicated through body language and tone of voice. Whether you agree with the customer or not, you can communicate respect for his or her feelings. This will help to calm the irate customer and show that you are listening. For example, "I appreciate that this is very frustrating for you, Mr. Smith," or "I know it can be confusing when changes are made."

If your organization has kept the customer waiting or made a mistake, give a sincere apology. For example, "I apologize for the wait, Ms. Brown." Then move on to doing something to resolve the issue.

If you must deny a customer's request, explain the reasons. If more than one solution is available, present the options to the customer. When suggesting solutions, be creative, but within the limits of your customer-service policies.

The following guidelines provide further suggestions for dealing with customer concerns.

1. If the customer is angry, maintain self-control. This is not a personal attack on you. Upset customers need you to listen so that they can express their feelings. Having done so, they will be more amenable and ready to let you solve the problem.
2. Express interest in and an understanding of the caller's problem.
3. Clarify any misunderstandings that may have occurred.
4. Don't blame someone else for the problem.
5. Take enough time to help the customer. If the customer senses that you are rushed, he or she will think that you consider the contact unimportant.
6. Tell the customer what action you will take. If the customer has experienced problems, make repairs and exchanges cheerfully. Provide whatever relief is available through warranties and company policy.
7. If you cannot make the adjustment yourself, refer the caller to someone who can and explain the situation so that the customer does not have to repeat the entire story to someone else.
8. Thank the customer for bringing the situation to your attention.
9. Follow up to make sure that the customer is satisfied.

Customers who have their problems resolved effectively and promptly will provide free publicity by telling others about the good customer service. Alternatively, customers who do not receive a satisfactory remedy will communicate their dissatisfaction to others, and may do so by using the Internet. This phenomenon is called **e-whining.** Several Web sites exist that will list the customer's complaints. Other Web sites will send an anonymous e-mail letting companies know that someone is dissatisfied with a product or a service. Aim to provide the best customer service available to avoid this kind of publicity.

Keeping Communications Positive

Use positive language in your communications with customers. Never engage in negative statements such as "Business has really been slow lately." Express information in positive ways. State what you know, and what you can do, for the customer, not what you can't do. For example, avoid negative statements such as, "It's not our policy to give cash refunds." Instead, use a positive statement, such as, "What we can do for you, Ms. Jones, is exchange this for another item."

Use **discretion** in your communications with customers. Protect the privacy of your employer and demonstrate loyalty by being discreet in your comments. Avoid making inappropriate conversation about company business or personnel. If the subject comes up, be noncommittal and change the topic of conversation.

To the customer, you are the company; you represent the organization for which you work and may be the only person with whom that person has contact. It is essential that you communicate in a prompt, respectful way, and take action to answer questions and solve issues.

Review of Key Terms

1. What is *empathy*? Give an example of a situation in which using empathy with a customer would be appropriate, and write down what you would say.
2. It is important to keep your comments to customers positive. Explain how you would use *discretion* to keep your comments about your employer and colleagues positive.

Practical Application

1. Describe a situation in which you had a positive experience as a customer. What was said or done to show respect?
2. Describe a situation in which you had a negative customer experience because your situation was not handled promptly or effectively. What should have been done differently to satisfy your needs?
3. The following negative statements should not be made to customers. Replace each item with a positive statement.
    a. It's not our fault.
    b. No, you don't qualify for the 10 per cent discount. You only qualify for a 5 per cent discount because you spent less than $200.
4. Identify a product or service that you would like to have more information about. Make a list of questions you will ask and then telephone the company to obtain the information. Analyze how your call was handled and write a summary of the favourable and unfavourable aspects of this experience.
5. Review the case at the beginning of the chapter and list the ways in which respect was or was not shown for Patrice. Develop a role play for this situation in which employees provide speed and convenience, treat Patrice with respect, resolve her issue, and keep the communication positive. Present your role play to the class and ask them to identify each of the positive customer service elements.

TEAMWORK

Editing Practice

Eliminate the unnecessary repetitions in the following sentences.

1. We are planning to revert back to personal contacts as our main sales strategy.
2. What prerequisites are required for this course?
3. Please repeat the instructions again so that everyone understands them.
4. What files are stored inside of this cabinet?
5. Past experience shows that Michael is reliable.

Discussion Points

1. What are some appropriate ways to deal with irate customers or customers who need to exchange an item?

2. Imagine that a customer has just asked you a question and that you do not have the answer. What will you say and do?

Chapter 11 Wrap-Up

SUMMARY

▶ Customer service is a complex function that involves all employees in an organization. Customer service involves not only reacting to customers' requests and complaints, but also being proactive. This means anticipating customers' needs and seeking to constantly improve service by learning from customer feedback.

▶ To be successful, a business must build customer loyalty by developing successful relationships with customers. This requires employees who can communicate effectively with customers both orally and in writing, because customers will choose from a variety of contact methods such as telephone, e-mail, and text chat.

▶ External customers are people from outside the organization who purchase its goods or services. Internal customers are co-workers and supervisors—people within the company who depend on goods or services from another department.

▶ Customers want convenient, speedy communications. We must respond promptly to all methods of customer contact. Making a business accessible to customers is an important part of providing convenience and speed.

▶ Customers want to be treated with respect. This means acknowledging customers promptly, using their names, giving them your full attention, and being courteous.

▶ Customers want their questions and concerns handled efficiently and effectively. Employees must be knowledgeable about their organization's products and services, as well as its policies.

▶ When dealing with customers' complaints, you must listen carefully and allow the customer to vent his or her feelings. Respond with empathy to show that you appreciate how the customer is feeling. Apologize when your organization has made a mistake.

▶ Keep communications with customers positive. Never engage in negative statements about your organization or colleagues. To the customer, you are the organization, and it is essential that you communicate in a prompt, respectful way, and take action to answer questions and solve issues.

CASE 11.1

Jerry and Sue drive up to Crustee's to order lunch. The woman at the drive-through window says, "What is your order?" Jerry says, "I would like two hamburgers, two orders of fries, and a large cola." The woman repeats back the order by saying, "OK, two hamburgers, two fries, and two colas." Jerry says, "No, one large cola," very loudly. Sounding offended, the woman says, "Sir, you don't have to yell at me! We're under enough pressure here! Pull around to the drive-through window."

Jerry and Sue are behind another car waiting to pick up their order and pay, but the line is not moving. There seems to be a problem with the order for the car in front of them. After waiting five minutes, Sue goes inside and talks to a cashier. The cashier says, "It's too bad you had to wait, but we're short staffed today, so someone new is on the takeout. She hasn't finished her training yet. Your order should be out there soon." Sue says, "Why can't you just get me the order here?" The cashier replies, "I can't do that. Our system doesn't work that way." Very upset, Sue returns to the car, and the order finally arrives. After driving away, Sue and Jerry find that they only have one order of fries.

Sue calls Crustee's head office the next day and gets the name and address of the owner of the franchise. She writes the owner a letter about her bad experience. The owner decides to develop specific customer-service policies at his franchise.

If you were hired to develop these policies, what specific items would you include? How do these items relate to the information in this chapter?

CASE 11.2

Kristin Anderson and Ron Zemke wrote *Delivering Knock Your Socks Off Service* published by AMACOM Books in 1998. According to the authors, a "Moment of Truth" occurs "anytime a customer comes in contact with any part of your organization" and uses that contact to judge the quality of the organization (p. 88).

Anderson and Zemke emphasize that managers and executives understand that they set the example. They report that Bill Marriott Jr., chairman of Marriott Hotels, "often takes a turn at the hotel registration desk checking in guests; he also empties ashtrays in the lobby and picks up trash in the parking lot" (p. 88).

Form groups of four or five students. You work at a Marriott hotel. Brainstorm what the Moments of Truth would be from the moment a guest calls or e-mails your hotel to the moment they leave the hotel at the end of their stay. Remember—these Moments of Truth may be positive or negative, depending on what happens each time the customer has an opportunity to form an opinion about your hotel. Come back together with the rest of the class to share what all the groups have generated.

Communicating in Your Career

You are the manager of a bank branch office. You decide to run a customer-service training session for your employees. Make notes of the major points you would cover in this session.

On the Web

Browse through indigo.ca, an on-line bookstore, at **http://www.indigo.ca**. Research books, videos, DVDs, and other products to explore the effects of on-line shopping. Ask questions using the Help button to measure their on-line customer service. What do you like or dislike about their services?

Key Terms

accessibility	506	discretion	509	external customer	502
auto responder	505	empathy	507	internal customer	502
customer service	501	e-whining	508	referrals	502

Chapter 12 Communicating in Employment Situations

Chapter Learning Outcomes

After successfully completing this chapter, you will have demonstrated the ability to:

▸ analyze job search methods and determine which ones best suit different job search situations;

▸ compose a resumé that markets your qualifications to prospective employers;

▸ outline strategies for preparing a scannable resumé and an employment portfolio;

▸ write employment-related letters, including a persuasive application letter;

▸ prepare for several types of interviews;

▸ use your communication skills effectively during a job interview;

▸ use communication skills appropriately when requesting a compensation increase or a promotion, or leaving a position.

H arold is one of ten graduates at East Coast Community College who were to be interviewed for two positions that would begin June 1 at HiTech Solutions Ltd., a local computer company. Edward Gajdel, HiTech's interviewer, met with all ten as a group at the college to tell them about the company and the two available positions.

Harold arrived late for the group meeting and took a seat near the door. Mr. Gajdel was telling the group about HiTech and the two available positions. Harold felt uncomfortable as he glanced around the room because everyone else wore a business suit while he had on jeans, a school sweatshirt, and a baseball cap.

Harold was determined to dress appropriately and to arrive early for the interview—two tasks that he hadn't accomplished at the group meeting. On the day of the interview, Harold was running late. He stopped at a self-service gas station and filled up his gas tank. In his haste, Harold spilled some gas on his shoes.

In the reception area, Harold sat down beside his classmate Kyo Maclear and started a conversation. The receptionist asked, "Sir, may I help you?" From his seat, Harold identified himself and told the receptionist he had an appointment with Mr. Gajdel.

What would have been your first impression of Harold? As you read Chapter 12, consider how Harold could have been better prepared for his interview.

Job Search Skills

Your work parallels your life—but in the sense of a glass full of water where people look at it and say: 'Oh, the water's the same shape as the glass!'

—Francis Ford Coppola, film director

Finding the position you want is similar to taking a comprehensive final exam. You must review everything you have learned and apply it to a specific situation. The information and related assignments in this chapter will prepare you for your job search. The process will be easier if you approach it systematically in separate steps. You need to:

1. Analyze yourself and your professional qualifications.
2. Assess the job market.
3. Develop personal packaging information, including resumés and application letters.

Analyzing Yourself and Your Qualifications

The first step in the job search process is to analyze yourself and your professional qualifications. You need to consider what kind of work interests you and what qualifications you have that would help you perform that particular work.

Career Goals

To determine your career goals, ask yourself these questions: What professional position, if any, do I have now? What position do I want when I complete my course of study? What position do I want two years from now? What position do I want five years from now? Answers to these questions are the basis of what many refer to as a five-year plan, a fundamental building block in life planning.

Education

Think about how education affects your career goals by asking yourself these questions: What courses, degrees, or training have prepared me for my career goals? Can I achieve my career goals with the education I now have? Do I need additional courses to qualify me for the position I want? Will I need additional education and training for the position I want in the future?

Experience

Analyze your work experience by asking yourself these questions: What experience do I have that is related to the position I want? How is this experience specifically related to my career goals? If I do not have related experience, how can I acquire such experience? Do I have additional—though unrelated—experience that will demonstrate a successful work history?

Personal Characteristics

Define your personal characteristics by asking yourself these questions: What are my major strengths and weaknesses? Do I enjoy working with data, computers, or people, or a combination of these? Do I like variety? Do I want responsibility? Do I like challenges and problem solving? Would I accept a position that offers advancement but frequently requires overtime?

Your Ideal Job

The next step is to become very specific. Begin by describing your ideal potential employer and the position you would want with that firm. This description helps you determine exactly what you want. Here are some questions to consider when writing the description of your ideal job:

- Which products or services am I interested in providing?
- Do I want to work in a small community or a large city? In Canada or abroad?
- Would I like to work for a small, medium, or large company?
- Which position do I want?
- What salary range would I be looking for?
- How important are benefits such as a flexible schedule, child care, vacation policy, health insurance, or retirement options?
- Am I prepared to travel as part of my job?
- Am I looking for a career opportunity that offers promotions, transfers, additional education, and training?

Compare your description of your ideal company and position with your analyses of your goals, education, experience, and personal characteristics to see how the two sets of information fit. If almost everything is in agreement, proceed to the next step. If your personal assessment and the description of your ideal position and company do not agree, work through both sets of information again to decide where you should make changes.

For example, you may learn that the type of job you want as a network specialist exists, but that the available positions are in another province and you were hoping to work near your home. Should you stick to your original plan or rethink your choices? You must consider your choices and establish your priorities. This leads to the second step in the job search: assessing the job market.

Assessing the Job Market

After you have analyzed yourself and your qualifications and identified the type of employment you want, begin looking for positions that meet your specifications. Many convenient sources of information about job opportunities are at your disposal. Traditionally, listings on college bulletin boards, newspaper classifieds, chambers of commerce, and library reference books offer up-to-date information and reliable resources. Depending on the size and geographic region of your desired location, some sources of information may be more accessible than others.

Use the Internet to find potential employers. Many companies use their Web site to post general information about their purpose and goals, the locations of their branches, and current employment opportunities. The Internet also has a number of job search engines that offer listings of professional openings in numerous fields. Also, using a standard search engine to search for job openings in many categories is helpful. More information on searching for jobs on the Internet is given later in this chapter.

Your Personal Contact Network

Your personal contact network of friends, relatives, and college instructors can be effective sources of employment opportunities, particularly in a small community. Employees of a company often know when positions will become available because of transfers, promotions, resignations, and retirement and the creation of new positions. Inform people in your personal contact network about the kind of job you are seeking and the date when you will be available to accept a position. Even if your personal contacts do not know of an available position, they may know others who do.

Your Professional Contact Network

You can establish your own professional contact network of friends and acquaintances in the business world using the following tips.

Arrange to Meet Professionals Who Are Affiliated in Some Way with Your College.   Find out if the department in your program area has a board of advisors or a similar group. You might suggest holding a reception that gives students the opportunity to interact with members of this group.

Acquire Work Experience Through Internships, Summer Jobs, and Part-Time Employment.   In addition to the work experience positions like this provide, you develop relationships with professionals who can serve as mentors and sources of recommendation. You also develop links to other employers who might have positions available that match your qualifications. Internships and temporary employment situations give you a chance to see if a career in a particular field is right for you.

Build Cordial Relationships with the Business Professionals with Whom You Work.   Through your job performance, impress upon the employer your willingness to accept new assignments and to work as a team member. Many employers use internships and temporary employment situations to determine the potential of temporary employees for permanent employment. Employers particularly look for traits that are complex to measure, such as the ability to work in teams, a positive attitude, and creativity in coming up with new ideas or suggestions for solving problems.

College Placement Centres

Most educational institutions have placement offices whose career counsellors can assist you in finding a position. Visit your school's placement centre to see what services are available. Besides listing employment requests from area businesses, career counsellors also arrange job fairs that bring potential employers to the campus to interview students. Many career placement centres offer software programs that help you make career decisions, as well as books, pamphlets, and magazines related to current employment trends.

A comprehensive placement centre would offer workshops on resumé preparation and interviewing techniques. Often, career counsellors can help you get a part-time job while you are in school. Many college placement centres offer to help students even after they graduate.

Newspaper Advertisements

The classified advertisement section of newspapers carries announcements of job openings in many types of business positions. If you want to apply for a position in a distant city, you should start checking the classified advertisements several months in advance for job openings in that location. Your college library, local library, or bookstore may subscribe to or sell a newspaper for the city you have chosen. If not, you may need to take out a short-term subscription to the newspaper. You should also check to see if this newspaper is available on the Internet.

Specialized Journals

Another place to look for employment opportunities is in specialized journals, such as those for accountants, medical personnel, office personnel, teachers, and other professionals. *The College Placement Annual*, which offers information on a variety of employment opportunities, is available through college placement centres. This publication lists employers alphabetically and geographically. It also gives general background information about the companies and lists anticipated position openings.

Hidden Job Market

The **hidden job market** is not really a new concept, but today it seems to be used more and more. The hidden job market refers to job opportunities that are not advertised in the traditional venues such as newspapers or journals. This market, which represents a majority of available jobs in some fields, should not be overlooked. Most of these job openings are filled through word-of-mouth contacts, or sometimes through on-line announcements that encourage submission of applications and resumés. Word-of-mouth contacts take place through networking. **Networking** involves developing a wide range of contacts through family, friends, and social and business contacts, and then using this network to assist you in your job search.

You can develop business contacts for your network by conducting informational interviews. In an informational interview you talk to someone already employed in the type of job you are seeking. The purpose is to gather information about a job from someone with firsthand experience. It is also an excellent way to gain confidence in meeting people and preparing for an actual job interview. Prepare for this meeting by researching the job in other ways, and the company, so that you can ask intelligent questions. Prepare a short list of questions. For example, you could ask the interviewee to describe a typical day at work. Arrive on time, keep to the time allotted for the interview, dress professionally, and send a follow-up thank-you note.

For additional information on networking and to access an Informational Interviewing Tutorial, go to **http://www.quintcareers.com/networking_guide.html**.

On-Line Searching for Employment

The many employment-related sites on the Internet and the World Wide Web make it possible to conduct an on-line employment search. Many companies have home pages on the World Wide Web that provide information about the company and its employment opportunities. Also, on-line services provide job postings, and employer profiles, and resumés for review by employers. Many of these sites allow you to post your resumé electronically, either free of charge or for a fee. In the next section, you will learn how to write an electronic resumé.

Listed below are a number of on-line employment services and their addresses that were current at the time of publication.

CareerBuilder Inc.	**http://www.careerbuilder.com** (Choose International to find Canada)
Monster.com	**http://www.monster.com**
Workopolis	**http://www.workopolis.com**
Canjobs.com	**http://canjobs.com**
Canada Work Infonet	**http://www.canadawork.com**

Placement Agencies and Employment Contractors

Private employment agencies exist in most metropolitan areas. Some of these placement agencies fill job openings in a wide range of occupations, while

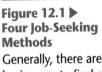

Figure 12.1 ▶
Four Job-Seeking Methods
Generally, there are four basic ways to find a job. The hidden job market is, by far, the most successful. By looking at the pie chart for these job-seeking methods, you can determine how to best use your time and energy in your own job search.

Thinking Critically. Why do you think the hidden job market is a better place to find a job than want ads?

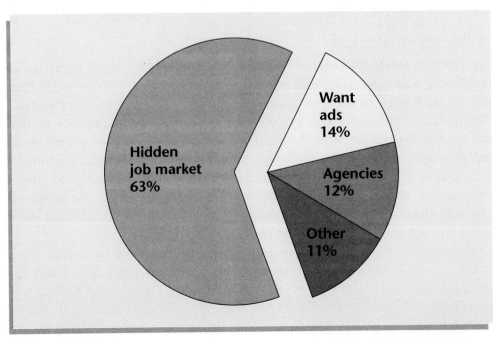

others focus on one area of employment such as management, construction, or office personnel. These agencies charge a fee, which is usually a percentage of the annual salary for the position. The fee is paid either by the company seeking to fill a vacancy or by the person who gets the job.

Employment contractors, also known as temporary agencies, supply personnel on a temporary basis for a given company's specific requests and needs. Temporary workers gain valuable workplace experience, establish a positive relationship with a company, and possibly attain permanent employment.

Review of Key Terms

1. How can you find out about employment in a *hidden job market*?
2. What are some advantages and some disadvantages of using private *employment agencies*?

Practical Application

1. Make a list of your personal characteristics and your work experience. Use this list to write a description of your ideal job.

2. Research the job market in your area by visiting your college placement centre, a local employment agency, or an on-line Web site such as workopolis.com. What kinds of openings are most available in your area? What markets are tight? Write a report of the team's findings for your instructor.

Editing Practice

Rewrite the following sentences for clarity and correctness.

1. Having arranged for a seminar, the conference room was reserved by Laurel.
2. Each of the 3 applicants are qualified.
3. Its company policy to conduct drug screening on all new employees'.
4. Our team was asked to develope a schedule for the Spring projects.
5. The report is up-to-date, and will be distributed tommorow.

Discussion Points

1. Discuss how internships and summer jobs are valuable employment contacts.
2. How could you develop a network to help you in your job search? Hold brainstorming sessions in groups and then compile a list of specific suggestions for your class.

Resumés

TOPICS

▶ Resumé Content

▶ Resumé Parts

▶ Resumé Types

▶ Formatting a Resumé

▶ Scannable Resumés

▶ **Key Terms**

▶ resumé

▶ chronological resumé

▶ functional resumé

▶ combination resumé

▶ scannable resumé

The only place where success comes before work is in a dictionary.

—Vidal Sassoon, founder of an international business for hairdressing services and products

---

After deciding what position you want and are qualified for, you begin the application process. You can answer advertisements, or you can apply directly to companies in which you are interested. Your resumé, application letter, list of references, and portfolio are the items you use to market yourself to prospective employers. These four items present your qualifications and assets to a prospective employer.

Resumé Content

The **resumé** is an outline, or summary, of your background and qualifications for the kind of job you want. As you prepare your resumé, remember that the care in its preparation and the information it supplies often determine whether you will be invited for an interview. Proofread and edit your resumé carefully to make sure that the spelling, grammar, and facts are correct and that the wording is clear. Ask several people to proofread your resumé as well. Your resumé must be error-free to make the all-important first impression a favourable one.

Always be honest when listing your qualifications on a resumé. Falsifying your credentials or application documents is grounds for immediate termination in many companies.

Employers are prohibited by law from asking the age, sex, marital status, religion, or race of applicants. Therefore, supplying such information is optional. If you consider any of this data an asset, you can include it on your resumé. However, most people prefer to omit such information.

Resumé Parts

Resumés usually have sections. This makes it easy for prospective employers to review a job candidate's credentials. You can individualize the information in these standard sections to present your qualifications in the best light. Include the following major sections in your resumé.

Identification

Begin with your name, address, and telephone number. If applicable, include a fax number and/or e-mail address. If you have a temporary address while you are in college, be sure to include your temporary as well as your permanent address information. You may want to have a heading such as the following above your temporary address: Address Until May 10, 2004.

Career Objective

Your career objective should express your employment goal. If you prepare your resumé in response to an advertised position, you may want to reflect the specifics noted in the ad, such as "A position as a paralegal in the area of wills and estates." If you are preparing a resumé to send to many companies, your career objective should be more general, such as "A position as a nursing assistant in a clinic." You also have the option of not including a career objective.

Education

List your most recent education first, and work back from that if there is previous education to include. In detailing your education, you must decide how far back you need to go, depending on the amount of education you have and the job for which you are applying. If you are a recent college or university graduate, or soon will be, it is usually sufficient to give information about your college or university education.

If you have not yet received a diploma or degree, list the date it will be awarded. "Diploma in Accounting and Finance to be awarded May 2004." As a prospective college graduate, your education can be your strongest selling point. List some of your major and related courses. Be specific about course titles: "Accounting 3206" is not informative; "Managerial Accounting" is quite descriptive.

Special Skills

Use this optional category to list distinctive competencies such as proficiency in another language, ability to interpret for the hearing-impaired, or experience with specific software programs.

Experience

You have several options in listing work experience. You may choose to list all past jobs, even though they may be unrelated to the position for which you are applying. Past experience can demonstrate important qualities such as acceptance of responsibility and interacting with customers.

List your current or most recent work experience first and continue backward. Give the months and years of employment, such as *May 1997-June 1999*, along with the company name, city, province, and postal code. Include brief, specific descriptions of your job responsibilities using active verbs. For example:

Managed store during supervisor's absence.

Prepared weekly staff schedules.

Developed employee awards program.

Trained new employees on telephone system.

If you have had many jobs, you may use the heading "Selected Experience" or "Related Experience" and include only the jobs most related to the posi-

Use action verbs in your resumé to describe your work responsibilities:

achieved	developed	initiated	reduced
arranged	evaluated	managed	researched
completed	expanded	minimized	simplified
coordinated	implemented	organized	solved
created	improved	presented	supervised
designed	increased	programmed	trained

tion you seek. These headings indicate that your resumé does not include your entire employment history.

Activities

List your participation in school and community organizations, sports, and volunteer activities. Specify any offices you held in organizations, such as president, secretary, or treasurer. This section demonstrates your leadership abilities and community involvement, qualities that many employers look for in job candidates. You can expand the section on activities to include special recognitions such as dean's list, academic scholarships, and so on. If you expand this list, use a heading such as "Activities and Awards."

◀ **Figure 12.2**
Reference List

Thinking Critically.
What kinds of information did Janet provide in her reference list?

JANET HARDIMAN

148 Davis Drive
Regina, SK S4N 2B3

Telephone: 306-555-3284
Fax: 306-555-3429
E-mail: janeth@sympatico.ca

Reference List

EMPLOYMENT REFERENCE

Mr. Steve Roscoe
Roscoe Accounting Services
P. O. Box 3389
Regina, SK S2B 4J7
306-555-8293

ACADEMIC REFERENCE

Dr. Phyllis Jamison
Prairie Community College
812 Regal Avenue
Saskatoon, SK S9L 2W9
306-555-9923

CHARACTER REFERENCE

Ms. Selma Braxton
5234 East 33rd Street
Regina, SK S2A 4J2
306-555-2394

References.   Use the statement "References supplied upon request" to indicate you will provide references when a prospective employer requests them. As part of the resumé preparation process, you should create a reference list. The stationery for the reference list should match the stationery for the application letter and the resumé. See Figure 12.2 for an example of a reference list.

You should carefully select three individuals who know you well and who will communicate with prospective employers on your behalf. You could choose an instructor in your major field, a former or current employer or supervisor, and someone who knows you personally but is not a relative. Give the name, job title (if applicable), complete address, and telephone number of each reference.

As a courtesy, you should ask each person before you give his or her name as a reference. Although you can request permission by telephone or in person, you may also request this information in writing, as in the following example.

Would you be willing to serve as a reference for me in my job search? As you are aware, I will graduate in May 2004 from Central Community College with a Diploma in Hospitality Management. Enclosed is a copy of my resumé for your reference.

Please indicate your answer in the space provided and return this letter to me in the enclosed envelope by March 15. Thank you.

Note that this person is giving a copy of his/her resumé to people supplying references. This will help them to supply relevant information during a reference check. Remember to follow up with people who provide you with a reference to thank them and to inform them of your progress.

Resumé Types

Resumé formats are usually chronological, functional, or a combination of these two types. Scannable resumés are discussed later in this section.

Chronological Resumés

A **chronological resumé** lists work experience in reverse chronological order, with the most recent work experience listed first, as shown in Figure 12.3. Chronological resumés are appropriate when you have a steady work history and work experience in your field of interest.

Functional Resumés

Unlike chronological resumés, **functional resumés**, which are also called skills resumés, highlight professional skills and related accomplishments and de-emphasize work history. A functional resumé, as shown in Figure 12.4, is appropriate for recent graduates who wish to emphasize their education and training over their work experience.

Combination Resumés

These resumés employ the best features of chronological and functional resumés to present a prospective employee's qualifications. As shown in Figure 12.5, a **combination resumé** emphasizes skills while also mentioning work experience.

Be sure not to mispell words on a resumé.

(misspell)

BLAKE RODCHESTER
418 Barton Street
Ajax, ON L2N 4B4
905-555-2841
brodchester@hotmail.com

OBJECTIVE	To obtain a position as an accountant with opportunities for advancement based on performance.
EXPERIENCE	Accountant and Sales Associate Great Brands Outlet Store, Pickering, Ontario May 2000 to Present • Developed home page for Great Brands Internet site • Established computerized record keeping system • Completed all end-of-quarter reports Customer-Service Representative Atkins Jewelry Store, Oshawa, Ontario January 1998 to April 2000 • Handled billing inquiries from customers • Inputted data for credit reports Sales Associate Capers Department Store, Oshawa, Ontario January 1996 to December 1998 • Simplified inventory procedures for the children's department • Designed sales displays
EDUCATION	Associate of Arts Degree to be awarded May 9, 2002 Durham Community College, Oshawa, Ontario • Emphasis in Accounting • Additional hours in Management Information Systems • 3.8 overall GPA/4.0 Scale
SPECIAL SKILLS	Bilingual in English and French Proficient in Microsoft Word, PowerPoint, Access, and Excel Experienced in accounting procedures
HONORS AND ACTIVITIES	Dean's List all semesters Top Sales Award, Great Brands Outlet Store, 2000
REFERENCES	Provided on request

Devote time and effort to preparing your resumé. A sloppy, poorly written, or incomplete resumé will be set aside by a potential employer—and with it your chance for a job. If you are just beginning your academic career, start building your resumé by acquiring work experience, doing volunteer work, and participating in appropriate campus or community organizations. Establishing a solid work history can assist you in your job search by providing sources for excellent recommendations on your job performance. Having a sufficient work background in your field of interest and being involved in a variety of activities certainly makes writing your resumé much easier.

Formatting a Resumé

Once you have identified the information to include in your resumé, you need to arrange and format the information for the most attractive, professional, and eye-catching appearance. Use the guidelines in the accompanying box to help you.

Guidelines for Formatting a Resumé

- Limit your resumé to two pages. While your resumé should contain all pertinent information, it should not be crowded.

- Place your resumé attractively on the page. Include an eye-appealing combination of printed information and white space to make the resumé easy to read.

- Use 5 cm (1-inch) side and bottom margins and a 7.5 cm (1 1/2-inch) top margin.

- Use headings with bold or capital letters to identify your sections of work experience, education, activities, and skills.

- Select a readable font in 11- or 12-point type for your text and a somewhat larger font, such as 14-point type, for headings. The smallest acceptable font is a 10-point size. It should be used sparingly and reserved for less important details.

- Select a good-quality paper with matching envelopes. Ideally, your matching envelopes should be large enough to accommodate your resumé and application letter unfolded. Use the same type and colour stationery for your resumé, application letter, and list of references. White stationery is used most often, but light colours such as cream, buff, or grey are acceptable.

Figure 12.4 ▶
Functional Resumé

Thinking Critically.
Why did Brenda choose a functional format for her resumé?

BRENDA BIZAL
7 Stone Avenue
Ottawa, ON K1S 4W4
613-555-1688
bbizal@sympatico.ca

Objective: An Administrative Assistant position where my computer skills can be used.

Qualifications: Computer Skills:

Word 97 and 2000	WordPerfect 6.1
Excel 97 and 2000	Access 97 and 2000
PowerPoint 2000	PageMaker 6.5

Enter, edit, and revise data and text
Create spreadsheets, graphs, and charts
Compose business letters, memos, and reports

Administrative Skills:
Perform general office duties and reception duties
Handle complex switchboard
Maintain calendar and appointments
Keyboarding—60 words per minute

Organizational Skills:
Process incoming and outgoing mail
Work efficiently without close supervision
Supervise part-time office workers

Experience: Davis Community College Data Services Department
Logged equipment problems
Completed work orders on equipment problems
Assisted with new software loading on campus computers

Barnett's Ice Cream Shop
Waited on customers
Maintained records of company operations

Education: Davis Community College
Office Administration Diploma to be awarded May 2002

References: Available on Request

Figure 12.5
Combination Resumé
This combination resumé emphasizes Wendy's blend of experience, skills, and education.

Thinking Critically.
What is the purpose of the Profile section?

Wendy Zhao

543 West Woodland Avenue
Saskatoon, SK S7H 4W2

Telephone: 304-555-3284
E-Mail: Zhao@sask.ca

OBJECTIVE	To obtain a supervisory positon in a customer service environment.
PROFILE	Excellent customer service skills Strong communication and interpersonal skills Ability to work under pressure Proven ability to build rapport and customer loyalty
EXPERIENCE	**Customer Service Agent**, Saskatchewan Telepower Co., Saskatoon, 2002 – present • Assist customers with billing enquiries • Liaise with other departments to resolve customer issues • Participate in orientation for new employees • Deal with escalated calls during supervisor's absence
ACHIEVEMENTS	Customer Satisfaction Award, 2002 and 2003 Initiated Team Participation awards scheme at Saskatchewan Telepower
EDUCATION	**Customer Relationship Certificate**, Western College, Calgary, Albera, May 2002 Course work included • Customer Relationship Management • Communications • Computers • Team Building
VOLUNTEER WORK	Habitat for Humanity Community Shelter – Out of the Cold Program
REFERENCES	Available on request

Scannable Resumés

To take advantage of all the employment opportunities available today, job applicants must consider how to prepare a resumé to be viewed electronically. Resumés may be scanned by a computer, entered in a database, posted on the Internet, sent via e-mail, or faxed. A **scannable resumé** is one that has been written to enhance the writer's chances of being selected when computers, using a data tracking system, scan for specific keywords and nouns.

Computers are programmed to scan resumés for specific keywords or nouns associated with a particular industry and specific positions within that industry. If a resumé contains enough keywords or nouns to match an advertised job opening, the applicant is selected for further consideration. To prepare a scannable resumé, use keywords such as those listed in the Memory Hook to describe your accomplishments and responsibilities.

Besides the traditional method of submitting resumés by mail, job applicants now have the opportunity to post resumés on the Internet. These postings can be viewed 24 hours a day, 365 days of the year and are available to Internet users in Canada and in over 100 other countries. Many on-line services offer tips for writing a resumé that can be scanned or searched for keywords.

Lagging behind in technological skills poses a treat to job security.

(threat)

Keywords for Scannable Resumés.

ability to delegate	customer oriented	problem solving
ability to implement	detail minded	public speaking
accurate	flexibility	relocation
adaptable	industrious	self-starter
analytical ability	leadership	team player
communication skills	multi-tasking	willing to travel

In the box below are some guidelines to help you correctly prepare your resumé in a way that will be compatible with computers, fax machines, photocopiers, and scanners.

It is a good idea to follow up an electronically sent resumé with a printed resumé, application letter, and list of references for any job that you feel is a possible match for you. You should, however, exercise caution in sending personal information and your list of references over the Internet to employers that you do not know by reputation.

Guidelines for a Scannable Resumé

* The applicant's name should be the first line of text on the resumé.

* Put your career objective on the second line of text.

* Use keywords and nouns, not action verbs, to describe your responsibilities and accomplishments. Refer to the Memory Hook on this page for some sample keywords.

* Place keywords within the text of your resumé, or group them in a separate paragraph at the end.

* Align text at the left margin.

* Avoid centering text or using right justification.

* Do not use tabs or indenting.

* Single-space the text.

* Remove hard returns to allow the text to wrap.

* Do not condense the spacing between letters.

* Use asterisks instead of bullets.

* Do not use italic, script, or underlined text.

* Use a font size of 11 to 14 points.

* Use a readable typeface such as Times New Roman, Arial, or Comic Sans MS.

* Avoid using horizontal or vertical lines, which are difficult for computers to read.

* Do not use two-column text.

* Send an original of your resumé, not a copy.

* Use letter-size paper in a light colour such as white, eggshell, beige, or light grey.

* Print your resumé on a laser printer for the best quality.

* Do not staple or fold your resumé.

* Use the high-resolution or detailed mode when faxing your resumé to make it easier to read.

If you send a printed resumé to a prospective employer, remember it may be scanned electronically, hence the type font you choose and color of paper can either help or hinder you in your job quest. Dark or colored stationery and exotic type fonts may render your document electronically unreadable and hence unintentionally remove you from consideration.

Today's business organizations are trying to be efficient as they strive to identify people who can do specific jobs. Computers—not human resource people—screen resumés to identify potential employees. This reduces the cost and time involved in assessing job applicants.

In traditional resumés, the emphasis is on action verbs. With the scannable resumés, the emphasis is on keywords and nouns. Scanned resumés, because they are stored in large databases, remain active longer than traditional resumés.

Scanning equipment can select potential employees who can do the jobs specified. However, only the judgments made in a personal interview can determine if the person will actually do the job and fit into the organization.

Review of Key Terms

1. What is the difference between a *chronological resumé* and a *functional resumé*?
2. What is a *scannable resumé*? Why are these resumés used?

Practical Application

1. Based on your education, work experience, and skills, determine which resumé style is best for you. Explain your choice. Then, make a list of people you could use as references. Remember to contact them to make sure they agree to speak on your behalf.
2. Write your resumé using the style you selected in item 1 above. Use one of the sample resumés as a guide. Once your resumé is completed, do peer editing in your team. Make a checklist, noting use of action words, clarity, organization, spelling, grammar, and mechanics. Make sure the formatting is professional. Prepare your final resumé on good-quality paper.

   TEAMWORK
3. Turn your traditional resumé into a scannable resumé. Edit your resumé by replacing action words with keywords and nouns that describe your responsibilities and accomplishments. Then, format the resumé following the guidelines listed for scannable resumés given in this section. Remember to make an electronic copy of both your traditional resumé and your scannable resumé. Once your scannable resumé is finished, seek peer editing within your team. Use the guidelines on page 530 to make sure the resumé is ready for scanning. Remember to check spelling, grammar, and mechanics. Turn the final copy in to your instructor.

   TEAMWORK

Editing Practice

Correct any spelling errors in the following sentences.

1. The employment agency reccommended me for the job.
2. We were asked to print the address lables for the company newsletter.
3. I was truely shocked to learn about the factory lay-off.
4. Make sure the colour of your stationery and envelops match.
5. We have a vacency for an adminstrative assistant.

Discussion Points

1. Some people "pad" their skills and work experience on a resumé. Why is it important for you to be honest when listing qualifications in a resumé?
2. If you have little work experience, how can you build your resumé? Who could you use for references?
3. What effect has technology had on job searching? How can lagging behind in technological skills affect your career?

Application Documents—
Letter, Form, and Portfolio

Custom is second nature, and no less powerful.

—Michel Eyquem Montaigne, sixteenth-century French essayist

Application Letter

After you have prepared your resumé and targeted prospective employers, you are ready to organize your application letter, often called a cover letter. The **application letter** is a companion document to your resumé and list of references; to show this connection, use the same stationery and typeface for all three documents.

Remember, the application letter is intended to highlight your most important qualifications and to persuade the employer to grant you a personal interview. Your resumé will help the employer determine whether you have the education and skills required for the job. A sample application letter appears in Figure 12.6.

Get to the Point Immediately

The first paragraph of your application letter should:

• State your intent to apply for a position with the company.

• Describe the position for which you are applying.

• Indicate how you learned about the position.

If you are submitting a resumé to a company that has no advertised openings in your field of interest, identify the type of position you seek.

There is no one best opening for an application letter. The following opening sentences are suggestions that have been used successfully. Adapt them to suit your needs.

For Newspaper Ads.

Please consider me an applicant for the position of management trainee, as advertised in the June 25 issue of *The Globe and Mail*.

The position of paralegal, which you advertised in the April 1 issue of the *Gazette*, matches my qualifications and experience. Please consider me an applicant for this position.

From an actual job application letter –

"I would like to set up a meating to discust possible job opportunities with …"

[meeting; discuss]

Figure 12.6 ▶
Application Letter

Thinking Critically.
What four things does
Nasreen do in this
application letter?

Nasreen Hamali
227 Oak Bay Road, Apt. 31
Calgary, Alberta T4V 6J6
(403) 555-7355

January 20, 2001

Ms. Sophia Bergart
Human Resources Consultant
Able & Wise Building Supplies Limited
72 Mountain View Road
Edmonton, AB T9A 4J7

Dear Ms. Bergart:

Please consider me a candidate for the position of Sales Associate as advertised in
the January 16 issue of *Alberta News*.

I graduated in December 20-- from Alberta Business College with a diploma in
Business Studies — Marketing. While pursuing my studies over the last three
years, I have also worked part time as a sales associate for two firms that sell
building products.

I have letters of reference from both employers outlining my excellent work record.

In a recent issue of *Business News* I read that Able & Wise is expected to grow
rapidly in the near future. As a member of your expansion team, I can offer you:

• Strong interpersonal and communication skills
• The ability to work as a team player
• A customer-service focus
• Knowledge of the current Building Code
• Eagerness to work hard, to learn, and to excel

I would welcome the opportunity to discuss my potential contribution to your
company. Thank you for considering my application.

Sincerely,

Nasreen Hamali

(Ms.) Nasreen Hamali

For Referrals.

A mutual friend, Marvin Klein, suggested that I contact you concerning a position
as administrative assistant with your company.

Your company has been recommended to me by Mrs. Ana Perez, the placement
director of Maritime College, as one with exceptional opportunities for accountants.
Might you have a position for a self-starter who has two years of experience in
accounts payable?

For Applications Made Directly to a Company.

I believe my qualifications for a position as insurance adjuster will interest you.

I am interested in working for a progressive real estate firm such as yours. My enclosed resumé lists my qualifications for the position.

Here are five reasons why I think you will be interested in interviewing me for a sales position with Kramer and Associates.

Explain Why You Should Be Considered

In the second paragraph of your application letter, state how your skills and accomplishments make you a desirable candidate for the position referred to in the first paragraph. For example:

As you can see from my enclosed resumé, my coursework in accounting, human resource management, and economics has prepared me to assess a variety of financial and personnel needs. In all my courses, I consistently ranked in the top 5 per cent of my class.

Of course, the nature of the second paragraph will depend on what you have to sell. If your work experience is limited and unlikely to impress the employer, you should emphasize your education. In such a case, you might follow the above paragraph with a statement such as this:

Of particular interest to me in the accounting courses I completed were the applications of accounting theory to computerized procedures and equipment. Working for a large organization such as Johnson Associates would allow me to implement my training with spreadsheets and databases on a wide scale.

The writer of the following paragraph lacks business experience but compensates for this lack by demonstrating interest and enthusiasm.

I am very interested in working as a paralegal for Dunn and Kellerman. As a result of conversations with Yukio Tanaka, a paralegal with your firm, I feel the varied duties and opportunities for advancement fit well with my legal research background. With my willingness to learn and attention to detail, I can be an asset to Dunn and Kellerman within a short period of time.

If you have had experience related to the position for which you are applying, make the most of it as in the following example.

As an intern with Evans-Henshaw & Company last summer, I participated on the total quality management team that drafted information-processing procedures. This opportunity gave me valuable experience in team problem solving that I could put to use for your company.

Show a Willingness to Work and Learn

The employer who hires you is taking a risk that you may not be suitable for the position. One of the best ways to convince the employer of your suitability is to demonstrate a willingness to learn and to express genuine interest in the job. The following are examples of ways you can convey your enthusiasm:

As a self-starter who absorbs new information quickly, you will find me willing to learn and eager to improve.

I am not afraid of hard work; in fact, I enjoy it.

I pride myself on my punctuality, accuracy, and dependability.

You will find I am adept at problem solving and a quick learner.

These claims should not, of course, be made unless they are true.

Point Out How Your Qualifications Meet the Employer's Needs

The reason a position is open is that the employer has a need. The employer does not want just any employee but an employee who can fulfill that need. When an ad specifies particular qualifications needed for a position, be sure you underscore your own qualifications in your cover letter and/or resumé that will fulfill that need.

Make It Easy for the Employer to Ask You for an Interview

Write the last paragraph of your application letter with the aim of obtaining an invitation for an interview. Make it easy for the employer to contact you by including your telephone number and the best time to reach you if you do not have voice mail.

I look forward to meeting with you to discuss the paralegal position available with your firm. You may contact me at 314-555-7613 or at the address at the top of the letter. I am available to meet with you between 11 a.m. and 3 p.m. Monday through Thursday.

Application Form

Most companies require prospective employees to fill out an **application form**. You may be asked to complete the form at the company office, to take the form home to complete, or to fill in an on-line form.

Be Prepared

When applying for a job, take the information you will need with you to complete an application form. Most application forms ask for details about your education, work experience, and references. You should have this detailed information with you, along with a copy of your resumé and a list of your references. These documents will help you complete the application form accurately and completely. These tips will help you be prepared:

- Read the application form before you start.
- Take two working pens, preferably black.
- Write legibly.
- Follow any directions given on the application form. If the instructions say "print," don't use cursive writing.

The Hidden Questions

A prospective employer can tell a great deal about you by the way you complete the application form. Your completed application shows if you:

- are sloppy in your work habits,
- can follow written directions,
- are detail oriented,
- can accurately complete a task.

The Job-Related Questions

The basic categories of information on an application form include:

- your name, mailing address, and phone number, so the employer can contact you;
- your educational background, including schools attended, dates attended, mailing addresses, and phone numbers;
- your work experience, including names and addresses of employers, dates employed, job duties, reasons for leaving, and—sometimes—beginning and ending salaries;
- references, including names, mailing addresses, and phone numbers.

Some application forms include questions you are expected to answer in complete sentences. The purpose of these questions is to test your ability to communicate clearly in writing; your knowledge of spelling, punctuation, and grammar rules; and your proofreading skills.

Tips for Completing the Application Form

Keep these suggestions in mind the next time you fill out an application form:

- Read the application before filling it out so you know what information is requested.
- Use black ink because it photocopies better than blue ink.
- Keyboard the form, if possible; otherwise, use your neatest printing. If the job requires a great deal of keyboarding, you should key the application.
- Double-check your answers to be sure all the dates match what's on your resumé.
- If the form asks for "Salary Desired" or "Salary Requirement," never include a figure; answer "Open" or "Negotiable." The job interview is the appropriate time and place to discuss salary.
- Don't leave anything blank. If the category does not apply, write "N/A" or put a line in the blank to show you read the question. The only exception to this would be if the answer is very negative and you believe it might eliminate you from consideration for the position. In that case, leave the answer blank and be prepared to discuss it in the job interview.
- Never state a negative reason for leaving a job. Use reasons such as better job opportunity, career advancement, return to school, and summer/seasonal job. Obviously, negative reasons will reflect poorly on you.

The Signature

Application forms have a place at the end for your signature. A paragraph above the signature line often states that the information you have put on the application is true and accurate to the best of your knowledge. You are expected to sign that statement. If you lie or significantly misrepresent yourself on an application form and the employer finds out, the employer has a legal right to terminate you—even if you are doing a good job.

Remember that your application form becomes part of your permanent record at your company.

Employment Portfolio

A **portfolio** is a folder or notebook containing evidence and examples of your achievements and skills. Portfolios are gaining in popularity and acceptance in the job search arena. For many years, artists, models, and advertising associates have used portfolios to display examples of their work during interviews. Prospective employees in other fields have noted the value of this method and are using it too.

Portfolio Contents

A resumé and a list of references form the basis of the portfolio, but your creativity and your prospective employment position determine the contents of your portfolio. For example, potential sales representatives might include pictures and scripts or videos of mock sales presentations they have developed. Administrative assistants might include examples of non-confidential correspondence and spreadsheets they have prepared. Medical personnel might include copies of their licence and certificates.

Every item in your portfolio should be of high quality. Start with an attractive binder that has pockets for odd-shaped items such as a video tape. Documents such as your resumé, transcripts, and certificates should be placed in plastic sheet protectors.

Portfolios become a conversation piece during an interview. Thus, you should include items that you want to talk about because they accentuate your strengths. Professional portfolios are built over time. As you complete a course or master a new skill, select and accumulate class- or work-related projects that could be used in your portfolio.

The following items could be included in a portfolio, if applicable:

- title page
- divider pages with labelled tabs
- resumé
- references
- a copy of diplomas and certificates
- transcript of grades, if your grades were good
- perfect attendance awards
- software examples that you've created in class
- document examples from a job
- anything else that will serve as "proof" of your ability

Presenting Your Portfolio

Find the right time to introduce your portfolio during a job interview. Few interviewers will ask to see your portfolio; they expect you to present it to them. Here are ways to introduce it.

When Discussing Your Educational or Work Background.
You might reply: "I learned a great deal at XYZ College about how to prepare professional-looking documents in a timely manner. I've brought my portfolio with some samples of what I learned. Would you care to look at it?"

When Answering Specific Questions About Your Computer Skills.
You might say as you open your portfolio to the appropriate section: "Here's

a PowerPoint presentation I prepared for my supervisor. I enjoy working with presentation software."

When You Have an Opportunity to Ask Questions. If you have not found an opportunity during the interview to present your portfolio, you can do it as the interviewer asks if you have any questions. After your questions, you could say: "I'm very interested in this position, and I believe I have the qualifications you are looking for. Would you care to look at my portfolio and see the kinds of work I'm capable of doing?"

When You Are Asked to Take a Test or Complete Additional Paperwork. If the interviewer asks you to take tests or to complete additional paperwork, say: "Would you like to look at my portfolio while I'm taking the test?"

Review of Key Terms

1. What is the purpose of an *application letter*?
2. What are some tips to follow when completing an *application form*?
3. What is a *portfolio*? How can a portfolio help you in a job interview?

Practical Application

1. From the "Help Wanted" advertisements in your local newspaper, select a position that appeals to you and for which you are qualified, or will be upon graduation. Write an application letter answering the advertisement, and enclose a resumé targeted specifically for this job.
2. Make a list of some items you can include in your work portfolio. Then, begin to collect these items, making sure that everything looks professional. Write a summary about what you will include in your portfolio.
3. Complete an Internet search for sites that advertise job openings. Select two or three companies that interest you and have this feature. Then, make a list of current listings and qualifications needed for those openings, and find out if they have on-line applications. Compose a short presentation for your class, and share URLs for these companies.

Editing Practice

Correct any errors in the use of pronouns in the following sentences.

1. The article was written by she last summer.
2. Lori and him volunteered to work overtime during inventory.
3. Are you going to give your expense report to Gordon or I?
4. With who did you have your appointment?
5. Mr. Wallace stated that it was the operator and them who made the shipping error.

Discussion Points

1. Interviewers often read the application letter before looking at the resumé. What can you do to ensure that your application letter and resumé get you an interview?
2. What does an application form communicate about you to a prospective employer?
3. When should you present your portfolio to the interviewer? Should you let your portfolio do the talking, or should you provide narration as the interviewer flips through the pages?

The Effective Employment Interview

Luck is what happens when preparation meets opportunity.

—Anonymous

▶ **Key Terms**

▶ screening interview

▶ one-on-one interview

▶ panel (committee) interview

▶ group interview

▶ stress interview

▶ unstructured interview

▶ behavioural interview

▶ situational interview

The job interview is always a critical factor in determining whether or not a person is hired. For that reason, it is essential for you to be well prepared for each interview in which you participate. No matter how impressive your background, your resumé, and your application letter, you may fail to be hired if you cannot "sell" yourself when you meet a prospective employer face to face. In Section 12.1, you learned that a resumé and application letter are the first phase in marketing yourself to potential employers. The interview is the second phase of the marketing process.

During an interview, you have an opportunity to sell yourself. Your responses to questions, your descriptions of experiences and activities, your explanations of procedures and methods—all contribute to the interviewer's impression of you. Therefore, you must prepare thoroughly to interview well.

Mental Preparation for the Interview

Although you were not conscious of it at the time, you began preparing for a job interview quite some time ago. You chose the type of work you wanted to do; then you acquired the education and training necessary for your chosen career. You then targeted prospective employers, compiled a resumé and a list of references, wrote an application letter, and obtained the interview. Now you must prepare for the job interview itself.

Remember the Goal of the Interview

Remember that your goal is twofold: first, to sell yourself; and second, to find out if the job draws on your qualifications and fits your career plans.

Research the Prospective Employer

Conduct some research on your prospective employer. Find out about the company's products, services, and history. Knowing something about the organization will help you decide whether it is a place you would like to work.

Having this background knowledge will also help you effectively answer the often-asked question, "Why are you interested in working for our company?" Your answer should demonstrate that you know something about the company. "I have always been interested in investments, and I know that your company is one of the leading investment firms in this area." Or, "I'm interested in the telecommunications industry, and I know that your company has recently developed a wireless fourth generation cellular phone that has the potential to revolutionize the way we use cellular phones."

Most employers agree that thoroughly researching the employer's company is one of the most important things you can do to prepare for an interview. Follow these guidelines, therefore, in researching a company:

- Speak with the person who referred you to the organization or to an employee of the organization to gather information.
- Explore the Internet for information about the company or organization. Many companies have home pages on the World Wide Web that provide background information about the company, including the type of business and a description of its products and services.
- Search print or computerized databases in the library for information about local, national, or international companies.
- Obtain a copy of the company's annual report.
- Contact the chamber of commerce for information on companies in the area—the type of business, years of operation, and number of employees.

Remember that printed material may not be current. Always check the date of the information.

When researching an organization, find answers to as many of the following questions as possible:

- How long has the company been in business?
- Is the company publicly or privately owned?
- Is the company a subsidiary or a division?
- Where is the corporate headquarters located (if applicable)?
- What services and products does the company offer?
- How many people does the company employ?
- Who are the company's competitors in the industry?
- Does the company show a certain pattern of growth in the past 10 to 20 years?
- What are the company's annual sales?
- What are the company's assets and earnings for the previous year?
- Does the firm have divisions and subdivisions?
- Are there offices in more than one province?
- What vision does the company have for new products and services?
- Are there any international operations and/or plans for expansion into other countries?

Job applicants who have researched the company they are interviewing with (1) are better able to discuss how their experiences and qualifications match the company's needs, and (2) can also talk about how they can make an immediate contribution to the organization. The ability to do these two things makes a very positive impression in a job interview.

Prepare Questions to Ask the Interviewer

During an interview you will be asked many questions designed to help the employer find out about your specific skills and qualifications for the job. Remember: the interview is also your opportunity to find out more about the company. Prepare a list of questions you would like to ask and take the list with you to the interview.

Research-Related Questions. Researching a company will help you prepare intelligent questions to ask the interviewer. Here are some examples:

I read that your company exports products to South America. What percentage of your product is shipped abroad?

I know that your company has eight branch offices. Which office is experiencing the most growth?

Job-Related Questions. After you are comfortably into the interview, plan to ask some questions related to the prospective job. Questions you might ask the interviewer include:

- Could you please describe the type of person who does best in your company?
- What would my primary duties be? How will these change over time?
- Could you please tell me how my work in this position fits into the whole operation of your company?
- What are the opportunities for advancement?
- Would travel be required for this position?
- What is your company's dress code?
- What is the most difficult part of the job?
- Who would I be working with, and what do they do?
- How will my work be evaluated, and how often?
- Are internal candidates being considered for this position?
- How soon will the decision for this position be made?

Questions About Salary and Benefits. After the company shows an interest in hiring you, it is permissible to ask questions that deal with salary, benefits, vacation, or job security. If you ask these questions too early in the interview, an employer may interpret them as self-centered questions that reveal that you're more concerned about yourself than you are about what you can offer the company.

Examples of these types of questions are:

- Does the company provide training and additional education for employees who want to develop their skills?
- What health insurance benefits do you provide for employees?
- What is the salary for this position? Sometimes, a job applicant knows the salary offered for a position before the interview. However, if you do not know the salary, you should ask about the salary near the end of the interview. The best time to negotiate for salary and benefits is *after* you've been offered the job.
- Listen closely during the job interview and take notes. You don't want to ask a question that was answered earlier in the interview.

Know Your Strengths and Weaknesses

As a job applicant, you are a sales representative, and the product you are selling is you. Preparing a resumé gives you an excellent opportunity to put on paper what you have to sell—to emphasize your strengths and to present your education, experience, and special interests and skills in a way that makes you a strong candidate for the job. You should know your qualifications so well that you can communicate them orally without hesitation.

Anticipate Questions

Anticipate questions that the interviewer may ask about your education, work experience, and personal qualities. Interview questions are discussed in the next section. You should practice answering these questions out loud to prepare for the actual interview. Ways to practice include: recording your questions and answers and then evaluating the recording, and watching your facial expressions and eye contact by answering the questions as you sit in front of a mirror. The best way to practice is to have a friend or family member ask you interview questions and videotape the mock interview. The videotape will show any nervous habits that you don't realize you have.

Become Knowledgeable About Industry Trends and Current Events

Acquire a working knowledge of trends and issues in the industry in which the company does business. Also, keep up-to-date about local and national current events. Read a local newspaper to learn about issues as well as cultural and civic events. Such knowledge demonstrates interest in the business and thoroughness in preparing for the interview.

Physical Preparation for the Interview

Make sure you have the information and materials you need to keep your appointment and to do well.

Confirm Your Appointment

One or two days before the interview, make a telephone call to confirm the appointment time, date, and place.

Get Directions to the Interview Site

Ask for directions to the interview site. If you are taking public transportation, double-check the departure times and travel times. If your interview is in a city or town with which you are unfamiliar, get a map of that city and study it. If you are driving, make sure you know where you can park. If possible, travel to the interview site the day before the interview to determine the travel time, route, and exact location of the building. Make sure you have enough gas or money for the trip.

Identify Items to Take

Take the following items to an interview:

- Two good pens.
- A professional-looking folder with a letter-sized pad of paper.

- Three or four copies of your resumé and list of references, placed in a the folder. Often you will interview with more than one person. Each interviewer may not have a copy of your resumé. You can also use an extra copy of your resumé as a reference when completing a job application form.

- A list of questions to ask the interviewer. Keep this list in the folder with your resumé. You should not read the list to the interviewer, but have it available to refresh your memory. Review the list while waiting for your appointment.

- A portfolio, if appropriate, that contains documents or projects that demonstrate your knowledge and qualifications.

Types of Interviews

The questions you are asked during a job interview will be determined by the type of interview that you are given. There are several types of interviews.

Screening Interview

A **screening interview** is conducted to determine if you have the skills and qualifications for the job. This type of interview may be conducted over the telephone and may also serve as a preliminary screening of your communication skills and interpersonal skills. Keep your responses concise.

One-on-One Interview

As the label implies, in a **one-on-one interview** you will be interviewed by one person only. The interviewer wants to see if you will fit in with the company and determine how your skills will benefit the company.

Panel or Committee Interview

An interview with several people is fairly common today as companies look for ways to make better hiring decisions. This is called a **panel (committee) interview**. The interview team members usually take turns asking questions. When answering questions, focus your attention on the person who asked the question rather than the whole group.

Group Interview

In a **group interview**, several applicants meet with one or two interviewers. This type of interview is designed to uncover leadership potential among the applicants and to see how you interact with others.

Stress Interview

A **stress interview** is a deliberate attempt to put you under stress to test how you react under pressure. Some techniques used in stress interviewing are rapidly firing questions at you, attempting to place you on the defensive with irritating questions or comments, or long periods of silence after you answer a question. Do not attempt to "fill up" this silence by talking. Doing so will indicate that you feel uncomfortable with the silence. Also, in these circumstances, people often say something unfortunate. Remain calm during this type of interview by remembering that the interviewers are simply looking at your ability to handle stress.

Unstructured Interview

An **unstructured interview** usually consists of one or two broad questions, such as, "Why don't you tell me about yourself?" The purpose is to find out if the applicant is wise enough to focus on his or her qualifications for the job and to assess oral communication skills.

Behavioural Interview

In a **behavioural interview**, the idea is to see how a candidate handled a situation in the past. The theory is that past behaviour is a good predictor of future behaviour. The interviewer uses questions and statements to get applicants to relate specific examples of how they have successfully used the skills required in the job. An example of a behavioural interview question is, "Tell me about a conflict you had with another student and how you handled it."

To prepare for a behavioural interview, list the key attributes required for the job outlined in the job description. Think about potential questions for each of these attributes and based on your experience develop brief responses. For example if a requirement is "ability to work in a team," put yourself in the interviewer's place and frame some questions. "Describe a time when you made a significant contribution to a team project," or "Tell me about a time when you worked on a team project and one member of the team did not contribute. How did you handle this?" Draw on your experience and develop your answers to highlight your team skills.

Other attributes for which you could prepare behavioural responses are:

- ability to handle stress
- customer service skills
- dealing with an angry customer
- showing initiative
- perseverance
- sensitivity to cultural differences
- communication skills

Your examples do not have to be limited to business or school experiences, unless the interviewer specifically requests this. You can draw on experience in clubs, volunteer work, sports teams, etc.

Situational Interview

A **situational interview** is similar to a behavioural interview. Instead of asking candidates to relate past experiences, the applicant is given a situation and then asked, "How would you handle this?"

Interview Questions

There are literally hundreds of questions you might be asked during the course of an interview. Here are examples of possible interview questions you should be prepared to answer.

Sample Standard Interview Questions

1. Why did you select this particular course of study?
2. Which of these courses did you like best? Why? Which course did you like the least? Why?

3. Tell me something about your course in communications (or other subject).
4. I see by your application that you were a co-op student at ABC Company for one semester. Describe the work you did. What did you like most about your job? What did you like least?
5. What hobbies or activities do you enjoy in your spare time?
6. Were you active in school organizations? Which ones?
7. Do you like to write? How would you rate your English skills?
8. Tell me about yourself. (This request will give you a chance to emphasize your most salable features, such as what you do best. Never discuss your family, marital status, financial problems, or health problems.)
9. If I talked to your teachers/class mates/the office staff/your present supervisor, what do you think they would say about you?
10. What have you accomplished lately that makes you feel proud?
11. What motivates you?
12. How would you rate your communication skills and what have you done to improve them?
13. What else besides your school studies and job experience qualifies you for this job?
14. What have you read lately and what are you reading now?
15. Do you prefer to work independently or as part of a team?
16. What are some of the things you like to avoid in a job? Why?
17. What are some of the things that you feel have done particularly well in a present or previous job?
18. What does success mean to you? How do you judge it?
19. Who or what in your life has influenced you most with regard to your career objectives?
20. What kinds of things do you feel most confident in doing? Somewhat less confident in doing?
21. What are some of the things you are doing now, or have thought about doing, that are self-development activities?
22. What kinds of pressures have you experienced in a job? How do you cope with these pressures?
23. Do you make decisions quickly, or do you take time?
24. Do you become involved, or hold back, when you see coworkers disagreeing?
25. Do you prefer a job with clear tasks and responsibilities, or one where things change frequently?
26. What have been your experiences in dealing with customers? When have people really tried your patience?
27. What goals have you set in the past and how successful have you been in attaining them?
28. What gives you the greatest satisfaction?
29. How would you describe yourself?
30. What has been your most rewarding experience in life?
31. What do you know about our company?
32. If you were hiring someone for this job, what qualities would you look for? Why?
33. What does two-way communication mean to you?
34. Describe a time when you had to set priorities.

35. Describe a very busy day and explain how you scheduled your time.
36. Do you like to try new things, or do you prefer to stay with established routines?
37. If you were a supervisor, and a staff member regularly came to work late, what would you do?
38. What are some things about school/your present job that you like? What do you dislike?
39. Summarize your college courses and your work experience. (Emphasize the college courses or work experience that will best support your qualifications for this job.)
40. What are your strongest points? Your weakest points?
41. Why should you be hired for this position?
42. Why do you want to work for our company?
43. Why did you leave your last job?
44. What job would you like to have five years from now?
45. Would you be willing to work overtime if necessary?
46. Would you be willing to travel?
47. Would you be willing to relocate?
48. What do you do on your days off?

Sample Surprise Interview Questions

1. If you could be an animal, what animal would you be, and why?
2. Give me three words that describe you.
3. What is the worst mistake you ever made?
4. What was the last book you read?
5. Why do you think manhole covers are round?

Sample Behavioural Interview Questions

1. Describe a situation in which you recognized a potential problem as an opportunity. What did you do?
2. How have you built and maintained successful relationships at school or work? Give me examples.
3. Tell me about a time when you failed to meet a deadline. What happened? What did you learn?
4. Describe a time when you got co-workers or classmates who dislike each other to work together. How did you do this?
5. Give me an example of a time when you set a goal and were able to meet or achieve it.
6. Tell me about a time when you had to go above and beyond the call of duty to get a job done.
7. What is your typical way of dealing with conflict? Give me an example.
8. Tell me about a recent situation in which you had to deal with a very upset customer or co-worker.
9. Describe a time when you were under a lot of pressure and how you dealt with this.
10. Tell me about a time when you used your communication skills to achieve something worthwhile.

Your answers to interview questions will help the interviewer assess your qualifications for the position, determine how quickly you would adjust to the job, and gauge your potential for growth.

Use this strategy when answering behavioral interview questions:

Remember the acronym SAR when responding to a behavioral interview question.
1. Situation—Describe the specific situation or event.
2. Action—Describe the action you took.
3. Results—Describe the outcome. What happened?

The Interview

When you arrive at the interview site, state your name and the purpose of your visit. While you wait, review your resumé, check your completed application form, and read any literature about the company that is available in the reception area. Always convey a professional image.

Interviewing—From the Interviewer's Perspective

Most interviewers have three standard goals for an interview:

1. To give the applicant general information about the company and specific information on the position. Sometimes the interviewer will give the applicant printed information about the company and a printed job description.

2. To establish a positive rapport that makes the interview comfortable for the applicant. A skilled interviewer will try to put the applicant at ease to facilitate the interview process.

3. To get enough information from the candidate to make a decision about the person's suitability for employment with the company.

Making a Positive First Impression

Your punctuality and appearance contribute to the impression you make. Follow these suggestions to create a positive first impression.

Arrive Early. Plan to arrive for your appointment at least 15 minutes early. Traffic problems, weather, or simply getting lost could result in your being late. Last-minute traffic delays can cause you to feel frustrated, apprehensive, and stressed. Allow an extra 30 minutes to arrive at the interview site on time and relaxed.

Ensure a Businesslike Appearance. It is most important to look your best at an employment interview. Therefore:
- Make sure your hair, nails, and shoes are neat and clean.
- Avoid wild coloured clothing. Stick to more neutral or conservative colours.
- You want the interviewer to perceive you as a professional, and a suit or other business outfit definitely contributes to that image. Men should wear a tie. Women must remember that short skirts and sleeveless tops are not appropriate.
- Put your car keys and any other essentials in a pocket or a briefcase that contains your resumé.
- Be conservative about accessories. Avoid dangling and gaudy jewelry.

- Watch your personal grooming. Ensure that you have no body odor or bad breath. Be cautious about wearing too much cologne or after-shave. Avoid smoking before going into an interview because the smoke smell will be on your clothes and your breath. Don't chew gum during an interview.

Check Your Appearance.   While you are waiting to be called in for the interview, visit the restroom and make sure your hair and clothes are neat.

Demonstrate Your Self-Confidence.   The impression you make when you first walk into the room will very likely influence the interviewer's attitude toward you throughout the entire interview. Stand up straight, smile, and project an air of self-confidence. Preparing yourself, as outlined in this chapter, is the key to building self-confidence.

Beginning the Interview.   When you are ushered into the interviewer's office, try to be relaxed—but not casual or arrogant—and to look pleasant. Greet your interviewer with a firm handshake, a smile, and good eye contact. Introduce yourself and express your interest in employment with the company. Seat yourself only when you are invited to do so.

Keep with you the materials you have brought. Don't place anything on the interviewer's desk unless you are invited to do so. When asked about your education and work experience, give the interviewer your resumé if you haven't already done so. Say something like: "Here is my resumé, which summarizes the information. I also have completed the application form." Then hand both to the interviewer.

Follow the interviewer's lead. The interviewer may ask most of the questions or prefer that you take the initiative.

During the Interview

During the interview, conduct yourself in a professional manner. Follow these suggestions:

Be Attentive and Speak Clearly.   Face the interviewer directly and speak to him or her. It is fine to shift your gaze occasionally, but don't stare at the floor or out the window while either of you is talking.

Speak Slowly and Enunciate Carefully.   Give your answers and statements in a straightforward manner. This shows that you have thought them through and that you can speak with precision. Give short answers that sufficiently answer the questions. For example, if you are asked this question, "I see you had one course in accounting. Did you like it?" it is not enough simply to say yes. You might add, "I enjoyed the course very much, and I plan to take more accounting in evening school."

Be Specific and Honest About Your Qualifications.   "My accounting courses consisted of principles, cost, and tax. I also had the opportunity to learn two accounting packages on microcomputers." Or, "I consistently received high grades in communication courses, and I particularly liked writing letters." Or, "One of the most interesting things I did during my summers at Laverty's was to verify the cash balance each day. It wasn't easy to make everything balance, since we had so many people handling the cash, but I was successful and learned a lot from the experience." When asked about your achievements or experiences, show the interviewer appropriate items from your portfolio.

Be Noncommittal About Controversial Matters. Try to respond positively to questions that ask you to critique yourself or someone else. If you are asked your opinion about your previous supervisor or place of work, and your opinion isn't especially favourable, reply diplomatically: "My work there gave me some valuable experience, and I enjoyed much of it."

- *Be objective when you must explain why you left a previous position.* If you make negative comments about the people or the company policies of former employers, you may give the impression that you are a complainer. Say something like, "I found it difficult to adjust to some of the procedures and to the unusual hours at XYZ Company."
- *When you are asked about your strengths, respond by identifying your strongest point without bragging about it.* "I am very task oriented and work diligently until the project is completed."
- *When asked about your biggest weakness, answer the question truthfully and positively.* "I sometimes take on too many tasks, which can lead to a lot of stress. I've recently set up a new diary system so that I can see at a glance what my commitments are. It's already starting to help me be more realistic."

Express Confidence

If you're asked about leisure activities, mention interests that involve either physical energy or mental capabilities. Good answers would include jogging, playing tennis, reading, and working on your computer. Avoid giving poor answers such as watching television, shopping, and sleeping. Develop constructive leisure activities if you don't have any, because many interviewers ask this question to find out if you have initiative.

Relax, and smile occasionally. Remember: the interviewer needs someone to fill an open position and is just as eager to make a decision in your favour as you are to get the job. Avoid nervous habits such as brushing lint off clothing, fussing with hair, toying with an object such as a pen or a paper clip, or putting your hand to your face. Give your full attention to the interviewer.

Avoid the temptation to read materials on the interviewer's desk. He or she would likely view you as being nosy and unprofessional.

If your interview involves dining, follow the lead of your interviewer. Ask for suggestions on menu items, but don't order the most expensive meal. Avoid foods such as spaghetti that are messy to eat. Let your interviewer begin eating first. Enjoy your meal, but remember that you are still under scrutiny. Be sure to thank the interviewer for your meal.

Ending the Interview

The interviewer generally will let you know when the interview is over. The usual sign is to rise. As soon as the interviewer stands, you should also rise. The exchange that takes place might be something like the following conversation.

Interviewer (rising): I enjoyed meeting and talking with you.

Applicant (rising): Thank you, Mr. Higashi. I enjoyed meeting you and appreciate the opportunity to interview with your company.

Interviewer: We have your telephone number, and we will call you just as soon as we have reached a decision.

Applicant : Thank you. I'll look forward to hearing from you. Do you know when you will make a decision?

Interviewer: You should hear from us by the end of next week. Good-bye.

Applicant : Good-bye.

Leave quickly and thank the receptionist as you depart.

Following Up the Interview

As soon as possible after the interview, jot down the names and titles of the people with whom you talked. Write a summary based on your notes and your opinions about what you learned regarding the company and the job during the interview. If you are interviewing for jobs in several different companies, these written summaries will prove an excellent way to refresh your memory about an interview when you are trying to make your final job choice.

Post-Interview Thank-You Letters

After you have been interviewed, it is good strategy—and common courtesy—to write the interviewer a thank-you letter. Getting the follow-up letter on the interviewer's desk a day or two after the interview will create a good impression. The thank-you letter puts your name before the interviewer again and it gives you a second opportunity to sell yourself by mentioning pertinent qualifications. A basic follow-up letter might take this form:

Dear Ms. Tsui:

Thank you for meeting with me on April 15 to discuss the medical assistant position at Rose Valley Clinic.

Your description of the position gave me a clear picture of the responsibilities that a medical assistant has at your facility. The duties you discussed fit well with my training and my internship experience at Belmont Manor.

After visiting your clinic, I am convinced I could make a positive contribution to your patient-care team. I look forward to hearing from you soon.

Sincerely

Follow-up Letter

If you have not heard from the company within the time frame indicated at the interview, write a follow-up letter to each person with whom you interviewed. Express your continued interest in the position and ask that your application remain on file.

Dear Mr. Swanson:

On April 2 I interviewed with you for the position of computer operator. During the interview, you indicated that you would make a decision within two to three weeks.

I am still very interested in the position and would like you to keep my application current. Please contact me at 216-555-4253 if you need additional information about my qualifications.

Sincerely,

Accepting a Job Offer

Suppose that you receive a letter offering you a position for which you applied and interviewed. You decide to take the job. If you are to start work almost immediately, or if a reply has been requested by a certain date, you should probably telephone to inform the employer of your decision. Writing a letter is appropriate if your reporting date is two or more weeks away or if the representative is out of town.

Dear Mrs. Kunze:

I am pleased to accept the position as editorial assistant with the catalogue department of Herr's Exports. I know that I will enjoy working with you in designing and producing your promotional and sales materials.

As you requested, I shall report to work on Monday, September 18. Thank you for the confidence you have expressed in me by giving me this opportunity.

Sincerely,

Declining a Job Offer

You may decide not to take the position, however. Declining a job offer should be done tactfully, not only because it is the right thing to do, but also because you may be interested in working for that firm later in your career.

Dear Dr. Wolzinki:

Thank you for offering me the position of office manager for your medical practice. Since we last talked, I have been offered and have accepted a position as office manager in a real estate company.

Working in a real estate office will help me achieve my long-term goal of becoming a commercial real estate sales representative. My new employer is already encouraging me to begin studying for the licensing exam.

Thank you, Dr. Wolzinki, for your time and courtesy in interviewing me. I very much appreciate that you considered me worthy of the position in your office.

Sincerely,

Thank-You Letters to Others

After you have accepted a job, you should personally thank each person who helped you get the job. You should write a brief note or letter to the people who provided job leads, introductions to potential employers, or personal references.

Dear Mr. Trower:

You will be pleased to learn that I have accepted a position as medical technologist with Durham Region Medical Centre in Oshawa. The staff of the Durham Region Medical Centre performs diagnostic tests for eight large hospitals. I start work next week, and I am eager to begin my new position. The job fits well with my qualifications.

Thank you very much for letting me list you as a character reference. I am sure that your recommendation was instrumental in my being hired.

Sincerely,

Handling Rejections

Be positive, but be realistic. You may get the job for which you interview, but you may not. Whether you are turned down once or many times, don't take the rejection personally. View each interview as a learning experience. Take note of the strategies that worked well and use them again. Eliminate or improve the strategies that were ineffective.

Review of Key Terms

1. Explain the difference between a *behavioural interview* and a *situational interview*.
2. What are the reasons for using a *group interview*?
3. Compare and contrast how you would prepare for a *one-on-one interview* with preparing for a *committee interview*.

Practical Application

1. Each of the following questions or statements may be used during an employment interview. Prepare written answers.

   Why do you think you would like this job?

   What are your job goals for the next five-year period?

   What are your strengths and weaknesses?

   Tell me about yourself.

   Summarize your college courses and your work experience.

   What is your typical way of dealing with a conflict? Give me an example.

2. Make a list of the questions you might like to ask the interviewer about the position for which you are applying, or the company for which you wish to work.

3. Assume you are being interviewed at Data Bytes, Inc. The interviewer begins by expressing two opposing opinions about a topic and then asks for your opinion. What should you do? Then he asks that you list the strengths and weaknesses of your former supervisor. What would you say?

4. Assume you just interviewed with Worldwide Telecommunications.
   a. Write a thank-you letter to Patricia L. Carmichael, director of the company.
   b. Now assume you have been offered the job. Write an acceptance letter.

5. Form pairs and take turns being the interviewer and the applicant. Each pair should prepare a list of questions to be asked by the interviewer. Videotape the interview. Then, write an analysis of your performance as an applicant—address areas of strengths and weaknesses.

TEAMWORK

Editing Practice

The following sentences lack writing polish. Edit and rewrite them.
1. Nothing should be done to change the procedure. You must see to it that it doesn't.
2. The ruling which takes effect today is the one concerning tardiness.

3. The reason Mel was late is because he had to pick up a report from another branch.
4. I have difficulty in distinguishing one to the other.

Discussion Points

1. Would you be better prepared to answer standard interview questions or behavioural interview questions? Please explain your answer.
2. Why is it important to research the company you are interviewing with? How can you obtain this information?
3. Other than researching the company, how can you prepare for an interview? What are some of the errors that people make during an interview?
4. Discuss the do's and don'ts in dressing for an interview.

Other Employment Situations

▶ **Key Terms**

▶ salary trends
▶ work ethic
▶ resignation letter

The quality of a person's life is in direct proportion to their commitment to excellence, regardless of their chosen field of endeavor.

—Vincent Lombardi, former coach of the Green Bay Packers

Requesting a Compensation Increase

Ideally, you will receive a periodic performance review or assessment and an adequate pay increase on a regular and timely basis. Unfortunately, in many organizations, the routine work tasks totally occupy the supervisors, and they simply forget that it is time for a compensation increase. Here are some tips for bringing this to your supervisor's attention in a tactful way.

Research the Competitive Salary

Do some research on **salary trends** for employees with your job responsibilities. Using job titles for comparison purposes will not get you the data you need because there is no standard for job titles. An administrative assistant in one organization may perform only receptionist duties, whereas in another organization, this is a lower-level management position. Try to find out the salary range at your company for your job classification and where your current salary falls within that range.

Salary information may be available from your Chamber of Commerce, Career Services office at your school, and private employment firms. You can also gather salary figures by visiting on-line employment services such as those listed earlier in this chapter, reading help wanted ads, and magazine or newspaper articles that contain references and facts about salaries.

Prepare a Written Proposal

Your supervisor will probably have to justify and "sell" the idea of a pay raise for you to his or her supervisor. Prepare a written rationale that your supervisor can use when requesting a pay increase for you. List specific examples of your major accomplishments in addition to the work you completed that was "above and beyond" what your job description requires. Give measurable comparisons where possible, such as, "increased sales 8 per cent over previous year" or "handled 5 per cent more customer service calls since January 1."

List skills that are indispensable to your company, as well as any new technical skills you have learned—either by attending training sessions or on your own.

Also state what you are doing to help the company meet its corporate goals. Include future goals you plan to achieve on behalf of the company. Review recent performance evaluations and other progress and periodic reports you've prepared to help you list these goals.

Anticipate Objections

You should anticipate the objections and problems that your supervisor will have with your request for a raise. Address these objections and problems in your written proposal and tell how they can be overcome. Be cautious about listing problems for which you have no solutions. You may be giving your supervisor the reasons he or she needs to deny your request for a raise.

Watch Your Timing

The best time to ask for a raise is right after you've either completed a major project successfully or taken on additional responsibility. You should also be aware of the financial status of your organization. It's not good timing to ask for a raise when business is down.

You may also want to hold off if your supervisor is new to your department or the organization. Your supervisor will need to establish his or her own credibility in the job before seeking raises for subordinates.

Set a Meeting

After you've done your research and prepared your written proposal, schedule a meeting with your supervisor—do not "drop in."

Plan this meeting to demonstrate that you are organized. Speak respectfully and assertively, but avoid any hint of "or else" threats. Review your accomplishments and share any salary comparison information you've gathered. Caution: Do not ask for a raise because of your personal financial situation; raises are given based on your job performance and the value you bring to your company.

Don't ask for a raise in general; have a specific amount in mind and ask for it. Also have some alternatives in mind that you would find acceptable. For instance, if your supervisor can't approve an 8 per cent raise, perhaps you can get a 4 per cent raise now and another 4 per cent in six months.

Be open-minded about taking perks such as more paid vacation days, flexible scheduling, telecommuting opportunities, company paid parking, travel allowance, subsidized child care, new technology training, formal education reimbursement, bonuses, and permission to attend company-paid seminars and workshops in lieu of a salary increase.

If your supervisor asks for time to think it over, ask for another meeting in two weeks. Don't leave the meeting with an open-ended time limit.

How to React When the Boss Says "No"

If your supervisor turns down your request for a raise because "the timing is not right," ask, "Could we discuss my proposal again at a more appropriate time?" Then try to find out what conditions would need to be present to qualify as a better time to revisit the request.

If your supervisor tells you "the request cannot be justified," ask, "What can I do to earn an increase in salary?" Make notes of what the boss suggests, then start immediately to accomplish those objectives.

End the Meeting with a Thank You

If you get the raise, end the meeting with a verbal thank you, but be sure to follow up with a written thank-you note or card. If you do not get the raise, you should still say thank you. Let your supervisor know you appreciate his or her honesty and that you appreciate him or her taking the time to meet with you.

Requesting a Promotion

Many of the same principles discussed in getting a pay raise apply when you are seeking a promotion. You should start thinking about a promotion the day you start work. Be sure you develop a reputation for being dependable by getting your job done on time and correctly—the first time.

Once you learn your job, start taking on additional responsibilities. Take advantage of any opportunities to cross-train in other related areas, including some of your supervisor's job responsibilities. Volunteer for more difficult and responsible assignments.

Demonstrate a strong **work ethic** by showing up for work punctually every day. Have a customer service attitude toward everyone, both internal and external customers, and maintain a friendly, cheerful, and enthusiastic manner. Dress for the job you want, not the job you have. This makes it easier for your supervisor(s) to visualize you in a higher level job.

Following the tips in this section will prepare you to apply for a higher-level position when one becomes available. Another option for a promotion is to make a case for having your job level and job title raised because of the additional responsibilities you've assumed. Prepare a written rationale for promotion using the same guidelines that were explained in the preceding section on justifying a salary increase.

Leaving a Position

You may be terminated. Your job may be eliminated because of restructuring, downsizing, or the company going out of business.

Resigning from a Position

Most people change jobs several times in the course of their careers. You may leave a position for another job or for personal reasons.

Resigning from a job requires almost as much tact, diplomacy, and care as applying for a job. You should leave on good terms with your employer for two key reasons. You might want to work for this company again, and you may need references. Your **resignation letter** should contain three elements: the date of your resignation, a positive explanation for your resignation, and a thank you for the experience. This letter will become part of your permanent employment file.

Follow these guidelines when you resign from a job:

1. Make an appointment with your immediate supervisor, and hand your letter of resignation to him or her.

2. In your letter and in the comments you make during the appointment, indicate that you enjoyed working for the organization. You might mention that the experience gained with the company has definitely moved you forward in your career.

3. Give at least a two-week advance notice that you are leaving, unless your company handbook or employment agreement specifies a longer time period.

4. If you are leaving due to job dissatisfaction, express your reasons in a positive way. For example, "I feel that City Realty will offer me some new challenges and a greater opportunity for advancement."

5. Make certain that all your work is up-to-date and that your papers and files are clearly marked and well organized.

6. Leave a list of instructions or suggestions that may be helpful for your successor.

Here is a sample letter of resignation.

Last week, I received an offer from Computer Consultants. They have offered me a position as senior systems analyst, which represents a major career advancement for me. I have accepted the position.

Please accept my resignation effective April 1. I would be happy to help you train a replacement for my position.

Working with you has been a pleasure. You gave me my first job after college, and you helped me grow personally and develop professionally. I have learned a great deal through working with you and the other programmers in our department. I appreciate Data Trac's investment in my career development.

Being Downsized

The economy has a great deal to do with whether companies need employees or must downsize to survive. Be aware of what's going on with the local and national economy. Always keep your resumé up to date. If you lose your job, follow these three steps:

- Stay calm. Don't show your anger or frustration. Try to negotiate continued health insurance for a transition period, a severance payment, outplacement services, etc. Always remain professional.
- Seek the support of family and friends. Eat properly and get adequate rest. Take advantage of job counselling offered by the company.
- Network. Let people know that you are looking for a job, and ask the people you know to suggest others to contact.

As you have learned in this chapter, communication skills of all types play a critical role in the job application and interview processes. In other words, the written and oral communication skills you learn in school form the basis for the skills you will use throughout your career.

Review of Key Terms

1. What can you do to demonstrate a strong *work ethic*?
2. Choose a job that interests you and explain how you could research *salary trends* for this job.

Practical Application

1. Assume you are a manager with The Overland, a province-wide restaurant. You have worked there two years and have not yet received a raise. Write a list of some of your accomplishments and skills that make you an exceptional employee. If you are not familiar with what a restaurant manager does, interview a manager at a local restaurant.

2. Assume you have worked for Treasured Vacations, a local travel agency, for five years. You have been offered a job at specialized travel agency, Cruises Unlimited. Write a resignation letter to your supervisor, André Garcia, and notify him of the day you are leaving, why you are leaving, and any other pertinent information you think would be appropriate.

3. **TEAMWORK** Writing a list of accomplishments is easy. Verbalizing your accomplishments is often more difficult. With your list that you created above for Question 1, take turns asking for this raise. One team member can be the supervisor, while the others provide feedback about your communication skills.

4. **TEAMWORK** Assume your team is being downsized. Make a list of proactive steps you should take. Ask friends and family if they know of anyone who is hiring, and document your findings. Investigate if your school or local employment agency offers any counselling to those who have lost their jobs. Write a summary of support groups your team discovered.

Editing Practice

Rewrite the following sentences, correcting the grammatical errors.

At tomorrow's meeting, we will be discussed the proposed manufacturing of several of our products. Many new issues will be risen that will be sensitive to some committee members. Piease put your personal feelings aside, and look for the better outcome for the company. Incidentally, several members will be sitting in from management on our meeting to get suggestions and answering questions.

Discussion Points

1. Before asking for a raise or a promotion, what background work should you do?
2. Discuss why it is important to leave on good terms with an employer. Provide examples of this in your own life.

Chapter 12 Wrap-Up

SUMMARY

▶ A successful job search requires you, the applicant, to analyze your wants and qualifications, to assess the job market, and finally, to market yourself.

▶ As the candidate, you should consider the following resources in your job search: your personal contact network, professional contact network, professional organizations, faculty, college placement centres, newspapers, the Internet, summer employment, word-of-mouth from colleagues at work, and employment agencies and contractors.

▶ Whether chronological, functional, or a combination of these two, resumés are summaries of your qualifications for the job you want. Include identification, career objective, educational background, special skills, experience, and references on your resumé. The phrases describing your experience should be concise. Action verbs should be used to articulate results produced during employment. When formatting your resumé, follow the formatting guidelines in this chapter, as well as those for preparing a scannable resumé because many employers use this method.

▶ When writing the application letter, briefly describe the purpose of the letter, highlight your most important qualifications, tell the employer why you should be considered, and specify how your qualifications meet the particular employer's needs. Give specific content information. Application forms must be neat, accurate, and complete.

▶ In any employment interview, the objective is to sell yourself and to see if the job meets your qualifications. To prepare for the interview, a job candidate should research the company, prepare questions for the interview, and know his or her strengths and weaknesses. Managing the details is crucial. A job candidate should confirm all the logistics prior to the interview and dress appropriately for the position they are applying for. Conduct a mock interview, asking typical interview questions, surprise questions, and behavioural questions appropriate to the position. During the interview be clear in your answers and be confident. Express your gratitude to the interviewer in a thank-you note.

▶ Inform the employer promptly of your decision to accept a job. Use tact when declining an offer.

▶ Research salary compensation resources when asking for a promotion and follow the specific company guidelines for the request. If you choose to leave a job, give enough notice and make sure that all the details of your projects are completed and communicated to someone else.

CASE 12.1

Study the information in the Employability Skills Profile (see Appendix).

1. What information is contained in your resumé about each of the main sections of this profile—Academic Skills, Personal Management Skills, and Teamwork Skills?

2. What examples could you give an interviewer of your "Positive Attitudes and Behaviours?"

CASE 12.2

After working as an accountant for seven years, you decide to return to school. You are enrolled at a community college with a major in marketing. You wish to find an internship with Procter and Gamble because of their international marketing.

1. What type of resumé would you choose to submit based on your lack of experience in the field?

2. What would you emphasize in your application letter to the company?

Communicating in Your Career

You are a Human Resource Director with Coca-Cola. You have been asked to speak at a community college about interviewing. The students are particularly interested in some pointers from a professional perspective about what to say in an interview. They are also curious about approaches to phone interviewing and follow-up after an interview. What tips would you give the students?

On the Web

Visit **www.umanitoba.ca/student/employment** for additional information about resumé writing and the interview process.

Key Terms

Appendix

Employability Skills 2000+

Employability Skills 2000+ was developed by the Conference Board of Canada and outlines the skills you need to enter, stay in, and progress in the world of work—whether you work on your own or as part of a team. These skills can also be applied and used beyond the workplace in a range of daily activities.

Communicating in the Workplace, Sixth Canadian Edition will help you develop skills in several major areas found in Employability Skills 2000+. Your **communication** and **critical thinking** abilities will be enhanced with each Section and Chapter studied, and your **teamwork skills** can be developed through group projects and class discussion.

Employability Skills 2000+

Fundamental Skills

The skills needed as a base for further development.

You will be better prepared to progress in the world of work when you can:

Communicate

- Read and understand information presented in a variety of forms (e.g., words, graphs, charts, diagrams)
- Write and speak so others pay attention and understand
- Listen and ask questions to understand and appreciate the points of view of others
- Share information using a range of information and communications technologies (e.g., voice, email, computers)
- Use relevant scientific, technological, and mathematical skills to explain or clarify ideas

Manage Information

- Locate, gather, and organize information using appropriate technology and information systems
- Access, analyze, and apply knowledge and skills from various disciplines (e.g., the arts,

languages, science, technology, mathematics, social sciences, and the humanities)

Use Numbers

- Decide what needs to be measured or calculated
- Observe and record data using appropriate methods, tools, and technology
- Make estimates and verify calculations

Think & Solve Problems

- Assess situations and identify problems
- Seek different points of view and evaluate them based on facts
- Recognize the human, interpersonal, technical, scientific, and mathematical dimensions of a problem
- Identify the root cause of a problem
- Be creative and innovative in exploring possible solutions
- Readily use science, technology, and mathematics as ways to think, gain and share knowledge, solve problems, and make decisions
- Evaluate solutions to make recommendations or decisions
- Implement solutions
- Check to see if a solution works, and act on opportunities for improvement

Personal Management Skills

The personal skills, attitudes, and behaviours that drive one's potential for growth.

You will be able to offer yourself greater possibilities for achievement when you can:

Demonstrate Positive Attitudes & Behaviours

- Feel good about yourself and be confident
- Deal with people, problems, and situations with honesty, integrity, and personal ethics
- Recognize your worth and other people's good efforts
- Take care of your personal health
- Show interest, initiative, and effort

● *Employability Skills 2000+* Brochure 2000 E/F (Ottawa: The Conference Board of Canada, 2000).

Be Responsible

- Set goals and priorities balancing work and personal life
- Plan and manage time, money, and other resources to achieve goals
- Assess, weigh, and manage risk
- Be accountable for your actions and the actions of your group
- Be socially responsible and contribute to your community

Be Adaptive

- Work independently or as part of a team
- Carry out multiple tasks or projects
- Be innovative and resourceful; identify and suggest alternate ways to achieve goals and get the job done
- Be open and respond constructively to change
- Learn from your mistakes and accept feedback
- Cope with uncertainty

Learn Continuously

- Be willing to continuously learn and grow
- Assess personal strengths and areas for development
- Set your own learning goals
- Identify and assess learning sources and opportunities
- Plan for and achieve your learning

Work Safely

Be aware of personal and group health and safety procedures, and act in accordance with these

Teamwork Skills

The skills and attributes needed to contribute productively.

You will be better prepared to add value to the outcome of a task, project, or team when you can:

Work with Others

- Understand and work within the dynamics of a group
- Ensure that a team's purpose and objectives are clear
- Be flexible: respect, be open to and supportive of the thoughts, opinions, and contributions of others in a group
- Recognize and respect people's diversity, individual differences, and perspectives
- Accept and provide feedback in a constructive and considerate manner
- Contribute to a team by sharing information and expertise
- Lead or support when appropriate, motivating a group for high performance
- Understand the role of conflict in a group to reach solutions
- Manage and resolve conflict when appropriate

Participate in Projects & Tasks

- Plan, design, or carry out a project or task from start to finish with well-defined objectives and outcomes
- Develop a plan, seek feedback, test, revise, and implement
- Work to agreed quality standards and specifications
- Select and use appropriate tools and technology for a task or project
- Adapt to changing requirements and information
- Continuously monitor the success of a project or task and identify ways to improve

Employability Skills 2000+ Brochure 2000 E/F (Ottawa: The Conference Board of Canada, 2000). ●

Checkup Answers

Section 2.2 Checkup 1
1. F
2. T
3. F
4. T
5. F
6. F
7. T
8. T
9. T
10. T

Section 2.3 Checkup 1
1. T
2. T
3. F
4. T
5. F
6. F
7. F
8. T
9. T
10. T

Section 3.1 Checkup 1
1. we (P) tickets (N) play (N) Toronto (N)
2. I (P) Jasmin Lee (N) our (P) reservation (N) we (P) her (P)
3. They (P) software (N) Ottawa (N) month (N)
4. You (P) I (P) Tuesday (N) budget (N)
5. She (P) Edmonton (N) Banff (N) sights (N)
6. Sol (N) Chris (N) me (P) Maritimes (N) their (P) part (N) country (N)

Section 3.1 Checkup 2
1. seems
2. was planning
3. hired, promoted
4. has been
Answers may vary for questions 5–8.
5. completed/finished/received (action), started/began (action)
6. is (being)
7. studied (action)
8. were/are (being), attended (action)

Section 3.1 Checkup 3
1. adjective
2. adjective, adverb, adjective
3. adverb, adjective
4. adjective, adverb
5. adjective, adverb, adjective
6. adjective, adverb

Section 3.1 Checkup 4
1. (P) (P)
2. (C) (P) (P) (P)
3. (P) (C) (P)
4. (P) (C) (P) (P)
5. (P) (P) (C)

Section 3.2 Checkup 1
1. Amir Gammal (person spoken about)
2. William Ko-Chen (person spoken about)
3. I (person speaking)
4. reports (thing spoken about)
5. Emilio and Dana (persons spoken about)

Section 3.2 Checkup 2
1. employees (simple)
2. participant (simple)
3. Harrison or Margaret (compound)
4. folders (simple)
5. salons and store (compound)

Section 3.2 Checkup 3
1. attended the conference in Victoria.
2. offers an excellent benefits package to all employees.
3. is the manager of our Legal Department.
4. expires next month.
5. uses colour-coded labels.

Section 3.2 Checkup 4
Note: simple subjects are underscored
1. Eve and Eric Norton (complete subject; compound subject)
2. the basement (complete subject), the Nortons (complete subject)
3. the renovation (complete subject), the Nortons (complete subject)
4. The only other houses on Saugeen Road are located at the top of the hill (normal order); The only other houses on Saugeen Road (complete subject)
5. A bridge and a lake (complete subject) are on the south border of the property (normal order); bridge and lake (compound subject)

Section 3.2 Checkup 5
1. INT
2. IMP
3. D
4. E
5. D

Section 3.2 Checkup 6
1. sentence
2. sentence
Suggested completions on 3, 4, and 5 will vary.
3. dependent (, they review all the medical reports.)
4. dependent (, the current staff will be asked to work overtime.)
5. dependent (, she will explain the new schedule.)

Section 3.2 Checkup 7
1. PP, PP, PP
2. IP, PP, PP
3. IP, PP, VP, PP
4. VP, PP
5. IP, VP, IP, PP

Section 3.2 Checkup 8
Completions for 1, 2, and 4 will vary.
1. fragment (, we must complete the work by September 30.)
2. fragment (, I will ask Samantha and Joel to sign.)
3. sentence
4. fragment (, it has now expired and must be renewed.)
5. sentence

Section 3.3 Checkup 1
1. invited (action)
2. wants (condition)
3. are (being)
4. has accepted (action)
5. seemed (condition)
6. was (being)

Section 3.3 Checkup 2
1. talked, talked, talking
2. elect, elected, electing
3. order, ordered, ordering
4. indicate, indicated, indicated
5. remembered, remembered, remembering
6. respond, responded, responding
7. trusted, trusted, trusting
8. use, used, using
9. marry, married, marrying
10. answer, answered, answered

Section 3.3 Checkup 3
Main verbs are underscored.
1. will be checking
2. can complete
3. will enter
4. Have … approved
5. have been hoping
6. want

Section 3.3 Checkup 4

Answers will vary.

1. We have remembered your birthday!
2. They are listening to all of the explanations.
3. By now James will have noticed that John is absent.
4. Our company will be inspecting the elevators tomorrow.
5. I have asked Susan if I can leave early today.
6. Ralf wanted to buy a bike.
7. The union has rejected management's latest offer.
8. Every month my team leader reviews our performance.

Section 3.3 Checkup 5

1. had known / has known
2. had begun
3. came
4. who has taken / who took
5. OK
6. grown
7. has seen

Section 3.3 Checkup 6

1. has been evaluating (B)
2. was (B)
3. have been (B) (*been* is the main verb; *have* is a helper.)
4. is (B)
5. is (B)
6. have been siding (B)

Section 3.3 Checkup 7

1. OK
2. as if he were
3. were younger
4. as if he were
5. OK

Section 3.3 Checkup 8

1. had been appointed (T)
2. will be (B)
3. will be televised (T)
4. has told (T)
5. have left (I)
6. has been (B)

Section 3.3 Checkup 9

1. raise
2. sits
3. raised
4. set
5. set
6. lay
7. laid
8. rise

Section 3.4 Checkup 1

1. does, its
2. are, their, them
3. wants, her
4. has, its
5. is, its
6. is, her, she

Section 3.4 Checkup 2

1. there are
2. there are
3. is to be
4. is affected
5. There are
6. there are

Section 3.4 Checkup 3

Simple subjects are given in parentheses.

1. has submitted (Nobody)
2. wants (Each)
3. OK (Anyone)
4. if he or she shows his or her pass (Using plurals could make this sentence more readable.)
5. has (Neither)
6. his or her (manager) (or All managers ... are ... their)

Section 3.4 Checkup 4

1. OK
2. are used
3. has been criticized
4. is printed
5. are
6. are
7. is leaving
8. OK

Section 3.4 Checkup 5

1. has risen
2. OK
3. OK
4. are unhappy
5. were not
6. have already begun

Section 3.4 Checkup 6

1. are
2. is
3. OK
4. has
5. is
6. is

Section 3.4 Checkup 7

1. likes, his
2. have
3. have, their
4. are, their
5. is

Section 3.4 Checkup 8

1. OK
2. OK
3. OK
4. double-checks his
5. OK
6. wants

Section 4.1 Checkup 1

1. editors in chief
2. sons-in-law
3. OK
4. supplies
5. lenses
6. communities counties
7. secretaries
8. OK
9. attorneys
10. major generals

Section 4.1 Checkup 2

1. Miss Smiths *or* Misses Smith
2. OK
3. I's
4. OK
5. women companies
6. OK
7. shelves
8. women, Messrs Hill and Ryan, Mses. Kramer and Sung

Section 4.1 Checkup 3

1. tomatoes, mosquitoes *or* mosquitos
2. logos, dittos
3. leaves, thieves
4. loaves, knives
5. solos, videos
6. wives, gulfs
7. bailiffs, handkerchiefs
8. volcanos, concertos
9. radios, trios
10. watches, brushes

Section 4.1 Checkup 4

1. stimuli
2. civics
3. OK
4. OK *or* alumnae
5. thousand
6. bacteria
7. discos
8. analysis

Section 4.2 Checkup 1

1. Riley's
2. actress's or actresses' (pl.)
3. father's
4. women's

5. applicants'
6. representatives'
7. OK
8. supervisors'

Section 4.2 Checkup 2
1. OK
2. else's
3. presidents'
4. Neil and Anne's
5. OK
6. OK
7. mother-in-law's
8. Anita's

Section 4.2 Checkup 3
1. Who's *or* Who is
2. there's *or* there is
3. it's *or* it is
4. you're *or* you are
5. its
6. their boss
7. Who's *or* Who is
8. there's *or* there is

Section 4.3 Checkup 1
1. they
2. OK
3. change *me* to *I*
4. OK
5. change *him* to *he*

Section 4.3 Checkup 2
1. whom
2. who
3. whomever
4. whom
5. Whoever
6. who

Section 4.3 Checkup 3
1. to us
2. Dr. Humphreys or me
3. Tanya and him
4. as she?
5. than I
6. asked us
7. OK
8. Radmila or he
9. none of us
10. OK

Section 4.3 Checkup 4
1. OK
2. Elaine and I
3. she herself wants
4. OK
5. he said
6. Sean and I will call

Section 5.1 Checkup 1
1. first(L) realty(D) major(D) our(P)
2. special(D) new(D) these(DM) important(D)
3. Two(L) well-known(C/D) this(DM) large(D) Brian's(P/PR)
4. two(L) her(P) older(D) this(DM) Regina(PR)
5. Harry's(P/PR) two-year(L/C) accurate(D)
6. Vancouver(PR) that(DM) our(P) additional(L) Henderson's(P/PR)
7. Kelly's(P/PR) crucial(D) new(D) Vancouver(PR)
8. These(DM) tax-free(D/C) their(P) new(D)

Section 5.1 Checkup 2
1. was empty
2. uses more electricity
3. is happier
4. is the larger
5. is unique
6. more nearly full
7. are quieter and bigger
8. OK

Section 5.1 Checkup 3
1. three-time winner
2. any other
3. court-appointed lawyer
4. any other
5. anyone
6. 15-minute question-and-answer session
7. word-of-mouth advertising
8. OK
9. OK
10. well-known public speaker

Section 5.1 Checkup 4
1. PA
2. PN
3. PA, PA
4. PN
5. PN

Section 5.2 Checkup 1
1. quickly
2. hard
3. quietly, efficiently
4. very
5. soon
6. quite
7. always, diligently, usually, early
8. late
9. specifically
10. very

Section 5.2 Checkup 2
1. SA; SC
2. SC; SA; SA
3. SA; CA; SA
4. SC; SA
5. SC
6. CA
7. SC
8. SA; SA; CA

Section 5.2 Checkup 3
1. somewhat
2. really
3. OK
4. surely
5. well
6. angry
7. OK
8. really
9. bad
10. OK

Section 5.3 Checkup 1
1. <u>for</u> the delay
2. <u>on</u> my desk, <u>to</u> the Accounting Department
3. <u>of</u> our members, <u>with</u> the new meeting schedule
4. <u>in</u> a rush, <u>to</u> the airport
5. <u>in</u> my file cabinet
6. <u>between</u> you and me, <u>out</u> of college
7. <u>into</u> the conference room, <u>with</u> her guest
8. <u>on</u> the site, <u>of</u> the new mall, <u>by</u> the planning board

Section 5.3 Checkup 2
1. angry with
2. plans to open
3. OK
4. in regard to
5. OK
6. different from
7. discrepancy between
8. OK
9. retroactive to
10. identical with

Section 5.3 Checkup 3
1. the two of them are
2. cannot help talking
3. has gone?
4. OK
5. into the new hotel
6. within working hours
7. divided among
8. into the garage
9. beside

10. all these chairs
11. Both the
12. like him

Section 5.4 Checkup 1
1. as soon as (S)
2. While (S)
3. both ...and (correlative)
4. and (coordinating)
5. if (S)
6. Unless (S)
7. whether (S)
8. that (S)
9. or (coordinating)
10. or (coordinating)

Section 5.4 Checkup 2
1. sit around as if
2. because she's taking
3. but she is
4. is that
5. who would be
6. It seems as if *or* as though
7. unless you get
8. OK
9. seems as if *or* as though
10. unless I specifically ask

Section 5.4 Checkup 3
1. and apply
2. but exercising
3. and courteous
4. or in person
5. and studying
6. helpful to everyone,

Section 5.4 Checkup 4
1. either to form
2. opened by either
3. surfing the Internet
4. went neither
5. generally given either to
6. and colourfully illustrated

Section 6.1 Checkup 1
1. Tuesday?
2. appointment.
3. Monday?
4. afternoon.
5. opening.
6. month.
7. December 31.
8. December 31?

Section 6.1 Checkup 2
1. $600
2. Inc.
3. Frazer II
4. OK
5. $39
6. OK

Section 6.1 Checkup 3
1. OK
2. hours when
3. meeting, we
4. noon. We (*or* noon, because we)
5. ago,
6. Monday. He (*or* Monday, because he)
7. deposit. He (*or* After the cashier)
8. hour, she

Section 6.1 Checkup 4
1. ready.
2. OK
3. he?
4. quickly.
5. they?
6. OK
7. report.
8. OK.

Section 6.2 Checkup 1
1. offer but
2. Samantha;
3. team,
4. month,
5. December but
6. morning and
7. OK
8. drove and

Section 6.2 Checkup 2
1. plants, etc.
2. Starr &
3. etc.,
4. agendas,
5. or messenger; or,
6. Andrea,
7. advertising;
8. backpack,

Section 6.2 Checkup 3
1. tomorrow,
2. received,
3. software took
4. OK
5. therefore,
6. plan,
7. cafeteria,
8. days,
9. business requires
10. approved, moreover,

Section 6.2 Checkup 4
1. recruiter who
2. Anna, ... office,
3. alternative, ...yesterday,
4. OK
5. lawyer whom ... consult is

6. received, ... principal,
7. staff who ... CA is
8. supplies if
9. alternative, ... think,
10. OK

Section 6.2 Checkup 5
1. Salinger,
2. Gander, Newfoundland,
3. July 2000,
4. OK
5. Davidovitch,
6. 2001,
7. divisions, Simco Chemicals,
8. England,
9. Friday,
10. OK

Section 6.2 Checkup 6
1. outlet, ... West,
2. products that
3. cleaning products that ... Web site may
4. magazine, which ... Society,
5. office are
6. OK

Section 6.2 Checkup 7
1. brilliant, reliable,
2. OK
3. OK
4. solid,
5. OK
6. creative,

Section 6.2 Checkup 8
1. Doyle,
2. long, long
3. Dartmouth office, August ... Summerside office, August
4. risky, risky
5. OK
6. Larry,

Section 6.2 Checkup 9
1. 2007,
2. 2 hours 45 minutes
3. 1232 ... 1336
4. 4840
5. OK
6. 80876
7. Toronto, Ontario M4E 2E6
8. 2 kilograms 25 grams

Section 6.3 Checkup 1
1. week;
2. line;
3. projects;
4. OK
5. informative;

6. factory;
7. month;
8. Printers;

Section 6.3 Checkup 2
1. areas:
2. procedure:
3. OK
4. Matthias: namely,
5. meeting: my
6. errors: Use

Section 6.3 Checkup 3
1. galleries—these
2. offer—at
3. OK
4. shape—but
5. booklet—all

Section 6.3 Checkup 4
1. she?—
2. OK
3. OK
4. prices—
5. prize—
6. OK

Section 6.4 Checkup 1
1. April 11,"
2. catalogue," said Victor, "will
3. session," ... Caruso, "because
4. announced, ... afternoon."
5. window of opportunity
6. "Fragile,"
7. 'Handle With Care'."
8. "Barbara Myers,"

Section 6.4 Checkup 2
1. overstated";
2. models"?
3. Taken."
4. "Waste not, want not"
5. OK
6. performers":
7. courier!"
8. OK

Section 6.4 Checkup 3
1. memorandum),
2. Industries (formerly ...Services") is
3. July 15.)
4. move)?
5. OK
6. (we ... so),
7. photocopies),
8. OK

Section 6.5 Checkup 1
1. "Sincerely"
2. Substantially

3. Always
4. –Management ... and How to
5. OK
6. Servers ... Printers ... Notebook
7. No,
8. Business and Pleasure ... Business and Industry
9. All's
10. a report

Section 6.5 Checkup 2
1. Mexican
2. City
3. Inn ... Lake
4. in Business ... A Guide for
5. Association of Canadian Community Colleges ... Centre
6. Day ... Hoffman
7. in Japan—An Up-to-Date
8. Monday ... October ... spring

Section 6.5 Checkup 3
1. Aid
2. west
3. president
4. cars
5. Federal
6. supervisor ... auditorium
7. OK
8. president
9. crackers
10. agency

Section 6.6 Checkup 1
1. Mr. Bradley has not
2. Professor
3. OK
4. Dr. Lucretia T. Harper *or* Lucretia T. Harper, M.D.
5. Mr.
6. Jessica W. Taft, Ph.D. *or* Ms. Jessica W. Taft

Section 6.6 Checkup 2
1. UAW
2. 10:15 a.m.
3. Tuesday, March 7
4. centimetres
5. New Brunswick,
6. kilograms
7. British Columbia
8. Number

Section 6.7 Checkup 1
1. eight
2. 1970s
3. one-third
4. Forty-seven
5. OK

6. 3 1/2 or 3.5
7. Sixteen
8. thousand
9. OK
10. seventeenth-century

Section 6.7 Checkup 2
1. OK (significant statistics)
2. 270
3. 14
4. 12th
5. $4 million
6. $495,
7. OK
8. 5 ... 7

Section 6.7 Checkup 3
1. July 1,
2. 3 o'clock
3. March 15,
4. 5 1/2 *or* 5.5 ... 2 parts
5. OK
6. OK *or* 5th
7. OK
8. 2 metres ... 4 metres

Section 7.3 Checkup 1
Answers will vary. Suggested answers are:
1. The samples you requested in your April 5 letter are enclosed.
2. Material on the Thornton account is in three large files.
3. Please include your payment with the completed order form.
4. Please give me your response by Friday.
5. To be successful, you should try harder.

Section 7.3 Checkup 2
1. Although some additional options were presented, the manager ...
2. Because the report is due March 4, Jeff ...
3. Despite the costs involved, we are committed ...
4. Because our accounting department is understaffed, we propose ...
5. Save the files in a new directory, and print a copy of each file.

Section 7.3 Checkup 3
1. as well as,
2. than that of
3. OK
4. copies were sent
5. or did you e-mail her assistant? (or did her assistant send the e-mail?)

Section 7.4 Checkup 1
1. Our children's bargain Christmas sale
2. were carefully selected
3. hurriedly discussed
4. rotating tennis schedule

Section 7.4 Checkup 2
1. can be operated in a few minutes
2. fax machine at the repair shop
3. program for your personal computer
4. advertisement in the local newspaper

Section 7.4 Checkup 3
1. Until our annual profits are satisfactory, our
2. sweater, which is on sale for $35.99, on
3. Because she misplaced her glasses, Meghan
4. Because he was worried about the board meeting, Hugo

Section 7.5 Checkup 1
1. exceeded
2. dessert
3. averse
4. ingenious
5. edition

Section 7.5 Checkup 2
1. We have received your cheque for $120.
2. has experience
3. my opinion, ... co-operated well.
4. our practice ... the same
5. Until now, *or* So far, ... the facts

Section 7.5 Checkup 3
1. modern
2. capture
3. aggravate
4. unrelated
5. meagre

Section 7.6 Checkup 1
1. scraping
2. OK
3. territories
4. momentous
5. monkeys
6. believe
7. necessarily
8. envious
9. scarring
10. transmitted

Section 7.6 Checkup 2
1. purpose
2. defendant
3. returnable
4. maintenance
5. OK
6. permanent

Section 7.6 Checkup 3
1. conscientious
2. OK
3. beneficial
4. OK
5. ambitious
6. anxious

Section 7.6 Checkup 4
1. calendar
2. realtor
3. preceding
4. particles
5. inventory, stationery
6. technical ... statistical

Index

possessive forms of personal pronouns
   described, 160
   its, it's, 160
   special cases, 160–161
   their, there, they're, 160
   theirs, there's, 161
   whose, who's, 161
   your, you're, 161
post-interview thank-you letters, 552
postscript, 390
posture, 48
predicate adjectives, 181
predicate agreement
   basic agreement rule, 131–132
   in clauses introduced by relative
      pronouns, 138–139
   collective-noun simple subjects,
      135
   with compound subjects, 137–138
   foreign-noun subjects, 135
   number, 136
   part, portion or amount subjects,
      136
   pronoun-subject agreement, 132
   simple-subject agreement prob-
      lems, 132–134
   simple subjects, 131–134
   with special subjects, 134–136
   subject-verb agreement, 131
   subjects joined by *and,* 137
   subjects joined by *or* or *nor,* 138
predicate nominatives, 181
predicates, 106, 115, 227
prejudice, 24
prepositional phrases, 101–102, 109,
   195, 232
prepositions
   commonly confused, 199–200
   defined, 99
   frequently used combinations,
      99–101
   identification of, 195–196
   idiomatic usage, 196–198
   necessary, 101–102
   object of, 195
   superfluous, 101
preprinted response, 409
present participle, 116–117
present perfect tense, 119
present progressive tense, 120
present tense, 116–117, 118–119
presentation software, 87–88
presentations
   audience analysis, 79
   delivery of, 83–86
   develop your speech, 79–81
   evaluation of, 85
   fielding questions, 84

getting ready, 81–82
importance of presentation skills,
   77
introduction of speaker, 78–79
preparation, 79–83
professional image, 82–83
rhetorical question, 79
stage fright, 84–85
thanking speaker, 78–79
visual aids. *See* visual aids
pretend that, 208
primary sources
   defined, 459
   interviews, 459–460
   observations, 460
   questionnaires, 459
   telephone surveys, 459
procedures book, 399, 481
professional contact network, 518
professional image, 82–83
progress report, 453
progressive tenses, 120
projectors, 87
promotion requests, 559
promotions, 437–438
prompt reply, 408–409
pronoun phrases, 167
pronoun-subject agreement, 132
pronouns
   with *as,* 167
   agreement with common-gender
      nouns, 133
   case forms, 164–168
   in compound subjects or objects,
      167
   confusing pronoun references,
      334–335
   described, 96
   ending in *self,* 168–169
   indefinite-pronoun subject, 134
   nominative case, 164–165
   objective case, 165–166
   possessive forms of personal pro-
      nouns, 160–161
   as predicate nominatives, 181
   relative pronouns, 138–139
   with *than,* 167
pronunciation, 52, 339–340
proofreaders' marks, 298, 299–300
proofreading
   checklist, 307
   defined, 305
   importance of, 307–308
   spell checkers, 306
   for yourself and others, 306
proper adjectives, 176
proper nouns, 97, 147, 176
proposals, 454

province names, 236
pseudo-homonyms, 343, 344
public distance, 49
public relations
   campaigns, 431
   defined, 431
   everyday public relations opportu-
      nities, 433–434
   new business promotion, 432–433
   news release, 492–495
   special public relations opportuni-
      ties, 431–433
   specialist, 431
punctuation
   apostrophes, 262
   colons, 247–248
   commas. *See* commas
   dashes, 249–251
   end-of-sentence, 218–223
   exclamation points, 222–223
   open punctuation in business let-
      ters, 390
   parenthesis, 260–261
   periods, 218–221
   question marks, 221–222
   quotation marks, 256–259
   semicolons. *See* semicolons
   standard punctuation in business
      letters, 390
purpose of report, 478
purposes, 311

Q
question marks, 221–222
questionnaires, 459
questions, 132
quorum, 491
quotation marks
   certain titles, 258
   definitions, 257
   direct quotations, 256–257
   punctuation marks at end of quota-
      tions, 258–259
   quotations within quotations, 257
   slang, 257
   special expressions, 257
   translations, 257
   unfamiliar terms, 257

R
readability, 314
readers. *See* audience
reading skills, 10
real, really, 189–190
reason is that, 208
recommendations, 439–440, 482–484
recording, 39
reference initials, 390